Fundamentals of Artificial Neural Networks

Fundamentals of Artificial Neural Networks

Mohamad H. Hassoun

A Bradford Book

The MIT Press
Cambridge, Massachusetts
London, England

This book was set in Times Roman by Asco Trade Typesetting Ltd., Hong Kong and was printed and bound in the United States of America.

Library of Congress Cataloging-in-Publication Data
Hassoun, Mohamad H.
    Fundamentals of artificial neural networks / Mohamad H. Hassoun.
      p. cm.
    "A Bradford book."
    Includes bibliographical references and index.
    ISBN 0-262-08239-X
    1. Neural networks (Computer science) 2. Artificial intelligence. I. Title.
QA76.87.H374   1995
006.3—dc20

94-47300
CIP

The author may be contacted by e-mail at the following address:
hassoun@brain.eng.wayne.edu

To Amal,
Lamees, and Tarek

Contents

Preface

My purpose in writing this book has been to give a systematic account of major concepts and methodologies of *artificial* neural networks and to present a unified framework that makes the subject more accessible to students and practitioners. This book emphasizes fundamental theoretical aspects of the computational capabilities and learning abilities of artificial neural networks. It integrates important theoretical results on artificial neural networks and uses them to explain a wide range of existing empirical observations and commonly used heuristics.

The main audience is first-year graduate students in electrical engineering, computer engineering, and computer science. This book may be adapted for use as a senior undergraduate textbook by selective choice of topics. Alternatively, it may also be used as a valuable resource for practicing engineers, computer scientists, and others involved in research in artificial neural networks.

This book has evolved from lecture notes of two courses on artificial neural networks, a senior-level course and a graduate-level course, which I have taught during the last 6 years in the Department of Electrical and Computer Engineering at Wayne State University.

The background material needed to understand this book is general knowledge of some basic topics in mathematics, such as probability and statistics, differential equations and linear algebra, and multivariate calculus. The reader is also assumed to have enough familiarity with the concept of a system and the notion of "state," as well as with the basic elements of Boolean algebra and switching theory. The required technical maturity is that of a senior undergraduate in electrical engineering, computer engineering, or computer science.

Artificial neural networks are viewed here as parallel computational models, with varying degrees of complexity, comprised of densely interconnected adaptive processing units. These networks are fine-grained parallel implementations of nonlinear static or dynamic systems. A very important feature of these networks is their adaptive nature, where "learning by example" replaces traditional "programming" in solving problems. This feature makes such computational models very appealing in application domains where one has little or incomplete understanding of the problem to be solved but where training data is readily available. Another key feature is the intrinsic parallelism that allows for fast computations of solutions when these networks are implemented on parallel digital computers or, ultimately, when implemented in customized hardware.

Artificial neural networks are viable computational models for a wide variety of problems, including pattern classification, speech synthesis and recognition, adaptive interfaces between humans and complex physical systems, function approximation, image data compression, associative memory, clustering, forecasting and prediction, combinatorial optimization, nonlinear system modeling, and control. These networks are "neural" in the sense that they may have been inspired by neuroscience, but not because they are faithful models of biologic neural or cognitive phenomena. In fact, the majority of the network models covered in this book are more closely related to traditional mathematical and/or statistical models such as optimization algorithms, nonparametric pattern classifiers, clustering algorithms, linear and nonlinear filters, and statistical regression models than they are to neurobiologic models.

The theories and techniques of artificial neural networks outlined here are fairly mathematical, although the level of mathematical rigor is relatively low. In my exposition I have used mathematics to provide insight and understanding rather than to establish rigorous mathematical foundations.

The selection and treatment of material reflect my background as an electrical and computer engineer. The operation of artificial neural networks is viewed as that of nonlinear systems: Static networks are viewed as mapping or static input/output systems, and recurrent networks are viewed as dynamical systems with an evolving "state." The systems approach is also evident when it comes to discussing the stability of learning algorithms and recurrent network retrieval dynamics, as well as in the adopted classifications of neural networks as discrete-state or continuous-state and discrete-time or continuous-time. The neural network paradigms (architectures and their associated learning rules) treated here were selected because of their relevence, mathematical tractability, and/or practicality. Omissions have been made for a number of reasons, including complexity, obscurity, and space.

This book is organized into eight chapters. Chapter 1 introduces the reader to the most basic artificial neural net, consisting of a single linear threshold gate (LTG). The computational capabilities of linear and polynomial threshold gates are derived. A fundamental theorem, the function counting theorem, is proved and is applied to study the capacity and the generalization capability of threshold gates. The concepts covered in this chapter are crucial because they lay the theoretical foundations for justifying and exploring the more general artificial neural network architectures treated in later chapters.

Chapter 2 mainly deals with theoretical foundations of multivariate function approximation using neural networks. The function counting theorem of Chapter 1 is employed to derive upper bounds on the capacity of various feedforward nets of LTGs. The necessary bounds on the size of LTG-based multilayer classifiers for the cases of training data in general position and in arbitrary position are derived. Theoretical results on continuous function approximation capabilities of feedforward nets, with units employing various nonlinearities, are summarized. The chapter concludes with a discussion of the computational effectiveness of neural net architectures and the efficiency of their hardware implementations.

Learning rules for single-unit and single-layer nets are covered in Chapter 3. More than 20 basic discrete-time learning rules are presented. Supervised rules are considered first, followed by reinforcement, Hebbian, competitive, and feature mapping rules. The presentation of these learning rules is unified in the sense that they may all be viewed as realizing incremental steepest-gradient-descent search on a suitable criterion function. Examples of single-layer architectures are given to illustrate the application of unsupervised learning rules (e.g., principal-component analysis, clustering, vector quantization, and self-organizing feature maps).

Chapter 4 is concerned with the theoretical aspects of supervised, unsupervised, and reinforcement learning rules. The chapter starts by developing a unifying framework for the characterization of various learning rules (supervised and unsupervised). Under this framework, a continuous-time learning rule is viewed as a first-order stochastic differential equation/dynamical system whereby the state of the system evolves so as to minimize an associated instantaneous criterion function. Statistical approximation techniques are employed to study the dynamics and stability, in an "average" sense, of the stochastic system. This approximation leads to an "average learning equation" that, in most cases, can be cast as a globally, asymptotically stable gradient system whose stable equilibria are minimizers of a well-defined criterion function. Formal analysis is provided for supervised, reinforcement, Hebbian, competitive, and topology-preserving learning. Also, the generalization properties of deterministic and stochastic neural nets are analyzed. The chapter concludes with an investigation of the complexity of learning in multilayer neural nets.

Chapter 5 deals with learning in multilayer artificial neural nets. It extends the gradient descent-based learning to multilayer feedforward nets, which results in the back error propagation learning rule (or backprop). An extensive number of methods and heuristics for improving backprop's convergence speed and solution quality are presented, and an attempt is made to give a theoretical basis for such methods and heuristics. Several significant applications of backprop-trained multilayer nets are described. These applications include conversion of English text to speech, mapping of hand gestures to speech, recognition of handwritten ZIP codes, continuous vehicle navigation, medical diagnosis, and image compression. The chapter also extends backprop to recurrent networks capable of temporal association, nonlinear dynamical system modeling, and control.

Chapter 6 is concerned with other important adaptive multilayer net architectures, such as the radial basis function (RBF) net and the cerebeller model articulation controller (CMAC) net, and their associated learning rules. These networks often have similar computational capabilities to feedforward multilayer nets of sigmoidal units, but with the potential for faster learning. Adaptive mulilayer unit-allocating nets such as hyperspherical classifiers, restricted Coulomb energy (RCE) net, and cascade-correlation net are discussed. The chapter also addresses the issue of unsupervised learning in multilayer nets, and it describes two specific networks [adaptive resonance theory (ART) net and the autoassociative clustering net] suitable for adaptive data clustering. The clustering capabilities of these nets are demonstrated through examples, including the decomposition of complex electromyogram signals.

Chapter 7 discusses associative neural memories. Various models of associative learning and retrieval are presented and analyzed, with emphasis on recurrent models. The stability, capacity, and error-correction capabilities of these models are analyzed. The chapter concludes by describing the use of one particular recurrent model (the Hopfield continuous model) for solving combinatorial optimization problems.

Global search methods for optimal learning and retrieval in multilayer neural networks is the topic of Chapter 8. It covers the use of simulated annealing, mean-field annealing, and genetic algorithms for optimal learning. Simulated annealing is also discussed in the context of local-minima-free retrievals in recurrent neural networks (Boltzmann machines). Finally, a hybrid genetic algorithm/gradient-descent-search method that combines optimal and fast learning is described.

Each chapter concludes with a set of problems designed to allow the reader to further explore the concepts discussed. More than 200 problems of varying degrees of difficulty are provided. The problems can be divided roughly into three categories. The first category consists of problems that are relatively easy to solve. These problems are designed to directly reinforce the topics discussed in the book. The second category of problems, marked with an asterisk (*), is relatively more difficult. These problems normally involve mathematical derivations and proofs and are intended to be thought provoking. Many of these problems include reference to technical papers in the literature that may give complete or partial solutions. This second category of problems is intended mainly for readers interested in exploring advanced topics for the purpose of stimulating original research ideas. Problems marked with a dagger (†) represent a third category of problems that are numerical in nature and require the use of a computer. Some of these problems are mini programming projects, which should be especially useful for students.

This book contains enough material for a full semester course on artificial neural networks at the first-year graduate level. I have also used this material selectively to teach an upper-level undergraduate introductory course. For the undergraduate course, one may choose to skip all or a subset of the following material: Sections

1.4–1.6, 2.1–2.2, 4.3–4.8, 5.1.2, 5.4.3–5.4.5, 6.1.2, 6.2–6.4, 6.4.2, 7.2.2, 7.4.1–7.4.4, 8.3.2, 8.4.2, and 8.6.

I hope that this book will prove useful to those students and practicing professionals who are interested not only in understanding the underlying theory of artificial neural networks but also in pursuing research in this area. A list of about 700 relevent references is included with the aim of providing guidance and direction for the readers' own search of the research literature. Even though this reference list may seem comprehensive, the published literature is too extensive to allow such a list to be complete.

Acknowledgments

First and foremost, I acknowledge the contributions of the many researchers in the area of artificial neural networks on which most of the material in this text is based. It would have been extremely difficult (if not impossible) to write this book without the support and assistance of a number of organizations and individuals. I would first like to thank the National Science Foundation, Electric Power Research Institute (EPRI), Ford Motor Company, Mentor Graphics, Sun Micro Systems, Unisys Corporation, Whitaker Foundation, and Zenith Data Systems for supporting my research. I am also grateful for the support I have received for this project from Wayne State University through a Career Development Chair Award.

I thank my students, who have made classroom use of preliminary versions of this book and whose questions and comments have definitely enhanced it. In particular, I would like to thank Raed Abu Zitar, David Clark, Mike Finta, Jing Song, Agus Sudjianto, Chuanming (Chuck) Wang, Hui Wang, Paul Watta, and Abbas Youssef. I also would like to thank my many colleagues in the artificial neural networks community and at Wayne State University, especially Dr. A. Robert Spitzer, for many enjoyable and productive conversations and collaborations.

I am in debt to Mike Finta, who very capably and enthusiastically typed the complete manuscript and helped with most of the artwork, and to Dr. Paul Watta of the Computation and Neural Networks Laboratory, Wayne State University, for his critical reading of the manuscript and assistance with the simulations that led to Figures 5.3.8 and 5.3.9.

My deep gratitude goes to the reviewers for their critical and constructive suggestions. They are Professors Shun-Ichi Amari of the University of Tokyo, James Anderson of Brown University, Thomas Cover of Stanford University, Richard Golden of the University of Texas–Dallas, Laveen Kanal of the University of Maryland, John G. Taylor of King's College London, Francis T. S. Yu of the University of Pennsylvania, Dr. Granino Korn of G. A. and T. M. Korn Industrial Consultants, and other anonymous reviewers.

Finally, let me thank my wife Amal, daughter Lamees, and son Tarek for their quiet patience through the many lonely hours during the preparation of the manuscript.

Mohamad H. Hassoun
Detroit, 1994

Abbreviations

AHK	adaptive Ho-Kashyap
ART	adaptive resonance theory
backprop	back error propagation
BAM	bidirectional associative memory
BSB	brain-state-in-a-box
CCN	cascade-correlation net
CMAC	cerebeller model articulation controller
DAM	dynamic associative memory
DHK	direct Ho-Kashyap
erf	error function
exp	exponential
FIR	finite-duration impulse response
GA	genetic algorithm
GD	gradient descent
GSH	Gallent-Smith-Hassoun
IIR	infinite-duration impulse response
K-map	Karnaugh map
LAM	linear associative memory
LMS	least mean square
ln	natural logarithm
$\log_2$	base 2 logarithm
LTG	linear threshold gate
max	maximum
min	minimum
MSE	mean square error
OLAM	optimal linear associative memory
PTC	polynomial-time classifier
PTG	polynomial threshold gate
QTG	quadratic threshold gate
RCE	restricted Coulomb energy
RBF	radial basis function

RTRL   real-time recurrent learning
sgn   signum or sign function
SOFM   self-organizing feature map
SSE   sum of square error
tanh   hyperbolic tangent
VLSI   very large scale integration
XOR   exclusive-OR Boolean function
XNOR   equivalence Boolean function (complement of XOR)

Symbols

$\mathbf{a}$	column vector
$\mathbf{a}^T$	transpose of vector $\mathbf{a}$, signified by the superscript T
$\mathbf{a}^T\mathbf{b}$	inner product of vectors $\mathbf{a}$ and $\mathbf{b}$
$\mathbf{a}\mathbf{b}^T$	outer product of vectors $\mathbf{a}$ and $\mathbf{b}$
AND	logical "and" operation
$\mathbf{a}\wedge\mathbf{b}$	component-wise ANDing of vectors $\mathbf{a}$ and $\mathbf{b}$
$A(m,d)$	probability of ambiguous response of a d-parameter threshold gate given m points
$\mathbf{b}$	margin vector
b_i	ith component of margin vector $\mathbf{b}$
$\mathbf{B}_{ij}$	ijth element of matrix $\mathbf{B}$
$\mathbf{B}_n$	number of LTG-realizable Boolean functions of n variables
$\mathbf{B}_n(r)$	number of PTG(r)-realizable Boolean functions
$\mathbf{c}^{(i)}$	ith eigenvector of matrix $\mathbf{C}$
$\mathbf{C}$	autocorrelation matrix
$\mathbf{C}^{-1}$	inverse of matrix $\mathbf{C}$
$C(m,n)$	number of linearly separable dichotomies of m points in general position in R^n
$\mathbf{d}^k$	desired target vector associated with input vector $\mathbf{x}$
d_i	ith component of target vector $\mathbf{d}$
$D_{\mathbf{x}}$	see $D(\mathbf{x}',\mathbf{x}'')$
$D(\mathbf{x}',\mathbf{x}'')$	normalized Hamming distance between two binary vectors $\mathbf{x}'$ and $\mathbf{x}''$
$E, E(\mathbf{w}), E(t)$	error or energy function
E_l^k	residual error for unit l at the kth time step
$\nabla E(t)$	gradient of E at time t
$f(net)$	differentiable activation function, usually a sigmoid function
$f'(net)$	derivative of f with respect to net
F	activation function vector operator
h	constant threshold field
$\mathbf{H}$	Hessian matrix
i^*	label of a winning neuron in a competitive net
$\mathbf{I}$	identity matrix

I_i	ith component of the bias vector $\boldsymbol{\theta}$
$J(\mathbf{w})$	criterion (objective) function
$K\left(\dfrac{\|\mathbf{x} - \boldsymbol{\mu}\|}{\sigma^2}\right)$	radially symmetric kernel with center $\boldsymbol{\mu}$ and width σ
$L(m, n)$	number of linearly separable dichotomies of m points in arbitrary position in R^n
m	number of training pairs
$\mathbf{M}_i^k$	cluster membership matrix
n	number of components in a vector
net	weighted-sum or $\mathbf{w}^T\mathbf{x}$
OR	logical "or" operation
$O(\cdot)$	denotes "order of"
P_e	probability of an extreme point
P_{error}	probability of error
$P(i|\mathbf{x})$	conditional probability of unit i winning the competition upon the presentation of $\mathbf{x}$
$P(y = 1)$	probability of y taking the value 1
$P_{LS}(m, n)$	probability of linear separation of m points in general position in R^n
$p(\mathbf{x})$	probability density function of $\mathbf{x}$
$p(d, \mathbf{w})$	joint probability density function of d and $\mathbf{w}$
$p(y|\mathbf{w})$	conditional probability density function of y, given vector $\mathbf{w}$
$\|P(\mathbf{w})\|^2$ or J_R	regularization term
$\mathbf{r}$	position vector of a unit in a neural field
R^n	space of n-dimensional real-valued numbers, also used to designate Euclidean space
$\text{rank}(\mathbf{A})$	rank of matrix $\mathbf{A}$
$r^k, r(y, \mathbf{x}^k)$	reinforcement signal
$r(\mathbf{w}, \mathbf{x}, z)$	learning signal; also appears as $r(\mathbf{w}^T\mathbf{x}, z)$
$\mathbf{s}^k$	learning vector evaluated at the kth time step
$s(\mathbf{r}, \mathbf{x})$	total stimulus at position $\mathbf{r}$ in a neural field, due to input $\mathbf{x}$
t	time, continuous or discrete depending on context
T	threshold constant; also used in Chapter 8 to signify "temperature"

$\text{Tr}(\mathbf{C})$	trace of matrix $\mathbf{C}$
$u(\mathbf{r})$, $u(\mathbf{r}, t)$	neural field potential at position $\mathbf{r}$
$u^*(\mathbf{r})$	equilibrium neural field potential
$u(\xi)$	unit step function
$\mathbf{w}$	weight vector
$\mathbf{w(r)}$	weight vector of a unit at position $\mathbf{r}$ in a neural field
$\mathbf{w}_i^*$	weight vector of winning unit i
$\dot{\mathbf{w}}$	time derivative of vector $\mathbf{w}$
$\mathbf{w}^*$	solution weight vector
$\mathbf{W}$	weight matrix
$\mathbf{x}$	input vector or state vector
$\mathbf{x}^k$	kth input vector
$\hat{\mathbf{x}}$	noisy input vector
$\mathbf{X}^\dagger$	pseudo- or generalized inverse
$\bar{x}$	binary complement
$|x|$	absolute value of x
$\|\mathbf{x}\|$	Euclidean norm of vector $\mathbf{x}$
y	unit (neuron) output
$z!$	z factorial
α	momentum rate, also used as a constant parameter or a label
$\alpha(\mathbf{r}, \mathbf{r}')$	neural field lateral weight distribution
Δ	unit-delay
$\Delta \mathbf{w}$	small change applied to $\mathbf{w}$
∇	gradient operator
$\nabla J(\mathbf{w})$ or $\nabla_{\mathbf{w}} J$	gradient of J with respect to vector $\mathbf{w}$
$\nabla \nabla J(\mathbf{w})$	Hessian of J
ε	positive constant, usually arbitrarily small
ε^k	error vector at the kth step of the AHK algorithm
$\phi_i(\mathbf{x})$	ith component of the ϕ-mapping realized by a PTG
$\Phi_j(\mathbf{x})$	element of an orthonormal set
$\Phi(\mathbf{r}_i, \mathbf{r}_{i*})$	discrete neighborhood function with center $\mathbf{r}_{i*}$

$\Phi(\mathbf{r}, \mathbf{r}^*)$	continuous neighborhood function with center at $\mathbf{r}^*$
λ_i	ith eigenvalue of matrix $\mathbf{C}$
$\boldsymbol{\mu}$	mean vector
$\boldsymbol{\theta}$	bias vector
φ	sigmoid activation function
ϑ	general activation function
ρ	learning rate; also used to denote vigilance parameter or basin of attraction radius
$\rho^k, \rho(t)$	learning rate at iteration k and time t, respectively
$\rho(\mathbf{w})$	weight vector probability density function
σ^2	variance
$\sigma_{\mathbf{w}}^2$	variance of the components of vector $\mathbf{w}$
Σ	compact subset in multidimensional Euclidean space
τ, τ'	time constant
$\binom{m}{k}$	binomial coefficient
$\prod_{k=1}^{n} x_k$	product of the n terms x_1 through x_n
$\in$	symbol for "belongs to"
$\subset$	symbol for "subset of"
$\cup$	symbol for "union of"
$\cap$	symbol for "intersection of"
$\langle \cdot \rangle$	mathematical expectation or mean
$[a, b]$	closed interval of real-valued numbers between a and b
$\{0, 1\}^n$	n-dimensional binary hypercube
$\{\mathbf{x}^k, d^k\}$	kth training pairs

1 Threshold Gates

Artificial neural networks are parallel computational models comprised of densely interconnected adaptive processing units.[1] These networks are fine-grained parallel implementations of nonlinear static or dynamic systems. A very important feature of these networks is their adaptive nature, where "learning by example" replaces "programming" in solving problems. This feature makes such computational models very appealing in application domains where one has little or incomplete understanding of the problem to be solved but where training data is readily available. Another key feature is the intrinsic parallel architecture that allows for fast computation of solutions when these networks are implemented on parallel digital computers or, ultimately, when implemented in customized hardware.

Artificial neural networks are viable computational models for a wide variety of problems. These include pattern classification, speech synthesis and recognition, adaptive interfaces between humans and complex physical systems, function approximation, image compression, associative memory, clustering, forecasting and prediction, combinatorial optimization, nonlinear system modeling, and control. These networks are "neural" in the sense that they may have been inspired by neuroscience but not necessarily because they are faithful models of biologic neural or cognitive phenomena. In fact, the majority of the networks covered in this book are more closely related to traditional mathematical and/or statistical models such as non-parametric pattern classifiers, clustering algorithms, nonlinear filters, and statistical regression models than they are to neurobiologic models.

The "artificial neuron" is the basic building block/processing unit of an artificial neural network. It is necessary to understand the computational capabilities of this processing unit as a prerequisite for understanding the function of a network of such units. The artificial neuron model considered here is closely related to an early model used in threshold logic (Winder, 1962; Brown, 1964; Cover, 1964; Dertouzos, 1965; Hu, 1965; Lewis and Coates, 1967; Sheng, 1969; Muroga, 1971). Here, an approximation to the function of a biologic neuron is captured by the linear threshold gate (McCulloch and Pitts, 1943).

This chapter investigates the computational capabilities of a linear threshold gate (LTG). Also in this chapter, the polynomial threshold gate (PTG) is developed as a generalization of the LTG, and its computational capabilities are studied. An important theorem, known as the *function counting theorem*, is proved and is used to determine the statistical capacity of LTGs and PTGs. Then a method for minimal parameter PTG synthesis is developed for the realization of arbitrary binary

---

1. The history of the development of the field of artificial neural networks has been told and retold in many books. The interested reader may refer to the nice introduction found in the book by Hecht-Nielsen (1990).

mappings (switching functions). The chapter concludes by defining the concepts of ambiguous and extreme points and applying them to study the generalization capability of threshold gates and to determine the average amount of information necessary for characterizing large data sets by threshold gates.

1.1   Threshold Gates

1.1.1   Linear Threshold Gates

The basic function of a linear threshold gate (LTG) is to discriminate between labeled points (vectors) belonging to two different classes. An LTG maps a vector of input data $\mathbf{x}$ into a single binary output y. The transfer function of an LTG is given analytically by

$$y = \begin{cases} 1 & \text{if } \mathbf{w}^T\mathbf{x} = \sum_{i=1}^{n} w_i x_i \geq T \\ 0 & \text{otherwise} \end{cases} \tag{1.1.1}$$

where $\mathbf{x} = [x_1\, x_2 \ldots x_n]^T$ and $\mathbf{w} = [w_1\, w_2 \ldots w_n]^T$ are the input and weight (column) vectors, respectively, and T is a threshold constant.[2] Figure 1.1.1a shows a symbolic representation of an LTG with n inputs. A graphic representation of Equation (1.1.1) is shown in Figure 1.1.1b. The vector $\mathbf{x}$ in Equation (1.1.1) is n dimensional with

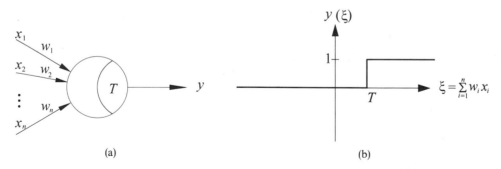

(a)   (b)

Figure 1.1.1
(a) Symbolic representation of a linear threshold gate and (b) its transfer function.

2. The term $\sum_{i=1}^{n} w_i x_i$ in Equation (1.1.1) will be referred to as the *weighted sum* and is usually denoted by the vector inner product $\mathbf{w}^T\mathbf{x}$ or $\mathbf{x}^T\mathbf{w}$. Here, the superscript T signifies the transpose of a vector.

binary or real components (i.e., $\mathbf{x} \in \{0, 1\}^n$ or $\mathbf{x} \in R^n$) and $\mathbf{w} \in R^n$. Thus the LTG output y may assume either of the following mapping forms:

$$\mathbf{x} \in \{0, 1\}^n \Rightarrow y: \{0, 1\}^n \to \{0, 1\}$$

or

$$\mathbf{x} \in R^n \quad \Rightarrow y: R^n \to \{0, 1\}$$

An LTG performs a linear weighted-sum operation followed by a nonlinear hard-clipping/thresholding operation, as described in Equation (1.1.1). Figure 1.1.2 shows an example of an LTG that realizes the Boolean function[3] y given by

$$y(x_1, x_2, x_3) = \bar{x}_1 x_2 + x_2 \bar{x}_3 \tag{1.1.2}$$

where x_1, x_2 and x_3 belong to $\{0, 1\}$. Equation (1.1.2) reads $y = [(\text{NOT } x_1) \text{ AND } x_2]$ OR $[x_2 \text{ AND } (\text{NOT } x_3)]$. Here, the weight vector $\mathbf{w} = [-1 \quad 2 \quad -1]^T$ and threshold

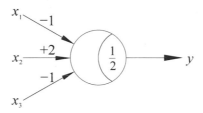

Figure 1.1.2
Example of an LTG realization of the Boolean function $y(x_1, x_2, x_3) = \bar{x}_1 x_2 + x_2 \bar{x}_3$.

3. A Boolean function (or a switching function) is a logic expression formed with binary variables, the two binary operators OR and AND, and the unary operator NOT. This logic expression is based on an algebraic system known as *switching algebra*, developed by Shannon (1938), which builds on the pioneering work of George Boole (1854). An n-variable Boolean function also may be represented by a *truth table*. Here, we need a list of the 2^n combinations of 1s and 0s of the n binary variables and a column showing the combination for which the function is equal to 1 or 0. For example, the first row in a truth table for the Boolean function in Equation (1.1.2) has the combination (0, 0, 0) associated with a function value of 0, the third row has the combination (0, 1, 0) associated with a function value of 1, and so on. The truth table may be used to derive a canonical sum-of-products algebraic expression for Boolean functions. This is done by finding the sum (ORing) of all terms that correspond to those combinations (i.e., rows) for which the function assumes the value 1. Each term is a product (ANDing) of the variables on which the function depends. Variable x_i appears in uncomplemented form in the product if it has the value 1 in the corresponding combination, and it appears in complemented form if it has the value 0. The product term which contains each of the n variables in either complemented or uncomplemented form is called a *minterm*. As an example, the following is the canonical sum-of-products expression for the Boolean function in Equation (1.1.2):

$$y(x_1, x_2, x_3) = \bar{x}_1 x_2 x_3 + \bar{x}_1 x_2 \bar{x}_3 + x_1 x_2 \bar{x}_3$$

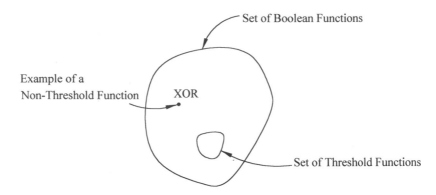

Figure 1.1.3
Pictorial representation depicting the set of threshold functions as a small subset of the set of all Boolean functions.

$T = \frac{1}{2}$ lead to a correct realization of y. One way of directly arriving at such a solution for **w** and T is to determine a solution for the following set of eight inequalities:

$$0 < T \qquad\qquad w_1 + w_2 \geq T$$

$$w_1 < T \qquad\qquad w_1 + w_3 < T$$

$$w_2 \geq T \qquad\qquad w_2 + w_3 \geq T$$

$$w_3 < T \qquad w_1 + w_2 + w_3 < T$$

These inequalities are obtained by substituting all eight binary input combinations (x_1, x_2, x_3) and their associated y values from Equation (1.1.2) into Equation (1.1.1). For example, for input $(x_1, x_2, x_3) = (0, 0, 0)$, the output y [using Equation (1.1.2)] is given by $y = 0$. Hence, for a proper operation of the LTG, we require $0w_1 + 0w_2 + 0w_3 < T$, which gives the first of the above eight inequalities: $0 < T$. The other seven inequalities are obtained similarly for each of the remaining cases: $(x_1, x_2, x_3) = (0, 0, 1)$ through $(1, 1, 1)$. It should be noted that the solution given in Figure 1.1.2 is one of an infinite number of possible solutions for the preceding set of inequalities.

There are 2^n combinations of n independent binary variables that lead to 2^{2^n} unique ways of labeling these 2^n combinations into two distinct categories (i.e., 0 or 1); hence, there exists a total of 2^{2^n} unique Boolean functions (switching functions) of n variables. It can be shown (see Section 1.2) that a single n-input LTG is capable of realizing only a small subset of these 2^{2^n} Boolean functions (refer to Figure 1.1.3). A Boolean function that can be realized by a single LTG is known as a *threshold*

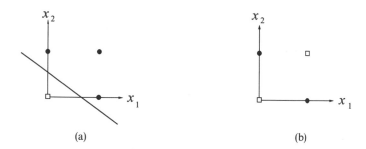

Figure 1.1.4
Linear versus nonlinear separability: (*a*) Linearly separable function, and
(*b*) nonlinearly separable function. Filled circles and open squares designate points in the first and second classes, respectively.

function. A threshold function is a linearly separable function, i.e., a function with
inputs belonging to two distinct categories (classes) such that the inputs corresponding to one category may be geometrically separated from the inputs corresponding to
the other category by a hyperplane. Any function that is not linearly separable, such
as the exclusive-OR (XOR) function $[y(x_1, x_2) = \bar{x}_1 x_2 + x_1 \bar{x}_2]$, cannot be realized
using a single LTG and is termed a *nonthreshold function*. Linear and nonlinear
separability are illustrated in Figure 1.1.4*a* and *b*, respectively.

Threshold functions have been exhaustively enumerated for small n (Cameron,
1960; Muroga, 1971) as shown in Table 1.1.1. This table shows the limitation of a
single LTG with regard to the realization of an arbitrary Boolean function. Here, as
$n \to \infty$, the ratio of the number of LTG-realizable Boolean functions B_n to the total
number of Boolean functions approaches zero; formally,

Table 1.1.1
Comparison of the Number of Threshold Functions vs. the Number of All Possible Boolean Functions for
Selected Values of n

n	Number of Threshold Functions B_n	Total Number of Boolean Functions (2^{2^n})
1	4	4
2	14	16
3	104	256
4	1,882	65,536
5	94,572	$\sim 4.3 \times 10^9$
6	15,028,134	$\sim 1.8 \times 10^{19}$
7	8,378,070,864	$\sim 3.4 \times 10^{38}$
8	17,561,539,552,946	$\sim 1.16 \times 10^{77}$

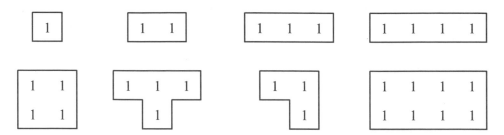

Figure 1.1.5
Admissible Karnaugh map threshold patterns for $n = 3$.

$$\lim_{n \to \infty} \left(\frac{B_n}{2^{2^n}} \right) = 0 \qquad (1.1.3)$$

This result is verified in Section 1.2.

Although a single LTG cannot represent all Boolean functions, it is capable of realizing the universal NAND (or NOR) logic operation ($x_1 \text{ NAND } x_2 = \overline{x_1 x_2} = \bar{x}_1 + \bar{x}_2$ and $x_1 \text{ NOR } x_2 = \overline{x_1 + x_2} = \bar{x}_1 \bar{x}_2$). Hence the LTG is a universal logic gate; any Boolean function is realizable using a network of LTGs (only two logic levels are needed). Besides the basic NAND and NOR functions, though, an LTG is capable of realizing many more Boolean functions. Therefore, a single n-input LTG is a much more powerful gate than a single n-input NAND or NOR gate.

For $n \leq 5$, a Karnaugh map[4] (or K-map) may be employed to identify threshold functions or to perform the decomposition of nonthreshold functions into two or more factors, each of which will be a threshold function. This decomposition allows for obtaining an LTG network realization for Boolean functions, as illustrated later in Section 2.1.1. Figure 1.1.5 shows the admissible K-map threshold patterns for

4. The Karnaugh map (also known as the *Veitch diagram*) was first proposed by Veitch (1952) and slightly modified by Karnaugh (1953). It provides a practical procedure for minimizing the number of terms and/or variables in the algebraic expression of a Boolean function with a small number of variables. A Karnaugh map is actually a modified form of a truth table (see footnote 3) in which the arrangement of the combinations is particularly convenient. The map for the three-variable function $y(x_1, x_2, x_3) = \bar{x}_1 x_2 + x_2 \bar{x}_3$ is shown in Figure 1.1.6. The column headings are labeled with the four combinations of the variables x_2 and x_3. The row headings correspond to the binary values of x_1 (an example of a four-variable Karnaugh map is shown in Figure 2.1.2). Each n-variable map consists of 2^n cells (squares) representing all possible combinations of these variables. The "cyclic" code used in listing the combinations as column and row headings is of particular importance. According to this coding, adjacent cells correspond to combinations that differ by the value of just a single variable and play a major role in the simplification process of Boolean expressions. For the purpose of determining all adjacencies, it is useful to regard the three-variable map as the surface of a cylinder formed by joining the left and right sides of the map [for further details, see Kohavi (1978) or Mano (1979)].

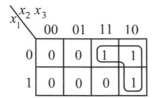

Figure 1.1.6
A Karnaugh map representation for the threshold
function $y(x_1, x_2, x_3) = \bar{x}_1 x_2 + x_2 \bar{x}_3$. The 1s of this
function can be grouped as shown to form one of the
threshold patterns depicted in Figure 1.1.5.

$n = 3$. The K-map for the threshold function in Equation (1.1.2) is shown in Figure
1.1.6 along with its corresponding threshold pattern. Each admissible pattern may be
in any position on the map, provided that its basic topologic structure is preserved.
Note that the complements of such patterns also represent admissible threshold patterns (refer to Example 1.2.1 in Section 1.2 for an example). Admissible patterns of
Boolean functions of n variables are also admissible for functions of $n + 1$ or more
variables (Kohavi, 1978).

1.1.2   Quadratic Threshold Gates

Given that for large n the number of threshold functions is very small compared to the
total number of available Boolean functions, one might try to design a yet more
powerful "logic" gate that can realize nonthreshold functions. This can be accomplished by expanding the number of inputs to an LTG. For example, one can do this
by feeding the products or ANDings of inputs as new inputs to the LTG. In this case,
we require a fixed preprocessing layer of AND gates that artificially increases the
dimensionality of the input space. We expect that the resulting Boolean function
(which is now only partially specified) becomes a threshold function and hence realizable using a single LTG. This phenomenon is illustrated through an example (Example 1.2.1) given in the next section.

The realization of a Boolean function by the preceding process leads to a *quadratic
threshold gate* (QTG). The general transfer characteristics for an n-input QTG are
given by

$$y = \begin{cases} 1 & \text{if } \sum_{i=1}^{n} w_i x_i + \sum_{i=1}^{n} \sum_{j=i}^{n} w_{ij} x_i x_j \geq T \\ 0 & \text{otherwise} \end{cases} \qquad (1.1.4)$$

for $\mathbf{x} \in R^n$ and

$$
y = \begin{cases} 1 & \text{if } \sum_{i=1}^{n} w_i x_i + \sum_{i=1}^{n} \sum_{j=i+1}^{n} w_{ij} x_i x_j \geq T \\ 0 & \text{otherwise} \end{cases} \tag{1.1.5}
$$

for $\mathbf{x} \in \{0, 1\}^n$. Note that the only difference between Equations (1.1.4) and (1.1.5) is the range of the index j of the second summation in the double-summation term. The bounds on the double summations in Equations (1.1.4) and (1.1.5) eliminate the $w_{ij} x_i x_j$ and $w_{ji} x_j x_i$ duplications. QTGs greatly increase the number of realizable Boolean functions as compared with LTGs. By comparing the number of degrees of freedom (number of weights plus threshold) listed in Table 1.1.2, we find an increased flexibility of a QTG over an LTG.

1.1.3   Polynomial Threshold Gates

Although the QTG greatly increases the number of functions that can be realized, a single QTG still cannot realize all Boolean functions of n variables. Knowing that a second order polynomial expansion of inputs offers some improvement, it makes sense to extend this concept to r-order polynomials. This results in a *polynomial threshold gate* denoted PTG(r). Note that the LTG and QTG are special cases, where LTG $\equiv$ PTG(1) and QTG $\equiv$ PTG(2). The general transfer equation for a PTG(r) is given by

$$
y = \begin{cases} 1 & \text{if } \sum_{i_1=1}^{n} w_{i_1} x_{i_1} + \sum_{i_1=1}^{n} \sum_{i_2=i_1}^{n} w_{i_1 i_2} x_{i_1} x_{i_2} + \cdots \\ & + \sum_{i_1=1}^{n} \sum_{i_2=i_1}^{n} \cdots \sum_{i_r=i_{r-1}}^{n} w_{i_1 i_2 \cdots i_r} x_{i_1} x_{i_2} \cdots x_{i_r} \geq T \\ 0 & \text{otherwise} \end{cases} \tag{1.1.6}
$$

Table 1.1.2
Comparison of the Number of Degrees of Freedom in an LTG vs. a QTG

Threshold Gate	Number of Degrees of Freedom/Parameters (Including Threshold)
LTG	$n + 1$
QTG	$\dfrac{(n + 1)(n + 2)}{2}$ $\quad \mathbf{x} \in R^n$
	$\dfrac{n(n + 1)}{2} + 1$ $\quad \mathbf{x} \in \{0, 1\}^n$

In this case, the number of degrees of freedom is given by

$$d = \sum_{i=1}^{r} \begin{bmatrix} n \\ i \end{bmatrix} + 1 = \sum_{i=0}^{r} \begin{bmatrix} n \\ i \end{bmatrix} = \sum_{i=0}^{r} \frac{n!}{(n-i)!\,i!} \tag{1.1.7}$$

for $\mathbf{x} \in \{0, 1\}^n$ and

$$d = \sum_{i=1}^{r} \begin{bmatrix} n + i - 1 \\ i \end{bmatrix} + 1 = \begin{bmatrix} n + r \\ r \end{bmatrix} = \frac{(n+r)!}{n!\,r!} \tag{1.1.8}$$

for $\mathbf{x} \in R^n$. Here, the term $\begin{bmatrix} m \\ k \end{bmatrix}$ gives the number of different combinations of m different things, k at a time, without repetitions. The PTG appears to be a powerful gate. It is worthwhile to investigate its capabilities.

1.2   Computational Capabilities of Polynomial Threshold Gates

Next, we consider the capabilities of PTGs in realizing arbitrary Boolean functions. Let us start with a theorem which establishes the universality of a single n-input PTG(r) in the realization of arbitrary Boolean functions.

THEOREM 1.2.1 (Nilsson, 1965; Krishnan, 1966)   Any Boolean function of n variables can be realized using a PTG of order $r \leq n$.

The proof of this theorem follows from the discussion in Section 1.4. Theorem 1.2.1 indicates that $r = n$ is an upper bound on the order of the PTG for realizing arbitrary Boolean functions. It implies that the most difficult n-variable Boolean function to implement by a PTG(r) requires $r = n$, and this may require

$$d = \sum_{i=1}^{n} \begin{bmatrix} n \\ i \end{bmatrix} + 1 = 2^n$$

parameters. Therefore, in the worst case, the number of required parameters increases exponentially in n.

Winder (1963) gave the following upper bound on the number of realizable Boolean functions $B_n(r)$ of n variables by a PTG(r), $r \leq n$ (see Section 1.3.4 for details):

$$B_n(r) \leq C(2^n, d - 1) \tag{1.2.1}$$

where d is given by Equation (1.1.7) and

$$C(m, d - 1) = 2 \sum_{i=0}^{d-1} \begin{bmatrix} m - 1 \\ i \end{bmatrix} \tag{1.2.2}$$

A couple of special cases are interesting to examine. The first occurs when $r = n$. From Theorem 1.2.1, any n-variable Boolean function is realizable using a single PTG(n). This means that the right-hand side of Equation (1.2.1) should not exceed the number of n-variable Boolean functions 2^{2^n} if it is to be a tight upper bound. Indeed, this can be shown to be the case by first starting with Equation (1.2.1) and then finding the limit of $C(2^n, d - 1)$ as r approaches n. Since

$$\lim_{r \to n} \sum_{i=1}^{r} \begin{bmatrix} n \\ i \end{bmatrix} + 1 = 2^n,$$

we have

$$B_n(n) \le C(2^n, 2^n - 1) \tag{1.2.3}$$

or

$$B_n(n) \le 2 \sum_{i=0}^{2^n-1} \begin{bmatrix} 2^n - 1 \\ i \end{bmatrix} = 2(2^{2^n-1}) = 2^{2^n} \tag{1.2.4}$$

which is the desired result.

The other interesting case is for $r = 1$, which leads to the case of an LTG. Employing Equation (1.2.1) with $d = n + 1$, $n \ge 2$, gives the following upper bound on the number of n-input threshold functions:

$$B_n(1) \le C(2^n, n) < 2^{n^2} \tag{1.2.5}$$

It can be shown (Winder, 1963) that a yet tighter upper bound on $B_n(1)$ is $2(2^{n^2}/n!)$ (see Problem 1.3.3). Equation (1.2.5) allows us to validate Equation (1.1.3) by taking the following limit:

$$\lim_{n \to \infty} \frac{B_n(1)}{2^{2^n}} \le \lim_{n \to \infty} \frac{2^{n^2}}{2^{2^n}} = 0 \tag{1.2.6}$$

Table 1.2.1 extends Table 1.1.1 by evaluating the preceding upper bounds on the number of threshold functions. Note that despite the pessimistic fact implied by Equation (1.2.6), a single LTG remains a powerful logic gate by being able to realize a very large number of Boolean functions. This can be seen from the enumerated results in Table 1.2.1 [see the column labeled $B_n(1)$]. In fact, $B_n(1)$ scales exponentially in n, as can be deduced from the following lower bound (Muroga, 1965):

$$B_n(1) > 2^{\frac{n^2}{3}} \tag{1.2.7}$$

Table 1.2.1
Enumeration of Threshold Functions and Evaluations of Various Upper Bounds for $n \leq 8$

n	Number of Threshold Functions $[B_n(1)]$	Total Number of Boolean Functions (2^{2^n})	Upper Bounds for $B_n(1)$		
			$2\sum_{i=0}^{n}\binom{2^n-1}{i}$	$2\left(\dfrac{2^{n^2}}{n!}\right)$	2^{n^2}
1	4	4	4	4	2
2	14	16	14	16	16
3	104	256	128	~ 170	512
4	1,882	65,536	3,882	$\sim 5,461$	65,536
5	94,572	$\sim 4.3 \times 10^9$	412,736	$\sim 559,240$	33,554,432
6	15,028,134	$\sim 1.8 \times 10^{19}$	$\sim 1.5 \times 10^8$	$\sim 1.9 \times 10^8$	$\sim 6.9 \times 10^{10}$
7	8,378,070,864	$\sim 3.4 \times 10^{38}$	$\sim 1.9 \times 10^{11}$	$\sim 2.2 \times 10^{11}$	$\sim 5.6 \times 10^{14}$
8	17,561,539,552,946	$\sim 1.16 \times 10^{77}$	$\sim 8.2 \times 10^{14}$	$\sim 9.2 \times 10^{14}$	$\sim 1.8 \times 10^{19}$

By its very definition, a PTG may be thought of as a two-layer network with a fixed preprocessing layer followed by a high-fan-in LTG. Kaszerman (1963) showed that a PTG(r) with binary inputs can be realized as the cascade of a layer of $\sum_{i=1}^{r}\binom{n}{i} - n$ AND gates, each having a fan-in between two and r input lines and a single LTG with $\sum_{i=1}^{r}\binom{n}{i}$ inputs (representing the inputs received from the AND gates plus the original n inputs). The resulting architecture is shown in Figure 1.2.1.

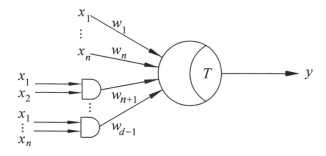

Figure 1.2.1
PTG realization as a cascade of one layer of AND gates and a single LTG.

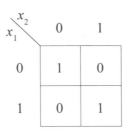

Figure 1.2.2
Karnaugh map of the XNOR function.

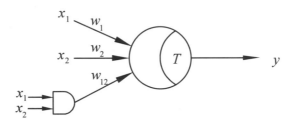

Figure 1.2.3
A PTG(2) (or QTG) with binary inputs.

Example 1.2.1 Consider the XNOR function (also known as the *equivalence function*):

$$y(x_1, x_2) = x_1 x_2 + \bar{x}_1 \bar{x}_2$$

Using a Karnaugh map (shown in Figure 1.2.2), it can be verified that this function is not a threshold function; therefore, it cannot be realized using a single 2-input LTG (a diagonal pattern of 1s in the K-map is a nonthreshold pattern and indicates a nonthreshold/nonlinearly separable function).

Since $n = 2$, Theorem 1.2.1 implies that a PTG(2) is sufficient; i.e., the QTG with three weights, shown in Figure 1.2.3, should be sufficient to realize the XNOR function. By defining $x_3 = x_1 x_2$, we can treat the PTG as a 3-input LTG and generate the K-map shown in Figure 1.2.4.

Since x_3 is defined as $x_1 x_2$, there are some undefined states which we will refer to as "don't care" states; these states can be assigned either a 1 or 0, to our liking, and give us the flexibility to identify the threshold pattern shown in Figure 1.2.5 (this pattern is the complement of one of the threshold patterns shown in Figure 1.1.5, and therefore, it is an admissible threshold pattern).

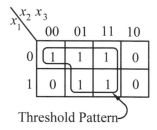

Figure 1.2.4
Karnaugh map for XNOR in expanded input space.
d signifies a "don't care" state.

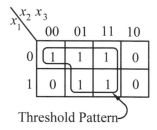

Threshold Pattern

Figure 1.2.5
Karnaugh map after an appropriate assignment of 1s and 0s to the
"don't care" states of the map in Figure 1.2.4.

The preceding K-map verifies that $y(x_1, x_2, x_3)$ is realizable using a single LTG. The QTG in Figure 1.2.3 will realize the desired XNOR function with weight assignments as shown in Figure 1.2.6. Dertouzos (1965) describes a tabular method for determining weights for LTGs with small n. This method works well here but will not be discussed. The topic of adaptive weight computation for LTGs is treated in Chapter 3.

A geometric interpretation of the synthesized QTG may be obtained by first employing Equation (1.1.5), which gives

$$y = \begin{cases} 1 & \text{if } -x_1 - x_2 + 3x_1x_2 \geq -\frac{1}{2} \\ 0 & \text{otherwise} \end{cases} \tag{1.2.8}$$

In arriving at this result, we took the liberty of interpreting the AND operation as multiplication. Note that this interpretation does not affect the QTG in Figure 1.2.6 when the inputs are in $\{0, 1\}$. Next, Equation (1.2.8) may be used to define a separating surface g that discriminates between the 1 and 0 vertices according to

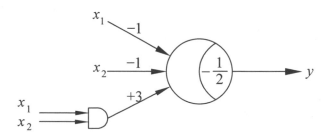

Figure 1.2.6
Weight assignment for a QTG for realizing the XNOR function.

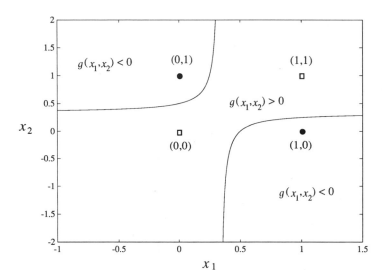

Figure 1.2.7
Separating surface realized by the QTG of Equation (1.2.9).

$$g(x_1, x_2) \triangleq -x_1 - x_2 + 3x_1x_2 + \tfrac{1}{2} = 0 \qquad (1.2.9)$$

(here, $\triangleq$ is the symbol for "defined as"). A plot of this function is shown in Figure 1.2.7, which illustrates how the QTG employs a nonlinear separating surface in order to correctly classify all vertices of the XNOR problem.

Another way of geometrically interpreting the operation of the QTG described by Equation (1.2.8) is possible if we define the product x_1x_2 as a new input x_3. Now we can visualize the surface of Equation (1.2.9) in three dimensions as a plane that properly separates the four vertices (patterns) of the XNOR function (see Problem 1.2.4 for an exploration of this idea).

1.3   General Position and the Function Counting Theorem

In this section we try to answer the following fundamental question: Given m points in $\{0, 1\}^n$, how many dichotomies[5] of these m points are realizable with a single PTG(r), for $r = 1, 2, \ldots, n$? We are also interested in answering the question for the more general case of m points in R^n. But first we present a theorem from classical analysis on the capability of polynomials as approximators of continuous functions.

1.3.1   Weierstrass's Approximation Theorem

THEOREM 1.3.1 (WEIERSTRASS'S APPROXIMATION THEOREM)   Let g be a continuous real-valued function defined on a closed interval $[a, b]$. Then, given any ε positive, there exists a polynomial y (which may depend on ε) with real coefficients such that

$$|g(x) - y(x)| < \varepsilon \tag{1.3.1}$$

for every $x \in [a, b]$.

The proof of this theorem can be found in Apostol (1957).

Theorem 1.3.1 is described by the statement: "Every continuous function can be 'uniformly approximated' by a polynomial." Note that the order of the polynomial depends on the function being approximated and the desired accuracy of the approximation. Weierstrass's approximation theorem also applies for the case of a continuous multivariate function g which maps a compact set $\Sigma \subset R^n$ to a compact set $Y \subset R$ (Narendra and Parthasarathy, 1990). Thus a single PTG of unrestricted order r which employs no thresholding is a universal approximator for continuous functions $g: \Sigma \to Y$.

Theorem 1.3.1 can also be extended to nonpolynomial functions. Let $\{\Phi_1(\mathbf{x}), \ldots, \Phi_d(\mathbf{x})\}$ be a complete *orthonormal set*.[6] Then any g satisfying the requirements of Theorem 1.3.1 can be approximated by a function

---

5. A *dichotomy* is a labeling of m points or objects into two distinct categories.

6. The functions $y_1(x), y_2(x), \ldots$ are *orthogonal* on some interval $[a, b]$ (possibly infinite) if

$$\int_a^b y_i(x) y_j(x)\, dx = 0 \qquad \text{for } i \neq j$$

And these functions are called *orthonormal* on $[a, b]$ if they are orthogonal there and all have norm

$$\|y_i\| = \sqrt{\int_a^b y_i^2(x)\, dx}$$

equal to 1. The set $\{y_i : i = 1, 2, \ldots\}$ is a complete *orthonormal set* if the functions y_i are orthonormal and if

$$y = \sum_{j=1}^{d} w_j \Phi_j(\mathbf{x}) \tag{1.3.2}$$

where the w_j coefficients are real constants.

Polynomials also may be used to approximate binary-valued functions defined on a finite set of points. Examples of such functions are Boolean functions and functions of the form $g: S \rightarrow \{0, 1\}$, where S is a finite set of arbitrary points in R^n. A PTG differs from a polynomial in that it has an intrinsic quantifier (threshold nonlinearity) for the output state. This gives the PTG the natural capability for realizing Boolean functions and complex dichotomies of arbitrary points in R^n. The remainder of this section develops some theoretical results needed to answer the questions raised at the beginning of this section.

1.3.2   Points in General Position

Let us calculate the number of dichotomies of m points in R^n (ways of labeling m points into two distinct categories) achieved by a linear separating surface (i.e., an LTG). We call each of these dichotomies a *linear dichotomy*. For m n-dimensional patterns, the number of linear dichotomies is equal to twice the number of ways in which the m points can be partitioned by an $(n-1)$-dimensional hyperplane (for each distinct partition, there are two different classifications).

As an example, consider the case $m = 4$ and $n = 2$. Figure 1.3.1 shows four points in a two-dimensional space. The lines l_i, $i = 1, \ldots, 7$, give all possible linear partitions of these four points. In particular, consider l_5. It could be the decision surface implementing either of the following: (1) $\mathbf{x}^1$ and $\mathbf{x}^4$ in class 1 and $\mathbf{x}^2$ and $\mathbf{x}^3$ in class 2 or (2) $\mathbf{x}^1$ and $\mathbf{x}^4$ in class 2 and $\mathbf{x}^2$ and $\mathbf{x}^3$ in class 1. Thus one may enumerate all possible linear dichotomies to be equal to 14. If three of the points belong to the same line (Figure 1.3.2), there are only six linear partitions. For $m > n$, we say that a set of m points is in general position in R^n if and only if no subset of $n + 1$ points lies on an $(n-1)$-dimensional hyperplane; for $m \leq n$, a set of m points is in general position if no $(m-2)$-dimensional hyperplane contains the set. Thus the four points of Figure 1.3.1 are in general position, whereas the four points of Figure 1.3.2 are not. Equivalently, a set of m points in R^n is in general position if every subset of n or fewer points (vectors) is linearly independent, which implies that

---

there is no (nontrivial) function orthogonal to each y_i. As an example of a complete orthonormal set in $[0, \pi]$, consider the following family of sinusoids:

$$\left\{ \frac{\sin nx}{\sqrt{\pi}} : n = 1, 2, \ldots \right\}$$

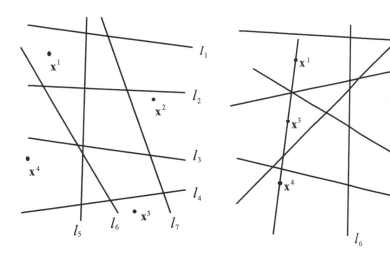

Figure 1.3.1
Points in general position.

Figure 1.3.2
Points not in general position.

$$\text{rank}[\mathbf{x}^1 \quad \mathbf{x}^2 \quad \cdots \quad \mathbf{x}^m] = n \qquad (1.3.3)$$

Note that general position requires a stringent rank condition on the matrix $[\mathbf{x}^1 \quad \mathbf{x}^2 \quad \cdots \quad \mathbf{x}^m]$ (the matrix $[\mathbf{x}^1 \quad \mathbf{x}^2 \quad \cdots \quad \mathbf{x}^m]$ has maximal rank n if at least one $n \times n$ submatrix has a nonzero determinant).

It can be shown (see Section 1.3.3) that for m points in general position with $m \le n + 1$, the total number of linear dichotomies is 2^m. This means that a hyperplane is not constrained by the requirement of correctly classifying $n + 1$ or fewer points in general position. Note that as $n \to \infty$, a set of m random points in R^n is in general position with probability approaching 1.

1.3.3 Function Counting Theorem

The so-called function counting theorem, which counts the number of linearly separable dichotomies of m points in general position in R^d, is essential for estimating the separating capacity of an LTG or a PTG and is considered next. This theorem is also useful in giving an upper bound on the number of linear dichotomies for points in arbitrary position.

THEOREM 1.3.2 (FUNCTION COUNTING THEOREM) (Cover, 1965)   The number of linearly separable dichotomies of m points in general position in Euclidean d-space is

$$C(m,d) = \begin{cases} 2 \displaystyle\sum_{i=0}^{d} \begin{bmatrix} m-1 \\ i \end{bmatrix} & m > d+1 \\ \\ 2^m & m \leq d+1 \end{cases} \qquad (1.3.4)$$

The general position requirement on the m points is a necessary and sufficient condition.

Proof of Theorem 1.3.2   Consider a set of m points $X = \{x^1, x^2, \ldots, x^m\}$ in general position in R^d. Let $C(m,d)$ be the number of linearly separable dichotomies $\{X^+, X^-\}$ of X. Here, X^+ (X^-) is a subset of X consisting of all points which lie above (below) the separating hyperplane.

Consider a new point x^{m+1} such that the set of $m+1$ points $X' = \{x^1, x^2, \ldots, x^{m+1}\}$ is in general position. Now some of the linear dichotomies of the set X can be achieved by hyperplanes which pass through x^{m+1}. Let the number of such dichotomies be D. For each of these D linear dichotomies there will be two new dichotomies, $\{X^+, X^- \cup \{x^{m+1}\}\}$ and $\{X^+ \cup \{x^{m+1}\}, X^-\}$. This occurs because when the points are in general position, any hyperplane through x^{m+1} that realizes the dichotomy $\{X^+, X^-\}$ can be shifted infinitesimally to allow arbitrary classification of x^{m+1} without affecting the separation of the dichotomy $\{X^+, X^-\}$. For the remaining $C(m,d) - D$ dichotomies, either $\{X^+ \cup \{x^{m+1}\}, X^-\}$ or $\{X^+, X^- \cup \{x^{m+1}\}\}$ must be separable. Therefore, there will be one new linear dichotomy for each old one. Thus the number $C(m+1,d)$ of linear dichotomies of X' is given by

$$C(m+1,d) = C(m,d) - D + 2D = C(m,d) + D$$

Again, D is the number of linear dichotomies of X that could have had the dividing hyperplane drawn through x^{m+1}. But this number is simply $C(m, d-1)$, because constraining the hyperplane to go through a particular point x^{m+1} makes the problem effectively $d-1$ dimensional. This observation allows us to obtain the recursion relation

$$C(m+1,d) = C(m,d) + C(m,d-1)$$

The repeated iteration of this relation for $m, m-1, m-2, \ldots, 1$ yields

$$C(m,d) = \sum_{i=0}^{d} \begin{bmatrix} m-1 \\ i \end{bmatrix} C(1,d-1)$$

from which the theorem follows immediately on noting that $C(1,N) = 2$ (one point can be linearly separated into one category or the other) and

$$2 \sum_{i=0}^{d} \begin{bmatrix} m-1 \\ i \end{bmatrix} = 2 \sum_{i=0}^{m-1} \begin{bmatrix} m-1 \\ i \end{bmatrix} = 2^m \text{ for } m \le d+1.$$

Theorem 1.3.2 may now be employed to study the ability of a single LTG to separate m points in general position in R^n. Since the total number of possible dichotomies of m points is 2^m, the probability of a single n-input LTG to separate m points in general position (assuming equal probability for the 2^m dichotomies) is

$$P_{LS}(m,n) = \frac{C(m,n)}{2^m} = \begin{cases} (\tfrac{1}{2})^{m-1} \sum_{i=0}^{n} \begin{bmatrix} m-1 \\ i \end{bmatrix} & m > n+1 \\ \\ 1 & m \le n+1 \end{cases} \tag{1.3.5}$$

Equation (1.3.5) is plotted in Figure 1.3.3. Note that if $m < 2(n+1)$, then as n approaches infinity, P_{LS} approaches 1; i.e., the LTG almost always separates the m points. At $m = 2(n+1)$, exactly one-half of all possible dichotomies of the m points are linearly separable. We refer to $m = 2(n+1)$ as the *statistical capacity* of the LTG.

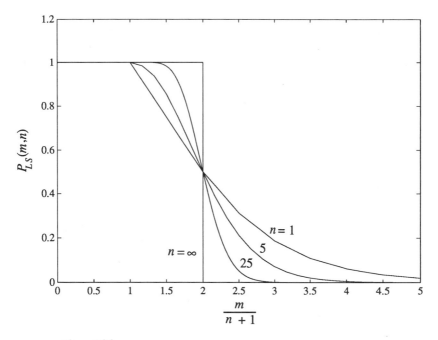

Figure 1.3.3
Probability of linear separability of m points in general position in R^n.

It is noted from Figure 1.3.3 that a single LTG is essentially not capable of handling the classification of m points in general position when $m > 3(n + 1)$.

1.3.4   Separability in ϕ-Space

A PTG(r) with labeled inputs $\mathbf{x} \in R^n$ may be viewed as an LTG with $d - 1$ pre-processed inputs (see Figure 1.3.4), where

$$
d = \begin{bmatrix} n + r \\ r \end{bmatrix} = \frac{(n + r)!}{n!\,r!}.
$$

We refer to the mapping $\phi(\mathbf{x})$ from the input space R^n to the ϕ-space R^{d-1} as the ϕ-mapping. A dichotomy of m points in R^n is said to be "ϕ-separable" by a PTG(r) if there exists a set of $d - 1$ PTG weights and a threshold that correctly classify all m points, i.e., if there exists a $(d - 2)$-dimensional hyperplane in ϕ-space which correctly classifies all m points. The inverse image of this hyperplane in the input space R^n defines a polynomial separating surface of order r, which will be referred to as the ϕ-surface. Note that the function counting theorem still holds true if the set of m points $\{\phi(\mathbf{x}^1), \phi(\mathbf{x}^2), \ldots, \phi(\mathbf{x}^m)\}$ is in general position in ϕ-space or, equivalently for the case $d \leq m$, if no d points lie on the same ϕ-surface in the input space. Here we say $X = \{\mathbf{x}^1, \mathbf{x}^2, \ldots, \mathbf{x}^m\}$ is in ϕ-general position. Therefore, the probability of a single PTG with d degrees of freedom (including threshold) to separate m points in ϕ-general

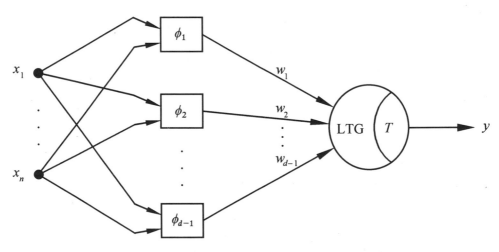

Figure 1.3.4
Block diagram of a PTG represented as the cascade of a fixed preprocessing layer and a single LTG.

position is given by

$$
P_{LS}(m, d-1) = \frac{C(m, d-1)}{2^m} = \begin{cases} (\frac{1}{2})^{m-1} \displaystyle\sum_{i=0}^{d-1} \begin{bmatrix} m-1 \\ i \end{bmatrix} & m > d \\ 1 & m \le d \end{cases} \tag{1.3.6}
$$

Since for an arbitrary set of m points in R^n, the number of ϕ-separable dichotomies $L(m, d-1)$ is less than or equal to the number of ϕ-separable dichotomies of m points in ϕ-general position, we may write

$$
L(m, d-1) \le C(m, d-1) \tag{1.3.7}
$$

Thus the number of Boolean functions $B_n(r)$ of n variables which can be realized by an n-input PTG(r) satisfies

$$
B_n(r) \le C \left[2^n, \sum_{i=1}^{r} \begin{bmatrix} n \\ i \end{bmatrix} \right] \tag{1.3.8}
$$

which is exactly the inequality of Equation (1.2.1).

1.4   Minimal PTG Realization of Arbitrary Switching Functions

THEOREM 1.4.1 (Kashyap, 1966)   Any n-variable switching (Boolean) function of m points with $m \le 2^n$ is realizable using a PTG(r) with m or less terms (degrees of freedom).

Proof of Theorem 1.4.1   Let $g(\mathbf{x})$ represent the weighted-sum signal (the signal just before thresholding) for a PTG with m degrees of freedom (here, the threshold T will be set to zero),

$$
g(\mathbf{x}) = \sum_{i=0}^{m-1} w_i \phi_i(\mathbf{x}) \tag{1.4.1}
$$

where

$$
\phi_i(\mathbf{x}) = \prod_{k=1}^{n} (x_k)^{x_k^i} \tag{1.4.2}
$$

For example, if $n = 4$, $\mathbf{x} = [x_1 \, x_2 \, x_3 \, x_4]^T$, and $\mathbf{x}^i = [1\,1\,0\,1]^T$, Equation (1.4.2) gives $\phi_i(\mathbf{x}) = x_1 x_2 x_4$. Note that by convention $0^0 = 1$. Next, we rearrange the m points (vertices) of a given switching function as $\mathbf{x}^{(0)}, \mathbf{x}^{(1)}, \ldots, \mathbf{x}^{(m-1)}$ so that the number of 1s in $\mathbf{x}^{(i)}$ is larger than or equal to those in $\mathbf{x}^{(j)}$ if $i > j$. To find the separating surface $g(\mathbf{x}) = 0$ that separates the m points into the two designated classes (0 and 1), the function $g(\mathbf{x})$ must satisfy

$$g(\mathbf{x}^{(i)}) = (\mathbf{y}^i)^{\mathsf{T}}\mathbf{w} \begin{cases} \geq 0 & \text{if } \mathbf{x}^{(i)} \in \text{class } 1 \\ < 0 & \text{if } \mathbf{x}^{(i)} \in \text{class } 0 \end{cases} \quad \text{for } i = 0, 1, \ldots, m-1 \qquad (1.4.3)$$

where

$$y_j^i = \phi_j(\mathbf{x}^{(i)}) = \prod_{k=1}^{n} (x_k^{(i)})^{x_k^{(j)}} \qquad (1.4.4)$$

and $\mathbf{w} = [w_0\, w_1\, w_2 \cdots w_{m-1}]^{\mathsf{T}}$ is the PTG weight vector. If the vector $\mathbf{y}$ is normalized by multiplying patterns of class 0 by -1, then Equation (1.4.3) may be rewritten in the following compact form:

$$\mathbf{A}\mathbf{w} = \mathbf{b} > 0 \qquad (1.4.5)$$

where $\mathbf{b}$ is an arbitrary positive margin vector. Here, $\mathbf{A} = \mathbf{TB}$, where $\mathbf{B}$ is defined as the $m \times m$ matrix

$$\mathbf{B} = \begin{bmatrix} (\mathbf{y}^0)^{\mathsf{T}} \\ (\mathbf{y}^1)^{\mathsf{T}} \\ \vdots \\ (\mathbf{y}^{m-1})^{\mathsf{T}} \end{bmatrix} \qquad (1.4.6)$$

and $\mathbf{T}$ is an $m \times m$ diagonal matrix given by

$$\mathbf{T}_{ii} = \begin{cases} 1 & \text{if } \mathbf{x}^i \in \text{class } 1 \\ -1 & \text{if } \mathbf{x}^i \in \text{class } 0 \end{cases} \qquad (1.4.7)$$

The $\mathbf{A}$ matrix is a square matrix, and its singularity depends on the $\mathbf{B}$ matrix. Using Equations (1.4.4) and (1.4.6), the ijth component of $\mathbf{B}$ is given by

$$\mathbf{B}_{ij} = \prod_{k=1}^{n} (x_k^{(i)})^{x_k^{(j)}} \qquad (1.4.8)$$

Since we have assumed that $0^0 = 1$, Equation (1.4.8) gives $\mathbf{B}_{ii} = 1$, for $i = 0, 1, \ldots,$ $m - 1$. Now, since $\mathbf{x}^{(i)}$ has more 1s than $\mathbf{x}^{(j)}$ when $i > j$, then $\mathbf{B}_{ij} = 0$ for $i < j$. Hence $\mathbf{B}$ is a lower triangular and nonsingular matrix. Accordingly, $\mathbf{A}$ is a triangular non-singular matrix; thus the solution vector $\mathbf{w}$ exists and can be easily calculated by forward substitution (e.g., see Gerald, 1978) in Equation (1.4.5). (Note that some of the components of the solution vector $\mathbf{w}$ may be forced to zero with proper selection of the margin vector $\mathbf{b}$). This completes the proof of Theorem 1.4.1.

Example 1.4.1   Consider the partially specified nonthreshold Boolean function in Table 1.4.1. The patterns in Table 1.4.1 are shown sorted in an ascending order in terms of the number of 1s in each pattern. From Equation (1.4.8), the $\mathbf{B}$ matrix is computed as

Table 1.4.1
A Partially Specified Boolean Function for Example 1.4.1

Ordered Patterns	x_1	x_2	x_3	Class
$\mathbf{x}^{(0)}$	0	0	0	1
$\mathbf{x}^{(1)}$	1	0	0	0
$\mathbf{x}^{(2)}$	0	1	0	0
$\mathbf{x}^{(3)}$	1	1	0	1
$\mathbf{x}^{(4)}$	0	1	1	1
$\mathbf{x}^{(5)}$	1	1	1	1

$$\mathbf{B} = \begin{bmatrix} 1 & 0 & 0 & 0 & 0 & 0 \\ 1 & 1 & 0 & 0 & 0 & 0 \\ 1 & 0 & 1 & 0 & 0 & 0 \\ 1 & 1 & 1 & 1 & 0 & 0 \\ 1 & 0 & 1 & 0 & 1 & 0 \\ 1 & 1 & 1 & 1 & 1 & 1 \end{bmatrix}$$

and from Equation (1.4.7), the $\mathbf{T}$ matrix is given by

$$\mathbf{T} = \begin{bmatrix} 1 & 0 & 0 & 0 & 0 & 0 \\ 0 & -1 & 0 & 0 & 0 & 0 \\ 0 & 0 & -1 & 0 & 0 & 0 \\ 0 & 0 & 0 & 1 & 0 & 0 \\ 0 & 0 & 0 & 0 & 1 & 0 \\ 0 & 0 & 0 & 0 & 0 & 1 \end{bmatrix}$$

Thus $\mathbf{A} = \mathbf{T}\mathbf{B}$ is given as

$$\mathbf{A} = \mathbf{T}\mathbf{B} = \begin{bmatrix} 1 & 0 & 0 & 0 & 0 & 0 \\ -1 & -1 & 0 & 0 & 0 & 0 \\ -1 & 0 & -1 & 0 & 0 & 0 \\ 1 & 1 & 1 & 1 & 0 & 0 \\ 1 & 0 & 1 & 0 & 1 & 0 \\ 1 & 1 & 1 & 1 & 1 & 1 \end{bmatrix}$$

Now, using forward substitution in Equation (1.4.5) with $\mathbf{b} = [1 \quad 1 \quad 1 \quad 1 \quad 1 \quad 1]^T$, we arrive at the solution:

$$\mathbf{w} = [1 \quad -2 \quad -2 \quad 4 \quad 2 \quad -2]^T$$

Substituting this $\mathbf{w}$ in Equation (1.4.1) allows us to write the equation for the separating surface (ϕ-surface) realized by the above PTG as

$$g(\mathbf{x}) = 1 - 2x_1 - 2x_2 + 4x_1x_2 + 2x_2x_3 - 2x_1x_2x_3 = 0$$

In general, the margin vector may be chosen in such a way that some of the components of the weight vector $\mathbf{w}$ are forced to zero, thus resulting in a simpler realization of the PTG. Experimental evidence (Kashyap, 1966) indicates that the number of nonzero components of vector $\mathbf{w}$ varies roughly from $m/5$ to about $m/2$. Note also that for $m = 2^n$, Theorem 1.4.1 is equivalent to Theorem 1.2.1. To prove this, we note that according to Theorem 1.4.1, a PTG with

$$d = \sum_{i=1}^{r} \binom{n}{i} + 1 = m$$

is sufficient for guaranteed realizability of m arbitrary points in $\{0, 1\}^n$. Now, for $r = n$, d takes on its largest possible value of 2^n, which is the largest possible value for m. Therefore, any Boolean function of n variables is realizable by a single PTG($r \leq n$) (this proves Theorem 1.2.1).

1.5   Ambiguity and Generalization

Consider the training set $\{\mathbf{x}^1, \mathbf{x}^2, \ldots, \mathbf{x}^m\}$ and a class of decision (separating) surfaces [e.g., ϕ-surfaces associated with a PTG(r)] that separate this set. The classification of a new pattern $\mathbf{y}$ is *ambiguous* relative to the given class of decision surfaces and with respect to the training set if there exist two decision surfaces that both correctly classify the training set but yield different classifications of the new pattern. In Figure 1.5.1, points $\mathbf{y}^1$ and $\mathbf{y}^3$ are unambiguous, but point $\mathbf{y}^2$ is ambiguous for the class of linear decision surfaces. In the context of a single threshold gate, it can be shown (Cover, 1965) that the number of training patterns must exceed the statistical capacity of a threshold gate before ambiguity is eliminated.

Generalization is the ability of a network (here, a PTG) to correctly classify new patterns. Consider the problem of generalizing from a training set with respect to a given admissible family of decision surfaces (e.g., the family of surfaces that can be implemented by a PTG). During the training phase, a decision (separating) surface from the admissible class is synthesized which correctly assigns members of the train-

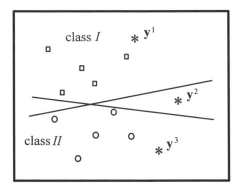

Figure 1.5.1
Ambiguous generalization. The points $\mathbf{y}^1$ and $\mathbf{y}^3$ are
uniquely classified regardless of which of the two lin-
ear decision surfaces shown is used. The point $\mathbf{y}^2$ has
an ambiguous classification.

ing set to the desired categories. The new pattern will be assigned to the category lying
on the same side of the decision surface. Clearly, for some dichotomies of the training
set, the assignment of category will not be unique. However, it is generally known that
if a large number of training patterns are used, the decision surface will be sufficiently
constrained to yield a unique response to a new pattern. Next, we show that the
number of training patterns must exceed the statistical capacity of the PTG before
unique response becomes probable.

THEOREM 1.5.1 (Cover, 1965)   Let $X \cup \{\mathbf{y}\} = \{\mathbf{x}^1, \mathbf{x}^2, \ldots, \mathbf{x}^m, \mathbf{y}\}$ be in ϕ-general position in R^{d-1}. Then $\mathbf{y}$ is ambiguous with respect to $C(m, d-2)$ dichotomies of X
relative to the class of all ϕ-surfaces.

Proof of Theorem 1.5.1   The point $\mathbf{y}$ is ambiguous with respect to a dichotomy
$\{X^+, X^-\}$ of $X = \{\mathbf{x}^1, \mathbf{x}^2, \ldots, \mathbf{x}^m\}$ if and only if there exists a ϕ-surface containing $\mathbf{y}$
that separates $\{X^+, X^-\}$. This is so because when X is in ϕ-general position, any
ϕ-surface through $\mathbf{y}$ that realizes the dichotomy $\{X^+, X^-\}$ can be shifted infinitesimally to allow arbitrary classification of $\mathbf{y}$ without affecting the separation of
$\{X^+, X^-\}$. Equivalently, since ϕ-general position of $X \cup \{\mathbf{y}\}$ implies that the set of
points $Z \cup \{\phi(\mathbf{y})\} = \{\phi(\mathbf{x}^1), \phi(\mathbf{x}^2), \ldots, \phi(\mathbf{x}^m), \phi(\mathbf{y})\}$ is in general position in R^{d-1}, the
point $\phi(\mathbf{y})$ is ambiguous with respect to the linear dichotomy $\{Z^+, Z^-\}$ (here each
linear dichotomy of Z, $\{Z^+, Z^-\}$, corresponds to a unique ϕ-separable dichotomy
$\{X^+, X^-\}$ in the input space). Hence the point $\phi(\mathbf{y})$ is ambiguous with respect to D
linear dichotomies $\{Z^+, Z^-\}$ that can be separated by a $(d-2)$-dimensional hyperplane constrained to pass through $\phi(\mathbf{y})$. Constraining the hyperplane to pass through

a point effectively reduces the dimension of the space by 1. Thus, by Theorem 1.3.2, $D = C(m, d - 2)$. Now, by noting the one-to-one correspondence between the linear separable dichotomies in ϕ-space and the ϕ-separable dichotomies in the input space, we establish that $\mathbf{y}$ is ambiguous with respect to $C(m, d - 2)$ ϕ-separable dichotomies of X.

Now, if each of the ϕ-separable dichotomies of X has equal probability, then the probability $A(m, d)$ that $\mathbf{y}$ is ambiguous with respect to a random ϕ-separable dichotomy of X is

$$A(m, d) = \frac{C(m, d - 2)}{C(m, d - 1)} = \begin{cases} \dfrac{\displaystyle\sum_{i=0}^{d-2} \begin{bmatrix} m - 1 \\ i \end{bmatrix}}{\displaystyle\sum_{i=0}^{d-1} \begin{bmatrix} m - 1 \\ i \end{bmatrix}} & m \geq d \\[4ex] 1 & m < d \end{cases} \qquad (1.5.1)$$

Example 1.5.1   Let us apply the preceding theorem to a problem with $m = 10$ points in general position in R^2. A new point $\mathbf{y}$ is ambiguous with respect to $C(10, 1) = 20$ dichotomies of the m points relative to the class of all lines in the plane (here, $d = 3$). Now, $C(10, 2) = 92$ dichotomies of the m points are separable by the class of all lines in the plane. Thus a new point $\mathbf{y}$ is ambiguous with respect to a random, linearly separable dichotomy of the m points with probability

$$A(10, 3) = \frac{C(10, 1)}{C(10, 2)} = \frac{5}{23}$$

The behavior of $A(m, d)$ for large d is given by (Cover, 1965)

$$A^*(\beta) = \lim_{\substack{m = \beta d \\ d \to \infty}} A(m, d) = \begin{cases} 1 & 0 \leq \beta \leq 2 \\ \dfrac{1}{\beta - 1} & \beta > 2 \end{cases} \qquad (1.5.2)$$

where $\beta = m/d$. The function $A^*(\beta)$ is plotted in Figure 1.5.2. It is interesting to note that according to Equation (1.5.2), ambiguous response is reduced only when $\beta > 2$; i.e., when m is larger than the statistical capacity of the PTG (or more generally, the separating surface used).

To eliminate ambiguity, we need $\beta \gg 2$ or $m \gg 2d$; i.e., a large number of training samples is required. If we define $0 \leq \varepsilon \leq 1$ as the probability of generalization error, then we can determine the number of samples required to achieve a desired ε. Assume that we choose m points (patterns) from a given distribution such that these points are

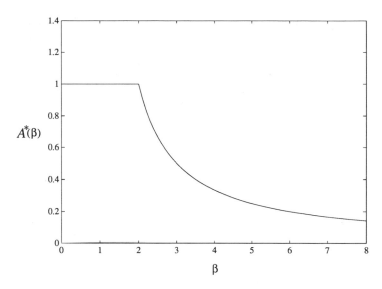

Figure 1.5.2
Asymptotic probability of ambiguous response.

in general position and they are classified independently with equal probability into one of two categories. Then the probability of generalization error on a new pattern similarly chosen, conditioned on the separability of the entire set, is equal to $\frac{1}{2}A(m,d)$. Therefore, as $d \to \infty$, one can employ Equation (1.5.2) and show that m must satisfy

$$m \geq \frac{1+2\varepsilon}{2\varepsilon}d \qquad (1.5.3)$$

in order to bound the probability of generalization error below ε. Thus we find that the probability of generalization error for a single threshold gate with d degrees of freedom approaches zero as fast as $d/2m$ in the limit of $m \gg d$.

1.6 Extreme Points

For any linear dichotomy $\{X^+, X^-\}$ of a set of points, there exists a minimal sufficient subset of *extreme points* such that any hyperplane correctly separating this subset must separate the entire set correctly. From this definition, it follows that a point is an extreme point of the linear dichotomy $\{X^+, X^-\}$ if and only if it is ambiguous with respect to $\{X^+, X^-\}$. Thus, for a set of m points in general position in R^d, each of the

m points is ambiguous with respect to precisely $C(m-1, d-1)$ linear dichotomies of the remaining $m-1$ points. Here, each of the $C(m-1, d-1)$ dichotomies is the restriction of two linearly separable dichotomies of the original m points; the two dichotomies differ only in the classification of the remaining point. Therefore, each of the m points is an extreme point with respect to $2C(m-1, d-1)$ dichotomies. Since there are a total of $C(m, d)$ linearly separable dichotomies, the probability P_e of a point being an extreme point with respect to a randomly generated dichotomy is (assuming equiprobable dichotomies)

$$P_e(m, d) = \frac{2C(m-1, d-1)}{C(m, d)} \tag{1.6.1}$$

Then the expected number of extreme points in a set of m points in general position in R^d is equal to the sum of the m probabilities that each point is an extreme point. Since these probabilities are equal, the expected number of extreme points can be written as

$$mP_e(m, d) = \frac{2mC(m-1, d-1)}{C(m, d)} \tag{1.6.2}$$

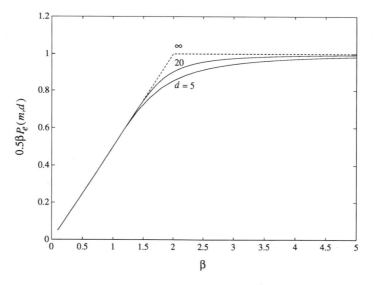

Figure 1.6.1
Normalized expected number of extreme points for $d = 5, 20$, and ∞ as a function of $\beta = m/d$.

Figure 1.6.1 illustrates the effect of the size of the training set m on the normalized expected number of extreme points $\dfrac{mP_e(m,d)}{2d} = \dfrac{1}{2}\beta P_e(m,d)$. For large d, the normalized expected number of extreme points is given by (Cover, 1965)

$$\lim_{\substack{m=\beta d \\ d\to\infty}} \tfrac{1}{2}\beta P_e(m,d) = \begin{cases} \dfrac{\beta}{2} & 0 \leq \beta \leq 2 \\[2mm] 1 & \beta > 2 \end{cases} \tag{1.6.3}$$

which agrees with the simulation results in Figure 1.6.1 for $d \to \infty$. The preceding limit on the expected number of extreme points implies, roughly, that for a random separable set of m patterns, the average number of patterns (information) that need to be stored for a complete characterization of the whole set is only twice the number of degrees of freedom of the class of separating surfaces being used. The implication for pattern recognition is that the essential information in an infinite training set can be expected to be loaded into a network of finite capacity (e.g., a PTG of finite order or a finite network of simple gates).

1.7 Summary

This chapter introduces the LTG as the basic computational unit in a binary-state neural network and analyzes its computational capabilities in realizing binary mappings. The LTG is then extended to the more powerful PTG. A single LTG can only realize threshold (linearly separable) functions. On the other hand, a PTG with order $r \leq n$ is capable of realizing any Boolean function of n inputs. The impressive computational power of a PTG comes at the expense of increased implementation complexity.

The notion of a separating surface is introduced and is used to describe the operation of a threshold gate as a two-class classifier. It is found that a single LTG is characterized by a linear separating surface (hyperplane). On the other hand, a single PTG is capable of realizing a highly flexible nonlinear (polynomial) separating surface. The flexibility of a PTG's separating surface is due to a dimensionality expanding polynomial mapping (ϕ-mapping) realized by a preprocessing layer intrinsic to the PTG.

A fundamental theorem, known as the function counting theorem, is proved and is used to derive the following important properties of threshold gates. First, the statistical capacity of a single LTG, assuming data in general position in R^n, is equal to twice the number of its degrees of freedom (weights). This result is also true for a PTG.

Second, a threshold gate with d degrees of freedom trained to correctly classify m patterns will, on average, respond ambiguously to a new input pattern as long as $m \leq 2d$. In this context, it is found that the probability of generalization error approaches zero asymptotically as $d/2m$. Finally, in the limit as $d \to \infty$, we find that the average number of patterns needed for complete characterization of a given training set is only twice the number of degrees of freedom d of a threshold gate, assuming the separability of this training set by the threshold gate.

Problems

1.1.1 Verify that the patterns in Figure 1.1.5 are admissible threshold patterns.

1.1.2 Derive the formulas given in Table 1.1.2 for degrees of freedom for real and binary input QTGs.

1.1.3 Prove that a PTG(r) with n binary inputs has

$$\sum_{i=1}^{r} \begin{bmatrix} n \\ i \end{bmatrix}$$

degrees of freedom, not including threshold.

1.1.4 Derive the closed-form expression for the number of degrees of freedom for a PTG(r) given in Equation (1.1.8).

1.2.1 Show that

$$\lim_{r \to n} \sum_{i=1}^{r} \begin{bmatrix} n \\ i \end{bmatrix} + 1 = 2^n.$$

Also, show that

$$2 \sum_{i=0}^{m-1} \begin{bmatrix} m-1 \\ i \end{bmatrix} = 2^m.$$

1.2.2 a. Prove algebraically that

$$\begin{bmatrix} n+1 \\ i \end{bmatrix} = \begin{bmatrix} n \\ i-1 \end{bmatrix} + \begin{bmatrix} n \\ i \end{bmatrix},$$

for $1 \leq i \leq n$.

b. Prove by induction, using the recursion relation in part a, the binomial theorem:

$$(\alpha + \beta)^n = \sum_{i=0}^{n} \binom{n}{i} \alpha^i \beta^{n-i}$$

where α and β are real numbers and n is an integer.

c. Use the binomial theorem to prove that $\displaystyle\sum_{i=0}^{n} \binom{n}{i} (-1)^i = 0.$

1.2.3 Verify the inequality in Equation (1.2.5) by showing that $C(2^n, n) < 2^{n^2}$ for $n \geq 2$.

1.2.4 Plot the function

$$g(x_1, x_2) = -x_1 - x_2 + ax_1 x_2 + \tfrac{1}{2} = 0$$

for $a = 2$ and 3. Now let $x_3 = x_1 x_2$. Plot $g(x_1, x_2, x_3) = 0$. Show that the four patterns of the XNOR function of Example 1.2.1 are properly separated by g.

*1.3.1 Prove that

$$\lim_{\substack{n \to \infty \\ m < 2(n+1)}} (\tfrac{1}{2})^{m-1} \sum_{i=0}^{n} \binom{m-1}{i} = 1$$

and that

$$\lim_{\substack{n \to \infty \\ m > 2(n+1)}} (\tfrac{1}{2})^{m-1} \sum_{i=0}^{n} \binom{m-1}{i} = 0.$$

Also, show that if $m = 2(n + 1)$, then

$$(\tfrac{1}{2})^{m-1} \sum_{i=0}^{n} \binom{m-1}{i} = \frac{1}{2}.$$

1.3.2 Assuming that

$$n < m \leq d = \binom{n+r}{r},$$

is it true that m points in general position in R^n are mapped by the ϕ-mapping of a PTG(r) into points in general position in R^{d-1} space (i.e., ϕ-general position)? Why? Can this PTG map m arbitrary points in R^n into m points in ϕ-general position? Explain.

*1.3.3 Given m arbitrary points in R^n space, show that for $m \geq 3n + 2$ and $n \geq 2$, the number of dichotomies of the m points that are realizable with a single LTG is bounded from above by $2m^n/n!$. [*Hint*: Use Equation (1.3.7) adapted for the LTG case, with $d - 1 = n$.] Note that this bound reduces to $2^{n^2+1}/n!$ for $m = 2^n$, which represents a tighter upper bound than that of Equation (1.2.5). Use this result to show that

$$\lim_{n \to \infty} \frac{\log_2 B_n(1)}{n^2} = 1$$

1.3.4 Consider a mapping $f: R \to R$, defined as the set of input/output pairs $\{x^i, y^i\}$, $i = 1, 2, \ldots, m$. Assume that $x^i \neq x^j$ for all $i \neq j$. Show that this mapping can be exactly realized by a polynomial of order $r = m - 1$ (this is referred to as "strict" interpolation). *Hint*: The determinant

$$D_m = \begin{vmatrix} 1 & 1 & \cdots & 1 \\ z_1 & z_2 & \cdots & z_m \\ z_1^2 & z_2^2 & \cdots & z_m^2 \\ \vdots & \vdots & \ddots & \vdots \\ z_1^{m-1} & z_2^{m-1} & \cdots & z_m^{m-1} \end{vmatrix}$$

is the Vandermonde's determinant, which is nonzero if $z_i \neq z_j$, for all $i \neq j = 1$, $2, \ldots, m$.

*1.3.5 Consider the mapping from $\{0, 1, 2, 3, 4\}$ to $\{0, 1\}$ defined by the input/output pairs $(0, 0)$, $(1, 1)$, $(2, 0)$, $(3, 0)$, and $(4, 1)$. Use the result of Problem 1.3.4 to synthesize a polynomial $g(x)$ of minimal order that realizes the preceding mapping. Plot $g(x)$ to verify your solution. Next, assume that a PTG(r) is used to realize the same mapping. Is it possible for the order r of this PTG to be smaller than that of the polynomial $g(x)$? If the answer is yes, then synthesize the appropriate weights for this PTG (assume a zero threshold), and plot the weighted sum (i.e., the PTG output without thresholding) versus x.

1.3.6 Derive Equation (1.3.4) from the recursion relation

$$C(m + 1, d) = C(m, d) + C(m, d - 1).$$

1.3.7 Let $y(x) = a + bx$, where $a, b \in R$. Find the parameters a and b which minimize

a. $\displaystyle\int_{-1}^{+1} [x^2 - y(x)]^2\, dx$

b. $\displaystyle\int_{0}^{1/2} [e^x - y(x)]^2\, dx$

1.3.8 Find the polynomial $y(x) = ax + bx^3$ that approximates the function $g(x) = \sin x$ over $[0, \alpha]$ by minimizing $\displaystyle\int_{0}^{\alpha} [g(x) - y(x)]^2\, dx$. Compare graphically the function $g(x)$, its approximation $y(x)$, and its power series approximation $g(x) \approx x - \dfrac{x^3}{6}$ for $\alpha = \pi/4$ and $\pi/2$.

1.4.1 Find the solution vector **w** in Example 1.4.1 if $\mathbf{b} = [1 \quad 1 \quad 1 \quad 1 \quad 1 \quad 3]^T$. Use the K-map technique to show that the Boolean function in Table 1.4.1 is not a threshold function. Does a $\mathbf{b} > \mathbf{0}$ exist which leads to a solution vector **w** with four or fewer nonzero components?

1.4.2 Use the method of Section 1.4 to synthesize a PTG for realizing the Boolean function $y = \bar{x}_1 x_3 + \bar{x}_2 x_3$. Use a margin vector **b** that results in the minimal number of nonzero PTG weights.

***1.5.1** Derive Equation (1.5.2). See Cover (1965) for hints.

†**1.5.2** Plot the probability of ambiguous response $A(m, d)$ given in Equation (1.5.1) versus $\beta = m/d$, for $d = 2, 10$, and 20.

1.5.3 Derive Equation (1.5.3).

***1.6.1** Derive Equation (1.6.3), starting from Equation (1.6.2).

2 Computational Capabilities of Artificial Neural Networks

In the preceding chapter, the computational capabilities of single LTGs and PTGs were investigated. This chapter considers networks of LTGs and investigates their mapping capabilities. The function-approximating capabilities of networks of units (artificial neurons) with continuous nonlinear activation functions are also investigated. In particular, some important theoretical results on the approximation of arbitrary multivariate continuous functions by feedforward multilayer neural networks are presented. This chapter concludes with a brief section on neural network computational complexity and the efficiency of neural network hardware implementation. In the remainder of this book, the terms *artificial neural network*, *neural network*, *network*, and *net* will be used interchangeably unless otherwise noted.

Before proceeding any further, note that the n-input PTG(r) of Chapter 1 can be considered as a form of a neural network with a "fixed" preprocessing (hidden) layer feeding into a single LTG in its output layer, as was shown in Figure 1.3.4. Furthermore, Theorems 1.2.1 and 1.3.1 (extended to multivariate functions) establish the "universal" realization capability of this architecture for continuous functions of the form $f: \Sigma \subset R^n \to Y \subset R$ (assuming that the output unit has a linear activation function) and for Boolean functions of the form $f: \{0, 1\}^n \to \{0, 1\}$, respectively. Here, universality means that the approximation of an arbitrary continuous function can be made to any degree of accuracy. Note that for continuous functions, the order r of the PTG may become very large. On the other hand, for Boolean functions, universality means that the realization is exact. Here, $r \leq n$ is sufficient. The following sections consider other more interesting neural net architectures and present important results on their computational capabilities.

2.1 Some Preliminary Results on Neural Network Mapping Capabilities

This section defines some basic LTG network architectures and derives bounds on the number of arbitrary functions they can realize. The realizations of both Boolean and multivariate functions of the form $f: R^n \to \{0, 1\}$ are considered.

2.1.1 Network Realization of Boolean Functions

A well-known result from switching theory [e.g., see Kohavi (1978)] is that any switching function (Boolean function) of n variables can be realized using a two-layer network with at most 2^{n-1} AND gates in the first (hidden) layer and a single OR gate in the second (output) layer, assuming that the input variables and their complements are available as inputs. This network is known as the *AND-OR network* and is shown in Figure 2.1.1. The parity function is a Boolean function that requires the largest

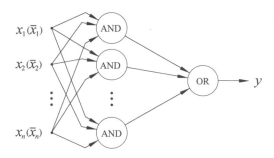

Figure 2.1.1
AND-OR network structure.

	00	01	11	10
00	0	1	0	1
01	1	0	1	0
11	0	1	0	1
10	1	0	1	0

$x_3\ x_4$

$x_1\ x_2$

Figure 2.1.2
K-map for the four-input parity function.

network, i.e., the network with 2^{n-1} AND gates. For the case $n = 4$, the K-map of the parity function is shown in Figure 2.1.2.

It was shown in Chapter 1 that a single LTG is a more powerful logic gate than a single AND (or OR) gate. Thus one may replace the hidden layer AND gates in Figure 2.1.1 with LTGs and still retain the universal logic property of the AND-OR network. [The universality of a properly interconnected network of simple threshold gates was first noted in a classic paper by McCulloch and Pitts (1943).] The resulting net with the LTGs does not require the complements of the input variables as inputs, as for the AND-OR net. This LTG net will be referred to as a *threshold-OR net*. Given the same switching function, the threshold-OR net may require a smaller number of gates compared with an AND-OR net. The parity function, though, is an example where the required number of AND gates is equal to the number of threshold gates in both nets, i.e., 2^{n-1} gates. Note that a fewer number of hidden LTGs than AND gates are needed if the LTG net employs an LTG for the output unit. However, it can be shown (see Section 2.2.1) that $2^n/n^2$ hidden LTGs would still be necessary for realizing arbitrary Boolean functions in the limit of large n. Another interesting result is that a two-hidden-layer net with $(1/\sqrt{n})2^{n/2+1}$ LTGs is necessary for realizing arbitrary Boolean functions (see Section 2.2.2 for details). Here, $2^{n/2+1}$ LTGs are sufficient.

The synthesis of threshold-OR and other LTG nets for the realization of arbitrary switching functions was studied extensively in the sixties and early seventies. A recommended brief introduction to this subject appears in the book by Kohavi (1978). In fact, several books and Ph.D. dissertations have been written on threshold logic networks and their synthesis (refer to the introduction of Chapter 1 for references). This section gives only a simple illustrative example employing the K-map technique (the K-map was introduced in Section 1.1.1) to realize the Boolean function $f(\mathbf{x})$ in Figure 2.1.3a. Figure 2.1.3b shows one possible decomposition of $f(\mathbf{x})$ into a minimal number of threshold patterns (single LTG realizable patterns) $f_1(\mathbf{x})$ and $f_2(\mathbf{x})$. The corresponding architecture for the threshold-OR net realization is depicted in Figure 2.1.3c. This K-map-based synthesis technique may be extended to multiple output nets (see Problem 2.1.2) but is only practical for $n \leq 5$.

The following theorem establishes an upper bound on the size of a feedforward net of LTGs for realizing arbitrary, partially specified switching functions.

THEOREM 2.1.1 Consider a partially specified switching function $f(\mathbf{x})$ defined on a set of m arbitrary points in $\{0, 1\}^n$, with $m \leq 2^n$. Then, a two-layer net of LTGs employing m LTGs in its hidden layer, feeding into a single output LTG, is sufficient to realize $f(\mathbf{x})$.

Proof of Theorem 2.1.1 This theorem can be viewed as a corollary of Theorem 1.4.1 (see Problem 2.1.3).

Theorem 2.1.1 can be easily extended to the case of multiple output switching functions of the form $f: \{0, 1\}^n \rightarrow \{0, 1\}^L$. Here, the worst-case scenario is to duplicate the preceding network L times, where L is the number of output functions. This leads to a sufficient LTG net realization having mL LTGs in its hidden layer and L LTGs in its output layer.

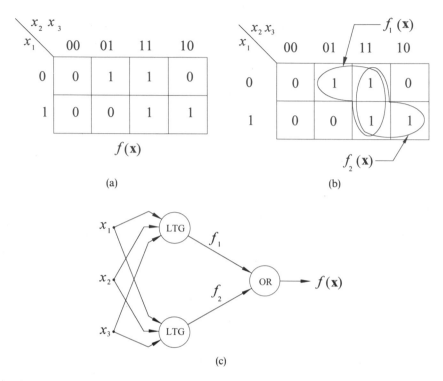

Figure 2.1.3
Threshold-OR realization of a three-input switching function $f(\mathbf{x})$: (a) K-map for $f(\mathbf{x})$; (b) K-map decomposition of $f(\mathbf{x})$ into two threshold functions; and (c) threshold-OR realization of $f(\mathbf{x})$.

2.1.2 Bounds on the Number of Functions Realizable by a Feedforward Network of LTGs

Consider the following question: "How many functions $f: R^n \to \{0, 1\}$ defined on m arbitrary points in R^n are realizable by a layered net of k LTGs?" In the discussion that follows, this question is answered for three different network architectures: (1) a single-hidden-layer feedforward network, (2) an arbitrarily interconnected net with no feedback, and (3) a two-hidden-layer feedforward network. All three nets are assumed to be fully interconnected.

Consider a feedforward net with k LTGs in its hidden layer, all feeding into a single LTG in the output layer, as shown in Figure 2.1.4. We can show that for m arbitrary points in R^n, with $m \geq 3n + 2$ and $n \geq 2$, this net can realize at most $F_1(n, m, k)$ functions, with F_1 given by (Winder, 1963)

$$F_1(n, m, k) = \frac{2^{k+1} m^{(n+1)k}}{(n!)^k k!} \tag{2.1.1}$$

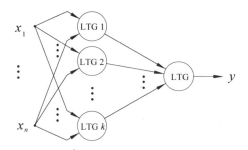

Figure 2.1.4
A two-layer feedforward net with k hidden LTGs feeding into a single-output LTG.

Proof   Each of the k LTGs can realize at most (Winder, 1963; also recall Problem 1.3.3)

$$\frac{2m^n}{n!}$$

functions (dichotomies), and the final LTG can realize at most

$$\frac{2m^k}{n!}$$

functions. Therefore, the network can realize no more than

$$\left(\frac{2m^n}{n!}\right)^k \frac{2m^k}{k!} \qquad \text{or} \qquad \frac{2^{k+1}m^{(n+1)k}}{(n!)^k k!}$$

functions.

Another interesting type of network is the generally fully interconnected net of k LTGs with no feedback, as shown in Figure 2.1.5. This type of network can realize at most $G(n, m, k)$ functions with G given by

$$G(n, m, k) = \frac{2^k m^{[nk + k(k-1)/2]}}{(n!)^k} \tag{2.1.2}$$

Proof   Since there is no feedback, the gates (LTGs) can be ordered as first gate, second gate, $\ldots$, kth gate so that the jth gate only receives inputs from the n independent input variables and the $j - 1$ gates labeled $1, 2, \ldots, j - 1$ (see Figure 2.1.5). The jth gate can then realize at most

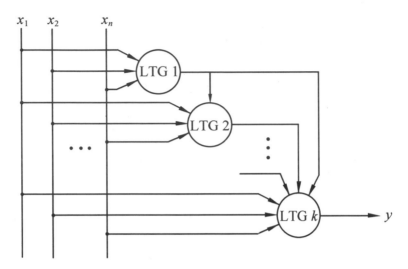

Figure 2.1.5
Generally fully interconnected net of k LTGs with no feedback.

$$\frac{2m^{(n+j-1)}}{(n+j-1)!}$$

functions. The total network can realize at most

$$\left(\frac{2m^n}{n!}\right)\left[\frac{2m^{n+1}}{(n+1)!}\right]\cdots\left[\frac{2m^{(n+j-1)}}{(n+j-1)!}\right]\cdots\left[\frac{2m^{(n+k-1)}}{(n+k-1)!}\right]$$

functions, which is less than

$$2^k\frac{m^n m^{n+1}\cdots m^{n+j-1}\cdots m^{n+k-1}}{(n!)^k}$$

This last result can be simplified to

$$\frac{2^k m^{[nk+k(k-1)/2]}}{(n!)^k}$$

Similarly, it can be shown that the feedforward net shown in Figure 2.1.6 with two hidden layers of $k/2$ LTGs each and with a single-output LTG is capable of realizing at most

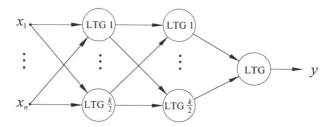

Figure 2.1.6
A three-layer LTG net having $k/2$ units in each of the two hidden layers and a single-output LTG.

$$F_2(n, m, k) = \left(\frac{2m^n}{n!}\right)^{k/2} \left[\frac{2m^{k/2}}{(k/2)!}\right]^{k/2} \left[\frac{2m^{k/2}}{(k/2)!}\right] = \left[\frac{4m^{n+k/2+1}}{n!\,(k/2)!}\right]^{k/2} \frac{2}{(k/2)!} \qquad (2.1.3)$$

functions.

Similar bounds can be derived for points in general position simply by replacing the $2m^d/d!$ bound on the number of realizable functions by the tighter bound $2^{2(d+1)}$ for input units (units receiving direct connections from all components of the input vector), since the statistical capacity of a single d-input LTG is $2(d + 1)$ points, for large d (refer to Section 1.3.3).

2.2   Necessary Lower Bounds on the Size of LTG Networks

In this section we derive necessary lower bounds on the number of gates k in a network of LTGs for realizing any function $f\colon R^n \to \{0, 1\}$ of m points arbitrarily chosen in R^n. For the case of functions defined on m points in general position, similar bounds are also derived. Again, we consider the three network architectures of Section 2.1.2.

2.2.1   Two-Layer Feedforward Networks

Case 1: m Arbitrary Points   Consider the function $f\colon R^n \to \{0, 1\}$ defined on m arbitrary points in R^n. Here, we show that a two-layer feedforward net with less than $m/[n \log_2 (me/n)]$ LTGs in its hidden layer is not sufficient to realize such an arbitrary function (in the limit of large n). Recalling Equation (2.1.1) and requiring that $F_1(n, m, k)$ be larger than or equal to the total number of possible binary functions of

m points, we get (assuming $m \geq 3n + 2$ and $n \geq 2$)

$$2^m \leq \frac{2^{k+1} m^{(n+1)k}}{(n!)^k k!} = \frac{2(2m^{n+1}/n!)^k}{k!} \tag{2.2.1}$$

We may solve for k as a function of m and n. Taking the logarithm (base 2) of Equation (2.2.1) and rearranging terms, we get

$$k \geq \frac{m - 1 + \log_2 k!}{1 + (n + 1)\log_2 m - \log_2 n!} \tag{2.2.2}$$

By employing Sterling's approximation $n! \approx \sqrt{2\pi n}(n/e)^n$, we can write

$$\log_2 n! \approx \log_2 \sqrt{2\pi n} + n \log_2 \frac{n}{e}$$

$$\approx n \log_2 \frac{n}{e}$$

where a large n is assumed. Similarly, we employ the approximation $\log_2 k! \approx k \log_2 (k/e) + \log_2 \sqrt{2\pi k}$. Now, Equation (2.2.2) reduces to

$$k \geq \frac{m - 1 + \log_2 \sqrt{2\pi k}}{1 + n \log_2 \dfrac{me}{n} + \log_2 \dfrac{me}{k}} \approx \frac{m}{n \log_2 \dfrac{me}{n}} \tag{2.2.3}$$

with $m \geq 3n$ and $n \to \infty$. Equation (2.2.3) gives a necessary condition on the size of the net for realizing any function of m arbitrary points in R^n. It is interesting to note the usefulness of this bound by comparing it with the sufficient net constructed by Baum (1988), which requires $4m/[n \log_2 (m/n)]$ hidden LTGs.

As a special case, we may consider an arbitrary completely specified ($m = 2^n$) Boolean function with $\mathbf{x} \in \{0, 1\}^n$. Here, Equation (2.2.3) with $m = 2^n$ gives

$$k \geq \frac{2^n}{n^2 - n \log_2 \dfrac{n}{e}} \approx \frac{2^n}{n^2} \tag{2.2.4}$$

which means that as $n \to \infty$, an infinitely large net is required. A limiting case of Equation (2.2.3) is for $m/n \to \infty$, which leads to the bound

$$k \geq \frac{m}{n \log_2 m} \tag{2.2.5}$$

Case 2: m Points in General Position   Recalling Equation (1.3.5) and the discussion in Section 1.3.3 on the statistical capacity of a single LTG, one can determine an upper bound F_{GP} on the number of possible functions (dichotomies) on m points in general position in R^n for a two-layer feedforward net with k hidden units as

$$F_{GP} = (2^{2(n+1)})^k \frac{2m^k}{k!} \tag{2.2.6}$$

for $n \to \infty$. The first term on the right-hand side of Equation (2.2.6) represents the total number of functions realizable by the k-hidden-layer LTGs, where each LTG is capable of realizing $2^{2(n+1)}$ functions. On the other hand, the term $2m^k/k!$ in Equation (2.2.6) represents an upper bound on the number of functions realized by the output LTG. It assumes that the hidden layer transforms the m points in general position in R^n to points that are not necessarily in general position in the hidden space R^k.

   For the net to be able to realize any one of the preceding functions, its hidden layer size k must satisfy

$$2^m \le F_{GP} \le \frac{2m^k 2^{2k(n+1)}}{\left(\dfrac{k}{e}\right)^k} \tag{2.2.7}$$

or

$$k \ge \frac{m-1}{2n + \log_2 \dfrac{me}{k}} \approx \frac{m}{2n} \tag{2.2.8}$$

This bound is tight for m close to $2n$; it gives $k = 1$, which is the optimal net (recall that any dichotomy of m points in general position in R^n has a probability approaching 1 to be realized by a single LTG as long as $m \le 2n$ for large n). Note that when there is only a single LTG in the hidden layer, the output LTG becomes redundant.

   Equation (2.2.8) agrees with the early experimental results reported by Widrow and Angell (1962). Also, it is interesting to note that in the limit as $m/n \to \infty$, Equation (2.2.8) gives a lower bound on k, which is equal to one-half the number of hidden LTGs of the optimal net reported by Baum (1988). It is important to note that the bounds on k derived using this approach are relatively tighter for the m points in the general position case than for the case of m points in arbitrary position. This is because we are using the actual statistical capacity of an LTG for the general position case as opposed to the upper bound on the number of dichotomies being used for the arbitrary position case. This observation is also valid for the bounds derived in the remainder of this section.

2.2.2 Three-Layer Feedforward Networks

Case 1: *m* Arbitrary Points   Consider a two-hidden-layer net having $k/2$ (k is even) LTGs in each of its hidden layers and a single LTG in its output layer. From Equation (2.1.3), the net is capable of realizing at most

$$F_2(n, m, k) = \left(\frac{2m^n}{n!}\right)^{k/2} \left[\frac{2m^{k/2}}{(k/2)!}\right]^{k/2} \frac{2m^{k/2}}{(k/2)!}$$

arbitrary functions. Following earlier derivations, we can bound the necessary net size by

$$2^m \leq F_2(n, m, k) \tag{2.2.9}$$

for $m \geq 3n$ and $n \rightarrow \infty$. Next, taking the logarithm of both sides of Equation (2.2.9) and employing Sterling's approximation gives

$$m \leq \frac{k}{2}\left[\left(n + \frac{k}{2}\right)\log_2 \frac{me}{n} + \left(\frac{k}{2} + 1\right)\log_2 \frac{2me}{k}\right] \approx \frac{k}{2}\left(n + \frac{k}{2}\right)\log_2 \frac{me}{n} \tag{2.2.10}$$

which can be solved for k as

$$k \geq -n + \sqrt{n^2 + \frac{4m}{\log_2 \dfrac{me}{n}}} \tag{2.2.11}$$

Assuming that $m \gg n^2$, Equation (2.2.11) can be approximated as

$$k \geq 2\sqrt{\frac{m}{\log_2 \dfrac{me}{n}}} \approx 2\sqrt{\frac{m}{\log_2 m}} \tag{2.2.12}$$

For the special case of arbitrary Boolean functions with $m = 2^n$, Equation (2.2.12) gives a lower bound of $(1/\sqrt{n})2^{n/2+1}$ hidden LTGs. An upper bound of $2^{n/2+1}$ on the number of hidden LTGs was reported by Muroga (1959).

Case 2: *m* Points in General Position   Here, we start from the relation

$$2^m \leq 2^{2(n+1)(k/2)} 2^{2(k/2+1)(k/2)} 2^{2(k/2+1)} = 2^{k(n+k/2+3)+2} \tag{2.2.13}$$

which assumes that k is large and that the two-hidden-layer mappings preserve the general position property of the m points. Now, in the limit of $m \gg n^2$ and $n \rightarrow \infty$, Equation (2.2.13) can be solved for k to give

$$k \geq \sqrt{2m} \tag{2.2.14}$$

2.2.3   Generally Interconnected Networks with No Feedback

It is left as an exercise for the reader to verify that the necessary size of an arbitrarily fully interconnected network of LTGs (with no feedback) for realizing any function $f: R^n \to \{0, 1\}$ defined on m arbitrary points is given by (see Problem 2.2.3)

$$k > \sqrt{\frac{2m}{\log_2 m}} \qquad \text{for } m \gg n^2 \text{ and } n \to \infty \qquad (2.2.15)$$

and for points in general position

$$k > \sqrt{m} \qquad \text{for } m \gg n^2 \text{ and } n \to \infty \qquad (2.2.16)$$

It is of interest to compare Equations (2.2.12) and (2.2.14) with Equations (2.2.15) and (2.2.16), respectively. Note that for these two seemingly different network architectures, the number of necessary LTGs for realizing arbitrary functions is of the same order. This agrees with the results of Baum (1988), who showed that these bounds are of the same order for any layered feedforward net with two or more hidden layers and the same number of units, irrespective of the number of layers used. This suggests that if one were able to compute an arbitrary function using a two-hidden-layer net with only $O(\sqrt{m})$ units, there would not be much to gain, in terms of random or arbitrary function realization capability, by using more than two hidden layers! Also, comparing Equations (2.2.3), (2.2.12), and (2.2.15) [or Equations (2.2.8), (2.2.14), and (2.2.16)] shows that when the size of the training set is much larger than the dimension of the input exemplars, then networks with two or more hidden layers may require substantially fewer units than networks with a single hidden layer.

Table 2.2.1
Lower Bounds on the Size of a Net of LTGs for Realizing Any Function of m Points, $f: R^n \to \{0, 1\}$, in the Limit of Large n

Network Architecture	Lower Bounds on the Size of an LTG Net		
	Arbitrary Points		Points in General Position
One-hidden-layer feedforward net with k hidden units	$\dfrac{m}{n \log_2 \dfrac{me}{n}}$	$(m \geq 3n)$	$\dfrac{m}{2n}$
Two-hidden-layer feedforward net with $k/2$ units in each layer	$2\sqrt{\dfrac{m}{\log_2 m}}$	$(m \gg n^2)$	$\sqrt{2m} \quad (m \gg n^2)$
Generally interconnected net with k units (no feedback)	$\sqrt{\dfrac{2m}{\log_2 m}}$	$(m \gg n^2)$	$\sqrt{m} \quad (m \gg n^2)$

In practice, the actual points (patterns) that we want to discriminate between are not arbitrary or random; rather, they are likely to have natural regularities and redundancies. This may make them easier to realize with networks having substantially smaller size than these enumerational statistics would indicate. For convenience, the results of this section are summarized in Table 2.2.1.

2.3   Approximation Capabilities of Feedforward Neural Networks for Continuous Functions

This section summarizes some fundamental results, in the form of theorems, on continuous function approximation capabilities of feedforward nets. The main result is that a two-layer feedforward net with a sufficient number of hidden units, of the sigmoidal activation type, and a single linear output unit is capable of approximating any continuous function $f : R^n \to R$ to any desired accuracy. Before formally stating this result, let us consider some early observations on the implications of a classic theorem on function approximation, Kolmogorov's theorem, which motivates the use of layered feedforward nets as function approximators.

2.3.1   Kolmogorov's Theorem

It has been suggested (Hecht-Nielsen, 1987, 1990; Lippmann, 1987; Spreecher, 1993) that Kolmogorov's theorem concerning the realization of arbitrary multivariate functions provides theoretical support for neural networks that implement such functions.

THEOREM 2.3.1 (Kolmogorov, 1957) Any continuous real-valued functions $f(x_1, x_2, \ldots, x_n)$ defined on $[0, 1]^n$, $n \geq 2$, can be represented in the form

$$f(x_1, x_2, \ldots, x_n) = \sum_{j=1}^{2n+1} g_j \left[\sum_{j=1}^{n} \phi_{ij}(x_i) \right] \qquad (2.3.1)$$

where the g_j terms are properly chosen continuous functions of one variable, and the ϕ_{ij} functions are continuous monotonically increasing functions independent of f.

   The basic idea in Kolmogorov's theorem is captured in the network architecture of Figure 2.3.1, where a universal transformation M maps R^n into several unidimensional transformations. The theorem states that one can express a continuous multivariate function on a compact set in terms of sums and compositions of a finite number of single variable functions.

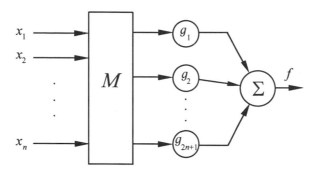

Figure 2.3.1
Network representation of Kolmogorov's theorem.

Others, such as Girosi and Poggio (1989), have criticized this interpretation of Kolmogorov's theorem as irrelevant to neural networks by pointing out that the ϕ_{ij} functions are highly nonsmooth and the functions g_j are not parameterized. On the other hand, Kůrková (1992) supported the relevance of this theorem to neural nets by arguing that nonsmooth functions can be approximated as sums of infinite series of smooth functions; thus one should be able to approximately implement ϕ_{ij} and g_j with parameterized networks. More recently, Lin and Unbehauen (1993) argued that an "approximate" implementation of g_i does not, in general, deliver an approximate implementation of the original function $f(\mathbf{x})$. As this debate continues, the importance of Kolmogorov's theorem might not be in its direct application to proving the universality of neural nets as universal function approximators, in as much as it points to the feasibility of using parallel and layered network structures for multivariate function mappings.

2.3.2 Single-Hidden-Layer Neural Networks Are Universal Approximators

Rigorous mathematical proofs for the universality of feedforward layered neural nets employing continuous sigmoid type, as well as other more general, activation units were given, independently, by Cybenko (1989), Hornik et al. (1989), and Funahashi (1989). Cybenko's proof is distinguished by being mathematically concise and elegant [it is based on the Hahn-Banach theorem (Luenberger, 1969)]. The following is the statement of Cybenko's theorem [the reader is referred to the original paper by Cybenko (1989) for the proof].

THEOREM 2.3.2 (Cybenko, 1989)   Let φ be any continuous sigmoid-type function [e.g., $\varphi(\xi) = 1/(1 + e^{-\xi})$]. Then, given any continuous real-valued function f on $[0,1]^n$ (or any other compact subset of R^n) and $\varepsilon > 0$, there exists vectors $\mathbf{w}_1, \mathbf{w}_2, \ldots, \mathbf{w}_N$, $\boldsymbol{\alpha}$, and $\boldsymbol{\theta}$ and a parameterized function $G(\cdot, \mathbf{w}, \boldsymbol{\alpha}, \boldsymbol{\theta}): [0,1]^n \to R$ such that

$$|G(\mathbf{x}, \mathbf{w}, \boldsymbol{\alpha}, \boldsymbol{\theta}) - f(\mathbf{x})| < \varepsilon \qquad \text{for all } \mathbf{x} \in [0,1]^n$$

where

$$G(\mathbf{x}, \mathbf{w}, \boldsymbol{\alpha}, \boldsymbol{\theta}) = \sum_{i=1}^{N} \alpha_j \varphi(\mathbf{w}_j^T \mathbf{x} + \theta_j) \qquad (2.3.2)$$

and $\mathbf{w}_j \in R^n$, α_j, $\theta_j \in R$, $\mathbf{w} = (\mathbf{w}_1, \mathbf{w}_2, \ldots, \mathbf{w}_N)$, $\boldsymbol{\alpha} = (\alpha_1, \alpha_2, \ldots, \alpha_N)$, and $\boldsymbol{\theta} = (\theta_1, \theta_2, \ldots, \theta_N)$.

Hornik et al. (1989) [employing the Stone-Weierstrass theorem (Rudin, 1976)] and Funahashi (1989) [using an integral formula presented by Irie and Miyake (1988)] independently proved similar theorems stating that a one-hidden-layer feedforward neural network is capable of approximating uniformly any continuous multivariate function to any desired degree of accuracy. This implies that any failure of a function mapping by a multilayer network must arise from inadequate choice of parameters (i.e., poor choices for $\mathbf{w}_1, \mathbf{w}_2, \ldots, \mathbf{w}_N$, $\boldsymbol{\alpha}$, and $\boldsymbol{\theta}$) or an insufficient number of hidden nodes. Hornik et al. (1990) proved another important result relating to the approximation capability of multilayer feedforward neural nets employing sigmoidal hidden unit activations. They showed that these networks can approximate not only an unknown function but also its derivative. In fact, Hornik et al. (1990) also showed that these networks can approximate functions that are not differentiable in the classic sense but possess a generalized derivative, as in the case of piecewise differentiable functions.

Using a theorem by Sun and Cheney (1992), Light (1992a) extended Cybenko's results to any continuous function f on R^n and showed that integer weights and thresholds are sufficient for accurate approximation. In another version of the theorem, Light shows that the sigmoid can be replaced by any continuous function ϑ on R satisfying:

$$1. \quad \int_0^\infty |\vartheta(\xi)\xi^{n-1}| \, dt < \infty$$

$$2. \quad \int_{-\infty}^{+\infty} \vartheta(\xi)\xi^{2j} \, dt = 0 \qquad 0 \le j \le \frac{n-3}{2} \qquad (2.3.3)$$

$$3. \quad \int_{-\infty}^{+\infty} \vartheta(\xi)\xi^{n-1} \, dt \ne 0$$

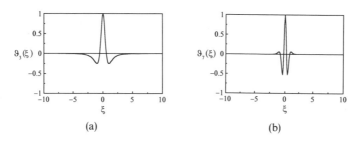

Figure 2.3.2
Activation function $\vartheta_n(\xi)$ for the case (a) $n = 3$ and (b) $n = 7$.

where n is odd and $n \geq 3$. A similar result can be established for n even. Examples of activation functions satisfying the preceding conditions are given by the family of functions

$$\vartheta_n(\xi) = \frac{1}{\sqrt{(1 + \xi^2)^n}} \cos\left(n \cos^{-1} \frac{1}{\sqrt{1 + \xi^2}}\right) \qquad (2.3.4)$$

Note that the cosine term is the Chebyshev polynomial of degree n. Figure 2.3.2 shows two plots of this activation function for $n = 3$ and $n = 7$, respectively.

The universality of single-hidden-layer nets with units having nonsigmoidal activation functions was formally proved by Stinchcombe and White (1989). Baldi (1991) showed that a wide class of continuous multivariate functions can be approximated by a weighted sum of bell-shaped functions (multivariate Bernstein polynomials); i.e., a single-hidden-layer net with bell-shaped activations for its hidden units and a single linear output unit is a possible approximator of functions $f: R^n \rightarrow R$. Hornik (1991) proved that a sufficient condition for universal approximation can be obtained by using continuous, bounded, and nonconstant hidden unit activation functions. Leshno et al. (1993; see also Hornik, 1993) extended these results by showing that the preceding neural network with locally bounded piecewise continuous activation functions for hidden units is a universal approximator if and only if the network's activation function is not a polynomial. Ito (1991) showed that any function belonging to the class of rapidly decreasing continuous functions in R^n [i.e., functions $f(\mathbf{x})$ satisfying $\lim_{\|\mathbf{x}\| \to \infty} |x_1^{k_1} x_2^{k_2} \cdots x_n^{k_n} f(\mathbf{x})| = 0$ for any $k_j \geq 0$] can be approximated arbitrarily well by a two-layer architecture with a finite number of LTGs in the hidden layer. Here, the requirement of rapid decrease in f is not necessary and can be weakened.

2.3.3   Single-Hidden-Layer Neural Networks Are Universal Classifiers

Theorem 2.3.2 also may be extended to classifier-type mappings (Cybenko, 1989) of the form

$$f(\mathbf{x}) = j \quad \text{iff } \mathbf{x} \in P_j \tag{2.3.5}$$

where $f: A^n \to \{1, 2, \ldots, k\}$. A^n is a compact (closed and bounded) subset of R^n, and $P_1, P_2, \ldots, P_k$ partition A^n into k disjoint measurable subsets, i.e., $A^n = \bigcup_{j=1}^{k} P_j$ and $P_i \cap P_j$ is empty for $i \neq j$.

Thus a single-hidden-layer net with sigmoidal activation units and a single linear output unit is a universal classifier. This result was confirmed empirically by Huang and Lippmann (1988) on several examples, including the ones shown in Figure 2.3.3 for $n = 2$ and $k = 2$ (i.e., two-class problems in a two-dimensional space).

This section concludes with a note that in Equation (2.3.5) the class label is explicitly generated as the output of a linear unit. This representation of class labels via quantized levels of a single linear output unit, although useful for theoretical considerations, is not practical; it imposes unnecessary constraints on the hidden layer, which, in turn, leads to a large number of hidden units for the realization of complex map-

Figure 2.3.3
Ten complex decision regions formed by a neural net classifier with a single hidden layer. [Adapted from Huang and Lippmann (1988) with the permission of the American Institute of Physics.]

pings. In practical implementations, a local encoding of classes is more commonly used (Rumelhart et al., 1986b). This relaxes the constraints on the hidden layer mapping by adding several output units, each of which is responsible for representing a unique class. Here, LTGs or sigmoid type units may be used as output units.

2.4   Computational Effectiveness of Neural Networks

2.4.1   Algorithmic Complexity

A general way of looking at the efficiency of embedding a problem in a neural network comes from a computational complexity point of view (Abu-Mostafa, 1986a, b). Solving a problem on a sequential computer requires a certain number of steps (time complexity), a certain memory size (space complexity), and a certain length of algorithm (Kolmogorov complexity). In a neural net simulation, the number of computations is a measure of time complexity, the number of units is a measure of space complexity, and the number of weights (degrees of freedom) where the algorithm is "stored" is a measure of Kolmogorov complexity. In formulating neural network solutions for practical problems, we seek to minimize, simultaneously, the resulting time, space, and Kolmogorov complexities of the network. If a given problem is very demanding in terms of space complexity, then the required network size is large and thus the number of weights is large, even if the Kolmogorov complexity of the algorithm is very modest. This spells inefficiency: Neural net solutions of problems with short algorithms and high space complexity are very inefficient. The same is true for problems in which time complexity is very demanding, while the other complexities may not be.

The preceding complexity discussion leads us to identify certain problems that best match the computational characteristics of artificial neural networks. Problems that require a very long algorithm if run on sequential machines make the most use of neural nets, since the capacity of the net grows faster than the number of units. Such problems are called *random problems* (Abu-Mostafa, 1986b). Examples are pattern recognition problems in natural environments and artificial intelligence (AI) problems requiring huge databases. These problems make the most use of the large capacity of neural nets. It is interesting to note that humans are very good at such random problems but not at structured ones. The other interesting property of random problems is that we do not have explicit algorithms for solving them. A neural net can develop one by learning from examples, as will be shown in Chapters 5 and 6.

At this point one may recall the results of Chapter 1, based on Cover's concept of extreme patterns/inequalities, which point to the effectiveness of threshold units in loading a large set of labeled patterns (data/prototypes) by only learning on extreme patterns. These results and those presented here show that neural networks can be very efficient classifiers.

2.4.2 Computational Energy

For any computational device, be it biologically based, microprocessor-based, etc., the cost per computation, or *computational energy*, of the device can be measured directly in terms of the energy required (in units of Joules) to perform the computation. From this point of view, one may then compare computational devices in terms of the total energy required to solve a given problem.

As technology evolved, it always moved in the direction of lower energy per unit computation in order to allow for more computations per unit time in a practically sized computing machine (note the trend from vacuum tubes, to transistors, to integrated circuits). A typical microprocessor chip can perform about 10 million operations per second and uses about 1 W of power. In round numbers, it costs about 10^{-7} J to do one operation on such a chip. The ultimate silicon technology that can be envisioned today will dissipate on the order of 10^{-9} J of energy for each operation at the single-chip level.

The brain, on the other hand, has about 10^{15} synapses. A nerve impulse arrives at each synapse on the average of 10 times per second. Therefore, the brain accomplishes roughly 10^{16} complex operations per second. Since the power dissipation is a few watts, each operation costs only 10^{-16} J. The brain is more efficient, by a factor of 10 million, than the best digital technology that we can hope to attain.[1]

One reason for the inefficiency in computation energy is the way in which devices are used in a system. In a typical silicon implementation, we switch about 10^4 transistors to do one operation. Using the physics of the device (e.g., analog computing in a single transistor) can save us these four orders of magnitude in computation energy. For example, analog addition is done for free at a node, and nonlinear activations (sigmoids) can be realized using a single MOS transistor operating in its subthreshold region. Similarly, multiplication may be performed with a small MOS transistor circuit. Therefore, one can very efficiently realize analog artificial neurons with existing technology employing device physics (Hopfield, 1990; Mead, 1991). Carver Mead (1991) wrote: "We pay a factor of 10^4 for taking all of the beautiful physics that is built

---

1. Obviously, we are comparing the brain and digital computing machines on the kind of problems (e.g., cognitive tasks) which are routinely performed by the brain. This comparison is meaningless if the problem is one which involves arithmetic computations requiring the execution of a short "program" with high precision (e.g., finding the square root of several thousand randomly chosen real numbers!).

into these transistors, mashing it down into a one or a zero, and then painfully building it back, with AND and OR gates to reinvent the multiply. We then string together those multiplications and additions to get an exponential. But we neglected a basic fact: the transistor does an exponential all by itself."

Based on the preceding, the type of computations required by neural networks may lend themselves nicely to efficient implementation with current analog VLSI technology; there is a potential for effectively and efficiently realizing very large analog neural nets on single chips. Analog optical implementations of neural networks also could have a competitive advantage over digital implementations. Optics have the unique advantage that beams of light can cross each other without affecting their information contents. Thus optical interconnections may be used in conjunction with electronic VLSI chips to efficiently implement very large and richly interconnected neural networks. The richness of optical device physics, such as holograms, analog spatial light modulators, optical filters, and Fourier lenses, suggests that optical implementation of analog neural nets could be very efficient. [For examples of very large optical neural networks, the reader is referred to the works of Paek and Psaltis (1987), Abu-Mostafa and Psaltis (1987), and Anderson and Erie (1987).]

2.5 Summary

Lower bounds on the size of multilayer feedforward neural networks for the realization of arbitrary dichotomies of points are derived. It is found that networks with two or more hidden layers are potentially more size efficient than networks with a single hidden layer. However, the derived bounds suggest that no matter what network architecture is used (assuming no feedback), the size of such networks must always be on the order $O(\sqrt{m/\log_2 m})$ or larger for the realization of arbitrary or random functions of m points in R^n, in the limit $m \gg n^2$. Fortunately, though, the functions encountered in practice are likely to have natural regularities and redundancies which make them easier to realize with substantially smaller networks than these bounds would indicate.

Single-hidden-layer feedforward neural networks are universal approximators for arbitrary multivariate continuous functions. These networks are also capable of implementing arbitrarily complex dichotomies; thus they are suitable as pattern classifiers. However, it is crucial that the parameters of these networks be chosen carefully in order to exploit the full function approximation potential of these networks. In the next chapter we explore learning algorithms that may be used to adaptively discover optimal values for these parameters.

Finally, we find that from an algorithmic complexity point of view, neural networks are best fit for solving random problems such as pattern-recognition problems in noisy environments. We also find such networks appealing from a computational energy point of view when implemented in analog VLSI and/or optical technologies that utilize the properties of device physics.

Problems

2.1.1 Use the K-map-based threshold-OR synthesis technique illustrated in Figure 2.1.3 to identify all possible decompositions of the Boolean function $f(x_1, x_2, x_3) = x_1 x_3 + x_2 x_3 + \bar{x}_1 \bar{x}_3$ into the ORing of two threshold functions. (*Hint*: Recall the admissible K-map threshold patterns of Figure 1.1.5.)

2.1.2 Find a minimal threshold-OR network realization for the switching function $f: \{0,1\}^3 \to \{0,1\}^2$ given by the K-maps in Figure P2.1.2.

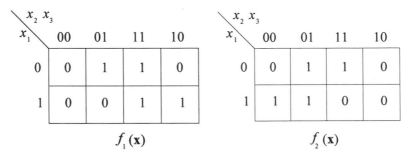

Figure P2.1.2
A three-input, two-output switching function.

2.1.3 Employ Theorem 1.4.1 and the equivalence of the two nets in Figures 1.3.4 and 1.2.1, for $\mathbf{x} \in \{0,1\}^n$, to show that a two-layer LTG net with m LTGs in the hidden layer feeding into a single-output LTG is sufficient for realizing any Boolean function of m points in $\{0,1\}^n$. Is the requirement of full interconnectivity between the input vector and the hidden LTG layer necessary? Why?

*__2.2.1__ Estimate the maximum number of functions $f: R^n \to \{0,1\}$, defined on m points in general position, that can be realized using the generally interconnected LTG network shown in Figure 2.1.5.

2.2.2 Derive the bound on k in Equation (2.2.14).

*2.2.3 Derive the bound on k in Equation (2.2.15). [*Hint*: Use Equation (2.1.2).]

2.2.4 Consider an arbitrarily fully interconnected network of LTGs with no feedback. Show that this network must have more than $(1/\sqrt{n})2^{(n+1)/2}$ LTGs for realizing arbitrary, completely specified Boolean functions of n variables.

*2.2.5 Derive the bound on k in Equation (2.2.16). (*Hint*: Use the result of Problem 2.2.1.)

2.3.1 Plot Equation (2.3.4) for $n = 9$.

*2.3.2 Show that the activation in Equation (2.3.4) with $n = 3$ satisfies the three conditions in Equation (2.3.3).

3 Learning Rules

One of the most significant attributes of a neural network is its ability to learn by interacting with its environment or with an information source. Learning in a neural network is normally accomplished through an adaptive procedure, known as a *learning rule* or *algorithm*, whereby the weights of the network are incrementally adjusted so as to improve a predefined performance measure over time.

In the context of artificial neural networks, the process of learning is best viewed as an optimization process. More precisely, the learning process can be viewed as "search" in a multidimensional parameter (weight) space for a solution, which gradually optimizes a prespecified objective (criterion) function. This view is adopted in this chapter, and it allows us to unify a wide range of existing learning rules which otherwise would have looked more like a diverse variety of learning procedures.

This chapter presents a number of basic learning rules for supervised, reinforced, and unsupervised learning tasks. In *supervised learning* (also known as *learning with a teacher* or *associative learning*), each input pattern/signal received from the environment is associated with a specific desired target pattern. Usually, the weights are synthesized gradually, and at each step of the learning process they are updated so that the error between the network's output and a corresponding desired target is reduced. On the other hand, *unsupervised learning* involves the clustering of (or the detection of similarities among) unlabeled patterns of a given training set. The idea here is to optimize (maximize or minimize) some criterion or performance function defined in terms of the output activity of the units in the network. Here, the weights and the outputs of the network are usually expected to converge to representations that capture the statistical regularities of the input data. *Reinforcement learning* involves updating the network's weights in response to an "evaluative" teacher signal; this differs from supervised learning, where the teacher signal is the "correct answer." Reinforcement learning rules may be viewed as stochastic search mechanisms that attempt to maximize the probability of positive external reinforcement for a given training set.

In most cases, these learning rules are presented in the basic form appropriate for single-unit training. Exceptions are cases involving unsupervised (competitive or feature mapping) learning schemes in which an essential competition mechanism necessitates the use of multiple units. For such cases, simple single-layer architectures are assumed. Later chapters in this book (Chapters 5, 6, and 7) extend some of the learning rules discussed here to networks with multiple units and multiple layers.

3.1 Supervised Learning in a Single-Unit Setting

Supervised learning is treated first. Here, two groups of rules are discussed: error-correction rules and gradient-descent-based rules. By the end of this section it will be established that all these learning rules can be systematically derived as minimizers of an appropriate criterion function.

3.1.1   Error Correction Rules

Error-correction rules were proposed initially as ad hoc rules for single-unit training. These rules essentially drive the output error of a given unit to zero. This section starts with the classic perceptron learning rule and gives a proof for its convergence. Then other error correction rules such as Mays' rule and the α-LMS rule are covered. Throughout this section an attempt is made to point out criterion functions that are minimized by using each rule. These learning rules also will be cast as relaxation rules, thus unifying them with the other gradient-based search rules such as the ones presented in Section 3.1.2.

Perceptron Learning Rule   Consider the linear threshold gate shown in Figure 3.1.1, which will be referred to as the *perceptron*. The perceptron maps an input vector $\mathbf{x} = [x_1 \quad x_2 \quad \cdots \quad x_{n+1}]^T$ to a bipolar binary output y, and thus it may be viewed as a simple two-class classifier. The input signal x_{n+1} is usually set to 1 and plays the role of a bias to the perceptron. We will denote by $\mathbf{w}$ the vector $\mathbf{w} = [w_1 \quad w_2 \quad \cdots \quad w_{n+1}]^T \in R^{n+1}$ consisting of the free parameters (weights) of the perceptron. The input/output relation for the perceptron is given by $y = \text{sgn}(\mathbf{x}^T\mathbf{w})$, where sgn is the "sign" function, which returns $+1$ or -1 depending on whether the sign of its scalar argument is positive or negative, respectively.

Assume we are training this perceptron to load (learn) the training pairs $\{\mathbf{x}^1, d^1\}$, $\{\mathbf{x}^2, d^2\}, \ldots, \{\mathbf{x}^m, d^m\}$, where $\mathbf{x}^k \in R^{n+1}$ is the kth input vector and $d^k \in \{-1, +1\}$,

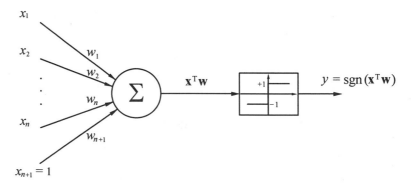

Figure 3.1.1
The perceptron computational unit.

$k = 1, 2, \ldots, m$, is the desired target for the kth input vector (usually the order of these training pairs is random). The entire collection of these pairs is called the *training set*. The goal, then, is to design a perceptron such that for each input vector $\mathbf{x}^k$ of the training set, the perceptron output y^k matches the desired target d^k; that is, we require $y^k = \text{sgn}(\mathbf{w}^T\mathbf{x}^k) = d^k$, for each $k = 1, 2, \ldots, m$. In this case we say that the perceptron correctly classifies the training set. Of course, "designing" an appropriate perceptron to correctly classify the training set amounts to determining a weight vector $\mathbf{w}^*$ such that the following relations are satisfied:

$$\begin{cases} (\mathbf{x}^k)^T\mathbf{w}^* > 0 & \text{if } d^k = +1 \\ (\mathbf{x}^k)^T\mathbf{w}^* < 0 & \text{if } d^k = -1 \end{cases} \tag{3.1.1}$$

Recall that the set of all $\mathbf{x}$ which satisfy $\mathbf{x}^T\mathbf{w}^* = 0$ defines a hyperplane in R^n. Thus, in the context of the preceding discussion, finding a solution vector $\mathbf{w}^*$ to Equation (3.1.1) is equivalent to finding a separating hyperplane that correctly classifies all vectors $\mathbf{x}^k$, $k = 1, 2, \ldots, m$. In other words, we desire a hyperplane $\mathbf{x}^T\mathbf{w}^* = 0$ that partitions the input space into two distinct regions, one containing all points $\mathbf{x}^k$ with $d^k = +1$ and the other region containing all points $\mathbf{x}^k$ with $d^k = -1$.

One possible incremental method for arriving at a solution $\mathbf{w}^*$ is to invoke the perceptron learning rule (Rosenblatt, 1962):

$$\begin{cases} \mathbf{w}^1 & \text{arbitrary} \\ \mathbf{w}^{k+1} = \mathbf{w}^k + \rho(d^k - y^k)\mathbf{x}^k, & k = 1, 2, \ldots \end{cases} \tag{3.1.2}$$

where ρ is a positive constant called the *learning rate*. The incremental learning process given in Equation (3.1.2) proceeds as follows: First, an initial weight vector $\mathbf{w}^1$ is selected (usually at random) to begin the process. Then, the m pairs $\{\mathbf{x}^k, d^k\}$ of the training set are used to successively update the weight vector until (hopefully) a solution $\mathbf{w}^*$ is found that correctly classifies the training set. This process of sequentially presenting the training patterns is usually referred to as *cycling* through the training set, and a complete presentation of the m training pairs is referred to as a *cycle* (or *pass*) through the training set. In general, more than one cycle through the training set is required to determine an appropriate solution vector. Hence, in Equation (3.1.2), the superscript k in $\mathbf{w}^k$ refers to the iteration number. On the other hand, the superscript k in $\mathbf{x}^k$ (and d^k) is the label of the training pair presented at the kth iteration. To be more precise, if the number of training pairs m is finite, then the superscripts in $\mathbf{x}^k$ and d^k should be replaced by $[(k - 1) \bmod m] + 1$. Here, $a \bmod b$ returns the remainder of the division of a by b (e.g., $5 \bmod 8 = 5$, $8 \bmod 8 = 0$, and $19 \bmod 8 = 3$). This observation is valid for all incremental learning rules presented in this chapter.

Notice that for $\rho = 0.5$, the perceptron learning rule can be written as

$$\begin{cases} \mathbf{w}^1 & \text{arbitrary} \\ \mathbf{w}^{k+1} = \mathbf{w}^k + \mathbf{z}^k & \text{if } (\mathbf{z}^k)^T\mathbf{w}^k \leq 0 \\ \mathbf{w}^{k+1} = \mathbf{w}^k & \text{otherwise} \end{cases} \tag{3.1.3}$$

where

$$\mathbf{z}^k = \begin{cases} +\mathbf{x}^k & \text{if } d^k = +1 \\ -\mathbf{x}^k & \text{if } d^k = -1 \end{cases} \tag{3.1.4}$$

That is, a correction is made if and only if a misclassification, indicated by

$$(\mathbf{z}^k)^T\mathbf{w}^k \leq 0 \tag{3.1.5}$$

occurs. The addition of vector $\mathbf{z}^k$ to $\mathbf{w}^k$ in Equation (3.1.3) moves the weight vector directly toward and perhaps across the hyperplane $(\mathbf{z}^k)^T\mathbf{w}^k = 0$. The new inner product $(\mathbf{z}^k)^T\mathbf{w}^{k+1}$ is larger than $(\mathbf{z}^k)^T\mathbf{w}^k$ by the amount of $\|\mathbf{z}^k\|^2$, and the correction $\Delta\mathbf{w}^k = \mathbf{w}^{k+1} - \mathbf{w}^k$ is clearly moving $\mathbf{w}^k$ in a good direction, the direction of increasing $(\mathbf{z}^k)^T\mathbf{w}^k$, as can be seen from Figure 3.1.2.[1] Thus the perceptron learning rule attempts to find a solution $\mathbf{w}^*$ for the following system of inequalities:

$$(\mathbf{z}^k)^T\mathbf{w} > 0 \qquad \text{for } k = 1, 2, \ldots, m \tag{3.1.6}$$

In an analysis of any learning algorithm, and in particular the perceptron learning algorithm of Equation (3.1.2), there are two main issues to consider: (1) the existence of solutions and (2) convergence of the algorithm to the desired solutions (if they exist). In the case of the perceptron, it is clear that a solution vector (i.e., a vector $\mathbf{w}^*$ that correctly classifies the training set) exists if and only if the given training set is

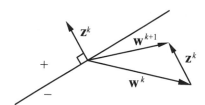

Figure 3.1.2
Geometric representation of the perceptron learning
rule with $\rho = 0.5$.

---

1. The quantity $\|\mathbf{z}\|^2$ is given by $\mathbf{z}^T\mathbf{z}$ and is sometimes referred to as the *energy* of $\mathbf{z}$. $\|\mathbf{z}\|$ is the Euclidean norm (length) of vector $\mathbf{z}$ and is given by the square root of the sum of the squares of the components of $\mathbf{z}$ [note that $\|\mathbf{z}\| = \|\mathbf{x}\|$ by virtue of Equation (3.1.4)].

linearly separable. Assuming, then, that the training set is linearly separable, we may proceed to show that the perceptron learning rule converges to a solution (Novikoff, 1962; Ridgway, 1962; Nilsson, 1965) as follows: Let $\mathbf{w}^*$ be any solution vector so that

$$(\mathbf{z}^k)^{\mathrm{T}}\mathbf{w}^* > 0 \qquad \text{for } k = 1, 2, \ldots, m \tag{3.1.7}$$

Then, from Equation (3.1.3), if the kth pattern is misclassified, we may write

$$\mathbf{w}^{k+1} - \alpha\mathbf{w}^* = \mathbf{w}^k - \alpha\mathbf{w}^* + \mathbf{z}^k \tag{3.1.8}$$

where α is a positive scale factor, and hence

$$\|\mathbf{w}^{k+1} - \alpha\mathbf{w}^*\|^2 = \|\mathbf{w}^k - \alpha\mathbf{w}^*\|^2 + 2(\mathbf{z}^k)^{\mathrm{T}}(\mathbf{w}^k - \alpha\mathbf{w}^*) + \|\mathbf{z}^k\|^2 \tag{3.1.9}$$

Since $\mathbf{z}^k$ is misclassified, we have $(\mathbf{z}^k)^{\mathrm{T}}\mathbf{w}^k \leq 0$, and thus

$$\|\mathbf{w}^{k+1} - \alpha\mathbf{w}^*\|^2 \leq \|\mathbf{w}^k - \alpha\mathbf{w}^*\|^2 - 2\alpha(\mathbf{z}^k)^{\mathrm{T}}\mathbf{w}^* + \|\mathbf{z}^k\|^2 \tag{3.1.10}$$

Now, let $\beta^2 = \max_i \|\mathbf{z}^i\|^2$ and $\gamma = \min_i(\mathbf{z}^i)^{\mathrm{T}}\mathbf{w}^*$ [γ is positive because $(\mathbf{z}^i)^{\mathrm{T}}\mathbf{w}^* > 0$] and substitute into Equation (3.1.10) to get

$$\|\mathbf{w}^{k+1} - \alpha\mathbf{w}^*\|^2 \leq \|\mathbf{w}^k - \alpha\mathbf{w}^*\|^2 - 2\alpha\gamma + \beta^2 \tag{3.1.11}$$

If we choose α sufficiently large, in particular $\alpha = \beta^2/\gamma$, we obtain

$$\|\mathbf{w}^{k+1} - \alpha\mathbf{w}^*\|^2 \leq \|\mathbf{w}^k - \alpha\mathbf{w}^*\|^2 - \beta^2 \tag{3.1.12}$$

Thus the square distance between $\mathbf{w}^k$ and $\alpha\mathbf{w}^*$ is reduced by at least β^2 at each correction, and after k corrections, we may write Equation (3.1.12) as

$$0 \leq \|\mathbf{w}^{k+1} - \alpha\mathbf{w}^*\|^2 \leq \|\mathbf{w}^1 - \alpha\mathbf{w}^*\|^2 - k\beta^2 \tag{3.1.13}$$

It follows that the sequence of corrections must terminate after no more than k_0 corrections, where

$$k_0 = \frac{\|\mathbf{w}^1 - \alpha\mathbf{w}^*\|^2}{\beta^2} \tag{3.1.14}$$

Therefore, if a solution exists, it is achieved in a finite number of iterations. When corrections cease, the resulting weight vector must classify all the samples correctly, since a correction occurs whenever a sample is misclassified, and since each sample appears infinitely often in the sequence. In general, a linearly separable problem admits an infinite number of solutions. The perceptron learning rule in Equation (3.1.2) converges to one of these solutions. This solution, though, is sensitive to the value of the learning rate ρ used and to the order of presentation of the training pairs.

This sensitivity is responsible for the varying quality of the perceptron-generated separating surface observed in simulations.

The bound on the number of corrections k_0 given by Equation (3.1.14) depends on the choice of the initial weight vector $\mathbf{w}^1$. If $\mathbf{w}^1 = 0$, we get

$$k_0 = \frac{\alpha^2 \|\mathbf{w}^*\|^2}{\beta^2} = \frac{\beta^2 \|\mathbf{w}^*\|^2}{\gamma^2} \qquad \text{or} \qquad k_0 = \frac{\max_i \|\mathbf{x}^i\|^2 \|\mathbf{w}^*\|^2}{[\min_i (\mathbf{x}^i)^\mathsf{T} \mathbf{w}^*]^2} \qquad (3.1.15)$$

Here, k_0 is a function of the initially unknown solution weight vector $\mathbf{w}^*$. Therefore, Equation (3.1.15) is of no help for predicting the maximum number of corrections. However, the denominator of Equation (3.1.15) implies that the difficulty of the problem is essentially determined by the samples most nearly orthogonal to the solution vector.

Generalizations of the Perceptron Learning Rule The perceptron learning rule may be generalized to include a variable increment ρ^k and a fixed positive margin b. This generalized learning rule updates the weight vector whenever $(\mathbf{z}^k)^\mathsf{T}\mathbf{w}^k$ fails to exceed the margin b. Here, the algorithm for weight vector update is given by

$$\begin{cases} \mathbf{w}^1 \quad \text{arbitrary} \\ \mathbf{w}^{k+1} = \mathbf{w}^k + \rho^k \mathbf{z}^k & \text{if } (\mathbf{z}^k)^\mathsf{T}\mathbf{w}^k \leq b \\ \mathbf{w}^{k+1} = \mathbf{w}^k & \text{otherwise} \end{cases} \qquad (3.1.16)$$

The margin b is useful because it gives a dead-zone robustness to the decision boundary. That is, the perceptron's decision hyperplane is constrained to lie in a region between the two classes such that sufficient clearance is realized between this hyperplane and the extreme points (boundary patterns) of the training set. This makes the perceptron robust with respect to noisy inputs. It can be shown (Duda and Hart, 1973) that if the training set is linearly separable and if the following three conditions are satisfied:

$$1. \quad \rho^k \geq 0 \qquad\qquad\qquad\qquad\qquad\qquad\qquad\qquad (3.1.17a)$$

$$2. \quad \lim_{m \to \infty} \sum_{k=1}^{m} \rho^k = \infty \qquad\qquad\qquad\qquad\qquad\qquad (3.1.17b)$$

$$3. \quad \lim_{m \to \infty} \frac{\sum_{k=1}^{m} (\rho^k)^2}{\left(\sum_{k=1}^{m} \rho^k\right)^2} = 0 \qquad\qquad\qquad\qquad\qquad (3.1.17c)$$

(e.g., $\rho^k = \rho/k$ or even $\rho^k = \rho k$), then $\mathbf{w}^k$ converges to a solution $\mathbf{w}^*$ that satisfies $(\mathbf{z}^i)^T\mathbf{w}^* > b$, for $i = 1, 2, \ldots, m$. Furthermore, when ρ^k is fixed at a positive constant ρ, this learning rule converges in finite time.

Another variant of the perceptron learning rule is given by the *batch update* procedure

$$\begin{cases} \mathbf{w}^1 & \text{arbitrary} \\ \mathbf{w}^{k+1} = \mathbf{w}^k + \rho \sum_{\mathbf{z} \in Z(\mathbf{w}^k)} \mathbf{z} \end{cases} \tag{3.1.18}$$

where $Z(\mathbf{w}^k)$ is the set of patterns $\mathbf{z}$ misclassified by $\mathbf{w}^k$. Here, the weight vector change $\Delta\mathbf{w} = \mathbf{w}^{k+1} - \mathbf{w}^k$ is along the direction of the resultant vector of all misclassified patterns. In general, this update procedure converges faster than the perceptron rule, but it requires more storage.

In the nonlinearly separable case, the preceding algorithms do not converge. Few theoretical results are available on the behavior of these algorithms for nonlinearly separable problems [see Minsky and Papert (1969) and Block and Levin (1970) for some preliminary results]. For example, it is known that the length of $\mathbf{w}$ in the perceptron rule is bounded, i.e., tends to fluctuate near some limiting value $\|\mathbf{w}^*\|$ (Efron, 1964). This information may be used to terminate the search for $\mathbf{w}^*$. Another approach is to average the weight vectors near the fluctuation point $\mathbf{w}^*$. Butz (1967) proposed the use of a reinforcement factor γ, $0 \leq \gamma \leq 1$, in the perceptron learning rule. This reinforcement places $\mathbf{w}$ in a region that tends to minimize the probability of error for nonlinearly separable cases. Butz's rule is as follows:

$$\begin{cases} \mathbf{w}^1 & \text{arbitrary} \\ \mathbf{w}^{k+1} = \mathbf{w}^k + \rho\mathbf{z}^k & \text{if } (\mathbf{z}^k)^T\mathbf{w}^k \leq 0 \\ \mathbf{w}^{k+1} = \mathbf{w}^k + \rho\gamma\mathbf{z}^k & \text{if } (\mathbf{z}^k)^T\mathbf{w} > 0 \end{cases} \tag{3.1.19}$$

The Perceptron Criterion Function It is interesting to see how the preceding error-correction rules can be derived by a gradient descent on an appropriate criterion (objective) function. For the perceptron, we may define the following criterion function (Duda and Hart, 1973):

$$J(\mathbf{w}) = -\sum_{\mathbf{z} \in Z(\mathbf{w})} \mathbf{z}^T\mathbf{w} \tag{3.1.20}$$

where $Z(\mathbf{w})$ is the set of samples misclassified by $\mathbf{w}$ (i.e., $\mathbf{z}^T\mathbf{w} \leq 0$). Note that if $Z(\mathbf{w})$ is empty, then $J(\mathbf{w}) = 0$; otherwise, $J(\mathbf{w}) > 0$. Geometrically, $J(\mathbf{w})$ is proportional to the sum of the distances from the misclassified samples to the decision boundary. The smaller J is, the better the weight vector $\mathbf{w}$ will be.

Given this objective function $J(\mathbf{w})$, the search point $\mathbf{w}^k$ can be incrementally improved at each iteration by sliding downhill on the surface defined by $J(\mathbf{w})$ in $\mathbf{w}$ space. Specifically, we may use J to perform a discrete gradient-descent search that updates $\mathbf{w}^k$ so that a step is taken downhill in the "steepest" direction along the search surface $J(\mathbf{w})$ at $\mathbf{w}^k$. This can be achieved by making $\Delta \mathbf{w}^k$ proportional to the gradient of J at the present location $\mathbf{w}^k$; formally, we may write[2]

$$\mathbf{w}^{k+1} = \mathbf{w}^k - \rho \nabla J(\mathbf{w})|_{\mathbf{w}=\mathbf{w}^k} = \mathbf{w}^k - \rho \left[\frac{\partial J}{\partial w_1} \; \frac{\partial J}{\partial w_2} \; \cdots \; \frac{\partial J}{\partial w_{n+1}} \right]^T \Bigg|_{\mathbf{w}=\mathbf{w}^k} \qquad (3.1.21)$$

Here, the initial search point $\mathbf{w}^1$ and the learning rate (step size) ρ are to be specified by the user. Equation (3.1.21) can be called the *steepest gradient descent search rule* or, simply, *gradient descent*. Next, substituting the gradient

$$\nabla J(\mathbf{w}^k) = - \sum_{\mathbf{z} \in Z(\mathbf{w}^k)} \mathbf{z} \qquad (3.1.22)$$

into Equation (3.1.21) leads to the weight update rule

$$\mathbf{w}^{k+1} = \mathbf{w}^k + \rho \sum_{\mathbf{z} \in Z(\mathbf{w}^k)} \mathbf{z} \qquad (3.1.23)$$

The learning rule given in Equation (3.1.23) is identical to the multiple-sample (batch) perceptron rule of Equation (3.1.18). The original perceptron learning rule of Equation (3.1.3) can be thought of as an "incremental" gradient descent search rule for minimizing the perceptron criterion function in Equation (3.1.20). Following a similar

---

2. Discrete gradient-search methods are generally governed by the following equation:

$$\mathbf{w}^{k+1} = \mathbf{w}^k - \alpha \mathbf{A} \nabla J|_{\mathbf{w}=\mathbf{w}^k}$$

Here, $\mathbf{A}$ is an $n \times n$ matrix and α is a real number, both are functions of $\mathbf{w}^k$. Numerous versions of gradient-search methods exist, and they differ in the way in which $\mathbf{A}$ and α are selected at $\mathbf{w} = \mathbf{w}^k$. For example, if $\mathbf{A}$ is taken to be the identity matrix, and if α is set to a small positive constant, the gradient "descent" search in Equation (3.1.21) is obtained. On the other hand, if α is a small negative constant, gradient "ascent" search is realized which seeks a local maximum. In either case, though, a saddle point (nonstable equilibrium) may be reached. However, the existence of noise in practical systems prevents convergence to such nonstable equilibria.

It also should be noted that in addition to its simple structure, Equation (3.1.21) implements "steepest" descent (refer to Section 8.1 for additional qualitative analysis of gradient-based search). It can be shown (e.g., Kelley, 1962) that starting at a point $\mathbf{w}^0$, the gradient direction $\nabla J(\mathbf{w}^0)$ yields the greatest incremental increase of $J(\mathbf{w})$ for a fixed incremental distance $\Delta \mathbf{w}^0 = \mathbf{w} - \mathbf{w}^0$. The speed of convergence of steepest descent search is affected by the choice of α, which is normally adjusted at each time step to make the most error correction subject to stability constraints. This topic is explored in Sections 5.2.2 and 5.2.3. Lapidus et al. (1961) compares six ways of choosing α, each slightly different, by applying them to a common problem.

Finally, it should be pointed out that setting $\mathbf{A}$ equal to the inverse of the Hessian matrix $[\nabla \nabla J]^{-1}$ and α to 1 results in the well-known Newton's search method.

procedure as in Equations (3.1.21) through (3.1.23), it can be shown that

$$J(\mathbf{w}) = - \sum_{\mathbf{z}^T\mathbf{w} \leq b} (\mathbf{z}^T\mathbf{w} - b) \tag{3.1.24}$$

is the appropriate criterion function for the modified perceptron rule in Equation (3.1.16).

Before moving on, it should be noted that the gradient of J in Equation (3.1.22) is not mathematically precise. Owing to the piecewise linear nature of J, sudden changes in the gradient of J occur every time the perceptron output y goes through a transition at $(\mathbf{z}^k)^T\mathbf{w} = 0$. Therefore, the gradient of J is not defined at "transition" points $\mathbf{w}$ satisfying $(\mathbf{z}^k)^T\mathbf{w} = 0$, $k = 1, 2, \ldots, m$. However, because of the discrete nature of Equation (3.1.21), the likelihood of $\mathbf{w}^k$ overlapping with one of these transition points is negligible, and thus we may still express ∇J as in Equation (3.1.22). The reader is referred to Problem 3.1.3 for further exploration into gradient descent on the perceptron criterion function.

Mays' Learning Rule   The criterion functions in Equations (3.1.20) and (3.1.24) are by no means the only functions that are minimized when $\mathbf{w}$ is a solution vector. For example, an alternative function is the quadratic function

$$J(\mathbf{w}) = \tfrac{1}{2} \sum_{\mathbf{z}^T\mathbf{w} \leq b} (\mathbf{z}^T\mathbf{w} - b)^2 \tag{3.1.25}$$

where b is a positive constant margin. Like the previous criterion functions, the function $J(\mathbf{w})$ in Equation (3.1.25) focuses attention on the misclassified samples. Its major difference is that its gradient is continuous, whereas the gradient of the perceptron criterion function, with or without the use of margin, is not. Unfortunately, the present function can be dominated by the input vectors with the largest magnitudes. We may eliminate this undesirable effect by dividing by $\|\mathbf{z}\|^2$:

$$J(\mathbf{w}) = \tfrac{1}{2} \sum_{\mathbf{z}^T\mathbf{w} \leq b} \frac{(\mathbf{z}^T\mathbf{w} - b)^2}{\|\mathbf{z}\|^2} \tag{3.1.26}$$

The gradient of $J(\mathbf{w})$ in Equation (3.1.26) is given by

$$\nabla J(\mathbf{w}) = \sum_{\mathbf{z}^T\mathbf{w} \leq b} \frac{\mathbf{z}^T\mathbf{w} - b}{\|\mathbf{z}\|^2} \mathbf{z} \tag{3.1.27}$$

which, upon substituting in Equation (3.1.21), leads to the following learning rule

$$\begin{cases} \mathbf{w}^1 \quad \text{arbitrary} \\ \\ \mathbf{w}^{k+1} = \mathbf{w}^k + \rho \sum_{\mathbf{z}^{\mathrm{T}}\mathbf{w} \leq b} \dfrac{b - \mathbf{z}^{\mathrm{T}}\mathbf{w}^k}{\|\mathbf{z}\|^2} \mathbf{z} \end{cases} \qquad (3.1.28)$$

If we consider the incremental update version of Equation (3.1.28), we arrive at Mays' rule (Mays, 1964):

$$\begin{cases} \mathbf{w}^1 \quad \text{arbitrary} \\ \\ \mathbf{w}^{k+1} = \mathbf{w}^k + \rho \dfrac{b - (\mathbf{z}^k)^{\mathrm{T}}\mathbf{w}^k}{\|\mathbf{z}^k\|^2} \mathbf{z}^k \qquad \text{if } (\mathbf{z}^k)^{\mathrm{T}}\mathbf{w}^k \leq b \\ \\ \mathbf{w}^{k+1} = \mathbf{w}^k \qquad \qquad \qquad \qquad \text{otherwise} \end{cases} \qquad (3.1.29)$$

If the training set is linearly separable, Mays' rule converges in a finite number of iterations, for $0 < \rho < 2$ (Duda and Hart, 1973). In the case of a nonlinearly separable training set, the training procedure in Equation (3.1.29) will never converge. To fix this problem, a decreasing learning rate such as $\rho^k = \rho/k$ may be used to force convergence to some approximate separating surface (Duda and Singleton, 1964).

Widrow-Hoff (α-LMS) Learning Rule   Another example of an error correcting rule with a quadratic criterion function is the Widrow-Hoff rule (Widrow and Hoff, 1960). This rule was originally used to train the linear unit, also known as the *adaptive linear combiner element* (ADALINE), shown in Figure 3.1.3. In this case, the output of the linear unit in response to the input $\mathbf{x}^k$ is simply $y^k = (\mathbf{x}^k)^{\mathrm{T}}\mathbf{w}$. The Widrow-Hoff rule was proposed originally as an ad hoc rule which embodies the so-called minimal disturbance principle. Later, it was discovered (Widrow and Stearns, 1985) that this rule converges in the mean square to the solution $\mathbf{w}^*$ that corresponds to the least-

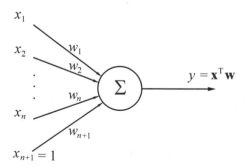

Figure 3.1.3
Adaptive linear combiner element (ADALINE).

mean-square (LMS) output error if all input patterns are of the same length (i.e., $\|\mathbf{x}^k\|$ is the same for all k). Therefore, this rule is sometimes referred to as the α-*LMS rule* (the α is used here to distinguish this rule from another very similar rule that is discussed in Section 3.1.2).

The α-LMS rule is given by

$$\begin{cases} \mathbf{w}^1 = \mathbf{0} \text{ or arbitrary} \\ \\ \mathbf{w}^{k+1} = \mathbf{w}^k + \alpha(d^k - y^k)\dfrac{\mathbf{x}^k}{\|\mathbf{x}^k\|^2} \end{cases} \qquad (3.1.30)$$

where $d^k \in R$ is the desired response, and $\alpha > 0$. Equation (3.1.30) is similar to the perceptron rule if one sets ρ in Equation (3.1.2) as

$$\rho = \rho^k = \frac{\alpha}{\|\mathbf{x}^k\|^2} \qquad (3.1.31)$$

However, the error in Equation (3.1.30) is measured at the linear output, not after the nonlinearity, as in the perceptron. The constant α controls the stability and speed of convergence (Widrow and Stearns, 1985; Widrow and Lehr, 1990). If the input vectors are independent over time, stability is ensured for most practical purposes if $0 < \alpha < 2$.

As for Mays' rule, this rule is self-normalizing in the sense that the choice of α does not depend on the magnitude of the input vectors. Since the α-LMS rule selects $\Delta\mathbf{w}^k$ to be collinear with $\mathbf{x}^k$, the desired error correction is achieved with a weight change of the smallest possible magnitude. Thus, when adapting to learn a new training sample, the responses to previous training samples are, on average, minimally disturbed. This is the basic idea behind the minimal disturbance principle on which the α-LMS is founded. Alternatively, one can show that the α-LMS learning rule is a gradient descent minimizer of an appropriate quadratic criterion function (see Problem 3.1.4).

3.1.2   Other Gradient-Descent-Based Learning Rules

In the following, additional learning rules for single-unit training are derived. These rules are derived systematically by first defining an appropriate criterion function and then optimizing such a function by an iterative gradient search procedure.

μ-LMS Learning Rule   The μ-LMS learning rule (Widrow and Hoff, 1960) represents the most analyzed and most applied simple learning rule. It is also of special importance due to its possible extension to learning in multiple unit neural nets. Therefore, special attention is given to this rule in this chapter. In the following, the μ-LMS rule is described in the context of the linear unit in Figure 3.1.3.

Let

$$J(\mathbf{w}) = \tfrac{1}{2} \sum_{i=1}^{m} (d^i - y^i)^2 \tag{3.1.32}$$

be the sum of squared error (SSE) criterion function, where

$$y^i = (\mathbf{x}^i)^{\mathrm{T}} \mathbf{w} \tag{3.1.33}$$

Now, using steepest gradient-descent search to minimize $J(\mathbf{w})$ in Equation (3.1.32) gives

$$\mathbf{w}^{k+1} = \mathbf{w}^k - \mu \nabla J(\mathbf{w})$$

$$= \mathbf{w}^k + \mu \sum_{i=1}^{m} (d^i - y^i)\mathbf{x}^i \tag{3.1.34}$$

The criterion function $J(\mathbf{w})$ in Equation (3.1.32) is quadratic in the weights because of the linear relation between y^i and $\mathbf{w}$. In fact, $J(\mathbf{w})$ defines a convex[3] hyperparaboloidal surface with a single minimum $\mathbf{w}^*$ (the global minimum). Therefore, if the positive constant μ is chosen sufficiently small, the gradient-descent search implemented by Equation (3.1.34) will asymptotically converge toward the solution $\mathbf{w}^*$ regardless of the setting of the initial search point $\mathbf{w}^1$. The learning rule in Equation (3.1.34) is sometimes referred to as the *batch LMS rule*.

The incremental version of Equation (3.1.34), known as the *μ-LMS* or *LMS rule*, is given by

$$\begin{cases} \mathbf{w}^1 = \mathbf{0} \text{ or arbitrary} \\ \mathbf{w}^{k+1} = \mathbf{w}^k + \mu(d^k - y^k)\mathbf{x}^k \end{cases} \tag{3.1.35}$$

Note that this rule becomes identical to the α-LMS learning rule in Equation (3.1.30) upon setting μ as

$$\mu = \mu^k = \frac{\alpha}{\|\mathbf{x}^k\|^2} \tag{3.1.36}$$

---

3. A function of the form $f: R^n \to R$ is said to be *convex* if the following condition is satisfied:

$$(1 - \lambda)f(\mathbf{u}) + \lambda f(\mathbf{v}) \geq f[(1 - \lambda)\mathbf{u} + \lambda \mathbf{v}]$$

for any pair of vectors $\mathbf{u}$ and $\mathbf{v}$ in R^n and any real number λ in the closed interval $[0, 1]$.

Also, when the input vectors have the same length, as would be the case when $\mathbf{x} \in \{-1, +1\}^n$, then the α-LMS rule becomes identical to the μ-LMS rule. Since the α-LMS learning algorithm converges when $0 < \alpha < 2$, we can start from Equation (3.1.36) and calculate the required range on μ for ensuring the convergence of the μ-LMS rule for "most practical purposes":

$$0 < \mu < \frac{2}{\max_i \|\mathbf{x}^i\|^2} \tag{3.1.37}$$

For input patterns independent over time and generated by a stationary process, convergence of the mean of the weight vector $\langle \mathbf{w}^k \rangle$ is ensured if the fixed learning rate μ is chosen to be smaller than $2/\langle \|\mathbf{x}\|^2 \rangle$ (Widrow and Stearns, 1985) (also see Problem 4.3.8 in the next chapter for further exploration). Here, $\langle \cdot \rangle$ signifies the "mean" or expected value. In this case, $\langle \mathbf{w}^k \rangle$ approaches a solution $\mathbf{w}^*$ as $k \to \infty$. Note that the bound $2/\langle \|\mathbf{x}\|^2 \rangle$ is less restrictive than the one in Equation (3.1.37). Horowitz and Senne (1981) showed that the bound $(2/3)\langle \|\mathbf{x}\|^2 \rangle$ on μ guarantees the convergence of $\mathbf{w}$ in the mean square (i.e., $\langle \|\mathbf{w}^k - \mathbf{w}^*\|^2 \rangle \to 0$ as $k \to \infty$) for input patterns generated by a zero-mean Gaussian process independent over time. It should be noted that convergence in the mean square implies convergence in the mean; however, the converse is not necessarily true. The assumptions of decorrelated patterns and stationarity are not necessary conditions for the convergence of μ-LMS (Widrow et al., 1976; Farden, 1981). For example, Macchi and Eweda (1983) have a much stronger result regarding convergence of the μ-LMS rule which is even valid when a finite number of successive training patterns are strongly correlated.

In practical problems, $m > n + 1$; hence it becomes impossible to satisfy all requirements $(\mathbf{x}^k)^T \mathbf{w} = d^k$, $k = 1, 2, \ldots, m$. Therefore, Equation (3.1.35) never converges. Thus, for convergence, μ is set to $\mu_0/k > 0$, where μ_0 is a small positive constant. In applications such as linear filtering, though, the decreasing step size is not very valuable, because it cannot accommodate nonstationarity in the input signal. Indeed, $\mathbf{w}^k$ will essentially stop changing for large k, which precludes the tracking of time variations. Thus the fixed-increment (constant μ) LMS learning rule has the advantage of limited memory, which enables it to track time fluctuations in the input data.

When the learning rate μ is sufficiently small, the μ-LMS rule becomes a "good" approximation to the gradient-descent rule in Equation (3.1.34). This means that the weight vector $\mathbf{w}^k$ will tend to move toward the global minimum $\mathbf{w}^*$ of the convex SSE criterion function. Next, we show that $\mathbf{w}^*$ is given by

$$\mathbf{w}^* = \mathbf{X}^\dagger \mathbf{d} \tag{3.1.38}$$

where $\mathbf{X} = [\mathbf{x}^1 \quad \mathbf{x}^2 \quad \cdots \quad \mathbf{x}^m]$, $\mathbf{d} = [d^1 \quad d^2 \quad \cdots \quad d^m]^T$, and $\mathbf{X}^\dagger = (\mathbf{XX}^T)^{-1}\mathbf{X}$ is the generalized inverse or pseudoinverse (Penrose, 1955) of $\mathbf{X}$ for $m > n + 1$.

The extreme points (minima and maxima) of the function $J(\mathbf{w})$ are solutions to the equation

$$\nabla J(\mathbf{w}) = \mathbf{0} \tag{3.1.39}$$

Therefore, any minimum of the SSE criterion function in Equation (3.1.32) must satisfy

$$\nabla J(\mathbf{w}) = -\sum_{i=1}^{m} [d^i - (\mathbf{x}^i)^T\mathbf{w}]\mathbf{x}^i = \mathbf{X}(\mathbf{X}^T\mathbf{w} - \mathbf{d}) = \mathbf{0} \tag{3.1.40}$$

Equation (3.1.40) can be rewritten as

$$\mathbf{XX}^T\mathbf{w} = \mathbf{Xd} \tag{3.1.41}$$

which for a nonsingular matrix $\mathbf{XX}^T$ gives the solution in Equation (3.1.38), or explicitly

$$\mathbf{w}^* = (\mathbf{XX}^T)^{-1}\mathbf{Xd} \tag{3.1.42}$$

Recall that just because $\mathbf{w}^*$ in Equation (3.1.42) satisfies the condition $\nabla J(\mathbf{w}^*) = \mathbf{0}$, this does not guarantee that $\mathbf{w}^*$ is a local minimum of the criterion function J. It does, however, considerably narrow the choices in that such $\mathbf{w}^*$ represents (in a local sense) either a point of minimum, maximum, or saddle point of J. To verify that $\mathbf{w}^*$ is actually a minimum of $J(\mathbf{w})$, we may evaluate the second derivative or Hessian matrix

$$\nabla\nabla J = \left[\frac{\partial^2 J}{\partial w_i \, \partial w_j} \right]$$

of J at $\mathbf{w}^*$ and show that it is positive definite.[4] But this result follows immediately after noting that $\nabla\nabla J$ is equal to the positive-definite matrix $\mathbf{XX}^T$. Thus $\mathbf{w}^*$ is a minimum of J.[5]

The LMS rule also may be applied to synthesize the weight vector $\mathbf{w}$ of a perceptron for solving two-class classification problems. Here, one starts by training the linear unit in Figure 3.1.3 with the given training pairs $\{\mathbf{x}^k, d^k\}$, $k = 1, 2, \ldots, m$, using the LMS rule. During training, the desired target d^k is set to $+1$ for one class and to

---

4. An $n \times n$ real symmetric matrix $\mathbf{A}$ is positive-definite if the quadratic form $\mathbf{x}^T\mathbf{Ax}$ is strictly positive for all nonzero column vectors $\mathbf{x}$ in R^n [for further details, see Gantmacher (1990)].

5. Of course, the same result could have been achieved by noting that the convex, unconstrained quadratic nature of $J(\mathbf{w})$ admits one extreme point $\mathbf{w}^*$, which must be the global minimum of $J(\mathbf{w})$.

−1 for the other class. (In fact, any positive constant can be used as the target for one class, and any negative constant can be used as the target for the other class.) After convergence of the learning process, the solution vector obtained may now be used in the perceptron for classification. Because of the thresholding nonlinearity in the perceptron, the output of the classifier will now be properly restricted to the set $\{-1, +1\}$.

When used as a perceptron weight vector, the minimum SSE solution in Equation (3.1.42) does not generally minimize the perceptron classification error rate. This should not be surprising, since the SSE criterion function is not designed to constrain its minimum inside the linearly separable solution region. Therefore, this solution does not necessarily represent a linear separable solution, even when the training set is linearly separable (this is further explored in Section 3.1.5). However, when the training set is nonlinearly separable, the solution arrived at may still be a useful approximation. Therefore, by employing the LMS rule for perceptron training, linear separability is sacrificed for good compromise performance on both separable and nonseparable problems.

The μ-LMS as a Stochastic Process   Stochastic approximation theory may be employed as an alternative to the deterministic gradient-descent analysis presented thus far. It has the advantage of naturally arriving at a learning-rate schedule ρ^k for asymptotic convergence in the mean square. Here, one starts with the mean-square error (MSE) criterion function:

$$J(\mathbf{w}) = \tfrac{1}{2}\langle(\mathbf{x}^T\mathbf{w} - d)^2\rangle \tag{3.1.43}$$

where again $\langle\cdot\rangle$ denotes the mean (expectation) over all training vectors. Now one may compute the gradient of J as

$$\nabla J(\mathbf{w}) = \langle(\mathbf{x}^T\mathbf{w} - d)\mathbf{x}\rangle \tag{3.1.44}$$

which upon setting to zero allows us to find the minimum $\mathbf{w}^*$ of J in Equation (3.1.43) as the solution of

$$\langle\mathbf{x}\mathbf{x}^T\rangle\mathbf{w}^* = \langle d\mathbf{x}\rangle$$

which gives

$$\mathbf{w}^* = \mathbf{C}^{-1}\mathbf{P} \tag{3.1.45}$$

where $\mathbf{C} \triangleq \langle\mathbf{x}\mathbf{x}^T\rangle$ and $\mathbf{P} \triangleq \langle d\mathbf{x}\rangle$. Note that the expected value of a vector or a matrix is found by taking the expected values of its components. We refer to $\mathbf{C}$ as the *auto-correlation matrix* of the input vectors and to $\mathbf{P}$ as the *cross-correlation vector* between the input vector **x** and its associated desired target d (more to follow on the properties of **C** in Section 3.3.1). In Equation (3.1.45), the determinant of **C**, $|C|$, is assumed different from zero. The solution **w*** in Equation (3.1.45) is sometimes called the *Wiener weight vector* (Widrow and Stearns, 1985). It represents the minimum MSE solution, also known as the *least-mean-square (LMS) solution.*

It is interesting to note here the close relation between the minimum SSE solution in Equation (3.1.42) and the LMS or minimum MSE solution in Equation (3.1.45). In fact, one can show that when the size of the training set m is large, the minimum SSE solution converges to the minimum MSE solution.

First, let us express $\mathbf{X}\mathbf{X}^T$ as the sum of vector outer products $\sum_{k=1}^{m} \mathbf{x}^k(\mathbf{x}^k)^T$. We can also rewrite $\mathbf{X}\mathbf{d}$ as $\sum_{k=1}^{m} d^k\mathbf{x}^k$. This representation allows us to express Equation (3.1.42) as

$$\mathbf{w}^* = \left[\sum_{k=1}^{m} \mathbf{x}^k(\mathbf{x}^k)^T \right]^{-1} \left(\sum_{k=1}^{m} d^k\mathbf{x}^k \right)$$

Now, multiplying the right-hand side of the preceding equation by m/m allows us to express it as

$$\mathbf{w}^* = \left[\frac{1}{m} \sum_{k=1}^{m} \mathbf{x}^k(\mathbf{x}^k)^T \right]^{-1} \left(\frac{1}{m} \sum_{k=1}^{m} d^k\mathbf{x}^k \right)$$

Finally, if m is large, the averages

$$\frac{1}{m} \sum_{k=1}^{m} \mathbf{x}^k(\mathbf{x}^k)^T \qquad \text{and} \qquad \frac{1}{m} \sum_{k=1}^{m} d^k\mathbf{x}^k$$

become very good approximations of the expectations $\mathbf{C} = \langle \mathbf{x}\mathbf{x}^T \rangle$ and $\mathbf{P} = \langle d\mathbf{x} \rangle$, respectively. Thus we have established the equivalence of the minimum SSE and minimum MSE for a large training set.

Next, in order to minimize the MSE criterion, one may employ a gradient-descent procedure where, instead of the expected gradient in Equation (3.1.44), the instantaneous gradient $[(\mathbf{x}^k)^T\mathbf{w}^k - d^k]\mathbf{x}^k$ is used. Here, at each learning step the input vector **x** is drawn at random. This leads to the stochastic process

$$\mathbf{w}^{k+1} = \mathbf{w}^k + \rho^k[d^k - (\mathbf{x}^k)^T\mathbf{w}^k]\mathbf{x}^k \tag{3.1.46}$$

which is the same as the μ-LMS rule in Equation (3.1.35) except for a variable learning rate ρ^k. It can be shown that if $|C| \neq 0$ and ρ^k satisfies the three conditions

$$1. \ \rho^k \geq 0 \tag{3.1.47a}$$

$$2. \ \lim_{m \to \infty} \sum_{k=1}^{m} \rho^k = +\infty \tag{3.1.47b}$$

$$3. \ \lim_{m \to \infty} \sum_{k=1}^{m} (\rho^k)^2 < \infty \tag{3.1.47c}$$

then $\mathbf{w}^k$ converges to $\mathbf{w}^*$ in Equation (3.1.45) asymptotically in the mean square; i.e.,

$$\lim_{k \to \infty} \langle \| \mathbf{w}^k - \mathbf{w}^* \|^2 \rangle = 0 \tag{3.1.48}$$

The criterion function in Equation (3.1.43) is of the form $\langle g(\mathbf{w}, \mathbf{x}) \rangle$ and is known as a *regression function*. The iterative algorithm in Equation (3.1.46) is also known as a *stochastic approximation procedure* (or Kiefer-Wolfowitz or Robbins-Monro procedure). For a thorough discussion of stochastic approximation theory, the reader is referred to Wasan (1969).

Example 3.1.1 This example presents the results of a set of simulations that should help give some insight into the dynamics of the batch and incremental LMS learning

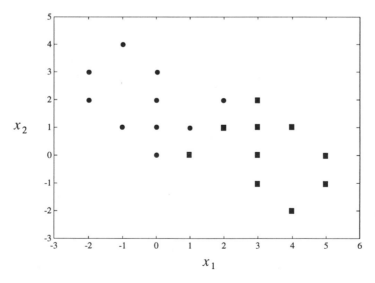

Figure 3.1.4
A 20-sample training set used in the simulations associated with Example 3.1.1. Points signified by a square and a filled circle should map into $+1$ and -1, respectively.

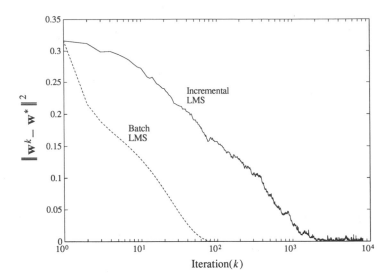

Figure 3.1.5
Plots (learning curves) for the square of the distance between the search point
$\mathbf{w}^k$ and the minimum SSE solution $\mathbf{w}^*$ generated using two versions of the LMS
learning rule. The dashed line corresponds to the batch LMS rule in Equation
(3.1.34). The solid line corresponds to the incremental LMS rule in Equation
(3.1.35) with a random order of presentation of the training patterns. In both
cases, $\mathbf{w}^1 = \mathbf{0}$ and $\mu = 0.005$ are used. Note the logarithmic scale for the iteration number k.

rules. Specifically, we are interested in comparing the convergence behavior of the
discrete-time dynamical systems in Equations (3.1.34) and (3.1.35). Consider the training set depicted in Figure 3.1.4 for a simple mapping problem. The 10 squares and 10
filled circles in this figure are positioned at the points whose coordinates (x_1, x_2)
specify the two components of the input vectors. The squares and circles are to be
mapped to the targets $+1$ and -1, respectively. For example, the left-most square in
the figure represents the training pair $\{[1, 0]^T, 1\}$. Similarly, the right most circle
represents the training pair $\{[2, 2]^T, -1\}$. Figure 3.1.5 shows plots for the evolution of
the square of the distance between the vector $\mathbf{w}^k$ and the (computed) minimum SSE
solution $\mathbf{w}^*$ for batch LMS (dashed line) and incremental LMS (solid line). In both
simulations, the learning rate (step size) μ was set to 0.005. The initial search point $\mathbf{w}^1$
was set to $[0, 0]^T$. For the incremental LMS rule, the training examples are selected
randomly from the training set. The batch LMS rule converges to the optimal solution $\mathbf{w}^*$ in less than 100 steps. Incremental LMS requires more learning steps, on the
order of 2000 steps, to converge to a small neighborhood of $\mathbf{w}^*$. The fluctuations in

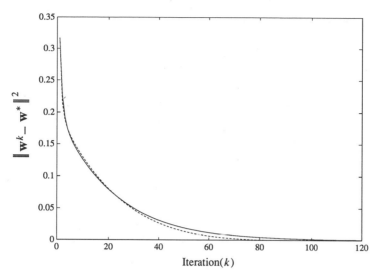

Figure 3.1.6
Learning curves for the batch LMS (dashed line) and incremental LMS (solid line) learning rules for the data in Figure 3.1.4. The result for the batch LMS rule shown here is identical to the one shown in Figure 3.1.5 (this result looks different only because of the present use of a linear scale for the horizontal axis). The incremental LMS rule results shown assume a deterministic, fixed order of presentation of the training patterns. Also, for the incremental LMS case, $\mathbf{w}^k$ represents the weight vector after the completion of the kth learning "cycle." Here, one cycle corresponds to 20 consecutive learning iterations.

$\|\mathbf{w}^k - \mathbf{w}^*\|^2$ in this neighborhood are less than 0.02, as can be seen from Figure 3.1.5. The effect of a deterministic order of presentation of the training examples on the incremental LMS rule is shown by the solid line in Figure 3.1.6. Here, the training examples are presented in a predefined order, which did not change during training. The same initialization and step size are used as before. In order to allow for a more meaningful comparison between the two LMS rule versions, one learning step of incremental LMS is taken to mean a full cycle through the 20 samples. For comparison, the simulation result with batch LMS learning is plotted in the figure (see dashed line). These results indicate a very similar behavior in the convergence characteristics of incremental and batch LMS learning. This is so because of the small step size used. Both cases show asymptotic convergence toward the optimal solution $\mathbf{w}^*$, but with a relatively faster convergence of the batch LMS rule near $\mathbf{w}^*$. This is attributed to the use of more accurate gradient information.

Correlation Learning Rule   The *correlation learning rule* is derived by starting from the criterion function

$$J(\mathbf{w}) = -\sum_{i=1}^{m} y^i d^i \tag{3.1.49}$$

where $y^i = (\mathbf{x}^i)^{\mathsf{T}}\mathbf{w}$, and performing gradient descent to minimize J. Note that minimizing $J(\mathbf{w})$ is equivalent to maximizing the correlation between the desired target and the corresponding linear unit's output for all $\mathbf{x}^i$, $i = 1, 2, \ldots, m$. Now, employing steepest gradient descent to minimize $J(\mathbf{w})$ leads to the learning rule:

$$\begin{cases} \mathbf{w}^1 = \mathbf{0} \\ \mathbf{w}^{k+1} = \mathbf{w}^k + \rho\, d^k \mathbf{x}^k \end{cases} \tag{3.1.50}$$

By setting ρ to 1 and completing one learning cycle using Equation (3.1.50), we arrive at the weight vector $\mathbf{w}^*$ given by

$$\mathbf{w}^* = \sum_{i=1}^{m} d^i \mathbf{x}^i = \mathbf{X}\mathbf{d} \tag{3.1.51}$$

where $\mathbf{X}$ and $\mathbf{d}$ are as defined on page 70. Note that Equation (3.1.51) leads to the minimum SSE solution in Equation (3.1.38) if $\mathbf{X}^{\dagger} = \mathbf{X}$. This is only possible if the training vectors $\mathbf{x}^k$ are encoded such that $\mathbf{X}\mathbf{X}^{\mathsf{T}}$ is the identity matrix (i.e., the $\mathbf{x}^k$ vectors are orthonormal). Correlation learning is further explored in Section 7.1.1.

Another version of this type of learning is the *covariance learning rule*. This rule is obtained by steepest gradient descent on the criterion function

$$J(\mathbf{w}) = -\left|\sum_{i=1}^{m} (y^i - \langle y\rangle)(d^i - \langle d\rangle)\right|.$$

Here, $\langle y\rangle$ and $\langle d\rangle$ are computed averages, over all training pairs, for the unit's output and the desired target, respectively. Covariance learning provides the basis of the cascade-correlation net presented in Section 6.3.2.

3.1.3 Extension of μ-LMS Rule to Units with Differentiable Activation Functions: Delta Rule

The following rule is similar to the μ-LMS rule except that it allows for units with a differentiable nonlinear activation function f. Figure 3.1.7 illustrates a unit with a sigmoidal activation function. Here, the unit's output is $y = f(net)$, with *net* defined as the vector inner product $\mathbf{x}^{\mathsf{T}}\mathbf{w}$.

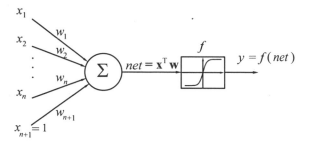

Figure 3.1.7
A computational unit with a differentiable sigmoidal activation
function.

Again, consider the training pairs $\{\mathbf{x}^i, d^i\}$, $i = 1, 2, \ldots, m$, with $\mathbf{x}^i \in R^{n+1}$ ($x_{n+1}^i = 1$ for all i) and $d^i \in [-1, +1]$. Performing gradient descent on the instantaneous SSE criterion function $J(\mathbf{w}) = \frac{1}{2}(d - y)^2$, whose gradient is given by

$$\nabla J(\mathbf{w}) = -(d - y)f'(net)\mathbf{x} \tag{3.1.52}$$

leads to the delta rule:

$$\begin{cases} \mathbf{w}^1 & \text{arbitrary} \\ \mathbf{w}^{k+1} = \mathbf{w}^k + \rho[d^k - f(net^k)]f'(net^k)\mathbf{x}^k = \mathbf{w}^k + \rho\delta^k\mathbf{x}^k \end{cases} \tag{3.1.53}$$

where $net^k = (\mathbf{x}^k)^T\mathbf{w}^k$ and $f' = \dfrac{df}{d\,net}$. If f is defined by $f(net) = \tanh(\beta\,net)$, then its derivative is given by $f'(net) = \beta[1 - f^2(net)]$. For the "logistic" function, $f(net) = 1/(1 + e^{-\beta\,net})$, the derivative is $f'(net) = \beta f(net)[1 - f(net)]$. Figure 3.1.8 plots f and f' for the hyperbolic tangent activation function with $\beta = 1$. Note how f asymptotically approaches $+1$ and -1 in the limit as net approaches $+\infty$ and $-\infty$, respectively.

One disadvantage of the delta learning rule is immediately apparent upon inspection of the graph of $f'(net)$ in Figure 3.1.8. In particular, notice how $f'(net) \approx 0$ when net has large magnitude (i.e., $|net| > 3$); these regions are called *flat spots* of f'. In these flat spots, we expect the delta learning rule to progress very slowly (i.e., very small weight changes even when the error $(d - y)$ is large), because the magnitude of the weight change in Equation (3.1.53) directly depends on the magnitude of $f'(net)$. Since slow convergence results in excessive computation time, it would be advantageous to try to eliminate the flat spot phenomenon when using the delta learning rule. One common flat spot elimination technique involves replacing f' by f' plus a small

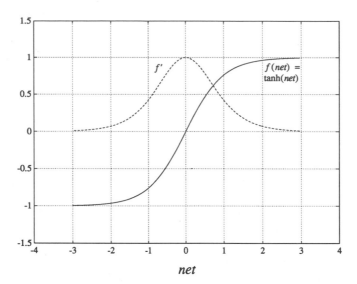

Figure 3.1.8
Hyperbolic tangent activation function f and its derivative f', plotted for
$-3 \leq net \leq +3$.

positive bias ε. In this case, the weight update equation reads as

$$\mathbf{w}^{k+1} = \mathbf{w}^k + \rho[d^k - f(net^k)][f'(net^k) + \varepsilon]\mathbf{x}^k \tag{3.1.54}$$

One of the primary advantages of the delta rule is that it has a natural extension
that may be used to train multilayered neural nets. This extension, known as *error
back propagation*, will be discussed in Chapter 5.

3.1.4   Adaptive Ho-Kashyap (AHK) Learning Rules

Hassoun and Song (1992) proposed a set of adaptive learning rules for classification
problems as enhanced alternatives to the LMS and perceptron learning rules. In the
following, three learning rules, AHK I, AHK II, and AHK III, are derived based on
gradient-descent strategies on an appropriate criterion function. Two of the proposed
learning rules, AHK I and AHK II, are well suited for generating robust decision
surfaces for linearly separable problems. The third training rule, AHK III, extends
these capabilities to find "good" approximate solutions for nonlinearly separable
problems. The three AHK learning rules preserve the simple incremental nature
found in the LMS and perceptron learning rules. The AHK rules also possess additional processing capabilities, such as the ability to automatically identify critical

cluster boundaries and place a linear decision surface in such a way that it leads to enhanced classification robustness.

Consider a two-class $\{c_1, c_2\}$ classification problem with m labeled feature vectors (training vectors) $\{\mathbf{x}^i, d^i\}$, $i = 1, 2, \ldots, m$. Assume that $\mathbf{x}^i$ belongs to R^{n+1} (with the last component of $\mathbf{x}^i$ being a constant bias of value 1) and that $d^i = +1\,(-1)$ if $\mathbf{x}^i \in c_1\,(c_2)$. Then, a single perceptron can be trained to correctly classify the preceding training pairs if an $(n + 1)$-dimensional weight vector $\mathbf{w}$ is computed that satisfies the following set of m inequalities (the sgn function is assumed to be the perceptron's activation function):

$$(\mathbf{x}^i)^T\mathbf{w} \begin{cases} > 0 & \text{if } d^i = +1 \\ < 0 & \text{if } d^i = -1 \end{cases} \quad \text{for } i = 1, 2, \ldots, m \tag{3.1.55}$$

Next, if we define a set of m new vectors $\mathbf{z}^i$ according to

$$\mathbf{z}^i = \begin{cases} +\mathbf{x}^i & \text{if } d^i = +1 \\ -\mathbf{x}^i & \text{if } d^i = -1 \end{cases} \quad \text{for } i = 1, 2, \ldots, m \tag{3.1.56}$$

and we let

$$\mathbf{Z} = [\mathbf{z}^1 \quad \mathbf{z}^2 \quad \cdots \quad \mathbf{z}^m] \tag{3.1.57}$$

then Equation (3.1.55) may be rewritten as the single matrix equation

$$\mathbf{Z}^T\mathbf{w} > \mathbf{0} \tag{3.1.58}$$

Now, defining an m-dimensional positive-valued margin vector $\mathbf{b}$ ($\mathbf{b} > \mathbf{0}$) and using it in Equation (3.1.58), we arrive at the following equivalent form of Equation (3.1.55):

$$\mathbf{Z}^T\mathbf{w} = \mathbf{b} \tag{3.1.59}$$

Thus the training of the perceptron is now equivalent to solving Equation (3.1.59) for $\mathbf{w}$, subject to the constraint $\mathbf{b} > \mathbf{0}$. Ho and Kashyap (1965) proposed an iterative algorithm for solving Equation (3.1.59). In the Ho-Kashyap algorithm, the components of the margin vector are first initialized to small positive values, and the pseudoinverse is used to generate a solution for $\mathbf{w}$ (based on the initial guess of $\mathbf{b}$) that minimizes the SSE criterion function $J(\mathbf{w}, \mathbf{b}) = \frac{1}{2}\|\mathbf{Z}^T\mathbf{w} - \mathbf{b}\|^2$:

$$\mathbf{w} = \mathbf{Z}^\dagger\mathbf{b} \tag{3.1.60}$$

where $\mathbf{Z}^\dagger = (\mathbf{Z}\mathbf{Z}^T)^{-1}\mathbf{Z}$, for $m > n + 1$. Next, a new estimate for the margin vector is computed by performing the constrained ($\mathbf{b} > \mathbf{0}$) gradient descent

$$\mathbf{b}^{k+1} = \mathbf{b}^k + \frac{1}{2}[\boldsymbol{\varepsilon} + |\boldsymbol{\varepsilon}|] \qquad \text{with } \boldsymbol{\varepsilon}^k = \mathbf{Z}^T\mathbf{w}^k - \mathbf{b}^k \tag{3.1.61}$$

where $|\cdot|$ denotes the absolute value of the components of the argument vector, and $\mathbf{b}^k$ is the "current" margin vector. A new estimate of $\mathbf{w}$ can now be computed using Equation (3.1.60) and employing the updated margin vector from Equation (3.1.61). This process continues until all the components of ε are zero (or are sufficiently small and positive), which is an indication of linear separability of the training set, or until $\varepsilon < 0$, which is an indication of nonlinear separability of the training set (no solution is found). It can be shown (Ho and Kashyap, 1965; Slansky and Wassel, 1981) that the Ho-Kashyap procedure converges in a finite number of steps if the training set is linearly separable. For simulations comparing the preceding training algorithm with the LMS and perceptron training procedures, the reader is referred to Hassoun and Clark (1988), Hassoun and Youssef (1989), and Hassoun (1989a). This algorithm will be referred to here as the *direct Ho-Kashyap (DHK) algorithm*.

The direct synthesis of the $\mathbf{w}$ estimate in Equation (3.1.60) involves a one-time computation of the pseudoinverse of $\mathbf{Z}$. However, such computation can be computationally expensive and requires special treatment when $\mathbf{ZZ}^\mathrm{T}$ is ill-conditioned (i.e., the determinant $|\mathbf{ZZ}^\mathrm{T}|$ close to zero). An alternative algorithm that is based on gradient-descent principles and which does not require the direct computation of $\mathbf{Z}^\dagger$ can be derived. This derivation is presented next.

Starting with the criterion function $J(\mathbf{w}, \mathbf{b}) = \frac{1}{2}\|\mathbf{Z}^\mathrm{T}\mathbf{w} - \mathbf{b}\|^2$, gradient descent may be performed (Slansky and Wassel, 1981) with respect to $\mathbf{b}$ and $\mathbf{w}$ so that J is minimized subject to the constraint $\mathbf{b} > \mathbf{0}$. The gradient of J with respect to $\mathbf{w}$ and $\mathbf{b}$ is given by

$$\nabla_\mathbf{b} J(\mathbf{w}, \mathbf{b})|_{\mathbf{w}^k, \mathbf{b}^k} = -(\mathbf{Z}^\mathrm{T}\mathbf{w}^k - \mathbf{b}^k) \qquad (3.1.62a)$$

$$\nabla_\mathbf{w} J(\mathbf{w}, \mathbf{b})|_{\mathbf{w}^k, \mathbf{b}^{k+1}} = \mathbf{Z}(\mathbf{Z}^\mathrm{T}\mathbf{w}^k - \mathbf{b}^{k+1}) \qquad (3.1.62b)$$

where the superscripts k and $k + 1$ represent current and updated values, respectively. One analytic method for imposing the constraint $\mathbf{b} > \mathbf{0}$ is to replace the gradient in Equation (3.1.62a) by $-0.5(\varepsilon + |\varepsilon|)$, with ε as defined in Equation (3.1.61). This leads to the following gradient-descent formulation of the Ho-Kashyap procedure:

$$\mathbf{b}^{k+1} = \mathbf{b}^k + \frac{\rho_1}{2}(|\varepsilon^k| + \varepsilon^k) \qquad \text{with } \varepsilon^k = \mathbf{Z}^\mathrm{T}\mathbf{w}^k - \mathbf{b}^k \qquad (3.1.63a)$$

and

$$\mathbf{w}^{k+1} = \mathbf{w}^k - \rho_2 \mathbf{Z}(\mathbf{Z}^\mathrm{T}\mathbf{w}^k - \mathbf{b}^{k+1})$$

$$= \mathbf{w}^k + \frac{\rho_1 \rho_2}{2} \mathbf{Z}\left[|\varepsilon^k| + \varepsilon^k\left(1 - \frac{2}{\rho_1}\right)\right] \qquad (3.1.63b)$$

where ρ_1 and ρ_2 are strictly positive constant learning rates. Because of the requirement that all training vectors $\mathbf{z}^k$ (or $\mathbf{x}^k$) be present and included in $\mathbf{Z}$, this procedure is called the *batch-mode adaptive Ho-Kashyap (AHK) procedure*. It can be easily shown that if $\rho_1 = 0$ and $\mathbf{b}^1 = \mathbf{1}$, Equation (3.1.63) reduces to the μ-LMS learning rule. Furthermore, convergence can be guaranteed (Duda and Hart, 1973) if $0 < \rho_1 < 2$ and $0 < \rho_2 < 2/\lambda_{max}$, where λ_{max} is the largest eigenvalue of the positive definite matrix $\mathbf{ZZ}^T$.

A completely adaptive Ho-Kashyap procedure for solving Equation (3.1.59) is arrived at by starting from the instantaneous criterion function

$$J(\mathbf{w}, \mathbf{b}) = \tfrac{1}{2}[(\mathbf{z}^i)^T\mathbf{w} - b_i],$$

which leads to the following incremental update rules:

$$b_i^{k+1} = b_i^k + \frac{\rho_1}{2}(|\varepsilon_i^k| + \varepsilon_i^k) \qquad \text{with } \varepsilon_i^k = (\mathbf{z}^i)^T\mathbf{w}^k - b_i^k \qquad (3.1.64a)$$

and

$$\mathbf{w}^{k+1} = \mathbf{w}^k - \rho_2\mathbf{z}^i[(\mathbf{z}^i)^T\mathbf{w}^k - b_i^{k+1}]$$

$$= \mathbf{w}^k + \frac{\rho_1\rho_2}{2}\left[|\varepsilon_i^k| + \varepsilon_i^k\left(1 - \frac{2}{\rho_1}\right)\right]\mathbf{z}^i \qquad (3.1.64b)$$

Here, b_i represents a scalar margin associated with the $\mathbf{x}^i$ input. In all the preceding Ho-Kashyap learning procedures, the margin values are initialized to small positive values, and the perceptron weights are initialized to zero (or small random) values. If full margin error correction is assumed in Equation (3.1.64a), i.e., $\rho_1 = 1$, the incremental learning procedure in Equation (3.1.64) reduces to the heuristically derived procedure reported in Hassoun and Clark (1988). An alternative way of writing Equation (3.1.64) is

$$\Delta b_i = \rho_1\varepsilon_i^k \qquad \text{and} \qquad \Delta\mathbf{w} = \rho_2(\rho_1 - 1)\varepsilon_i^k\mathbf{z}^i \qquad \text{if } \varepsilon_i^k > 0 \qquad (3.1.65a)$$

$$\Delta b_i = 0 \qquad \text{and} \qquad \Delta\mathbf{w} = -\rho_2\varepsilon_i^k\mathbf{z}^i \qquad \text{if } \varepsilon_i^k \leq 0 \qquad (3.1.65b)$$

where Δb and $\Delta\mathbf{w}$ signify the difference between the updated and current values of b and $\mathbf{w}$, respectively. This procedure is called the *AHK I learning rule*. For comparison purposes, it may be noted that the μ-LMS rule in Equation (3.1.35) can be written as $\Delta\mathbf{w} = -\mu\varepsilon_i^k\mathbf{z}^i$, with b_i held fixed at $+1$.

The implied constraint $b_i > 0$ in Equations (3.1.64) and (3.1.65) was realized by starting with a positive initial margin and restricting the change Δb to positive real values. An alternative, more flexible way to realize this constraint is to allow both positive and negative changes in Δb, except for the cases where a decrease in b_i results in a negative margin. This modification results in the following alternative AHK II learning rule:

$$\Delta b_i = \rho_1 \varepsilon_i^k \quad \text{and} \quad \Delta \mathbf{w} = \rho_2(\rho_1 - 1)\varepsilon_i^k \mathbf{z}^i \quad \text{if } b_i^k + \rho_1 \varepsilon_i^k > 0 \quad (3.1.66a)$$

$$\Delta b_i = 0 \quad \text{and} \quad \Delta \mathbf{w} = -\rho_2 \varepsilon_i^k \mathbf{z}^i \quad \text{if } b_i^k + \rho_1 \varepsilon_i^k \le 0 \quad (3.1.66b)$$

In the general case of an adaptive margin, as in Equation (3.1.66), Hassoun and Song (1992) showed that a sufficient condition for the convergence of the AHK rules is given by

$$0 < \rho_2 < \frac{2}{\max_i \|\mathbf{z}^i\|^2} \tag{3.1.67a}$$

$$0 < \rho_1 < 2 \tag{3.1.67b}$$

Another variation results in the AHK III rule, which is appropriate for both linearly separable and nonlinearly separable problems. Here, $\Delta \mathbf{w}$ is set to $\mathbf{0}$ in Equation (3.1.66b). The advantages of the AHK III rule are that (1) it is capable of adaptively identifying difficult-to-separate class boundaries and (2) it uses such information to discard nonseparable training vectors and speed up convergence (Hassoun and Song, 1992). The reader is invited to apply the AHK III rule in Problem 3.1.7 for gaining insight into the dynamics and separation behavior of this learning rule.

Example 3.1.2   In this example the perceptron, LMS, and AHK learning rules are compared in terms of the quality of the solutions they generate. Consider the simple two-class linearly separable problem shown earlier in Figure 3.1.4. The μ-LMS rule of Equation (3.1.35) is used to obtain the solution shown as a dashed line in Figure 3.1.9. Here, the initial weight vector was set to $\mathbf{0}$ and a learning rate $\mu = 0.005$ is used. This solution is not one of the linearly separable solutions for this problem. Four examples of linearly separable solutions are shown as solid lines in the figure. These solutions are generated using the perceptron learning rule of Equation (3.1.2), with varying order of input vector presentations and with a learning rate of $\rho = 0.1$. Here, it should be noted that the most robust solution, in the sense of tolerance to noisy input, is given by $x_2 = x_1 + \frac{1}{2}$, which is shown as a dotted line in Figure 3.1.9. This robust solution was in fact automatically generated by the AHK I learning rule of Equation (3.1.65).

3.1.5   Other Criterion Functions

The SSE criterion function in Equation (3.1.32) is not the only possible choice. We have already seen other alternative functions such as the ones in Equations (3.1.20),

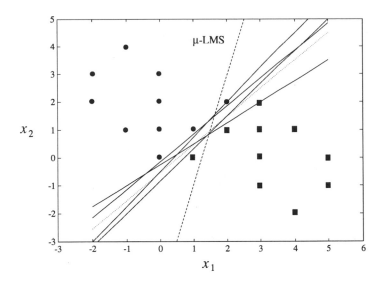

Figure 3.1.9
LMS-generated decision boundary (dashed line) for a two-class linearly separable problem. For comparison, four solutions generated using the perceptron learning rule are shown (solid lines). The dotted line is the solution generated by the AHK I rule.

(3.1.24), and (3.1.25). In general, any differentiable function that is minimized upon setting $y^i = d^i$, for $i = 1, 2, \ldots, m$, could be used. One possible generalization of SSE is the Minkowski-r criterion function (Hanson and Burr, 1988) given by

$$J(\mathbf{w}) = \frac{1}{r} \sum_{i=1}^{m} |d^i - y^i|^r \tag{3.1.68}$$

or its instantaneous version

$$J(\mathbf{w}) = \frac{1}{r} |d - y|^r \tag{3.1.69}$$

Figure 3.1.10 shows a plot of $|d - y|^r$ for $r = 1, 1.5, 2$, and 20. The general form of the gradient of this criterion function is given by

$$\nabla J(\mathbf{w}) = -\operatorname{sgn}(d - y)|d - y|^{r-1} f'(net)\mathbf{x} \tag{3.1.70}$$

Note that for $r = 2$ this reduces to the gradient of the SSE criterion function given by Equation (3.1.52). If $r = 1$, then $J(\mathbf{w}) = |d - y|$ with the gradient [note that the gradient of $J(\mathbf{w})$ does not exist at the solution points $d = y$]

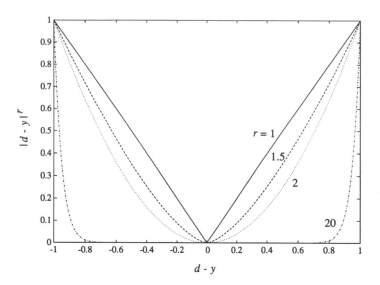

Figure 3.1.10
A family of instantaneous Minkowski-r criterion functions.

$$\nabla J(\mathbf{w}) = -\operatorname{sgn}(d - y)f'(net)\mathbf{x} \tag{3.1.71}$$

In this case, the criterion function in Equation (3.1.68) is known as the *Manhattan norm*. For $r \to \infty$, a supremum error measure is approached.

A small r gives less weight for large deviations and tends to reduce the influence of the outer-most points in the input space during learning. It can be shown, for a linear unit with normally distributed inputs, that $r = 2$ is an appropriate choice in the sense of both minimum SSE and minimum probability of prediction error (maximum likelihood). The proof is as follows.

Consider the training pairs $\{\mathbf{x}^i, d^i\}$, $i = 1, 2, \ldots, m$. Assume that the vectors $\mathbf{x}^i$ are drawn randomly and independently from a normal distribution. Then a linear unit with a fixed but unknown weight vector $\mathbf{w}$ outputs the estimate $\hat{d}^i = \mathbf{w}^T\mathbf{x}^i$ when presented with input $\mathbf{x}^i$. Since a weighted sum of independent normally distributed random variables is itself normally distributed [e.g., see Mosteller et al. (1970)], then $\hat{d}^i$ is normally distributed. Thus the prediction error $\varepsilon = d^i - \hat{d}^i = d^i - \mathbf{w}^T\mathbf{x}^i$ is normally distributed with mean zero and some variance σ^2. This allows us to express the conditional probability density for observing target d^i, given $\mathbf{w}$, upon the presentation of $\mathbf{x}^i$ as

$$p(d^i | \mathbf{w}, \mathbf{x}^i) = \frac{1}{\sqrt{2\pi}\sigma} \exp\left[-\tfrac{1}{2}\left(\frac{d^i - \mathbf{w}^\mathsf{T}\mathbf{x}^i}{\sigma} \right)^2 \right] \tag{3.1.72}$$

This function is also known as the likelihood of $\mathbf{w}$ with respect to observation d^i. The maximum likelihood estimate of $\mathbf{w}$ is that value of $\mathbf{w}$ which maximizes the probability of occurrence of observation d^i for input $\mathbf{x}^i$. The likelihood of $\mathbf{w}$ with respect to the whole training set is the joint distribution

$$p(d^1, d^2, \ldots, d^m | \mathbf{w}) = \left(\frac{1}{\sqrt{2\pi}\sigma} \right)^m \prod_{i=1}^{m} \exp\left[-\tfrac{1}{2}\left(\frac{d^i - \mathbf{w}^\mathsf{T}\mathbf{x}^i}{\sigma} \right)^2 \right] \tag{3.1.73}$$

This likelihood function may be maximized by maximizing the log-likelihood function:

$$\ln\left\{ \left(\frac{1}{\sqrt{2\pi}\sigma} \right)^m \prod_{i=1}^{m} \exp\left[-\tfrac{1}{2}\left(\frac{d^i - \mathbf{w}^\mathsf{T}\mathbf{x}^i}{\sigma} \right)^2 \right] \right\} = m\ln\left(\frac{1}{\sqrt{2\pi}\sigma} \right) - \tfrac{1}{2}\sum_{i=1}^{m}\left(\frac{d^i - \mathbf{w}^\mathsf{T}\mathbf{x}^i}{\sigma} \right)^2 \tag{3.1.74}$$

Since the $m\ln(1/\sqrt{2\pi}\sigma)$ term is a constant, maximizing the log-likelihood function in Equation (3.1.74) is equivalent to minimizing the SSE criterion:

$$J(\mathbf{w}) = \frac{1}{2\sigma^2}\sum_{i=1}^{m}(d^i - \mathbf{w}^\mathsf{T}\mathbf{x}^i)^2 \tag{3.1.75}$$

Therefore, with the assumption of a linear unit (ADALINE) with normally distributed inputs, the SSE criterion is optimal in the sense of minimizing prediction error. However, if the input distribution is non-Gaussian, then the SSE criterion will not possess maximum likelihood properties. See Mosteller and Tukey (1980) for a more thorough discussion on the maximum likelihood estimation technique.

If the distribution of the training patterns has a heavy tail such as the Laplace-type distribution, $r = 1$ will be a better criterion function choice. This criterion function is known as *robust regression* because it is more robust to an outlier training sample than $r = 2$. Finally, $1 < r < 2$ is appropriate to use for pseudo-Gaussian distributions where the distribution tails are more pronounced than in the Gaussian distributions.

Another criterion function that can be used (Baum and Wilczek, 1988; Hopfield, 1987; Solla et al., 1988) is the instantaneous relative entropy error measure (Kullback, 1959) defined by

$$J(\mathbf{w}) = \tfrac{1}{2}\left[(1 + d)\ln\left(\frac{1 + d}{1 + y} \right) + (1 - d)\ln\left(\frac{1 - d}{1 - y} \right) \right] \tag{3.1.76}$$

where d belongs to the open interval $(-1, +1)$. As before, $J(\mathbf{w}) \geq 0$, and if $y = d$, then $J(\mathbf{w}) = 0$. If $y = f(net) = \tanh(\beta\, net)$, the gradient of Equation (3.1.76) is

$$\nabla J(\mathbf{w}) = -\beta(d - y)\mathbf{x} \tag{3.1.77}$$

The factor $f'(net)$ in Equations (3.1.53) and (3.1.70) is missing from Equation (3.1.77). This eliminates the flat spot encountered in the delta rule and makes the training here more like μ-LMS [note, however, that y here is given by $y = f(net) \neq net$]. This entropy criterion is "well formed" in the sense that gradient descent over such a function will result in a linearly separable solution, if one exists (Wittner and Denker, 1988; Hertz et al., 1991). On the other hand, gradient descent on the SSE criterion function does not share this property, since it may fail to find a linearly separable solution, as demonstrated in Example 3.1.2.

In order for gradient-descent search to find a solution $\mathbf{w}^*$ in the desired linearly separable region, we need to use a well-formed criterion function. Consider the following general criterion function:

$$J(\mathbf{w}) = \sum_{i=1}^{m} g(\mathbf{z}^T\mathbf{w}) \tag{3.1.78}$$

where

$$\mathbf{z} = \begin{cases} +\mathbf{x} & \text{if } \mathbf{x} \in \text{class } c_1 \\ -\mathbf{x} & \text{if } \mathbf{x} \in \text{class } c_2 \end{cases}$$

Let $s = \mathbf{z}^T\mathbf{w}$. The criterion function $J(\mathbf{w})$ is said to be *well formed* if $g(s)$ is differentiable and satisfies the following conditions (Wittner and Denker, 1988):

1. For all s, $-\dfrac{dg(s)}{ds} \geq 0$; i.e., g does not push in the wrong direction.

2. There exists $\varepsilon > 0$ such that $-\dfrac{dg(s)}{ds} \geq \varepsilon$ for all $s \leq 0$; i.e., g keeps pushing if there is a misclassification.

3. $g(s)$ is bounded from below.

For a single unit with weight vector $\mathbf{w}$, it can be shown (Wittner and Denker, 1988) that if the criterion function is well formed, then gradient descent is guaranteed to enter the region of linearly separable solutions $\mathbf{w}^*$, provided that such a region exists.

Example 3.1.3 The perceptron criterion function in Equation (3.1.20) is a well-formed criterion function because it satisfies the three preceding conditions:

1. $J(\mathbf{w}) = \sum\limits_{\mathbf{z}^T\mathbf{w} \leq 0} -(\mathbf{z}^T\mathbf{w})$; thus $g(s) = -s$ and $-\dfrac{dg(s)}{ds} = 1 > 0$ for all s.

2. $-\dfrac{dg(s)}{ds} = 1 \geq \varepsilon > 0$ for all $s \leq 0$.

3. $g(s)$ is bounded from below, since $g(s) = -s = -\mathbf{z}^T\mathbf{w} \geq 0$.

3.1.6 Extension of Gradient-Descent-Based Learning to Stochastic Units

The linear threshold gate, perceptron, and ADALINE are examples of deterministic units; for a given input, the unit always responds with the same output. On the other hand, a stochastic unit has a binary-valued output which is a probabilistic function of the input activity *net*, as depicted in Figure 3.1.11.

Formally, y is given by

$$y = \begin{cases} +1 \text{ with probability } P(y = +1) \\ -1 \text{ with probability } P(y = -1) = 1 - P(y = +1) \end{cases} \qquad (3.1.79)$$

One possible probability function is $P(y = +1) = 1/(1 + e^{-2\beta\,net})$. Therefore, $P(y = -1) = 1 - P(y = +1) = 1/(1 + e^{+2\beta\,net})$. Also, note that the expected value of y, $\langle y \rangle$, is given by

$$\langle y \rangle = (+1)P(y = +1) + (-1)P(y = -1) = \tanh(\beta\,net) \qquad (3.1.80)$$

Stochastic units are the basis for reinforcement learning networks, as is shown in the next section. Also, these units allow for a natural mapping of optimal stochastic learning and retrieval methods onto neural networks, as discussed in Section 8.3.

Let us now define an SSE criterion function in terms of the mean output of the stochastic unit:

$$J = \tfrac{1}{2}\sum_{i=1}^{m}(d^i - \langle y^i \rangle)^2 = \tfrac{1}{2}\sum_{i=1}^{m}[d^i - \tanh(\beta\,net^i)]^2 \qquad (3.1.81)$$

Employing gradient descent, we arrive at the following update rule:

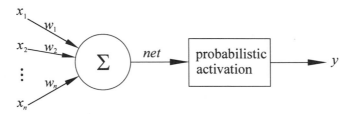

Figure 3.1.11
A stochastic unit.

$$\mathbf{w}^{k+1} = \mathbf{w}^k + \rho \sum_{i=1}^{m} (d^i - \langle y^i \rangle)\beta \operatorname{sech}^2(\beta \, net^i)\mathbf{x}^i \qquad (3.1.82)$$

In the incremental update mode, we have the following update rule:

$$\mathbf{w}^{k+1} = \mathbf{w}^k + \rho\beta[d^k - \tanh(\beta \, net^k)][1 - \tanh^2(\beta \, net^k)]\mathbf{x}^k$$

$$= \mathbf{w}^k + \rho\beta(d^k - \langle y^k \rangle)(1 - \langle y^k \rangle^2)\mathbf{x}^k \qquad (3.1.83)$$

This learning rule is identical in form to the delta learning rule that is given in Equation (3.1.53), which used a deterministic unit with an activation function $f(net) = \tanh(\beta \, net)$. Therefore, in an average sense, the stochastic unit learning rule in Equation (3.1.83) leads to a weight vector that is equal to that obtained using the delta rule for a deterministic unit with a hyperbolic tangent activation function.

3.2   Reinforcement Learning

Reinforcement learning is a process of trial and error designed to maximize the expected value of a criterion function known as a *reinforcement signal*. The basic idea of reinforcement learning has its origins in psychology in connection with experimental studies of animal learning (Thorndike, 1911). In its simplest form, reinforcement learning is based on the idea that if an action is followed by an "improvement" in the state of affairs, then the tendency to produce that action is strengthened, i.e., reinforced. Otherwise, the tendency of the system to produce that action is weakened (Barto and Singh, 1991; Sutton et al., 1991).

Given a training set of the form $\{\mathbf{x}^k, r^k\}$, $k = 1, 2, \ldots, m$, where $\mathbf{x}^k \in R^n$ and r^k is an evaluative signal (normally $r \in \{-1, +1\}$) supplied by a "critic," the idea here is not to associate $\mathbf{x}^k$ with r^k as in supervised learning. Rather, r^k is a reinforcement signal that informs the unit being trained about its performance on the input $\mathbf{x}^k$. Therefore, r^k evaluates the "appropriateness" of the unit's output y^k due to the input $\mathbf{x}^k$. Usually, r^k gives no indication as to what the output y^k should be. It is therefore important for the unit to be stochastic so that a mechanism of exploration of the output space is present.

One may view supervised learning in a stochastic unit as an extreme case of reinforcement learning, where the output of the unit is binary and there is one correct output for each input. Here, r^k becomes the desired target d^k. Also, we may use the gradient-descent learning rule of Equation (3.1.83) to train the stochastic unit. In general, the reinforcement signal itself may be stochastic such that the pair $\{\mathbf{x}^k, r^k\}$

only provides the "probability" of positive reinforcement. In the most general formulation of the reinforcement learning problem (and the most difficult), the reinforcement signal and the input patterns depend arbitrarily on the past history of the stochastic unit's output. An example would be the stabilization of an unstable dynamical system or even a game of chess where the reinforcement signal arrives at the end of a sequence of player moves.

3.2.1   Associative Reward-Penalty Reinforcement Learning Rule

This subsection presents a reinforcement learning rule due to Barto and Anandan (1985) known as the *associative reward-penalty* (A_{rp}) *algorithm*. This rule is discussed here in the context of a single stochastic unit. Motivated by Equation (3.1.83), the A_{rp} reinforcement rule may be expressed as

$$\mathbf{w}^{k+1} = \mathbf{w}^k + \rho(r^k)(d^k - \langle y^k \rangle)(1 - \langle y^k \rangle^2)\mathbf{x}^k \tag{3.2.1}$$

where

$$d^k = \begin{cases} y^k & \text{if } r^k = +1 \text{ (reward)} \\ -y^k & \text{if } r^k = -1 \text{ (penalty)} \end{cases} \tag{3.2.2}$$

and

$$\rho(r^k) = \begin{cases} \rho^+ & \text{if } r^k = +1 \\ \rho^- & \text{if } r^k = -1 \end{cases} \tag{3.2.3}$$

with $\rho^+ \gg \rho^- > 0$. The derivative term $(1 - \langle y^k \rangle^2)$ in Equation (3.2.1) may be eliminated without affecting the general behavior of this learning rule. In this case, the resulting learning rule corresponds to steepest descent on the relative entropy criterion function. The setting of d^k according to Equation (3.2.2) guides the unit to do what it just did if y^k is "good" and to do the opposite if not (Widrow et al., 1973). In general, this makes the dynamics of $\mathbf{w}^k$ in Equation (3.2.1) substantially different from that of $\mathbf{w}^k$ in the supervised stochastic learning rule in Equation (3.1.83). When learning converges, the expected output $\langle y^k \rangle$ approaches ± 1, making the unit effectively deterministic; the unit's output approaches the state providing the largest average reinforcement on the training set.

One variation of A_{rp} (Barto and Jordan, 1987) utilizes a continuous-valued or graded reinforcement signal, $0 \le r \le 1$, and has the form

$$\mathbf{w}^{k+1} = \mathbf{w}^k + \rho(r^k)[r^k(y^k - \langle y^k \rangle) - (1 - r^k)(y^k + \langle y^k \rangle)]\mathbf{x}^k \tag{3.2.4}$$

Another variation uses $r^k = \pm 1$ and has the simple form

$$\mathbf{w}^{k+1} = \mathbf{w}^k + \rho r^k [y^k - \langle y^k \rangle]\mathbf{x}^k \tag{3.2.5}$$

This latter rule is more amenable to theoretical analysis, as is shown in Section 4.5, where it will be shown that the rule tends to maximize the average reinforcement signal $\langle r \rangle$. Reinforcement learning speed may be improved if batch mode training is used (Barto and Jordan, 1987; Ackley and Littman, 1990). Here, a given pattern $\mathbf{x}^k$ is presented several times, and the accumulation of all the weight changes is used to update $\mathbf{w}^k$. Then, pattern $\mathbf{x}^{k+1}$ is presented several times, and so on. For an overview treatment of the theory of reinforcement learning, see Barto (1985) and Williams (1992). Also see the "Special Issue on Reinforcement Learning" of *Machine Learning*, edited by Sutton (1992), for theoretical and practical considerations.

3.3   Unsupervised Learning

In *unsupervised learning*, there is no teacher signal. We are given a training set $\{\mathbf{x}^i; i = 1, 2, \ldots, m\}$ of unlabeled vectors in R^n. The objective is to categorize or discover features or regularities in the training data. In some cases, the input vectors $\mathbf{x}^i$ must be mapped into a lower-dimensional set of patterns such that any topological relations existing among the $\mathbf{x}^i$ are preserved among the new set of patterns. Normally, the success of unsupervised learning hinges on some appropriately designed network that encompasses a task-independent criterion of the quality of representation the network is required to learn. Here, the weights of the network are to be optimized with respect to this criterion.

The interest here is in training networks of simple units to perform the preceding tasks. In the remainder of this chapter, some basic unsupervised learning rules for a single unit and for simple networks are introduced. The following three classes of unsupervised rules are considered: Hebbian learning, competitive learning, and self-organizing feature-map learning. Hebbian learning is treated first. Then competitive learning and self-organizing feature-map learning are covered in Sections 3.4 and 3.5, respectively.

3.3.1   Hebbian Learning

The rules considered in this section are motivated by the classic Hebbian synaptic modification hypothesis (Hebb, 1949). Hebb suggested that biological synaptic efficaces ($\mathbf{w}$) change in proportion to the correlation between the pre- and postsynaptic signals $\mathbf{x}$ and y, respectively, which may be stated (for a single unit) formally as (Stent, 1973; Changeux and Danchin, 1976)

$$\mathbf{w}^{k+1} = \mathbf{w}^k + \rho y^k \mathbf{x}^k \tag{3.3.1}$$

where $\rho > 0$, $\mathbf{x}^k$ is the unit's input, and $y^k = (\mathbf{x}^k)^T \mathbf{w}^k$ is the unit's output.

Let us now assume that the input vectors are drawn from an arbitrary probability distribution $p(\mathbf{x})$. Let us also assume that the network being trained consists of a single unit. At each time k, we will present a vector $\mathbf{x}$, randomly drawn from $p(\mathbf{x})$, to this unit. We will employ the Hebbian rule in Equation (3.3.1) to update the weight vector $\mathbf{w}$. The expected weight change $\langle \Delta \mathbf{w} \rangle$ can be evaluated by averaging Equation (3.3.1) over all inputs $\mathbf{x}$. This gives

$$\langle \Delta \mathbf{w} \rangle = \rho \langle y\mathbf{x} \rangle = \rho \langle \mathbf{x}\mathbf{x}^T \mathbf{w} \rangle \tag{3.3.2}$$

or, assuming that $\mathbf{x}$ and $\mathbf{w}$ are statistically independent,

$$\langle \Delta \mathbf{w} \rangle = \rho \langle \mathbf{x}\mathbf{x}^T \rangle \langle \mathbf{w} \rangle \tag{3.3.3}$$

Since, at equilibrium $\langle \Delta \mathbf{w} \rangle = \mathbf{0}$, Equation (3.3.3) leads to $\mathbf{Cw} = \mathbf{0}$, and thus $\mathbf{w}^* = \mathbf{0}$ is the only equilibrium state. Here, $\mathbf{C} = \langle \mathbf{x}\mathbf{x}^T \rangle$ is known as the *autocorrelation matrix* and is given by

$$\mathbf{C} = \begin{bmatrix} \langle x_1^2 \rangle & \langle x_1 x_2 \rangle & \cdots & \langle x_1 x_n \rangle \\ \langle x_2 x_1 \rangle & \langle x_2^2 \rangle & \cdots & \langle x_2 x_n \rangle \\ \vdots & \vdots & \ddots & \vdots \\ \langle x_n x_1 \rangle & \langle x_n x_2 \rangle & \cdots & \langle x_n^2 \rangle \end{bmatrix} \tag{3.3.4}$$

The terms on the main diagonal of $\mathbf{C}$ are the mean squares of the input components, and the cross terms are the cross-correlations among the input components. $\mathbf{C}$ is a Hermitian matrix (real and symmetric). Thus its eigenvalues λ_i, $i = 1, 2, \ldots, n$, are positive real or zero, and it has orthogonal eigenvectors $\mathbf{c}^{(i)}$. From the definition of an eigenvector, each $\mathbf{c}^{(i)}$ satisfies the relation $\mathbf{C}\mathbf{c}^{(i)} = \lambda_i \mathbf{c}^{(i)}$.

It can be shown that the solution $\mathbf{w}^* = \mathbf{0}$ is not stable (see Section 4.3.1). Therefore, Equation (3.3.3) is unstable, and it drives $\mathbf{w}$ to infinite magnitude, with a direction parallel to that of the eigenvector of $\mathbf{C}$ with the largest eigenvalue. It will be shown in Section 4.3.1 that this learning rule tends to maximize the mean square of y, i.e., $\langle y^2 \rangle$. In other words, this rule is driven to maximize the variance of the output of a linear unit, assuming that y has zero mean. A zero-mean y can be achieved if the unit inputs are independent random variables with zero mean. One way to prevent the divergence of the Hebbian learning rule in Equation (3.3.1) is to normalize $\|\mathbf{w}\|$ to 1 after each learning step (von der Malsburg, 1973; Rubner and Tavan, 1989). This leads to the following update rule[6]:

$$\begin{cases} \mathbf{w}^1 \quad \text{arbitrary} \\ \\ \mathbf{w}^{k+1} = \dfrac{\mathbf{w}^k + \rho y^k \mathbf{x}^k}{\|\mathbf{w}^k + \rho y^k \mathbf{x}^k\|} \end{cases} \tag{3.3.5}$$

The following subsections briefly describe additional stable Hebbian-type learning rules. The detailed analysis of these rules is deferred to Chapter 4.

3.3.2   Oja's Rule

An alternative approach for stabilizing the Hebbian rule is to modify it by adding a weight decay proportional to y^2 (Oja, 1982). This results in Oja's rule:

$$\begin{cases} \mathbf{w}^1 \quad \text{arbitrary} \\ \mathbf{w}^{k+1} = \mathbf{w}^k + \rho y^k \mathbf{x}^k - \rho (y^k)^2 \mathbf{w}^k \\ \qquad\; = \mathbf{w}^k + \rho (\mathbf{x}^k - y^k \mathbf{w}^k) y^k \end{cases} \tag{3.3.6}$$

Oja's rule converges in the mean to a state $\mathbf{w}^*$ that maximizes the mean value of y^2, i.e., $\langle y^2 \rangle$, subject to the constraint $\|\mathbf{w}\| = 1$. It also can be shown that the solution $\mathbf{w}^*$ is the principal eigenvector (the one with the largest corresponding eigenvalue) of $\mathbf{C}$ (Oja, 1982; Oja and Karhunen, 1985). The analysis of this rule is covered in Chapter 4.

3.3.3   The Yuille et al. Rule

Other modifications to the Hebbian rule have been proposed to prevent divergence. Yuille et al. (1989) proposed the following rule:

$$\begin{cases} \mathbf{w}^1 \quad \text{arbitrary} \\ \mathbf{w}^{k+1} = \mathbf{w}^k + \rho (y^k \mathbf{x}^k - \|\mathbf{w}^k\|^2 \mathbf{w}^k) \end{cases} \tag{3.3.7}$$

It can be shown that, in an average sense, the weight vector update is given by gradient descent on the criterion function:

$$J(\mathbf{w}) = -\tfrac{1}{2}\langle y^2 \rangle + \tfrac{1}{4}\|\mathbf{w}\|^4 = -\tfrac{1}{2}\mathbf{w}^{\mathrm{T}}\mathbf{C}\mathbf{w} + \tfrac{1}{4}\|\mathbf{w}\|^4 \tag{3.3.8}$$

---

6. The "average" version of the weight update rule in Equation (3.3.5) can be written as

$$\langle \mathbf{w}^{k+1} \rangle = \frac{\langle \mathbf{w}^k \rangle + \rho \mathbf{C} \langle \mathbf{w}^k \rangle}{\|\langle \mathbf{w}^k \rangle + \rho \mathbf{C} \langle \mathbf{w}^k \rangle\|}$$

which for large ρ reduces to $\langle \mathbf{w}^{k+1} \rangle = \mathbf{C} \langle \mathbf{w}^k \rangle / \|\mathbf{C} \langle \mathbf{w}^k \rangle\|$. It is interesting to note that this last result has the form $\mathbf{c}^{k+1} = \mathbf{A}\mathbf{c}^k / \|\mathbf{A}\mathbf{c}^k\|$, which is the standard "power method" for extracting the eigenvector of $\mathbf{A}$ with the largest eigenvalue [e.g., see Carnahan et al. (1969)].

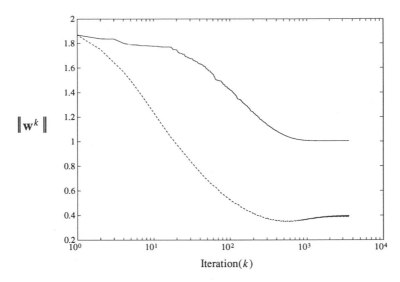

Figure 3.3.1
Weight vector magnitude versus time for Oja's rule (solid curve) and for the Yuille
et al. rule (dashed curve) with $\rho = 0.02$. The training set consists of sixty 15-dimen-
sional real-valued vectors whose components are generated according to a uniform
random distribution in the range $[-0.5, +0.5]$.

In Section 4.3.4 it is shown that Equation (3.3.7) converges to a vector $\mathbf{w}^*$ that points
in the same (or opposite) direction as the principal eigenvector of $\mathbf{C}$ and whose norm
is given by the square root of the largest eigenvalue of $\mathbf{C}$.

Example 3.3.1   In this example the convergence behaviors of the Oja and the Yuille
et al. learning rules are demonstrated on zero-mean random data. Figures 3.3.1
through 3.3.4 show two sets of simulation results for the evolution of the weight
vector of a single linear unit trained with Oja's rule and with the Yuille et al. rule.
Figures 3.3.1 and 3.3.2 show the behavior of the norm and the direction (cosine of
the angle θ between $\mathbf{w}$ and the eigenvector of $\mathbf{C}$ with the largest eigenvalue) of the
weight vector $\mathbf{w}$ as a function of iteration number k, respectively. In this simulation,
the data (training set) consists of sixty 15-dimensional vectors whose components are
generated randomly and independently from a uniform distribution in the range
$[-0.5, +0.5]$. In this particular case, the data set leads to a correlation matrix having
its two largest eigenvalues equal to 0.1578 and 0.1515, respectively. During learning,
the training vectors are presented in a fixed, cyclic order, and a learning rate $\rho = 0.02$
is used. As can be seen from Figure 3.3.1, the length of $\mathbf{w}^k$ (practically) converges after

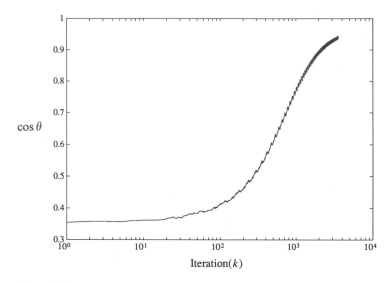

Figure 3.3.2
Evolution of the cosine of the angle between the weight vector and the principal eigenvector of the correlation matrix for Oja's rule (solid curve) and for the Yuille et al. rule (dashed curve) with $\rho = 0.02$ (the dashed line is hard to see because it overlaps with the solid line). The training set is the same as for Figure 3.3.1.

3000 iterations. Here, both the Oja and Yuille et al. rules converge to the theoretically predicted values of 1 and $\sqrt{0.1578}$, respectively. The two rules exhibit an almost identical weight vector direction evolution as depicted in Figure 3.3.2. The figure shows an initial low overlap between the starting weight vector and the principal eigenvector of the data correlation matrix. This overlap increases slowly at first but then increases fast toward 1. As the direction of $\mathbf{w}$ approaches that of the principal eigenvector (i.e., $\cos\theta$ approaches 1), the convergence becomes slow again. Note that Figure 3.3.2 only shows the evolution of $\cos\theta$ over the first 3600 iterations. Beyond this point, the convergence becomes very slow. This is due to the uniform nature of the data, which does not allow for the principal eigenvector to dominate all other eigenvectors. Thus a strong competition emerges among several eigenvectors, each attempting to align $\mathbf{w}^k$ along its own direction, which results in the slow convergence of $\cos\theta$.

The second set of simulations involves a training set of sixty 15-dimensional vectors drawn randomly from a normal distribution with zero mean and variance of 1. This data leads to a correlation matrix $\mathbf{C}$ with a dominating eigenvector relative to that of

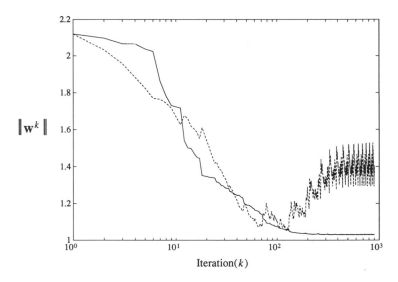

Figure 3.3.3
Weight vector magnitude versus time for Oja's rule (solid curve) and for the Yuille et al. rule (dashed curve) with $\rho = 0.01$. The training set consists of sixty 15-dimensional real-valued vectors whose components are generated according to $N(0, 1)$.

the previous data set. Here, the largest two eigenvalues of $\mathbf{C}$ are equal to 2.1172 and 1.6299, respectively. Again, the Oja and Yuille et al. rules are used, but with a learning rate of 0.01. Figure 3.3.3 shows a better-behaved convergence for Oja's rule as compared with the Yuille et al. rule. The latter rule exhibits an oscillatory behavior in $\|\mathbf{w}^k\|$ about its theoretical asymptotic value, $\sqrt{2.1172}$. As for the convergence of the direction of $\mathbf{w}$, Figure 3.3.4 shows a comparable behavior for both rules. Here, the existence of a dominating eigenvector for $\mathbf{C}$ is responsible for the relatively faster convergence of $\cos \theta$ as compared with the earlier simulation in Figure 3.3.2. Finally, note that the oscillatory behavior in Figures 3.3.3 and 3.3.4 can be significantly reduced by resorting to smaller constant learning rates or by using a decaying learning rate of the form $\rho^k = \rho_0/k$. This, however, leads to slower convergence speeds for both $\|\mathbf{w}^k\|$ and $\cos \theta$.

3.3.4   Linsker's Rule

Linsker (1986, 1988) proposed and studied the general unsupervised learning rule:

$$\Delta \mathbf{w} = \rho(y\mathbf{x} + a\mathbf{x} + b y + \mathbf{d}) \tag{3.3.9}$$

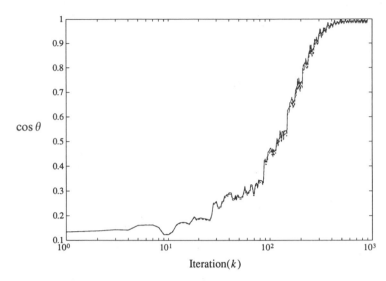

Figure 3.3.4
Evolution of the cosine of the angle between the weight vector and the principal
eigenvector of the correlation matrix for Oja's rule (solid curve) and for the
Yuille et al. rule (dashed curve) with $\rho = 0.01$. The training set is the same as for
Figure 3.3.3.

subject to bounding constraints on the weights $w^- \leq w_i \leq w^+$, with $y = \mathbf{w}^T\mathbf{x}$ and $\mathbf{x}, \mathbf{b},$
and $\mathbf{d} \in R^n$. The average weight change in Equation (3.3.9) is given by

$$\langle \Delta \mathbf{w} \rangle = \rho(\mathbf{C}\mathbf{w} + a\boldsymbol{\mu} + b\mathbf{w}^T\boldsymbol{\mu} + \mathbf{d}) \tag{3.3.10}$$

where $\boldsymbol{\mu} = \langle \mathbf{x} \rangle$. If we set $a > 0$, $b_i = -a$ for $i = 1, 2, \ldots, n,$ and $\mathbf{d} = \mathbf{0}$ in Equation
(3.3.10), we get

$$\langle \Delta \mathbf{w} \rangle = \rho[\mathbf{C}\mathbf{w} + a(\boldsymbol{\mu} - \mathbf{w}^T\boldsymbol{\mu}\mathbf{1})] \tag{3.3.11}$$

where $\mathbf{1}$ is an n-dimensional column vector of ones. Equation (3.3.11) gives the ith
average weight change:

$$\langle \Delta \mathbf{w}_i \rangle = \rho\left[\mathbf{C}_i\mathbf{w} + a\left(\mu_i - \sum_{j=1}^{n} \mu_j w_j \right) \right] \tag{3.3.12}$$

where $\mathbf{C}_i$ is the ith row of $\mathbf{C}$. If we assume that the components of $\mathbf{x}$ are random and
are drawn from the same probability distribution with mean μ, then $\mu_i = \mu$ for all $i,$
and Equation (3.3.11) reduces to

$$\langle \Delta \mathbf{w} \rangle = \rho \left[\mathbf{Cw} + \lambda \left(1 - \sum_{j=1}^{n} w_j \right) \mathbf{1} \right] \tag{3.3.13}$$

where $\lambda = a\mu$ was used. Here it can be easily shown that Equation (3.3.13) has the following associated criterion function:

$$J(\mathbf{w}) = -\tfrac{1}{2} \mathbf{w}^{\mathrm{T}} \mathbf{Cw} + \frac{\lambda}{2} \left(1 - \sum_{j=1}^{n} w_j \right)^2 \tag{3.3.14}$$

Therefore, by noting that $\mathbf{w}^{\mathrm{T}}\mathbf{Cw}$ is the mean square of the unit's output activity, i.e., $\langle y^2 \rangle$, the simplified form of $\langle \Delta \mathbf{w} \rangle$ in Equation (3.3.13) corresponds to maximizing $\langle y^2 \rangle$ subject to the constraint $\sum_{j=1}^{n} w_j = 1$. It can be shown that this rule is unstable, but with the restriction $w^- \leq w_i \leq w^+$, the final state will be clamped at a boundary value, $w_i = w^-$ or $w_i = w^+$. If λ is large enough, $w^- = -1$, $w^+ = +1$, and n is odd, then the preceding rule converges to a weight vector with $(n + 1)/2$ weights equal to w^+ and the remaining weights equal to w^-. The weight vector configuration is such that $\langle y^2 \rangle$ is maximized. For the n even case, one of the weights at w^- will be pushed toward zero so that $\sum_j w_j = 1$ is maintained.

3.3.5   Hebbian Learning in a Network Setting: Principal-Component Analysis (PCA)

Hebbian learning can lead to more interesting computational capabilities when applied to a network of units. This subsection applies unsupervised Hebbian learning in a simple network setting to extract the m principal directions of a given set of data (i.e., the leading eigenvector directions of the input vectors' autocorrelation matrix).

Amari (1977a) and later Linsker (1988) pointed out that principal-component analysis (PCA) is equivalent to maximizing the information content in the outputs of a network of linear units. The aim of PCA is to extract m normalized orthogonal vectors $\mathbf{u}_i$, $i = 1, 2, \ldots, m$, in the input space that account for as much of the data's variance as possible. Subsequently, the n-dimensional input data (vectors $\mathbf{x}$) may be transformed to a lower m-dimensional space without losing essential intrinsic information. This can be done by projecting the input vectors onto the m-dimensional subspace spanned by the extracted orthogonal vectors $\mathbf{u}_i$ according to the inner products $\mathbf{x}^{\mathrm{T}}\mathbf{u}_i$. Since m is smaller than n, a dimensionality reduction of the data is achieved. This, in turn, makes subsequent processing of the data (e.g., clustering or classification) much easier to handle.

The following is an outline for a *direct* optimization-based method for determining the $\mathbf{u}_i$ vectors. Let $\mathbf{x} \in R^n$ be an input vector generated according to a zero-mean probability distribution $p(\mathbf{x})$. Let $\mathbf{u}$ denote a vector in R^n onto which the input vectors are to be projected. The projection $\mathbf{x}^T\mathbf{u}$ is the linear sum of n zero-mean random variables, which is itself a zero-mean random variable. Here, the objective is to find the solution(s) $\mathbf{u}^*$ that maximizes $\langle(\mathbf{x}^T\mathbf{u})^2\rangle$, the variance of the projection $\mathbf{x}^T\mathbf{u}$ with respect to $p(\mathbf{x})$, subject to $\|\mathbf{u}\| = 1$. In other words, we are interested in finding the maxima $\mathbf{w}^*$ of the criterion function

$$J(\mathbf{w}) = \left\langle \left(\mathbf{x}^T \frac{\mathbf{w}}{\|\mathbf{w}\|} \right)^2 \right\rangle \tag{3.3.15}$$

from which the unity norm solution(s) $\mathbf{u}^*$ can be computed as $\mathbf{u}^* = \mathbf{w}^*/\|\mathbf{w}^*\|$, with $\|\mathbf{w}^*\| \neq 0$. Now, by noting that $\langle(\mathbf{x}^T\mathbf{w})^2\rangle = \langle(\mathbf{x}^T\mathbf{w})(\mathbf{x}^T\mathbf{w})\rangle = \mathbf{w}^T\langle\mathbf{xx}^T\rangle\mathbf{w}$ and recalling that $\langle\mathbf{xx}^T\rangle$ is the autocorrelation matrix $\mathbf{C}$, Equation (3.3.15) may be expressed as

$$J(\mathbf{w}) = \frac{\mathbf{w}^T\mathbf{Cw}}{\|\mathbf{w}\|^2} \tag{3.3.16}$$

The extreme points of $J(\mathbf{w})$ are the solutions to $\nabla J(\mathbf{w}) = \mathbf{0}$, which gives

$$\nabla J(\mathbf{w}) = \frac{\mathbf{Cw}\|\mathbf{w}\|^2 - (\mathbf{w}^T\mathbf{Cw})\mathbf{w}}{\|\mathbf{w}\|^4} = \mathbf{0} \quad \text{or} \quad \mathbf{Cw} = \frac{(\mathbf{w}^T\mathbf{Cw})}{\|\mathbf{w}^2\|}\mathbf{w} \tag{3.3.17}$$

The solutions to Equation (3.3.17) are $\mathbf{w} = a\mathbf{c}^{(i)}$, $i = 1, 2, \ldots, n$, $a \in R$. In other words, the maxima $\mathbf{w}^*$ of $J(\mathbf{w})$ must point in the same or opposite direction as one of the eigenvectors of $\mathbf{C}$. Upon careful examination of the Hessian of $J(\mathbf{w})$ (as in Section 4.3.2), we find that the only maximum exists at $\mathbf{w}^* = a\mathbf{c}^{(1)}$ for some finite real-valued a [in this case $J(\mathbf{w}^*) = \lambda_1$]. Therefore, the variance of the projection $\mathbf{x}^T\mathbf{u}$ is maximized for $\mathbf{u} = \mathbf{u}_1 = \mathbf{w}^*/\|\mathbf{w}^*\| = \pm\mathbf{c}^{(1)}$. Next, we repeat the preceding maximization of $J(\mathbf{w})$ in Equation (3.3.15) but with the additional requirement that the vector $\mathbf{w}$ be orthogonal to $\mathbf{c}^{(1)}$. Here, it can be readily seen that the maximum of $J(\mathbf{w})$ is equal to λ_2 and occurs at $\mathbf{w}^* = a\mathbf{c}^{(2)}$. Thus $\mathbf{u}_2 = \mathbf{c}^{(2)}$. Similarly, the solution $\mathbf{u}_3 = \mathbf{c}^{(3)}$ maximizes J under the constraint that $\mathbf{u}_3$ be orthogonal to $\mathbf{u}_1$ and $\mathbf{u}_2$ simultaneously. Continuing this way, we arrive at the m principal directions $\mathbf{u}_1$ through $\mathbf{u}_m$. Again, these vectors are ordered so that $\mathbf{u}_1$ points in the direction of the maximum data variance, and the second vector $\mathbf{u}_2$ points in the direction of maximum variance in the subspace orthogonal to $\mathbf{u}_1$, and so on. The projections $\mathbf{x}^T\mathbf{u}_i$, $i = 1, 2, \ldots, m$, are called the *principal components* of the data; these projections are equivalent to the ones obtained by the classic Karhunen-Loève transformation of statistics (Karhunen, 1947; Loève, 1963). Note that the previous Hebbian rules discussed in the single linear unit setting all maximize $\langle y^2\rangle$, the output signal variance, and hence they extract the first principal component of the zero-mean data. If the data set has a non-zero mean, then we subtract that mean from it before extracting the principal components.

PCA in a Network of Interacting Units   Here, an m-output network is desired that is capable of incrementally and efficiently computing the first m principal components of a given set of vectors in R^n. Consider a network of m linear units, $m < n$. Let $\mathbf{w}_i$ be the weight vector of the ith unit. Oja (1989) extended his learning rule in Equation (3.3.6) to the m-unit network according to (we will drop the k superscript here for clarity)

$$\Delta w_{ij} = \rho \left(x_j - \sum_{k=1}^{m} w_{kj} y_k \right) y_i \qquad (3.3.18)$$

where w_{ij} is the jth weight for unit i, and y_i is its output. Another rule proposed by Sanger (1989) is given by

$$\Delta w_{ij} = \rho \left(x_j - \sum_{k=1}^{i} w_{kj} y_k \right) y_i \qquad (3.3.19)$$

Equations (3.3.18) and (3.3.19) require communication between the units in the network during learning. Equation (3.3.18) requires the jth input signal x_j, as well as the output signals y_k of all units, to be available when adjusting the jth weight of unit i. Each signal y_k is modulated by the jth weight of unit k and is fed back as an inhibitory input to unit i. Thus unit i can be viewed as employing the original Hebbian rule of Equation (3.3.1) to update its jth weight, but with an effective input signal whose jth component is given by the term inside parentheses in Equation (3.3.18). Sanger's rule employs similar feedback except that the ith unit only receives modulated output signals generated by units with index k, where $k \leq i$.

The preceding two rules are identical to Oja's rule in Equation (3.3.6) for $m = 1$. For $m > 1$, they only differ by the upper limit on the summation. Both rules converge to weight vectors $\mathbf{w}_i$ that are orthogonal. Oja's rule does not generally find the eigenvector directions of $\mathbf{C}$. However, in this case, the m weight vectors converge to span the same subspace as the first m eigenvectors of $\mathbf{C}$. Here, the weight vectors depend on the initial conditions and on the order of presentation of the input data and therefore differ individually from trial to trial. On the other hand, Sanger's rule is insensitive to initial conditions and to the order of presentation of input data. It converges to $\mathbf{w}_i^* = \pm \mathbf{c}^{(i)}$ in order, where the first unit ($i = 1$) has $\mathbf{w}_1 = \pm \mathbf{c}^{(1)}$. Some insights into the convergence behavior of this rule/PCA net can be gained by exploring the analysis in Problems 3.3.5 and 3.3.6. Additional analysis is given in Section 4.4.

Sanger (1989) gave a convergence proof of the preceding PCA net employing Equation (3.3.19) under the assumption $\rho = \rho^k$ with $\lim_{k \to \infty} \rho^k = 0$ and $\sum_{k=0}^{\infty} \rho^k = \infty$. The significance of this proof is that it guarantees the dynamics in Equation (3.3.19) to find the first m eigenvectors of the autocorrelation matrix $\mathbf{C}$ (assuming that the eigenvalues λ_1 through λ_m are distinct). An equally important property of Sanger's PCA net is that there is no need to compute the full correlation matrix $\mathbf{C}$. Rather, the first eigenvectors of $\mathbf{C}$ are computed by the net adaptively and directly from the input vectors. This property can lead to significant savings in computational effort if the dimension of the input vectors is very large compared with the desired number of principal components to be extracted. For an interesting application of PCA to image coding/compression, the reader is referred to Gonzalez and Wintz (1987) and Sanger (1989). See also Section 5.3.6.

PCA in a Single-Layer Network with Adaptive Lateral Connections   Another approach for PCA is to use a single-layer network with m linear units and trainable lateral connections between units, as shown in Figure 3.3.5 (Rubner and Tavan, 1989). The lateral connections u_{ij} are present from unit j to unit i only if $i > j$. The weights w_{ij} connecting the inputs $\mathbf{x}^k$ to the units are updated according to the simple normalized Hebbian learning rule:

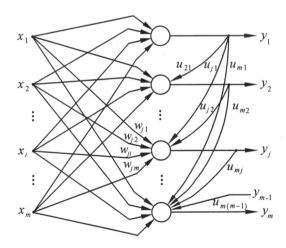

Figure 3.3.5
PCA network with adaptive lateral connections.

$$\mathbf{w}_i^{k+1} = \frac{\mathbf{w}_i^k + \rho \mathbf{x}^k y_i^k}{\|\mathbf{w}_i^k + \rho \mathbf{x}^k y_i^k\|} \tag{3.3.20}$$

On the other hand, the lateral weights employ anti-Hebbian learning in the form

$$\Delta u_{ij} = -\eta y_i^k y_j^k \tag{3.3.21}$$

where $\eta > 0$. Note that the first unit with index 1 extracts $\mathbf{c}^{(1)}$. The second unit tries to do the same, except that the lateral connection u_{21} from unit 1 inhibits y_2 from approaching $\mathbf{c}^{(1)}$; hence y_2 is forced to settle for the second principal direction, namely, $\mathbf{c}^{(2)}$, and so on. Thus this network extracts the first m principal data directions in descending order, just as Sanger's network. Since the principal directions are orthogonal, the correlation's $y_i y_j$ approach zero as convergence is approached, and thus the u_{ij} weights are driven to zero.

3.3.6   Nonlinear PCA

PCA networks, such as those just discussed, extract principal components that provide an optimal *linear* mapping from the original input space to a lower-dimensional output space whose dimensions are determined by the number of linear units in the network. The optimality of this mapping is with respect to the second-order statistics of the training set $\{\mathbf{x}^k\}$.

Optimal PCA mappings based on more complex statistical criteria are also possible if nonlinear units are used (Oja, 1991; Taylor and Coombes, 1993). Here, the extracted principal components can be thought of as the eigenvectors of the matrix of higher-order statistics which is a generalization of the second-order statistics matrix (correlation matrix $\mathbf{C}$). The nonlinearities implicitly introduce higher-order moments into the optimal solution.

Two natural ways of introducing nonlinearities into the PCA net are via higher-order units or via units with nonlinear activations. In order to see how higher-order units lead to higher-order statistics PCA, consider the case of a simple network of a single quadratic unit of n-inputs x_i, $i = 1, 2, \ldots, n$. The input/output relation for this quadratic unit is given by

$$y = \sum_{i=1}^n \left(w_i + \sum_{j=i}^n w_{ij} x_j \right) x_i \tag{3.3.22}$$

Another way of interpreting Equation (3.3.22) is to write it in the form of a linear unit, such as

$$y = \sum_{i=1}^n w_i x_i + \sum_{i=1}^n \sum_{j=i}^n w_{ij} x_i x_j = \mathbf{w}^T \mathbf{z} \tag{3.3.23}$$

where

$$\mathbf{z} = [x_1 \quad x_2 \quad x_3 \quad \cdots \quad x_n \quad x_1^2 \quad x_1 x_2 \quad \cdots \quad x_1 x_n \quad x_2^2 \quad x_2 x_3 \quad \cdots \quad x_n^2]^{\mathrm{T}}$$

and

$$\mathbf{w} = [w_1 \quad w_2 \quad \cdots \quad w_n \quad w_{11} \quad w_{12} \quad \cdots \quad w_{1n} \quad w_{22} \quad w_{23} \quad \cdots \quad w_{nn}]^{\mathrm{T}}$$

is a vector of real-valued parameters. Therefore, the n-input quadratic unit is equivalent to a linear unit receiving its $[(n + 1)(n + 2)/2] - 1$ inputs from a fixed preprocessing layer. This preprocessing layer transforms the original input vectors $\mathbf{x}^k$ into higher-dimensional vectors $\mathbf{z}^k$, as in a QTG (refer to Section 1.1.2).

Now, if stable Hebbian learning is used to adapt the $\mathbf{w}$ parameter vector, this vector will stabilize at the principal eigenvector of the correlation matrix $\mathbf{C}_\mathbf{z} = \langle \mathbf{z}\mathbf{z}^{\mathrm{T}} \rangle$. This matrix can be written in terms of the inputs x_i as

$$\mathbf{C}_\mathbf{z} = \begin{bmatrix} \mathbf{C}_1 & \mathbf{C}_2 \\ \mathbf{C}_3 & \mathbf{C}_4 \end{bmatrix}$$

$$= \left[\begin{array}{cccc|cccc} \langle x_1^2 \rangle & \langle x_1 x_2 \rangle & \cdots & \langle x_1 x_n \rangle & \langle x_1^3 \rangle & \langle x_1^2 x_2 \rangle & \cdots & \langle x_1 x_n^2 \rangle \\ \langle x_2 x_1 \rangle & \langle x_2^2 \rangle & \cdots & \langle x_2 x_n \rangle & \langle x_2 x_1^2 \rangle & \langle x_1 x_2^2 \rangle & \cdots & \langle x_2 x_n^2 \rangle \\ \vdots & \vdots & \ddots & \vdots & \vdots & \vdots & \ddots & \vdots \\ \langle x_n x_1 \rangle & \langle x_n x_2 \rangle & \cdots & \langle x_n^2 \rangle & \langle x_n x_1^2 \rangle & \langle x_1 x_2 x_n \rangle & \cdots & \langle x_n^3 \rangle \\ \hline \langle x_1^3 \rangle & \langle x_2 x_1^2 \rangle & \cdots & \langle x_n x_1^2 \rangle & \langle x_1^4 \rangle & \langle x_1^3 x_2 \rangle & \cdots & \langle x_1^2 x_n^2 \rangle \\ \langle x_2 x_1^2 \rangle & \langle x_2^2 x_1 \rangle & \cdots & \langle x_2 x_1 x_n \rangle & \langle x_2 x_1^3 \rangle & \langle x_2^2 x_1^2 \rangle & \cdots & \langle x_1 x_2 x_n^2 \rangle \\ \vdots & \vdots & \ddots & \vdots & \vdots & \vdots & \ddots & \vdots \\ \langle x_n^2 x_1 \rangle & \langle x_n^2 x_2 \rangle & \cdots & \langle x_n^3 \rangle & \langle x_n^2 x_1^2 \rangle & \langle x_n^2 x_2 x_1 \rangle & \cdots & \langle x_n^4 \rangle \end{array} \right]$$

$$(3.3.24)$$

Note that $\mathbf{C}_1 = \langle \mathbf{x}\mathbf{x}^{\mathrm{T}} \rangle$, as in Equation (3.3.4), and that $\mathbf{C}_2 = \mathbf{C}_3^{\mathrm{T}}$. The matrices $\mathbf{C}_2$ and $\mathbf{C}_3$ reflect third-order statistics, and $\mathbf{C}_4$ reflects fourth-order statistics. Yet higher-order statistics can be realized by allowing for higher-order terms of the x_i components in $\mathbf{z}$.

Extraction of higher-order statistics is also possible if units with nonlinear activation functions are used (e.g., sigmoidal activation units). This can be seen by employing Taylor series expansion of the output of a nonlinear unit $y = f(\mathbf{w}^{\mathrm{T}}\mathbf{x})$ at $\mathbf{w}^{\mathrm{T}}\mathbf{x} = 0$. Here, it is assumed that all derivatives of f exist. This expansion allows us to write this unit's output as

$$y = f(0) + \frac{\mathbf{w}^{\mathrm{T}}\mathbf{x}}{1!} f'(0) + \frac{(\mathbf{w}^{\mathrm{T}}\mathbf{x})^2}{2!} f''(0) + \frac{(\mathbf{w}^{\mathrm{T}}\mathbf{x})^3}{3!} f'''(0) + \cdots \qquad (3.3.25)$$

which may be interpreted as the output of a high-order (polynomial) unit (see Problem 3.3.7). Therefore, higher-order (nonlinear) principal-component extraction is expected when Hebbian-type learning is applied to this unit. For further exploration in nonlinear PCA, the reader may consult Karhunen (1994), Sudjianto and Hassoun (1994), and Xu (1994). Also, see Section 5.3.6.

3.4 Competitive Learning

The preceding section considered simple Hebbian-based networks of linear units that employed some degree of competition through lateral inhibition in order for each unit to capture a principal component of the training set. This section extends this notion of competition among units and specialization of units to tackle a different class of problems involving clustering of unlabeled data or vector quantization. Here, a network of binary-valued outputs, with only one "on" at a time, is used to classify as to which of several categories an input belongs. These categories are to be discovered by the network on the basis of correlations in the input data. The network would then classify each cluster of "similar" input data as a single output class.

3.4.1 Simple Competitive Learning

Because this section deals with competition, it only makes sense to consider a group of interacting units. The simplest architecture is assumed, where there is a single layer of units, each receiving the same input $\mathbf{x} \in R^n$ and producing an output y_i. It is also assumed that only one unit is active at a given time. This active unit is called the *winner* and is determined as the unit with the largest weighted-sum net_i^k, where

$$net_i^k = \mathbf{w}_i^T \mathbf{x}^k \qquad (3.4.1)$$

and $\mathbf{x}^k$ is the current input. Thus unit i is the winning unit if

$$\mathbf{w}_i^T \mathbf{x}^k \geq \mathbf{w}_j^T \mathbf{x}^k \qquad \text{for all } j \neq i \qquad (3.4.2)$$

which may be written as

$$\|\mathbf{w}_i - \mathbf{x}^k\| \leq \|\mathbf{w}_j - \mathbf{x}^k\| \qquad \text{for all } j \neq i \qquad (3.4.3)$$

if $\|\mathbf{w}_i\| = 1$, for all $i = 1, 2, \ldots, m$. Thus the winner is the node with the weight vector closest (in a Euclidean distance sense) to the input vector. It is interesting to note that lateral inhibition may be employed here in order to implement the "winner take all" operation in Equation (3.4.2) or (3.4.3). This is similar to what was described in the preceding section with a slight variation: Each unit inhibits all other units and self-excites itself, as shown in Figure 3.4.1.

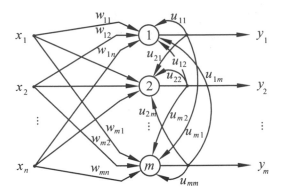

Figure 3.4.1
Single layer competitive network.

In order to ensure winner-take-all operation, a proper choice of lateral weights and unit activation functions must be made [e.g., see Grossberg (1976) and Lippmann (1987)]. One possible choice for the lateral weights is

$$u_{ij} = \begin{cases} 1 & i = j \\ -\varepsilon & i \neq j \end{cases} \tag{3.4.4}$$

where $0 < \varepsilon < 1/m$, and m is the number of units in the network. An appropriate activation function for this type of network is shown in Figure 3.4.2, where T is chosen such that the outputs y_i do not saturate at 1 before convergence of the winner-take-all competition; after convergence, only the winning unit will saturate at 1, with all other units having zero outputs. Note, however, that if one is training the net as part of a computer simulation, there is no need for the winner-take-all net to be implemented explicitly; it is more efficient from a computation point of view to perform the winner selection by direct search for the maximum net_i. Thus far this section has only described the competition mechanism of the competitive learning technique. A learning equation for weight updating is presented next.

For a given input $\mathbf{x}^k$ drawn from a random distribution $p(\mathbf{x})$, the weights of the winning unit are updated (the weights of all other units are left unchanged) according to (Grossberg, 1969; von der Malsburg, 1973; Rumelhart and Zipser, 1985)

$$\Delta\mathbf{w}_i = \begin{cases} \rho(\mathbf{x}^k - \mathbf{w}_i) & \text{if } \mathbf{w}_i \text{ is the weight vector of the winning unit} \\ \mathbf{0} & \text{otherwise} \end{cases} \tag{3.4.5}$$

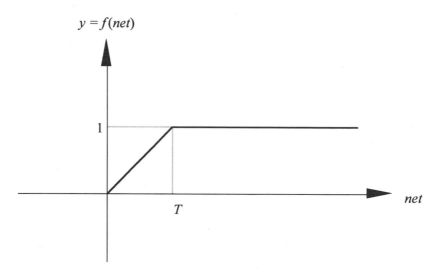

Figure 3.4.2
Activation function for units in the competitive network of Figure 3.4.1.

If the magnitudes of the input vectors contain no useful information, a more appropriate rule to use is

$$\Delta\mathbf{w}_i = \rho\left(\frac{\mathbf{x}^k}{\|\mathbf{x}^k\|} - \mathbf{w}_i\right) \tag{3.4.6}$$

The preceding rules tend to tilt the weight vector of the current winning unit in the direction of the current input. The cumulative effect of the repetitive application of these rules can be described as follows: If one views the input and weight vectors as points scattered on the surface of a hypersphere (or a circle, as in Figure 3.4.3), the effect of the application of the competitive learning rule is to sensitize certain units toward neighboring clusters of input data. Ultimately, some units (frequent winner units) will evolve so that their weight vector points toward the "center of mass" of the nearest significant dense cluster of data points. This effect is illustrated pictorially for a simple example in Figure 3.4.3.

At the onset of learning, one does not know the number of clusters in the data set. Normally, therefore, this number is overestimated by including excess units in the network. This means that after convergence, some units will be redundant in the sense that they do not evolve significantly and thus do not capture any data clusters. This can be seen, for example, in Figure 3.4.3 where the weight vector $\mathbf{w}_1$ does not significantly evolve throughout the computation. These are typically the units that are

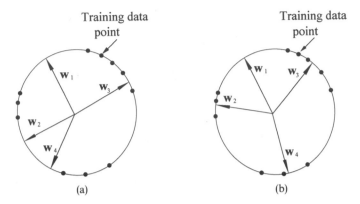

Figure 3.4.3
Simple competitive learning. (*a*) initial weight vectors; (*b*) weight vector
configuration after performing simple competitive learning.

initialized to points in the weight space that have relatively low overlap with the
training data points; such units may still be desirable, since they may capture new
clusters if the underlying distribution $p(\mathbf{x})$ changes in time, or if desired, their probability of occurrence may be reduced by using some of the following heuristics: (1)
initialize the weight vectors to randomly selected sample input vectors, (2) use "leaky
learning" (Rumelhart and Zipser, 1985) (here, all loser units are also updated in response to an input vector, but with a learning rate much smaller than the one used for
the winner unit), (3) update the neighboring units of the winner unit, and/or (4) smear
the input vectors with added noise using a long-tailed distribution (Szu, 1986).

After learning has converged, it is necessary to "calibrate" the preceding clustering
network in order to determine the number of units representing the various learned
clusters and cluster membership. Here, the weights of the net are held fixed, and the
training set is used to interrogate the network for sensitized units. The following
example demonstrates these ideas for a simple data clustering problem.

Example 3.4.1   Consider the set of unlabeled two-dimensional data points plotted in
Figure 3.4.4. This example demonstrates the typical solution (cluster formation) generated by a four-unit competitive net, which employs Equations (3.4.2) and (3.4.5). No
normalization of either the weight vectors or the input vectors is used. During training, the input samples (data points) are selected uniformly at random from the data
set. The four weight vectors are initialized to random values close to the center of
the plot in Figure 3.4.4. Training with $\rho = 0.01$ is performed for 1000 iterations.
The resulting weight vector trajectories are plotted in Figure 3.4.5a, with the initial

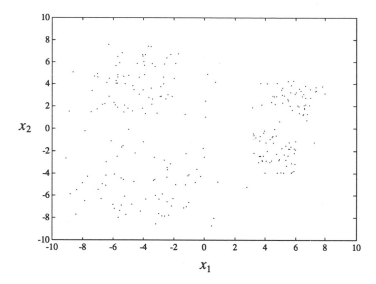

Figure 3.4.4
Unlabeled two-dimensional data used in training the simple competitive net
of Example 3.4.1.

weights marked by an asterisk. Note how one of the units never evolved beyond its
initial weight vector. This occurred because this unit never became a winner. Each of
the remaining three units evolved its weight vector to a distinct region in the input
space. Since ρ is small, the weight vectors are shown to enter and stay inside "tiny"
neighborhoods; the weight vectors fluctuate inside their respective terminal neighborhoods. These fluctuations are amplified if a relatively larger ρ ($\rho = 0.05$) value is used,
as demonstrated in Figure 3.4.5b. Finally, the trained network is calibrated by assigning a unique cluster label for any unit that becomes a winner for one or more training
samples. Here, Equation (3.4.2) is used to determine the winning unit. During calibration, only three units are found to ever become winners. Figure 3.4.6 depicts the result
of the calibration process. Here, the symbols +, ∘, and × are used to tag the three
winner units, respectively. The figure shows a +, ∘, or × printed at the exact position
of the training sample **x** if **x** causes the unit with label +, ∘, or × to be a winner,
respectively. We should note that the exact same clusters in Figure 3.4.6 are generated
by the net with $\rho = 0.05$. The cluster labeled × looks interesting because of its obvious bimodal structure. Intuitively speaking, one would have expected this cluster to
be divided by the competitive net into two distinct clusters. In fact, if one carefully
looks at Figure 3.4.5b, this is what the net attempted to do but failed. However, very
few simulations out of a large number of simulations that were attempted, but are not

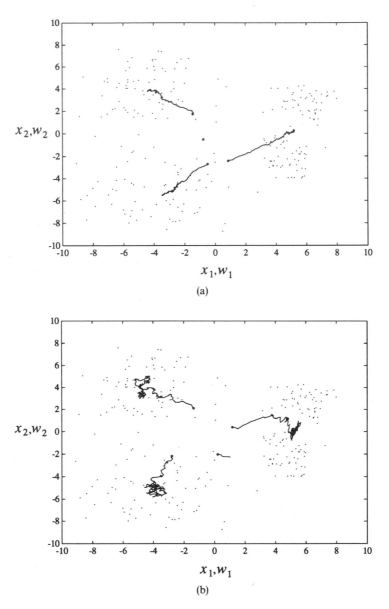

Figure 3.4.5
Weight vector evolution trajectories for a four-unit competitive net employing
Equations (3.4.2) and (3.4.5). These trajectories are shown superimposed on the
plane containing the training data. An asterisk is used to indicate the initial
setting of the weights for each of the four units. (*a*) Learning rate equals 0.01. (*b*)
Learning rate equals 0.05.

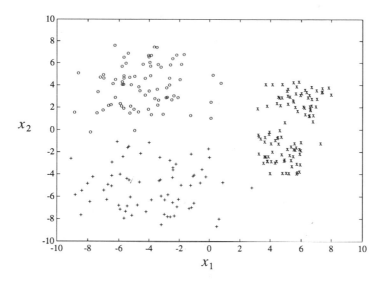

Figure 3.4.6
A three-cluster solution for the data shown in Figure 3.4.4. This solution represents a typical cluster formation generated by the simple four-unit competitive net of Example 3.4.1.

shown here, did in fact result in this "intuitive" solution. In Chapter 4 the competitive learning rule in Equation (3.4.5) is shown to correspond to stochastic gradient descent on the criterion $J(\mathbf{w}) = \frac{1}{2} \sum_k \|\mathbf{x}^k - \mathbf{w}_{i*}\|^2$, where $\mathbf{w}_{i*}$ is the weight vector of the winner unit. Therefore, one may explain the three-cluster solution in this example as representing a suboptimal solution that corresponds to a local minimum of $J(\mathbf{w})$.

3.4.2   Vector Quantization

One of the common applications of competitive learning is adaptive vector quantization for data compression (e.g., speech and image data). In this approach, a given set of $\mathbf{x}^k$ data points (vectors) is categorized into m "templates" so that later one may use an encoded version of the corresponding template of any input vector to represent the vector, as opposed to using the vector itself. This leads to efficient quantization (compression) for storage and for transmission purposes (albeit at the expense of some distortion).

Vector quantization is a technique whereby the input space is divided into a number of distinct regions, and for each region a "template" (reconstruction vector) is defined (Linde et al., 1980; Gray, 1984). When presented with a new input vector $\mathbf{x}$,

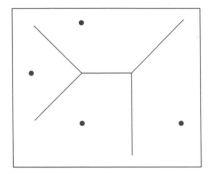

Figure 3.4.7
Input space partitions realized by a Voronoi quantizer
with four reconstruction vectors. The four reconstruction vectors are shown as filled circles in the figure.

a vector quantizer first determines the region in which the vector lies. Then the
quantizer outputs an encoded version of the reconstruction vector $\mathbf{w}_i$ representing
that particular region containing $\mathbf{x}$. The set of all possible reconstruction vectors $\mathbf{w}_i$ is
usually called the *codebook* of the quantizer. When the Euclidean distance similarity
measure is used to decide on the region to which the input $\mathbf{x}$ belongs, the quantizer is
called a *Voronoi quantizer*. The Voronoi quantizer partitions its input space into
Voronoi cells (Gray, 1984), and each cell is represented by one of the reconstruction
vectors $\mathbf{w}_i$. The ith Voronoi cell contains those points of the input space which are
closer (in a Euclidean sense) to the vector $\mathbf{w}_i$ than to any other vector $\mathbf{w}_j, j \neq i$. Figure
3.4.7 shows an example of the input space partitions of a Voronoi quantizer with four
reconstruction vectors.

The competitive learning rule in Equation (3.4.5) with a winning unit determination
based on the Euclidean distance as in Equation (3.4.3) may now be used to allocate
a set of m reconstruction vectors $\mathbf{w}_i \in R^n$, $i = 1, 2, \ldots, m$, to the input space of n-
dimensional vectors $\mathbf{x}$. Let $\mathbf{x}$ be distributed according to the probability density function $p(\mathbf{x})$. Initially, we set the starting values of the vectors $\mathbf{w}_i$ to the first m randomly
generated samples of $\mathbf{x}$. Additional samples $\mathbf{x}$ are then used for training. Here, the
learning rate ρ in Equation (3.4.5) is selected as a monotonically decreasing function
of the number of iterations k. Based on empirical results, Kohonen (1989) conjectured
that, in an average sense, the asymptotic local point density of the vector $\mathbf{w}_i$ (i.e., the
number of $\mathbf{w}_i$ falling in a small volume of R^n centered at $\mathbf{x}$) obtained by the preceding
competitive learning process takes the form of a continuous, monotonically increas-
ing function of $p(\mathbf{x})$. Thus this competitive learning algorithm may be viewed as an

"approximate" method for computing the reconstruction vectors $\mathbf{w}_i$ in an unsupervised manner.

Kohonen (1989) designed supervised versions of vector quantization (called *learning vector quantization*, or LVQ) for adaptive pattern classification. Here, class information is used to fine-tune the reconstruction vectors in a Voronoi quantizer so as to improve the quality of the classifier decision regions. In pattern-classification problems, it is the decision surface between pattern classes and not the inside of the class distribution that should be described most accurately. The preceding quantizer process can be easily adapted to optimize placement of the decision surface between different classes. Here, one would start with a trained Voronoi quantizer and calibrate it using a set of labeled input samples (vectors). Each calibration sample is assigned to that $\mathbf{w}_i$ which is closest. Each $\mathbf{w}_i$ is then labeled according to the majority of classes represented among those samples which have been assigned to $\mathbf{w}_i$. Here, the distribution of the calibration samples to the various classes, as well as the relative numbers of the $\mathbf{w}_i$ assigned to these classes, must comply with the a priori probabilities of the classes, if such probabilities are known. Next, the tuning of the decision surfaces is accomplished by rewarding correct classifications and punishing incorrect ones. Let the training vector $\mathbf{x}^k$ belong to the class c_j. Assume that the closest reconstruction vector $\mathbf{w}_i$ to $\mathbf{x}^k$ carries the label of class c_l. Then, only vector $\mathbf{w}_i$ is updated according to the following supervised rule (LVQ rule):

$$\Delta \mathbf{w}_i = \begin{cases} +\rho^k(\mathbf{x}^k - \mathbf{w}_i) & \text{if } c_j = c_l \\ -\rho^k(\mathbf{x}^k - \mathbf{w}_i) & \text{if } c_j \neq c_l \end{cases} \tag{3.4.7}$$

where ρ^k is assumed to be a monotonically decreasing function of the number of iterations k. After convergence, the input space R^n is again partitioned by a Voronoi tessellation corresponding to the tuned $\mathbf{w}_i$ vectors. The primary effect of the reward/punish rule in Equation (3.4.7) is to minimize the number of misclassifications. At the same time, however, the vectors $\mathbf{w}_i$ are pulled away from the zones of class overlap where misclassifications persist.

The convergence speed of LVQ can be improved if each vector $\mathbf{w}_i$ has its own adaptive learning rate ρ_i^k given by (Kohonen, 1990)

$$\rho_i^k = \begin{cases} \dfrac{\rho_i^{k-1}}{1 + \rho_i^{k-1}} & \text{if } c_j = c_l \\[3mm] \dfrac{\rho_i^{k-1}}{1 - \rho_i^{k-1}} & \text{if } c_j \neq c_l \end{cases} \tag{3.4.8}$$

This recursive rule causes ρ_i to decrease if $\mathbf{w}_i$ classifies $\mathbf{x}^k$ correctly. Otherwise, ρ_i increases. Equations (3.4.7) and (3.4.8) define what is known as an *optimized learning rate* LVQ (OLVQ). Another improved algorithm named LVQ2 also has been suggested by Kohonen et al. (1988) that approaches the optimal performance predicted by Bayes decision theory (Duda and Hart, 1973).

Some theoretical aspects of competitive learning are considered in the next chapter. More general competitive networks with stable categorization behavior have been proposed by Carpenter and Grossberg (1987a, b). One of these networks, called ART1, is described in Chapter 6.

3.5   Self-Organizing Feature Maps: Topology-Preserving Competitive Learning

Self-organization is a process of unsupervised learning whereby significant patterns or features in the input data are discovered. In the context of a neural network, self-organization learning consists of adaptively modifying the synaptic weights of a network of locally interacting units in response to input excitations and in accordance with a learning rule until a final useful configuration develops. The local interaction of units means that the changes in the behavior of a unit only (directly) affect the behavior of its immediate neighborhood. The key question here is how could a useful configuration evolve from self-organization. The answer lies essentially in a naturally observed phenomenon whereby global order can arise from local interactions (Turing, 1952). This phenomenon applies to neural networks (biological and artificial) where man, originally random local interactions between neighboring units (neurons) of a network couple and coalesce into states of global order. This global order leads to coherent behavior, which is the essence of self-organization.

In the following, a modified version of the simple competitive learning network discussed in Section 3.4.1 is presented that exhibits self-organization features. This network attempts to map a set of input vectors $\mathbf{x}^k$ in R^n onto an array of units (normally one- or two-dimensional) such that any topological relationships among the $\mathbf{x}^k$ patterns are preserved and are represented by the network in terms of a spatial distribution of unit activities. The more related two patterns are in the input space, the closer one can expect the position in the array of the two units representing these patterns. In other words, if $\mathbf{x}^1$ and $\mathbf{x}^2$ are "similar" or are topological neighbors in R^n, and if $\mathbf{r}_1$ and $\mathbf{r}_2$ are the locations of the corresponding winner units in the net/array, then the Euclidean distance $\|\mathbf{r}_1 - \mathbf{r}_2\|$ is expected to be small. Also, $\|\mathbf{r}_1 - \mathbf{r}_2\|$ approaches zero as $\mathbf{x}^1$ approaches $\mathbf{x}^2$. The idea is to develop a topographic map of the input vectors so that similar input vectors would trigger nearby units. Thus a global organization of the units is expected to emerge.

An example of such topology-preserving self-organizing mappings that exist in animals is the somatosensory map from the skin onto the somatosensory cortex, where there exists an image of the body surface. The retinotopic map from the retina to the visual cortex is another example. It is believed that such biological topology-preserving maps are not entirely preprogrammed by the genes and that some sort of (unsupervised) self-organizing learning phenomenon exists that tunes such maps during development. Two early models of topology-preserving competitive learning were proposed by von der Malsburg (1973) and Willshaw and von der Malsburg (1976) for the retinotopic map problem. This section presents a detailed topology-preserving model due to Kohonen (1982a) that is commonly referred to as the *self-organizing feature map* (SOFM).

3.5.1 Kohonen's SOFM

The purpose of Kohonen's self-organizing feature map is to capture the topology and probability distribution of input data (Kohonen, 1982a and 1989). This model generally involves an architecture consisting of a two-dimensional structure (array) of linear units, where each unit receives the same input $\mathbf{x}^k \in R^n$. Each unit in the array is characterized by an n-dimensional weight vector. The ith unit weight vector $\mathbf{w}_i$ is sometimes viewed as a position vector that defines a "virtual position" for unit i in R^n. This, in turn, will allow interpretation of changes in $\mathbf{w}_i$ as movements of unit i. However, one should keep in mind that no physical movements of units take place.

The learning rule is similar to that of simple competitive learning in Equation (3.4.5) and is defined by

$$\Delta \mathbf{w} = \rho \Phi(\mathbf{r}_i, \mathbf{r}_{i*})(\mathbf{x}^k - \mathbf{w}_i) \qquad \text{for all } i = 1, 2, \ldots \qquad (3.5.1)$$

where $i*$ is the index of the winner unit. The winner unit is determined according to the Euclidean distance as in Equation (3.4.3), with no weight vector normalization. The major difference between this update rule and that of simple competitive learning is the presence of the neighborhood function $\Phi(\mathbf{r}_i, \mathbf{r}_{i*})$ in the former. This function is very critical for the successful preservation of topological properties. It is normally symmetric [i.e., $\Phi(\mathbf{r}_i, \mathbf{r}_{i*}) = \Phi(\mathbf{r}_i - \mathbf{r}_{i*})$] with values close to 1 for units i close to $i*$ and decreases monotonically with the Euclidean distance $\|\mathbf{r}_i - \mathbf{r}_{i*}\|$ between units i and $i*$ in the array.

At the onset of learning, $\Phi(\mathbf{r}_i, \mathbf{r}_{i*})$ defines a relatively large neighborhood whereby all units in the net are updated for any input $\mathbf{x}^k$. As learning progresses, the neighborhood is shrunk down until it ultimately goes to zero, where only the winner unit is updated. The learning rate also must follow a monotonically decreasing schedule in order to achieve convergence. One may think of the initial large neighborhood as effecting an exploratory global search which is then continuously refined to a local search as the variance of $\Phi(\mathbf{r}_i, \mathbf{r}_{i*})$ approaches zero. The following is one possible choice for $\Phi(\mathbf{r}_i, \mathbf{r}_{i*})$:

$$\Phi(\mathbf{r}, \mathbf{r}_{i*}) = e^{-\frac{\|\mathbf{r}_i - r_i*\|^2}{2\sigma^2}} \tag{3.5.2}$$

where the variance σ^2 controls the width of the neighborhood. Here, σ and ρ may be set proportional to $1/k^{\alpha}$ ($0 < \alpha \leq 1$) with k representing the learning step. Ritter and Schulten (1988a) proposed the following update schedule for ρ:

$$\rho^k = \rho_0 \left(\frac{\rho_f}{\rho_0}\right)^{k/k_{\max}} \tag{3.5.3}$$

and for σ:

$$\sigma^k = \sigma_0 \left(\frac{\sigma_f}{\sigma_0}\right)^{k/k_{\max}} \tag{3.5.4}$$

where $\rho_0(\sigma_0)$ and $\rho_f(\sigma_f)$ control the initial and final values of the learning rate (neighborhood width), respectively, and $k_{\max}$ is the maximum number of learning steps anticipated.

At present there is no theory to guide the selection of values for these learning schedules parameters for arbitrary training data. However, practical values are $0 < \rho_0 \leq 1$ (typically 0.8), $\rho_f \ll 1$, $\sigma_0 \approx m_d/2$ (m_d is the number of units along the largest diagonal of the array) or an equivalent value that will permit $\Phi(i, i^*, k = 0)$ to reach all units when i^* is set close to the center of the array, and $\sigma_f = 0.5$. Finally $k_{\max}$ is usually set to 2 or more orders of magnitude larger than the total number of units in the net.

Let the input vector $\mathbf{x}$ be a random variable with a stationary probability density function $p(\mathbf{x})$. Then the basis for Equation (3.5.1) and various other self-organizing algorithms is captured by the following two-step process: (1) locate the best-matching unit for the input vector $\mathbf{x}$, and (2) increase matching at this unit and its topological neighbors. The computation achieved by a repetitive application of this process is rather surprising and is captured by the following proposition due to Kohonen (1989): "The $\mathbf{w}_i$ vectors tend to be ordered according to their mutual similarity, and the asymptotic local point density of the $\mathbf{w}_i$, in an average sense, is of the form $g(p(\mathbf{x}))$, where g is some continuous, monotonically increasing function." This proposition is tested by the following experiments.

3.5.2 Examples of SOFMs

Figure 3.5.1 shows an example of mapping uniform random points inside the positive unit square onto a 10×10 planar array of units with rectangular topology. Here,

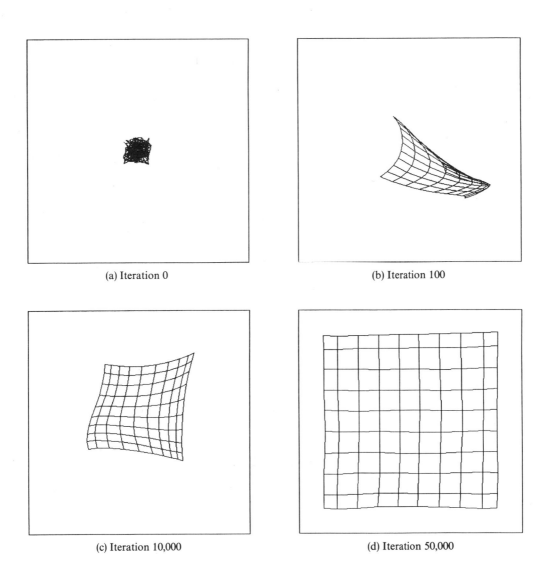

(a) Iteration 0

(b) Iteration 100

(c) Iteration 10,000

(d) Iteration 50,000

Figure 3.5.1
Mapping uniform random points from the unit square using 10×10 planar array of units ($\rho_0 = 0.8, \rho_f = 0.01$, $\sigma_0 = 5, \sigma_f = 1$, and $k_{\max} = 50,000$).

each unit i has four immediate neighboring units, which are located symmetrically at a (normalized) distance of 1 from unit i. In general, however, other array topologies such as hexagonal topology may be assumed. In the figure, the weight vectors of all units are shown as points superimposed on the input space. Connections are shown between points corresponding to topologically neighboring units in the array for improved visualization. Thus a line connecting two weight vectors $\mathbf{w}_i$ and $\mathbf{w}_j$ is only used to indicate that the two corresponding units i and j are adjacent (immediate neighbors) in the array. The weights are initialized randomly near $(0.5, 0.5)$, as shown in Figure 3.5.1a. During training, the inputs to the units in the array are selected randomly and independently from a uniform distribution $p(\mathbf{x})$ over the unit square. Figure 3.5.1b through d shows snapshots of the time evolution of the feature map. Initially, the map untangles and orders its units as in parts b and c of the figure. Ultimately, as shown in Figure 3.5.1d, the map spreads to fill all the input space except for the border region, which shows a slight contraction of the map. Figures 3.5.2 through 3.5.4 show additional examples of mapping uniformly distributed points from a disk, a triangle, and a hollow disk, respectively, onto a 15×15 array of units. The initial weight distribution is shown in part a of each of these figures. Learning rule parameters are provided in the figure captions.

The feature maps in Figures 3.5.1 through 3.5.4 all share the following properties: First, it is useful to observe that there are two phases in the formation of the map: an ordering phase and a convergence phase. The ordering phase involves the initial formation of the correct topological ordering of the weight vectors. This is roughly accomplished during the first several hundred iterations of the learning algorithm. The fine-tuning of the map is accomplished during the convergence phase, where the map converges asymptotically to a solution that approximates $p(\mathbf{x})$. During this phase, the neighborhood width σ^2 and the learning rate ρ take on very small values, thus contributing to slow convergence. For good results, the convergence phase may take 10 to 1000 times as many steps as the ordering phase. Another common property in these SOFMs is a border aberration effect that causes a slight contraction of the map and a higher density of weight vectors at the borders.[7] This aberration is due to the "pulling" by the units inside the map. The important thing, though, is to observe how in all cases the $\mathbf{w}$ vectors are ordered according to their mutual similarity, which preserves the topology of the Euclidean input space. Another important result is that the density of the weight vectors in the weight space follows the uniform probability

---

7. This contraction effect diminishes with increasing size of the array (Kohonen, 1989).

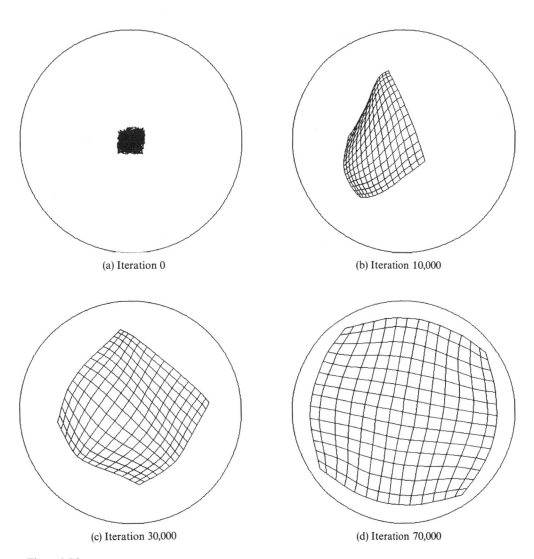

(a) Iteration 0

(b) Iteration 10,000

(c) Iteration 30,000

(d) Iteration 70,000

Figure 3.5.2
Mapping uniform random points from a disk onto a 15×15 array of units ($\rho_0 = 0.8, \rho_f = 0.01, \sigma_0 = 8$, $\sigma_f = 1$, and $k_{max} = 70,000$).

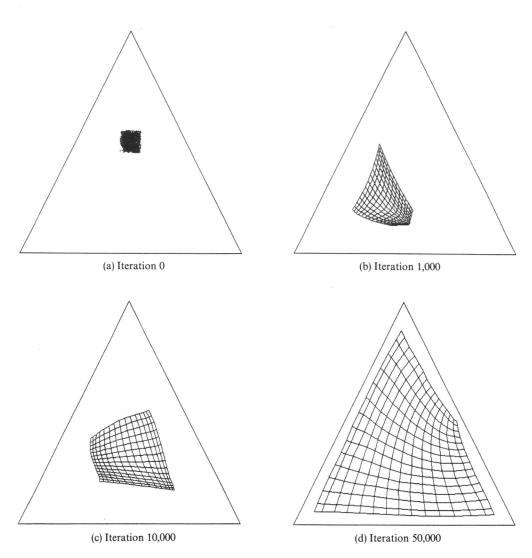

(a) Iteration 0

(b) Iteration 1,000

(c) Iteration 10,000

(d) Iteration 50,000

Figure 3.5.3
Mapping uniform random points from a triangle onto a 15×15 array of units ($\rho_0 = 0.8, \rho_f = 0.01, \sigma_0 = 8,$ $\sigma_f = 1$, and $k_{\max} = 50,000$).

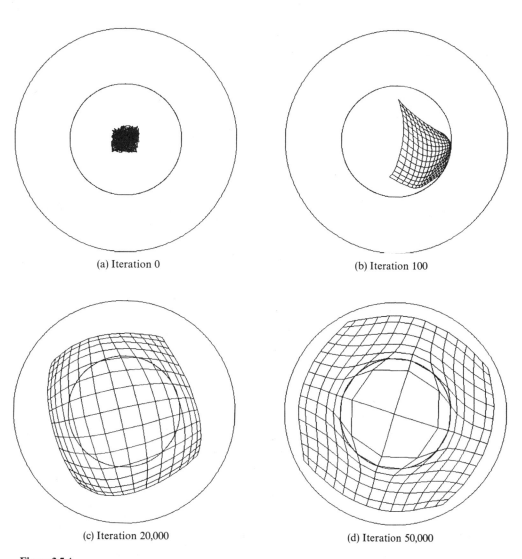

(a) Iteration 0

(b) Iteration 100

(c) Iteration 20,000

(d) Iteration 50,000

Figure 3.5.4
Mapping uniform random points from a hollow disk onto a 15×15 array of units ($\rho_0 = 0.8, \rho_f = 0.01,$ $\sigma_0 = 8, \sigma_f = 1,$ and $k_{max} = 50,000$).

distribution of the input vectors.[8] If the distribution $p(\mathbf{x})$ had been nonuniform, we would have found more grid points of the map where $p(\mathbf{x})$ was high (this is explored in Problem 3.5.5).

Mappings from higher to lower dimensions are also possible with a SOFM and are in general useful for dimensionality reduction of input data. An illustrative example is shown in Figure 3.5.5, in which a mapping from a hollow disk region to a linear array (chain) of 60 units is performed using Kohonen's feature-map learning in Equation (3.5.1). Here, the units self-organize such that they cover the largest region possible (space-filling curve).

Two additional interesting simulations of SOFMs, due to Ritter and Schulten (1988a), are considered next. The first simulation involves the formation of a somato-sensory map between the tactile receptors of a hand surface and an "artificial cortex" formed by a 30 × 30 planar square array of linear units. The training set consisted of the activity patterns of the set of tactile receptors covering the hand surface. Figure 3.5.6 depicts the evolution of the feature map from an initial random map. Here, random points are selected according to the probability distributions defined by regions D, L, M, R, and T shown in Figure 3.5.6a. It is interesting to note the boundaries developed (shown as dotted regions in the maps of Figure 3.5.6c and d) between the various sensory regions. Also note the correlations between the sensory regions sizes of the input data and their associated regions in the converged map.

The second simulation is inspired by the work of Durbin and Willshaw (1987) [see also Angeniol et al. (1988) and Hueter (1988)] related to solving the traveling salesman problem (TSP) by an elastic net. Here, 30 random city locations are chosen in the unit square with the objective of finding the path with minimal length that visits all cities, where each city is visited only once. A linear array (chain) of 100 units is used for the feature map. The initial neighborhood size used is 20, and the initial learning rate is 1. Figure 3.5.7a shows the 30 randomly chosen city locations (filled circles) and the initial location and shape of the chain (open squares). The generated solution path is shown in Figure 3.5.7b, c, and d after 5000, 7500, and 10,000 steps, respectively.

Applications of SOFMs can be found in many areas, including trajectory planning for a robot arm (Kohonen, 1989; Ritter and Schulten, 1988a) and combinatorial optimization (Angeniol et al., 1988; Hueter, 1988; Ritter and Schulten, 1988a). In

8. In Figure 3.5.4d, there are nine grid points (weight vectors) in a region of zero probability. But it is difficult to find a better solution without clustering a lot of points inside this region. An extension of Kohonen's SOFM to maps with dynamically evolving array structure and size can be found in Fritzke (1991). This extension allows for a problem-dependent array structure to be learned, which gives the SOFM the capability of modeling more accurately a far wider range of distributions of input vectors, such as the one in Figure 3.5.4.

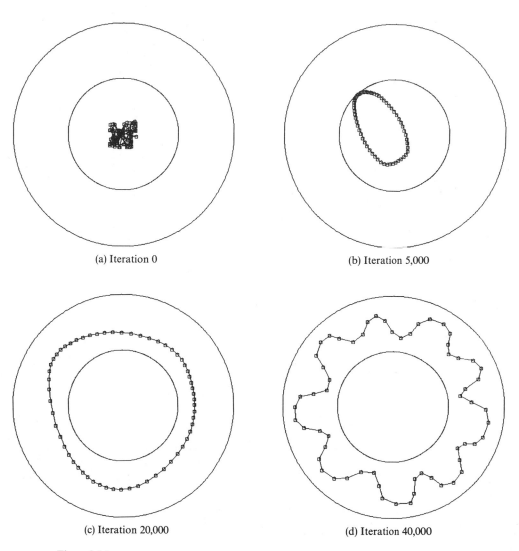

(a) Iteration 0

(b) Iteration 5,000

(c) Iteration 20,000

(d) Iteration 40,000

Figure 3.5.5
Mapping from a hollow disk region onto a linear array (chain) of 60 units using a SOFM.

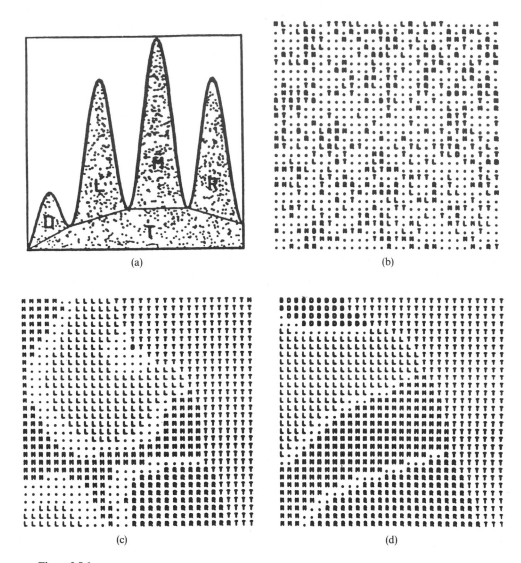

(a)   (b)

(c)   (d)

Figure 3.5.6
An example of somatosensory map formation on a planar array of 30 × 30 units. (From H. Ritter and
K. Schulten, Kohonen's self-organizing maps: Exploring their computational capabilities, *Proceedings
of the IEEE International Conference on Neural Networks*, vol. I, Son Diego, IEEE Press, pp. 109–116,
© 1988 IEEE.)

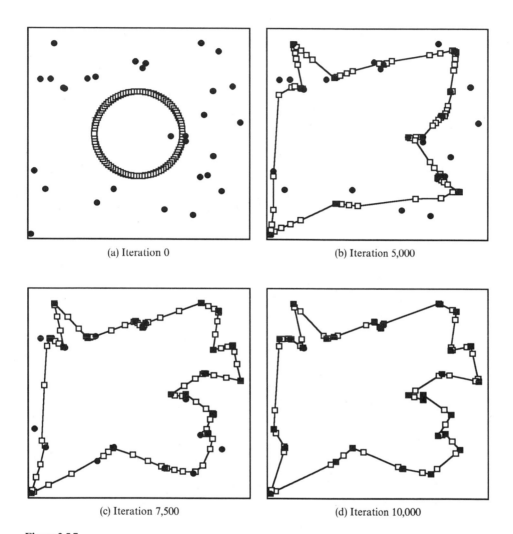

(a) Iteration 0

(b) Iteration 5,000

(c) Iteration 7,500

(d) Iteration 10,000

Figure 3.5.7
Solving 30-city TSP using a SOFM consisting of a "chain" of 100 units. Filled circles correspond to fixed city locations. Open squares correspond to weight vector coordinates of units forming the chain.

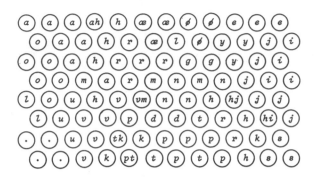

Figure 3.5.8
Phonotopic feature map for Finnish speech. Units, shown as
circles, are labeled with the symbols of the phonemes to which
they adapted to give the best responses. Some units are shown
to respond to two phonemes. (From T. Kohonen, The "neural"
phonetic typewriter, *IEEE Computer Magazine*, **21**(3), pp. 11–
22, 1988; © 1988 IEEE.)

practical applications of self-organizing feature maps, input vectors are often high
dimensional. Such is the case in speech processing. This section concludes by high-
lighting an interesting practical application of feature maps as phonotopic maps for
continuous speech processing (Kohonen, 1988).

In speech processing (transcription, recognition, etc.), a microphone signal is first
digitally preprocessed and converted into a 15-channel spectral representation that
covers the range of frequencies from 200 Hz to 5 kHz. Let these channels together
constitute the 15-dimensional input vector $\mathbf{x}(t)$ to a feature map (normally, each
vector is preprocessed by subtracting the average from all components and normalizing its length). Here, an 8×12 hexagonal array of units is assumed as depicted in
Figure 3.5.8; note how each unit in this array has six immediate neighbors. The
self-organizing process of Equation (3.5.1) is used to create a "topographic" two-
dimensional map of speech elements onto the hexagonal array.

The input vectors $\mathbf{x}(t)$, representing a short-time spectrum of the speech waveform,
are computed every 9.83 msec. These inputs are presented in their natural order as
inputs to the units in the array. After training on sufficiently large segments of continuous speech (Finnish speech in this case) and subsequent calibration of the resulting
map with standard reference phoneme spectra, the phonotopic map of Figure 3.5.8
emerges. Here, the units are labeled with the symbols of the phonemes to which they
"learned" to give the best responses. A striking result is that the various units in the
array become sensitized to spectra of different phonemes and their variations in a

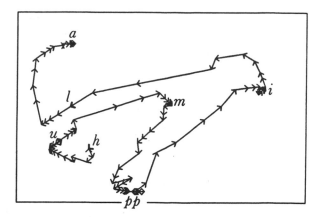

Figure 3.5.9
Sequence of the responses of units obtained from the phonotopic map when the Finnish word *humpilla* was uttered. The arrows correspond to intervals of 9.83 ms. (From T. Kohonen, The "neural" phonetic typewriter, *IEEE Computer Magazine*, **21**(3), pp. 11–22, 1988; © 1998 IEEE.)

two-dimensional order, although teaching was not done using the phonemes. One can attribute this to the fact that the input spectra are clustered around phonemes, and the self-organizing process finds these clusters. Some of the units in the array have double labels, which implies units that respond to two phonemes. For example, the distinction of "*k*," "*p*," and "*t*" from this map is not reliable [a solution for such a problem is described in Kohonen (1988)]. This phonotopic map can be used as the basis for isolated-word recognition. Here, the signal $\mathbf{x}(t)$ corresponding to an uttered word induces an ordered sequence of responses in the units in the array. Figure 3.5.9 shows the sequence of responses obtained from the phonotopic map when the Finnish word *Humpilla* (name of a place) was uttered. This sequence of responses defines a phonemic transcription of the uttered word. Then this transcription can be recognized by comparing it with reference transcriptions collected from a great many words. Also, these phonemic trajectories provide the means for the visualization of the phonemes of speech, which may be useful for speech training therapy. Further extensions of the use of SOFMs in automatic speech recognition can be found in Tattersal et al. (1990).

Kohonen (1988) employed the phonotopic map in a speech transcription system implemented in hardware in a PC environment. This system is used as a "phonetic typewriter" that can produce text from arbitrary dictation. When trained on speech from half a dozen speakers using office text, names, and the most frequent words of the language (this amounts to several thousand words), the phonetic typewriter had a transcription accuracy between 92 and 97 percent depending on the speaker and difficulty of text. This system can be adapted on-line to new speakers by fine-tuning the phonotopic map on a dictation of about 100 words.

3.6   Summary

This chapter describes a number of basic learning rules for supervised, reinforcement, and unsupervised learning. It presents a unifying view of these learning rules for the single-unit setting. Here, the learning process is viewed as steepest-gradient-based search for a set of weights that optimizes an associated criterion function. This is true for all learning rules regardless of the usual taxonomy of these rules as supervised, reinforcement, or unsupervised. Preliminary characterizations of some learning rules are given, with the in depth mathematical analysis deferred to the next chapter.

Various forms of criterion functions are discussed, including the perceptron, SSE, MSE, Minkowski-r, and relative entropy criterion functions. The issue of which learning rules are capable of finding linearly separable solutions led to the definition of the class of well-formed criterion functions. These functions, when optimized by an iterative search process, guarantee that the search will enter the region in the weight space that corresponds to linearly separable solutions.

Steepest-gradient-based learning is extended to the stochastic unit, which serves as the foundation for reinforcement learning. Reinforcement learning is viewed as a stochastic process that attempts to maximize the average reinforcement.

Unsupervised learning is treated in the second half of the chapter. Here, Hebbian learning is discussed, and examples of stable Hebbian-type learning rules are presented along with illustrative simulations. It is pointed out that Hebbian learning applied to a single linear unit tends to maximize the unit's output variance. Finally, simple single-layer networks of multiple interconnected units are considered in the context of competitive learning, learning vector quantization, principal-component analysis, and self-organizing feature maps. Simulations are also included which are designed to illustrate the powerful emerging computational properties of these simple networks and their application. It is demonstrated that local interactions in a competitive net can lead to global order. A case in point is the SOFM, where simple incremental interactions among locally neighboring units lead to a global map that preserves the topology and density of the input data.

Table 3.6.1 summarizes all learning rules considered in this chapter. It gives a quick reference to the learning equations and their associated criterion functions, appropriate parameter initializations, type of unit activation function employed, and some remarks on convergence behavior and the nature of the obtained solution.

Table 3.6.1
Summary of Basic Learning Rules

Learning Rule (Type)	Criterion Function[a]	Learning Vector[b]	Conditions	Activation Function[c]	Remarks
Perceptron rule (supervised)	$J(\mathbf{w}) = -\sum\limits_{\mathbf{z}^T\mathbf{w}\leq 0} \mathbf{z}^T\mathbf{w}$	$\begin{cases} \mathbf{z}^k & \text{if } (\mathbf{z}^k)^T\mathbf{w}^k \leq 0 \\ \mathbf{0} & \text{otherwise} \end{cases}$	$\rho > 0$	$f(net) = \text{sgn}(net)$	Finite convergence time if training set is linearly separable. $\|\mathbf{w}\|$ stays bounded for arbitrary training sets.
Perceptron rule with variable learning rate and fixed margin (supervised)	$J(\mathbf{w}) = -\sum\limits_{\mathbf{z}^T\mathbf{w}\leq b} (\mathbf{z}^T\mathbf{w} - b)$	$\begin{cases} \mathbf{z}^k & \text{if } (\mathbf{z}^k)^T\mathbf{w}^k \leq b \\ \mathbf{0} & \text{otherwise} \end{cases}$	$b > 0$ ρ^k satisfies: 1. $\rho^k \geq 0$ 2. $\sum\limits_{k=1}^{\infty} \rho^k = \infty$ 3. $\dfrac{\sum\limits_{k=1}^{\infty} (\rho^k)^2}{\left(\sum\limits_{k=1}^{\infty} \rho^k\right)^2} = 0$	$f(net) = \text{sgn}(net)$	Converges to $\mathbf{z}^T\mathbf{w} > b$ if training set is linearly separable. Finite convergence if $\rho^k = \rho$, where ρ is a finite positive constant.
Mays' rule (supervised)	$J(\mathbf{w}) = \dfrac{1}{2}\sum\limits_{\mathbf{z}^T\mathbf{w}\leq b} \dfrac{(\mathbf{z}^T\mathbf{w} - b)^2}{\|\mathbf{z}\|^2}$	$\begin{cases} \dfrac{b - (\mathbf{z}^k)^T\mathbf{w}^k}{\|\mathbf{z}^k\|^2} \mathbf{z}^k & \text{if } (\mathbf{z}^k)^T\mathbf{w}^k \leq b \\ \mathbf{0} & \text{otherwise} \end{cases}$	$0 < \rho < 2$ $b > 0$	$f(net) = \text{sgn}(net)$	Finite convergence to the solution $\mathbf{z}^T\mathbf{w} \geq b > 0$ if the training set is linearly separable.

Table 3.6.1 (continued)
Summary of Basic Learning Rules

Learning Rule (Type)	Criterion Function[a]	Learning Vector[b]	Conditions	Activation Function[c]	Remarks
Butz's rule (supervised)	$J(\mathbf{w}) = -\sum_i (\mathbf{z}^i)^\mathrm{T}\mathbf{w}$	$\begin{cases}\mathbf{z}^k & \text{if } (\mathbf{z}^k)^\mathrm{T}\mathbf{w}^k \leq 0 \\ \gamma \mathbf{z}^k & \text{otherwise}\end{cases}$	$0 \leq \gamma \leq 1$ $\rho > 0$	$f(net) = \mathrm{sgn}(net)$	Finite convergence if training set is linearly separable. Places $\mathbf{w}$ in a region that tends to minimize the probability of error for non-linearly separable cases.
Widrow-Hoff rule (α-LMS) (supervised)	$J(\mathbf{w}) = \dfrac{1}{2}\sum_i \dfrac{[d^i - (\mathbf{x}^i)^\mathrm{T}\mathbf{w}]^2}{\|\mathbf{x}^i\|^2}$	$[d^k - (\mathbf{x}^k)^\mathrm{T}\mathbf{w}^k]\mathbf{x}^k$	$\rho^k = \dfrac{\alpha}{\|\mathbf{x}^k\|^2}$ $0 < \alpha < 2$	$f(net) = net$	Converges in the mean square to the minimum SSE or LMS solution if $\|\mathbf{x}^i\| = \|\mathbf{x}^j\|$ for all i, j.
μ-LMS (supervised)	$J(\mathbf{w}) = \dfrac{1}{2}\sum_i [d^i - (\mathbf{x}^i)^\mathrm{T}\mathbf{w}]^2$	$[d^k - (\mathbf{x}^k)^\mathrm{T}\mathbf{w}^k]\mathbf{x}^k$	$0 < \rho < \dfrac{2}{3\langle\|\mathbf{x}\|^2\rangle}$	$f(net) = net$	Converges in the mean square to the minimum SSE or LMS solution.
Stochastic μ-LMS rule (supervised)	$J(\mathbf{w}) = \dfrac{1}{2}\langle [d^i - (\mathbf{x}^i)^\mathrm{T}\mathbf{w}]^2 \rangle$	$[d^k - (\mathbf{x}^k)^\mathrm{T}\mathbf{w}^k]\mathbf{x}^k$	ρ^k satisfies: 1. $\rho^k \geq 0$ 2. $\sum_{k=1}^{\infty} \rho^k = +\infty$ 3. $\sum_{k=1}^{\infty} (\rho^k)^2 < \infty$	$f(net) = net$	$\langle \cdot \rangle \equiv$ mean operator. (At each leaning step the training vector $\mathbf{x}^k$ is drawn at random.) Converges in the mean square to the minimum SSE or LMS solution.

Rule	$J(\mathbf{w})$	Update	Parameters	Activation	Comments
Correlation rule (supervised)	$J(\mathbf{w}) = -\sum_i d^i(\mathbf{x}^i)^\mathrm{T}\mathbf{w}$	$d^k\mathbf{x}^k$	$\rho > 0$	$f(net) = net$	Converges to the minimum SSE solution if the vectors $\mathbf{x}^k$ are mutually orthonormal.
Delta rule (supervised)	$J(\mathbf{w}) = \dfrac{1}{2}\sum_i (d^i - y^i)^2$ $y^i \triangleq (\mathbf{x}^i)^\mathrm{T}\mathbf{w}$	$(d^k - y^k)f'(net^k)\mathbf{x}^k$	$0 < \rho < 1$	$y = f(net)$ where f is a sigmoid function.	Extends the μ-LMS rule to cases with differentiable non-linear activations.
Minkowski-r delta rule (supervised)	$J(\mathbf{w}) = \dfrac{1}{r}\sum_i |d^i - y^i|^r$	$sgn(d^k - y^k)|d^k - y^k|^{r-1}f'(net^k)\mathbf{x}^k$	$0 < \rho < 1$	$y = f(net)$ where f is a sigmoid function.	$1 < r < 2$ for pseudo-Gaussian distribution $p(\mathbf{x})$ with pronounced tails. $r = 2$ gives delta rule. $r = 1$ arises when $p(\mathbf{x})$ is a Laplace distribution.
Relative entropy delta rule (supervised)	$J(\mathbf{w})$ $= \dfrac{1}{2}\sum_i\left[(1+d^i)\ln\left(\dfrac{1+d^i}{1+y^i}\right) \right.$ $\left. + (1-d^i)\ln\left(\dfrac{1-d^i}{1-y^i}\right) \right]$	$\beta(d^k - y^k)\mathbf{x}^k$	$0 < \rho < 1$	$y = \tanh(\beta\, net)$	Eliminates the flat spot suffered by the delta rule. Converges to a linearly separable solution if one exists.
AHK I (supervised)	$J(\mathbf{w},\mathbf{b}) = \dfrac{1}{2}\sum_i [(\mathbf{z}^i)^\mathrm{T}\mathbf{w} - b_i]^2$ with margin vector $\mathbf{b} > 0$	Magin $\Delta b_i = \begin{cases} \rho_1\varepsilon_i^k & \text{if } \varepsilon_i^k > 0 \\ 0 & \text{otherwise} \end{cases}$ Weight vector: $\begin{cases} \rho_2(\rho_1-1)\varepsilon_i^k\mathbf{z}^i & \text{if } \varepsilon_i^k > 0 \\ -\rho_2\varepsilon_i^k\mathbf{z}^i & \text{if } \varepsilon_i^k \leq 0 \end{cases}$ $\varepsilon_i^k = (\mathbf{z}^i)^\mathrm{T}\mathbf{w} - b_i^k$	$\mathbf{b}^1 > \mathbf{0}$ $0 < \rho_1 < 2$ $0 < \rho_2 < \dfrac{2}{\max\limits_i \|\mathbf{z}^i\|^2}.$	$f(net) = sgn(net)$	b_i values can only increase from their initial values. Converges to a robust solution for linearly separable problems.

Table 3.6.1 (continued)
Summary of Basic Learning Rules

Learning Rule (Type)	Criterion Function[a]	Learning Vector[b]	Conditions	Activation Function[c]	Remarks
AHK II (supervised)	$J(\mathbf{w}, \mathbf{b}) = \dfrac{1}{2} \sum_i [(\mathbf{z}^i)^T \mathbf{w} - b_i]^2$ with margin vector $\mathbf{b} > 0$	Margin Δb_i^k $= \begin{cases} \rho_1 \varepsilon_i^k & \text{if } \varepsilon_i^k > \dfrac{-b_i^k}{\rho_1} \\ 0 & \text{otherwise} \end{cases}$ Weight vector: $\begin{cases} \rho_2(\rho_1 - 1)\varepsilon_i^k \mathbf{z}^i & \text{if } \varepsilon_i^k > \dfrac{-b_i^k}{\rho_1} \\ -\rho_2 \varepsilon_i^k \mathbf{z}^i & \text{if } \varepsilon_i^k \leq \dfrac{-b_i^k}{\rho_1} \end{cases}$ $\varepsilon_i^k = (\mathbf{z}^i)^T \mathbf{w}^k - b_i^k$	$\mathbf{b}^1 > 0$ $0 < \rho_1 < 2$ $0 < \rho_2 < \dfrac{2}{\max\limits_i \|\mathbf{z}^i\|^2}.$	$f(net) = \text{sgn}(net)$	b_i values can take any positive value. Converges to a robust solution for linearly separable problems.
AHK III (supervised)	$J(\mathbf{w}, \mathbf{b}) = \dfrac{1}{2} \sum_i [(\mathbf{z}^i)^T \mathbf{w} - b_i]^2$ with margin vector $\mathbf{b} > 0$	Margin Δb_i^k $= \begin{cases} \rho_1 \varepsilon_i^k & \text{if } \varepsilon_i^k > \dfrac{-b_i^k}{\rho_1} \\ 0 & \text{otherwise} \end{cases}$ Weight vector: $\begin{cases} \rho_2(\rho_1 - 1)\varepsilon_i^k \mathbf{z}^i & \text{if } \varepsilon_i^k > \dfrac{-b_i^k}{\rho_1} \\ 0 & \text{otherwise} \end{cases}$ $\varepsilon_i^k = (\mathbf{z}^i)^T \mathbf{w}^k - b_i^k$	$\mathbf{b}^1 > 0$ $0 < \rho_1 < 2$ $0 < \rho_2 < \dfrac{2}{\max\limits_i \|\mathbf{z}^i\|^2}.$	$f(net) = \text{sgn}(net)$	Converges for linearly separable as well as nonlinearly separable cases. It automatically identifies and discards the critical points affecting the nonlinear separability, and results in a solution which tends to minimize misclassifications.

Rule	$J(\mathbf{w})$	Learning rule	Conditions	Activation	Comments
Delta rule for stochastic units (supervised)	$J(\mathbf{w}) = \frac{1}{2}\sum_i (d^i - \langle y^i \rangle)^2$	$\beta[d^k - \tanh(\beta\,net^k)] \cdot [1 - \tanh^2(\beta\,net^k)]\mathbf{x}^k$	$0 < \rho < 1$	Stochastic activation: $y = \begin{cases} +1 & \text{with} & P(y=+1) \\ -1 & \text{with} & 1 - P(y=+1) \end{cases}$ $P(y=1) = \dfrac{1}{1 + e^{-2\beta\,net}}$	Performance in the average is equivalent to the delta rule applied to a unit with deterministic activation: $f(net) = \tanh(\beta\,net)$.
Simple associative reward penalty rule (reinforcement)	$J(\mathbf{w}) = -\langle r \rangle$	$r^k(y^k - \langle y^k \rangle)\mathbf{x}^k$	$\rho > 0$ $r^k = \begin{cases} +1 & \text{reward} \\ -1 & \text{penalize} \end{cases}$	Stochastic activation (as above)	$\mathbf{w}^k$ evolves so as to maximize the average reinforcement signal $\langle r \rangle$.
Hebbian rule (unsupervised)	$J(\mathbf{w}) = -\frac{1}{2}\langle y^2 \rangle$	$y^k\mathbf{x}^k$	$\rho \geq 0$	$f(net) = net$	$\|\mathbf{w}^*\| \to \infty$ with $\mathbf{w}^*$ pointing in the direction of $\mathbf{c}^{(1)}$ (see comment d).
Oja's rule (unsupervised)	Does not have an exact $J(\mathbf{w})$. However, this rule tends to maximize $\langle y^2 \rangle$ subject to the constraint $\|\mathbf{w}\| = 1$.	$y^k\mathbf{x}^k - (y^k)^2\mathbf{w}^k$	$0 < \rho < \dfrac{1}{\lambda_{\max}}$	$f(net) = net$	Converges in the mean to $\mathbf{w}^* = \mathbf{c}^{(1)}$, which maximizes $\langle y^2 \rangle$.
Yuille et al. rule (unsupervised)	$J(\mathbf{w}) = -\frac{1}{2}\langle y^2 \rangle + \dfrac{\|\mathbf{w}\|^4}{4}$	$y^k\mathbf{x}^k - \|\mathbf{w}\|^2\mathbf{w}^k$	$0 < \rho < \dfrac{1}{\lambda_{\max}}$	$f(net) = net$	Converges in the mean to $\|\mathbf{w}^*\| = \lambda_{\max}$ with $\mathbf{w}^*$ in the direction of $\mathbf{c}^{(1)}$; $\mathbf{w}^*$ maximizes $\langle y^2 \rangle$.

Table 3.6.1 (continued)
Summary of Basic Learning Rules

Learning Rule (Type)	Criterion Function[a]	Learning Vector[b]	Activation Function[c]	Conditions	Remarks
Linsker's rule (unsupervised)[e]	$J(\mathbf{w}) = -\frac{1}{2}\langle y^2\rangle + \frac{\lambda}{2}\left(1 - \sum_j w_j\right)^2$	$y^k\mathbf{x}^k + \lambda\left(1 - \sum_j w_j^k\right)\mathbf{1}$	$f(net) = net$	$\sum_j w_j = 1$ $0 < \rho \ll 1$ $w^- \le w_i^k \le w^+$ $\lambda > 0$	Maximizes $\langle y^2\rangle$ subject to $\sum_j w_j = 1$. Converges to $\mathbf{w}^*$ whose components are clamped at w^- or w^+, when λ is large.
Hassoun's rule (unsupervised)[e]	$J(\mathbf{w}) = -\frac{1}{2}\langle y^2\rangle + \frac{\lambda}{2}(1 - \|\mathbf{w}\|)^2$	$y^k\mathbf{x}^k - \lambda\mathbf{w}^k\left(1 - \frac{1}{\|\mathbf{w}^k\|}\right)$ For $\rho\lambda = 1$ this rule reduces to $\mathbf{w}^{k+1} = \frac{\mathbf{w}^k}{\|\mathbf{w}^k\|} + \rho y^k\mathbf{x}^k$	$f(net) = net$	$\lambda \gg \lambda_{max}$ $0 < \rho \le \frac{2}{\lambda}$	Converges in the mean to $\|\mathbf{w}^*\| = \dfrac{\lambda}{\lambda - \lambda_{max}}$ with $\mathbf{w}^*$ parallel to $\mathbf{c}^{(1)}$. For $\lambda \gg \lambda_{max}$, $\mathbf{w}^*$ approaches $\mathbf{c}^{(1)}$ (see Section 4.3.5 for details).
Standard competitive learning rule (unsupervised)[e]	$J(\mathbf{w}) = \frac{1}{2}\sum_k\|\mathbf{x}^k - \mathbf{w}_{i^*}\|^2$ i^* is the index of the winning unit: $\mathbf{w}_{i^*}^T\mathbf{x}^k \ge \mathbf{w}_j^T\mathbf{x}^k$	$\mathbf{x}^k - \mathbf{w}_{i^*}$	$f(net) = net$	ρ^k satisfies: 1. $\rho^k \ge 0$ 2. $\sum_{k=1}^\infty (\rho^k)^2 < \infty$ 3. $\sum_{k=1}^\infty \rho^k = \infty$	Converges to a local minima of J representing some clustering configuration.

Kohonen's feature map rule (unsupervised)[e]

$$J(\mathbf{w}) = \frac{1}{2}\sum_{k,i}\Phi(\mathbf{r},\mathbf{r}_{i\bullet})\|\mathbf{x}^k - \mathbf{w}_i\|^2$$

$$\left(\text{e.g., } \Phi(\mathbf{r},\mathbf{r}_{i\bullet}) = e^{-\frac{\|\mathbf{r}_i - \mathbf{r}_{i\bullet}\|^2}{2\sigma^2}}\right)$$

$$\Phi(\mathbf{r},\mathbf{r}_{i\bullet})(\mathbf{x}^k - \mathbf{w}_i)$$

ρ^k and σ^k evolve according to: $k^{-\alpha}$ with $0 < \alpha \le 1$

or

$a\left(\dfrac{b}{a}\right)^{k/k_{max}}$ with

$0 < b < a < 1$

$f(net) = net$

The weight vectors evolve to a solution which tends to preserve the topology of the input space. The local point density of this solution is of the form $g(p(\mathbf{x}))$, where g is a continuous monotonically increasing function and $p(\mathbf{x})$ is a stationary probability density function governing $\mathbf{x}^k$.

---

[a] Note: $\mathbf{z}^k = \begin{cases} \mathbf{x}^k & \text{if } d^k = +1 \\ -\mathbf{x}^k & \text{if } d^k = -1 \end{cases}$

[b] The general form of the learning equation is $\mathbf{w}^{k+1} = \mathbf{w}^k + \rho^k\mathbf{s}^k$, where ρ^k is the learning rate and $\mathbf{s}^k$ is the learning vector.

[c] $net = \mathbf{x}^T\mathbf{w}$

[d] $\mathbf{c}^{(i)}$ is the ith normalized eigenvector of the autocorrelation matrix $\mathbf{C}$ with a corresponding eigenvalue λ_i ($\lambda_1 \geq \lambda_2 \geq \cdots \geq \lambda_n \geq 0$ and $\lambda_{max} = \lambda_1$).

[e] The criterion functions associated with these rules are discussed in Chapter 4.

Problems

3.1.1 Show that the choice $\alpha = \beta^2/\gamma$ in the convergence proof for the perceptron learning rule minimizes the maximum number of corrections k_0 if $\mathbf{w}^1 = \mathbf{0}$.

3.1.2 This problem explores an alternative convergence proof (Kung, 1993) for the perceptron learning rule in Equation (3.1.2). Here, we follow the notation in Section 3.1.1.

   a. Show that if $\mathbf{x}^k$ is misclassified by a perceptron with weight vector $\mathbf{w}^k$, then

$$\|\mathbf{w}^{k+1} - \mathbf{w}^*\|^2 = \|\mathbf{w}^k - \mathbf{w}^*\|^2 + 4\rho^2\|\mathbf{x}^k\|^2 + 2\rho(d^k - y^k)(\mathbf{w}^k - \mathbf{w}^*)^{\mathrm{T}}$$

$$= \|\mathbf{w}^k - \mathbf{w}^*\|^2 + 4\rho^2\|\mathbf{x}^k\|^2 - 4\rho(|\mathbf{w}^{*\mathrm{T}}\mathbf{x}^k| + |\mathbf{w}^{k\mathrm{T}}\mathbf{x}^k|) \quad (1)$$

where $\mathbf{w}^*$ is a solution that separates all patterns $\mathbf{x}^k$ correctly.

   b. Show that if we restrict ρ to sufficiently small values, then $\mathbf{w}^{k+1}$ converges in a finite number of steps (recall that no weight update is needed if all $\mathbf{x}^k$ are classified correctly). Does $\mathbf{w}^{k+1}$ have to converge to the particular solution $\mathbf{w}^*$? Explain.

   c. Show that if $\mathbf{x}^k$ is misclassified, then $\|\mathbf{w}^{k+1} - \mathbf{w}^*\|^2$ is minimized by setting ρ to its optimal value

$$\rho_{\mathrm{opt}} = \frac{|\mathbf{w}^{*\mathrm{T}}\mathbf{x}^k| + |\mathbf{w}^{k\mathrm{T}}\mathbf{x}^k|}{2\|\mathbf{x}^k\|^2}$$

   d. Show that the choice $\rho = \rho_{\mathrm{opt}}$ guarantees the convergence of the perceptron learning rule in a finite number of steps. In other words, show that if the choice $\rho = \rho_{\mathrm{opt}}$ is made, then $\mathbf{w}^{k+1}$ in Equation (1) stops changing after a finite number of corrections.

   e. Show that the use of $\rho = \rho_{\mathrm{opt}}$ in Equation (3.1.2) leads to the learning rule

$$\mathbf{w}^{k+1} = \begin{cases} \mathbf{w}^k + \dfrac{(\mathbf{w}^* - \mathbf{w}^k)^{\mathrm{T}}\mathbf{x}^k}{2\|\mathbf{x}^k\|^2}\mathbf{x}^k & \text{if } \mathbf{x}^k \text{ is misclassified} \\\\ \mathbf{w}^k & \text{otherwise} \end{cases}$$

   (Note that this learning rule is impractical, since it requires a solution, $\mathbf{w}^*$, to be known!)

3.1.3 Show that the perceptron criterion function J in Equation (3.1.20) is piecewise linear. Next, consider the four training pairs $\{-4, -1\}$, $\{-2, -1\}$, $\{-1, +1\}$, and $\{+1, +1\}$. Note that these pairs take the form $\{x, d\}$, where

x, $d \in R$. The following is a guided exploration into the properties of the function J for this linearly separable training set. This exploration should give some additional insights into the convergence process of the perceptron learning rule.

a. Plot the criterion function J for a two-input perceptron with weights w_1 and w_2 over the range $-1 \le w_1 \le +4$ and $-3 \le w_2 \le +3$. Here, w_2 is the weight associated with the bias input (assume a bias of $+1$).

b. Identify the solution region in the weight space containing all linearly separable solutions $\mathbf{w}^*$. What is the value of J in this region?

c. Based on the preceding results, describe the evolution process of the weight vector in Equation (3.1.23), starting from an arbitrary initial weight vector.

d. For comparative purposes, plot the quadratic criterion function in Equation (3.1.25) with $b = 0$. Comment on the differentiability of this function.

3.1.4 Show that the α-LMS rule in Equation (3.1.30) can be obtained from an incremental gradient descent on the criterion function

$$J(\mathbf{w}) = \tfrac{1}{2} \sum_i \frac{(d^i - y^i)^2}{\|\mathbf{x}^i\|^2}$$

† **3.1.5** For the simple two-dimensional linearly separable two-class problem in Figure P3.1.5, compute and plot the dynamic margins (b_i) versus learning cycles

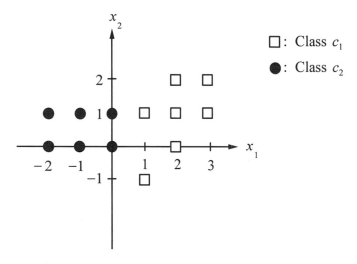

Figure P3.1.5
A simple two-class linearly separable pattern for Problem 3.1.5.

using the AHK I learning rule with the following initial values and parameters: $\mathbf{w}^1 = \mathbf{0}$, $\rho_1 = 0.1$, $\rho_2 = 0.05$, and initial margins of 0.1. Repeat using the AHK II rule. Compare the convergence speed and quality of the solution of these two rules.

3.1.6   Draw the two decision surfaces for Problem 3.1.5 and compare them with the decision surfaces generated by the perceptron rule, μ-LMS learning rule (use $\mu = 0.05$), and Butz's rule (use $\rho = 0.1$ and a reinforcement factor $\gamma = 0.2$). Assume $\mathbf{w}^1 = \mathbf{0}$ for these rules.

† 3.1.7   Repeat Problem 3.1.5 for the two-class problem in Figure P3.1.7 using the AHK III rule.

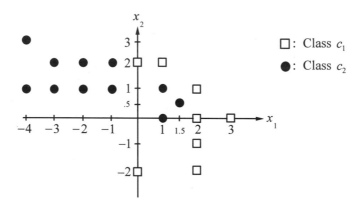

Figure P3.1.7
A simple two-class nonlinearly separable training set for Problem 3.1.7.

3.1.8   Draw the decision surface for Problem 3.1.7 and compare it with the decision surfaces generated by the perceptron rule, μ-LMS learning rule (use $\mu = 0.05$), and Butz's rule (use $\rho = 0.1$ and a reinforcement factor $\gamma = 0.2$). Assume $\mathbf{w}^1 = \mathbf{0}$ for these rules.

3.1.9   Check the "well-formedness" of the criterion functions of the following learning rules:
a.   Mays' rule.
b. μ-LMS rule.
c.   AHK I rule.

3.1.10 Is there a value for r for which the Minkowski-r criterion function is well formed? Is the relative entropy criterion function well formed?

3.1.11 Consider the training set $\{\mathbf{x}^k, d^k\}$, $k = 1, 2, \ldots, m$, with $\mathbf{x}^k \in R^n$. Define a stability measure for pattern k as

$$\gamma^k = d^k (\mathbf{x}^k)^T \mathbf{w}$$

where $\mathbf{w}$ is a perceptron weight vector that is constrained to have a constant length $\|\mathbf{w}\| = \sqrt{n}$. Employing statistical mechanics arguments, it is possible to show (Gordon et al., 1993) that the mean number of errors made by the perceptron on the training set at "temperature" T (T is a monotonically decreasing positive function of training time) is

$$J(\mathbf{w}) = \sum_{k=1}^{m} \frac{1}{1 + \exp\left[-\dfrac{(\gamma^k - b)}{T} \right]}$$

where b ($b \geq 0$) is an imposed stability factor specified by the user. Employing gradient descent on $J(\mathbf{w})$, show that an appropriate update rule for the ith weight is given by

$$\Delta w_i = \frac{\rho}{4T} \sum_{k=1}^{m} \frac{d^k x_i^k}{\left[\cosh\left(\dfrac{\gamma^k - b}{2T} \right) \right]^2}$$

Give a qualitative analysis of the behavior of this learning rule and compare it with the correlation and AHK III rules. Explain the effects of b and T on the placement of the separating hyperplane. How would this rule behave for nonlinearly separable training sets?

3.1.12 Consider the learning procedure (Polyak, 1990)

$$\hat{\mathbf{w}}^{k+1} = \hat{\mathbf{w}}^k + \mu(d^k - y^k)\mathbf{x}^k$$

$$\mathbf{w}^{k+1} = \mathbf{w}^k + \rho^k(\hat{\mathbf{w}}^{k+1} - \mathbf{w}^k)$$

where $y^k = (\hat{\mathbf{w}}^k)^T \mathbf{x}^k$ and $\rho^k = 1/(1 + k)$. Discuss qualitatively the difference between this learning procedure and the μ-LMS learning rule (Equation 3.1.35).

3.1.13 Consider the Minkowski-r criterion function in Equation (3.1.68). If no prior knowledge is available about the distribution of the training data, then extensive experimentation with various r values must be done in order to estimate an appropriate value for r. Alternatively, an automatic method for estimating r is possible by adaptively updating r in the direction of decreasing E. Employ steepest gradient descent on $E(r)$ in order to derive an update rule for r.

†**3.2.1** Use the A_{rp} rule in Equation (3.2.1) with $\beta = 1$ to find the stochastic unit separating surface $\mathbf{w}^T\mathbf{x} = 0$, arrived at after 10, 50, 100, and 200 cycles through the training set in Figure P3.2.1. Start with $\mathbf{w} = [1 \quad 0 \quad -2]^T$, and assume $x_3 = +1$. Use reinforcement r^k equal to $+1$ if $\mathbf{x}^k$ is correctly classified and -1 otherwise. Assume $\rho^+ = 0.1$ and $\rho^- = 0.01$. Repeat by subjectively assigning a $+1$ or a -1 to r^k based on whether the movement of the separating surface after each presentation is good or bad, respectively. Use $\rho^+ = 0.6$ and $\rho^- = 0.06$, and plot the generated separating surface after the first 20 presentations.

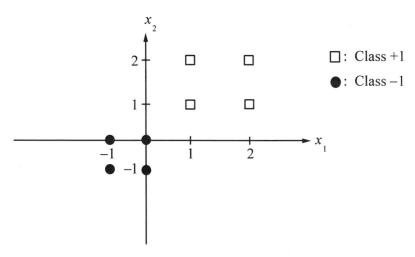

Figure P3.2.1
Two-class linearly separable training set for Problem 3.2.1.

†**3.3.1** Consider a data set of two-dimensional vectors $\mathbf{x}$ generated as follows: x_1 and x_2 are distributed randomly and independently according to the normal distributions $N(0, 0.1)$ and $N(0, 0.01)$, respectively. Generate and plot 1000 data points $\mathbf{x}$ in the input plane. Compute and plot (in the input plane) the solution trajectories $\mathbf{w}^k$ generated by the normalized Hebbian rule, Oja's rule, and the Yuille et al. rule upon training a single linear unit with weight vector $\mathbf{w}$ on samples $\mathbf{x}$ drawn randomly and independently from the preceding distribution. In your simulations, assume $\rho = 0.01$ and stop training after 1500 iterations. Also assume $\mathbf{w}^1 = [1.5, 1]^T$ in all simulations. Verify graphically that, for large k, the average direction of $\mathbf{w}^k$ is that of the maximum data variance. Study, via simulation, the effects of larger learning rates (e.g., $\rho = 0.05, 0.1$) and various initial weight vectors on the $\mathbf{w}^k$ trajectories.

3.3.2 Show that the average Oja rule has as its equilibria the eigenvectors of $\mathbf{C}$. Start by showing that $\langle \Delta \mathbf{w} \rangle = \rho(\mathbf{C}\mathbf{w} - \mathbf{w}^T\mathbf{C}\mathbf{w}\mathbf{w})$ is the average of Oja's rule in Equation (3.3.6).

*3.3.3 Starting from $\langle \Delta \mathbf{w} \rangle = -\rho \nabla J$, show that $\nabla J = -\mathbf{C}\mathbf{w} + \mathbf{w}^T\mathbf{C}\mathbf{w}\mathbf{w}$ for Oja's rule. Evaluate the Hessian matrix $\nabla \nabla J$ at the equilibria found in Problem 3.3.2. Study the stability of these equilibria states in terms of the eigenvalues of the Hessian matrix.

3.3.4 Show that the average weight change $\langle \Delta \mathbf{w} \rangle$ in the Yuille et al. rule is given by steepest gradient descent on the criterion function

$$J(\mathbf{w}) = -\tfrac{1}{2}\mathbf{w}^T\mathbf{C}\mathbf{w} + \tfrac{1}{4}\|\mathbf{w}\|^4$$

3.3.5 Consider Sanger's rule (Equation 3.3.19) with $m = 2$ units. Assume that the first unit has already converged to $\mathbf{c}^{(1)}$, the principal eigenvector of $\mathbf{C}$. Show that the second unit's update equation for the average weight vector change is given by

$$\langle \Delta \mathbf{w}_2 \rangle = \rho[(\mathbf{I} - \mathbf{c}^{(1)}\mathbf{c}^{(1)^T})\mathbf{C}\mathbf{w}_2 - (\mathbf{w}_2^T\mathbf{C}\mathbf{w}_2)\mathbf{w}_2]$$

and that $\mathbf{c}^{(1)}$ is not an equilibrium point.

*3.3.6 Show that the average weight change $\langle \Delta \mathbf{w}_i \rangle$ of the ith unit for Sanger's rule is given by (Hertz et al., 1991)

$$\langle \Delta \mathbf{w}_i \rangle = \rho \left[\mathbf{C}\mathbf{w}_i - \sum_{k=1}^{i-1} (\mathbf{w}_k^T\mathbf{C}\mathbf{w}_i)\mathbf{w}_k - (\mathbf{w}_i^T\mathbf{C}\mathbf{w}_i)\mathbf{w}_i \right]$$

Now assume that the weight vectors for the first $i - 1$ units have already converged to their appropriate eigenvectors, so $\mathbf{w}_k = \pm\mathbf{c}^{(k)}$, for $k < i$. Show that the first two terms in $\langle \Delta \mathbf{w}_i \rangle$ give the projection of $\mathbf{C}\mathbf{w}_i$ onto the space orthogonal to the first $i - 1$ eigenvectors of $\mathbf{C}$. Employ these results to show that $\mathbf{w}_i$ converges to $\pm\mathbf{c}^{(i)}$.

3.3.7 Approximate the output of a sigmoid unit having the transfer characteristics $y = \tanh(\beta \mathbf{w}^T \mathbf{x})$ by the first four terms in a Taylor series expansion. Show that this unit approximates a third-order unit if it is operated near $\mathbf{w}^T \mathbf{x} = 0$. Comment on the effects of the saturation region on the quality of the higher-order principal component analysis realized when the unit is trained using Hebbian learning.

3.4.1 Let $\mathbf{x}^k \in \{0, 1\}^n$ and the initial weights $\sum_{j=1}^{n} w_{ij} = 1$, for all i, in a single-layer competitive network. Assume the following learning rule for the ith unit:

$$
w_{ij}^{k+1} = \begin{cases} w_{ij}^k & \text{unit } i \text{ is a loser} \\[2em] w_{ij}^k + \rho \left[\dfrac{x_j^k}{\sum_{l=1}^{n} x_l^k} - w_{ij}^k \right] & \text{unit } i \text{ is a winner} \end{cases}
$$

Show that this rule preserves $\sum_{i=1}^{n} w_{ij}^k = 1$ for all k.

3.4.2 Consider the 200-sample two-dimensional data set $\{\mathbf{x}^k\}$ generated randomly and independently as follows: 50 samples generated according to the normal distribution $N([-5, +5]^T, 1)$, 75 samples generated according to $N([+5, +5]^T, 2)$, and 75 samples generated according to a uniform distribution in the region $|x_1| \leq 2.5$ and $-7.5 \leq x_2 \leq -2.5$. Use a five-unit competitive net to discover the underlying clusters in this data set, as in Example 3.4.1 [use Equations (3.4.5) and (3.4.2)]. Assume a learning rate $\rho = 0.01$, and start with random weight vectors distributed uniformly in the region $|w_1| \leq 10$ and $|w_2| \leq 10$. Stop training after 2000 iterations (steps); at each iteration, the vector $\mathbf{x}^k$ is to be chosen from the data set at random. Depict the evolution of the weight vectors of all five units as in Figure 3.4.5. Finally, plot the clusters discovered by the net (as in Figure 3.4.6) and compare this solution with the known solution.

† **3.4.3** Repeat Problem 3.4.2 using the similarity measure in Equation (3.4.3), with no weight vector normalization, for determining the winning unit. Make sure that you use the same initial weight vectors as in the previous problem. Discuss any differences in the number and/or shape of the generated clusters compared with the solution in Problem 3.4.2.

†**3.4.4** Consider a Voronoi quantizer with the following 10 reconstruction vectors: $[0, 0]^T$, $[1, 0]^T$, $[-1, 0]^T$, $[0, -1]^T$, $[0, 1]^T$, $[3, 3]^T$, $[4, 3]^T$, $[2, 3]^T$, $[3, 2]^T$, and $[3, 4]^T$.

a. Draw the input space partitions (Voronoi tessellation) realized by this quantizer.

b. Starting with the Voronoi quantizer of part a, use the LVQ method described in Section 3.4.2 in order to design a two-class classifier for data generated randomly according to the probability density functions $p_1(\mathbf{x}) = N([0, 0]^T, 1)$ and $p_2(\mathbf{x}) = N([3, 3]^T, 2)$ for classes 1 and 2, respectively. Assume equal *a priori* probability of the two classes. During training, use the adaptive learning rates in Equation (3.4.8), initialized to $\rho_i^0 = 0.1$. Stop training after 1000 iterations.

c. Draw the Voronoi tessellations realized by the weight vectors (reconstruction vectors) that resulted from the LVQ training in part b. Compare these tessellations with the ones drawn in part a.

d. Draw the decision boundary for the classifier in part b.

*3.5.1 Consider the following criterion function, suitable for solving the TSP in an elastic net architecture (Durbin and Willshaw, 1987):

$$J(\mathbf{w}_i) = -\sigma^2 \sum_k \ln\left(\sum_{i=1}^{m} e^{-\|\mathbf{x}^k - \mathbf{w}_i\|^2/2\sigma^2}\right) + \frac{\eta}{2} \sum_{i=1}^{m} \|\mathbf{w}_{i+1} - \mathbf{w}_i\|^2$$

where m is the number of units in the net and $\eta > 0$. Here, $\mathbf{x}^k$ represents the position of city k and $\mathbf{w}_i$ represents the ith stop.

a. Show that gradient descent on J leads to the update rule:

$$\Delta\mathbf{w}_i = \rho\left[\sum_k \phi_i^k(\mathbf{x}^k - \mathbf{w}_i) + \eta(\mathbf{w}_{i+1} - 2\mathbf{w}_i + \mathbf{w}_{i-1})\right]$$

where

$$\phi_i^k = \frac{e^{\frac{-\|\mathbf{x}^k - \mathbf{w}_i\|^2}{2\sigma^2}}}{\sum_{j=1}^{m} e^{\frac{-\|\mathbf{x}^k - \mathbf{w}_j\|^2}{2\sigma^2}}}$$

b. Give qualitative interpretations for the various terms in J and $\Delta\mathbf{w}_i$.

c. Show that J is bounded below, and that as $\sigma \to 0$ and $m \to \infty$, J is minimized by the shortest possible tour.

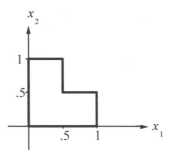

Figure P3.5.2
L-shaped region representing a uniform distribution
of inputs for the feature map of Problems 3.5.2 and
3.5.3.

† **3.5.2** Consider the L-shaped region shown in Figure P3.5.2. Train a two-dimensional Kohonen feature map on points generated randomly and uniformly from this region. Assume a 15×15 array of units and the following learning parameters, $k_{max} = 80,000$, $\rho_0 = 0.8$, $\rho_f = 0.01$, $\sigma_0 = 8$, and $\sigma_f = 0.5$. Choose all initial weights randomly inside the region. Display the trained net as in Figure 3.5.1 at times 0, 1000, 20,000, 40,000, and 80,000.

† **3.5.3** Repeat Problem 3.5.2 (but with $\sigma_0 = 20$) for a one-dimensional chain consisting of 60 units and initialized randomly inside the L-shaped region. Display the trained map as in Figure 3.5.5 at various training times.

† **3.5.4** The self-organizing map simulation in Figure 3.5.5 employs $\rho_0 = 0.8$, $\rho_f = 0.01$, $\sigma_0 = 20$, $\sigma_f = 0.1$, and $k_{max} = 70,000$. Repeat the simulation and plot the map (chain) at iterations 50,000 and 70,000. (*Note*: The chain configuration in Figure 3.5.5*d* is not a stable configuration for these parameters.) Repeat the simulation with $\sigma_f = 1$, and compare the resulting chain configuration at 70,000 iterations with that in the previous simulation. Discuss your results.

† **3.5.5** Repeat the SOFM simulation in Figure 3.5.1 (see Section 3.5.2 for details) assuming $p(\mathbf{x}) = N([0,0]^T, 0.1)$, $|x_1| \le 1$, and $|x_2| \le 1$. Use the learning parameters given in the caption of Figure 3.5.1. What is the general shape of the point distribution $p(\mathbf{w})$ of the weight vectors? Estimate the variance of $p(\mathbf{w})$. Is $p(\mathbf{w})$ proportional to $p(\mathbf{x})$?

4 Mathematical Theory of Neural Learning

This chapter deals with theoretical aspects of learning in artificial neural networks. It investigates mathematically the nature and stability of the asymptotic solutions obtained using the basic supervised, Hebbian, and reinforcement learning rules, which were introduced in the preceding chapter. Formal analysis is also given for simple competitive learning and self-organizing feature-map learning.

A unifying framework for the characterization of various learning rules is presented. This framework is based on the notion that learning in general neural networks can be viewed as a search, in a multidimensional space, for a solution that optimizes a prespecified criterion function with or without constraints. Under this framework, a continuous-time learning rule is viewed as a first-order, stochastic differential equation/dynamical system, whereby the state of the system evolves so as to minimize an associated instantaneous criterion function. Approximation techniques are employed to determine, in an average sense, the nature of the asymptotic solutions of the stochastic system. This approximation leads to an *average learning equation*, which, in most cases, can be cast as a globally, asymptotically stable gradient system whose stable equilibria are minimizers of a well-defined average criterion function. Finally, and subject to certain assumptions, these stable equilibria can be taken as the possible limits (attractor states) of the stochastic learning equation.

The chapter also treats two important issues associated with learning in a general feedforward neural network. These are learning generalization and learning complexity. The section on generalization presents a theoretical method for calculating the asymptotic probability of correct generalization of a neural network as a function of the training set size and the number of free parameters in the network. Here, generalization in deterministic and stochastic nets is investigated. The chapter concludes by reviewing some significant results on the complexity of learning in neural networks.

4.1 Learning as a Search/Approximation Mechanism

Learning in an artificial neural network, whether it is supervised, reinforcement, or unsupervised, can be viewed as a process of searching a multidimensional parameter space for a state that optimizes a predefined *criterion function J* (J is also commonly referred to as an *error function*, a *cost function*, or an *objective function*). In fact, all the learning rules considered in Chapter 3, except Oja's rule (refer to Table 3.1), have well-defined analytical criterion functions. These learning rules implement local search mechanisms (i.e., gradient search) to obtain weight vector solutions which (locally) optimize the associated criterion function. Therefore, it is the criterion function that determines the nature of a learning rule. For example, supervised learning rules are designed so as to minimize an error measure between the network's output and the corresponding desired output, unsupervised Hebbian learning is designed to maximize the variance of the output of a given unit, and reinforcement learning is designed to maximize the average reinforcement signal.

Supervised learning can be related to classical approximation theory (Poggio and Girosi, 1990). Here, the idea is to approximate or interpolate a continuous multivariate function $g(\mathbf{x})$, from samples $\{\mathbf{x}, g(\mathbf{x})\}$, by an approximation function (or class of functions) $G(\mathbf{w}, \mathbf{x})$, where $\mathbf{w} \in R^d$ is a parameter vector with d degrees of freedom, and $\mathbf{x}$ belongs to a compact set $\Sigma \subset R^n$. In this case, the set of samples $\{\mathbf{x}, g(\mathbf{x})\}$, $\mathbf{x} \in \Sigma$, is referred to as a *training set*. The approximation problem is to find an optimal parameter vector that provides the "best" approximation of g on the set Σ for a given class of functions G. Formally stated, we desire a solution $\mathbf{w}^* \in R^d$ such that

$$\|G(\mathbf{w}^*, \mathbf{x}) - g(\mathbf{x})\| \leq \varepsilon \quad \text{for all } \mathbf{x} \in \Sigma \tag{4.1.1}$$

where the tolerance ε is a positive real number, and $\|\cdot\|$ is any appropriate norm. For the case where $\|\cdot\|$ is the Euclidean norm, it is well known that an appropriate criterion function J is

$$J(\mathbf{w}) = \sum_{\mathbf{x} \in \Sigma} [G(\mathbf{w}, \mathbf{x}) - g(\mathbf{x})]^2 \tag{4.1.2}$$

whose global minimum represents the minimum sum of square error (SSE) solution. The choice of approximation function G, the criterion function J, and the search mechanism for $\mathbf{w}^*$ all play critical roles in determining the quality and properties of the resulting solution/approximation.

Usually we know our objective, and this knowledge is translated into an appropriate criterion function J. In terms of search mechanisms, gradient-based search is appropriate (and is simple to implement) for cases where it is known that J is differentiable and bounded. Of course, if gradient search is used, we must be willing to accept locally optimal solutions. In general, only global search mechanisms, which are computationally intensive, may lead to globally optimal solutions (global search –based learning is the subject of Chapter 8). Among the preceding three factors, the most critical in terms of affecting the quality of the approximation in Equation (4.1.1) is the choice of approximation function G.

In classical analysis, polynomials and rational functions are typically used for function approximation. On the other hand, for artificial neural networks, the approximation functions are usually chosen from the class of smooth sigmoidal-type functions, and the approximation is constructed as a superposition of such sigmoidal functions. In general, there are two important issues in selecting an appropriate class of approximation (basis) functions: universality and generalization. By *universality*, we mean the ability of G to represent, to any desired degree of accuracy, the class of functions g being approximated; in Chapter 2 we established the universality of feedforward layered neural nets. On the other hand, *generalization* means the ability of G to correctly map new points $\mathbf{x}$, drawn from the same underlying input distribution $p(\mathbf{x})$, that were not seen during the learning phase. Thus an interesting question here is how well does a neural network compare with other universal approximation functions in terms of generalization (some insight into answering this question is given in Section 5.2.5). Later in this chapter it will be shown that for feedforward neural networks, the number of degrees of freedom (weights) in G plays a critical role in determining the degree of data overfitting, which directly affects generalization quality.

Another way to control generalization is through criterion function conditioning. A *regularization* term (Poggio and Girosi, 1990) may be added to an initial criterion function $\hat{J}$ according to

$$J(\mathbf{w}) = \hat{J}(\mathbf{w}) + \lambda \|P(\mathbf{w})\|^2 \tag{4.1.3}$$

The $\|P(\mathbf{w})\|^2$ term in Equation (4.1.3) is used to embed a priori information about the function g, such as smoothness, invariance, etc. In this case, $\hat{J}$ is the quantity to be minimized subject to the regularization constraint that $\|P(\mathbf{w})\|^2$ is kept "small," with the Lagrange multiplier λ determining the degree of regularization. These ideas also can be extended to unsupervised learning, where the $\lambda \|P(\mathbf{w})\|^2$ term may be thought of as a constraint-satisfaction term; such a term may help condition the criterion $\hat{J}$ so that the search process is stabilized. Examples of this regularization strategy have already been encountered in the unsupervised Hebbian-type learning rules presented in Chapter 3 [e.g., refer to Equation (3.3.8)].

4.2   Mathematical Theory of Learning in a Single-Unit Setting

Instead of dealing separately with the various learning rules proposed in the preceding chapter, this section seeks to study a single learning rule, called the *general learning equation* (Amari, 1977a and 1990), that captures the salient features of several of the different single-unit learning rules. Two forms of the general learning equation will be presented: a discrete-time version, in which the weight vector evolves according to a discrete dynamical system of the form $\mathbf{w}(k + 1) = g(\mathbf{w}(k))$, and a continuous-time version, in which the weight vector evolves according to a smooth dynamical system of the form $\dot{\mathbf{w}} = g(\mathbf{w}(t))$. Statistical analysis of the continuous-time version of the general learning equation is then performed for selected learning rules, including correlation, LMS, and Hebbian learning rules.

4.2.1   General Learning Equation

Consider a single unit characterized by a weight vector $\mathbf{w} \in R^n$, an input vector $\mathbf{x} \in R^n$, and, in some cases, a scalar teacher signal z. In a supervised learning setting, the teacher signal is taken as the desired target associated with a particular input vector. The input vector (signal) is assumed to be generated by an environment or an information source according to the probability density $p(\mathbf{x}, z)$, or $p(\mathbf{x})$ if z is missing (as in unsupervised learning). Now consider the following discrete-time dynamical process that governs the evolution of the unit's weight vector $\mathbf{w}$:

$$\Delta \mathbf{w} = \rho r(\mathbf{w}, \mathbf{x}, z)\mathbf{x} - \lambda \mathbf{w} \qquad (4.2.1)$$

Also consider the continuous-time version:

$$\dot{\mathbf{w}} = \rho r(\mathbf{w}, \mathbf{x}, z)\mathbf{x} - \lambda \mathbf{w} \qquad (4.2.2)$$

where λ and ρ are positive real numbers, and $\dot{\mathbf{w}} = \dfrac{d\mathbf{w}}{dt}$. Here, $r(\mathbf{w}, \mathbf{x}, z)$ is referred to as a *learning signal*. One can easily verify that these two equations lead to the discrete-time and continuous-time versions, respectively, of the perceptron learning rule in Equation (3.1.2) if $\lambda = 0$, $y = \text{sgn}(\mathbf{w}^T\mathbf{x})$, and $r(\mathbf{w}, \mathbf{x}, z) = z - y$ (here z is taken as bipolar binary). The μ-LMS (or Widrow-Hoff) rule of Equation (3.1.35) can be obtained by setting $\lambda = 0$ and $r(\mathbf{w}, \mathbf{x}, z) = z - \mathbf{w}^T\mathbf{x}$ in Equation (4.2.1). Similarly, substituting $\lambda = 0$, $\rho = 1$, and $r(\mathbf{w}, \mathbf{x}, z) = z$ in Equation (4.2.1) leads to the simple correlation rule in Equation (3.1.50), and $\lambda = 0$ and $r(\mathbf{w}, \mathbf{x}, z) = y$ leads to the Hebbian rule in Equation (3.3.1). In the remainder of this section Equation (4.2.2) is adopted and is referred to as the *general learning equation*. Note that in Equation (4.2.2) the state $\mathbf{w}^* = \mathbf{0}$ is an asymptotically stable equilibrium point if either $r(\mathbf{w}, \mathbf{x}, z)$ and/or $\mathbf{x}$ is identically zero. Thus the term $-\lambda \mathbf{w}$ in Equation (4.2.2) plays the role of a *forgetting term* that tends to "erase" those weights not receiving sufficient reinforcement during learning.

From the point of view of analysis, it is useful to think of Equation (4.2.2) as implementing a fixed-increment steepest-gradient-descent search of an instantaneous criterion function J, or formally,

$$\dot{\mathbf{w}} = -\rho \nabla_{\mathbf{w}} J(\mathbf{x}, \mathbf{w}, z) = \rho r(\mathbf{w}, \mathbf{x}, z)\mathbf{x} - \lambda \mathbf{w} \qquad (4.2.3)$$

For the case $r(\mathbf{w}, \mathbf{x}, z) = r(\mathbf{w}^T\mathbf{x}, z) = r(u, z)$, the right-hand side of Equation (4.2.2) can be integrated to yield

$$J(\mathbf{w}) = -\int_0^{\mathbf{w}^T\mathbf{x}} r(u, z)\, du + \frac{1}{2}\varepsilon\|\mathbf{w}\|^2 \qquad (4.2.4)$$

where $\varepsilon = \lambda/\rho$. This type of criterion function (which has the classic form of a potential function) is appropriate for learning rules such as perceptron, LMS, Hebbian, and correlation rules. In the most general case, however, $r(\mathbf{w}, \mathbf{x}, z) \neq r(\mathbf{w}^T\mathbf{x}, z)$, and a suitable criterion function J satisfying Equation (4.2.3) may not as readily be determined (or may not even exist). It is interesting to note that finding the equilibrium points $\mathbf{w}^*$ of the general learning equation does not require the knowledge of J explicitly if the gradient of J is known.

The criterion function J in Equation (4.2.4) fits the general form of the constrained criterion function in Equation (4.1.3). Therefore, we may view the task of minimizing J as an optimization problem with the objective of minimizing $\hat{J}(\mathbf{w}) = -\int_0^{\mathbf{w}^T\mathbf{x}} r(u, z)\, du$ subject to regularization, which penalizes solution vectors $\mathbf{w}^*$ with large norms. It is interesting to note that by minimizing $\hat{J}(\mathbf{w})$, one is actually maximizing the amount of information learned from a given example pair $\{\mathbf{x}, z\}$. In other words, the general learning equation is designed so that it extracts the maximum amount of "knowledge" present in the learning signal $r(\mathbf{w}, \mathbf{x}, z)$.

4.2.2   Analysis of the Learning Equation

In a stochastic environment where the information source is ergodic,[1] the sequence of inputs $\mathbf{x}(t)$ is an independent stochastic process governed by $p(\mathbf{x})$. The general learning equation in Equation (4.2.2) then becomes a stochastic differential equation or a stochastic approximation algorithm. The weight vector $\mathbf{w}$ is changed in random directions depending on the random variable $\mathbf{x}$. From Equation (4.2.3), the average value of $\dot{\mathbf{w}}$ becomes proportional to the average gradient of the instantaneous criterion function J. Formally, we write

$$\langle \dot{\mathbf{w}} \rangle = -\rho \langle \nabla J \rangle \qquad (4.2.5)$$

where $\langle \cdot \rangle$ implies averaging over all possible inputs $\mathbf{x}$ with respect to the probability distribution $p(\mathbf{x})$. This equation will be referred to as the *average learning equation*. Equation (4.2.5) may be viewed as a steepest-gradient-descent search for $\mathbf{w}^*$ that (locally) minimizes the expected criterion function $\langle J \rangle$ because the linear nature of the averaging operation allows us to express Equation (4.2.5) as

$$\langle \dot{\mathbf{w}} \rangle = -\rho \nabla \langle J \rangle \qquad (4.2.6)$$

It is interesting to note that finding $\mathbf{w}^*$ does not require the knowledge of J explicitly

---

1. The information source generating the vectors $\mathbf{x}$ is *ergodic* if the temporal average over a typical sequence $\mathbf{x}(t)$ is the same as the average over the probability distribution $p(\mathbf{x})$.

if the gradient of J is known. Equation (4.2.6) is useful from a theoretical point of view in determining the equilibrium state(s) and in characterizing the stochastic learning equation [Equation (4.2.3)] in an "average" sense. In practice, the stochastic learning equation is implemented, and its average convergence behavior is characterized by the average learning equation given as

$$\langle \dot{\mathbf{w}} \rangle = -\rho \nabla \langle J \rangle = \rho \langle r(\mathbf{w}, \mathbf{x}, z)\mathbf{x} \rangle - \lambda \langle \mathbf{w} \rangle \qquad (4.2.7)$$

The gradient system in Equation (4.2.6) has special properties that make its dynamics rather simple to analyze. First, note that the equilibria $\mathbf{w}^*$ are solutions of the equation $\nabla \langle J \rangle = \mathbf{0}$. This means that the equilibria $\mathbf{w}^*$ are local minima, local maxima, and/or saddle points of $\langle J \rangle$. Furthermore, it is a well-established result that for any $\rho > 0$, these local minima are asymptotically stable points (attractors) and that the local maxima are unstable points (Hirsch and Smale, 1974). Thus one would expect the stochastic dynamics of the system in Equation (4.2.3), with sufficiently small ρ, to approach a local minimum[2] of $\langle J \rangle$.

In practice, discrete-time versions of the stochastic dynamical system in Equation (4.2.3) are used for weight adaptation. Here, the stability of the corresponding discrete-time average learning equation (discrete-time gradient system) is ensured if $0 < \rho < (2/\lambda_{\max})$, where $\lambda_{\max}$ is the largest eigenvalue of the Hessian matrix[3] $\mathbf{H} = \nabla\nabla J$ evaluated at the current point in the search space (the proof of this statement is outlined in Problem 4.3.8). These discrete-time "learning rules" and their associated average learning equations have been studied extensively in a more general context than that of neural networks. The book by Tsypkin (1971) gives an excellent treatment of these iterative learning rules and their stability.

4.2.3 Analysis of Some Basic Learning Rules

Using Equation (4.2.7) allows us to analyze some basic learning rules. These are the correlation, LMS, and Hebbian learning rules.

Correlation Learning   Here, $r(\mathbf{w}, \mathbf{x}, z) = z$, which represents the desired target associated with the input $\mathbf{x}$. From Equation (4.2.2) we have the stochastic equation

$$\dot{\mathbf{w}} = \rho z\mathbf{x} - \lambda \mathbf{w} \qquad (4.2.8)$$

---

2. Note that the continuous-time gradient system in Equation (4.2.6) may also converge to a saddle point. Fortunately, though, the stochastic nature of the corresponding learning rule in Equation (4.2.3) prevents the system from staying at such saddle points, and convergence to local minima is achieved.

3. The *Hessian matrix* is defined as the symmetric matrix $\mathbf{H}(\mathbf{w}) = \nabla\nabla J(\mathbf{w}) = \left[\dfrac{\partial^2 J}{\partial w_i \partial w_j} \right]$.

which leads to the average learning equation

$$\langle \dot{\mathbf{w}} \rangle = \rho \langle z\mathbf{x} \rangle - \lambda \langle \mathbf{w} \rangle \tag{4.2.9}$$

Now, by setting $\langle \dot{\mathbf{w}} \rangle = \mathbf{0}$, one arrives at the (only) equilibrium point

$$\mathbf{w}^* = \frac{\rho}{\lambda} \langle z\mathbf{x} \rangle \tag{4.2.10}$$

The stability of $\mathbf{w}^*$ may now be studied systematically through the "expected" Hessian matrix $\langle \mathbf{H}(\mathbf{w}^*) \rangle$, which is computed, by first employing Equations (4.2.5) and (4.2.9) to identify $\langle \nabla J \rangle$, as

$$\langle H(\mathbf{w}^*) \rangle = \langle \nabla\nabla J \rangle|_{\mathbf{w}^*} = \nabla \left(-\langle z\mathbf{x} \rangle + \frac{\lambda}{\rho} \langle \mathbf{w} \rangle \right) \Bigg|_{\langle \mathbf{w} \rangle = \mathbf{w}^*} = \frac{\lambda}{\rho} \mathbf{I} \tag{4.2.11}$$

This equation shows that the Hessian of $\langle J \rangle$ is positive definite; i.e., its eigenvalues are strictly positive or, equivalently, the eigenvalues of $-\nabla \langle \nabla J(\mathbf{w}^*) \rangle$ are strictly negative. This makes the system $\langle \dot{\mathbf{w}} \rangle = -\rho \langle \nabla J(\mathbf{w}) \rangle$ locally asymptotically stable at the equilibrium solution $\mathbf{w}^*$ by virtue of Liapunov's first method[4] [see Gill et al. (1981) and Dickinson (1991)]. Thus $\mathbf{w}^*$ is a stable equilibrium of Equation (4.2.9). In fact, the positive definite Hessian implies that $\mathbf{w}^*$ is a minimum of $\langle J \rangle$, and therefore, the gradient system $\langle \dot{\mathbf{w}} \rangle = -\rho \langle \nabla J(\mathbf{w}) \rangle$ converges globally and asymptotically to $\mathbf{w}^*$, its only minimum from any initial state.[5] Thus the trajectory $\mathbf{w}(t)$ of the stochastic system

4. Consider the dynamical system

$$\dot{\mathbf{x}}(t) = \mathbf{f}(\mathbf{x}) = [f_1(\mathbf{x}) \quad f_2(\mathbf{x}) \quad \cdots \quad f_n(\mathbf{x})]^{\mathrm{T}}$$

where $\mathbf{f}$ is continuous and differentiable in a neighborhood of $\mathbf{x}^*$ with derivative $\mathbf{f}'(\mathbf{x}) = \dfrac{d\mathbf{f}}{d\mathbf{x}} = \left[\dfrac{\partial f_i}{\partial x_j} \right]$. Here, $\mathbf{f}'(\mathbf{x})$ is called the *Jacobian matrix*. Now, assume that $\mathbf{x}^*$ is an equilibrium point; i.e., $\mathbf{f}(\mathbf{x}^*) = \mathbf{0}$. Then, by the Liapunov theorem (also known as *Liapunov's first method*), if all the eigenvalues of $\mathbf{f}'(\mathbf{x}^*)$ have nonzero negative real parts [i.e., $\mathbf{f}'(\mathbf{x}^*)$ is negative definite], $\mathbf{x}^*$ is asymptotically stable. Alternatively, if one or more eigenvalues of $\mathbf{f}'(\mathbf{x}^*)$ have positive real part, $\mathbf{x}^*$ is an unstable equilibrium. Note that in certain cases, such as the systems discussed in this section, the vector function $\mathbf{f}(\mathbf{x})$ may be written as the negative of the gradient of a scalar function, namely, $\mathbf{f}(\mathbf{x}) = -\nabla J$. In this case,

$$\mathbf{f}'(\mathbf{x}) = -\frac{d^2 J(\mathbf{x})}{d\mathbf{x}^2} = -\nabla\nabla J(\mathbf{x}) = -\left[\frac{\partial^2 J(\mathbf{x})}{\partial x_i \partial x_j} \right] = -\mathbf{H}(\mathbf{x}),$$

and the equilibrium $\mathbf{x}^*$ is asymptotically stable if the Hessian matrix $\mathbf{H}(\mathbf{x}^*)$ is positive definite; i.e., all eigenvalues of the symmetric matrix $\mathbf{H}$ have nonzero positive real part.

5. Note that the average gradient $\langle \nabla J \rangle = (\lambda/\rho)\langle \mathbf{w} \rangle - \langle z\mathbf{x} \rangle$ corresponds to the average criterion function $\langle J \rangle = (\lambda/2\rho)\langle \mathbf{w}^{\mathrm{T}} \rangle\langle \mathbf{w} \rangle - \langle \mathbf{w}^{\mathrm{T}} \rangle\langle z\mathbf{x} \rangle$, where we have made the assumption that the weights are uncorrelated with the inputs and with themselves. Here, $\langle J \rangle$ may be put in a quadratic form $\langle J \rangle = (\lambda/2\rho)\langle \mathbf{w}^{\mathrm{T}} \rangle \mathbf{I} \langle \mathbf{w} \rangle - \langle \mathbf{w}^{\mathrm{T}} \rangle\langle z\mathbf{x} \rangle$, where $\mathbf{I}$ is the identity matrix. Now, since $(\lambda/2\rho)\mathbf{I}$ is a positive definite matrix, then $\langle J \rangle$ is convex with a global minimum at $\mathbf{w}^* = (\rho/\lambda)\langle z\mathbf{x} \rangle$. Therefore, continuous-time steepest gradient descent on $\langle J \rangle$ is

in Equation (4.2.8) is expected to approach and then fluctuate about the state $(\rho/\lambda)\langle z\mathbf{x}\rangle$.

From Equation (4.2.4), the underlying instantaneous criterion function J is given by

$$J(\mathbf{w}) = -z\mathbf{w}^{\mathrm{T}}\mathbf{x} + \frac{\lambda}{2\rho}\|\mathbf{w}\|^2 = -zy + \frac{\lambda}{2\rho}\|\mathbf{w}\|^2 \qquad (4.2.12)$$

which may be minimized by maximizing the correlation zy subject to the regularization term $(\lambda/2\rho)\|\mathbf{w}\|^2$. Here, the regularization term is needed in order to keep the solution bounded.

LMS Learning   For $r(\mathbf{w}, \mathbf{x}, z) = z - \mathbf{w}^{\mathrm{T}}\mathbf{x}$ (the output error due to input $\mathbf{x}$) and $\lambda = 0$, Equation (4.2.2) leads to the stochastic equation

$$\dot{\mathbf{w}} = \rho(z - \mathbf{w}^{\mathrm{T}}\mathbf{x})\mathbf{x} \qquad (4.2.13)$$

In this case, the average learning equation becomes

$$\langle\dot{\mathbf{w}}\rangle = \rho\langle(z - \mathbf{w}^{\mathrm{T}}\mathbf{x})\mathbf{x}\rangle = \rho\langle\mathbf{x}(z - \mathbf{x}^{\mathrm{T}}\mathbf{w})\rangle \qquad (4.2.14)$$

with equilibria satisfying

$$\langle\mathbf{x}\mathbf{x}^{\mathrm{T}}\mathbf{w}^*\rangle = \langle z\mathbf{x}\rangle \qquad \text{or} \qquad \langle\mathbf{x}\mathbf{x}^{\mathrm{T}}\rangle\mathbf{w}^* = \langle z\mathbf{x}\rangle \qquad (4.2.15)$$

Let $\mathbf{C}$ denote the positive semidefinite autocorrelation matrix $\langle\mathbf{x}\mathbf{x}^{\mathrm{T}}\rangle$, defined in Equation (3.3.4), and $\mathbf{P} = \langle z\mathbf{x}\rangle$. If we have $|\mathbf{C}| \neq 0$, then $\mathbf{w}^* = \mathbf{C}^{-1}\mathbf{P}$ is the equilibrium state. Note that $\mathbf{w}^*$ approaches the minimum SSE solution in the limit of a large training set and that this analysis is identical to the analysis of the μ-LMS rule in Chapter 3. Let us now check the stability of $\mathbf{w}^*$. The Hessian matrix is

---

guaranteed to converge globally to $\mathbf{w}^*$ (i.e., from any initial $\mathbf{w}$ vector). A formal proof can be given by employing the Liapunov theorem on global asymptotic stability [e.g., see D'Azzo and Houpis (1988)]. Here, one proceeds by showing that $V(\langle\mathbf{w}\rangle) = \langle J\rangle - \langle J(\mathbf{w}^*)\rangle$ is a Liapunov (energy) function for the dynamical system in Equation (4.2.9), as follows:

1. V is everywhere continuous with continuous first partial derivatives.
2. $V > 0$ for all $\langle\mathbf{w}\rangle \neq \mathbf{w}^*$.
3. $V(\mathbf{w}^*) = 0$.
4. $V \rightarrow \infty$ as $\|\langle\mathbf{w}\rangle\| \rightarrow \infty$.
5. $\dfrac{dV}{dt} = (\nabla\langle J\rangle)^{\mathrm{T}}\langle\dot{\mathbf{w}}\rangle = -\rho\|\nabla\langle J\rangle\|^2 \leq 0$.
6. $\dfrac{dV}{dt} \neq 0$ except at $\langle\mathbf{w}\rangle = \mathbf{w}^*$.

Now, according to Liapunov's theorem, existence of a function V which satisfies these six conditions makes the dynamics in Equation (4.2.9) globally asymptotically stable.

$$\langle \mathbf{H} \rangle = \nabla\nabla\langle J \rangle = \langle \nabla[\mathbf{x}(\mathbf{x}^T\mathbf{w} - z)] \rangle = \langle \mathbf{x}\mathbf{x}^T \rangle = \mathbf{C} \tag{4.2.16}$$

which is positive definite if $|\mathbf{C}| \neq 0$. Therefore, $\mathbf{w}^* = \mathbf{C}^{-1}\mathbf{P}$ is the only (asymptotically) stable solution for Equation (4.2.14), and the stochastic dynamics in Equation (4.2.13) are expected to approach this solution.

Finally, note that with $\lambda = 0$, Equation (4.2.4) leads to

$$J(\mathbf{w}) = -\int_0^{\mathbf{w}^T\mathbf{x}} (z - u)\,du = \tfrac{1}{2}(z - u)^2|_{u = \mathbf{w}^T\mathbf{x}}$$

or

$$J(\mathbf{w}) = \tfrac{1}{2}(z - \mathbf{w}^T\mathbf{x})^2 = \tfrac{1}{2}(z - y)^2 \tag{4.2.17}$$

which is the instantaneous SSE (or MSE) criterion function.[6]

Hebbian Learning Here, upon setting $r(\mathbf{w}, \mathbf{x}, z) = y = \mathbf{w}^T\mathbf{x}$, Equation (4.2.2) gives the Hebbian rule with decay

$$\dot{\mathbf{w}} = \rho y\mathbf{x} - \lambda\mathbf{w} \tag{4.2.18}$$

whose average is

$$\langle \dot{\mathbf{w}} \rangle = \rho\langle y\mathbf{x} \rangle - \lambda\langle \mathbf{w} \rangle = \rho\langle \mathbf{x}\mathbf{x}^T\mathbf{w} \rangle - \lambda\langle \mathbf{w} \rangle \tag{4.2.19}$$

Setting $\langle \dot{\mathbf{w}} \rangle = \mathbf{0}$ in Equation (4.2.19) leads to the equilibria

$$\mathbf{C}\mathbf{w}^* = \frac{\lambda}{\rho}\mathbf{w}^* \tag{4.2.20}$$

Therefore, if $\mathbf{C}$ happens to have λ/ρ as an eigenvalue, then $\mathbf{w}^*$ will be the eigenvector of $\mathbf{C}$ corresponding to λ/ρ. In general, though, λ/ρ will not be an eigenvalue of $\mathbf{C}$, so Equation (4.2.19) will have only one equilibrium at $\mathbf{w}^* = \mathbf{0}$. This equilibrium solution is asymptotically stable if λ/ρ is greater than the largest eigenvalue of $\mathbf{C}$, since this makes the Hessian

$$\langle \mathbf{H} \rangle = \nabla\langle \nabla J \rangle = \nabla\left[-\langle \mathbf{x}\mathbf{x}^T\mathbf{w} \rangle + \frac{\lambda}{\rho}\langle \mathbf{w} \rangle\right] = -\mathbf{C} + \frac{\lambda}{\rho}\mathbf{I} \tag{4.2.21}$$

positive definite. Now, employing Equation (4.2.4), we get the instantaneous criterion function minimized by the Hebbian rule in Equation (4.2.18):

---

6. It is interesting to note that the average criterion function $\tfrac{1}{2}\langle (z - y)^2 \rangle$ is the MSE criterion function, first encountered in Equation (3.1.43), which is globally minimized at $\mathbf{w}^* = \mathbf{C}^{-1}\mathbf{P}$.

$$J = \tfrac{1}{2}\left[-(\mathbf{w}^{\mathrm{T}}\mathbf{x})^2 + \frac{\lambda}{\rho}\|\mathbf{w}\|^2 \right] = -\tfrac{1}{2}y^2 + \frac{\lambda}{2\rho}\|\mathbf{w}\|^2 \tag{4.2.22}$$

The regularization term $(\lambda/2\rho)\|\mathbf{w}\|^2$ is not adequate here to stabilize the Hebbian rule at a solution that maximizes $\langle y^2 \rangle$. However, other more appropriate regularization terms can ensure stability, as we will see in the next section.

4.3   Characterization of Additional Learning Rules

Equation (4.2.5) [or (4.2.6)] is a powerful tool that can be used in the characterization of the average behavior of stochastic learning equations. This section will employ this equation to characterize some unsupervised learning rules that were discussed in Chapter 3. The following analysis is made easier if one assumes (as before) that $\mathbf{w}$ and $\mathbf{x}$ are uncorrelated, and that $\langle \nabla J \rangle$ is averaged with respect to $\mathbf{x}$ (denoted by $\langle \nabla J \rangle_{\mathbf{x}}$), with $\mathbf{w}$ replaced by its mean $\langle \mathbf{w} \rangle$. This assumption leads to the "approximate" average learning equation

$$\langle \dot{\mathbf{w}} \rangle = -\rho \langle \nabla J \rangle_{\mathbf{x}} \tag{4.3.1}$$

This approximation of the average learning equation is valid when the learning equation contains strongly mixing random processes (processes for which the "past" and the "future" are asymptotically independent) with the mixing rate high compared with the rate of change of the solution process; i.e., it can be assumed that the weights are uncorrelated with the patterns $\mathbf{x}$ and with themselves. Taking the expected (average) value of a stochastic equation, one obtains a deterministic equation whose solution approximates asymptotically the behavior of the original system, as described by the stochastic equation [here, $\rho = \rho(t) = 1/t$ is normally assumed]. Roughly, the higher the mixing rate, the better the approximation in Equation (4.3.1) (Kushner and Clark, 1978). Equation (4.3.1) will be employed frequently in the remainder of this chapter.

A more rigorous characterization of stochastic learning requires the more advanced theory of stochastic differential equations and will not be considered here [see Kushner (1977) and Ljung (1978)]. Rather, this section proceeds with a deterministic analysis using the "average versions" of the stochastic equations. It can be shown that a necessary condition for the stochastic learning rule to converge (in the mean-square sense) is that the average version of the learning rule must converge. In addition, and under certain assumptions, the exact solution of a stochastic equation is guaranteed to "stay close," in a probabilistic sense, to the solution $\langle \mathbf{w}(t) \rangle$ of the associated average equation. It has been shown (Geman, 1979) that under strong mixing conditions (and some additional assumptions), $\lim_{\rho \to 0} \max_{t \geq 0} \langle \|\mathbf{w}(t) - \langle \mathbf{w}(t) \rangle\|^2 \rangle = 0$. This result implies that if sufficiently small learning rates are used, the behavior of a stochastic learning equation may be well approximated, in a mean-square sense, by the deterministic dynamics of its corresponding average equation. Oja (1983) pointed out that the convergence of constrained gradient descent (or ascent)–based stochastic learning equations (the type of equations considered in this chapter) can be studied with averaging techniques; i.e., the asymptotically stable equilibria of the average equation are the possible limits of the stochastic equation. Several examples of applying the averaging technique to the characterization of learning rules can be found in Kohonen (1989).

Before proceeding with further analysis of learning rules, the following important observations regarding the nature of the learning parameter ρ in the stochastic learning equation are made (Heskes and Kappen, 1991). When a neural network interacts with a fixed and unchanging (stationary) environment, the aim of the learning algorithm is to adjust the weights of the network in order to produce an optimal response, i.e., an optimal representation of the environment. To produce such an optimal and static representation, it is necessary for the learning parameter, which controls the amount of learning, to eventually approach zero. Otherwise, fluctuations in the representation will persist, due to the stochastic nature of the learning equation, and asymptotic convergence to optimal representation is never achieved. For a large class of stochastic algorithms, asymptotic convergence can be guaranteed (with high probability) by using the learning parameter $\rho = \rho(t) = 1/t$ (Ljung, 1977; Kushner and Clark, 1978).

On the other hand, consider biologic neural nets. Human beings, of course, are able to learn continually throughout their entire lifetime. In fact, human learning is able to proceed on two different time scales; humans learn with age (very large time scale adaptation/learning) and are also capable of discovering regularities and are attentive for details (short time scale learning). This constant tendency to learn accounts for the adaptability of natural neural systems to a changing environment. Therefore, it is clear that the learning processes in biologic neural networks do not allow for asymptotically vanishing learning parameters.

In order for artificial neural networks to be capable of adapting to a changing (nonstationary) environment, the learning parameter ρ must take a sufficiently large nonzero value. The larger the learning parameter, the faster the response of the network to the changing environment. On the other hand, a large learning parameter has a negative effect on the accuracy of the network's representation of the environment at any given time; a large ρ gives rise to large fluctuations around the desired optimal representation. In practice, though, one might be willing to trade some degree of fluctuation about the optimal representation (solution) for adaptability to a nonstationary process. Similar ideas have been proposed in connection with stochastic adaptive linear filtering. Here, an adaptive algorithm with a constant step size is used because it has the advantage of a limited memory, which enables it to track time fluctuations in the incoming data. These ideas date back to Wiener (1956) in connection with his work on linear prediction theory.

4.3.1 Simple Hebbian Learning

One version of the Hebbian learning rule was already presented in the preceding subsection. However, this subsection considers the most simple form of Hebbian learning, which is given by Equation (4.2.18) with $\lambda = 0$, namely,

$$\dot{\mathbf{w}} = \rho y \mathbf{x} \tag{4.3.2}$$

This equation is a continuous-time version of the unsupervised Hebbian learning rule introduced in Chapter 3. Employing Equation (4.3.1) results in the approximate average learning equation

$$\langle \dot{\mathbf{w}} \rangle = -\rho \langle \nabla J \rangle = \rho \langle y \mathbf{x} \rangle \tag{4.3.3}$$

In Equation (4.3.3) and in the remainder of this chapter, the subscript $\mathbf{x}$ in $\langle \nabla J \rangle_{\mathbf{x}}$ is dropped in order to simplify notation. Now, the average gradient of J in Equation (4.3.3) may be written as

$$\langle \nabla J \rangle = -\langle y \mathbf{x} \rangle = -\mathbf{C} \langle \mathbf{w} \rangle \tag{4.3.4}$$

from which the average instantaneous criterion function may be determined:

$$\langle J \rangle = -\tfrac{1}{2} \langle y^2 \rangle = -\tfrac{1}{2} \langle \mathbf{w}^{\mathrm{T}} \rangle \mathbf{C} \langle \mathbf{w} \rangle \tag{4.3.5}$$

Note that $\langle J \rangle$ is minimized by maximizing the unit's output variance. Again, $\mathbf{C} = \langle \mathbf{x} \mathbf{x}^{\mathrm{T}} \rangle$ is the autocorrelation matrix, which is positive semidefinite, having orthonormal eigenvectors $\mathbf{c}^{(i)}$ with corresponding eigenvalues $\lambda_1 \geq \lambda_2 \geq \cdots \geq \lambda_i \geq \cdots \geq \lambda_n \geq 0$. That is, $\mathbf{C} \mathbf{c}^{(i)} = \lambda_i \mathbf{c}^{(i)}$, for $i = 1, 2, \ldots, n$. The dynamics of Equation (4.3.3) are unstable. To see this, one first finds the equilibrium points by setting $\langle \nabla J \rangle = \mathbf{0}$, giving $\mathbf{C} \langle \mathbf{w} \rangle = \mathbf{0}$ or $\mathbf{w}^* = \mathbf{0}$. $\mathbf{w}^*$ is unstable because the Hessian (in an average sense) $\langle \mathbf{H}(\mathbf{w}) \rangle = \langle \nabla \nabla J \rangle = -\mathbf{C}$ is nonpositive for all $\langle \mathbf{w} \rangle$. Therefore, Equation (4.3.3) is unstable and results in $\langle \|\mathbf{w}\| \rangle \to \infty$. Note, however, that the direction of $\langle \mathbf{w} \rangle$ is not arbitrary; it will tend to point in the direction of $\mathbf{c}^{(1)}$, since if one assumes a fixed weight vector magnitude, $\langle J \rangle$ is minimized when $\langle \mathbf{w} \rangle$ is parallel to the eigenvector with the largest corresponding eigenvalue.

The following subsections will characterize other versions of the Hebbian learning rule, some of which were introduced in Chapter 3. These rules are well behaved and hence solve the divergence problem encountered with simple Hebbian learning. For simplifying mathematical notation and terminology, the following subsections will use J, ∇J, and $\mathbf{H}$ to designate $\langle J \rangle$, $\langle \nabla J \rangle$, and $\langle \mathbf{H} \rangle$, respectively. Thus $\langle J \rangle$ will be referred to simply as the *criterion function*, $\langle \nabla J \rangle$ as the *gradient of J*, and $\langle \mathbf{H} \rangle$ as the *Hessian of J*. Also, the quantity $\mathbf{w}$ in the following average equations should be interpreted as the state of the average learning equation.

4.3.2   Improved Hebbian Learning

Consider the criterion function

$$J = -\tfrac{1}{2}\frac{\mathbf{w}^{\mathsf{T}}\mathbf{C}\mathbf{w}}{\|\mathbf{w}\|^2} = -\tfrac{1}{2}\frac{\langle y^2 \rangle}{\|\mathbf{w}\|^2} \tag{4.3.6}$$

It is a well-established property of quadratic forms that if $\mathbf{w}$ is constrained to the surface of the unit hypersphere, then Equation (4.3.6) is minimized when $\mathbf{w} = \mathbf{c}^{(1)}$ with $J(\mathbf{c}^{(1)}) = -\lambda_1/2$ [e.g., see Johnson and Wichern (1988)]. Also, for any real symmetric $n \times n$ matrix $\mathbf{A}$, the Rayleigh quotient $(\mathbf{x}^{\mathsf{T}}\mathbf{A}\mathbf{x})/\|\mathbf{x}\|^2$ satisfies $\lambda_n \le (\mathbf{x}^{\mathsf{T}}\mathbf{A}\mathbf{x})/\|\mathbf{x}\|^2 \le \lambda_1$, where λ_1 and λ_n are the largest and smallest eigenvalues of $\mathbf{A}$, respectively. Starting from this criterion, one can derive an average learning equation. Employing Equation (4.3.1), one obtains

$$\dot{\mathbf{w}} = -\rho\nabla J = \rho\frac{\mathbf{C}\mathbf{w}\|\mathbf{w}\|^2 - \mathbf{w}^{\mathsf{T}}\mathbf{C}\mathbf{w}\mathbf{w}}{\|\mathbf{w}\|^4} \tag{4.3.7}$$

which can be shown to be the average version of the nonlinear stochastic learning rule

$$\dot{\mathbf{w}} = \frac{\rho}{\|\mathbf{w}\|^2}\left(y\mathbf{x} - y^2\frac{\mathbf{w}}{\|\mathbf{w}\|^2}\right) \tag{4.3.8}$$

If one heuristically sets $\|\mathbf{w}\|^2$ to 1 for the two $\|\mathbf{w}\|^2$ terms in this equation, Equation (4.3.8) reduces to the continuous version of Oja's rule [refer to Equation (3.3.6)]. Let us continue with the characterization of Equation (4.3.8) and defer the analysis of Oja's rule to Section 4.3.3. At equilibrium, Equation (4.3.7) gives

$$\mathbf{C}\mathbf{w} = (\mathbf{w}^{\mathsf{T}}\mathbf{C}\mathbf{w})\frac{\mathbf{w}}{\|\mathbf{w}\|^2} \tag{4.3.9}$$

Hence the equilibria of Equation (4.3.7) are the solutions of Equation (4.3.9) given by $\mathbf{w}^* = \alpha\mathbf{c}^{(i)}$, $i = 1, 2, \ldots, n$. Here, J takes its smallest value of $-\frac{1}{2}\lambda_1$ at $\mathbf{w}^* = \alpha\mathbf{c}^{(1)}$. This can be verified easily by direct substitution in Equation (4.3.6).

Next, consider the Hessian of J at $\mathbf{w}^* = \mathbf{c}^{(i)}$ (assuming, without loss of generality, $\alpha = 1$), and multiply it by $\mathbf{c}^{(j)}$, namely, $\mathbf{H}(\mathbf{c}^{(i)})\mathbf{c}^{(j)}$. It can be shown that this quantity is given by [see Problem 4.3.1; for a reference on matrix differential calculus, the reader is referred to the book by Magnus and Neudecker (1988)]

$$\mathbf{H}(\mathbf{c}^{(i)})\mathbf{c}^{(j)} = \begin{cases} 0\mathbf{c}^{(i)} = \mathbf{0} & i = j \\ (\lambda_i - \lambda_j)\mathbf{c}^{(j)} & i \neq j \end{cases} \tag{4.3.10}$$

This equation implies that $\mathbf{H}(\mathbf{w}^*)$ has the same eigenvectors as $\mathbf{C}$ but with different eigenvalues. $\mathbf{H}(\mathbf{w}^*)$ is positive semidefinite only when $\mathbf{w}^* = \mathbf{c}^{(1)}$. Thus, by following the dynamics of Equation (4.3.7), $\mathbf{w}$ will eventually point in the direction of $\mathbf{c}^{(1)}$ (since none of the other directions $\mathbf{c}^{(i)}$ is stable). Although the direction of $\mathbf{w}$ will eventually stabilize, it is entirely possible for $\|\mathbf{w}\|$ to approach infinity, and Equation (4.3.7) will appear never to converge. $\|\mathbf{w}\|$ may be artificially constrained to finite values by normalizing $\mathbf{w}$ after each update of Equation (4.3.8). Alternatively, the two $\|\mathbf{w}\|^2$ terms in Equation (4.3.8) may be set equal to 1. This latter case is considered next.

4.3.3   Oja's Rule

Oja's rule was defined by Equation (3.3.6). Its continuous-time version is given by the nonlinear stochastic differential equation

$$\dot{\mathbf{w}} = \rho(y\mathbf{x} - y^2\mathbf{w}) \tag{4.3.11}$$

The corresponding average learning equation is thus (Oja, 1982, 1989)

$$\dot{\mathbf{w}} = \rho[\mathbf{C}\mathbf{w} - (\mathbf{w}^\mathsf{T}\mathbf{C}\mathbf{w})\mathbf{w}] \tag{4.3.12}$$

which has its equilibria at $\mathbf{w}$, satisfying

$$\mathbf{C}\mathbf{w} = (\mathbf{w}^\mathsf{T}\mathbf{C}\mathbf{w})\mathbf{w} \tag{4.3.13}$$

The solutions of Equation (4.3.13) are $\mathbf{w}^* = \pm\mathbf{c}^{(i)}$, $i = 1, 2, \ldots, n$. All these equilibria are unstable except for $\mathbf{w}^* = \pm\mathbf{c}^{(1)}$. This can be seen by noting that the Hessian

$$\mathbf{H} = \nabla\nabla J = \nabla[-\mathbf{C}\mathbf{w} + (\mathbf{w}^\mathsf{T}\mathbf{C}\mathbf{w})\mathbf{w}]$$

$$= -\mathbf{C} + \mathbf{w}^\mathsf{T}\mathbf{C}\mathbf{w}\mathbf{I} + 2\mathbf{w}\mathbf{w}^\mathsf{T}\mathbf{C} \tag{4.3.14}$$

is positive definite only at $\mathbf{w}^* = \mathbf{c}^{(1)}$ (or $-\mathbf{c}^{(1)}$). Note that Equation (4.3.14) is derived starting from $\nabla J = -(1/\rho)\dot{\mathbf{w}}$, with $\dot{\mathbf{w}}$ given in Equation (4.3.12). Although J is not known, the positive definiteness of $\mathbf{H}$ can be seen from

$$\mathbf{H}(\mathbf{c}^{(i)})\mathbf{c}^{(j)} = \begin{cases} 2\lambda_i\mathbf{c}^{(i)} & i = j \\ (\lambda_i - \lambda_j)\mathbf{c}^{(j)} & i \neq j \end{cases} \tag{4.3.15}$$

and by noting that the eigenvalues of $\mathbf{C}$ satisfy $\lambda_1 \geq \lambda_2 \geq \cdots \geq \lambda_n \geq 0$ (we assume $\lambda_1 \neq \lambda_2$). Therefore, Oja's rule is equivalent to a stable version of the Hebbian rule given in Equation (4.3.8). A formal derivation of Oja's rule is explored in Problem 4.3.7.

A single unit employing Oja's rule (Oja's unit) is equivalent to a linear matched filter. To see this, assume that for all $\mathbf{x}$, $\mathbf{x} = \bar{\mathbf{x}} + \mathbf{v}$, where $\bar{\mathbf{x}}$ is a fixed vector (without loss of generality, let $\|\bar{\mathbf{x}}\| = 1$) and $\mathbf{v}$ is a vector of symmetrically distributed zero-mean noise with uncorrelated components having variance σ^2. Then $\mathbf{C} = \bar{\mathbf{x}}\bar{\mathbf{x}}^T + \langle \mathbf{v}\mathbf{v}^T \rangle = \bar{\mathbf{x}}\bar{\mathbf{x}}^T + \sigma^2\mathbf{I}$. The largest eigenvalue of $\mathbf{C}$ is $1 + \sigma^2$, and the corresponding eigenvector is $\mathbf{c}^{(1)} = \bar{\mathbf{x}}$. Oja's unit then becomes a matched filter for the data, since $\lim_{t \to \infty} \mathbf{w}(t) = \mathbf{c}^{(1)} = \bar{\mathbf{x}}$ in Equation (4.3.12). Here, the unit responds maximally to the data mean. Further characterization of Oja's rule can be found in Xu (1993).

Oja's rule is interesting because it results in a local learning rule that is biologically plausible. The locality property is seen by considering the component weight adaptation rule of Equation (4.3.11), namely,

$$\dot{w}_i = \rho(yx_i - y^2w_i) \tag{4.3.16}$$

and by noting that the change in the ith weight is not an "explicit" function of any other weight except the ith weight itself. Of course, $\dot{w}_i$ does depend on $\mathbf{w}$ via $y = \mathbf{w}^T\mathbf{x}$. However, this dependence does not violate the concept of locality.

It is also interesting to note that Oja's rule is similar to Hebbian learning with weight decay as in Equation (4.2.18). For Oja's rule, though, the growth in $\|\mathbf{w}\|$ is controlled by a "forgetting" or weight-decay term $-\rho y^2\mathbf{w}$ that has nonlinear gain; the forgetting becomes stronger with stronger response, thus preventing $\|\mathbf{w}\|$ from diverging.

Example 4.3.1   This example shows typical simulation results comparing the evolution of the weight vector $\mathbf{w}$ according to the stochastic Oja rule in Equation (4.3.11) and its corresponding average rule in Equation (4.3.12).

Consider a training set $\{\mathbf{x}\}$ of forty 15-dimensional column vectors with independent random components generated by a normal distribution $N(0, 1)$. In the following simulations, the training vectors' autocorrelation matrix $\mathbf{C} = \frac{1}{40}\sum_{k=1}^{40} \mathbf{x}^k\mathbf{x}^{kT}$ has the following set of eigenvalues: $\{2.561, 2.254, 2.081, 1.786, 1.358, 1.252, 1.121, 0.963, 0.745, 0.633, 0.500, 0.460, 0.357, 0.288, 0.238\}$.

During training, one of the 40 vectors is selected at random and is used in the learning rule to compute the next weight vector. Discretized versions of Equations (4.3.11) and (4.3.12) are used where $\dot{\mathbf{w}}$ is replaced by $\mathbf{w}^{k+1} - \mathbf{w}^k$. A learning rate $\rho = 0.005$ is used. This is equivalent to integrating these equations with Euler's method [e.g., see Gerald (1978)] using a time step $\Delta t = 0.005$ and $\rho = 1$. The initial weight vector is set equal to one of the training vectors. Figure 4.3.1 shows the evolution of the cosine of the angle θ between $\mathbf{w}^k$ and $\mathbf{c}^{(1)}$ and the evolution of the norm of $\mathbf{w}^k$, respectively. The solid line corresponds to the stochastic rule, and the dashed line corresponds to the average rule.

This simulation is repeated, but with a fixed presentation order of the training set. Results are shown in Figures 4.3.2. Note that the results for the average learning equation (dashed line) are identical in both simulations because they are not affected by the order of presentation of input vectors. These simulations agree with the theoretical results on the appropriateness of using the average learning equation to approximate the limiting behavior of its corresponding stochastic learning equation. Note that a monotonically decreasing learning rate [say ρ proportional to $1/(1 + \ln k)$ or $1/k$ with $k \geq 1$] can be used to force the convergence of the direction of $\mathbf{w}^k$ in the first simulation. It is also interesting to note that better approximations are possible when the training vectors are presented in a fixed deterministic order (or in a random order but with each vector guaranteed to be selected once every training cycle of $m = 40$ presentations). Here, a sufficiently small, constant learning rate is sufficient for making the average dynamics approximate, in a practical sense, the stochastic dynamics for all time.

4.3.4   Yuille et al. Rule

The continuous-time version of the Yuille et al. (1989) learning rule is

$$\dot{\mathbf{w}} = \rho(y\mathbf{x} - \|\mathbf{w}\|^2\mathbf{w}) \tag{4.3.17}$$

and the corresponding average learning equation is

$$\dot{\mathbf{w}} = \rho(\mathbf{C}\mathbf{w} - \|\mathbf{w}\|^2\mathbf{w}) \tag{4.3.18}$$

with equilibria at

$$\mathbf{w}^{i*} = \sqrt{\lambda_i}\mathbf{c}^{(i)} \qquad i = 1, 2, \ldots, n \tag{4.3.19}$$

From Equation (4.3.18), the gradient of J is

$$\nabla J = -\mathbf{C}\mathbf{w} + \|\mathbf{w}\|^2\mathbf{w} \tag{4.3.20}$$

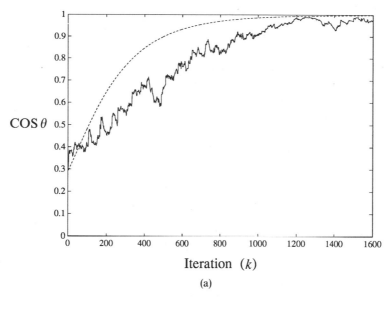

Iteration (k)

(a)

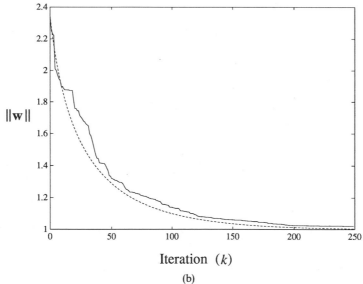

Iteration (k)

(b)

Figure 4.3.1
(a) Evolution of the cosine of the angle θ between the weight vector $\mathbf{w}^k$ and the principal eigenvector of the autocorrelation matrix $\mathbf{C}$ for the stochastic Oja rule (*solid line*) and for the average Oja rule (*dashed line*). (b) Evolution of the magnitude of the weight vector. The training set consists of forty 15-dimensional real-valued vectors whose components are independently generated according to a normal distribution $N(0, 1)$. The presentation order of the training vectors is random during training.

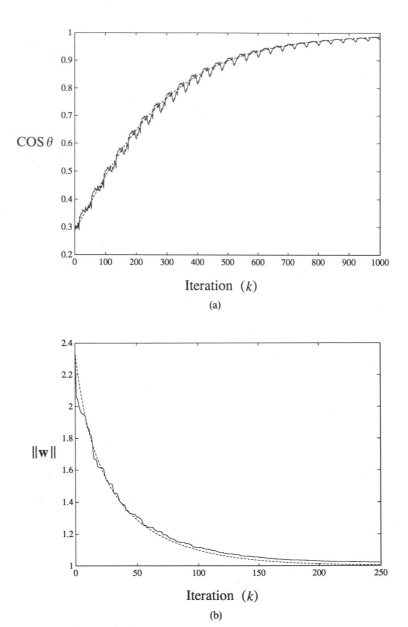

Figure 4.3.2
(a) Evolution of the cosine of the angle θ between the weight vector $\mathbf{w}^k$ and the principal eigenvector of the autocorrelation matrix $\mathbf{C}$ for the stochastic Oja rule (*solid line*) and for the average Oja rule (*dashed line*). (b) Evolution of the magnitude of the weight vector. The training set consists of forty 15-dimensional real-valued vectors whose components are independently generated according to a normal distribution $N(0, 1)$. The presentation order of the training vectors is fixed.

which leads to the Hessian

$$\mathbf{H} = -\mathbf{C} + \|\mathbf{w}\|^2 \mathbf{I} + 2\mathbf{w}\mathbf{w}^{\mathsf{T}} \qquad (4.3.21)$$

Note that one also could have computed $\mathbf{H}$ directly from the known criterion function:

$$J = -\tfrac{1}{2}\langle y^2 \rangle + \tfrac{1}{4}\|\mathbf{w}\|^4 = -\tfrac{1}{2}\mathbf{w}^{\mathsf{T}}\mathbf{C}\mathbf{w} + \tfrac{1}{4}\|\mathbf{w}\|^4 \qquad (4.3.22)$$

Now, evaluating $\mathbf{H}(\mathbf{w}^{i*})\mathbf{w}^{j*}$, one gets

$$\mathbf{H}(\mathbf{w}^{i*})\mathbf{w}^{j*} = \begin{cases} 2\lambda_i \mathbf{w}^{i*} & i = j \\ (\lambda_i - \lambda_j)\mathbf{w}^{j*} & i \neq j \end{cases} \qquad (4.3.23)$$

which implies that the $\mathbf{w}^{j*}$ are eigenvectors of $\mathbf{H}(\mathbf{w}^{i*})$ with eigenvalues $\lambda_i - \lambda_j$ for $i \neq j$ and $2\lambda_i$ for $i = j$. Therefore, $\mathbf{H}(\mathbf{w}^{i*})$ is positive definite if and only if $\lambda_i > \lambda_j$, for $i \neq j$. In this case, $\mathbf{w}^* = \pm\sqrt{\lambda_1}\mathbf{c}^{(1)}$ are the only stable equilibria, and the dynamics of the stochastic equation are expected to approach $\mathbf{w}^*$.

4.3.5   Hassoun's Rule

In the following, the unsupervised Hebbian-type learning rule

$$\dot{\mathbf{w}} = \rho\left[y\mathbf{x} - \lambda\mathbf{w}\left(1 - \frac{1}{\|\mathbf{w}\|}\right)\right] \qquad (4.3.24)$$

with $\|\mathbf{w}\| \neq 0$ is analyzed. Another way to stabilize Equation (4.3.2) is to start from a criterion function that explicitly penalizes the divergence of $\mathbf{w}$. For example, if $\|\mathbf{w}\| = 1$ is to be satisfied, one may utilize J given by

$$J = -\tfrac{1}{2}\mathbf{w}^{\mathsf{T}}\mathbf{C}\mathbf{w} + \frac{\lambda}{2}(1 - \|\mathbf{w}\|)^2 \qquad (4.3.25)$$

with $\lambda > 0$. It can be easily shown that steepest gradient descent on the preceding criterion function leads to the learning equation

$$\dot{\mathbf{w}} = \rho\left[\mathbf{C}\mathbf{w} - \lambda\mathbf{w}\left(1 - \frac{1}{\|\mathbf{w}\|}\right)\right] \qquad (4.3.26)$$

Equation (4.3.26) is the average learning equation for the stochastic rule of Equation (4.3.24). Its equilibria are solutions of the equation

$$\mathbf{C}\mathbf{w} = \lambda\left(1 - \frac{1}{\|\mathbf{w}\|}\right)\mathbf{w} \qquad (4.3.27)$$

Thus it can be seen that the solution vectors of Equation (4.3.27), denoted by $\mathbf{w}^{i*}$, must be parallel to one of the eigenvectors of $\mathbf{C}$, say $\mathbf{c}^{(i)}$, and satisfy

$$\lambda\left(1 - \frac{1}{\|\mathbf{w}^{i*}\|}\right) = \lambda_i \geq 0 \tag{4.3.28}$$

where λ_i is the ith eigenvalue of $\mathbf{C}$. From Equation (4.3.28) it can be seen that the norm of the ith equilibrium state is given by

$$\|\mathbf{w}^{i*}\| = \frac{\lambda}{\lambda - \lambda_i} > 0 \tag{4.3.29}$$

which requires $\lambda > \lambda_i$ for all i. Note that if $\lambda \gg \lambda_i$, then $\|\mathbf{w}^*\|$ approaches 1 for all equilibrium points. Thus the equilibria of Equation (4.3.26) approach unity norm eigenvectors of the correlation matrix $\mathbf{C}$ when λ is large.

Next, let us investigate the stability of these equilibria. Starting from the Hessian

$$\mathbf{H} = -\mathbf{C} + \lambda\left(1 - \frac{1}{\|\mathbf{w}\|}\right)\mathbf{I} + \frac{\lambda}{\|\mathbf{w}\|^3}\mathbf{w}\mathbf{w}^{\mathrm{T}} \tag{4.3.30}$$

one has

$$\mathbf{H}(\mathbf{w}^{i*})\mathbf{w}^{j*} = \begin{cases} (\lambda - \lambda_i)\mathbf{w}^{i*} & i = j \\ (\lambda_i - \lambda_j)\mathbf{w}^{j*} & i \neq j \end{cases} \tag{4.3.31}$$

which implies that $\mathbf{H}(\mathbf{w}^{i*})$ is positive definite if and only if $\mathbf{w}^{i*}$ is parallel to $\mathbf{c}^{(1)}$ and $\lambda > \lambda_1$. Therefore, the only stable equilibria of Equation (4.3.26) are $\mathbf{w}^* = [\pm\lambda/(\lambda - \lambda_i)]\mathbf{c}^{(1)}$, which approach $\pm\mathbf{c}^{(1)}$ for $\lambda \gg \lambda_1$. Like the Yuille et al. rule, this rule preserves the information about the size of λ_1 [λ_1 can be computed from Equation (4.3.29)].

For the discrete-time version, it is interesting to note that for the case $\lambda \gg \lambda_1$, and $\rho\lambda = 1$, Equation (4.3.24) reduces to

$$\mathbf{w}^{k+1} = \rho y^k \mathbf{x}^k + \frac{\mathbf{w}^k}{\|\mathbf{w}^k\|} \tag{4.3.32}$$

which is very similar to the discrete-time simple Hebbian learning rule with weight vector normalization of Equation (3.3.5) and expressed here as

$$\begin{cases} \tilde{\mathbf{w}}^{k+1} = \rho y^k \mathbf{x}^k + \mathbf{w}^k \\ \\ \mathbf{w}^{k+1} = \dfrac{\tilde{\mathbf{w}}^{k+1}}{\|\tilde{\mathbf{w}}^{k+1}\|} \end{cases} \tag{4.3.33}$$

Note that the weight vector in $y^k = (\mathbf{w}^k)^T \mathbf{x}^k$ in Equation (4.3.33) need not be normalized to prevent divergence.

In practice, discrete-time versions of the stochastic learning rules in Equations (4.3.11), (4.3.17), and (4.3.24) are used where $\dot{\mathbf{w}}$ is replaced by $\mathbf{w}^{k+1} - \mathbf{w}^k$ and $\mathbf{w}(t)$ by $\mathbf{w}^k$. Here, the stability of these discrete-time stochastic dynamical systems critically depends on the value of the learning rate ρ. Although the stability analysis is difficult, one can resort to the discrete-time versions of the average learning equations corresponding to these rules and derive conditions on ρ for asymptotic convergence (in the mean) in the neighborhood of equilibrium states $\mathbf{w}^*$. Such analysis is explored in Problems 4.3.8 and 4.3.9.

In concluding this section, another interpretation of the regularization effects on the stabilization of Hebbian-type rules is presented. In the stochastic learning Equations (4.2.18), (4.3.11), (4.3.17), and (4.3.24), regularization appears as weight decay terms $-\lambda\mathbf{w}$, $-\rho y^2 \mathbf{w}$, $-\rho\|\mathbf{w}\|^2\mathbf{w}$, and $-\rho\lambda[1 - (1/\|\mathbf{w}\|)]\mathbf{w}$, respectively. Therefore, one may think of weight decay as a way of stabilizing unstable learning rules. However, one should carefully design the gain coefficient in the weight decay term for proper performance. For example, it has been shown earlier that a simple positive constant gain λ in Equation (4.2.18) does not stabilize Hebb's rule. On the other hand, the nonlinear dynamic gains ρy^2, $\rho\|\mathbf{w}\|^2$, and $\rho\lambda[1 - (1/\|\mathbf{w}\|)]$ lead to stability. Note that the weight decay gain in Oja's rule utilizes more information, in the form of y^2, than the Yuille et al. rule or Hassoun's rule. The regularization in these latter rules is only a function of the current weight vector magnitude.

4.4   Principal-Component Analysis (PCA)

The PCA network of Section 3.3.5, employing Sanger's rule, is analyzed in this section. Recalling Sanger's rule [from Equation (3.3.19)] and writing it in vector form for the continuous-time case result in

$$\dot{\mathbf{w}}_i = \rho\left(\mathbf{x} - \sum_{j=1}^{i} \mathbf{w}_j y_j\right) y_i \tag{4.4.1}$$

with $i = 1, 2, \ldots, m$, where m is the number of units in the PCA network. We will assume, without any loss of generality, that $m = 2$. This leads to the following set of coupled learning equations for the two units:

$$\dot{\mathbf{w}}_1 = \rho(\mathbf{x} y_1 - \mathbf{w}_1 y_1^2) \tag{4.4.2}$$

and

$$\dot{\mathbf{w}}_2 = \rho[\mathbf{x} - (\mathbf{w}_1 y_1 + \mathbf{w}_2 y_2)] y_2 \tag{4.4.3}$$

Equation (4.4.2) is Oja's rule. It is independent of unit 2 and therefore converges to $\mathbf{w}_1^* = \mathbf{c}^{(1)}$, the principal eigenvector of the autocorrelation matrix of the input data (assuming zero mean input vectors). Equation (4.4.3) is Oja's rule with the added inhibitory term $\rho \mathbf{w}_1 y_1 y_2$. Next, a sequential operation of the two-unit net is assumed, where unit 1 is allowed to fully converge before evolving unit 2. This mode of operation is permissible because unit 1 is independent of unit 2.

With the sequential update assumption, Equation (4.4.3) becomes

$$\dot{\mathbf{w}}_2 = \rho(\mathbf{x} y_2 - y_2^2 \mathbf{w}_2 - \mathbf{c}^{(1)} y_1 y_2) \tag{4.4.4}$$

For clarity, the subscript on $\mathbf{w}$ will be dropped. Now, the average learning equation for unit 2 is given by

$$\dot{\mathbf{w}} = \rho[\mathbf{C}\mathbf{w} - (\mathbf{w}^{\mathrm{T}}\mathbf{C}\mathbf{w})\mathbf{w} - \mathbf{c}^{(1)}\mathbf{c}^{(1)^{\mathrm{T}}}\mathbf{C}\mathbf{w}] \tag{4.4.5}$$

which has equilibria satisfying

$$(\mathbf{I} - \mathbf{c}^{(1)}\mathbf{c}^{(1)^{\mathrm{T}}})\mathbf{C}\mathbf{w} = (\mathbf{w}^{\mathrm{T}}\mathbf{C}\mathbf{w})\mathbf{w} \tag{4.4.6}$$

Hence $\mathbf{w}^* = \mathbf{0}$ and $\mathbf{w}^* = \mathbf{c}^{(i)}$ with $i = 2, 3, \ldots, n$ are solutions. Note that the point $\mathbf{w} = \mathbf{c}^{(1)}$ is not an equilibrium. The Hessian is given by

$$\mathbf{H} = (\mathbf{c}^{(1)}\mathbf{c}^{(1)^{\mathrm{T}}} - \mathbf{I})\mathbf{C} + \mathbf{w}^{\mathrm{T}}\mathbf{C}\mathbf{w}\mathbf{I} + 2\mathbf{w}\mathbf{w}^{\mathrm{T}}\mathbf{C} \tag{4.4.7}$$

Since $\mathbf{H}(\mathbf{0}) = \lambda_1 \mathbf{c}^{(1)}\mathbf{c}^{(1)^{\mathrm{T}}} - \mathbf{C}$ is not positive definite, the equilibrium $\mathbf{w}^* = \mathbf{0}$ is not stable. For the remaining equilibria, we have

$$\mathbf{H}(\mathbf{c}^{(i)})\mathbf{c}^{(j)} = \begin{cases} 2\lambda_i \mathbf{c}^{(i)} & i = j \text{ and } j > 1 \\ (\lambda_i - \lambda_j)\mathbf{c}^{(j)} & i \neq j \text{ and } j > 1 \end{cases} \tag{4.4.8}$$

which is positive definite only at $\mathbf{w}^* = \mathbf{c}^{(2)}$, assuming $\lambda_2 \neq \lambda_3$. Thus Equation (4.4.5) converges asymptotically to the unique stable vector $\mathbf{w}^* = \mathbf{c}^{(2)}$, which is the eigenvector of $\mathbf{C}$ with the second largest eigenvalue λ_2. Similarly, for a network with m interacting units according to Equation (4.4.1), the ith unit ($i = 1, 2, \ldots, m$) will extract the ith eigenvector of $\mathbf{C}$.

The unit-by-unit description presented here helps simplify the explanation of the PCA net behavior. In fact, the weight vectors $\mathbf{w}_i$ approach their final values simultaneously, not one at a time. However, the preceding analysis still applies, asymptotically, to the end points. Note that the simultaneous evolution of the $\mathbf{w}_i$ is advantageous because it leads to faster learning than if the units are trained one at a time.

4.5   Theory of Reinforcement Learning

Recall the simplified stochastic reinforcement learning rule of Equation (3.2.5). The continuous-time version of this rule is given by

$$\dot{\mathbf{w}} = \rho r (y - \langle y \rangle) \mathbf{x} \qquad (4.5.1)$$

from which the average learning equation is given as

$$\langle \dot{\mathbf{w}} \rangle = \rho \langle r (y - \langle y \rangle) \mathbf{x} \rangle \qquad (4.5.2)$$

Here, $r = r(y, \mathbf{x})$. Now, employing Equation (4.2.6), Equation (4.5.2) may be seen as implementing a gradient search on an average instantaneous criterion function $\langle J \rangle$ whose gradient is given by

$$\nabla \langle J \rangle = \frac{-\langle \dot{\mathbf{w}} \rangle}{\rho} = -\langle r (y - \langle y \rangle) \mathbf{x} \rangle \qquad (4.5.3)$$

In Equations (4.5.1) through (4.5.3), the output y is generated by a stochastic unit according to the probability function $P(y | \mathbf{w}, \mathbf{x})$, given by

$$P(y = \pm 1 | \mathbf{w}, \mathbf{x}) = f(\pm \mathbf{w}^{\mathsf{T}} \mathbf{x}) = \frac{1}{1 + e^{\mp 2\beta \mathbf{w}^{\mathsf{T}} \mathbf{x}}} \qquad (4.5.4)$$

with the expected output

$$\langle y \rangle = \tanh (\beta \mathbf{w}^{\mathsf{T}} \mathbf{x}) \qquad (4.5.5)$$

as in Section 3.1.6. Next, it is shown that Equation (4.5.3) is proportional to the gradient of the expected reinforcement signal $\langle r \rangle$ (Williams, 1987; Hertz et al., 1991).

First, the expected (average) reinforcement signal $\langle r^{k} \rangle$ is expressed for the kth input vector with respect to all possible outputs y as

$$\langle r^{k} \rangle = \sum_{y = \pm 1} P(y | \mathbf{w}, \mathbf{x}^{k}) r(y, \mathbf{x}^{k}) \qquad (4.5.6)$$

and then its gradient is evaluated with respect to $\mathbf{w}$. The gradient of $P(y^{k} = \pm 1 | \mathbf{w}, \mathbf{x}^{k})$ is given by

$$\nabla P(y^{k} = \pm 1 | \mathbf{w}, \mathbf{x}^{k}) = \nabla f(\pm \mathbf{w}^{\mathsf{T}} \mathbf{x}^{k}) = 2\beta f(\pm \mathbf{w}^{\mathsf{T}} \mathbf{x}^{k})[\pm 1 \mp f(\pm \mathbf{w}^{\mathsf{T}} \mathbf{x}^{k})] \mathbf{x}^{k} \quad (4.5.7)$$

which follows from Equation (4.5.4). Also,

$$+1 - f(+\mathbf{w}^{\mathsf{T}} \mathbf{x}^{k}) = \tfrac{1}{2}(1 - \langle y^{k} \rangle) \qquad (4.5.8)$$

and

$$-1 + f(-\mathbf{w}^T\mathbf{x}^k) = -\tfrac{1}{2}(1 + \langle y^k \rangle) \tag{4.5.9}$$

which can be used in Equation (4.5.7) to give

$$\nabla P(y^k = \pm 1 | \mathbf{w}, \mathbf{x}^k) = \beta f(\pm \mathbf{w}^T\mathbf{x}^k)(\pm 1 - \langle y^k \rangle)\mathbf{x}^k$$

$$= \beta P(y^k = \pm 1 | \mathbf{w}, \mathbf{x}^k)(y^k - \langle y^k \rangle)\mathbf{x}^k \tag{4.5.10}$$

If the gradient of Equation (4.5.6) is taken and Equation (4.5.10) is used, one arrives at

$$\nabla \langle r^k \rangle = \beta \sum_y P(y | \mathbf{w}, \mathbf{x}^k) r(y, \mathbf{x}^k)(y^k - \langle y^k \rangle)\mathbf{x}^k \tag{4.5.11}$$

which also can be written as

$$\nabla \langle r^k \rangle = \beta \langle r(y, \mathbf{x}^k)(y^k - \langle y^k \rangle) \rangle \mathbf{x}^k \tag{4.5.12}$$

Finally, by averaging Equation (4.5.12) over all inputs $\mathbf{x}^k$, one gets

$$\nabla \langle r \rangle = \beta \langle r(y - \langle y \rangle)\mathbf{x} \rangle \tag{4.5.13}$$

where now the averages are across all patterns and all outputs. Note that $\nabla \langle r \rangle$ is proportional to $\nabla \langle J \rangle$ in Equation (4.5.3) and has an opposite sign. Thus Equation (4.5.2) can be written in terms of $\nabla \langle r \rangle$ as

$$\langle \dot{\mathbf{w}} \rangle = +\frac{\rho}{\beta} \nabla \langle r \rangle \tag{4.5.14}$$

which implies that the average weight vector converges to a local maximum of $\langle r \rangle$; i.e., Equation (4.5.1) converges, on average, to a solution that locally maximizes the average reinforcement signal.

Extensions of these results to a wider class of reinforcement algorithms can be found in Williams (1987). The characterization of the associative reward-penalty algorithm in Equation (3.2.1) is more difficult because it does not necessarily maximize $\langle r \rangle$. However, the preceding analysis should give some insight into the behavior of simple reinforcement learning.

4.6   Theory of Simple Competitive Learning

This section attempts to characterize simple competitive learning. Two approaches are described: one deterministic and the other statistical.

4.6.1 Deterministic Analysis

Consider a single layer of linear units, where each unit uses the simple continuous-time competitive rule [based on Equations (3.4.3) and (3.4.5)]:

$$\dot{\mathbf{w}}_i = \begin{cases} \rho(\mathbf{x}^k - \mathbf{w}_i) & \text{if unit } i \text{ is a winner for input } \mathbf{x}^k \\ 0 & \text{otherwise} \end{cases} \tag{4.6.1}$$

Also, consider the criterion function (Ritter and Schulten, 1988a)

$$J = \tfrac{1}{2} \sum_k \|\mathbf{x}^k - \mathbf{w}_{i*}\|^2 \tag{4.6.2}$$

where $\mathbf{w}_{i*}$ is the weight vector of the winner unit upon the presentation of the input vector $\mathbf{x}^k$. Here, all vectors $\mathbf{x}^k$ are assumed to be equally probable. In general, a probability of occurrence of $\mathbf{x}^k$, $P(\mathbf{x}^k)$, should be inserted inside the summation in Equation (4.6.2). An alternative way of expressing J in Equation (4.6.2) is through the use of a *cluster membership matrix* $\mathbf{M}$ defined for each unit $i = 1, 2, \ldots, n$ by

$$\mathbf{M}_i^k = \begin{cases} 1 & \text{if } \|\mathbf{w}_i - \mathbf{x}^k\| < \|\mathbf{w}_j - \mathbf{x}^k\| \quad \text{for all } i \neq j \\ 0 & \text{otherwise} \end{cases} \tag{4.6.3}$$

Here, $\mathbf{M}_i^k$ is a dynamically evolving function of k and i that specifies whether or not unit i is the winning unit upon the presentation of input $\mathbf{x}^k$. The cluster membership matrix allows the criterion function J to be written as

$$J = \tfrac{1}{2} \sum_k \sum_i \mathbf{M}_i^k \|\mathbf{x}^k - \mathbf{w}_i\|^2 \tag{4.6.4}$$

Now, performing gradient descent on J in Equation (4.6.4) yields

$$\dot{\mathbf{w}}_i = \rho \sum_k \mathbf{M}_i^k (\mathbf{x}^k - \mathbf{w}_i) \tag{4.6.5}$$

which is the batch-mode version of the learning rule in Equation (4.6.1). It was noted by Hertz et al. (1991) that this batch-mode competitive learning rule corresponds to the k-means clustering algorithm[7] when a finite training set is used. The local rule of

---

7. The popular k-means clustering algorithm is due to MacQueen (1967). It assumes a fixed number of clusters k and operates by associating a data point $\mathbf{x}$ to the cluster with the centroid closest to $\mathbf{x}$ and then updates centroids for the revised clusters. The basic k-means algorithm is initialized by assigning k randomly selected data points $\mathbf{x}$ as cluster centroids. The remaining data points are assigned to the cluster of the closest (in a Euclidean distance sense) centroid. Next, the k centroids are recomputed as the centroids of the vectors $\mathbf{x}$ in their cluster. This two-step process is invoked until convergence; i.e., until all centroids

Equation (4.6.1) may have an advantage over the batch-mode rule in Equation (4.6.5) because stochastic noise due to the random presentation order of the input patterns may kick the solution out of "poor" minima toward minima that are more optimal. However, only in the case of "sufficiently sparse" input data points can one prove stability and convergence theorems for the stochastic (incremental) competitive learning rule (Grossberg, 1976a, b). The data points are sparse enough if there exists a set of clusters so that the minimum overlap $(\mathbf{x}^i)^T\mathbf{x}^j$ within a cluster exceeds the maximum overlap between that cluster and any other cluster. In practice, a damped learning rate ρ^k is used (e.g., $\rho^k = \rho_0/k^\alpha$, where $0 < \alpha \le 1$ and ρ_0 is a positive constant) in order to stop weight evolution at one of the local solutions. Here, a relatively large initial learning rate allows for wide exploration during the initial phase of learning.

Criterion functions other than the one in Equation (4.6.4) may be employed that incorporate some interesting heuristics into the competitive rule for enhancing convergence speed or for altering the underlying "similarity measure" implemented by the learning rule. For an example, we may replace $\mathbf{M}_i^k$ by $2\mathbf{M}_i^k - 1$ in Equation (4.6.4). This causes the winning weight vector to be repelled by input vectors in other clusters while being attracted by its own cluster, which enhances convergence. Another example is to employ a different similarity measure (norm) in J such as the Minkowski-r norm of Equation (3.1.68), which has the ability to reduce the effects of outlier data points by proper choice of the exponent r. Other criterion functions also may be employed; the reader is referred to Bachmann et al. (1987) for yet another suitable criterion function.

4.6.2 Stochastic Analysis

The following is an analysis of simple competitive learning based on the stochastic approximation technique introduced in Section 4.3. Consider the following normalized discrete-time competitive rule (von der Malsberg, 1973; Rumelhart and Zipser, 1985):

$$
\Delta\mathbf{w}_i = \begin{cases} \rho\left(\dfrac{\mathbf{x}^k}{n^k} - \mathbf{w}_i\right) & \text{if unit } i \text{ is a winner for input } \mathbf{x}^k \\[2ex] \mathbf{0} & \text{otherwise} \end{cases}
\tag{4.6.6}
$$

---

stop changing. The convergence of the k-means clustering algorithm is ensured (Anderberg, 1973): Each (two-step) cycle of the algorithm decreases the sum of the squared distances from each data point to that data point's cluster centroid, and there are only finitely many partitions of the data points into k clusters. Note that the k-means algorithm converges to a locally optimal cluster configuration which is influenced by the initial assignment of the centroids.

where, again, the setting is a single-layer network of linear units. Here, $n^k = \sum_{j=1}^{n} x_j^k$, and typically, $\mathbf{x}^k \in \{0, 1\}^n$. Also, the weight normalization $\sum_{j=1}^{n} w_{ij} = 1$ is assumed for all units. It can be easily verified that Equation (4.6.6) preserves this weight normalization at any iteration (this was explored in Problem 3.4.1).

Let $P(\mathbf{x}^k)$ be the probability that input $\mathbf{x}^k$ is presented on any trial. Then, the average learning equation may be expressed as

$$\langle \Delta \mathbf{w}_i \rangle = \sum_k \Delta \mathbf{w}_i P(i|\mathbf{x}^k) P(\mathbf{x}^k) \qquad (4.6.7)$$

where $P(i|\mathbf{x}^k)$ is the conditional probability that unit i wins when input $\mathbf{x}^k$ is presented. Now, using Equation (4.6.6) in Equation (4.6.7), one obtains

$$\langle \Delta \mathbf{w}_i \rangle = \rho \sum_k \frac{\mathbf{x}^k}{n^k} P(i|\mathbf{x}^k) P(\mathbf{x}^k) - \rho \sum_k \mathbf{w}_i P(i|\mathbf{x}^k) P(\mathbf{x}^k) \qquad (4.6.8)$$

which implies that at equilibrium

$$\mathbf{w}_i = \frac{\sum_k \dfrac{\mathbf{x}^k}{n^k} P(i|\mathbf{x}^k) P(\mathbf{x}^k)}{\sum_k P(i|\mathbf{x}^k) P(\mathbf{x}^k)} \qquad (4.6.9)$$

Therefore, the jth component of vector $\mathbf{w}_i$ is given as

$$w_{ij} = \frac{\sum_k \dfrac{1}{n^k} x_j^k P(i|\mathbf{x}^k) P(\mathbf{x}^k)}{\sum_k P(i|\mathbf{x}^k) P(\mathbf{x}^k)} \qquad (4.6.10)$$

Now the following observations can be made. First, note that the denominator of Equation (4.6.10) is the probability that unit i wins averaged over all stimulus patterns. Note further that $\sum_k x_j^k P(i|\mathbf{x}^k) P(\mathbf{x}^k)$ is the probability that $x_j^k = 1$ (active) and unit i is a winner. Thus, assuming that all patterns have the same number of active bits (i.e., $n^k = n_0$ for all k), Bayes' rule $[P(A|B) = P(A, B)/P(B)]$ can be used, and Equation (4.6.10) can be written as

$$w_{ij} = \frac{1}{n_0} P(x_j^k = 1|i) \qquad (4.6.11)$$

which states that at equilibrium, w_{ij} is expected to be proportional to the conditional probability that the jth bit of input $\mathbf{x}^k$ is active given that unit i is a winner.

Next, upon the presentation of a new pattern $\mathbf{x}' \in \{0,1\}^n$ [assuming the equilibrium weight values given by Equation (4.6.9)], unit i will have a weighted sum (activity) of

$$y_i = \mathbf{w}_i^T \mathbf{x}' = \frac{\sum\limits_k \frac{1}{n^k}(\mathbf{x}^k)^T \mathbf{x}' P(i|\mathbf{x}^k) P(\mathbf{x}^k)}{\sum\limits_k P(i|\mathbf{x}^k) P(\mathbf{x}^k)} \tag{4.6.12}$$

or

$$y_i = \mathbf{w}_i^T \mathbf{x}' = \frac{\sum\limits_k z^k P(i|\mathbf{x}^k) P(\mathbf{x}^k)}{\sum\limits_k P(i|\mathbf{x}^k) P(\mathbf{x}^k)} \tag{4.6.13}$$

where $z^k = [(\mathbf{x}^k)^T \mathbf{x}']/n^k$ represents the overlap between stimulus $\mathbf{x}'$ and the kth training pattern $\mathbf{x}^k$. Thus, at equilibrium, a unit responds most strongly to patterns that overlap other patterns to which the unit responds and most weakly to patterns that are far from patterns to which it responds. Note that the conditional probability $P(i|\mathbf{x}^k)$ may be expressed according to the winner-take-all mechanism[8]

$$P(i|\mathbf{x}^k) = \begin{cases} 1 & \mathbf{w}_i^T \mathbf{x}^k > \mathbf{w}_j^T \mathbf{x}^k \qquad \text{for all } j \neq i \\ 0 & \text{otherwise} \end{cases} \tag{4.6.14}$$

Because of the dependency of $P(i|\mathbf{x}^k)$ on $\mathbf{w}_i$, there are many solutions that satisfy the equilibrium relation given in Equation (4.6.9).

Equation (4.6.6) leads the search to one of many stable equilibrium states satisfying Equations (4.6.9) and (4.6.14). In such a state, the ith unit activations $\mathbf{w}_i^T \mathbf{x}'$ become stable (fluctuate minimally), and therefore, $P(i|\mathbf{x}^k)$ becomes stable. A sequence of stimuli might, however, be presented in such a way as to introduce relatively large fluctuations in the $\mathbf{w}_i$ vectors. In this case, the system might move to a new equilibrium state that is, generally, more stable in the sense that $P(i|\mathbf{x}^k)$ becomes unlikely to change values for a very long period of time. Rumelhart and Zipser (1985) gave a measure of the stability of an equilibrium state as the average amount by which the output of the winning units is greater than the response of all the other units averaged over all patterns and all clusters. This stability measure is given by

8. It should be noted that the constraint $\sum\limits_{j=1}^{n} w_{ij} = 1$ realized by the competitive learning rule in Equation (4.6.6) forces the weight vectors of all units to have "approximately" the same length. Therefore, one may approximate the condition $\mathbf{w}_i^T \mathbf{x}^k > \mathbf{w}_j^T \mathbf{x}^k$ in Equation (4.6.14) by $\|\mathbf{w}_i - \mathbf{x}^k\| < \|\mathbf{w}_j - \mathbf{x}^k\|$. This allows us to interpret the probability $P(i, \mathbf{x}^k)$ in Equation (4.6.14) as the ikth component of the cluster membership matrix $\mathbf{M}$ given in Equation (4.6.3).

$$J = \sum_{i*,j} \langle y_{i*} - y_j \rangle \tag{4.6.15}$$

where the averaging is taken over all $\mathbf{x}^k$, and $i*$ is the index of winning units. Note that Equation (4.6.15) can be written as

$$J = \sum_{k} \left[P(\mathbf{x}^k) \sum_{i,j} P(i|\mathbf{x}^k)(\mathbf{w}_i^T - \mathbf{w}_j^T)\mathbf{x}^k \right] \tag{4.6.16}$$

The larger the value of J, the more stable the system is expected to be. Maximizing J can also be viewed as maximizing the overlap among patterns within a group (cluster) while minimizing the overlap among patterns between groups; this is exactly what is required for the clustering of unlabeled data. In geometric terms, J is maximized when the weight vectors point toward maximally compact stimulus (input) regions that are as distant as possible from other such regions.

4.7 Theory of Feature Mapping

The characterization of topological feature-preserving maps has received special attention in the literature (Kohonen, 1982a; Cottrell and Fort, 1986; Ritter and Schulten, 1986, 1988b; Tolat, 1990; Heskes and Kappen, 1993a; Lo et al., 1993; Kohonen, 1993b). In particular, Takeuchi and Amari (1979) and Amari (1980, 1983) have studied a continuous-time dynamical version of this map extensively to investigate the topological relation between the self-organized map and the input space governed by the density $p(\mathbf{x})$, the resolution and stability of the map, and convergence speed. The characterization of a general feature map is difficult, and much of the analysis has been done under simplifying assumptions.

In the following, a one-dimensional version of the self-organizing feature map of Kohonen is characterized following the approach of Ritter and Schulten (1986). A continuous-time dynamical version of Kohonen's map is also described and analyzed.

4.7.1 Characterization of Kohonen's Feature Map

Consider the criterion function $J(\mathbf{w})$ defined by (Ritter and Schulten, 1988a)

$$J(\mathbf{w}) = \tfrac{1}{2} \sum_{k} \sum_{i} \Phi(\mathbf{r}_j - \mathbf{r}_{i*}) \|\mathbf{x}^k - \mathbf{w}_i\|^2 \tag{4.7.1}$$

where $i*$ is the label of the winner unit upon presentation of stimulus (input) $\mathbf{x}^k$, and $\Phi(\mathbf{r}_i - \mathbf{r}_{i*})$ is the neighborhood function that was introduced in Section 3.5. It can be seen that Equation (4.7.1) is an extension of the competitive learning criterion function of Equation (4.6.2).[9] Performing gradient descent on Equation (4.7.1) yields

$$\Delta \mathbf{w}_i = -\rho \nabla J = \rho \sum_k \Phi(\mathbf{r}_i - \mathbf{r}_{i*})(\mathbf{x}^k - \mathbf{w}_i) \tag{4.7.2}$$

which is just the batch-mode version of Kohonen's self-organizing rule in Equation (3.5.1). Thus Kohonen's rule is a stochastic gradient-descent search that leads, on average and for small ρ, to a local minimum of J in Equation (4.7.1). These minima are given as solutions to

$$\Delta \mathbf{w}_i = \sum_k \Phi(\mathbf{r}_i - \mathbf{r}_{i*})(\mathbf{x}^k - \mathbf{w}_i) = 0 \tag{4.7.3}$$

This equation is not easy to solve; it depends on the choice of Φ and the distribution $p(\mathbf{x})$. Actually, what is desired is the global minimum of the criterion function J. Local minima of J are topological defects like kinks in one-dimensional maps and twists in two-dimensional maps (Kohonen, 1989; Geszti, 1990).

The analysis of feature maps becomes more tractable if one replaces Equation (4.7.3) with a continuous version that assumes a continuum of units and where the distribution $p(\mathbf{x})$ appears explicitly, namely,

$$\dot{\mathbf{w}} = \int \Phi(\mathbf{r} - \mathbf{r}^*)[\mathbf{x} - \mathbf{w}(\mathbf{r})]p(\mathbf{x}) \, d\mathbf{x} = 0 \tag{4.7.4}$$

where $\mathbf{r}^* = \mathbf{r}^*(\mathbf{x})$ is the coordinate vector of the winning unit upon presentation of input $\mathbf{x}$.

An implicit partial differential equation for $\mathbf{w}$ can be derived from Equation (4.7.4) (Ritter and Schulten, 1986). However, for the case of two- or higher-dimensional maps, no explicit solutions exist for $\mathbf{w}(\mathbf{r})$ given an arbitrary $p(\mathbf{x})$. On the other hand, solutions of Equation (4.7.4) are relatively easy to find for the one-dimensional map with scalar r and a given input distribution $p(x)$. Here, the equilibrium w^* satisfies (Ritter and Schulten, 1986)

$$\left| \frac{dw^*}{dr} \right| \propto [p(w)]^{-2/3} \tag{4.7.5}$$

which, in turn, satisfies the implicit differential equation corresponding to Equation (4.7.4), given by (assuming a sharply peaked symmetric Φ)

---

9. For other forms of criterion functions for self-organizing maps, the reader may consult Tolat (1990), Kohonen (1991), and Heskes and Kappen (1993a).

$$\frac{3}{2}p(w)\frac{d^2w}{dr^2} + \frac{dp(w)}{dw}\left(\frac{dw}{dr}\right)^2 = 0 \tag{4.7.6}$$

In Equations (4.7.5) and (4.7.6), the term $p(w)$ is given by $p(x)|_{x=w}$. Equation (4.7.5) shows that the density of the units in w space is proportional to $[p(w)]^{2/3}$ around point r. This verifies the density-preserving feature of the map. Ideally, however, we would have $\frac{dr}{dw} \propto p(w)$ for zero distortion. Therefore, a self-organizing feature map tends to undersample high-probability regions and oversample low-probability ones.

Finally, one may obtain the equilibria w^* by solving Equation (4.7.6). The local stability of some of these equilibria is ensured (with a probability approaching 1) if the learning coefficient $\rho = \rho(t)$ is sufficiently small, positive, and decays according to the following necessary and sufficient conditions (Ritter and Schulten, 1988b):

$$\lim_{t\to\infty}\int_0^t \rho(\tau)\,d\tau = \infty \tag{4.7.7a}$$

and

$$\lim_{t\to\infty}\rho(t) = 0 \tag{4.7.7b}$$

In particular, the decay law $\rho(t) \propto t^{-\alpha}$ with $0 < \alpha \leq 1$ ensures convergence. For laws with $\alpha > 1$ or exponential decay laws, Equation (4.7.7a) is not fulfilled, and some residual error remains even in the limit $t \to \infty$. It also can be shown that during convergence, the map first becomes untangled and fairly even and then moves into a *refinement phase* where it adapts to the details of $p(x)$. Occasionally, the "untangling" phase can slow convergence, because some types of tangles (e.g., kinks and twists) can take a long time to untangle. Geszti (1990) suggested the use of a strongly asymmetric neighborhood function Φ to speed up learning by breaking the symmetry effects responsible for slow untangling of kinks and twists.

4.7.2   Self-Organizing Neural Fields

Consider a continuum of units arranged as an infinite two-dimensional array (neural field). Each point (unit) on this array may be represented by a position vector $\mathbf{r}$ and has an associated potential $u(\mathbf{r})$. The output of the unit at $\mathbf{r}$ is assumed to be a nonlinear function of its potential $y(\mathbf{r}) = f[u(\mathbf{r})]$, where f is either a monotonically nondecreasing positive saturating activation function or a step function. Associated with each unit $\mathbf{r}$ is a set of input weights $\mathbf{w}(\mathbf{r})$ and another set of lateral weights $\alpha(\mathbf{r},\mathbf{r}') = \alpha(\mathbf{r} - \mathbf{r}')$. This lateral weight distribution is assumed to be of the on-center,

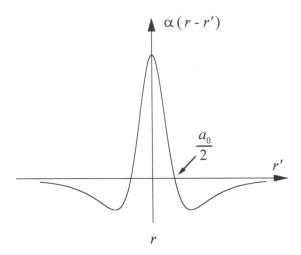

Figure 4.7.1
One-dimensional plot of a neural field's lateral weight distribution.

off-surround type, as shown in Figure 4.7.1 for the one-dimensional case. Here, a unit
at position $\mathbf{r}$ makes excitatory connections with all its neighbors located within a
distance $a_0/2$ from $\mathbf{r}$ and makes inhibitory connections with all other units.

The dynamics of the neural field potential $u(\mathbf{r}, t)$ are given by

$$\tau \dot{u}(\mathbf{r}, t) = -u(\mathbf{r}, t) + \alpha(\mathbf{r} - \mathbf{r}') \circ y(\mathbf{r}) + \mathbf{w}^T(\mathbf{r})\mathbf{x} + h \qquad (4.7.8)$$

where

$$\alpha \circ y \triangleq \int_{\text{neural field}} \alpha(\mathbf{r} - \mathbf{r}')f[u(\mathbf{r}', t)]\, d\mathbf{r}' \qquad (4.7.9)$$

and h is a constant-bias field. In Equation (4.7.8), it is assumed that the potential $u(\mathbf{r}, t)$
decays with time constant τ to the resting potential h in the absence of any stimula-
tion. Also, it is assumed that this potential increases in proportion to the total stimuli
$s(\mathbf{r}, \mathbf{x})$, which is the sum of the lateral stimuli $\alpha(\mathbf{r} - \mathbf{r}') \circ y(\mathbf{r})$ and the input stimuli $\mathbf{w}^T\mathbf{x}$
due to the input signal $\mathbf{x} \in R^n$. A conceptual diagram for this neural field is shown in
Figure 4.7.2.

In Equation (4.7.8), the rates of change of α and $\mathbf{w}$, if any, are assumed to be much
slower than that of the neural field potential. The input signal (pattern) $\mathbf{x}$ is a random
time sequence, and it is assumed that a pattern $\mathbf{x}$ is chosen according to probability
density $p(\mathbf{x})$. Also, it is assumed that inputs are applied to the neural field for a time
duration that is longer than the time constant τ of the neural field potential. On the

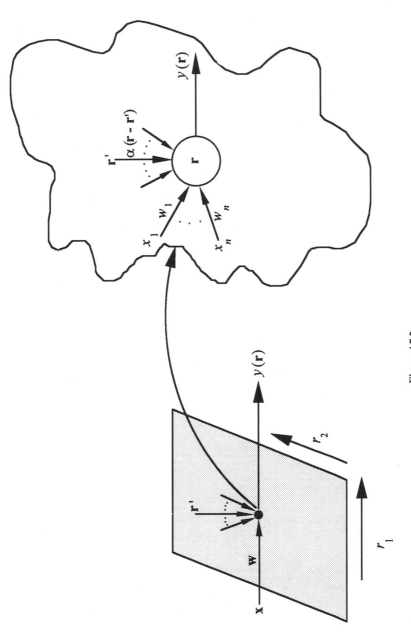

Figure 4.7.2
Self-organizing neural field.

other hand, the duration of stimulus $\mathbf{x}$ is assumed to be much shorter than the time constant τ' of the weight $\mathbf{w}$. Thus the potential distribution $u(\mathbf{r}, t)$ can be considered to change in a quasi-equilibrium manner denoted by $u(\mathbf{r}, \mathbf{x})$.

An initial excitation pattern applied to the neural field changes according to the dynamics given in Equation (4.7.8) and eventually converges to one of the equilibrium solutions. Stable equilibrium solutions are the potential fields $u(\mathbf{r})$ that the neural field can retain persistently under a constant input $\mathbf{x}$. The equilibria of Equation (4.7.8) must satisfy $\dot{u}(\mathbf{r}, t) = 0$ or

$$u^*(\mathbf{r}) = s(\mathbf{r}, u^*) + h \tag{4.7.10}$$

where $s(\mathbf{r}, u^*)$ is the total stimuli at equilibrium. When the lateral connections distribution $\alpha(\mathbf{r} - \mathbf{r}')$ is strongly off-surround inhibitory, given any $\mathbf{x}$, only a local excitation pattern is aroused as a stable equilibrium that satisfies Equation (4.7.10) (Amari, 1990). Here, a *local excitation* is a pattern where the excitation is concentrated on units in a small local region; i.e., $u^*(\mathbf{r})$ is positive only for a small neighborhood centered at a maximally excited unit $\mathbf{r}_0$. Thus $u^*(\mathbf{r}, \mathbf{x})$ represents a mapping from the input space onto the neural field.

Let us now look at the dynamics of the self-organizing process. It is best to start by assuming a particular update rule for the input weights of the neural field. One biologically plausible update rule is the Hebbian rule:

$$\tau' \dot{\mathbf{w}}(\mathbf{r}, \mathbf{x}, t) = -\lambda \mathbf{w} + \rho f(u^*)\mathbf{x} \tag{4.7.11}$$

where $f(u^*) = f[u^*(\mathbf{r}, \mathbf{x})]$ is the neural field's equilibrium output activity due to input $\mathbf{x}$. Equation (4.7.11) uses the earlier assumption $\tau' \gg \tau$. Next, strong mixing is assumed in Equation (4.7.11), which allows the average learning equation (absorbing τ' in ρ and in λ) to be expressed as

$$\dot{\mathbf{w}} = -\lambda \mathbf{w} + \rho \langle f(u^*)\mathbf{x} \rangle = -\lambda \mathbf{w} + \rho \int \mathbf{x}' f[u^*(\mathbf{r}, \mathbf{x}')] p(\mathbf{x}') \, d\mathbf{x}' \tag{4.7.12}$$

where the averaging is over all possible $\mathbf{x}$. The equilibria of Equation (4.7.12) are given by

$$\mathbf{w}^* = \frac{\rho}{\lambda} \langle f(u^*)\mathbf{x} \rangle \tag{4.7.13}$$

If Equation (4.7.12) is now transposed and multiplied by an arbitrary input vector $\mathbf{x}$, an equation for the change in input stimuli results:

$$\dot{\mathbf{w}}^T \mathbf{x} = -\lambda \mathbf{w}^T \mathbf{x} + \rho \int (\mathbf{x}^T \mathbf{x}') f[u^*(\mathbf{r}, \mathbf{x}')] p(\mathbf{x}') \, d\mathbf{x}' \tag{4.7.14}$$

The vector inner product $\mathbf{x}^T\mathbf{x}'$ represents the similarity of two input signals $\mathbf{x}$ and $\mathbf{x}'$ and hence the topology of the signal space (Takeuchi and Amari, 1979). Note how Equation (4.7.14) relates the topology of the input stimulus set $\{\mathbf{x}\}$ with that of the neural field.

On the other hand, if one assumes a learning rule where a unit $\mathbf{r}$ updates its input weight vector in proportion to the correlation of its equilibrium potential $u^*(\mathbf{r}, \mathbf{x})$ and the difference $\mathbf{x} - \mathbf{w}(\mathbf{r})$, one arrives at the average differential equation

$$\dot{\mathbf{w}}(\mathbf{r}, \mathbf{x}) = \rho \langle u^*(\mathbf{r}, \mathbf{x})[\mathbf{x} - \mathbf{w}(\mathbf{r})]\rangle \qquad (4.7.15)$$

This learning rule is equivalent to the averaged-continuum version of Kohonen's self-organizing feature map in Equation (4.7.2) if one views the potential distribution $u^*(\mathbf{r}, \mathbf{x})$ as the weighting neighborhood function Φ. Here, self-organization will emerge if the dynamics of the potential field evolve such that the quasi-stable equilibrium potential u^* starts positive for all $\mathbf{r}$ and then monotonically and slowly shrinks in diameter for positive time. This may be accomplished through proper control of the bias field h, as described below.

In general, it is difficult to solve Equations (4.7.8) and (4.7.12) [or Equation (4.7.15)]. However, some properties of the formation of feature maps are revealed from these equations for the special, but revealing, case of a one-dimensional neural field (Takeuchi and Amari, 1979; Amari, 1980, 1983). The dynamics of the potential field in Equation (4.7.8) for a one-dimensional neural field were analyzed in detail by Amari (1977b) and Kishimoto and Amari (1979) for a step-activation function and a continuous monotonically nondecreasing activation function, respectively. It was shown that with $\alpha(r - r')$ as shown in Figure 4.7.1 and $f(u) = \text{step}(u)$, there exist stable equilibrium solutions $u^*(r)$ for the $\mathbf{x} = 0$ case. The 0-solution potential field $u^*(r) < 0$ and the ∞-solution field $u^*(r) > 0$ are among these stable solutions. The 0-solution is stable if and only if $h < 0$. On the other hand, the ∞-solution is stable if and only if $h > -2A(\infty)$, where $A(\infty) = \lim\limits_{a \to \infty} A(a)$, with $A(a)$ as defined below. Local excitations (also known as a-solutions) where $u^*(r)$ is positive only over a finite interval $[a_1, a_2]$ of the neural field are also possible. An a-solution exists if and only if $h + A(a) = 0$. Here, $A(a)$ is the definite integral defined by

$$A(a) = \int_0^a \alpha(r)\, dr \qquad (4.7.16)$$

and plotted in Figure 4.7.3. Amari (see also Krekelberg and Kok, 1993) also showed that a single a-solution can exist for the case of a nonzero input stimulus and that the corresponding active region of the neural field is centered at the unit r receiving the

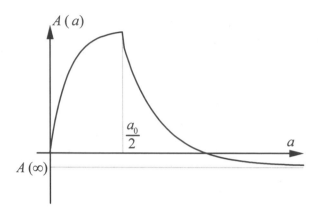

Figure 4.7.3
A plot of $A(a)$ of Equation (4.7.16).

maximum input. Furthermore, the width a of this active region is a monotonically decreasing function of the bias field h. Thus one may exploit the fact that the field potential/neighborhood function $u^*(r, \mathbf{x})$ is controlled by the bias field h in order to control the convergence of the self-organizing process. Here, the uniform bias field h is started at a positive value $h > -2A(\infty)$ and is slowly decreased toward negative values. This, in turn, causes u^* to start at the ∞-solution and then gradually move through a-solutions with decreasing width a until, ultimately, u^* becomes the 0-solution. For further analysis of the self-organizing process in a neural field, the reader is referred to Zhang (1991).

Kohonen (1993a, 1993b) proposed a self-organizing map model for which he gives physiologic justification. The model is similar to Amari's self-organizing neural field except that it uses a discrete two-dimensional array of units. The model assumes sharp self-on, off-surround lateral interconnections so that the neural activity of the map is stabilized where the unit receiving the maximum excitation becomes active and all other units are inactive. Kohonen's model employs unit potential dynamics similar to those of Equation (4.7.8). On the other hand, Kohonen uses a learning equation more complex than those in Equations (4.7.12) and (4.7.15). This equation is given for the ith unit weight vector by the pseudo-Hebbian learning rule

$$\dot{\mathbf{w}}_i = \left(\mathbf{x} - \lambda \mathbf{w}_i \sum_r w_{ir} x_r \right) \sum_l h_{il} y_l \qquad (4.7.17)$$

where λ is a positive constant. The term $\sum_l h_{il} y_l$ in Equation (4.7.17) models a natural "transient" neighborhood function. It represents a weighted sum of the output activities y_l of nearby units, which describes the strength of the diffuse chemical effect of cell l on cell i; h_{il} is a function of the distance of these units. This weighted sum of output activities replaces the output activity of the same cell y_i in Hebb's learning rule. On the other hand, the $-\lambda w_i \sum_r w_{ir} x_r$ term acts as a stabilizing term that models "forgetting" effects or disturbance due to adjacent synapses. Typically, forgetting effects in w_i are proportional to the weight w_i itself. In addition, if the disturbance caused by synaptic site r is mediated through the postsynaptic potential, the forgetting effect must further be proportional to $w_{ir} x_r$. This phenomenon is modeled by $\sum_r w_{ir} x_r$ in the forgetting term. Here, the summation is taken over a subset of the synapses of unit i that are located near the jth synapse w_{ij} and approximately act as one collectively interacting set. The major difference between the learning rules in Equations (4.7.17) and (4.7.12) is that, in the former, the neighborhood function is determined by a "transient" activity due to a diffusive chemical effect of nearby cell potentials, whereas it is determined by a stable region of neural field potential in the latter.

Under the assumption that the index r ranges over all components of the input signal $\mathbf{x}$, and regarding $\sum_l h_{il} y_l = \alpha$ as a positive scalar independent of $\mathbf{w}$ and $\mathbf{x}$, the vector form of Equation (4.7.18) takes the Riccati differential equation form

$$\dot{\mathbf{w}} = \alpha \mathbf{x} - \beta \mathbf{w}(\mathbf{w}^T \mathbf{x}) \qquad (4.7.18)$$

where $\beta = \alpha\lambda > 0$, Now, multiplying both sides of Equation (4.7.18) by $2\mathbf{w}^T$ leads to the differential equation

$$2\mathbf{w}^T \dot{\mathbf{w}} = \frac{d\|\mathbf{w}\|^2}{dt} = 2\mathbf{w}^T \mathbf{x}(\alpha - \beta\|\mathbf{w}\|^2) \qquad (4.7.19)$$

Thus, for arbitrary $\mathbf{x}$ with $\mathbf{w}^T \mathbf{x} > 0$, Equation (4.7.19) converges to $\|\mathbf{w}^*\| = \alpha/\beta$. On the other hand, the solution for the direction of $\mathbf{w}^*$ cannot be determined in closed form from the deterministic differential Equation (4.7.18). However, a solution for the expected value of $\mathbf{w}$ may be found if Equation (4.7.18) is treated as a stochastic differential equation with strong mixing in accordance to the discussion of Section 4.3. Taking the expected value of both sides of Equation (4.7.18) and solving for its equilibrium points (by setting $\langle \dot{\mathbf{w}} \rangle = 0$) gives

$$\mathbf{w}^* = \sqrt{\frac{\alpha}{\beta}} \frac{\langle \mathbf{x} \rangle}{\|\langle \mathbf{x} \rangle\|} \qquad (4.7.20)$$

Furthermore, this equilibrium point can be shown to be stable (Kohonen, 1989).

From the preceding analysis, it can be concluded that the synaptic weight vector $\mathbf{w}$ is automatically normalized to the length $\sqrt{\alpha/\beta}$ independent of the input signal $\mathbf{x}$ and that $\mathbf{w}$ rotates such that its average direction is aligned with the mean of $\mathbf{x}$. This is the expected result of a self-organizing map when a uniform nondecreasing neighborhood function is used. In general, though, the neighborhood term $\sum_l h_{il} y_l$ is nonuniform and time varying, which makes the analysis of Equation (4.7.17) much more difficult.

4.8 Generalization

Chapter 2 analyzed the capabilities of some neural network architectures for realizing arbitrary mappings. It was seen that a feedforward neural net with a single hidden layer having an arbitrary number of sigmoidal activation units is capable of approximating any mapping (or continuous multivariate function) to within any desired degree of accuracy. The results of Chapter 2 on the computational capabilities of layered neural networks say nothing about the synthesis/learning procedure needed to set the interconnection weights of these networks. What remains to be seen is whether such networks are capable of finding the necessary weight configuration for a given mapping by employing a suitable learning algorithm.

Later chapters in this book address the question of learning in specific neural network architectures by extending some of the learning rules covered in Chapter 3. The remainder of this chapter addresses two important issues related to learning in neural networks: generalization and complexity. The following discussion is general in nature, and thus it holds for a wide range of neural network paradigms.

Generalization is measured by the ability of a trained network to generate the correct output for a new randomly chosen input drawn from the same probability density $p(\mathbf{x})$ governing the training set. In this section, two cases are considered: average generalization and worst-case generalization. This section also considers the generalization capabilities of stochastic neural networks.

4.8.1 Generalization Capabilities of Deterministic Networks

One important performance measure of trainable neural networks is the size of the training set needed to bound their generalization error below some specified number. Schwartz et al. (1990) gave a theoretical framework for calculating the average probability of correct generalization for a neural net trained with a training set of size m. Here, the averaging is over all possible networks (of fixed architecture) consistent with the training set, and the only assumptions about the network's architecture are that it is deterministic (employs deterministic units) and that it is a universal architecture (or faithful model) of the class of functions/mappings being learned. It is assumed that these functions are of the form $f: R^n \to \{0, 1\}$, but the ideas can be extended to multiple and/or continuous-valued outputs as well.

The following analysis is based on the theoretical framework of Schwartz et al. (1990), and it also draws on some clarifications given by Hertz et al. (1991). The main result of this analysis is rather surprising: One can calculate the average probability of correct generalization for any training set of size m if one knows a certain function that can (in theory) be calculated before training begins. However, it should be kept in mind that this result is only meaningful when interpreted in an average sense and does not necessarily represent the typical situation encountered in a specific training scheme.

Consider a class of networks with a certain fixed architecture specified by the number of layers, the number of units within each layer, and the interconnectivity pattern between layers. The quantity V_0 can be defined as

$$V_0 = \int \rho(\mathbf{w}) \, d\mathbf{w} \tag{4.8.1}$$

which stands for the total "volume" of the weight space, where $\mathbf{w}$ represents the weights of an arbitrary network, and $\rho(\mathbf{w})$ is some a priori weight probability density function. Thus each network is represented as a point $\mathbf{w}$ in weight space that implements a function $f_{\mathbf{w}}(\mathbf{x})$. We may now partition the weight space into a set of disjoint regions, one for each function $f_{\mathbf{w}}$ that this class of networks can implement. The volume of the region of weight space that implements a particular function $f(\mathbf{x})$ is given by

$$V_0(f) = \int \rho(\mathbf{w}) \theta_f(\mathbf{w}) \, d\mathbf{w} \tag{4.8.2}$$

where

$$\theta_f(\mathbf{w}) = \begin{cases} 1 & \text{if } f_{\mathbf{w}}(\mathbf{x}) = f(\mathbf{x}) \quad \text{for all } \mathbf{x} \\ 0 & \text{otherwise} \end{cases}$$

Each time an example $\{\mathbf{x}^k, f_d(\mathbf{x}^k)\}$ of a desired function f_d is presented and is successfully learned (supervised learning is assumed), the weight vector $\mathbf{w}$ is modified so that it enters the region of weight space that is compatible with the presented example. If m examples are learned, then the volume of this region is given by

$$V_m = \int \rho(\mathbf{w}) \prod_{k=1}^{m} I(f_{\mathbf{w}}, \mathbf{x}^k) \, d\mathbf{w} \tag{4.8.3}$$

where

$$I(f_{\mathbf{w}}, \mathbf{x}^k) = \begin{cases} 1 & \text{if } f_{\mathbf{w}}(\mathbf{x}^k) = f_d(\mathbf{x}^k) \\ 0 & \text{otherwise} \end{cases}$$

The region V_m represents the total volume of weight space which realizes the desired function f_d as well as all other functions f that agree with f_d on the desired training set. Thus, if a new input is presented to the trained network, it will be ambiguous with respect to a number of functions represented by V_m (recall the discussion on ambiguity for the simple case of a single threshold gate in Section 1.5). As the number of learned examples m is increased, the expected ambiguity decreases.

Next, the volume of weight space consistent with both the training examples and a "particular" function f is given by

$$V_m(f) = \int \rho(\mathbf{w})\theta_f(\mathbf{w}) \prod_{k=1}^m I(f_{\mathbf{w}}, \mathbf{x}^k)\, d\mathbf{w}$$

$$= V_0(f) \prod_{k=1}^m I(f, \mathbf{x}^k) \tag{4.8.4}$$

where Equation (4.8.2) was used. Note that $f_{\mathbf{w}}$ in I has been replaced by f and that the product term factors outside the integral.[10] Now, assuming independent input vectors $\mathbf{x}^k$ generated randomly from distribution $p(\mathbf{x})$, the factors $I(f, \mathbf{x}^k)$ in Equation (4.8.4) are independent. Thus averaging $V_m(f)$ over all $\mathbf{x}^k$ gives

$$\langle V_m(f) \rangle = V_0(f)\langle I(f, \mathbf{x}) \rangle^m$$

$$= V_0(f)g(f)^m \tag{4.8.5}$$

The quantity $g(f)$ takes on values between 0 and 1. It is referred to as the *generalization ability* of f; i.e., $g(f)$ may be viewed as the probability that $f(\mathbf{x}) = f_d(\mathbf{x})$ for an input $\mathbf{x}$ randomly chosen from $p(\mathbf{x})$. As an example, for a completely specified n-input Boolean function f_d, $g(f)$ is given by (assuming that all 2^n inputs are equally likely)

$$g(f) = \frac{2^n - d_H(f, f_d)}{2^n}$$

where $d_H(f, f_d)$ is the number of bits by which f and f_d differ.

---

10. For the case of continuous-valued outputs, one would have to replace the sharp function $I(f, \mathbf{x}^k)$ in Equation (4.8.4) by a smooth function $\exp(-\beta\varepsilon^k)$ of the error ε^k in the kth example, $\varepsilon^k = [f_{\mathbf{w}}(\mathbf{x}^k) - f_d(\mathbf{x}^k)]^2$. This function falls off gradually from 1 if there is no error, to 0 for large error, and with a rate governed by the parameter β. In this case, the analysis can be performed based on statistical mechanics methods (Tishby et al., 1989)

Let us define the probability $P_m(f)$ that a particular function f can be implemented after training on m examples of f_d. This probability is equal to the average fraction of the remaining weight space that f occupies:

$$P_m(f) = \left\langle \frac{V_m(f)}{V_m} \right\rangle \approx \frac{\langle V_m(f) \rangle}{\langle V_m \rangle} \propto V_0(f)g(f)^m \tag{4.8.6}$$

The approximation in Equation (4.8.6) is based on the assumption that V_m does not vary much with the particular training sequence; i.e., $V_m \approx \langle V_m \rangle$ for each probable sequence. This assumption is expected to be valid as long as m is small compared with the total number of possible input combinations.

Good generalization requires that $P_m(f)$ be small. Let us use Equation (4.8.6) to compute the distribution of generalization ability $g(f)$ across all possible functions after successful training with m examples:

$$\rho_m(g) = \sum_f P_m(f)\delta[g - g(f)] \propto g^m \sum_f V_0(f)\delta[g - g(f)] \propto g^m\rho_0(g) \tag{4.8.7}$$

Note that an exact $\rho_m(g)$ can be derived by dividing the right-hand side of Equation (4.8.7) by $\int_0^1 g^m\rho_0(g)\,dg$. The preceding result is interesting because it allows one to compute, before learning, the distribution of generalization ability after training with m examples. The form of Equation (4.8.7) shows that the distribution $\rho_m(g)$ tends to get concentrated at higher and higher values of g as more and more examples are learned. Thus, during learning, although the allowed volume of weight (or function) space shrinks, the remaining regions tend to have large generalization ability.

Another useful measure of generalization is the average generalization ability $G(m)$ given by

$$G(m) = \int_0^1 g\rho_m(g)\,dg = \frac{\displaystyle\int_0^1 g^{m+1}\rho_0(g)\,dg}{\displaystyle\int_0^1 g^m\rho_0(g)\,dg} \tag{4.8.8}$$

which is the ratio between the $m + 1$ and the mth moments of $\rho_0(g)$ and can be computed if $\rho_0(g)$ is given or estimated. $G(m)$ gives the entire "learning curve"; i.e., it gives the average expected success rate as a function of m. Equation (4.8.8) allows us to predict the number of examples m necessary to train the network to a desired average generalization performance. We also may define the average prediction error as $1 - G(m)$. The asymptotic behavior $(m \to \infty)$ of the average prediction error is determined by the form of the initial distribution $\rho_0(g)$ near $g = 1$. If a finite gap γ between $g = 1$ and the next highest g for which $\rho_0(g)$ is nonzero exists, then the prediction error decays to 1 exponentially as $\exp(-m/\gamma)$. If, on the other hand, there is no such gap in $\rho_0(g)$, then the prediction error decays as $1/m$. These two behaviors of the learning curve have also been verified through numerical experiments. The nature of the gap in the distribution of generalizations near the region of perfect generalization ($g = 1$) is not completely understood. These gaps have been detected in experiments involving the learning of binary mappings (Cohn and Tesauro, 1991, 1992). It is speculated that such a gap could be due to the dynamic effects of the learning process, where the learning algorithm may, for some reason, avoid the observed near-perfect solutions. Another possibility is that the gap is inherent in the nature of the binary mappings themselves.

This approach, though theoretically interesting, is of little practical use for estimating m, since it requires knowledge of the distribution $\rho_0(g)$, whose estimation is computationally expensive. It also gives results that are only valid in an average sense and does not necessarily represent the typical situation encountered in a specific training scheme.

Next, let us summarize a result that explores the generalization ability of a deterministic feedforward neural network in the worst case. Here also, the case of learning a binary-valued output function $f: R^n \to \{0, 1\}$ is treated. Consider a set of m labeled training example pairs $(\mathbf{x}, y)$ selected randomly from some arbitrary probability distribution $p(\mathbf{x}, y)$, with $\mathbf{x} \in R^n$ and $y = f(\mathbf{x}) \in \{0, 1\}$. Also consider a single-hidden-layer feedforward neural net with k LTGs and d weights that has been trained on the m examples so that at least a fraction $1 - (\varepsilon/2)$, where $0 < \varepsilon \leq \frac{1}{8}$, of the examples are correctly classified. Then, with a probability approaching 1, this network will correctly classify the fraction $1 - \varepsilon$ of future random test examples drawn from $p(\mathbf{x}, y)$ as long as (Baum and Haussler, 1989)

$$m \geq O\left(\frac{d}{\varepsilon}\log_2\frac{k}{\varepsilon}\right) \tag{4.8.9}$$

Ignoring the log term, Equation (4.8.9) may be written, to a first-order approximation, as

$$\varepsilon \propto \frac{d}{m} \tag{4.8.10}$$

which requires $m \gg d$ for good generalization. It is interesting to note that this is the same condition for "good" generalization (low ambiguity) for a single LTG derived by Cover (1965) (refer to Section 1.5) and obtained empirically by Widrow (1987). Therefore, one may note that in the limit of large m, the architecture of the network is not important in determining the worst-case generalization behavior; what matters is the ratio of the number of degrees of freedom (weights) to the training set size. On the other hand, none of the preceding theories may hold for the case of a small training set. In this later case, the size and architecture of the network and the learning scheme all play a role in determining generalization quality (see the next chapter for more details). It should also be noted that the architecture of the net can play an important role in determining the speed of convergence of a given class of learning methods, as discussed later in Section 4.9.

Similar results for worst-case generalization are reported in Blumer et al. (1989). A more general learning curve based on statistical physics and VC dimension theories (Vapnik and Chervonenkis, 1971) that applies to a general class of networks can be found in Haussler et al. (1992). For generalization results with noisy target signals, the reader is referred to Amari et al. (1992).

4.8.2   Generalization in Stochastic Networks

This section deals with the asymptotic learning behavior of a general stochastic learning dichotomy machine (classifier). What is desired is a relation between the generalization error and the training error in terms of the number of free parameters of the machine (machine complexity) and the size of the training set. The results in this section are based on the work of Amari and Murata (1993) [see also Amari (1993)]. Consider a parametric family of stochastic machines where a machine is specified by a d-dimensional parameter vector $\mathbf{w}$ such that the probability of output y, given an input $\mathbf{x}$, is specified by $P(y|\mathbf{x}, \mathbf{w})$. As an example, one may assume the machine to be a stochastic multilayer neural network parameterized by a weight vector $\mathbf{w} \in R^d$, which, for a given input $\mathbf{x} \in R^n$, emits a binary output $y \in \{-1, 1\}$ with probability

$$P(y = 1|\mathbf{x}, \mathbf{w}) = f[g(\mathbf{x}, \mathbf{w})] \tag{4.8.11}$$

and

$$P(y = -1|\mathbf{x}, \mathbf{w}) = 1 - f[g(\mathbf{x}, \mathbf{w})]$$

where

$$f(g) = \frac{1}{1 + e^{-2\beta g}} \tag{4.8.12}$$

and $g(\mathbf{x}, \mathbf{w})$ may be considered as a smooth deterministic function (e.g., superposition of multivariate sigmoid functions typically employed in layered neural nets). Thus, in this example, the stochastic nature of the machine is determined by its stochastic output unit.

Assume that there exists a true machine that can be faithfully represented by one of the preceding family of stochastic machines with parameter $\mathbf{w}^0$. The true machine receives inputs $\mathbf{x}^k$, $k = 1, 2, \ldots, m$, which are randomly generated according to a fixed but unknown probability distribution $p(\mathbf{x})$, and emits y^k. The maximum likelihood estimator (refer to Section 3.1.5 for definition) characterized by the machine $\hat{\mathbf{w}}^m$ will be our first candidate machine. This machine predicts y for a given $\mathbf{x}$ with probability $P(y|\mathbf{x}, \hat{\mathbf{w}}^m)$. An entropic loss function is used to evaluate the generalization of a trained machine for a new example $(\mathbf{x}^{m+1}, y^{m+1})$.

Let ε_{gen} be the average predictive entropy (also known as the *average entropic loss*) of a trained machine parameterized by $\hat{\mathbf{w}}^m$ for a new example $(\mathbf{x}^{m+1}, y^{m+1})$:

$$\varepsilon_{\text{gen}}(m) = -\langle \log P(y^{m+1}|\mathbf{x}^{m+1}, \hat{\mathbf{w}}^m) \rangle \tag{4.8.13}$$

Similarly, $\varepsilon_{\text{train}}$ is defined as the average entropic loss over the training examples used to obtain $\hat{\mathbf{w}}^m$:

$$\varepsilon_{\text{train}}(m) = -\frac{1}{m} \sum_{k=1}^{m} \langle \log P(y^k|\mathbf{x}^k, \hat{\mathbf{w}}^m) \rangle \tag{4.8.14}$$

Finally, let H_0 be the average entropic error of the true machine:

$$H_0 = -\langle \log P(y|\mathbf{x}, \hat{\mathbf{w}}^0) \rangle \tag{4.8.15}$$

Amari and Murata proved the following theorem for training and generalization error.

THEOREM 4.8.1 (Amari and Murata, 1993)   The asymptotic learning curve for the entropic training error is given by

$$\varepsilon_{\text{train}}(m) = H_0 - \frac{d}{2m} \tag{4.8.16}$$

and for the entropic generalization error by

$$\varepsilon_{\text{gen}}(m) = H_0 + \frac{d}{2m} \tag{4.8.17}$$

The proof of Theorem 4.8.1 uses standard techniques of asymptotic statistics and is omitted here. [The reader is referred to the original paper by Amari and Murata (1993) for such proof.]

In general, H_0 is unknown, and it can be eliminated from Equation (4.8.17) by substituting its value from Equation (4.8.16). This gives

$$\varepsilon_{gen}(m) = \varepsilon_{train}(m) + \frac{d}{m} \qquad (4.8.18)$$

which shows that for a faithful stochastic machine and in the limit of $m \gg d$, the generalization error approaches that of the trained machine on m examples, which from Equation (4.8.16) is the classification error H_0 of the true machine.

Again, the particular network architecture is of no importance here as long as it allows for a faithful realization of the true machine and $m \gg d$. It is interesting to note that this result is similar to the worst-case learning curve for deterministic machines [Equation (4.8.10)] when the training error is zero. The result is also in agreement with Cover's result on classifier ambiguity in Equation (1.5.3), where the d/m term in Equation (4.8.18) may be viewed as the probability of ambiguous response on the $m + 1$ input. A number of techniques have been proposed in the literature in order to enhance the generalization ability of neural networks. These techniques include *weight decay*, *cross-validation*, and *weight sharing*, which are covered in Section 5.2.

4.9 Complexity of Learning

This section deals with the computational complexity of learning: How much computation is required to learn (exactly or approximately to some "acceptable" degree) an arbitrary mapping in a multilayer neural network? In other words, is there an algorithm that is computationally "efficient" for training layered neural networks? Here, it is assumed that the desired learning algorithm is a supervised one, which implies that the training set is labeled. Also, it is assumed that the neural network has an arbitrary architecture but with no feedback connections.

Learning in artificial neural networks is hard. More precisely, the loading of an arbitrary mapping onto a "faithful" neural network architecture requires exponential time irrespective of the learning algorithm used (batch or adaptive). Judd (1987, 1990) showed that the learning problem in neural networks is NP-complete, even for approximate learning; i.e., in the worst case, one will not be able to do much better than just randomly exhausting all combinations of weight settings to see if one happens to work. Therefore, as the problem size increases (i.e., as the input pattern dimension or the number of input patterns increases), the training time scales up exponentially in the size of the problem. Moreover, it has been shown (Blum and Rivest, 1989) that training a simple n-input, three-unit, two-layer net of LTG's can be NP-complete in the worst case when learning a given set of examples. Consider the class of functions $f: R^n \to \{0, 1\}$ defined on a collection of m arbitrary points in R^n. It has been shown that the problem of whether there exist two hyperplanes that separate them is

NP-complete (Megiddo, 1986); i.e., the training of a net with two-hidden n-input LTGs and a single-output LTG on examples of such functions is exponential in time, in the worst case, even if a solution exists. Blum and Rivest (1992) extend this result to the case of Boolean functions. They also showed that learning Boolean functions with a two-layer feedforward network of k-hidden units (k bounded by some polynomial in n) and one output unit (which computes the AND function) is NP-complete.

However, these theoretical results do not rule out the possibility of finding a polynomial-time algorithm for the training of certain classes of problems onto certain carefully selected architectures. Blum and Rivest (1992) gave an example of two networks trained on the same task such that training the first is NP-complete, but the second can be trained in polynomial time. Also, the class of linearly separable mappings can be trained in polynomial time if single-layer LTG nets are employed (only a single unit is needed if the mapping has a single output). This is easy to prove, since one can use linear programming (Karmarkar, 1984) to compute the weights and thresholds of such nets in polynomial time. One also can use this fact and construct layered networks that have polynomial learning time complexity for certain classes of nonlinearly separable mappings. This is illustrated next.

Consider a set F of nonlinearly separable functions $f: R^n \rightarrow \{0, 1\}$ or $f: \{0, 1\}^n \rightarrow \{0, 1\}$ that has the following two properties: (1) there exists at least one layered neural net architecture for which loading m training pairs $\{\mathbf{x}, y_d\}$ of $f(\mathbf{x})$ is NP-complete, and (2) there exists a fixed dimensionality expansion process D that maps points $\mathbf{x}$ in R^n to points $\mathbf{z}$ in R^d such that d is bounded by some polynomial in n [e.g., $d = O(n^2)$] and that the m training examples $\{\mathbf{z}, y_d\}$ representing $f(\mathbf{x})$ in the expanded space R^d are linearly separable. This set F is not empty; Blum and Rivest (1992) gave examples of functions in F. Figure 4.9.1 depicts a layered architecture that can realize any function in F. Here, a fixed preprocessing layer, labeled D in Figure 4.9.1, imple-

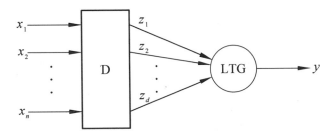

Figure 4.9.1
A layered architecture consisting of a fixed preprocessing layer D followed by an adaptive LTG.

ments the preceding dimensionality expansion process. The output node is a d-input LTG. It can be easily shown that the learning complexity of this network for functions in F is polynomial. This can be seen by noting that the training of the trainable part of this network (the output LTG) has polynomial complexity for m linearly separable examples in R^d and that as n increases, d remains polynomial in n.

The efficiency of learning linearly separable classification tasks in a single-threshold gate should not be surprising. Recall from Chapter 1 that the average amount of necessary and sufficient information for characterization of the set of separating surfaces for a random, separable dichotomy of m points grows slowly with m and asymptotically approaches $2d$ (twice the number of degrees of freedom of the class of separating surfaces). This implies that for a random set of linear inequalities in d unknowns, the expected number of extreme inequalities necessary and sufficient to cover the whole set tends to $2d$ as the number of consistent inequalities tends to infinity, thus bounding the (expected) necessary number of training examples for learning algorithms in separable problems. Moreover, this limit of $2d$ consistent inequalities is within the learning capacity of a single d-input LTG.

Another intuitive reason that the network in Figure 4.9.1 is easier to train than a fully adaptive two-layer feedforward net is that we are giving it predefined non-linearities. The former net does not have to start from scratch but instead is given more powerful building blocks to work with. However, there is a tradeoff. By using the network in Figure 4.9.1, we gain in a worst-case computational sense but lose in that the number of weights increases from n to $O(n^2)$ or higher. This increase in the number of weights implies that the number of training examples must increase so that the network can meaningfully generalize on new examples (recall the results of the previous section).

The problem of NP-complete learning in multilayer neural networks may be attributed to the use of fixed network resources (Baum, 1989). Learning an arbitrary mapping can be achieved in polynomial time for a network that allocates new computational units as more patterns are learned. Mukhopadhyay et al. (1993) gave a polynomial-time training algorithm for the general class of classification problems (defined by mappings of the form $f: R^n \to \{0, 1\}^L$) based on clustering and linear programming models. This algorithm simultaneously designs and trains an appropriate network for a given classification task. The basic idea of this method is to cover class regions with a minimal number of dynamically allocated hyperquadratic volumes (e.g., hyperspheres) of varying size. The resulting network has a layered structure consisting of a simple fixed preprocessing layer, a hidden layer of LTGs, and an output layer of logical OR gates. This and other efficiently trainable nets are considered in detail in Section 6.3.

4.10 Summary

Learning in artificial neural networks is viewed as a search for parameters (weights) that optimize a predefined criterion function. A general learning equation is presented that implements a stochastic steepest-gradient-descent search on a general criterion function with (or without) a regularization term. This learning equation serves to unify a wide variety of learning rules, regardless of whether they are supervised, unsupervised, or reinforcement rules.

The learning equation is a first-order stochastic differential equation. This allows one to employ an averaging technique to study its equilibria and its convergence characteristics. The use of averaging, under reasonable assumptions, allows one to approximate the stochastic learning equation by a deterministic first-order dynamical system. In most cases, a well-defined criterion function exists that allows one to treat the deterministic systems as a gradient system. In such case, the global stability property of gradient systems can be used to determine the nature of the solutions evolved by the average learning equation. These stable solutions are then taken to be the possible solutions sought by the associated stochastic learning equation. The averaging technique is employed in characterizing several basic rules for supervised, unsupervised, and reinforcement learning. For unsupervised learning, analysis and insights are presented into the theory of Hebbian, competitive, and self-organizing learning. In particular, self-organizing neural fields are introduced and analyzed.

The chapter also looks at some important results on generalization of learning in general feedforward neural architectures. The asymptotic behavior of generalization error is derived for deterministic and stochastic networks. Generalization in the average and in the worst case is considered. The main result here is that the number of training examples necessary for "good" generalization on test samples must far exceed the number of adjustable parameters of the network used.

Finally, the issue of complexity of learning in neural networks is addressed. It is found that learning an arbitrary mapping in a layered neural network is NP-complete in the worst case. However, it is also found that efficient (polynomial-time) learning is possible if appropriate network architectures and corresponding learning algorithms are found for certain classes of mappings/learning tasks.

Problems

4.1.1 Identify the "regularization" term, if any, in the learning rules that are listed in Table 3.1.

4.2.1 Characterize the LMS learning rule with weight decay ($\lambda \neq 0$) by analyzing its corresponding average differential equation as in Section 4.2. Find the underlying instantaneous criterion J and its expected value $\langle J \rangle$.

4.2.2 Employ Liapunov's first method (see footnote 4 on page 149) to study the stability of the nonlinear system

$$\begin{bmatrix} \dot{x}_1 \\ \dot{x}_2 \end{bmatrix} = \mathbf{f}(\mathbf{x}) = \begin{bmatrix} -x_1 + (x_1 + x_2 - 1)^2 \\ x_1 - 2x_2 + 2 + x_1^3 \end{bmatrix}$$

for the equilibrium point $\mathbf{x}^* = \begin{bmatrix} 0 & 1 \end{bmatrix}^T$. Is this an asymptotically stable point? Why?

4.2.3 Study the stability of the lossless pendulum system with the nonlinear dynamics

$$\begin{bmatrix} \dot{\theta} \\ \ddot{\theta} \end{bmatrix} = \begin{bmatrix} \dot{x}_1 \\ \dot{x}_2 \end{bmatrix} = \begin{bmatrix} x_2 \\ -\dfrac{g}{L} \sin x_1 \end{bmatrix}$$

about the equilibrium points $\mathbf{x}^* = \begin{bmatrix} 0 & 0 \end{bmatrix}^T$ and $\mathbf{x}^* = \begin{bmatrix} \pi & 0 \end{bmatrix}^T$. Here, θ measures the angle of the pendulum with respect to its vertical rest position, g is gravitational acceleration, and L is the length of the pendulum.

4.2.4 Liapunov's first method for studying the stability of nonlinear dynamical systems (see footnote 4) is equivalent to studying the asymptotic stability of a linearized version of these systems about an equilibrium point. Linearize the second-order nonlinear system in Problem 4.2.2 about the equilibrium point $\mathbf{x}^* = \begin{bmatrix} 0 & 1 \end{bmatrix}^T$, and write the system equations in the form $\dot{\mathbf{x}} = \mathbf{A}\mathbf{x}$. Show that the system matrix $\mathbf{A}$ is identical to the Jacobian matrix $\mathbf{f}'(\mathbf{x})$ at $\mathbf{x} = \begin{bmatrix} 0 & 1 \end{bmatrix}^T$ of the original nonlinear system and thus both matrices have the same eigenvalues. (Note that the asymptotic stability of a linear system requires the eigenvalues of its system matrix $\mathbf{A}$ to have strictly negative real parts.)

[†] **4.2.5** The linearization method for studying the stability of a nonlinear system at a given equilibrium point may fail when the linearized system is stable but not asymptotically, i.e., if all eigenvalues of the system matrix $\mathbf{A}$ have nonpositive real parts, and if the real part of one or more eigenvalues of $\mathbf{A}$ has zero real part. Demonstrate this fact for the nonlinear system

$$\dot{x}_1 = -x_2 + ax_1(x_1^2 + x_2^2)$$
$$\dot{x}_2 = +x_1 + ax_2(x_1^2 + x_2^2)$$

at the equilibrium point $\mathbf{x}^* = [0 \quad 0]^T$. [*Hint*: Simulate this dynamical system for the three cases: $a < 0$, $a = 0$, and $a > 0$, for an initial condition $\mathbf{x}(0)$ of your choice.]

*4.3.1 Show that the Hessian of J in Equation (4.3.6) is given by

$$\mathbf{H} = \frac{1}{\|\mathbf{w}\|^2}\left[-\mathbf{C} + \frac{2\mathbf{Cww}^T}{\|\mathbf{w}\|^2} + \frac{\mathbf{w}^T\mathbf{Cw}\mathbf{I} + 2\mathbf{ww}^T\mathbf{C}}{\|\mathbf{w}\|^2} - \frac{4(\mathbf{w}^T\mathbf{Cw})\mathbf{ww}^T}{\|\mathbf{w}\|^4} \right]$$

Also, show that

$$\mathbf{H}(\mathbf{c}^{(i)}) = \lambda_i\mathbf{I} - \mathbf{C} \qquad i = 1, 2, \ldots, n.$$

*4.3.2 Study the stability of the equilibrium point(s) of the dynamical system $\dot{\mathbf{w}} = -\rho\nabla J(\mathbf{w})$, where $J(\mathbf{w})$ is given by

$$J = -\tfrac{1}{2}\mathbf{w}^T\mathbf{Cw} + \frac{\lambda}{2}\left(1 - \sum_{j=1}^{n} w_j\right)^2$$

Note that this system corresponds to the average learning equation of Linsker's learning rule (see Section 3.3.4) without weight clipping.

4.3.3 Verify the Hessian matrices given in Section 4.3 for Oja's, the Yuille et al., and Hassoun's learning rules, given in Equations (4.3.14), (4.3.21), and (4.3.30), respectively.

4.3.4 Show that the average learning equation for Hassoun's rule is given by Equation (4.3.26).

4.3.5 Study the stability of the equilibrium points of the stochastic differential equation/learning rule (Riedel and Schild, 1992)

$$\dot{\mathbf{w}} = \rho(y\mathbf{x} - \|\mathbf{w}\|^\alpha\mathbf{w})$$

where α is a positive integer. (*Note*: This rule is equivalent to the Yuille et al. rule for $\alpha = 2$.)

†4.3.6 Study, via numerical simulations, the stability of the learning rule (Riedel and Schild, 1992)

$$\Delta\mathbf{w} = \rho(y\mathbf{x} - \mathbf{w}^{(3)})$$

where $\mathbf{w}^{(3)} = [w_1^3 \quad w_2^3 \quad \cdots \quad w_n^3]^T$. Assume a training set $\{\mathbf{x}\}$ of 20 vectors in R^{10} whose components are generated randomly and independently according to the normal distribution $N(0, 1)$. Is there a relation between the stable point(s) $\mathbf{w}^*$ [if such point(s) exist] and the eigenvectors of the input data autocorrelation matrix? Is this learning rule local? Why?

4.3.7 Show that the discrete-time version of Oja's rule is a good approximation of the normalized Hebbian rule in Equation (4.3.33) for small ρ values. *Hint*: Start by showing that

$$\|\tilde{\mathbf{w}}^{k+1}\|^{-1} \approx [1 + 2\rho(y^k)^2]^{-1/2} \approx 1 - \rho(y^k)^2$$

*4.3.8 Consider the general learning rule described by the following discrete-time gradient system:

$$\mathbf{w}^{k+1} = \mathbf{w}^k - \rho \nabla J(\mathbf{w}^k) \tag{1}$$

with $\rho > 0$. Assume that $\mathbf{w}^*$ is an equilibrium point for this dynamical system.
a. Show that in the neighborhood of $\mathbf{w}^*$, the gradient $\nabla J(\mathbf{w})$ can be approximated as

$$\nabla J(\mathbf{w}) \approx (\mathbf{w} - \mathbf{w}^*)\mathbf{H}(\mathbf{w}^*) \tag{2}$$

where $\mathbf{H}(\mathbf{w}^*)$ is the Hessian of J evaluated at $\mathbf{w}^*$.
b. Show that the gradient in Equation (2) is exact when $J(\mathbf{w})$ is quadratic; i.e., $J(\mathbf{w}) = \frac{1}{2}\mathbf{w}^T\mathbf{Q}\mathbf{w} + \mathbf{w}^T\mathbf{b}$, where $\mathbf{Q}$ is a symmetric matrix and $\mathbf{b}$ is a vector of constants.
c. Show that the linearized gradient system at $\mathbf{w}^*$ is given by

$$(\mathbf{w}^{k+1} - \mathbf{w}^*) = [\mathbf{I} - \rho \mathbf{H}(\mathbf{w}^*)](\mathbf{w}^k - \mathbf{w}^*) \tag{3}$$

where $\mathbf{I}$ is the identity matrix.
d. What are the conditions on $\mathbf{H}(\mathbf{w}^*)$ and ρ for local asymptotic stability of $\mathbf{w}^*$ in Equation (3)?
e. Use the preceding results to show that, in an average sense, the μ-LMS rule in Equation (3.1.35) converges asymptotically to the equilibrium solution in Equation (3.1.45) if $0 < \mu < 2/\lambda_{\max}$, where $\lambda_{\max}$ is the largest eigenvalue of the autocorrelation matrix $\mathbf{C}$ in Equation (3.3.4). [*Hint*: Start with the gradient system in Equation (1) and use Equation (3.1.44) for ∇J.] Now show that $0 < \mu < 2/\mathrm{trace}[\mathbf{C}] = 2/\langle\|\mathbf{x}\|^2\rangle$ is a sufficient condition for convergence of the μ-LMS rule. [*Hint*: The trace of a matrix (the sum of all diagonal elements) is equal to the sum of its eigenvalues.]

*4.3.9 Use the results from the preceding problem and Equation (4.3.14) to find the range of values for ρ for which the discrete-time Oja's rule is stable (in an average sense). Repeat for Hassoun's rule, which has the Hessian matrix given by Equation (4.3.30), and give a justification for the choice $\rho\lambda = 1$ which has led to Equation (4.3.32).

† **4.3.10** Consider a training set of forty 15-dimensional vectors whose components are independently generated according to a normal distribution N(0, 1). Employ the stochastic discrete-time version of Oja's, Yuille et al., and Hassoun's rules [replace $\dot{\mathbf{w}}$ by $\mathbf{w}^{k+1} - \mathbf{w}^k$ in Equations (4.3.11), (4.3.17), and (4.3.24), respectively] to extract the principal component of this training set. Use a fixed presentation order of the training vectors. Compare the convergence behavior of the three learning rules by generating plots similar to those in Figure 4.3.1. Use $\rho = 0.005$, $\lambda = 100$, and a random initial $\mathbf{w}$. Repeat using the corresponding discrete-time average learning equations with the same learning parameters and initial weight vector as before, and compare the two sets of simulations.

4.3.11 This problem illustrates an alternative approach to the one of Section 4.3 for proving the stability of equilibrium points of an average learning equation (Kohonen, 1989). Consider a stochastic first-order differential equation of the form $\dot{\mathbf{w}} = g(\mathbf{x}, \mathbf{w})$, where $\mathbf{x}(t)$ is governed by a stationary stochastic process. Furthermore, assume that the vectors $\mathbf{x}$ are statistically independent from each other and that strong mixing exists. Let $\mathbf{z}$ be an arbitrary constant vector having the same dimension as $\mathbf{x}$ and $\mathbf{w}$. Now, the "averaged" trajectories of $\mathbf{w}(t)$ are obtained by taking the expected value of $\dot{\mathbf{w}} = g(\mathbf{x}, \mathbf{w})$:

$$\langle\dot{\mathbf{w}}\rangle = \langle g(\mathbf{x}, \mathbf{w})\rangle$$

a. Show that

$$\frac{d\cos\theta}{dt} = \frac{\dfrac{d}{dt}(\mathbf{z}^{\mathsf{T}}\mathbf{w})}{\|\mathbf{z}\|\,\|\mathbf{w}\|} - \frac{\mathbf{z}^{\mathsf{T}}\mathbf{w}\dfrac{d\|\mathbf{w}\|}{dt}}{\|\mathbf{z}\|\,\|\mathbf{w}\|^2}$$

where θ is the angle between vectors $\mathbf{z}$ and $\mathbf{w}$.

b. Let $\mathbf{z} = \mathbf{c}^{(i)}$, the ith unity-norm eigenvector of the autocorrelation matrix $\mathbf{C} = \langle\mathbf{x}\mathbf{x}^{\mathsf{T}}\rangle$. Show that the average rate of change of the cosine of the angle between $\mathbf{w}$ and $\mathbf{c}^{(i)}$ for Oja's rule [Equation (4.3.12)] is given by

$$\left\langle\frac{d\cos\theta_i}{dt}\right\rangle = \rho\cos\theta_i\left(\lambda_i - \frac{\mathbf{w}^{\mathsf{T}}\mathbf{C}\mathbf{w}}{\|\mathbf{w}\|^2}\right)$$

where λ_i is the eigenvalue associated with $\mathbf{c}^{(i)}$. Note that the vectors $\mathbf{c}^{(i)}$ are the equilibria of Oja's rule.

   c. Use the result in part b to show that if $(\mathbf{c}^{(1)})^{\mathrm{T}}\mathbf{w}(0) \neq 0$, then $\mathbf{w}(t)$ will converge to the solution $\mathbf{w}^* = \pm\mathbf{c}^{(1)}$, where $\mathbf{c}^{(1)}$ is the eigenvector with the largest eigenvalue λ_1 (*Hint*: Recall the bounds on the Rayleigh quotient given in Section 4.3.2.)

*4.3.12 Use the technique outlined in Problem 4.3.11 to study the convergence properties (in the average) of the following stochastic learning rules which employ a generalized forgetting law:

   a. $\dot{\mathbf{w}} = \alpha\mathbf{x} - g(y)\mathbf{w}$.

   b. $\dot{\mathbf{w}} = \alpha y\mathbf{x} - g(y)\mathbf{w}$.

Assume that $\alpha > 0$ and $y = \mathbf{w}^{\mathrm{T}}\mathbf{x}$ and that $g(y)$ is an arbitrary scalar function of y such that $\langle g(y)\rangle$ exists. Note that Equation (4.7.18) and Oja's rule are special cases of the learning rules in parts a and b, respectively.

4.4.1 Show that Equation (4.4.7) is the Hessian for the criterion function implied by Equation (4.4.5).

4.6.1 Study (qualitatively) the competitive learning behavior that minimizes the criterion function

$$J(\mathbf{w}) = -\frac{1}{N}\sum_i \sum_k (2\mathbf{M}_i^k - 1)\|\mathbf{x}^k - \mathbf{w}_i\|^{-N}$$

where $\mathbf{M}_i^k$ is as defined in Equation (4.6.3). Can you think of a physical system (for some integer value of N) that is governed by this "energy" function J?

4.6.2 Derive a stochastic competitive learning rule whose corresponding average learning equation maximizes the criterion function in Equation (4.6.16).

*4.7.1 Show that for the one-dimensional feature map, Equation (4.7.6) can be derived from Equation (4.7.4). See Hertz et al. (1991) for hints.

4.7.2 Show that Equation (4.7.5) satisfies Equation (4.7.6).

4.7.3 Solve Equation (4.7.5) for $p(x) \propto x^{\alpha}$, where $\alpha \in R$. For which input distribution $p(x)$ do we have a zero-distortion feature map?

4.7.4 Prove the stability of the equilibrium point in Equation (4.7.20). (*Hint*: Employ the technique outlined in Problem 4.3.11.)

5 Adaptive Multilayer Neural Networks I

This chapter extends the gradient-descent-based delta rule of Chapter 3 to multilayer feedforward neural networks. The resulting learning rule is commonly known as *error backpropagation* (or *backprop*), and it is one of the most frequently used learning rules in many applications of artificial neural networks.

The backprop learning rule is central to much current work on learning in artificial neural networks. In fact, the development of backprop is one of the main reasons for the renewed interest in artificial neural networks. Backprop provides a computationally efficient method for changing the weights in a feedforward network, with differentiable activation function units, to learn a training set of input-output examples. Backprop-trained multilayer neural nets have been applied successfully to solve some difficult and diverse problems, such as pattern classification, function approximation, nonlinear system modeling, time-series prediction, and image compression and reconstruction. For these reasons, most of this chapter is devoted to the study of backprop, its variations, and its extensions.

Backpropagation is a gradient-descent search algorithm that may suffer from slow convergence to local minima. In this chapter, several methods for improving backprop's convergence speed and avoidance of local minima are presented. Whenever possible, theoretical justification is given for these methods. A version of backprop based on an enhanced criterion function with global search capability is described which, when properly tuned, allows for relatively fast convergence to good solutions. Several significant applications of backprop-trained multilayer neural networks are described. These applications include the conversion of English text into speech, mapping hand gestures to speech, recognition of hand-written ZIP codes, autonomous vehicle navigation, medical diagnoses, and image compression.

The last part of this chapter deals with extensions of backprop to more general neural network architectures. These include multilayer feedforward nets whose inputs are generated by a tapped delay-line circuit and fully recurrent neural networks. These adaptive networks are capable of extending the applicability of artificial neural networks to nonlinear dynamical system modeling and temporal pattern association.

5.1 Learning Rule for Multilayer Feedforward Neural Networks

Consider the two-layer feedforward architecture shown in Figure 5.1.1. This network receives a set of scalar signals $\{x_0, x_1, \ldots, x_n\}$ where x_0 is a bias signal equal to 1. This set of signals constitutes an input vector $\mathbf{x} \in R^{n+1}$. The layer receiving the input signal is called the *hidden layer*. Figure 5.1.1 shows a hidden layer having J units. The output of the hidden layer is a $(J + 1)$-dimensional real-valued vector $\mathbf{z} = [z_0, z_1, \ldots, z_J]^{\mathrm{T}}$. Again, $z_0 = 1$ represents a bias input and can be thought of as

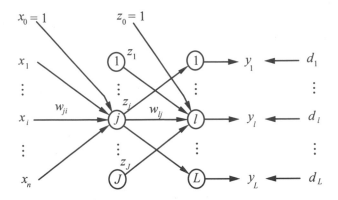

Figure 5.1.1
A two-layer fully interconnected feedforward neural network architecture. For clarity, only selected connections are drawn.

being generated by a "dummy" unit (with index zero) whose output z_0 is clamped at 1. The vector $\mathbf{z}$ supplies the input for the *output layer* of L units. The output layer generates an L-dimensional vector $\mathbf{y}$ in response to the input $\mathbf{x}$ which, when the network is fully trained, should be identical (or very close) to a "desired" output vector $\mathbf{d}$ associated with $\mathbf{x}$.

The activation function f_h of the hidden units is assumed to be a differentiable nonlinear function [typically, f_h is the logistic function defined by $f_h(net) = 1/(1 + e^{-\lambda net})$, or hyperbolic tangent function $f_h(net) = \tanh(\beta net)$, with values for λ and β close to unity]. Each unit of the output layer is assumed to have the same activation function, denoted f_o; the functional form of f_o is determined by the desired output signal/pattern representation or the type of application. For example, if the desired output is real valued (as in some function approximation applications), then a linear activation $f_o(net) = \lambda net$ may be used. On the other hand, if the network implements a pattern classifier with binary outputs, then a saturating nonlinearity similar to f_h may be used for f_o. In this case, the components of the desired output vector $\mathbf{d}$ must be chosen within the range of f_o. It is important to note that if f_h is linear, then one can always collapse the net in Figure 5.1.1 to a single-layer net and thus lose the universal approximation/mapping capabilities discussed in Chapter 2. Finally, we denote by w_{ji} the weight of the jth hidden unit associated with the input signal x_i. Similarly, w_{lj} is the weight of the lth output unit associated with the hidden signal z_j.

Next, consider a set of m input/output pairs $\{\mathbf{x}^k, \mathbf{d}^k\}$, where $\mathbf{d}^k$ is an L-dimensional vector representing the desired network output upon presentation of $\mathbf{x}^k$. The objective here is to adaptively adjust the $J(n + 1) + L(J + 1)$ weights of this network such that the underlying function/mapping represented by the training set is approximated or learned. Since the learning here is supervised (i.e., target outputs are available), an error function may be defined to measure the degree of approximation for any given setting of the network's weights. A commonly used error function is the SSE measure, but this is by no means the only possibility, and later in this chapter, several other error functions will be discussed. Once a suitable error function is formulated, learning can be viewed (as was done in Chapters 3 and 4) as an optimization process. That is, the error function serves as a criterion function, and the learning algorithm seeks to minimize the criterion function over the space of possible weight settings. For instance, if a differentiable criterion function is used, gradient descent on such a function will naturally lead to a learning rule. This idea was invented independently by Amari (1967, 1968), Bryson and Ho (1969), Werbos (1974), and Parker (1985). Next, this idea is illustrated by deriving a supervised learning rule for adjusting the weights w_{ji} and w_{lj} such that the following error function is minimized (in a local sense) over the training set (Rumelhart et al., 1986b):

$$E(\mathbf{w}) = \tfrac{1}{2} \sum_{l=1}^{L} (d_l - y_l)^2 \qquad (5.1.1)$$

Here, $\mathbf{w}$ represents the set of all weights in the network. Note that Equation (5.1.1) is the "instantaneous" SSE criterion of Equation (3.1.32) generalized for a multiple-output network.

5.1.1   Error Backpropagation Learning Rule

Since the targets for the output units are explicitly specified, one can use the delta rule directly, derived in Section 3.1.3 for updating the w_{lj} weights. That is,

$$\Delta w_{lj} = w_{lj}^{new} - w_{lj}^{c} = -\rho_0 \frac{\partial E}{\partial w_{lj}} = \rho_o(d_l - y_l)f_o'(net_l)z_j \qquad (5.1.2)$$

with $l = 1, 2, \ldots, L$ and $j = 0, 1, \ldots, J$. Here $net_l = \sum_{j=0}^{J} w_{lj}z_j$ is the weighted sum for the lth output unit, f_o' is the derivative of f_o with respect to net, and w_{lj}^{new} and w_{lj}^{c} represent the updated (new) and current weight values, respectively. The z_j values are computed by propagating the input vector $\mathbf{x}$ through the hidden layer according to

$$z_j = f_h\left(\sum_{i=0}^{n} w_{ji}x_i\right) = f_h(net_j) \qquad j = 1, 2, \ldots, J \qquad (5.1.3)$$

The learning rule for the hidden-layer weights w_{ji} is not as obvious as that for the output layer because we do not have available a set of target values (desired outputs) for hidden units. However, one may derive a learning rule for hidden units by attempting to minimize the output-layer error. This amounts to propagating the output errors $(d_l - y_l)$ back through the output layer toward the hidden units in an attempt to estimate "dynamic" targets for these units. Such a learning rule is termed *error backpropagation* or the *backprop learning rule* and may be viewed as an extension of the delta rule [Equation (5.1.2)] used for updating the output layer. To complete the derivation of backprop for the hidden-layer weights, and similar to the preceding derivation for the output-layer weights, gradient descent is performed on the criterion function in Equation (5.1.1), but this time, the gradient is calculated with respect to the hidden weights:

$$\Delta w_{ji} = -\rho_h \frac{\partial E}{\partial w_{ji}} \qquad j = 1, 2, \ldots, J; \qquad i = 0, 1, 2, \ldots, n \tag{5.1.4}$$

where the partial derivative is to be evaluated at the current weight values. Using the chain rule for differentiation, one may express the partial derivative in Equation (5.1.4) as

$$\frac{\partial E}{\partial w_{ji}} = \frac{\partial E}{\partial z_j} \frac{\partial z_j}{\partial \, net_j} \frac{\partial \, net_j}{\partial w_{ji}} \tag{5.1.5}$$

with

$$\frac{\partial \, net_j}{\partial w_{ji}} = x_i, \tag{5.1.6}$$

$$\frac{\partial z_j}{\partial \, net_j} = f'_h(net_j), \tag{5.1.7}$$

and

$$\frac{\partial E}{\partial z_j} = \frac{\partial}{\partial z_j} \left\{ \frac{1}{2} \sum_{l=1}^{L} [d_l - f_o(net_l)]^2 \right\}$$

$$= -\sum_{l=1}^{L} [d_l - f_o(net_l)] \frac{\partial f_o(net_l)}{\partial z_j}$$

$$= -\sum_{l=1}^{L} (d_l - y_l) f'_o(net_l) w_{lj} \tag{5.1.8}$$

Now, upon substituting Equations (5.1.6) through (5.1.8) into Equation (5.1.5) and using Equation (5.1.4), the desired learning rule is obtained:

$$\Delta w_{ji} = \rho_h \left[\sum_{l=1}^{L} (d_l - y_l) f_o'(net_l) w_{lj} \right] f_h'(net_j) x_i \tag{5.1.9}$$

By comparing Equation (5.1.9) with Equation (5.1.2), one can immediately define an "estimated target" d_j for the jth hidden unit implicitly in terms of the backpropagated error signal as follows:

$$d_j - z_j \triangleq \sum_{l=1}^{L} (d_l - y_l) f_o'(net_l) w_{lj} \tag{5.1.10}$$

It is usually possible to express the derivatives of the activation functions in Equations (5.1.2) and (5.1.9) in terms of the activations themselves. For example, for the logistic activation function,

$$f'(net) = \lambda f(net)[1 - f(net)] \tag{5.1.11}$$

and for the hyperbolic tangent function,

$$f'(net) = \beta[1 - f^2(net)] \tag{5.1.12}$$

These learning equations may also be extended to feedforward nets with more than one hidden layer and/or nets with connections that jump over one or more layers (see Problems 5.1.2 and 5.1.3). The complete procedure for updating the weights in a feedforward neural net utilizing these rules is summarized below for the two-layer architecture of Figure 5.1.1. This learning procedure will be referred to as *incremental backprop* or just *backprop*.

1. Initialize all weights and refer to them as "current" weights w_{lj}^c and w_{ji}^c (see Section 5.2.1 for details).

2. Set the learning rates ρ_o and ρ_h to small positive values (refer to Section 5.2.2 for additional details).

3. Select an input pattern $\mathbf{x}^k$ from the training set (preferably at random) and propagate it through the network, thus generating hidden- and output-unit activities based on the current weight settings.

4. Use the desired target $\mathbf{d}^k$ associated with $\mathbf{x}^k$, and employ Equation (5.1.2) to compute the output layer weight changes Δw_{lj}.

5. Employ Equation (5.1.9) to compute the hidden-layer weight changes Δw_{ji}. Normally, the current weights are used in these computations. In general, enhanced

error correction may be achieved if one employs the updated output-layer weights $w_{lj}^{new} = w_{lj}^c + \Delta w_{lj}$. However, this comes at the added cost of recomputing y_l and $f_o'(net_l)$.

6. Update all weights according to $w_{lj}^{new} = w_{lj}^c + \Delta w_{lj}$ and $w_{ji}^{new} = w_{ji}^c + \Delta w_{ji}$ for the output and hidden layers, respectively.

7. Test for convergence. This is done by checking some preselected function of the output errors[1] to see if its magnitude is below some preset threshold. If convergence is met, stop; otherwise, set $w_{ji}^c = w_{ji}^{new}$ and $w_{lj}^c = w_{lj}^{new}$, and go to step 3. It should be noted that backprop may fail to find a solution that passes the convergence test. In this case, one may try to reinitialize the search process, tune the learning parameters, and/or use more hidden units.

This procedure is based on *incremental learning*, which means that the weights are updated after every presentation of an input pattern. Another alternative is to employ *batch learning*, where weight updating is performed only after all patterns (assuming a finite training set) have been presented. Batch learning is formally stated by summing the right-hand sides of Equations (5.1.2) and (5.1.9) over all patterns $\mathbf{x}^k$. This amounts to gradient descent on the criterion function

$$E(\mathbf{w}) = \tfrac{1}{2} \sum_{k=1}^{m} \sum_{l=1}^{L} (d_l - y_l)^2 \tag{5.1.13}$$

Even though batch updating moves the search point $\mathbf{w}$ in the direction of the true gradient at each update step, the "approximate" incremental updating is more desirable for two reasons: (1) it requires less storage, and (2) it makes the search path in the weight space stochastic (here, at each time step, the input vector $\mathbf{x}$ is drawn at random), which allows for a wider exploration of the search space and, potentially, leads to better-quality solutions. When backprop converges, it converges to a local minimum of the criterion function (McInerny et al., 1989). This fact is true of any gradient-descent-based learning rule when the surface being searched is nonconvex (Amari, 1990); i.e., it admits local minima. Using stochastic approximation theory, Finnoff (1993, 1994) showed that for "very small" learning rates (approaching zero), incremental backprop approaches batch backprop and produces essentially the same results. However, for small constant learning rates there is a nonnegligible stochastic element in the training process that gives incremental backprop a quasi-annealing

---

1. A convenient selection is the root-mean-square (RMS) error given by $\sqrt{2E/(mL)}$, with E as in Equation (5.1.13). An alternative, and more sensible stopping test may be formulated by using cross-validation; see Section 5.2.6 for details.

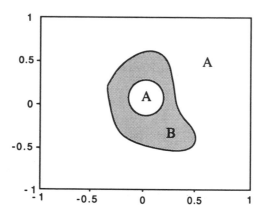

Figure 5.1.2
Decision regions for the pattern-classification problem in Example 5.1.1

character in which the cumulative gradient is continuously perturbed, allowing the
search to escape local minima with small and shallow basins of attraction. Thus
solutions generated by incremental backprop are often practical ones. The local minima problem can be eased further by heuristically adding random noise to the weights
(von Lehman et al., 1988) or by adding noise to the input patterns (Sietsma and Dow,
1988). In both cases, some noise-reduction schedule should be employed to dynamically reduce the added noise level toward zero as learning progresses.

Next, the incremental backprop learning procedure is applied to solve a two-
dimensional, two-class pattern-classification problem. This problem should help give
a good feel for what is learned by the hidden units in a feedforward neural network
and how the various units work together to generate a desired solution.

Example 5.1.1   Consider the two-class problem shown in Figure 5.1.2. The points
inside the shaded region belong to class B, and all other points are in class A. A
three-layer feedforward neural network with backprop training is employed that is
supposed to learn to distinguish between these two classes. The network consists of
an eight-unit first hidden layer, followed by a second hidden layer with four units,
followed by a one-unit output layer. Such a network is said to have an 8-4-1 architecture. All units employ a hyperbolic tangent activation function. The output unit
should encode the class of each input vector; a positive output indicates class B
and a negative output indicates class A. Incremental backprop was used with learning
rates set to 0.1. The training set consists of 500 randomly chosen points, 250 from

region A and another 250 from region B. In this training set, points representing class B and class A were assigned desired output (target) values of $+1$ and -1, respectively.[2] Training was performed for several hundred cycles over the training set.

Figure 5.1.3 shows geometric plots of all unit responses upon testing the network with a new set of 1000 uniformly (randomly) generated points inside the $[-1, +1]^2$ region. In generating each plot, a black dot was placed at the exact coordinates of the test point (input) in the input space if and only if the corresponding unit response was positive. The boundaries between the dotted and the white regions in the plots represent approximate decision boundaries learned by the various units in the network. Figure 5.1.3a–h represents the decision boundaries learned by the eight units in the first hidden layer. Figure 5.1.3i–l shows the decision boundaries learned by the four units of the second hidden layer. Figure 5.1.3m shows the decision boundary realized by the output unit. Note the linear nature of the separating surface realized by the first-hidden-layer units, from which complex nonlinear separating surfaces are realized by the second-hidden-layer units and ultimately by the output-layer unit. This example also illustrates how a single-hidden-layer feedforward net (counting only the first two layers) is capable of realizing convex, concave, as well as disjoint decision regions, as can be seen from Figure 5.1.3i–l. Here, we neglect the output unit and view the remaining net as one with an 8-4 architecture.

The present problem can also be solved with smaller networks (fewer numbers of hidden units or even a network with a single hidden layer). However, the training of such smaller networks with backprop may become more difficult. A smaller network with a 5-3-1 architecture utilizing a variant backprop learning procedure (Hassoun et al., 1990) is reported by Song (1992), and this network has a comparable separating surface to the one in Figure 5.1.3m.

Huang and Lippmann (1988) employed Monte Carlo simulations to investigate the capabilities of backprop in learning complex decision regions (see Figure 2.3.3). They reported no significant performance difference between two- and three-layer feedforward nets when forming complex decision regions using backprop. They also demonstrated that backprop's convergence time is excessive for complex decision regions and that the performance of such trained classifiers is similar to that obtained with the k-nearest neighbor classifier (Duda and Hart, 1973). Villiers and Barnard (1993) reported similar simulations but on data sets that consisted of a "distribution of

---

2. In fact, the actual targets used were offset by a small positive constant ε (say, $\varepsilon = 0.1$) away from the limiting values of the activation function. This resulted in replacing the $+1$ and -1 targets by $1 - \varepsilon$ and $-1 + \varepsilon$, respectively. Otherwise, backprop tends to drive the weights of the network to infinity and thereby slow the learning process.

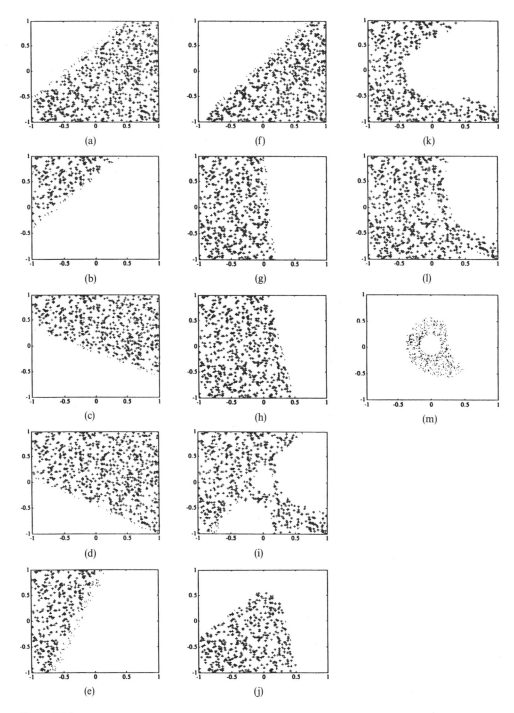

Figure 5.1.3
Separating surfaces generated by the various units in the 8-4-1 network of Example 5.1.1. (*a–h*) Separating surfaces realized by the units in the first hidden layer; (*i–l*) separating surface realized by the units in the second hidden layer; (*m*) separating surface realized by the output unit.

distributions" where a typical class is a set of clusters (distributions) in the feature space; each of which can be more or less spread out and which might involve some or all of the dimensions of the feature space; the distribution of distributions thus assigns a probability to each distribution in the data set. It was found for networks of equal complexity (same number of weights) that there is no significant difference between the quality of "best" solutions generated by two- and three-layer backprop-trained feedforward networks; actually, the two-layer nets demonstrated better performance, on average. As for the speed of convergence, three-layer nets converged faster if the number of units in the two hidden layers were roughly equal.

Gradient-descent search may be eliminated altogether in favor of a stochastic global search procedure that guarantees convergence to a global solution with high probability; genetic algorithms and simulated annealing are examples of such procedures and are considered in Chapter 8. However, the assured (in probability) optimality of these global search procedures comes at the expense of slow convergence. Next, a deterministic search procedure termed *global descent* is presented that helps backprop reach globally optimal solutions.

5.1.2 Global-Descent-Based Error Backpropagation

Here, a learning method is described in which the gradient-descent rule in batch backprop is replaced with a *global-descent rule* (Cetin et al., 1993a). This methodology is based on a global optimization scheme, acronymed TRUST (terminal repeller unconstrained subenergy tunneling), that formulates optimization in terms of the flow of a special deterministic dynamical system (Cetin et al., 1993b).[3]

Global descent is a gradient descent on a special criterion function $C(\mathbf{w}, \mathbf{w}^*)$ given by

$$C(\mathbf{w}, \mathbf{w}^*) = \ln\left(\frac{1}{1 + e^{-[E(\mathbf{w})-E(\mathbf{w}^*)+\sigma]}}\right) - \frac{3k}{4}\sum_i (w_i - w_i^*)^{4/3}\mathrm{u}[E(\mathbf{w}) - E(\mathbf{w}^*)] \quad (5.1.14)$$

where $\mathbf{w}^*$, with component values w_i^*, is a fixed-weight vector that can be a local minimum of $E(\mathbf{w})$ or an initial weight state $\mathbf{w}^0$, $\mathrm{u}[\cdot]$ is the unit step function, σ is a shifting parameter (typically set to 2), and k is a small positive constant. The first term in the right-hand side in Equation (5.1.14) is a monotonic transformation of the original criterion function (e.g., SSE criterion may be used) that preserves all critical

---

3. This method was originally designed for implementation in parallel analog VLSI circuitry, allowing implementation in a form whose computational complexity is only weakly dependent on problem dimensionality.

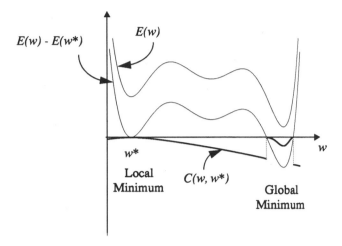

Figure 5.1.4
A plot of a one-dimensional criterion function $E(w)$ with local minimum at w^*. The function $E(w) - E(w^*)$ is plotted below, as well as the global-descent criterion function $C(w, w^*)$.

points of $E(\mathbf{w})$ and has the same relative ordering of the local and global minima of $E(\mathbf{w})$. It also flattens the portion of $E(\mathbf{w})$ above $E(\mathbf{w}^*)$ with minimal distortion elsewhere. On the other hand, the term $\sum_i (w_i - w_i^*)^{4/3}$ is a "repeller term," which gives rise to a convex surface with a unique minimum located at $\mathbf{w} = \mathbf{w}^*$. The overall effect of this energy transformation is schematically represented for a one-dimensional criterion function in Figure 5.1.4.

Performing gradient descent on $C(\mathbf{w}, \mathbf{w}^*)$ leads to the *global-descent update rule*:

$$\Delta w_i = -\rho \frac{\partial E(\mathbf{w})}{\partial w_i} \frac{1}{1 + e^{+[E(\mathbf{w}) - E(\mathbf{w}^*) + \sigma]}} + \rho k (w_i - w_i^*)^{1/3} \mathbf{u}[E(\mathbf{w}) - E(\mathbf{w}^*)] \quad (5.1.15)$$

The first term on the right-hand side of Equation (5.1.15) is a *subenergy gradient*, while the second term is a *non-Lipschitzian terminal repeller* (Zak, 1989). Upon replacing the gradient descent in Equations (5.1.2) and (5.1.4) by Equation (5.1.15), where w_i represents an arbitrary hidden-unit or output-unit weight, the modified backprop procedure may escape local minima of the original criterion function $E(\mathbf{w})$ given in Equation (5.1.13). Here, the batch training is required because Equation (5.1.15) necessitates a unique error surface for all patterns.

   The update rule in Equation (5.1.15) automatically switches between two phases: a tunneling phase and a gradient-descent phase. The tunneling phase is characterized by $E(\mathbf{w}) \geq E(\mathbf{w}^*)$. Since for this condition the subenergy gradient term is nearly zero in the vicinity of the local minimum $\mathbf{w}^*$, the terminal repeller term in Equation (5.1.15) dominates, leading to the dynamical system

$$\Delta w_i \approx \rho k (w_i - w_i^*)^{1/3} \tag{5.1.16}$$

This system has an unstable repeller equilibrium point at $w_i = w_i^*$, i.e., at the local minimum of $E(\mathbf{w})$. The "power" of this repeller is determined by the constant k. Thus the dynamical system given by Equation (5.1.15), when initialized with a small perturbation from $\mathbf{w}^*$, is repelled from this local minimum until it reaches a lower-energy region $E(\mathbf{w}) < E(\mathbf{w}^*)$; i.e., tunneling through portions of $E(\mathbf{w})$ where $E(\mathbf{w}) \geq E(\mathbf{w}^*)$ is accomplished. The second phase is a gradient-descent minimization phase characterized by $E(\mathbf{w}) < E(\mathbf{w}^*)$. Here, the repeller term is identically zero. Thus Equation (5.1.15) becomes

$$\Delta w_i = -\rho(\mathbf{w}) \frac{\partial E(\mathbf{w})}{\partial w_i} \tag{5.1.17}$$

where $\rho(\mathbf{w})$ is a dynamic learning rate (step size) equal to $\rho \{1 + \exp[E(\mathbf{w}) - E(\mathbf{w}^*) + \sigma]\}^{-1}$. Note that $\rho(\mathbf{w})$ is approximately equal to ρ when $E(\mathbf{w}^*)$ is large compared to $E(\mathbf{w}) + \sigma$.

   Initially, $\mathbf{w}^*$ is chosen as one corner of a domain in the form of a hyperparallelepiped of dimension $J(n + 1) + L(J + 1)$, which is the dimension of $\mathbf{w}$ in the architecture of Figure 5.1.1. A slightly perturbed version of $\mathbf{w}^*$, namely, $\mathbf{w}^* + \boldsymbol{\varepsilon}_\mathbf{w}$, is taken as the initial state of the dynamical system in Equation (5.1.15). Here $\boldsymbol{\varepsilon}_\mathbf{w}$ is a small perturbation that drives the system into the domain of interest. If $E(\mathbf{w}^* + \boldsymbol{\varepsilon}_\mathbf{w}) < E(\mathbf{w}^*)$, the system immediately enters a gradient-descent phase that equilibrates at a local minimum. Every time a new equilibrium is reached, $\mathbf{w}^*$ is set equal to this equilibrium, and Equation (5.1.15) is reinitialized with $\mathbf{w}^* + \boldsymbol{\varepsilon}_\mathbf{w}$, which ensures a necessary consistency in the search flow direction. Since $\mathbf{w}^*$ is now a local minimum, $E(\mathbf{w}) \geq E(\mathbf{w}^*)$ holds in the neighborhood of $\mathbf{w}^*$. Thus the system enters a repelling (tunneling) phase, and the repeller at $\mathbf{w}^*$ repels the system until it reaches a lower basin of attraction where $E(\mathbf{w}) < E(\mathbf{w}^*)$. As the dynamical system enters the next basin, the system automatically switches to gradient descent and equilibrates at the next lower local minimum. Then $\mathbf{w}^*$ is set equal to this new minimum, and the process is repeated. If, on the other hand, $E(\mathbf{w}^* + \boldsymbol{\varepsilon}_\mathbf{w}) \geq E(\mathbf{w}^*)$ at the onset of training, then the system is initially in a tunneling phase. The tunneling will proceed to a lower basin, at which point

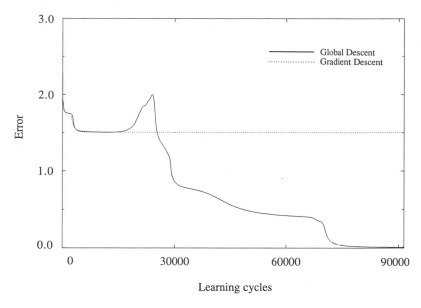

Figure 5.1.5
Learning curves for global-descent- and gradient-descent-based batch backprop for the
4-bit parity.

it enters the minimization phase and follows the behavior discussed above. Training
can be stopped when a minimum $\mathbf{w}^*$ corresponding to $E(\mathbf{w}^*) = 0$ is reached or when
$E(\mathbf{w}^*)$ becomes smaller than a preset threshold.

The global-descent method is guaranteed to find the global minimum for functions
of one variable but not for multivariate functions. However, in the multidimensional
case, the algorithm will always escape from one local minimum to another with a
lower or equal functional value. Figure 5.1.5 compares the learning curve for the
global-descent-based backprop with that of batch backprop for the 4-bit parity problem in a feedforward net with four hidden units and a single output unit. The same
initial random weights are used in both cases. The figure depicts one tunneling phase
for the global-descent algorithm before convergence to a (perfect) global-minimum
solution. In performing this simulation, it is found that the choice of the direction of
the perturbation vector $\boldsymbol{\varepsilon}_{\mathbf{w}}$ is very critical in regard to reaching a global minimum
successfully. On the other hand, batch backprop converges to the first local minimum
it reaches. This local solution represents a partial solution to the 4-bit parity problem
(i.e., mapping error is present). Simulations using incremental backprop with the
same initial weights as in the preceding simulations are also performed but are not

shown in the figure. Incremental backprop was able to produce both solutions shown in Figure 5.1.5; very small learning rates (ρ_0 and ρ_n) often lead to imperfect local solutions, while relatively larger learning rates may lead to a perfect solution.

5.2   Backprop Enhancements and Variations

In general, learning with backprop is slow (Sutton, 1986; Huang and Lippmann, 1988). Typically, this is due to the characteristics of the error surface. The surface is characterized by numerous flat and steep regions. In addition, it has many troughs that are flat in the direction of search. These characteristics are particularly pro-nounced in classification problems, especially when the size of the training set is small (Hush et al., 1991).

Many enhancements of and variations to backprop have been proposed. These are mostly heuristic modifications with goals of increased speed of convergence, avoidance of local minima, and/or improvement in the network's ability to generalize. This section presents some common heuristics that may improve these aspects of backprop learning in multilayer feedforward neural networks.

5.2.1   Weight Initialization

Owing to its gradient-descent nature, backprop is very sensitive to initial conditions. If the choice of the initial weight vector $\mathbf{w}^0$ (here $\mathbf{w}$ is a point in the weight space being searched by backprop) happens to be located within the attraction basin of a strong local minima attractor (one where the minima is at the bottom of a steep-sided valley of the criterion/error surface), then the convergence of backprop will be fast and the solution quality will be determined by the depth of the valley relative to the depth of the global minima. On the other hand, backprop converges very slowly if $\mathbf{w}^0$ starts the search in a relatively flat region of the error surface.

An alternative explanation for the sensitivity of backprop to initial weights (as well as to other learning parameters) is advanced by Kolen and Pollack (1991). Using Monte Carlo simulations on simple feedforward nets with incremental backprop learning of simple functions, they discovered a complex fractal-like structure for con-vergence as a function of initial weights. They reported regions of high sensitivity in the weight space where two very close initial points can lead to substantially different learning curves. Thus they hypothesize that these fractal-like structures arise in back-prop due to the nonlinear nature of the dynamic learning equations, which exhibit multiple attractors; rather than the gradient-descent metaphor with local valleys to get stuck in, they advance a many-body metaphor where the search trajectory is determined by complex interactions with the systems attractors.

In practice, the weights are normally initialized to small zero-mean random values (Rumelhart et al., 1986b). The motivation for starting from small weights is that large weights tend to prematurely saturate units in a network and render them insensitive to the learning process (Hush et al., 1991; Lee et al., 1991) (this phenomenon is known as *flat spot* and is considered in Section 5.2.4). On the other hand, randomness is introduced as a symmetry-breaking mechanism; it prevents units from adopting similar functions and becoming redundant.

A sensible strategy for choosing the magnitudes of the initial weights for avoiding premature saturation is to choose them such that an arbitrary unit i starts with a small and random weighted sum net_i. This may be achieved by setting the initial weights of unit i to be on the order of $1/\sqrt{f_i}$, where f_i is the number of inputs (fan-in) for unit i (Wessels and Barnard, 1992). It can be easily shown that for zero-mean random uniform weights in $[-r, +r]$ and assuming normalized inputs that are randomly and uniformly distributed in the range $[0, 1]$, net_i has zero mean and has standard deviation $\sigma_{net_i} = (r/3)\sqrt{f_i}$. Thus, by generating uniform random weights within the range $[-3/\sqrt{f_i}, +3/\sqrt{f_i}]$, the input to unit i (net_i) is a random variable with zero mean and a standard deviation of unity, as desired.

In simulations involving single-hidden-layer feedforward networks for pattern classification and function approximation tasks, substantial improvements in backprop convergence speed and avoidance of "bad" local minima are possible by initializing the hidden unit weight vectors to normalized vectors selected randomly from the training set (Denoeux and Lengellé, 1993).

5.2.2   Learning Rate

The convergence speed of backprop is directly related to the learning rate parameter ρ [ρ_o and ρ_h Equations (5.1.2) and (5.1.9), respectively]; if ρ is small, the search path will closely approximate the gradient path, but convergence will be very slow due to the large number of update steps needed to reach a local minima. On the other hand, if ρ is large, convergence initially will be very fast, but the algorithm will eventually oscillate and thus not reach a minimum. In general, it is desirable to have large steps when the search point is far away from a minimum, with decreasing step size as the search approaches a minimum. This section gives a sample of the various approaches for selecting the proper learning rate.

One early proposed heuristic (Plaut et al., 1986) is to use constant learning rates that are inversely proportional to the fan-in of the corresponding units. Extensions of the idea of fan-in dependence of the learning rate also have been proposed by (Tesauro and Janssens, 1988). The increased convergence speed of backprop as a result of using this method of setting the individual learning rates for each unit inversely proportional to the number of inputs to that unit has been theoretically justified by analyzing the eigenvalue distribution of the Hessian matrix of the criterion function, $\nabla^2 E$ (Le Cun et al., 1991a). Such learning rate normalization can be thought of intuitively as maintaining balance between the learning speed of units with different fan-in. Without this normalization, after each learning iteration, units with high fan-in have their input activity (*net*) changed by a larger amount than units with low fan-in. Thus, and due to the nature of the sigmoidal activation function used, the units with large fan-in tend to commit their output to a saturated state prematurely and are rendered difficult to adapt (see Section 5.2.4 for additional discussion). Therefore, normalizing the learning rates of the various units by dividing by their corresponding fan-in helps speed up learning.

The optimal learning rate for fast convergence of backprop/gradient-descent search is the inverse of the largest eigenvalue of the Hessian matrix $\mathbf{H}$ of the error function E evaluated at the search point $\mathbf{w}$. Computing the full Hessian matrix is prohibitively expensive for large networks with thousands of parameters involved. Therefore, finding the largest eigenvalue λ_{max} for speedy convergence seems rather inefficient. However, one may employ a shortcut to efficiently estimate λ_{max} (Le Cun et al., 1993). This shortcut is based on a simple method of approximating the product of $\mathbf{H}$ by an arbitrarily chosen (random) vector $\mathbf{z}$ through Taylor expansion: $\mathbf{Hz} = (1/\alpha)[\nabla E(\mathbf{w} + \alpha \mathbf{z}) - \nabla E(\mathbf{w})]$, where α is a small positive constant. Now, using the power method, which amounts to iterating the procedure

$$\mathbf{z} \leftarrow \frac{\mathbf{Hz}}{\|\mathbf{z}\|} = \frac{1}{\alpha}\left[\nabla E\left(\mathbf{w} + \alpha\frac{\mathbf{z}}{\|\mathbf{z}\|}\right) - \nabla E(\mathbf{w}) \right],$$

the vector $\mathbf{z}$ converges to $|\lambda_{max}|\mathbf{c}_{max}$, where $\mathbf{c}_{max}$ is the normalized eigenvector of $\mathbf{H}$ corresponding to λ_{max}. Thus the norm of the converged vector $\mathbf{z}$ gives a good estimate of $|\lambda_{max}|$, and its reciprocal may now be used as the learning rate in backprop. An on-line version of this procedure is reported by Le Cun et al. (1993).

Many heuristics have been proposed so as to adapt the learning rate automatically. Chan and Fallside (1987) proposed an adaptation rule for $\rho(t)$ that is based on the cosine of the angle between the gradient vectors $\nabla E(t)$ and $\nabla E(t-1)$ (here, t is an integer that represents iteration number). Sutton (1986) presented a method that can increase or decrease $\rho_i(t)$ for each weight w_i according to the number of sign changes observed in the associated partial derivative $\dfrac{\partial E}{\partial w_i}$. This method also was studied empirically by Jacobs (1988). Franzini (1987) investigated a technique that heuristically adjusts $\rho(t)$, increasing it whenever $\nabla E(t)$ is close to $\nabla E(t-1)$ and decreasing it otherwise. Cater (1987) suggested using separate parameters $\rho^k(t)$ one for each pattern $\mathbf{x}^k$.

Silva and Almeida (1990; see also Vogl et al., 1988) used a method where the learning rate for a given weight w_i is set to $a\rho_i(t)$ if $\dfrac{\partial E(t)}{\partial w_i}$ and $\dfrac{\partial E(t-1)}{\partial w_i}$ have the same sign, with $a > 1$; if the partial derivatives have different signs, then a learning rate of $b\rho_i(t)$ is used, with $0 < b < 1$. A similar, theoretically justified method for increasing the convergence speed of incremental gradient-descent search is to set $\rho(t) = \rho(t-1)$ if $\nabla E(t)$ has the same sign as $\nabla E(t-1)$, and $\rho(t) = \rho(t-1)/2$ otherwise (Pflug, 1990).

When the input vectors are assumed to be randomly and independently chosen from a probability distribution, we may view incremental backprop as a stochastic gradient-descent algorithm, along the lines of the theory in Section 4.2.2. Thus simply setting the learning rate ρ to a constant results in persistent residual fluctuations around a local minimum $\mathbf{w}^*$. The variance of such fluctuations depends on the size of ρ, the criterion function being minimized, and the training set. Based on results from stochastic approximation theory (Ljung, 1977), the "running average" schedule $\rho(t) = \rho_0/(1+t)$, with sufficiently small ρ, guarantees asymptotic convergence to a local minimum $\mathbf{w}^*$. However, this schedule leads to very slow convergence. Here, one would like to start the search with a learning rate faster than $1/t$ but then ultimately converge to the $1/t$ rate as $\mathbf{w}^*$ is approached. Unfortunately, increasing ρ_0 can lead to instability for small t. Darken and Moody (1991) proposed the "search then converge" schedule $\rho(t) = \rho_0/[1 + (t/\tau)]$, which allows for faster convergence without compromising stability. In this schedule, the learning rate stays relatively high for a "search time" τ during which it is hoped that the weights will hover about a good minimum. Then, for times $t \gg \tau$, the learning rate decreases as $\tau\rho_0/t$, and the learning converges. Note that for $\tau = 1$, this schedule reduces to the running average schedule. Therefore, a procedure for optimizing τ is needed. A completely automatic "search then converge" schedule can be found in Darken and Moody (1992).

5.2.3   Momentum

Another simple approach to speed up backprop is through the addition of a momentum term (Plaut et al., 1986) to the right-hand side of the weight update rules in Equations (5.1.2) and (5.1.9). Here, each weight change Δw_i is given some momentum so that it accelerates in the average downhill direction instead of fluctuating with every change in the sign of the associated partial derivative $\dfrac{\partial E}{\partial w_i}$. The addition of momentum to gradient search is stated formally as

$$\Delta w_i(t) = -\rho \frac{\partial E}{\partial w_i(t)} + \alpha \Delta w_i(t-1) \tag{5.2.1}$$

where α is a momentum rate normally chosen between 0 and 1 and $\Delta w_i(t-1) = w_i(t) - w_i(t-1)$. Equation (5.2.1) is a special case of multistage gradient methods that have been proposed for accelerating convergence (Wegstein, 1958) and escaping local minima (Tsypkin, 1971).

The momentum term also can be viewed as a way of increasing the effective learning rate in almost-flat regions of the error surface while maintaining a learning rate close to ρ (here $0 < \rho \ll 1$) in regions with high fluctuations. This can be seen by employing an N-step recursion and writing Equation (5.2.1) as

$$\Delta w_i(t) = -\rho \sum_{n=0}^{N-1} \alpha^n \frac{\partial E}{\partial w_i(t-n)} + \alpha^N \Delta w_i(t-N) \tag{5.2.2}$$

If the search point is caught in a flat region, then $\dfrac{\partial E}{\partial w_i}$ will be about the same at each time step, and Equation (5.2.2) can be approximated as (with $0 < \alpha < 1$ and N large)

$$\Delta w_i(t) \approx -\rho \frac{\partial E}{\partial w_i(t)} \sum_{n=0}^{N-1} \alpha^n = -\frac{\rho}{1-\alpha} \frac{\partial E}{\partial w_i(t)} \tag{5.2.3}$$

Thus, for flat regions, a momentum term leads to increasing the learning rate by a factor $1/(1-\alpha)$. On the other hand, if the search point is in a region of high fluctuation, the weight change will not gain momentum; i.e., the momentum effect vanishes. An empirical study of the effects of ρ and α on the convergence of backprop and on its learning curve can be found in Tollenaere (1990).

Adaptive momentum rates also may be employed. Fahlman (1989) proposed and extensively simulated a heuristic variation of backprop, called *quickprop*, that employs a dynamic momentum rate given by

$$\alpha(t) = \frac{\dfrac{\partial E}{\partial w_i(t)}}{\dfrac{\partial E}{\partial w_i(t-1)} - \dfrac{\partial E}{\partial w_i(t)}} \tag{5.2.4}$$

With this adaptive $\alpha(t)$ substituted in Equation (5.2.1), if the current slope is persistently smaller than the previous one but has the same sign, then $\alpha(t)$ is positive, and the weight change will accelerate. Here, the acceleration rate is determined by the magnitude of successive differences between slope values. If the current slope is in the opposite direction from the previous one, it signals that the weights are crossing over a minimum. In this case, $\alpha(t)$ has a negative sign, and the weight change starts to decelerate. Additional heuristics are used to handle the undesirable case where the current slope is in the same direction as the previous one but has the same or larger magnitude; otherwise, this scenario would lead to taking an infinite step or moving the search point backwards or up the current slope and toward a local maximum. Substituting Equation (5.2.4) in Equation (5.2.1) leads to the update rule

$$\Delta w_i(t) = -\rho \frac{\partial E}{\partial w_i(t)} - \frac{\dfrac{\partial E}{\partial w_i(t)}}{\left[\dfrac{\dfrac{\partial E}{\partial w_i(t)} - \dfrac{\partial E}{\partial w_i(t-1)}}{\Delta w_i(t-1)} \right]} \tag{5.2.5}$$

It is interesting to note that Equation (5.2.5) corresponds to steepest gradient-descent-based adaptation with a dynamically changing effective learning rate $\rho(t)$. This learning rate is given by the sum of the original constant learning rate ρ and the reciprocal of the denominator of the second term in the right-hand side of Equation (5.2.5).

The use of error gradient information at two consecutive time steps in Equation (5.2.4) to improve convergence speed can be justified as being based on approximations of second-order search methods such as Newton's method. Newton's method (e.g., Dennis and Schnabel, 1983) is based on a quadratic model $\tilde{E}(\mathbf{w})$ of the criterion $E(\mathbf{w})$ and hence uses only the first three terms in a Taylor series expansion of E about the "current" weight vector $\mathbf{w}^c$:

$$\tilde{E}(\mathbf{w}^c + \Delta \mathbf{w}) = E(\mathbf{w}^c) + \nabla E(\mathbf{w}^c)^{\mathrm{T}} \Delta \mathbf{w} + \tfrac{1}{2} \Delta \mathbf{w}^{\mathrm{T}} \nabla^2 E(\mathbf{w}^c) \Delta \mathbf{w}$$

This quadratic function is minimized by solving the equation $\nabla \tilde{E}(\mathbf{w}^c + \Delta \mathbf{w}) = \mathbf{0}$, which leads to Newton's method: $\Delta \mathbf{w} = -[\nabla^2 E(\mathbf{w}^c)]^{-1} \nabla E(\mathbf{w}^c) = -[\mathbf{H}(\mathbf{w}^c)]^{-1} \nabla E(\mathbf{w}^c)$. Here, $\mathbf{H}$ is the Hessian matrix with components $\mathbf{H}_{ij} = \dfrac{\partial^2 E}{\partial w_i \, \partial w_j}$.

Newton's algorithm iteratively computes the weight changes $\Delta \mathbf{w}$ and works well when initialized within a convex region of E. In fact, the algorithm converges quickly if the search region is quadratic or nearly so. However, this method is very computationally expensive, since the computation $\mathbf{H}^{-1}$ requires $O(N^3)$ operations at each iteration (here, N is the dimension of the search space). Several authors have suggested computationally efficient ways of approximating Newton's method (Parker, 1987; Ricotti et al., 1988; Becker and Le Cun, 1989). Becker and Le Cun proposed an approach whereby the off-diagonal elements of $\mathbf{H}$ are neglected, thus arriving at the approximation

$$\Delta w_i = -\frac{\partial E}{\partial w_i} \left(\frac{\partial^2 E}{\partial w_i^2} \right)^{-1} \tag{5.2.6}$$

which is a "decoupled" form of Newton's rule where each weight is updated separately. The second term in the right-hand side of Equation (5.2.5) can now be viewed as an approximation of Newton's rule, since its denominator is a crude approximation of the second derivative of E at step t. In fact, this suggests that the weight update rule in Equation (5.2.5) may be used with $\rho = 0$.

As with Equation (5.2.4), special heuristics must be used in order to prevent the search from moving in the wrong gradient direction and in order to deal with regions of very small curvature, such as inflection points and plateaus, which cause Δw_i in Equation (5.2.6) to blow up. A simple solution is to replace the $\dfrac{\partial^2 E}{\partial w_i^2}$ term in Equation (5.2.6) by $\left| \dfrac{\partial^2 E}{\partial w_i^2} \right| + \mu$, where μ is a small positive constant. The approximate Newton method just described is capable of scaling the descent step in each direction. However, because it neglects off-diagonal Hessian terms, it is not able to rotate the search direction as in the exact Newton's method. Thus this approximate rule is only efficient if the directions of maximal and minimal curvature of E happen to be aligned with the weight space axes. Bishop (1992) reported a somewhat efficient technique for computing the elements of the Hessian matrix exactly using multiple feedforward propagation through the network followed by multiple backward propagation.

Another approach for deriving theoretically justifiable update schedules for the momentum rate in Equation (5.2.1) is to adjust $\alpha(t)$ at each update step such that the gradient-descent search direction is "locally" optimal. In *optimal steepest descent* (also known as *best-step steepest descent*), the learning rate is set at time t such that it minimizes the criterion function E at time step $t + 1$; i.e., we desire a ρ that minimizes $E[\mathbf{w}(t + 1)] = E\{\mathbf{w}(t) - \rho \nabla E[\mathbf{w}(t)]\}$. Unfortunately, this optimal learning step is impractical because it requires computation of the Hessian $\nabla^2 E$ at each time step (refer to Problem 5.2.12 for an expression for the optimal ρ). However, one may still use some of the properties of the optimal ρ in order to accelerate the search, as demonstrated next.

When $\mathbf{w}(t)$ is specified, the necessary condition for minimizing $E[\mathbf{w}(t + 1)]$ is (Tompkins, 1956; Brown, 1959)

$$\frac{\partial E[\mathbf{w}(t + 1)]}{\partial \rho} = \nabla E[\mathbf{w}(t + 1)]^{\mathrm{T}} \frac{\partial \mathbf{w}(t + 1)}{\partial \rho}$$

$$= -\nabla E[\mathbf{w}(t + 1)]^{\mathrm{T}} \nabla E[\mathbf{w}(t)] = 0$$

(5.2.7)

This implies that the search direction in two successive steps of optimal steepest descent are orthogonal. The easiest method to enforce the orthogonal requirement is the Gram-Schmidt orthogonalization method. Suppose that the search direction at time $t - 1$ is known, denoted $\mathbf{d}(t - 1)$, and that the "exact" gradient $\nabla E(t)$ (used in batch backprop) can be computed at time step t [to simplify notation, we write $E[\mathbf{w}(t)]$ as $E(t)$]. Now, we can satisfy the condition of orthogonal consecutive search directions by computing a new search direction, employing Gram-Schmidt orthogonolization (Yu et al., 1993)

$$\mathbf{d}(t) = -\nabla E(t) + \frac{\nabla E(t)^{\mathrm{T}}\mathbf{d}(t - 1)}{\mathbf{d}(t - 1)^{\mathrm{T}}\mathbf{d}(t - 1)}\mathbf{d}(t - 1) \tag{5.2.8}$$

Performing descent search in the direction $\mathbf{d}(t)$ in Equation (5.2.8) leads to the weight vector update rule

$$\Delta\mathbf{w}(t) = -\rho\nabla E(t) + \frac{\nabla E(t)^{\mathrm{T}}\mathbf{d}(t - 1)}{\|\mathbf{d}(t - 1)\|^{2}}\Delta\mathbf{w}(t - 1) \tag{5.2.9}$$

where the relation $\Delta\mathbf{w}(t - 1) = \mathbf{w}(t) - \mathbf{w}(t - 1) = +\rho\mathbf{d}(t - 1)$ has been used. Comparing the component-wise weight update version of Equation (5.2.9) with Equation (5.2.1) reveals another adaptive momentum rate given by

$$\alpha(t) = \frac{\nabla E(t)^{\mathrm{T}}\mathbf{d}(t - 1)}{\|\mathbf{d}(t - 1)\|^{2}} = \rho\,\frac{\nabla E(t)^{\mathrm{T}}\Delta\mathbf{w}(t - 1)}{\|\Delta\mathbf{w}(t - 1)\|^{2}}$$

Another similar approach is to set the current search direction $\mathbf{d}(t)$ to be a compromise between the current "exact" gradient $\nabla E(t)$ and the previous search direction $\mathbf{d}(t - 1)$; i.e., $\mathbf{d}(t) = -\nabla E(t) + \beta\mathbf{d}(t - 1)$, with $\mathbf{d}(0) = -\nabla E(0)$. This is the basis for the conjugate gradient method in which the search direction is chosen (by appropriately setting β) so that it distorts as little as possible the minimization achieved by the previous search step. Here, the current search direction is chosen to be conjugate (with respect to $\mathbf{H}$) to the previous search direction. Analytically, we require $\mathbf{d}(t - 1)^{\mathrm{T}}\mathbf{H}(t - 1)\mathbf{d}(t) = 0$, where the Hessian $\mathbf{H}(t - 1)$ is assumed to be positive definite. In practice, β, which plays the role of an adaptive momentum, is chosen according to the Polack-Ribiére rule (Polack and Ribiére, 1969; Press et al., 1986):

$$\beta = \beta(t) = \frac{[\nabla E(t) - \nabla E(t - 1)]^{\mathrm{T}}\nabla E(t)}{\|\nabla E(t - 1)\|^{2}}$$

Thus the search direction in the conjugate gradient method at time t is given by

$$\mathbf{d}(t) = -\nabla E(t) + \beta\mathbf{d}(t - 1)$$

$$= -\nabla E(t) + \frac{[\nabla E(t) - \nabla E(t - 1)]^{\mathrm{T}}\nabla E(t)}{\|\nabla E(t - 1)\|^{2}}\mathbf{d}(t - 1)$$

Now, using $\mathbf{d}(t - 1) = (1/\rho)\Delta\mathbf{w}(t - 1)$ and substituting the preceding expression for $\mathbf{d}(t)$ in $\Delta\mathbf{w}(t) = \rho\mathbf{d}(t)$ leads to the weight update rule:

$$\Delta\mathbf{w}(t) = -\rho\nabla E(t) + \frac{[\nabla E(t) - \nabla E(t - 1)]^T\nabla E(t)}{\|\nabla E(t - 1)\|^2}\Delta\mathbf{w}(t - 1)$$

When E is quadratic, the conjugate gradient method theoretically converges in N or fewer iterations. In general, E is not quadratic, and therefore, this method would be slower than what the theory predicts. However, it is reasonable to assume that E is approximately quadratic near a local minimum. Therefore, conjugate gradient descent is expected to accelerate the convergence of backprop once the search enters a small neighborhood of a local minimum. As a general note, the basic idea of conjugate gradient search was introduced by Hestenes and Stiefel (1952). Beckman (1964) gives a good account of this method. Battiti (1992) and van der Smagt (1994) gave additional characterization of second-order backprop (such as conjugate gradient-based backprop) from the point of view of optimization. The conjugate gradient method has been applied to multilayer feedforward neural net training (Kramer and Sangiovanni-Vincentelli, 1989; Makram-Ebeid et al., 1989; van der Smagt, 1994) and is shown to outperform backprop in speed of convergence.

It is important to note that the preceding second-order modifications to backprop improve the speed of convergence of the weights to the "closest" local minimum. This faster convergence to local minima is the direct result of employing a better search direction as compared with incremental backprop. On the other hand, the stochastic nature of the search directions of incremental backprop and its fixed learning rates can be an advantage, since they allow the search to escape shallow local minima, which generally leads to better solution quality. These observations suggest the use of hybrid learning algorithms (Møller, 1990; Gorse and Shepherd, 1992), where one starts with incremental backprop and then switches to conjugate gradient-based backprop for the final convergence phase. This hybrid method has its roots in a technique from numerical analysis known as *Levenberg-Marquardt optimization* (Press et al., 1986).

As a historical note, it should be mentioned that the concept of gradient descent was first introduced by Cauchy (1847) for use in the solution of simultaneous equations; the method has enjoyed popularity ever since. It also should be noted that some of the preceding enhancements to gradient search date back to the fifties and sixties and are discussed in Tsypkin (1971). Additional modifications of the gradient-descent method that enhance its convergence to global minima are discussed in Section 8.1. For a good survey of gradient search, the reader is referred to the book by Polyak (1987).

5.2.4   Activation Function

As indicated earlier in this section, backprop suffers from premature convergence of
some units to flat spots. During training, if a unit in a multilayer network receives a
weighted signal *net* with a large magnitude, this unit outputs a value close to one of
the saturation levels of its activation function. If the corresponding target value (desired target value for an output unit or an unknown "correct" hidden target for a
hidden unit) is substantially different from that of the saturated unit, one can say that
the unit is incorrectly saturated or has entered a flat spot. When this happens, the size
of the weight update due to backprop will be very small, even though the error is
relatively large, and it will take an excessively long time for such incorrectly saturated
units to reverse their states. This situation can be explained by referring to Figure
5.2.1., where the activation function $f(net) = \tanh(\beta\, net)$ and its derivative f' [given
in Equation (5.1.12)] are plotted for $\beta = 1$. Here, when *net* has large magnitude, f'
approaches zero. Thus the weight change approaches zero in Equations (5.1.2) and
(5.1.9) even when there is a large difference between the actual and desired output for
a given unit.

A simple solution to the flat-spot problem is to bias the derivative of the activation
function (Fahlman, 1989); i.e., replace f'_o and f'_h in Equation (5.1.2) and (5.1.9) by
$f'_o + \varepsilon$ and $f'_h + \varepsilon$, respectively (a typical value for ε is 0.1). Hinton (1987a) suggested

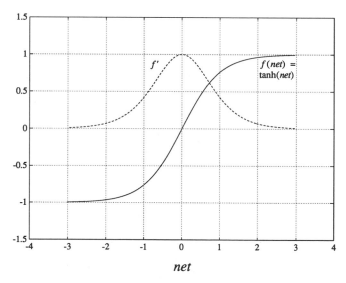

Figure 5.2.1
Plots of $f(net) = \tanh(net)$ and its derivative $f'(net)$.

the use of a nonlinear error function that goes to infinity at the points where f' goes to zero, resulting in a finite nonzero error value [see Franzini (1987) for an example of using such an error function]. The entropic criterion of Equation (3.1.76) is a good choice for the error function because it leads to an output unit update rule similar to that of Equation (5.1.2) but without the f_o' term [note, however, that the update rule for the hidden units would still have the derivative term; see Equation (5.2.18) in Section 5.2.7]. One also may modify the basic sigmoid activation function in backprop to reduce flat-spot effects. Use of the homotopy activation function $f_\alpha(net) = \alpha\, net + (1 - \alpha)f(net)$ is one such example (Yang and Yu, 1993). Here, $f_\alpha(net)$ forms a homotopy between a linear and a sigmoid function with $\alpha \in [0, 1]$. Initially, α is set to 1; i.e., all nodes have linear activations. Backprop is used to achieve a minimum in E, then α is decreased (monotonically), and backprop is continued until α is zero. That is, the activation function recovers its sigmoidal nature gradually as training progresses. Since $\dfrac{df_\alpha(net)}{d\,net} > \alpha$ and α is nonzero for most of the training phase, flat-spot effects are eliminated. Besides reducing the effects of flat spot, the homotopy function also helps backprop escape some local minima. This can be seen by noting that when $\alpha = 1$, the error function $E(\mathbf{w}, \alpha)$ is a polynomial of $\mathbf{w}$ that has a relatively smaller number of local minima than $E(\mathbf{w}, \alpha < 1)$. Because a minimum point of $E(\mathbf{w}, \alpha = 1)$ has been achieved, which can provide a relatively better initial point for minimizing $E(\mathbf{w}, \alpha < 1)$, many unwanted local minima are avoided. An alternative explanation of the effect of a gradually increasing activation function slope on the avoidance of local minima is given in Section 8.4 based on the concept of mean-field annealing.

Another method for reducing flat-spot effects involves dynamically updating the activation slope [λ and β in Equations (5.1.11) and (5.1.12), respectively] such that the slope of each unit is adjusted, independently, in the direction of reduced output error (Tawel, 1989; Kufudaki and Horejs, 1990; Rezgui and Tepedelenlioglu, 1990; Kruschke and Movellan, 1991; Sperduti and Starita, 1991, 1993). Gradient descent on the error surface in the activation function's slope space leads to the following update rules (assuming hyperbolic tangent activation functions):

$$\Delta\beta_l = -\eta_o\frac{\partial E}{\partial\beta_l} = +\eta_o(d_l - y_l)(1 - y_l^2)\,net_l \tag{5.2.10}$$

and

$$\Delta\beta_j = -\eta_h\frac{\partial E}{\partial\beta_j} = +\eta_h\left[\sum_l \beta_l w_{lj}(d_l - y_l)(1 - y_l^2)\right](1 - z_j^2)\,net_j \tag{5.2.11}$$

for the lth output unit and the jth hidden unit, respectively. Here, η_o and η_h are small positive constants. Typically, when initialized with slopes near unity, Equations (5.2.10) and (5.2.11) reduce the activation slopes toward zero, which increases the effective dynamic range of the activation function, which, in turn, reduces flat-spot effects and therefore allows the weights to update rapidly in the initial stages of learning. As the algorithm begins to converge, the slope starts to increase and thus restores the saturation properties of the units. It is important to note here that the slope adaptation process just described becomes a part of the backprop weight update procedure; the slopes are updated after every weight update step.

Other nonsigmoid activation functions may be used as long as they are differentiable (Robinson et al., 1989). From the discussion on the approximation capabilities of multilayer feedforward networks in Section 2.3, a wide range of activation functions may be employed without compromising the universal approximation capabilities of such networks. However, the advantages of choosing one particular class of activation functions (or a mixture of various functions) is not completely understood. Moody and Yarvin (1992) reported an empirical study where they have compared feedforward networks with a single-hidden-layer feeding into a single-linear-output unit, each network employing a different type of differentiable nonlinear activation function. The types of activation functions considered by Moody and Yarvin included the sigmoid logistic function, polynomials, rational functions (ratios of polynomials), and Fourier series (sums of cosines). Benchmark simulations on a few data sets representing noisy data with only mild nonlinearity and noiseless data with a high degree of nonlinearity were performed. It was found that the networks with nonsigmoidal activations attained superior performance on the highly nonlinear noiseless data. On the set of noisy data with mild nonlinearity, however, polynomials did poorly, whereas rationals and Fourier series showed better performance and were comparable with sigmoids.

Other methods for improving the training speed of feedforward multilayer networks involve replacing the sigmoid units by Gaussian or other units. These methods are covered in Chapter 6.

5.2.5 Weight Decay, Weight Elimination, and Unit Elimination

In Chapter 4 (Section 4.8), it was shown that in order to guarantee good generalization, the number of degrees of freedom or number of weights (which determines a network's complexity) must be considerably smaller than the amount of information available for training. Some insight into this matter can be gained from considering an analogous problem in curve fitting (Duda and Hart, 1973; Wieland and Leighton, 1987). For example, consider the rational function $g(x) = [(x - 2)(2x + 1)]/(1 + x^2)$,

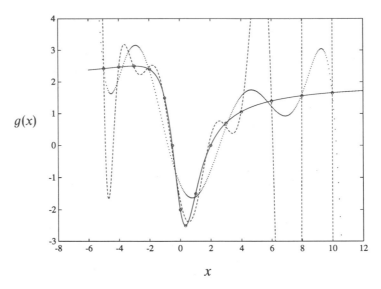

Figure 5.2.2
Polynomial approximation for the function $g(x) = [(x - 2)(2x + 1)]/(1 + x^2)$
(*solid line*) based on the 15 samples shown (*small circles*). The objective of the
approximation is to minimize the sum of squared error criterion. The dashed
line represents an eleventh-order polynomial. A better overall approximation for
$g(x)$ is given by an eighth-order polynomial (*dotted line*).

which is plotted in Figure 5.2.2 (solid line). And assume that we are given a set of 15
samples (shown as small circles) from which we are to find a "good" approximation
to $g(x)$. Two polynomial approximations are shown in Figure 5.2.2: an eleventh-order
polynomial (dashed line) and an eighth-order polynomial (dotted line). These approximations are computed by minimizing the SSE criterion over the sample points. The
higher-order polynomial has about the same number of parameters as the number of
training samples and thus is shown to give a very close fit to the data; this is referred
to as *memorization*. However, it is clear from the figure that this polynomial does not
provide good "generalization" (i.e., it does not provide reliable interpolation and/or
extrapolation) over the full range of data. On the other hand, fitting the data by an
eighth-order polynomial leads to relatively better overall interpolations over a wider
range of x values (refer to the dotted line in Figure 5.2.2). In this case, the number of
free parameters is equal to 9, which is smaller than the number of training samples.
This "underdetermined" nature leads to an approximation function that better
matches the "smooth" function $g(x)$ being approximated. Trying to use a yet lower-
order polynomial (e.g., fifth order or less) leads to a poor approximation because this

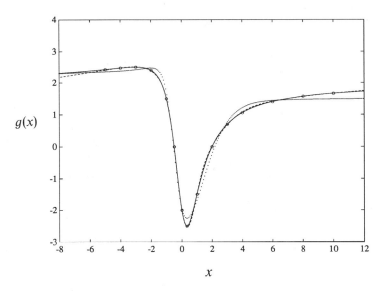

Figure 5.2.3
Neural network approximation for the function $g(x) = [(x - 2)(2x + 1)]/(1 + x^2)$
(*solid line*). The dotted line was generated by a 3-hidden-unit feedforward net.
The dashed line, which is shown to have substantial overlap with $g(x)$, was
generated by a 12-hidden unit feedforward net. In both cases, standard incremental backprop training was used.

polynomial would not have sufficient "flexibility" to capture the nonlinear structure
in $g(x)$.

The reader is advised to consider the nature and complexity of this simple approximation problem by carefully studying Figure 5.2.2. Here, the total number of possible
training samples of the form $(x, g(x))$ is uncountably infinite. From this huge set of
potential data, though, we chose only 15 samples to try to approximate the function.
In this case, the approximation involved minimizing an SSE criterion function over
these few sample points. Clearly, however, a solution that is globally (or near globally)
optimal in terms of sum-squared error over the training set (e.g., the eleventh-order
polynomial) may be hardly appropriate in terms of interpolation (generalization)
between data points. Thus one should choose a class of approximation functions that
penalizes unnecessary fluctuations between training sample points. Neural networks
satisfy this approximation property and are thus superior to polynomials in approximating arbitrary nonlinear functions from sample points (see further discussion given
below). Figure 5.2.3 shows the results of simulations involving the approximation of
the function $g(x)$, with the same set of samples used in the preceding simulations,

using single-hidden-layer feedforward neural nets. Here, all hidden units employ the hyperbolic tangent activation function (with a slope of 1), and the output unit is linear. These nets are trained using the incremental backprop algorithm [given by Equations (5.1.2) and (5.1.9)] with $\rho_o = 0.05$ and $\rho_h = 0.01$. Weights are initialized randomly and uniformly over the range $[-0.2, +0.2]$. The training was stopped when the rate of change of the SSE became insignificantly small. The dotted line in Figure 5.2.3 is for a net with three hidden units (which amounts to 10 degrees of freedom). Surprisingly, increasing the number of hidden units to 12 units (37 degrees of freedom) improved the quality of the fit, as shown by the dashed line in the figure. By comparing Figures 5.2.3 and 5.2.2, it is clear that the neural net approximation for $g(x)$ is superior to that of polynomials in terms of accurate interpolation and extrapolation.

The generalization superiority of the neural net can be attributed to the bounded and smooth nature of the hidden-unit responses as compared with the potentially divergent nature of polynomials. The bounded-unit response localizes the nonlinear effects of individual hidden units in a neural network and allows for the approximations in different regions of the input space to be independently tuned. This approximation process is similar in its philosophy to the traditional spline technique for curve fitting (Schumaker, 1981). Hornik et al. (1990) gave related theoretical justification for the usefulness of feedforward neural nets with sigmoidal hidden units in function approximation. They showed that in addition to approximating the training set, the derivative of the output of the network evaluated at the training data points is also a good approximation of the derivative of the unknown function being approximated.[4] This result explains the good extrapolation capability of neural nets observed in simulations. For example, the behavior of the neural net output shown in Figure 5.2.3 for $x > 10$ and $x < -5$ is a case in point. It should be noted, though, that in most practical situations the training data are noisy. Hence an exact fit of these data must be avoided, which means that the degrees of freedom of a neural net approximator must be constrained. Otherwise, the net will have a tendency for overfitting. This issue is explored next.

Once a particular approximation function or network architecture is decided on, generalization can be improved if the number of free parameters in the net is optimized. Since it is difficult to estimate the optimal number of weights (or units) a priori,

---

4. In addition, Hornik et al. (1990) showed that a multilayer feedforward network can approximate functions that are not differentiable in the classical sense but possess a generalized derivative, as in the case of piece-wise differentiable functions and functions with discontinuities. For example, a neural net with one hidden unit that employs the hyperbolic tangent function and a linear output unit can approximate very accurately the discontinuous function $g(x) = a\,\text{sgn}\,(x - b) + c$ (see Problem 5.2.16 for details).

there has been much interest in techniques that automatically remove excess weights and/or units from a network. These techniques are sometimes referred to as *network pruning algorithms* and are surveyed in Reed (1993).

One of the earliest and simplest approaches to remove excess degrees of freedom from a neural network is through the use of simple weight decay (Plaut et al., 1986; Hinton, 1986), in which each weight decays toward zero at a rate proportional to its magnitude so that connections disappear unless reinforced. Hinton (1987b) gave empirical justification by showing that such weight decay improves generalization in feedforward networks. Krogh and Hertz (1992) gave some theoretical justification for this generalization phenomenon.

Weight decay in the weight update equations of backprop can be accounted for by adding a complexity (regularization) term to the criterion function E that penalizes large weights:

$$J(\mathbf{w}) = E(\mathbf{w}) + \frac{\lambda}{2} \sum_i w_i^2 \qquad (5.2.12)$$

Here, λ represents the relative importance of the complexity term with respect to the error term $E(\mathbf{w})$ [note that the second term in Equation (5.2.12) is a regularization term as in Equation (4.1.3)]. Now, gradient search for minima of $J(\mathbf{w})$ leads to the following weight update rule:

$$\Delta w_i = -\rho \frac{\partial E}{\partial w_i} - \rho \lambda w_i \qquad (5.2.13)$$

which shows an exponential decay in w_i if no learning occurs. Because it penalizes more weights than necessary, the criterion function in Equation (5.1.12) overly discourages the use of large weights where a single large weight costs much more than many small ones. Weigend et al. (1991) proposed a procedure of weight elimination given by minimizing

$$J(\mathbf{w}) = E(\mathbf{w}) + \frac{\lambda}{2} \sum_i \frac{w_i^2}{w_0^2} \left(1 + \frac{w_i^2}{w_0^2} \right)^{-1} \qquad (5.2.14)$$

where the penalty term on the right-hand side helps regulate weight magnitudes and w_0 is a positive free parameter that must be determined. For large w_0, this procedure reduces to the weight decay procedure described above and hence favors many small weights, whereas if w_0 is small, fewer large weights are favored. Also note that when $|w_i| \gg w_0$, the cost of the weight approaches 1 (times λ), which justifies interpretation of the penalty term as a counter of large weights. In practice, a w_0 close to unity is used. It should be noted that this weight elimination procedure is very sensitive to the choice of λ. A heuristic for adjusting λ dynamically during learning is described in Weigend et al. (1991). For yet other forms of the complexity term, the reader is referred to Nowlan and Hinton (1992a, 1992b) and Section 5.2.7.

The preceding ideas have been extended to unit elimination [e.g., see Hanson and Pratt (1989), Chauvin (1989), Hassoun et al. (1990)]. Here, one would start with an excess of hidden units and dynamically discard redundant ones. As an example, one could penalize redundant units by replacing the weight decay term in Equation (5.2.13) by $-(\rho\lambda)/(1 + \sum_i w_{ji}^2)^2$ for all weights of hidden units, which leads to the hidden-unit update rule

$$\Delta w_{ji} = -\rho_h \frac{\partial E}{\partial w_{ji}} - \rho\lambda \frac{1}{\left(1 + \sum_i w_{ji}^2\right)^2} \qquad (5.2.15)$$

Generalization in feedforward networks also can be improved by using network construction procedures as opposed to weight or unit pruning. Here, one starts with a small network and allows it to grow gradually (add more units) in response to incoming data. The idea is to keep the network as small as possible. In Chapter 6 (Section 6.3), three adaptive networks having unit-allocation capabilities are discussed. Further details on network construction procedures can be found in Marchand et al. (1990), Frean (1990), Fahlman and Lebiere (1990), and Mézard and Nadal (1989).

5.2.6   Cross-Validation

An alternative or complementary strategy to the preceding methods for improving generalization in feedforward neural networks is suggested by findings based on empirical results (Morgan and Bourlard, 1990; Weigend et al., 1991; Hergert et al., 1992). In simulations involving backprop training of feedforward nets on noisy data, it is found that the validation (generalization) error decreases monotonically to a minimum but then starts to increase, even as the training error continues to decrease. This phenomenon is depicted in the conceptual plot in Figure 5.2.4 and is illustrated through the computer simulation given next.

Consider the problem of approximating the rational function $g(x)$ plotted in Figure 5.2.3 from a set of noisy sample points. This set of points is generated from the 15 perfect samples, shown in Figure 5.2.3, by adding zero-mean normally distributed random noise with variance of 0.25. A single-hidden-layer feedforward neural net is used with 12 sigmoidal hidden units and a single linear output unit. It employs incremental backprop training with $\rho_o = 0.05$, $\rho_h = 0.01$, and initial random weights in $[-0.2, +0.2]$. After 80 training cycles on the 15 noisy samples, the net is tested for

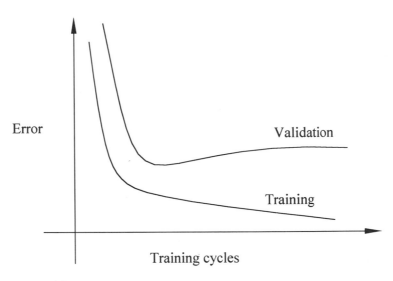

Figure 5.2.4
Training error and validation error encountered in training multilayer feedforward
neural nets using backprop.

uniformly sampled inputs x in the range $[-8, 12]$. The output of this 80-cycle net is
shown as a dashed line in Figure 5.2.5. Next, the training continued and then stopped
after 10,000 cycles. The output of the resulting net is shown as a dotted line in the
figure. Comparing the two approximations in Figure 5.2.5 leads to the conclusion that
the partially trained net is superior to the excessively trained net in terms of overall
interpolation and extrapolation capabilities. Further insight into the dynamics of the
generalization process for this problem can be gained from Figure 5.2.6. Here, the
validation RMS error is monitored by testing the net on a validation set of 294 perfect
samples, uniformly spaced in the interval $[-8, 12]$, after every 10 training cycles. This
validation error is shown as the dashed line in Figure 5.2.6. The training error (RMS
error on the training set of 15 points) is also shown in the figure as a solid line.
Note that the optimal net in terms of overall generalization capability is the one
obtained after about 80 to 90 training cycles.[5] Beyond this training point, the training

5. In general, the global minimum of the validation RMS error curve, which is being used to determine the
optimally trained net, is also a function of the number of hidden units/weights in the net. Therefore, the
possibility exists for a better approximation than the one obtained here, though, in order to find such an
approximation, one would need to repeat the preceding simulations for various numbers of hidden units.
The reader should be warned that this example is for illustrative purposes only. For example, if one has 294

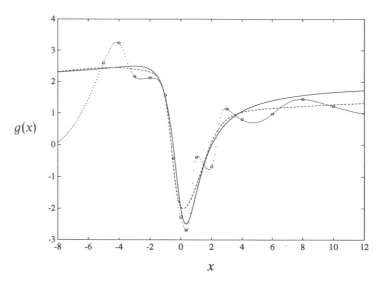

Figure 5.2.5
Two different neural network approximations (dashed lines and dotted lines) of the rational function $g(x)$ (*solid line*) from noisy samples. The training samples shown are generated from the 15 perfect samples in Figure 5.2.3 by adding zero-mean normally distributed random noise with 0.25 variance. Both approximations resulted from the same net with 12 hidden units and incremental backprop learning. The dashed line represents the output of the net after 80 learning cycles. After completing 10,000 learning cycles, the same net generates the dotted line output.

error keeps decreasing, while the validation error increases. It is interesting to note the nonmonotonic behavior of the validation error between training cycles 2000 and 7000. This suggests that, in general, multiple local minima may exist in the validation error curves of backprop-trained feedforward feedforward neural networks. The location of these minima is a complex function of the network size, weight initialization, and learning parameters. To summarize, when training with noisy data, excessive training usually leads to overfitting. On the other hand, partial training may lead to a better approximation of the unknown function in the sense of improved interpolation and, possibly, improved extrapolation.

(or fewer) "perfect" samples, one would not have to worry about validation; one would just train on the available perfect data! In practice, the validation set is noisy; usually having the same noise statistics as for the training set. Also, in practice, the size of the validation set is smaller than that of the training set. Thus the expected generalization capability of what is referred to as the "optimally trained" net may not be as good as those reported here.

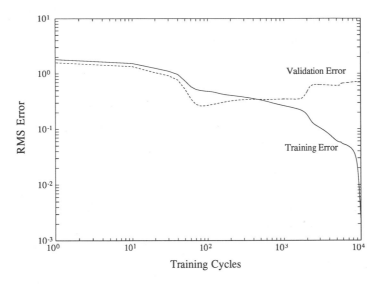

Figure 5.2.6
Training and validation RMS errors for the neural net approximation of the function $g(x)$. The training set consists of the 15 noisy samples in Figure 5.2.5. The validation set consists of 294 perfect samples uniformly spaced in the interval $[-8, 12]$. The validation error starts lower than the training error mainly because perfect samples are used for validation.

A qualitative explanation for the generalization phenomenon depicted in Figure 5.2.4 (and illustrated by the simulation in Figures 5.2.5 and 5.2.6) was advanced by Weigend et al. (1991). They explain that, to a first approximation, backprop initially adapts the hidden units in the network such that they all attempt to fit the major features of the data. Later, as training proceeds, some of the units then start to fit the noise in the data. This later process continues as long as there is error and as long as training continues (this is exactly what happens in the simulation of Figure 5.2.5). The overall process suggests that the effective number of free parameters (weights) starts small (even if the network is oversized) and gets larger, approaching the true number of adjustable parameters in the network as training proceeds. Baldi and Chauvin (1991) derived analytical results on the behavior of the validation error in LMS-trained single-layer feedforward networks learning the identity map from noisy autoassociation pattern pairs. Their results agree with the preceding generalization phenomenon in nonlinear multilayer feedforward nets. More recently, Wang et al. (1994) gave a formal justification for the phenomenon of improved generalization by stopping learning before the global minimum of the training error is reached. They showed that there exists a critical region in the training process where the trained network generalizes best, and after that the generalization error will increase. In this critical region, as long as the network is large enough to learn the examples, the size of the network has only a small effect on the best generalization performance of the network. All this means that stopping learning before the global minimum of the training error has the effect of network size (that is, network complexity) selection.

Therefore, a suitable strategy for improving generalization in networks of non-optimal size is to avoid "overtraining" by carefully monitoring the evolution of the validation error during training and stopping just before it starts to increase. This strategy is based on one of the early criteria in model evaluation known as *cross-validation* [e.g., see Stone (1978)]. Here, the whole available data set is split into three parts: training set, validation set, and prediction set. The training set is used to determine the values of the weights of the network. The validation set is used for deciding when to terminate training. Training continues as long as the performance on the validation set keeps improving. When it ceases to improve, training is stopped. The third part of the data, the prediction set, is used to estimate the expected performance (generalization) of the trained network on new data. In particular, the prediction set should not be used for validation during the training phase. Note that this heuristic requires the application to be data-rich. Some applications, though, suffer from scarcity of training data, which makes this method inappropriate. The reader is referred to Finnoff et al. (1993) for an empirical study of cross-validation–based generalization and its comparison to weight decay and other generalization-inducing methods.

5.2.7 Criterion Functions

As seen earlier in Section 3.1.5, other criterion/error functions can be used from which new versions of the backprop weight update rules can be derived. Here we consider two such criterion functions: (1) relative entropy and (2) Minkowski-r. Starting from the instantaneous entropy criterion (Baum and Wilczek, 1988)

$$E(\mathbf{w}) = \tfrac{1}{2} \sum_{l=1}^{L} \left[(1 + d_l)\ln\left(\frac{1 + d_l}{1 + y_l}\right) + (1 - d_l)\ln\left(\frac{1 - d_l}{1 - y_l}\right) \right] \qquad (5.2.16)$$

and employing gradient-descent search, the following learning equations are obtained:

$$\Delta w_{lj} = \rho_o \beta (d_l - y_l) z_j \qquad (5.2.17)$$

and

$$\Delta w_{ji} = \rho_h \beta^2 \left[\sum_{l=1}^{L} (d_l - y_l) w_{lj} \right] (1 - z_j^2) x_i \qquad (5.2.18)$$

for the output- and hidden-layer units, respectively. Equations (5.2.17) and (5.2.18) assume hyperbolic tangent activations at both layers.

From Equation (5.2.17) we see that the f'_o term present in the corresponding equation of standard backprop [Equation (5.1.2)] has now been eliminated. Thus the output units do not have a flat-spot problem; on the other hand, f'_h still appears in Equation (5.2.18) for the hidden units [this derivative appears implicitly as the $\beta(1 - z_j^2)$ term in the standard backprop equation]. Therefore, the flat-spot problem is only partially solved by employing the entropy criterion.

The entropy-based backprop is well suited to probabilistic training data. It has a natural interpretation in terms of learning the correct probabilities of a set of hypotheses represented by the outputs of units in a multilayer neural network. Here, the probability that the lth hypothesis is true given an input pattern $\mathbf{x}^k$ is determined by the output of the lth unit as $\frac{1}{2}(1 + y_l)$. The entropy criterion is a "well-formed" error function (Wittner and Denker, 1988); the reader is referred to Section 3.1.5 for a definition and discussion of "well-formed" error functions. Such functions have been shown in simulations to converge faster than standard backprop (Solla et al., 1988).

Another choice is the Minkowski-r criterion function (Hanson and Burr, 1988):

$$E(\mathbf{w}) = \frac{1}{r} \sum_{l=1}^{L} |d_l - y_l|^r \qquad (5.2.19)$$

which leads to the following weight update equations:

$$\Delta w_{lj} = \rho_o \, \text{sgn}\,(d_l - y_l)|d_l - y_l|^{r-1} f'_o(net_l) z_j \qquad (5.2.20)$$

and

$$\Delta w_{ji} = \rho_h \left[\sum_{l=1}^{L} \text{sgn}\,(d_l - y_l)|d_l - y_l|^{r-1} w_{lj} f'_o(net_l) \right] f'_h(net_j) x_i \qquad (5.2.21)$$

where sgn is the sign function. These equations reduce to those of standard backprop for the case $r = 2$. The motivation behind the use of this criterion is that it can lead to maximum-likelihood estimation of weights for Gaussian and non-Gaussian input data distributions by appropriately choosing r (e.g., $r = 1$ for data with Laplace distributions). A small r ($1 \leq r < 2$) gives less weight for large deviations and tends to reduce the influence of outlier points in the input space during learning. On the other hand, when noise is negligible, the sensitivity of the separating surfaces implemented by the hidden units to the geometry of the problem may be increased by employing $r > 2$. Here, fewer hidden units are recruited when learning complex nonlinearly separable mappings for larger r values (Hanson and Burr, 1988).

If no a priori knowledge is available about the distribution of the training data, it would be difficult to estimate a value for r without extensive experimentation with various r values (e.g., $r = 1.5, 2, 3$). Alternatively, an automatic method for estimating r is possible by adaptively updating r in the direction of decreasing E. Here, steepest gradient descent on $E(r)$ results in the update rule

$$\Delta r = \rho \frac{1}{r^2} \sum_l |d_l - y_l|^r - \rho \frac{1}{r} \sum_l |d_l - y_l|^r \ln|d_l - y_l| \qquad (5.2.22)$$

which when restricting r to be strictly greater than 1 (metric error measure case) may be approximated as

$$\Delta r \approx -\rho \frac{1}{r} \sum_l |d_l - y_l|^r \ln|d_l - y_l| \qquad (5.2.23)$$

Note that it is important that the r update rule be invoked much less frequently than the weight update rule (e.g., r is updated once every 10 training cycles of backprop).

The idea of increasing the learning robustness of backprop in noisy environments can be placed in a more general statistical framework (White, 1989) where the technique of robust statistics (Huber, 1981; Hampel et al., 1986) takes effect. Here, *robustness* of learning refers to insensitivity to small perturbations in the underlying probability distribution $p(\mathbf{x})$ of the training set. These statistical techniques motivate the replacement of the linear error $\varepsilon_l = d_l - y_l$ in Equations (5.1.2) and (5.1.9) by a nonlinear error suppressor function $f_e(\varepsilon_l)$ that is compatible with the underlying probability density function $p(\mathbf{x})$. One example is to set $f_e(\varepsilon_l) = \mathrm{sgn}(d_l - y_l)|d_l - y_l|^{r-1}$ with $1 \leq r < 2$. This error suppresser leads to the exact Minkowski-r weight update rule of Equations (5.2.20) and (5.2.21). In fact, the case $r = 1$ is equivalent to minimizing the summed absolute error criterion that is known to suppress outlier data points. Similarly, the selection $f_e(\varepsilon_l) = 2\varepsilon_l/(1 + \varepsilon_l^2)$ (Kosko, 1992) leads to robust backprop if $p(\mathbf{x})$ has long tails such as a Cauchy distribution or some other infinite variance density. [See Chen and Jain (1994) for a similar but more elaborate choice of $f_e(\varepsilon_l)$.]

Furthermore, regularization terms may be added to the preceding error functions $E(\mathbf{w})$ in order to introduce some desirable effects such as good generalization, smaller effective network size, smaller weight magnitudes, faster learning, etc. (Poggio and Girosi, 1990a; Mao and Jain, 1993). The regularization terms in Equations (5.2.12) and (5.2.14) used for enhancing generalization through weight pruning/elimination are examples. Another possible regularization term is $\lambda\|\nabla_x E\|^2$ (Drucker and Le Cun, 1992), which has been shown to improve backprop generalization by forcing the output to be insensitive to small changes in the input. It also helps speed up convergence by generating hidden-layer weight distributions that have smaller variances than those generated by standard backpropagation. (Refer to Problem 5.2.11 for yet another form of regularization.)

Weight sharing, a method where several weights in a network are controlled by a single parameter, is another way of enhancing generalization [Rumelhart et al. (1986b); also see Section 5.3.3 for an application]. It imposes equality constraints among weights, thus reducing the number of free (effective) parameters in the network, which leads to improved generalization. An automatic method for affecting weight sharing can be derived by adding the regularization term (Nowlan and Hinton, 1992a, 1992b)

$$J_R = -\sum_i \ln\left[\sum_j \alpha_j p_j(w_i)\right] \tag{5.2.24}$$

to the error function, where each $p_j(w_i)$ is a Gaussian density with mean μ_j and variance σ_j, the α_j is the mixing proportion of Gaussian p_j with $\sum_j \alpha_j = 1$, and w_i represents an arbitrary weight in the network. The α_j, μ_j, and σ_j parameters are assumed to adapt as the network learns. The use of multiple adaptive Gaussians allows the implementation of "soft weight sharing," in which the learning algorithm decides for itself which weights should be tied together. If the Gaussians all start with high variance, the initial grouping of weights into subsets will be very soft. As the network learns and the variance shrinks, the groupings become more and more distinct and converge to subsets influenced by the task being learned.

For gradient-descent-based adaptation, one may employ the partial derivatives

$$\frac{\partial J_R}{\partial w_i} = -\sum_j r_j(w_i)\left(\frac{\mu_j - w_i}{\sigma_j^2}\right), \tag{5.2.25}$$

$$\frac{\partial J_R}{\partial \mu_j} = +\sum_i r_j(w_i)\left(\frac{\mu_j - w_i}{\sigma_j^2}\right), \tag{5.2.26}$$

$$\frac{\partial J_R}{\partial \sigma_j} = -\sum_i r_j(w_i)\left[\frac{(\mu_j - w_i)^2 - \sigma_j^2}{\sigma_j^3}\right]. \tag{5.2.27}$$

and

$$\frac{\partial J_R}{\partial \alpha_j} = \sum_i \left[1 - \frac{r_j(w_i)}{\alpha_j}\right] \tag{5.2.28}$$

with

$$r_j(w_i) = \frac{\alpha_j p_j(w_i)}{\sum_k \alpha_k p_k(w_i)} \qquad\qquad (5.2.29)$$

It should be noted that the derivation of the partial of J_R with respect to the mixing proportions is less straightforward than those in Equations (5.2.25) through (5.2.27) because the sum of the α_j values must be maintained at 1. Thus the result in Equation (5.2.28) has been obtained by appropriate use of a Lagrange multiplier method and a bit of algebraic manipulation. The term $r_j(w_i)$ in Equations (5.2.25) through (5.2.29) is the posterior probability of Gaussian j given weight w_i; i.e., it measures the responsibility of Gaussian j for the ith weight. Equation (5.2.25) attempts to pull the weights toward the center of the "responsible" Gaussian. It realizes a competition mechanism among the various Gaussians for taking on responsibility for weight w_i. The partial derivative for μ_j drives μ_j toward the weighted average of the set of weights for which Gaussian j is responsible. Similarly, one may come up with simple interpretations for the derivatives in Equations (5.2.27) and (5.2.28). To summarize, the penalty term in Equation (5.2.24) leads to unsupervised clustering of weights (weight sharing) driven by the biases in the training set.

5.3   Applications

Backprop is by far the most popular supervised learning method for multilayer neural networks. Backprop and its variations have been applied to a wide variety of problems, including pattern recognition, signal processing, image compression, speech recognition, medical diagnosis, prediction, nonlinear system modeling, and control.

The most appealing feature of backprop is its adaptive nature, which allows complex processes to be modeled through learning from measurements or examples. This method does not require the knowledge of specific mathematical models for or expert knowledge of the problem being solved. The purpose of this section is to give the reader a flavor of the various areas of application of backprop and to illustrate some strategies that might be used to enhance the training process on some nontrivial real-world problems.

5.3.1   NETtalk

One of the earliest applications of backprop was to train a network to convert English text into speech (Sejnowski and Rosenberg, 1987). The system, known as NETtalk, consisted of two modules: a mapping network and a commercial speech synthesis module. The mapping network is a feedforward neural network having 80 units in the hidden layer and 26 units in the output layer. The output units form a 1-out-of-26 code that encodes phonemes. The output of the neural network drives the speech synthesizer, which in turn generates sounds associated with the input phonemes. The input to the neural network is a 203-dimensional binary vector that encodes a window of 7 consecutive characters (29 bits for each of the 7 characters, including punctuation; each character is encoded using a 1-out-of-29 binary code). The desired output was a phoneme code giving the pronunciation of the letter at the center of the input window.

A block diagram for NETtalk is shown in Figure 5.3.1. When trained on 1024 words from a set of English phoneme exemplars, NETtalk was capable of intelligible speech after only 10 training cycles, and it obtained an accuracy of 95 percent on the training set after 50 cycles. The network first learned to recognize the division points between words and then gradually learned to map phonemes, sounding rather like a child learning to talk. The network was capable of distinguishing between vowels and consonants, and when tested on new text, it achieved a generalization accuracy of 78 percent. Upon adding random noise to the weights or by removing a few units, the

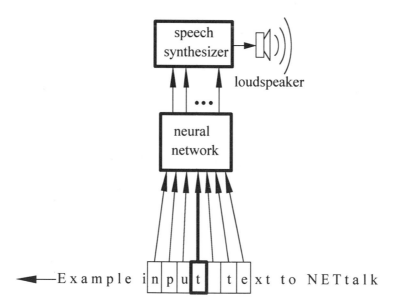

Figure 5.3.1
NETtalk: A backprop-trained neural network that converts English text to speech.

network's performance was found to degrade continuously as opposed to catastrophically (as is usually the case for faulty serial digital systems).

A similar commercially available rule-based system (DEC-talk) that employs an expert system of hand-coded linguistic rules performs better than NETtalk on the same task. However, the significance of NETtalk is in its relatively short development time; NETtalk simply learned from a limited set of examples, but DEC-talk embodies rules that are the result of several years of analysis by many linguists. This application illustrates the ease, relative to an expert-system approach, by which a neural network–based system can be developed even when a problem is not fully understood.

5.3.2 Glove-Talk

Using adaptive networks, it is possible to build device interfaces between a person's movements and a complex physical device. Such interfaces would simplify the process of designing a compatible mapping by adapting such a mapping automatically during a training phase and also allow the mapping to be tailored to individual users.

Glove-Talk is a neural network–based adaptive interface system that maps hand gestures to speech (Fels and Hinton, 1993). Here, a bank of five feedforward neural networks with single hidden layers and backprop training is used to map sensor signals generated by a data glove to appropriate commands (words), which in turn are sent to a speech synthesizer which then speaks the word. A block diagram of the Glove-Talk system is shown in Figure 5.3.2. The hand gesture data generated by the data glove consists of 16 parameters representing x, y, z, roll, pitch, and yaw of the hand relative to a fixed reference and 10 finger flex angles. These parameters are measured every 1/60 second.

Glove-Talk is designed to map complete hand gestures to whole words without mapping temporal constituents of the gesture. The trained system works as follows: The user forms a hand shape for a given root word (see Figure 5.3.3 for examples of root words/hand gestures). Then a movement of the hand forward and back in one of six directions determines the word ending: An up direction signifies an -s (plural) ending, toward user direction signifies an -ed ending, away from user direction signifies an -ing ending, to user's right direction signifies an -er ending, to user's left direction signifies an -ly ending, and down direction signifies no ending (normal). The duration and magnitude of the gesture determine the speech rate and stress. The exact time at which the word is spoken is determined by the hand trajectory network, which upon detecting a deceleration phase of forward movement sends a signal back to the preprocessor to enable it to pass appropriate buffered data to each of four neural networks to do the hand gesture to word mapping. The four neural networks are labeled

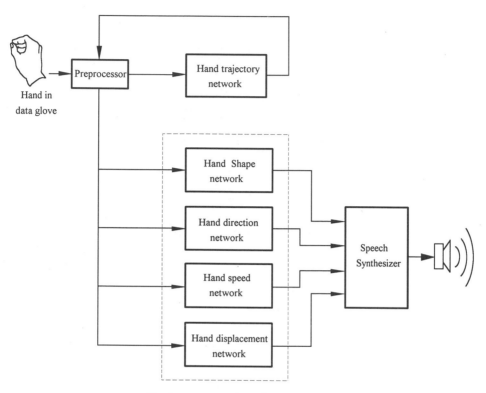

Hand-gesture to word mapping networks

Figure 5.3.2
Glove-Talk: A neural network–based system that maps hand gestures to speech. (From S. S. Fels and G. E. Hinton, Glove-Talk: A neural network interface between a data-glove and a speech synthesizer, *IEEE Transactions on Neural Networks*, **4**(1):2–8, 1993; © 1993 IEEE.)

in Figure 5.3.2 as hand shape, hand direction, hand speed, and hand displacement networks.

The hand shape network has 80 hidden units that are fully connected to 66 output units. The output units employ a 1-out-of-66 binary encoding to classify a vocabulary of 66 root words used by Glove-Talk. The input vector to this network consists of preprocessed versions of the finger's flex angles and the hand's roll, pitch, and yaw (the flex angles are linearly scaled to lie between 0 and 1, and the sines and cosines of the roll, pitch, and yaw are used). Full connectivity between the inputs and the 80 hidden units is assumed. Since the outputs of the units in the output layer may be viewed as representing probability distributions across mutually exclusive alternatives, the

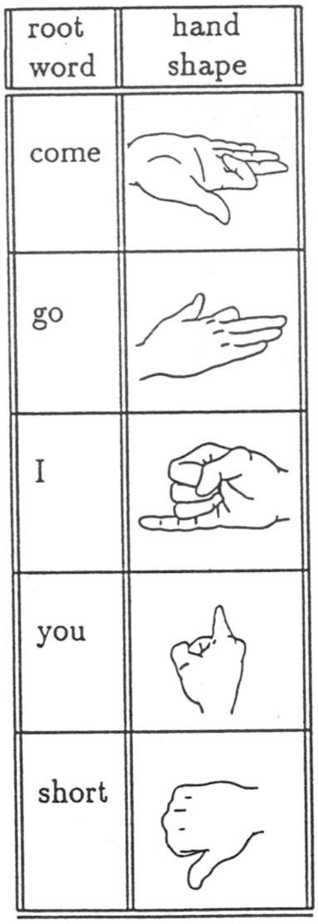

root word	hand shape
come	
go	
I	
you	
short	

Figure 5.3.3
Examples of root words for several hand gestures
(Adopted from S. S. Fels and G. E. Hinton, Glove-
Talk: A neural network interface between a data-
glove and a speech synthesizer, *IEEE Transactions on
Neural Networks*, **4**(1):2–8, 1993; © 1993 IEEE.)

activation function $f_o(net_l) = e^{net_l} \left(\sum_{s=1}^{L} e^{net_s} \right)^{-1}$ for the L output units. Also, the criterion/error function $E = -\sum_{l=1}^{L} d_l \ln(y_l)$ was used, which is appropriate for the preceding selected activations. This error function reduces to $E = -\ln(y_l)$ if binary targets d_l are used (recall the binary 1-out-of-L encoding for the output vector), where y_l is the output of the correct output unit. With these choices of output unit activation and error function, backprop is used to train the hand shape net.

The role of the hand direction network is to translate the direction of hand movement to one of the six possible endings of the word. This network used 10 hidden units
feeding into 6 output units. It employs output units whose activations and associated

error functions are similar to those in the hand shape network; the 6 output units used a 1-out-of-6 encoding to represent the 6 possible encodings. The input to this network is a 10-time-step window of Δx, Δy, and Δz values. The window includes the data at the "enable signal time" of the hand trajectory network and at the previous 9 times.

The hand speed network maps a 20-time-step window of directionless hand speed $(\Delta x^2 + \Delta y^2 + \Delta z^2)^{1/2}$ and acceleration (current speed minus previous speed), for a total of 40 inputs, to a real-valued speaking rate. This window is determined by the hand trajectory network enable signal time and the previous 19 time steps. Eight output units whose activities are in the range of 0 to 1 are used. Postprocessing is used to obtain a real-valued speaking rate (very fast, fast, slow, or very slow). This network has 15 hidden units. It employs standard backprop learning.

The hand displacement neural network of the hand gesture to word mapping of Glove-Talk maps the same inputs as in the hand speed network to the output of a single sigmoid output unit through 5 hidden units. Standard backprop is used for training. During retrieval, the value of the output unit was thresholded at 0.5 to decide whether to stress the word. Here, the amount of hand displacement determines whether a word is stressed.

Finally, the hand trajectory network has 10 hidden units feeding into a single sigmoidal unit that represents a binary decision about whether the most recent time is the right time to read the hand shape. The input data is a window of 10 time steps with 5 parameters at each time step, for a total of 50 inputs. The parameters are Δx, Δy, Δz, speed, and acceleration. The performance of this neural net is critical to the performance of the whole system; if the enable signal controlling the output of the preprocessor to the rest of the system is generated at the wrong time, the hand shape and direction of the movement may be wrong. Once the hand trajectory network is trained properly, the training of the other networks may be performed. Targets are presented to the user (as instructions), and he or she simply makes the appropriate hand gesture. An example of a target is "going fast (stressed)." Here, the user makes the second hand shape in Figure 5.3.3 and quickly moves his or her hand far away from him or her and back again. Since the input/output data required by each network differ, the neural networks were trained independently. Thus, when training the hand shape network, the user focused attention on getting the correct hand shape and paid less attention to his or her hand's trajectory. Similarly, when training the other networks, attention was focused on the relevant aspect of the gesture.

With a 203 gesture-to-word vocabulary (66 root words, each with up to 6 different endings), Glove-Talk produced the correct word more than 99 percent of the time, and no word (output) is produced about 5 percent of the time (this is due to a no response from the hand trajectory network).

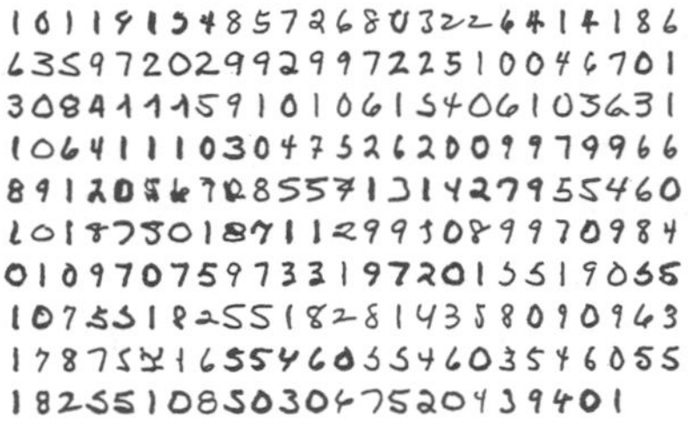

161191548572680322641418 6
635972029929972251007670 1
308411591010615+06103631
106411103047526200777996 6
891205678557131427955460
6018730187112991089970984
01097075973319720155190 65
10753182255182814358010963
1787521655460554603546055
182551085030675207394*01

Figure 5.3.4
Examples of normalized digits that were segmented
from handwritten U.S. ZIP codes. (From Y. Le Cun
et al., 1989, with permission of the MIT Press.)

The major lesson to learn from this project is that complex problems are sometimes best handled using a modular neural network architecture where separate networks are used for each defined subtask. However, this approach is only meaningful if the problem one is trying to solve admits naturally defined subtasks.

5.3.3 Handwritten ZIP Code Recognition

The recognition of handwritten digits is a classic problem in pattern recognition. Specifically, the Postal Service is interested in the recognition of handwritten ZIP codes on pieces of mail. A backprop network has been designed to recognize segmented numerals digitized from handwritten ZIP codes that appeared on U.S. mail (Le Cun et al., 1989). Figure 5.3.4 shows examples of such handwritten numerals.

The neural network was trained on 7291 examples and was tested on 2007 new examples. As can be seen from the figure, the data set contained numerous examples that are ambiguous, unclassifiable, or even misclassified. The examples are pre-processed through a simple linear transformation that makes the raw segmented digits fit in a 16 × 16 gray-level image. The transformation preserves the aspect ratios of the digits. The gray levels in each image were scaled and translated to fall within the range −1 to +1.

The network consisted of three hidden layers H1, H2, and H3 and an output layer. Layer H1 is connected to the input image, and layer H3 feeds its outputs into the output layer. The output layer has 10 units and uses 1-out-of-10 coding. Layer H3 has 30 units and is fully connected to H2. The output layer is fully connected to H3. On the other hand, "weight-sharing" interconnections are used between the inputs and layer H1 and between layers H1 and H2. The network is represented in Figure 5.3.5.

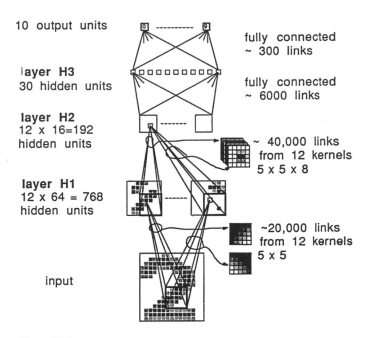

Figure 5.3.5
Network architecture for the handwritten ZIP code recognition neural network (From Y. Le Cun et al., 1989, with permission of the MIT Press.)

As mentioned in the previous section, *weight sharing* refers to having several connections controlled by a single weight (Rumelhart et al., 1986b). It imposes equality
constraints among connection strengths, thus reducing the number of free parameters
in the network, which leads to improved generalization. Another motivation for
employing weight sharing is to encourage the hidden layers H1 and H2 to develop
feature-selection properties that simplify the classification task ultimately implemented
by layer H3 and the output layer. This strategy is crucial for high-accuracy classification performance, since one is dealing here with low-level input images, as opposed to
using a relatively small-sized training set consisting of invariant features.

The first hidden layer (H1) is composed of "feature maps." All units in a feature map
share the same set of weights (except for the threshold, which may differ from unit to
unit). There are 12 groups of 8×8 feature maps (64 units per feature map). Each
unit in a feature map receives inputs from a 5×5 window of the input image. Two
neighboring units in a feature map in H1 have their receptive 5×5 field (in the input
layer) two pixels apart. Here, the motivation is that the exact position of a feature

need not be determined with high precision. Each of the 64 units in a given feature map performs the same operation on corresponding parts of the image. The function performed by a feature map can thus be interpreted as detecting the presence of 1 of 12 possible microfeatures at arbitrary positions in the input image.

Layer H2 is also composed of 12 feature maps, each containing 4×4 units. The connection scheme between layers H1 and H2 is quite similar to the one described above between H1 and the input layer, but with slightly more complications due to the multiple 8×8 feature maps in H1. Each unit in H2 receives input from a subset (8 in this case) of the 12 maps in H1. Its receptive field is composed of a 5×5 window centered at identical positions within each of the selected subset maps in H1. Again, all units in a given map in H2 share their weights.

As a result of this structure, the network has 1000 units, 64,660 connections, and 9760 independent weights. All units use a hyperbolic tangent activation function. Before training, the weights were initialized with a uniform random distribution between -2.4 and $+2.4$ and further normalized by dividing each weight by the fan-in of the corresponding unit.

Backprop based on the approximate Newton method (described in Section 5.2.3) was employed in an incremental mode. The network was trained for 23 cycles through the training set (which required 3 days of CPU time on a Sun SparcStation 1). The percentage of misclassified patterns was 0.14 percent on the training set and 5.0 percent on the test set. Another performance test was performed employing a rejection criterion, where an input pattern was rejected if the levels of the two most active units in the output layer exceeded a given threshold. For this given rejection threshold, the network classification error on the test patterns was reduced to 1 percent but resulted in a 12 percent rejection rate. Additional weight pruning based on information theoretical ideas in a four-hidden-layer architecture similar to the one described above resulted in a network with only about one-quarter as many free parameters as that described above and improved performance to 99 percent generalization error with a rejection rate of only 9 percent (Le Cun et al., 1990). For comparison, a fully interconnected feedforward neural network with 40 hidden units (10,690 free weights), employing no weight sharing, trained on the same task produced a 1.6 percent misclassification on the training set and 19.4 percent rejections for a 1 percent error rate on the test set.

Thus, when dealing with large amounts of low-level information (as opposed to carefully preprocessed feature data), proper constraints should be placed on the network so that the number of free parameters in the network is reduced as much as possible without overly reducing its computational power. Also, incorporating a priori knowledge about the task (such as the architecture for developing translation-invariant features implemented by layers H1 and H2 in the preceding network) can be very helpful in arriving at a practical solution to an otherwise difficult problem.

A similar experiment on handwritten digits scanned from real bank checks was reported by Martin and Pittman (1991). Digits were automatically presegmented and size normalized to a 15×24 gray-scale array, with pixel values from 0 to 1.0. A total of 35,200 samples were available for training and another 4000 samples for testing. Here, various nets were trained using backprop to error rates of 2 to 3 percent. All nets had 2 hidden layers and 10 units in their output layers, which employed 1-out-of-10 encoding. Three types of networks were trained. Global fully interconnected nets with 150 units in the first hidden layer and 50 units in the second layer were used, as well as local nets with 540 units in the first hidden layer receiving input from 5×8 local and overlapping regions (offset by 2 pixels) on the input array. These hidden units were fully interconnected to 100 units in the second hidden layer, which, in turn, were fully interconnected to units in the output layer. Finally, shared-weight nets also were used that had approximately the same number of units in each layer as in the local nets. These shared-weight nets employed a weight-sharing strategy similar to the one in Figure 5.3.5 between the input and the first hidden layer and between the first and second hidden layers. Full interconnectivity was assumed between the second hidden layer and the output layer.

With the full 35,200-sample training set, and with a rejection rate of 9.6 percent, the generalization errors were 1.7, 1.1, and 1.7 percent for the global, local, and local shared-weight nets, respectively. When the size of the training set was reduced to the 1000 to 4000 range, the local shared-weight net (with about 6500 independent weights) was substantially better than the global (at 63,000 independent weights) and local (at approximately 79,000 independent weights) nets. All these results suggest another way for achieving good generalization: Use a very large, "representative" training set. This works as long as the network is big enough to load the training set without too much effort to customize the interconnectivity patterns between hidden layers. However, a network that is about one order of magnitude smaller in terms of independent connections is easier to implement because of the reduced storage it requires.

Improved recognition performance can be achieved by training the preceding networks to reject the type of unclassifiable images ("rubbish") typically produced by the segmentation process by actually including images of rubbish in the training set (Bromley and Denker, 1993). Yet another approach for improving recognition performance involves integrating character segmentation and recognition within one neural network (Rumelhart, 1989; Martin, 1990, 1993; Keeler et al., 1991; Keeler and Rumelhart, 1992).

5.3.4   ALVINN: A Trainable Autonomous Land Vehicle

ALVINN (autonomous land vehicle in a neural network) is a backprop-trained feed-forward network designed to drive a modified Chevy van (Pomerleau, 1991). It is an example of a successful application using sensor data in real time to perform a real-world perception task. Using a real-time learning technique, ALVINN quickly learned to autonomously control the van by observing the reactions of a human driver.

ALVINN's architecture consists of a single-hidden-layer, fully interconnected feed-forward net with 5 sigmoidal units in the hidden layer and 30 linear output units. The input is a 30×32 pattern reduced from the image of an onboard camera. The steering direction generated by the network is taken to be the center of mass of the activity pattern generated by the output units. This allows finer steering corrections as compared with using the most active output unit.

During the training phase, the network is presented with road images as inputs and the corresponding steering signal generated by the human driver as the desired output. Backprop training is used with a constant learning rate for each weight that is scaled by the fan-in of the unit to which the weight projects. A steadily increasing momentum coefficient is also used during training. The desired steering angle is presented to the network as a Gaussian distribution of activation centered around the steering direction that will keep the vehicle centered on the road. The desired activation pattern was generated as $d_l = e^{-D_l^2/10}$, where d_l represents the desired output for unit l and D_l is the lth unit's distance from the correct steering direction point along the output vector. The variance 10 was determined empirically. The Gaussian target pattern makes the learning task easier than a 1-of-30 binary target pattern because slightly different road images require the network to respond with only slightly different output vectors.

Since the human driver tends to steer the vehicle down the center of the road, the network will not be presented with enough situations where it must recover from misalignment errors. A second problem may arise such that when training the network with only the current image of the road, one runs the risk of overlearning from repetitive inputs, thus causing the network to "forget" what it had learned from earlier training.

These two problems are handled by ALVINN as follows: First, each input image is laterally shifted to create 14 additional images in which the vehicle appears to be shifted by various amounts relative to the road center. These images are shown in Figure 5.3.6. A correct steering direction is then generated and used as the desired target for each of the shifted images. Second, in order to eliminate the problem of overtraining on repetitive images, each training cycle consisted of a pass through a

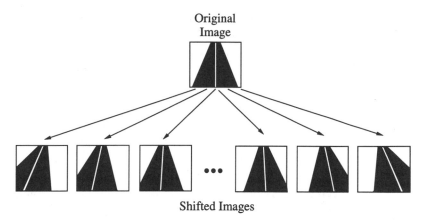

Original
Image

Shifted Images

Figure 5.3.6
Shifted video images from a single original video image used to enrich the training set used to train ALVINN. (From D. A. Pomerleau, 1991, with permission of the MIT Press.)

buffer of 200 images that includes the current original image and its 14 shifted versions. After each training cycle, a new road image and its 14 shifted versions are used to replace 15 patterns from the current set of 200 road scenes. Ten of the 15 patterns to be replaced are ones with the lowest error. The other 5 patterns are chosen randomly.

ALVINN requires approximately 50 iterations through this dynamically evolving set of 200 patterns to learn to drive on roads it had been trained to drive on (an onboard Sun-4 workstation took 5 minutes to do the training, during which a teacher driver drives at about 4 miles per hour over the test road). In addition to being able to drive along the same stretch of road it trained on, ALVINN also can generalize to drive along parts of the road it has never encountered, even under a wide variety of weather conditions. In the retrieval phase (autonomous driving), the system is able to process 25 images per second, allowing it to drive up to the van's maximum speed of 20 miles per hour (this maximum speed is due to constraints imposed by the hydraulic drive system.) This speed is over twice the speed of any other sensor-based autonomous system that was able to drive this van. Further refinements of ALVINN can be found in Pomerleau (1993).

In contrast to other traditional navigation systems (e.g., Dickmanns and Zapp, 1987), which are designed to track programmer-chosen features (such as lines painted on the road), ALVINN is able to learn for each new domain what road features are important and then develop its own steering strategy to stay on the road. When trained on multiple roads, the network developed hidden-unit feature detectors for the lines painted on the road, while in the absence of the painted lines, some hidden units became sensitive to road edges. As a result, ALVINN is able to drive in a wider variety of situations than any other autonomous navigation system.

5.3.5 Medical Diagnosis Expert Net

Clinical diagnosis is often fraught with great difficulty because multiple, often unrelated disease states can surface with very similar historical, symptomalogic, and clinical data. As a result, physicians' accuracy in diagnosing such diseases is often poor.

Feedforward multilayer neural networks trained with backprop have been reported to exhibit improved clinical diagnosis over physicians and traditional expert-system approaches (Bounds et al., 1988; Yoon et al., 1989; Baxt, 1990). This section describes a neural network–based medical diagnosis system that is applied to the diagnosis of coronary occlusion (Baxt, 1990).

Acute myocardial infarction (coronary occlusion) is an example of a disease that is difficult to diagnose. There have been a number of attempts to automate the diagnosis process. The most promising automated solution (Goldmann et al., 1988) is able to achieve a detection rate of 88 percent, which is about the same rate at which physicians are able to detect the disease, and a false-alarm rate of 26 percent, which is slightly better than the 29 percent false-alarm rate achieved by physicians. In the following study, a feedforward fully interconnected neural network with two hidden layers and a single output unit is trained to diagnose coronary occlusion. The two hidden layers have 10 units each. All units are assumed to have unipolar sigmoidal activation, and backprop is used to train the network.

The training set consisted of data on 356 patients who have been admitted to the coronary care unit. Of the 356 patients, 236 did not have the coronary disease and 120 did have it. The network was trained on a randomly chosen set of half the patients who had sustained infarction and half the patients who had not sustained infarction. The data on each patient consisted of 20 variables that were found to be predictive of the presence of acute myocardial infarction (examples of such variables are age, sex, nausea and vomiting, shortness of breath, diabetes, hypertension, and angina). These variables are a subset of 41 variables collected on all patients from the emergency department records of admitted patients to the coronary care unit. A procedure was subsequently used to confirm the presence of infarction (Goldman et al., 1988) in all 356 patients. Most of the clinical input variables were coded in binary such that 1 represented the presence of a finding and 0 represented the absence of a finding. Other variables such as patient age were coded as analog values between 0.0 and 1.0. The target value for the output was 1 for the subsequently confirmed presence of acute myocardial infarction and 0 for the confirmed absence of infarction.

After training, the network was tested on the remaining 178 patients (118 non-infarction, 60 infarction) to whom it had not been exposed. This resulted in about 92 percent correct identification of the presence of infarction and about 96 percent correct identification of the absence of infarction. These results did not change substantially when the training and subsequent testing of the network were repeated after swapping the original training and testing sets.

The 92 percent detection rate and 4 percent false-alarm rate for the neural network–based diagnosis of acute myocardial infarction show substantial improvements over physicians performance of 88 percent detection rate and 29 percent false alarms. The network used routinely available data that are used by physicians screening patients for the presence of infarction and was able to discover relationships in these data that are not immediately apparent to physicians.

5.3.6 Image Compression and Dimensionality Reduction

Image-compression techniques exploit the redundancy that naturally exists in most images for efficient storage and/or transmission purposes. Here, a picture is encoded with a much smaller number of bits than the total number of bits required to describe it exactly. After retrieval or at the receiver end of a transmission link, the encoded or "compressed" image may then be decoded into a full-sized picture. The compression of images can be posed as an optimization problem where, ideally, the encoding and decoding are done in a way that optimizes the quality of the decoded picture. A number of image-compression schemes have been reported in the literature [see, e.g., Gonzalez and Wintz (1987)]. In the following, a neural network–based solution to this problem is described.

Consider the architecture of the single-hidden-layer feedforward neural network shown in Figure 5.3.7. This network has the same number of units in its output layer as inputs, and the number of hidden units is assumed to be much smaller than the dimension of the input vector. The hidden units are assumed to be of the bipolar sigmoid type, and the output units are linear. This network is trained on a set of n-dimensional real-valued vectors (patterns) x^k such that each x^k is mapped to itself at the output layer in an autoassociative mode. Thus the network is trained to act as an encoder of real-valued patterns. Backprop may be used to learn such a mapping. Cottrell et al. (1987, 1989) proposed this architecture for image compression. One network they studied received inputs from an 8×8-pixel region ($n = 64$) and had 16 hidden units. Backprop was used to train the network to autoassociate randomly selected 8×8 patches (windows) of a given image. After training, the network was used to compress and then reconstruct the image, patch by patch, using a set of nonoverlapping patches that covered the whole image. Now, to store this image, one

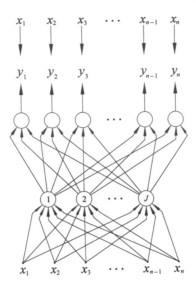

Figure 5.3.7
A two-layer feedforward autoassociative network for
image compression and dimensionality reduction.

need only store 16 data points for each 8×8 patch of the original image. This amounts
to a 4:1 compression ratio.

Next, the preceding method of image compression/encoding is illustrated for the
256×256-pixel (8 bits per pixel) image "Lenna" shown in Figure 5.3.8a. Following
the preceding training procedure, a 16-hidden-unit autoassociative net was trained on
random 8×8 patches of the image using incremental backprop learning. Here, all
pixel values are normalized in the range $[-1, +1]$. Typically, the learning consisted
of 50,000 to 100,000 iterations at a learning rate of 0.01 and 0.1 for the hidden and
output layer weights, respectively. Figure 5.3.8b shows the reproduced image by the
autoassociative net when tested on the training image. The reproduced image is quite
close (to the eye) to the training image in Figure 5.3.8a; hence the reconstructed image
is of good quality.

In order to achieve true compression for the purpose of efficient transmission over
a digital communication link, the outputs of the hidden units must be quantized.
Quantization consists of transforming the outputs of the hidden units [which are in
the open interval $(-1, +1)$] to some integer range corresponding to the number of
bits required for transmission. This effectively restricts the information in the hidden-
unit outputs to the number of bits used. In general, this transformation should be

(a)   (b)

(c)   (d)

Figure 5.3.8
(a) The original image "Lenna" used to train the autoassociative image compression net. (b) The reconstructed image using no quantization of the hidden unit outputs. (c) Reconstructed image using a 1.5-bits-per-pixel data rate. (d) Reconstructed image using a 1-bit-per-pixel data rate.

designed with care (Gonzalez and Wintz, 1987). However, in the preceding compression net, a simple uniformly spaced quantization may be used for two reasons. First, the squashing activation function forces all outputs into the range -1 to $+1$, so no scaling is necessary. Second, backprop tended to make the hidden-unit output variances about equal, so special block quantization (Huang and Schultheiss, 1963) is not needed here. The effects of quantization are tested for the training image in Figure 5.3.8a. Here, the hidden-unit outputs are restricted to 8 bits, i.e., 256 quantized values per output. This corresponds to a data rate of 2 bits per pixel (a total of 128 bits are needed to code each 8×8 patch of pixels, resulting in a data rate of 2 bits per pixel). That is, only 2 binary bits are transmitted for each pixel in the original image. The reconstructed image was as good to the eye as the one shown in Figure 5.3.8b; i.e., it was as good as the network does without any quantization. The network also was capable of respectable reconstructions of the training image with fewer quantized values for hidden-unit outputs. For example, Figure 5.3.8c and d shows image reconstructions with 64 quantization values (1.5 bits per pixel data rate) and 16 quantization values (1 bit per pixel data rate), respectively.

How does this autoassociative net perform on new (nontraining) images? Intuitively, one would not expect this net to generalize from a single training image since the network learns, in some sense, the statistics of the image it is trained on and different images have different statistics. Surprisingly, it turns out that the network does a respectable job of reproducing images that it was not trained on, even when quantization is used. For example, Figure 5.3.9b through d shows reproductions of the image "Amal" in Figure 5.3.9a using the preceding net (i.e., the autoassociative net trained with the image "Lenna" in Figure 5.3.8a). Figure 5.3.9b corresponds to the case with no quantization of hidden-layer outputs. On the other hand, Figure 5.3.9c and d corresponds to the cases of 1.5 and 1 bit per pixel data compression rates, respectively. Sonehara et al. (1989) reported similar simulations with an autoassociative image compression net. They showed that the reproduction of new images improves as the number of training images increases. They also showed, empirically, that the network achieves better reproduction when the quantized hidden-unit outputs are used during learning, as opposed to using quantization only during reproduction.

Since the input is forced to be reproduced through a narrow hidden layer, which is usually referred to as a *bottleneck*, backprop attempts to extract regularities (significant features) from the input vectors. Here, the hidden layer, which is also known as the *representation layer*, is expected to evolve an internal low-dimensional distributed representation of the training data. Empirical analysis of the trained compression network shows that the hidden-unit activities span the principal-component subspace

(a)   (b)

(c)   (d)

Figure 5.3.9
(a) The image "Amal" used to test the autoassociative image-compression net trained on the image in
Figure 5.3.8a. (b) Reconstructed test image using no quantization. (c) Reconstructed test image using a
1.5-bits-per-pixel data rate. (d) Reconstructed test image using a 1-bit-per-pixel data rate.

of the image vector(s), with some noise on the first principal component due to the nonlinear nature of the hidden unit activation's (Cottrell and Munro, 1988). In this net, the nonlinearity in the hidden units is theoretically of no help (Bourlard and Kamp, 1988), and indeed Cottrell et al. (1987) and Cottrell and Munro (1988) found that the nonlinearity has little added advantages in their simulations. These results are further supported by Baldi and Hornik (1989), who showed that if J linear hidden units are used, the network learns to project the input onto the subspace spanned by the first J principal components of the input. Thus the network's hidden units discard as little information as possible by evolving their respective weight vectors to point in the direction of the input's principal components. This means that autoassociative backprop learning in a two-layer feedforward neural network with linear units has no processing capability beyond those of the unsupervised Hebbian PCA nets of Section 3.3.5. [For an application of a Hebbian-type PCA net to image compression, the reader is referred to Sanger (1989).]

The addition of one or more encoding hidden layers with nonlinear units between the inputs and the representation layer and one or more decoding layers between the representation layer and the output layer provides a network that is capable of learning nonlinear representations (Kramer, 1991; Oja, 1991; Usui et al., 1991). Such networks can perform the nonlinear analog to principal-component analysis (recall the discussion of nonlinear PCA nets in Section 3.3.6) and extract *principal manifolds.* These principal manifolds can, in some cases, serve as low-dimensional representations of the data which are more useful than principal components.[6] A three-hidden-layer autoassociative net can, theoretically, compute any continuous mapping from the inputs to the second hidden layer (representation layer) and another mapping from the second hidden layer to the output layer. Thus a three-hidden-layer autoassociative net (with a linear or nonlinear representation layer) may in principle be considered as a universal nonlinear PCA net. However, such a highly nonlinear net may be problematic to train by backprop due to local minima.

Another way of interpreting the preceding autoassociative feedforward network is from the point of view of feature extraction (Kuczewski et al., 1987; Cottrell, 1991; Hassoun et al., 1992). Here, the outputs from the representation layer are taken as

---

6. When the data lie on a nonlinear submanifold of the feature space, then the principal components will overestimate the effective dimensionality of the data. For example, the covariance matrix of data sampled from a circle will have full rank, and thus the data appears two-dimensional for PCA. However, the circle is a one-dimensional manifold and can be effectively parameterized with a single parameter: the polar angle data. Kramer (1991) succeeded in training a three-hidden-layer autoassociative net which encodes the circle data in a single-unit representation and then smoothly reconstructs (decodes) the circle from the output of this single unit; i.e., the net finds an invertible one-dimensional representation of the data.

low-dimensional feature vectors associated with complete images (or any other high-dimensional raw data vectors) presented at the input layer, whereas the decoder (reconstruction) subnet is needed only during the training phase and is eliminated during retrieval. The output from the representation layer can now be used as an information-rich, low-dimensional feature vector that is easy to process/classify. Reducing dimensionality of data with minimal information loss is also important from the point of view of computational efficiency. Here, the high-dimensional input data can be transformed into "good" representations in a lower-dimensional space for further processing. Since many algorithms are exponential in the dimensionality of the input, a reduction by even a single dimension may provide significant computational savings.

DeMers and Cottrell (1993) presented impressive results whereby the encoder subnet of a four-hidden-layer autoassociative net is used to supply 5-dimensional inputs to a feedforward neural classifier. The classifier was trained to recognize the gender of a limited set of subjects. Here, the autoassociative net was first trained using backprop, with pruning of representation layer units, to generate a 5-dimensional representation from 50-dimensional inputs. The inputs were taken as the first 50 principal components of 64×64-pixel, 8-bit gray-scale images, each of which can be considered to be a point in a 4096-dimensional "pixel space." Here, the training set is comprised of 160 images of various facial impressions of 10 male and 10 female subjects, of which 120 images were used for training and 40 for testing. The images are captured by a frame grabber, and reduced to 64×64 pixels by averaging. Each image is then aligned along the axes of the eyes and mouth. All images are normalized to have equal brightness and variance in order to prevent the use of first-order statistics for discrimination. Finally, the grey levels of image pixels are linearly scaled to the range $[0, 0.8]$. The overall encoder/classifier system resulted in a 95 percent correct gender recognition on both training and test sets, which was found to be comparable with the recognition rate of human beings on the same images.

The high rate of correct classification in the preceding simulation is a clear indication of the "richness" and significance of the representations/feature vectors discovered by the nonlinear PCA autoassociative net. For another significant application of nonlinear PCA autoassociative nets, the reader is referred to Usui et al. (1991). A somewhat related recurrent multilayer autoassociative net for data clustering and signal decomposition is presented in Section 6.4.2.

5.4 Extensions of Backprop for Temporal Learning

Up to this point we have been concerned with "static" mapping networks that are trained to produce a spatial output pattern in response to a particular spatial input pattern. However, in many engineering, scientific, and economic applications, the need arises to model dynamical processes where a time sequence is required in response to certain temporal input signal(s). One such example is plant modeling in control applications. Here, it is desired to capture the dynamics of an unknown plant (usually nonlinear) by modeling a flexible-structured network that will imitate the plant by adaptively changing its parameters to track the plant's observable output signals when driven by the same input signals. The resulting model is referred to as a *temporal association network*.

Temporal association networks must have a recurrent (as opposed to static) architecture so as to handle the time-dependent nature of associations. Thus it would be very useful to extend the multilayer feedforward network and its associated training algorithm(s) (e.g., backprop) into the temporal domain. In general, this requires a recurrent architecture (nets with feedback connections) and proper associated learning algorithms.

Two special cases of temporal association networks are sequence-reproduction and sequence-recognition networks. For sequence reproduction, a network must be able to generate the rest of a sequence from a part of that sequence. This is appropriate, for example, for predicting the price trend of a given stock market from its past history or predicting the future course of a time series from examples. In sequence recognition, a network produces a spatial pattern or a fixed output in response to a specific input sequence. This is appropriate, for example, for speech recognition, where the output encodes the word corresponding to the speech signal. NETtalk and Glove-Talk of Section 5.3 are two other examples of sequence-recognition networks.

In the following, neural net architectures having various degrees of recurrency and their associated learning methods are introduced which are capable of processing time sequences.

5.4.1 Time-Delay Neural Networks

Consider the time-delay neural network architecture shown in Figure 5.4.1. This network maps a finite time sequence $\{x(t), x(t - \Delta), x(t - 2\Delta), \ldots, x(t - m\Delta)\}$ into a single output y (this architecture also can be generalized for the case when x and/or y are vectors). One may view this neural network as a discrete-time nonlinear filter (one also may use the borrowed terms *finite-duration impulse response* (FIR) *filter* or *nonrecursive filter* from the linear filtering literature).

The architecture in Figure 5.4.1 is equivalent to a single-hidden-layer feedforward neural network receiving the $(m + 1)$-dimensional "spatial" pattern $\mathbf{x}$ generated by a tapped-delay line preprocessor from a temporal sequence. Thus, if target values for

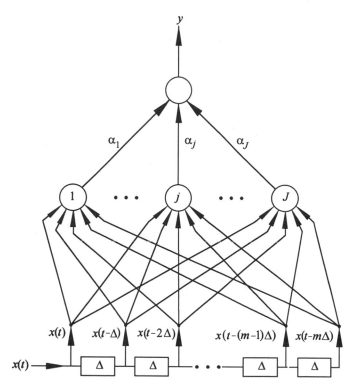

Figure 5.4.1
A time-delay neural network for one-dimensional input/output signals.

the output unit are specified for various times t, backprop may be used to train this network to act as a sequence recognizer.

The time-delay neural net has been applied successfully to the problem of speech recognition (e.g., Tank and Hopfield, 1987; Elamn and Zipser, 1988; Waibel, 1989; Waibel et al., 1989; Lippmann, 1989) and time series prediction (Lapedes and Farber, 1988; Weigend et al., 1991). Here, time-series prediction is discussed because it captures the spirit of the type of processing done by the time-delay neural net. Given observed values of the state x of a (nonlinear) dynamical system at discrete times less than t, the goal is to use these values to accurately predict $x(t + p)$, where p is some prediction time step into the future (for simplicity, a one-dimensional state x is assumed). Clearly, as p increases, the quality of the predicted value will degrade for any predictive method. A method is robust if it can maintain prediction accuracy for a wide range of p values.

As is normally done in linear signal processing applications (e.g., Widrow and Stearns, 1985), one may use the tapped delay line nonlinear filter of Figure 5.4.1 as the basis for predicting $x(t + p)$. Here, a training set is constructed of pairs $\{\mathbf{x}^k, x(t_k + p)\}$, where $\mathbf{x}^k = [x(t_k), x(t_k - \Delta), x(t_k - 2\Delta), \ldots, x(t_k - m\Delta)]^{\mathsf{T}}$. Backprop may now be employed to learn such a training set. Reported simulation results of this prediction method show comparable or better performance compared with other non-neural network–based techniques (Lapedes and Farber, 1988; Weigend et al., 1991; Weigend and Gershenfeld, 1993).

Theoretical justification for this approach is available in the form of a very powerful theorem by Takens (1981) which states that there exists a (smooth) functional relation of the form

$$x(t + p) = g[x(t), x(t - \Delta), \ldots, x(t - m\Delta)] \tag{5.4.1}$$

with $d < m \le 2d + 1$, as long as the trajectory $x(t)$ evolves toward compact attracting manifolds of dimension d. This theorem, however, provides no information on the form of g. The time-delay neural network approach provides a robust approximation for g in Equation (5.4.1) in the form of the continuous, adaptive parameter model

$$y = \sum_{j=1}^{J} \alpha_j f_h \left\{ \sum_{i=1}^{m+1} w_{ji} x[t - (i - 1)\Delta] \right\} \tag{5.4.2}$$

where a linear activation is assumed for the output unit, and f_h is the nonlinear activation of hidden units.

A simple modification to the time-delay net makes it suitable for sequence reproduction. The training procedure is identical to the one for the preceding prediction network. However, during retrieval, the output y [predicting $x(t + 1)$] is propagated through a single delay element, with the output of this delay element connected to the input of the time-delay net as is shown in Figure 5.4.2. This sequence reproduction net will only work if the prediction $y = \hat{x}(t + 1)$ is very accurate, since any error in the predicted signal has a multiplicative effect due to the iterated scheme employed.

Further generalization of these ideas can result in a network for temporal association. Such modifications are presented in the context of nonlinear dynamical plant identification/modeling of control theory. Consider the following general nonlinear single-input, single-output plant described by the difference equation

$$x(t + 1) = g[x(t), x(t - 1), \ldots, x(t - n); u(t), u(t - 1), \ldots, u(t - m)] \tag{5.4.3}$$

where $u(t)$ and $x(t)$ are, respectively, the input and output signals of the plant at time t, g is a nonlinear function, and $m \le n$. What is desired is to train a suitable-layered

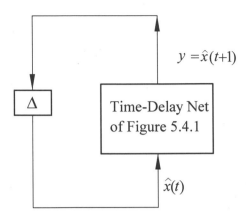

Figure 5.4.2
Sequence reproduction network.

neural network to capture the dynamics of the plant in Equation (5.4.3), thus modeling the plant. Here we assume that the order of the plant is known (m and n are known). The general form of Equation (5.4.3) suggests the use of a time-delay neural network, as shown inside the dashed rectangle in Figure 5.4.3. This also may be viewed as a (nonlinear) recursive filter, termed an *infinite-duration impulse response (IIR) filter* in the linear filtering literature.

During training, the neural network and the plant receive the same input $u(t)$. The neural network also receives the plant's output $x(t + 1)$ (switch S in the up position in Figure 5.4.3). Backprop can be used to update the weights of the neural network based on the "static" mapping pairs

$$\{[x(t) \quad x(t-1) \quad \cdots \quad x(t-n) \quad u(t) \quad u(t-1) \quad \cdots \quad u(t-m)]^{\mathrm{T}}, x(t+1)\}$$

for various values of t. This identification scheme is referred to as *series-parallel identification model* (Narendra and Parthasarathy, 1990). After training, the neural network with the switch S in the down position $[\hat{x}(t + 1)$ is fed back as the input to the top delay line in Figure 5.4.3] will generate (recursively) an output time sequence in response to an input time sequence. If the training were successful, one would expect the output $\hat{x}(t + 1)$ to approximate the actual output of the plant, $x(t + 1)$, for the same input signal $u(t)$ and the same initial conditions. Theoretical justifications for the effectiveness of this neural network identification method can be found in Levin and Narendra (1992).

Narendra and Parthasarathy (1990) reported successful identification of nonlinear plants by time-delay neural networks similar to the one in Figure 5.4.3. In one of their

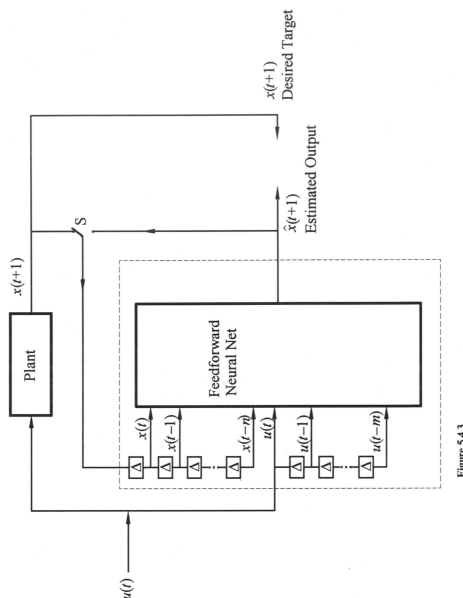

Figure 5.4.3
A time-delay neural network setup for the identification of a nonlinear plant.

simulations, the feedforward part of the neural network consisted of a two-hidden-layer network with five inputs and a single linear output unit. The two hidden layers consisted of 20 and 10 units with bipolar sigmoid activations, respectively. This network was used to identify the unknown plant

$$x(t + 1) = \frac{x(t)x(t - 1)x(t - 2)u(t - 1)[x(t - 2) - 1] + u(t)}{1 + x^2(t - 2) + x^2(t - 1)} \tag{5.4.4}$$

The inputs to the neural network during training were $x(t)$, $x(t - 1)$, $x(t - 2)$, $u(t)$, and $u(t - 1)$. Incremental backprop was used to train the network using a uniformly distributed random input signal whose amplitude was in the interval $[-1, +1]$. The training phase consisted of 100,000 training iterations, which amounts to one training cycle over the random input signal $u(t)$, for $0 < t \leq 100,000$. A learning rate of 0.25 was used. Figure 5.4.4a shows the output of the plant (solid line) and the model (dotted line) for the input signal

$$u(t) = \begin{cases} \sin\left(\dfrac{2\pi t}{250}\right) & \text{for } 0 \leq t \leq 500 \\[2ex] 0.8 \sin\left(\dfrac{2\pi t}{250}\right) + 0.2 \sin\left(\dfrac{2\pi t}{25}\right) & \text{for } t > 500 \end{cases} \tag{5.4.5}$$

It should be noted that in the preceding simulation no attempt has been made to optimize the network size or to tune the learning process. For example, Figure 5.4.4b shows simulation results with a single-hidden-layer net consisting of 20 bipolar sigmoid activation hidden units. Here, incremental backprop with a learning rate of 0.25 was used. The training phase consisted of 5×10^6 iterations. This amounts to 10,000 training cycles over a 500-sample input signal having the same characteristics as described above.

Other learning algorithms may be used for training the time-delay neural network discussed above, some of which are extensions of algorithms used in classical linear adaptive filtering or adaptive control. Nerrand et al. (1993) present examples of such algorithms.

5.4.2   Backpropagation Through Time

In the preceding section, a partially recurrent neural network was presented that was capable of temporal association. In general, however, a fully recurrent neural net is a more appropriate/economical alternative. Here, individual units may be input units, output units, or both. The desired targets are defined on a set of arbitrary units at certain predetermined times. Also, arbitrary interconnection patterns between units

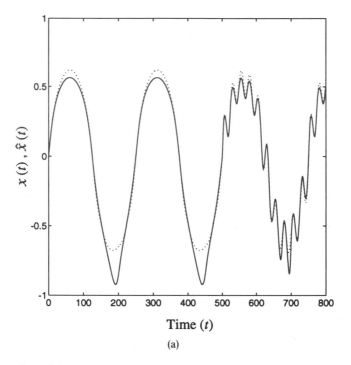

Time (*t*)

(a)

Figure 5.4.4
Identification results for the plant in Equation (5.4.4) using a time-delay neural network. Plant output $x(t)$ (*solid line*) and neural network output $\hat{x}(t)$ (*dotted line*) in response to the input signal in Equation (5.4.5). (*a*) The network has two hidden layers and is trained with incremental backprop for one cycle over a 100,000-sample random input signal. (Adapted from K. S. Narendra and K. Parthasarathy, Identification and control of dynamic systems containing neural networks, *IEEE Transactions on Neural Networks*, **1**(1):4–27, 1990; © 1990 IEEE.) (*b*) The network has a single hidden layer and is trained for 10,000 cycles over a 500-sample random input signal.

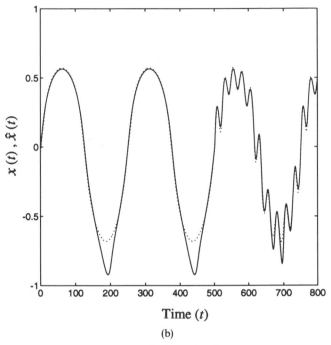

(b)

Figure 5.4.4 (continued)

can exist. An example of a simple two-unit fully interconnected network is shown in Figure 5.4.5a. The network receives an input sequence $x(t)$ at unit 1, and it is desired that the network generates the sequence $d(t)$ as the output $y_2(t)$ of unit 2.

A network that behaves identically to the preceding simple recurrent net over the time steps $t = 1, 2, 3,$ and 4 is shown in Figure 5.4.5b. This amounts to unfolding the recurrent network in time (Minsky and Papert, 1969) to arrive at a feedforward layered network. The number of resulting layers is equal to the unfolding time interval T. This idea is effective when T is small and limits the maximum length of sequences that can be generated. Here, all units in the recurrent network are duplicated T times so that a separate unit in the unfolded network holds the state $y_i(t)$ of the equivalent recurrent network at time t. Note that the connections w_{ij} from unit j to unit i in the unfolded network are identical for all layers.

The resulting unfolded network simplifies the training process of encoding the $x(t) \rightarrow d(t)$ sequence association because now backprop learning is applicable. However, we should note a couple of things here. First, targets may be specified for hidden

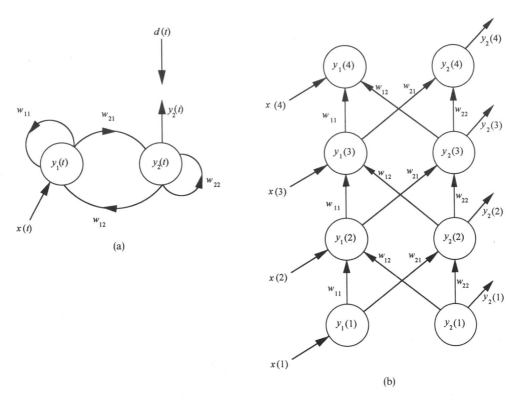

Figure 5.4.5
(a) A simple recurrent network. (b) A feedforward network generated by unfolding in time the recurrent net in part a. The two networks are equivalent over the four time steps $t = 1, 2, 3, 4$.

units. Thus errors at the output of hidden units, and not just the output errors, must be propagated backward from the layer in which they originate. Second, it is important to realize the constraint that all copies of each weight w_{ij} must remain identical across duplicated layers (backprop normally produces different increments Δw_{ij} for each particular weight copy). A simple solution is to add together the individual weight changes for all copies of a partial weight w_{ij} and then change all such copies by the total amount. Once trained, the weights from any layer of the unfolded net are copied into the recurrent network, which, in turn, is used for the temporal association task. Adapting backprop to training unfolded recurrent neural nets results in the so-called *backpropagation through time* learning method (Rumelhart et al., 1986b). There exist relatively few applications of this technique in the literature (Rumelhart et al., 1986b; Nowlan, 1988; Nguyen and Widrow, 1989). One reason is its inefficiency in

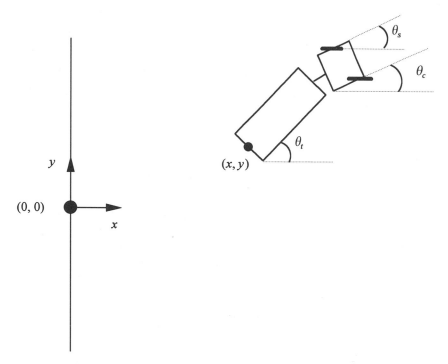

Figure 5.4.6
A pictorial representation of the truck backer-upper problem. The objective here is to design a controller that generates a steering signal θ_s which successfully backs up the truck so that the back of the trailer ends at the $(0,0)$ reference point, with the trailer perpendicular to the dock.

handling long sequences. Another reason is that other learning methods are able to solve the problem without the need for unfolding. These methods are treated next. First, however, one interesting application of backpropagation through time is described: the truck backer-upper problem.

Consider the trailer truck system shown in Figure 5.4.6. The goal is to design a controller that successfully backs up the truck so that the back of the trailer designated by coordinates (x, y) ends at $(0,0)$ with the trailer perpendicular to the dock (i.e., the trailer angle θ_t is zero) and where only backward movements of the cab are allowed. The controller receives the observed state $\mathbf{x} = [x, y, \theta_t, \theta_c]^{\mathrm{T}}$ (θ_c is the cab angle) and produces a steering signal (angle) θ_s. It is assumed that the truck backs up at a constant speed. The details of the trailer truck kinematics can be found in Miller et al. (1990a). The original application assumes six state variables, including the position of the back of the cab. However, the two variables associated with the position of the back of the cab may be eliminated if the length of the cab and that of the trailer are given.

Before the controller is designed, a feedforward single-hidden-layer neural network is trained, using backprop, to emulate the truck and trailer kinematics. This is accomplished by training the network on a large number of backup trajectories (corresponding to random initial trailer truck position configurations), each consisting of a set of association pairs $\{[\mathbf{x}(k-1)^{\mathrm{T}} \quad \theta_s(k-1)]^{\mathrm{T}}, \mathbf{x}(k)\}$, where $k = 1, 2, \ldots, T$, and T represents the number of backup steps until the trailer hits the dock or leaves some predesignated borders of the parking lot (T depends on the initial state of the truck and the applied steering signal θ_s). The steering signal was selected randomly during this training process. The general idea for training the neural net emulator for the identification of nonlinear dynamical systems is depicted in the block diagram of Figure 5.4.3. However, the tapped delay lines are not needed here because of the kinematic nature of the trailer truck system. Next, the trained emulator network is used to train the controller. Once trained, the controller is used to control the real system. The reason for training the controller with the emulator and not with the real system is justified below.

Figure 5.4.7 shows the controller/emulator system in a retrieval mode. The whole system is recurrent due to the external feedback loops (actually, the system exhibits partial recurrence, since the emulator is a feedforward network and it will be assumed

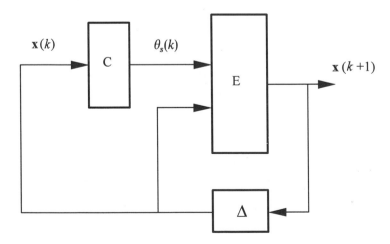

Figure 5.4.7
Controller/emulator retrieval system.

that the controller has a feedforward single-hidden-layer architecture). The controller and the emulator are labeled C and E, respectively, in the figure. The controller receives the input vector $\mathbf{x}(k)$ and responds with a single output $\theta_s(k)$, representing the control signal.

The idea of unfolding in time is applicable here. When initialized with state $\mathbf{x}(0)$, the system with the untrained, randomly initialized controller neural network evolves over T time steps until its state enters a restricted region (i.e., the trailer hits the borders). Unfolding the controller/emulator neural network T time steps results in the T-level feedforward network of Figure 5.4.8. This unfolded network has a total of $4T - 1$ layers of hidden units. The backpropagation through time technique can now be applied to adapt the controller weights. The only units with specified desired targets are the three units of the output layer at level T representing x, y, and θ_t. The desired target vector is the zero vector.

Once the output layer errors are computed, they are propagated back through the emulator network units and through the controller network units. Here, only the controller weights are adjusted (with equal increments for all copies of the same weight, as discussed earlier). The need to propagate the error through the plant block requires that a neural network–based plant emulator be used to replace the plant during training.

The trained controller is capable of backing the truck from any initial state, as long as it has sufficient clearance from the loading dock. Thousands of backups are required to train the controller. It is helpful (but not necessary) to start the learning with "easy" initial cases and then proceed to train with more difficult cases. Typical backup trajectories are shown in Figure 5.4.9.

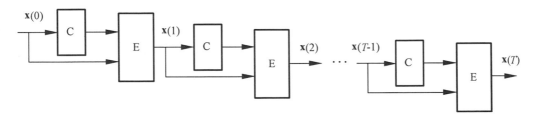

Figure 5.4.8
Unfolded trailer truck controller/emulator network over T time steps.

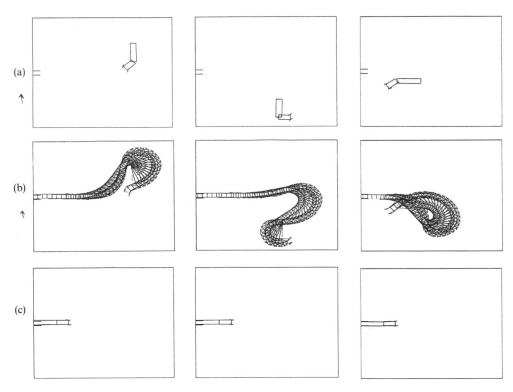

Figure 5.4.9
Typical backup trajectories for the trailer truck that resulted by employing a backpropagation through time trained controller. (*a*) Initial state, (*b*) trajectory, (*c*) final state. (Courtesy of Lee Feldkamp and Gint Puskorius of Ford Research Laboratory, Dearborn, Michigan.)

5.4.3 Recurrent Backpropagation

This section presents an extension of backprop to fully recurrent networks where the units are assumed to have continuously evolving states. The new algorithm is used to encode "spatial" input/output associations as stable equilibria of the recurrent network; i.e., after training on a set of $\{\mathbf{x}^k, \mathbf{d}^k\}$ pattern pairs, the presentation of $\mathbf{x}^k$ is supposed to drive the network's output $\mathbf{y}(t)$ toward the fixed attractor state $\mathbf{d}^k$. Thus the extension here is still restricted to learning "static" mappings as opposed to temporal association; however, it will serve as the basis for other extensions of backprop to sequence association that are discussed later in this section. The present extension, usually called *recurrent backpropagation*, was proposed independently by Pineda (1987, 1988) and Almeida (1987, 1988).

Consider a recurrent network of N units with outputs y_i, connections w_{ij}, and activations $f(net_i)$. A simple example ($N = 2$) of such a network is shown in Figure 5.4.5a. A unit is an input unit if it receives an element x_i^k of the input pattern $\mathbf{x}^k$. By definition, non-input units will be assigned an input $x_i^k = 0$. Output units are designated as units with prespecified desired outputs d_i^k. In general, a unit may belong to the set of input units and the set of output units simultaneously, or it may be "hidden" in the sense that it is neither an input nor an output unit. Henceforth, the pattern index k is dropped for convenience.

A biologically as well as electronically motivated choice for the state evolution of unit i is given by

$$\frac{dy_i}{dt} = -y_i + f\left(\sum_j w_{ij} y_j + x_i\right) = -y_i + f(net_i) \qquad i = 1, 2, \ldots, N \quad (5.4.6)$$

where net_i represents the total input activity of unit i, and $-y_i$ simulates natural signal decay. By setting $\dfrac{dy_i}{dt} = 0$, one arrives at the equilibrium points $\mathbf{y}^*$ of this system, given by

$$y_i^* = f(net_i^*) = f\left(\sum_j w_{ij} y_j^* + x_i\right) \tag{5.4.7}$$

The following is a derivation of a learning rule for the system/network in Equation (5.4.6) that assumes the existence and asymptotic stability of at least one equilibrium point $\mathbf{y}^* = [y_1^* \quad y_2^* \quad \cdots \quad y_N^*]^T$, in Equation (5.4.7). This equilibrium point represents the steady-state response of the network. Suppose that the network has converged to an equilibrium state $\mathbf{y}^*$ in response to an input $\mathbf{x}$. Then, if unit i is an output unit, it will respond with y_i^*. This output is compared with the desired response d_i, resulting in an error signal E_i. The goal is to adjust the weights of the network in such a way that the state $\mathbf{y}^*$ ultimately becomes equal to the desired response $\mathbf{d}$ associated with the input $\mathbf{x}$. In other words, our goal is to minimize the error function

$$E = \tfrac{1}{2} \sum_{i=1}^{N} (d_i - y_i^*)^2 = \tfrac{1}{2} \sum_{i=1}^{N} E_i^{*2} \qquad (5.4.8)$$

with $E_i^* = 0$ if unit i is not an output unit. Note that an instantaneous error function is used so that the resulting weight update rule is incremental in nature. Using gradient-descent search to update the weight w_{pq} gives

$$\Delta w_{pq} = -\rho \frac{\partial E}{\partial w_{pq}} = \rho \sum_i E_i^* \frac{\partial y_i^*}{\partial w_{pq}} \qquad (5.4.9)$$

with $\dfrac{\partial y_i^*}{\partial w_{pq}}$ given by differentiating Equation (5.4.7) to obtain

$$\frac{\partial y_i^*}{\partial w_{pq}} = f'(net_i^*) \left[\delta_{ip} y_q^* + \sum_j w_{ij} \frac{\partial y_j^*}{\partial w_{pq}} \right] \qquad (5.4.10)$$

where δ_{ip} is the Kronecker delta function ($\delta_{ip} = 1$ if $i = p$ and zero otherwise). Another way of writing Equation (5.4.10) is

$$\sum_j \mathbf{L}_{ij} \frac{\partial y_j^*}{\partial w_{pq}} = \delta_{ip} f'(net_i^*) y_q^* \qquad (5.4.11)$$

where

$$\mathbf{L}_{ij} = \delta_{ij} - f'(net_i^*) w_{ij} \qquad (5.4.12)$$

Now, one may solve for $\dfrac{\partial y_i^*}{\partial w_{pq}}$ by inverting the set of linear equations represented by Equation (5.4.11) and get

$$\frac{\partial y_i^*}{\partial w_{pq}} = (\mathbf{L}^{-1})_{ip} f'(net_p^*) y_q^* \tag{5.4.13}$$

where $(\mathbf{L}^{-1})_{ip}$ is the ipth element of the inverse matrix $\mathbf{L}^{-1}$. Hence substituting Equation (5.4.13) in Equation (5.4.9) gives the desired learning rule:

$$\Delta w_{pq} = \rho f'(net_p^*) \sum_i E_i^* (\mathbf{L}^{-1})_{ip} y_q^* \tag{5.4.14}$$

When the recurrent network is fully connected, then the matrix $\mathbf{L}$ is $N \times N$, and its inversion requires $O(N^3)$ operations using standard matrix inversion methods. Pineda and Almeida independently showed that a more economical local implementation, utilizing a modified recurrent neural network of the same size as the original network, is possible. This implementation has $O(N^2)$ computational complexity and is usually called *recurrent backpropagation*. To see this, consider the summation term in Equation (5.4.14) and define it as z_p^*:

$$z_p^* = \sum_i E_i^* (\mathbf{L}^{-1})_{ip} \tag{5.4.15}$$

Then, undoing the matrix inversion in Equation (5.4.15) leads to the set of linear equations for z_p^*, as shown by

$$\sum_p \mathbf{L}_{pi} z_p^* = E_i^* \tag{5.4.16}$$

or substituting for $\mathbf{L}$ from Equation (5.4.12), renaming the index p as j, and rearranging terms give

$$z_i^* = \sum_j f'(net_j^*) w_{ji} z_j^* + E_i^* \tag{5.4.17}$$

This equation can be solved using an analog network of units z_i with the dynamics

$$\frac{dz_i}{dt} = -z_i + \sum_j f'(net_j^*) w_{ji} z_j + E_i^* \qquad i = 1, 2, \ldots, N \tag{5.4.18}$$

Note that Equation (5.4.17) is satisfied by the equilibria of Equation (5.4.18). Thus a solution for $\mathbf{z}^* = [z_1^* \quad z_2^* \quad \cdots \quad z_N^*]^\mathrm{T}$, is possible if it is an attractor of the dynamics in Equation (5.4.18). It can be shown (see Problem 5.4.5) that $\mathbf{z}^*$ is an attractor of Equation (5.4.18) if $\mathbf{y}^*$ is an attractor of Equation (5.4.6).

The similarity between Equations (5.4.18) and (5.4.6) suggests that a recurrent network realization for computing $\mathbf{z}^*$ should be possible. In fact, such a network may be arrived at by starting with the original network and replacing the coupling weight w_{ij} from unit j to unit i by $f'(net_i^*)w_{ij}$ from unit i to unit j, assuming linear activations for all units, setting all inputs to zero, and feeding the error E_i^* as input to the ith output unit (of the original network). The resulting network is called the *error-propagation network* or the *adjoint* of the original net. Figure 5.4.10 shows the error-propagation network for the simple recurrent net given in Figure 5.4.5a.

We may now give a brief outline of the recurrent backpropagation learning procedure. An input pattern $\mathbf{x}^k$ is presented to the recurrent net, and a steady-state solution $\mathbf{y}^{*k}$ is computed by iteratively solving Equation (5.4.6). The steady-state outputs of the net are compared with the target $\mathbf{d}^k$ to find the output errors E_i^*. Then the z_i^{*k} values are computed by iteratively solving Equation (5.4.18). The weights are finally adjusted using Equation (5.4.14) or its equivalent form

$$\Delta w_{ij} = \rho f'(net_i^{*k})z_i^{*k}y_j^{*k} \tag{5.4.19}$$

where

$$net_i^{*k} = \sum_j w_{ij}y_j^{*k} + x_i^k$$

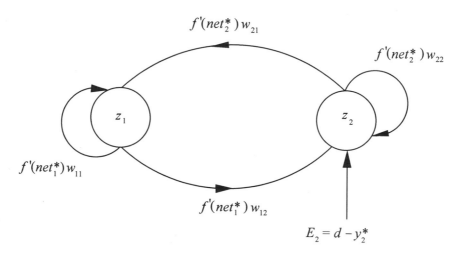

Figure 5.4.10
Error-propagation (adjoint) network for the simple recurrent net in Figure 5.4.5a.

Next, a new input pattern is presented to the network, and the preceding procedure is repeated, and so on. It should be noted that recurrent backpropagation reduces to incremental backprop for the special case of a net with no feedback.

The preceding analysis assumed that finite equilibria $\mathbf{y}^*$ exist and are stable. However, it has been shown (Simard et al., 1988, 1989) that for any recurrent neural network architecture there always exist divergent trajectories for Equation (5.4.6). In practice, though, if the initial weights are chosen to be small enough, the network almost always converges to a finite stable equilibrium $\mathbf{y}^*$.

One potential application of recurrent backpropagation networks is as associative memories (for definition and details of associative memories, refer to Chapter 7). This is so because these networks build attractors $\mathbf{d}^k$ that correspond to input/output association patterns $\{\mathbf{x}^k, \mathbf{d}^k\}$. That is, if a noisy and/or incomplete version of a trained pattern $\mathbf{x}^k$ is presented as input, it potentially causes the network to eventually converge to $\mathbf{d}^k$. These pattern-completion/error-correction features are superior to those of feedforward networks (Almeida, 1987). Other applications of recurrent backpropagation nets can be found in Qian and Sejnowski (1989).

5.4.4 Time-Dependent Recurrent Backpropagation

The recurrent backpropagation method just discussed can be extended to recurrent networks that produce time-dependent trajectories. One such extension is the time-dependent recurrent backpropagation method of Pearlmutter (1989a, 1989b) [see also Werbos (1988), and Sato (1990)]. In Pearlmutter's method, learning is performed as a gradient descent in the weights of a continuous recurrent network to minimize an error function E of the temporal trajectory of the states. It can be thought of as an extension of recurrent backpropagation to dynamic sequences. The following is a brief outline of this algorithm.

Here, we start with a recurrent net with units y_i having the dynamics

$$\tau_i \frac{dy_i}{dt} = -y_i + f(net_i) + x_i(t) \qquad i = 1, 2, \ldots, N \qquad (5.4.20)$$

Note that the inputs $x_i(t)$ are continuous functions of time. Similarly, each output unit y_l has a desired target signal $d_l(t)$ that is also a continuous function of time.

Consider minimizing a criterion $E(\mathbf{y})$, which is some function of the trajectory $\mathbf{y}(t)$ for t between 0 and t_1. Since the objective here is to teach the lth output unit to produce the trajectory $d_l(t)$ upon the presentation of $\mathbf{x}(t)$, an appropriate criterion (error) functional is

$$E = \frac{1}{2} \int_0^{t_1} \sum_l [d_l(t) - y_l(t)]^2 \, dt \qquad (5.4.21)$$

which measures the deviation of y_i from the function d_i. Now, the partial derivatives of E with respect to the weights may be computed as

$$\frac{\partial E}{\partial w_{ij}} = \frac{1}{\tau_i} \int_0^{t_1} f'[net_i(t)] z_i(t) y_j(t) \, dt \tag{5.4.22}$$

where $net_i(t) = \sum_j w_{ij} y_j(t)$, $y_j(t)$ is the solution to Equation (5.4.20), and $z_i(t)$ is the solution of the dynamical system given by

$$\frac{dz_i}{dt} = +\frac{1}{\tau_i} z_i - \sum_j \frac{1}{\tau_j} w_{ji} f'(net_j) z_j - E_i(t) \qquad i = 1, 2, \ldots, N \tag{5.4.23}$$

with the boundary condition $z_i(t_1) = 0$. Here, $E_i(t)$ is given by $d_i(t) - y_i(t)$ if unit i is an output unit, and zero otherwise. Simultaneously, one also may minimize E in the time-constant τ space by gradient descent utilizing

$$\frac{\partial E}{\partial \tau_i} = -\frac{1}{\tau_i} \int_0^{t_1} z_i(t) \frac{dy_i(t)}{dt} \, dt$$

$$= -\frac{1}{\tau_i^2} \int_0^{t_1} z_i(t) \{-y_i(t) + f[net_i(t)] + x_i(t)\} \, dt \tag{5.4.24}$$

Equations (5.4.22) and (5.4.24) may be derived by using a finite-difference approximation, as in Pearlmutter (1988). They also may be obtained using the calculus of variations and Lagrange multipliers, as in optimal control theory (Bryson and Denham, 1962).

Using numerical integration (e.g., first-order finite-difference approximations), one first solves Equation (5.4.20) for $t \in [0, t_1]$; then one sets the boundary condition $z_i(t_1) = 0$ and integrates the system in Equation (5.4.23) backward from t_1 to 0. Having determined $y_i(t)$ and $z_i(t)$, one may proceed with computing $\dfrac{\partial E}{\partial w_{ij}}$ and $\dfrac{\partial E}{\partial \tau_i}$ from Equations (5.4.22) and (5.4.24), respectively. Next, the weight changes Δw_{ij} and time-constant changes $\Delta \tau_i$ are computed from $\Delta w_{ij} = -\rho \dfrac{\partial E}{\partial w_{ij}}$ and $\Delta \tau_i = -\eta \dfrac{\partial E}{\partial \tau_i}$, respectively.

Because of its memory requirements and continuous-time nature, time-dependent recurrent backpropagation is more appropriate as an off-line training method. Some applications of this technique include learning limit cycles in two-dimensional space (Pearlmutter, 1989a), like the one shown in Figures 5.4.11 and 5.4.12. The trajectories in Figure 5.4.11b and c are produced by a network of 4 hidden units, 2 output units, and no input units after 1500 and 12,000 learning cycles, respectively. The desired

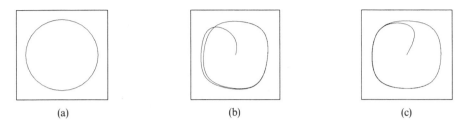

(a)   (b)   (c)

Figure 5.4.11
Learning performance of time-dependent recurrent backpropagation. (a) Desired trajectory $d_1(t)$ versus $d_2(t)$; (b) generated state space trajectory $y_1(t)$ versus $y_2(t)$ after 1500 cycles, (c) $y_1(t)$ versus $y_2(t)$ after 12,000 cycles. (From B. A. Pearlmutter, 1989a, with permission of the MIT Press.)

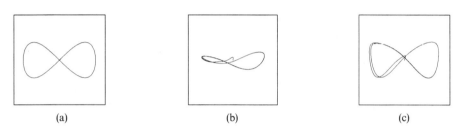

(a)   (b)   (c)

Figure 5.4.12
Learning the figure "eight" by a time-dependent recurrent backpropagation net. (a) Desired state space trajectory; (b) generated trajectory after 3182 cycles, (c) generated trajectory after 20,000 cycles. (From B. A. Pearlmutter, 1989a, with permission of the MIT Press.)

trajectory $[d_1(t)$ versus $d_2(t)]$ is the circle in Figure 5.4.11a. The state space trajectories in Figure 5.4.12b and c are generated by a network with 10 hidden units and 2 output units after 3182 and 20,000 cycles, respectively. The desired trajectory is shown in Figure 5.4.12a. This method has also been shown to work well in time-series prediction (Logar et al., 1993). Fang and Sejnowski (1990) reported improved learning speed and convergence of the preceding algorithm as the result of allowing independent learning rates for individual weights in the network (e.g., they report a better formed figure "eight" compared with the one in Figure 5.4.12c after only 2000 cycles).

Finally, an important property of the continuous-time recurrent net described by Equation (5.4.20) should be noted. It has been shown (Funahashi and Nakamura, 1993) that the output of a sufficiently large continuous-time recurrent net with hidden units can approximate any continuous state space trajectory to any desired degree of accuracy. This means that recurrent neural nets are universal approximators of dynamical systems. Note, however, that this says nothing about the existence of a learning procedure that will guarantee the synthesis of a recurrent net for a given desired continuous trajectory. What it implies, though, is that the failure of learning a given continuous trajectory by a sufficiently large recurrent net would be attributed to the learning algorithm used.

5.4.5 Real-Time Recurrent Learning

Another method that allows sequences to be associated is the real-time recurrent learning (RTRL) method[7] proposed by Williams and Zipser (1989a, 1989b). This method allows recurrent networks to learn tasks that require retention of information over time periods having either fixed or indefinite length. RTRL assumes recurrent nets with discrete-time states that evolve according to

$$y_i(t) = f[net_i(t-1)] = f\left[\sum_j w_{ij}y_j(t-1) + x_i(t-1)\right] \tag{5.4.25}$$

A desired target trajectory $\mathbf{d}(t)$ is associated with each input trajectory $\mathbf{x}(t)$. As before, the quadratic error measure is used:

$$E_{\text{total}} = \sum_{t=0}^{T} E(t) \tag{5.4.26}$$

where

$$E(t) = \tfrac{1}{2} \sum_l [d_l(t) - y_l(t)]^2$$

Thus gradient descent on E_{total} gives

$$\Delta w_{pq} = \sum_{t=0}^{T} \Delta w_{pq}(t) \tag{5.4.27}$$

with

$$\Delta w_{pq}(t) = -\rho \frac{\partial E(t)}{\partial w_{pq}} = \rho \sum_l [d_l(t) - y_l(t)] \frac{\partial y_l(t)}{\partial w_{pq}} \tag{5.4.28}$$

The partial derivative $\dfrac{\partial y_l}{\partial w_{pq}}$ in Equation (5.4.28) can now be computed from Equation (5.4.25) as

$$\frac{\partial y_l(t)}{\partial w_{pq}} = f'[net_l(t-1)]\left[\delta_{lp}y_q(t-1) + \sum_j w_{lj}\frac{\partial y_j(t-1)}{\partial w_{pq}}\right] \tag{5.4.29}$$

---

7. A similar method was first introduced by White (1975) in the context of infinite impulse response (IIR) linear filter adaptation.

Since Equation (5.4.29) relates the derivatives at time t to those at time $t-1$, we can iterate it forward [starting from some initial value for $\dfrac{\partial y_l(0)}{\partial w_{pq}}$; e.g., zero] and compute $\dfrac{\partial y_l(t)}{\partial w_{pq}}$ at any desired time while using Equation (5.4.25) to iteratively update states at each iteration. Each cycle of this algorithm requires time proportional to N^4, where N is the number of units in a fully interconnected net. Instead of using Equation (5.4.27) to update the weights, it was found (Williams and Zipser, 1989a) that updating the weights after each time step according to Equation (5.4.28) works well as long as the learning rate ρ is kept sufficiently small, thus the name *real-time recurrent learning*. This avoids the need for allocating memory proportional to the maximum sequence length and leads to simple on-line implementations. The power of this method was demonstrated through a series of simulations (Williams and Zipser, 1989b). In one particular simulation, a 12-unit recurrent net learned to detect whether a string of arbitrary length comprised of left and right parentheses consists entirely of sets of balanced parentheses by observing only the action of a Turing machine performing the same task. In some of the simulations, it was found that learning speed (and sometimes convergence) improved by setting the states of units $y_l(t)$ with known targets to their target values, but only after computing $E_l(t)$ and the derivatives in Equation (5.4.29). This heuristic is known as *teacher forcing*; it helps keep the network closer to the desired trajectory. The reader may refer to Robinson and Fallside (1988), Rohwer (1990), and Sun et al. (1992) for other methods for learning sequences in recurrent networks. (The reader is also referred to the special issue of the *IEEE Transactions on Neural Networks*, volume 5, number 2, 1994, for further exploration into recurrent neural networks and their applications.)

5.5 Summary

This chapter begins by deriving backprop, a gradient-descent-based learning procedure for minimizing the sum of squared error criterion function in a feedforward layered network of sigmoidal units. This result is a natural generalization of the delta learning rule given in Chapter 3 for single-layer networks. Also presented is a global-descent-based error backpropagation procedure that employs automatic tunneling through the error function for escaping local minima and converging toward a global minimum.

Various variations to backprop are introduced in order to improve convergence speed, avoid "poor" local minima, and enhance generalization. These variations include weight initialization methods, autonomous learning parameter adjustments, and the addition of regularization terms to the error function being minimized. The theoretical bases for several of these variations are presented.

A number of significant real-world applications are presented where backprop is used to train feedforward networks for realizing complex mappings between noisy sensory data and the corresponding desired classifications/actions. These applications include converting human hand movement to speech, handwritten digit recognition, autonomous vehicle control, medical diagnosis, and data compression.

Finally, extensions of the idea of backward error propagation learning to recurrent neural networks are given that allow for temporal association of time sequences. Time-delay neural networks, which may be viewed as nonlinear FIR or IIR filters, are shown to be capable of sequence recognition and association by employing standard backprop training. Backpropagation through time is introduced as a training method for fully recurrent networks. It employs a trick that allows backprop with weight sharing to be used to train an unfolded feedforward nonrecurrent version of the original network. Direct training of fully recurrent networks is also possible. A recurrent backpropagation method for training fully recurrent nets on static (spatial) associations is presented. This method is also extended to temporal association of continuous-time sequences (time-dependent recurrent backpropagation). Finally, a method of on-line temporal association of discrete-time sequences (real-time recurrent learning) is discussed.

Problems

5.1.1   Derive Equations (5.1.11) and (5.1.12).

5.1.2   Derive the backprop learning rule for the first hidden layer (layer directly connected to the input signal **x**) in a three-layer (two-hidden-layer) feedforward network. Assume that the first hidden layer has K units with weights w_{ki} and differentiable activations $f_{h1}(net_k)$, the second hidden layer has J units with weights w_{jk} and differentiable activations $f_{h2}(net_j)$, and the output layer has L units with weights w_{lj} and differentiable activations $f_o(net_l)$.

5.1.3   Consider the neural network in Figure 5.1.1 with full additional connections between the input vector **x** and the output layer units. Let the weights of these additional connections be designated as w_{li} (connection weights between the lth output unit and the ith input signal.) Derive a learning rule for these additional weights based on gradient-descent minimization of the instantaneous SSE criterion function.

5.1.4   Derive the batch backprop rule for the network in Figure 5.1.1.

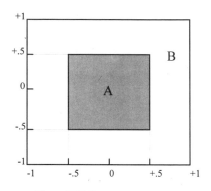

Figure P5.1.5
Two-class classification problem.

† **5.1.5** Use the incremental backprop procedure described in Section 5.1.1 to train a two-layer network with 12 hidden units and a single output unit to learn to distinguish between the class regions in Figure P5.1.5. Follow a similar training strategy to the one employed in Example 5.1.1. Generate and plot the separating surfaces learned by the various units in the network. Can you identify the function realized by the output unit?

*† **5.1.6** Derive and implement numerically the global-descent backprop learning algorithm for a single-hidden-layer feedforward network starting from Equation (5.1.15). Generate a learning curve (as in Figure 5.1.5) for the 4-bit parity problem using incremental backprop, batch backprop, and global-descent backprop. Assume a four-hidden-unit fully interconnected feedforward net with unipolar sigmoid activation units, and use the same initial weights and learning rates for all learning algorithms (use $\sigma = 2$ and $k = 0.001$ for global descent, and experiment with different directions of the perturbation vector $\varepsilon_{\mathbf{w}}$).

5.1.7 Consider the two-layer feedforward net in Figure 5.1.1. Assume that we replace the hidden-layer weights w_{ji} by nonlinear weights of the form $w_{ji}x_i^{r_{ji}}$, where $r_{ji} \in R$ is a parameter associated with hidden unit j and x_i is the ith component of the input vector $\mathbf{x}$. It has been shown empirically (Narayan, 1993) that this network is capable of faster and more accurate training when the weights and the r_{ji} exponents are adapted as compared with the same network with fixed $r_{ji} = 0$. Derive a learning rule for r_{ji} based on incremental gradient-descent minimization of the instantaneous SSE criterion of Equation (5.1.1). Are there any restrictions on the values of the inputs x_i? What would be a reasonable initial value for the r_{ji} exponents?

†**5.1.8** Consider the Feigenbaum (1978) chaotic time series generated by the non-linear iterated (discrete-time) map

$$x(t + 1) = 4x(t)[1 - x(t)]$$

Plot the time series $x(t)$ for $t \in [0, 20]$ starting from $x(0) = 0.2$. Construct (by inspection) an optimal net of the type considered in Problem 5.1.7 that will perfectly model this iterated map (assume zero biases and linear activation functions with unity slope for all units in the network). Now, vary all exponents and weights by $+1$ percent and -2 percent, respectively. Compare the time series predicted by this varied network to $x(t)$ over the range $t \in [0, 20]$. Assume $x(0) = 0.2$. Note that the output of the net at time $t + 1$ must serve as the new input to the net for predicting the time series at $t + 2$, and so on.

5.2.1 Given a unit with n weights w_i uniformly randomly distributed in the range $[-3/\sqrt{n}, +3/\sqrt{n}]$, and assuming that the components x_i of the input vector **x** are randomly and uniformly distributed in the interval $[0, 1]$, show that the random variable $net = \sum_{i=1}^{n} w_i x_i$ has a zero mean and unity standard deviation.

5.2.2 Explain qualitatively the characteristics of the approximate Newton's rule of Equation (5.2.6).

5.2.3 Complete the missing steps in the derivation of Equation (5.2.9).

5.2.4 Derive the activation function slope update rules of Equations (5.2.10) and (5.2.11).

5.2.5 Derive the incremental backprop learning rule [Equations (5.2.17) and (5.2.18)] starting from the entropy criterion function in Equation (5.2.16).

5.2.6 Derive the incremental backprop learning rule [Equations (5.2.20) and (5.2.21)] starting from the Minkowski-r criterion function in Equation (5.2.19).

5.2.7 Comment on the qualitative characteristics of the Minkowski-r criterion function for negative r.

5.2.8 Derive Equation (5.2.22).

*5.2.9 Derive the partial derivatives of J_R in Equations (5.2.25) through (5.2.28) for the soft weight-sharing regularization term in Equation (5.2.24). Use the appropriate partial derivatives to solve analytically for the optimal mixture parameters μ_j^* and σ_j^*, assuming fixed values for the "responsibilities" $r_j(w_i)$.

5.2.10 Give a qualitative explanation for the effect of adapting the Gaussian mixture parameters α_j, μ_j, and σ_j on learning in a feedforward neural net.

5.2.11 Consider the criterion function with entropy regularization (Kamimura, 1993)

$$E = \tfrac{1}{2} \sum_{l=1}^{L} (d_l - y_l)^2 - \lambda \sum_{j=1}^{J} \bar{z}_j \ln \bar{z}_j$$

where $\bar{z}_j = z_j \left(\sum_{i=1}^{J} z_i \right)^{-1}$ is a normalized output of hidden unit j, and $\lambda > 0$. Assume the same network architecture as in Figure 5.1.1 with logistic activations for all units, and derive backprop based on this criterion/error function. What are the effects of the entropy regularization term on the hidden-layer activity pattern of the trained net?

*5.2.12 The optimal-steepest-descent method employs a learning step $\rho = \rho_{opt}(t)$ defined as the smallest positive root of the equation

$$\frac{\partial E[\mathbf{w}(t+1)]}{\partial \rho} = \frac{\partial}{\partial \rho} E\{\mathbf{w}(t) - \rho \nabla E[\mathbf{w}(t)]\} = 0$$

Show that the optimal learning step is approximately given by (Tsypkin, 1971)

$$\rho_{opt}(t) \approx \frac{\|\nabla E[\mathbf{w}(t)]\|^2}{\nabla E[\mathbf{w}(t)]^T \nabla^2 E[\mathbf{w}(t)] \nabla E[\mathbf{w}(t)]}$$

†**5.2.13** Repeat the simulation in Figure 5.2.3 but with a 40-hidden-unit feedforward net. During training, use the noise-free training samples as indicated by the small circles in Figure 5.2.3; these samples have the following x values $\{-5, -4, -3, -2, -1, -\tfrac{1}{2}, 0, \tfrac{1}{3}, 1, 2, 3, 4, 6, 8, 10\}$. By comparing the number of degrees of freedom of this net with the size of the training set, what would your intuitive conclusions be about the net's approximation behavior? Does the result of your simulation agree with your intuitive conclusions? Explain. How would these results be affected if a noisy data set was used?

†**5.2.14** Repeat the simulations in Figure 5.2.5 using incremental backprop with
cross-validation–based stopping of training. Assume the net to be identical
to the one discussed in Section 5.2.6 in conjunction with Figure 5.2.5. Also
use the same weight initialization and learning parameters. Plot the validation and training RMS errors on a log-log scale for the first 10,000 cycles,
and compare them with Figure 5.2.6. Discuss the differences. Test the resulting "optimally trained" net on 200 points, x, generated uniformly in
$[-8, 12]$. Plot the output of this net versus x and compare it with the actual
function $g(x) = [(x - 2)(2x + 1)]/(1 + x^2)$ being approximated. Also compare the output of this net with the one in Figure 5.2.5 (dashed line), and give
the reason(s) for the difference (if any) in performance of the two nets. The
following training and validation sets are to be used in this problem. The
training set is the one plotted in Figure 5.2.5. The validation set has the same
noise statistics as for the training set.

Training set		Validation Set	
Input	Output	Input	Output
−5.0000	2.6017	−6.0000	2.1932
−4.0000	3.2434	−5.5000	2.5411
−3.0000	2.1778	−4.5000	1.4374
−2.0000	2.1290	−2.5000	2.8382
−1.0000	1.5725	−1.5000	1.7027
−0.5000	−0.4124	−0.7500	0.3688
0.0000	−2.2652	−0.2500	−1.1351
0.3333	−2.6880	0.4000	−2.3758
1.0000	−0.3856	0.8000	−2.5782
2.0000	−0.6755	1.5000	0.2102
3.0000	1.1409	2.5000	−0.3497
4.0000	0.8026	3.5000	1.5792
6.0000	0.9805	5.0000	1.1380
8.0000	1.4563	7.0000	1.9612
10.0000	1.2267	9.0000	0.9381

†**5.2.15** Repeat Problem 5.2.14 using, as your training set, all the available data
(i.e., both training and validation data). Here, cross-validation cannot be
used to stop training, since we have no independent (nontraining) data
to validate with. One (heuristic) way to help avoid overtraining in this case
would be to stop at the training cycle that led to the optimal net in Problem
5.2.14. Does the resulting net generalize better than the one in Problem
5.2.14? Explain.

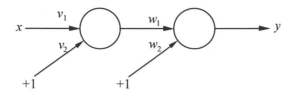

Figure P5.2.16
A neural network for approximating the function
$g(x) = a\,\text{sgn}\,(x - b) + c.$

5.2.16 Consider the simple neural net in Figure P5.2.16. Assume the hidden
unit has an activation function $f(\xi) = \tanh(\xi)$ and that the output unit
has a linear activation with unit slope. Show that there exists a set of
real-valued weights $\{w_1, w_2, v_1, v_2\}$ that approximates the discontinuous
function $g(x) = a\,\text{sgn}\,(x - b) + c$, for all x, a, b, and $c \in R$, to any degree of
accuracy.

†5.4.1 Consider the time series generated by the Mackey-Glass (Mackey and Glass,
1977) discrete-time equation

$$x(t + 1) = +0.9x(t) + \frac{0.2x(t - \tau)}{1 + x^{10}(t - \tau)}$$

Plot the time series $x(t)$ for $t \in [0, 1000]$ and $\tau = 17$. When solving this nonlinear difference delay equation, an initial condition specified by an initial
function defined over a strip of width τ is required. Experiment with several
different initial functions [e.g. $x(0) = 1.2$, $x(t) = 0$ for $t < 0$].

*†5.4.2 Use incremental backprop with sufficiently small learning rates to train the
network in Figure 5.4.1 to predict $x(t + 6)$ in the Glass-Mackey time series
of Problem 5.4.1 (assume $\tau = 17$). Use a collection of 500 training pairs
corresponding to different values of t generated randomly from the time
series for $t \in \{0, 1, 2, \ldots, 1000\}$. Assume training pairs of the form

$$\{[x(t) \quad x(t - 6) \quad x(t - 12) \quad \cdots \quad x(t - 60)]^T, x(t + 6)\}$$

Also assume 50 hidden units with hyperbolic tangent activation function (set
$\beta = 1$), and use a linear activation function for the output unit. Plot the
training RMS error versus the number of training cycles. Plot the signal $\hat{x}(t)$
predicted (recursively) by the trained network, and compare it with $x(t)$ for
$t = 0, 6, 12, 18, \ldots, 1200$. Repeat with a two-hidden-layer net having 30 units

in its first hidden layer and 15 units in its second hidden layer (use the learning equation derived in Problem 5.1.2 to train the weights of the first hidden layer). [For an interesting collection of time series and their prediction, the reader is referred to the edited volume by Weigend and Gershenfeld (1994)].

†**5.4.3** Employ the series-parallel identification scheme of Section 5.4.1 (refer to Figure 5.4.3) to identify the nonlinear discrete-time plant (Narendra and Parthasarathy, 1990)

$$x(t+1) = \frac{x(t)}{1 + x^2(t)} + u^3(t)$$

Use a feedforward neural network having 20 hyperbolic tangent activation units (set $\beta = 1$) in its hidden layer, feeding into a linear output unit. Use incremental backprop with sufficiently small learning rates to train the network. Assume the outputs of the delay lines (inputs to neural network in Figure 5.4.3) to be $x(t)$ and $u(t)$. Also assume uniform random inputs in the interval $[-2, +2]$ during training. Plot the output of the plant as well as the recursively generated output of the identification model for the input

$$u(t) = \sin\left(\frac{2\pi t}{25}\right) + \sin\left(\frac{2\pi t}{10}\right)$$

5.4.4 Derive Equations (5.4.10) and (5.4.13).

5.4.5 Show that if the state $\mathbf{y}^*$ is a locally asymptotically stable equilibrium of the dynamics in Equation (5.4.6), then the state $\mathbf{z}^*$ satisfying Equation (5.4.17) is a locally asymptotically stable equilibrium of the dynamics in Equation (5.4.18). (*Hint:* Start by showing that linearizing the dynamical equations about their respective equilibria gives

$$\tau \frac{d\Delta y_i}{dt} = -\sum_j \mathbf{L}_{ij} \Delta y_j$$

and

$$\tau \frac{d\Delta z_i}{dt} = -\sum_j \mathbf{L}_{ij}^\mathrm{T} \Delta z_j$$

where $\Delta y_i = y_i - y_i^*$ and $\Delta z_i = z_i - z_i^*$ are small perturbations added to y_i^* and z_i^*, respectively.)

* **5.4.6** Derive Equations (5.4.22) and (5.4.24). [See Pearlmutter (1988) for help.]

† **5.4.7** Employ time-dependent recurrent backpropagation learning to generate the trajectories shown in Figures 5.4.11a and 5.4.12a.

5.4.8 Show that the RTRL method applied to a fully recurrent network of N units has $O(N^4)$ computational complexity for each learning iteration.

6 Adaptive Multilayer Neural Networks II

The preceding chapter concentrated on multilayer architectures with sigmoidal-type units, both static (feedforward) and dynamic. The present chapter introduces several additional adaptive multilayer networks and their associated training procedures, as well as some variations. The majority of the networks considered here employ processing units that are not necessarily sigmoidal. A common feature of these networks is their fast training as compared with the backprop networks of the preceding chapter. The mechanisms leading to such increased training speed are emphasized.

All networks discussed in this chapter differ in one or more significant ways from those in the preceding chapter. One group of networks employs units with localized receptive fields, where units receiving direct input from input signals (patterns) can only "see" a part of the input pattern. Examples of such networks are the radial basis function network and the cerebellar model articulation controller.

A second group of networks employs resource allocation. These networks are capable of allocating units as needed during training. This feature enables the network size to be determined dynamically and eliminates the need for guessing the proper network size. This resource-allocating scheme is also shown to be the primary reason for efficient training. Examples of networks in this group are hyperspherical classifiers and the cascade-correlation network.

These two groups of networks mainly employ supervised learning. Some of these networks may be used as function interpolators/approximators, while others are best suited for classification tasks. The third and last group of adaptive multilayer networks treated in this chapter has the capability of unsupervised learning or clustering. Here, two specific clustering nets are discussed: the ART1 network and the auto-associative clustering network.

Throughout this chapter, fundamental similarities and differences among the various networks are stressed. In addition, significant extensions of these networks are pointed out, and the effects of these extensions on performance are discussed.

6.1 Radial Basis Function (RBF) Networks

This section describes an artificial neural network model motivated by the "locally tuned" response observed in biologic neurons. Neurons with locally tuned response characteristics can be found in many parts of biologic nervous systems. These nerve cells have response characteristics that are "selective" for some finite range of the input signal space. The cochlear stereocilia cells, for example, have a locally tuned response to frequency that is a consequence of their biophysical properties. The present model is also motivated by earlier work on radial basis functions (Medgassy, 1961) that were used for interpolation (Micchelli, 1986; Powell, 1987), probability density estimation (Parzen, 1962; Duda and Hart, 1973; Specht, 1990), and approximations of smooth multivariate functions (Poggio and Girosi, 1989). The model is commonly referred to as the *radial basis function (RBF) network*.

The most important feature that distinguishes the RBF network from earlier radial basis function–based models is its adaptive nature, which generally allows it to utilize a relatively smaller number of locally tuned units (RBFs). RBF networks were independently proposed by Broomhead and Lowe (1988), Lee and Kil (1988), Niranjan and Fallside (1988), and Moody and Darken (1989a, 1989b). Similar schemes were also suggested by Hanson and Burr (1987), Lapedes and Farber (1987), Casdagli (1989), Poggio and Girosi (1990b), and others. The following is a description of the basic RBF network architecture and its associated training algorithm.

The RBF network has a feedforward structure consisting of a single hidden layer of J locally tuned units which are fully interconnected to an output layer of L linear units, as shown in Figure 6.1.1. All hidden units simultaneously receive the n-dimensional real-valued input vector $\mathbf{x}$. Notice the absence of hidden-layer weights in Figure 6.1.1. This is because the hidden-unit outputs are not calculated using the weighted-sum/sigmoidal activation mechanism as in the preceding chapter. Rather, here, each hidden-unit output z_j is obtained by calculating the "closeness" of the input

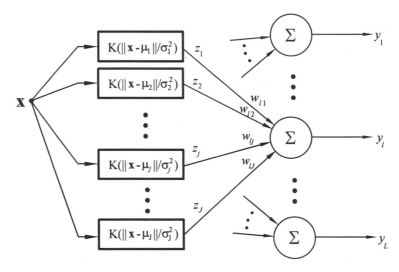

Figure 6.1.1
A radial basis function neural network consisting of a single hidden layer of locally tuned units that is fully interconnected to an output layer of linear units. For clarity, only hidden to output layer connections for the lth output unit are shown.

$\mathbf{x}$ to an n-dimensional parameter vector $\boldsymbol{\mu}_j$ associated with the jth hidden unit. Here, the response characteristics of the jth hidden unit are given by

$$z_j(\mathbf{x}) = K\left(\frac{\|\mathbf{x} - \boldsymbol{\mu}_j\|}{\sigma_j^2}\right) \tag{6.1.1}$$

where K is a strictly positive radially symmetric function (kernel) with a unique maximum at its "center" $\boldsymbol{\mu}_j$ and which drops off rapidly to zero away from the center. The parameter σ_j is the "width" of the receptive field in the input space for unit j. This implies that z_j has an appreciable value only when the "distance" $\|\mathbf{x} - \boldsymbol{\mu}_j\|$ is smaller than the width σ_j. Given an input vector $\mathbf{x}$, the output of the RBF network is the L-dimensional activity vector $\mathbf{y}$ whose lth component is given by[1]

$$y_l(\mathbf{x}) = \sum_{j=1}^{J} w_{lj} z_j(\mathbf{x}) \tag{6.1.2}$$

It is interesting to note here that for $L = 1$, the mapping in Equation (6.1.2) is similar in form to that employed by a polynomial threshold gate (PTG), as in Equation (1.4.1). However, in the RBF net, a choice is made to use radially symmetric kernels as "hidden units" as opposed to monomials.

RBF networks are best suited for approximating continuous or piecewise continuous real-valued mappings $f: R^n \to R^L$, where n is sufficiently small; these approximation problems include classification problems as a special case. According to Equations (6.1.1) and (6.1.2), the RBF network may be viewed as approximating a desired function $f(\mathbf{x})$ by superposition of nonorthogonal bell-shaped basis functions. The degree of accuracy can be controlled by three parameters: the number of basis functions used, their location, and their width. In fact, like feedforward neural networks with a single hidden layer of sigmoidal units, it can be shown that RBF networks are universal approximators (Poggio and Girosi, 1989; Hartman et al., 1990; Baldi, 1991; Park and Sandberg, 1991, 1993).

A special but commonly used RBF network assumes a Gaussian basis function for the hidden units:

$$z_j(\mathbf{x}) = \exp\left(-\frac{\|\mathbf{x} - \boldsymbol{\mu}_j\|^2}{2\sigma_j^2}\right) \tag{6.1.3}$$

where σ_j and $\boldsymbol{\mu}_j$ are the standard deviation and mean of the jth unit receptive field,

---

1. A bias can be added to the output units if needed. Here, one may treat the Jth hidden unit as a dummy unit by clamping its output z_J to $+1$. Thus w_{lJ} becomes the weight of the lth output unit associated with the bias input.

respectively, and the norm is the Euclidean norm. Another possible choice for the basis function is the logistic function of the form

$$z_j(\mathbf{x}) = \left[1 + \exp\left(\frac{\|\mathbf{x} - \boldsymbol{\mu}_j\|}{\sigma_j^2} - \theta_j \right) \right]^{-1} \tag{6.1.4}$$

where θ_j is an adjustable bias. In fact, with the basis function in Equation (6.1.4), the only difference between an RBF network and a feedforward neural network with a single hidden layer of sigmoidal units is the similarity computation performed by the hidden units. If we think of $\boldsymbol{\mu}_j$ as the parameter (weight) vector associated with the jth hidden unit, then it is easy to see that an RBF network can be obtained from a single-hidden-layer neural network with unipolar sigmoidal-type units and linear output units (like the one in Figure 5.1.1) by simply replacing the jth hidden-unit weighted-sum $net_j = \mathbf{x}^T \boldsymbol{\mu}_j$ by the negative of the normalized Euclidean distance $\|\mathbf{x} - \boldsymbol{\mu}_j\|/\sigma_j^2$. On the other hand, use of the Gaussian basis function in Equation (6.1.3) leads to hidden units with Gaussian-type activation functions and with a Euclidean distance similarity computation. In this case, no bias is needed.

Next, the training of RBF networks is addressed. Consider a training set of m labeled pairs $\{\mathbf{x}^i, \mathbf{d}^i\}$ that represent associations of a given mapping or samples of a continuous multivariate function. Also consider the SSE criterion function as an error function E to be minimized over the given training set. In other words, it is desired to develop a training method that minimizes E by adaptively updating the free parameters of the RBF network. These parameters are the receptive field centers (means $\boldsymbol{\mu}_j$ of the hidden layer Gaussian units), the receptive field widths (standard deviations σ_j), and the output layer weights (w_{lj}).

Because of the differentiable nature of the RBF network's transfer characteristics, one of the first training methods that comes to mind is a fully supervised gradient-descent method over E (Moody and Darken, 1989a; Poggio and Girosi, 1989). In particular, $\boldsymbol{\mu}_j$, σ_j, and w_{lj} are updated as follows: $\Delta\boldsymbol{\mu}_j = -\rho_{\boldsymbol{\mu}} \nabla_{\boldsymbol{\mu}_j} E$, $\Delta\sigma_j = -\rho_\sigma \dfrac{\partial E}{\partial \sigma_j}$, and $\Delta w_{lj} = -\rho_w \dfrac{\partial E}{\partial w_{lj}}$, where $\rho_{\boldsymbol{\mu}}$, ρ_σ, and ρ_w are small positive constants. This method, although capable of matching or exceeding the performance of backprop-trained networks, still gives training times comparable with those of sigmoidal-type networks (Wettschereck and Dietterich, 1992).

One reason for the slow convergence of the preceding supervised gradient-descent-trained RBF network is its inefficient use of the locally tuned representation of the hidden-layer units. When the hidden-unit receptive fields are narrow, only a small fraction of the total number of units in the network will be activated for a given input **x**; the activated units are the ones with centers very close to the input vector in the input space. Thus only those units which were activated need be updated for each input presentation. The preceding supervised learning method, though, places no restrictions on maintaining small values for σ_j. Thus the supervised learning method is not guaranteed to utilize the computational advantages of locality. One way to rectify this problem is to only use gradient-descent-based learning for the basis function centers and use a method that maintains small σ_j values. Examples of learning methods that take advantage of the locality property of the hidden units are presented below.

A training strategy that decouples learning at the hidden layer from that at the output layer is possible for RBF networks because of the local receptive field nature of the hidden units. This strategy has been shown to be very effective in terms of training speed; however, this advantage is generally offset by reduced generalization ability unless a large number of basis functions is used. In the following, efficient methods for locating the receptive field centers and computing receptive field widths are described. As for the output-layer weights, once the hidden units are synthesized, these weights can be computed easily using the delta rule [Equation (5.1.2)]. One may view this computation as finding the proper normalization coefficients of the basis functions. That is, the weight w_{lj} determines the amount of contribution of the jth basis function to the lth output of the RBF net.

Several schemes have been suggested to find proper receptive field centers and widths without propagating the output error back through the network. The idea here is to populate dense regions of the input space with receptive fields. One method places the centers of the receptive fields according to some coarse lattice defined over the input space (Broomhead and Lowe, 1988). Assuming a uniform lattice with k divisions along each dimension of an n-dimensional input space, this lattice would require k^n basis functions to cover the input space. This exponential growth renders this approach impractical for a high dimensional space. An alternative approach is to center k receptive fields on a set of k randomly chosen training samples. Here, unless there is prior knowledge about the location of prototype input vectors and/or the regions of the input space containing meaningful data, a large number of receptive fields would be required to adequately represent the distribution of the input vectors in a high dimensional space.

Moody and Darken (1989a) employed unsupervised learning of the receptive field centers μ_j in which a relatively small number of RBFs are used; the adaptive centers learn to represent only the parts of input space which are richly represented by clusters of data. The adaptive strategy also helps reduce sampling error because it allows the centers $\boldsymbol{\mu}$ to be determined by a large number of training samples. Here, the k-means clustering algorithm (MacQueen, 1967; Anderberg, 1973) is used to locate a set of k RBF centers that represents a local minimum of the SSE between the training set vectors $\mathbf{x}$ and the nearest of the k receptive field centers $\boldsymbol{\mu}_j$ [this SSE criterion function is given by Equation (4.6.4) with $\mathbf{w}$ replaced by $\boldsymbol{\mu}$]. In the basic k-means algorithm, the k RBFs are initially assigned centers $\boldsymbol{\mu}_j$, $j = 1, 2, \ldots, k$, which are set equal to k randomly selected training vectors. The remaining training vectors are assigned to class j of the closest center $\boldsymbol{\mu}_j$. Next, the centers are recomputed as the average of the training vectors in their class. This two-step process is invoked until all centers stop changing. An incremental version of this batch-mode process also may be used that requires no storage of past training vectors or cluster membership information. Here, at each time step, a random training vector $\mathbf{x}$ is selected and the center $\boldsymbol{\mu}_j$ of the nearest (in a Euclidean distance sense) receptive field is updated according to

$$\Delta\boldsymbol{\mu}_j = \rho(\mathbf{x} - \boldsymbol{\mu}_j) \tag{6.1.5}$$

where ρ is a small positive constant. Equation (6.1.5) is the simple competitive rule that was analyzed in Section 4.6.1. Similarly, learning vector quantization (LVQ) or one of its variants (see Section 3.4.2) may be used to effectively locate the k RBF centers (Vogt, 1993). Generally speaking, there is no formal method for specifying the required number k of hidden units in an RBF network. Cross-validation is normally used to decide on k.

Once the receptive field centers are found using one of the preceding methods, their widths can be determined by one of several heuristics in order to get smooth interpolation. Theoretically speaking, RBF networks with the same σ_j in each hidden kernel unit have the capability of universal approximation (Park and Sandberg, 1991, 1993). This suggests that one may simply use a single global fixed value σ for all σ_j values in the network. In order to preserve the local response characteristics of the hidden units, one should choose a relatively small (positive) value for this global width parameter. The actual value of σ for a particular training set may be found by cross-validation. Empirical results (Moody and Darken, 1989a) suggest that a "good" estimate for the global width parameter is the average width $\sigma = \langle \|\boldsymbol{\mu}_i - \boldsymbol{\mu}_j\| \rangle$, which represents a global average over all Euclidean distances between the center of each unit i and that of its nearest neighbor j. Other heuristics based on local computations may be used which yield individually tuned widths σ_j. For example, the width for unit j may be set to the distance $\alpha\|\boldsymbol{\mu}_i - \boldsymbol{\mu}_j\|$, where $\boldsymbol{\mu}_i$ is the center of the nearest neighbor to unit j (usually α is taken between 1.0 and 1.5). For classification tasks, one may make use of the category label of the nearest training vector. If that category label is different from that represented by the current RBF unit, it would be advisable to use a smaller width, which narrows the bell-shaped receptive field of the current unit. This leads to a sharpening of the class domains and allows for better approximation.

It has already been noted that the output layer weights w_{lj} can be adaptively computed using the delta rule

$$\Delta w_{lj} = \rho(d_l - y_l)f'(net_l)z_j \qquad l = 1, 2, \ldots, L; \quad j = 1, 2, \ldots, J \qquad (6.1.6)$$

once the hidden-layer parameters are obtained. Here, the term $f'(net_l)$ can be dropped for the case of linear units. Equation (6.1.6) drives the output layer weights to minimize the SSE criterion function [recall Equation (5.1.13)] for sufficiently small ρ. Alternatively, for the case of linear output units, one may formulate the problem of computing the weights as a set of simultaneous linear equations and employ the generalized-inverse method [recall Equation (3.1.42)] to obtain the minimum SSE solution. Without loss of generality, consider a single-output RBF net, and denote by $\mathbf{w} = [w_1 \quad w_2 \quad \cdots \quad w_J]^T$ the weight vector of the output unit. Now, recalling Equations (3.1.39) through (3.1.42), the minimum SSE solution for the system of equations $\mathbf{Z}^T\mathbf{w} = \mathbf{d}$ is given by (assuming an overdetermined system, i.e., $m \geq J$)

$$\mathbf{w}^* = \mathbf{Z}^\dagger\mathbf{d} = (\mathbf{Z}\mathbf{Z}^T)^{-1}\mathbf{Z}\mathbf{d} \qquad (6.1.7)$$

where $\mathbf{Z} = [\mathbf{z}^1 \quad \mathbf{z}^2 \quad \cdots \quad \mathbf{z}^m]$ is a $J \times m$ matrix, and $\mathbf{d} = [d^1 \quad d^2 \quad \cdots \quad d^m]^T$. Here, $\mathbf{z}^i$ is the output of the hidden layer for input $\mathbf{x}^i$. Therefore, the jith element of matrix $\mathbf{Z}$ may be expressed explicitly as

$$\mathbf{Z}_{ji} = K\left(\frac{\|\mathbf{x}^i - \boldsymbol{\mu}_j\|}{\sigma_j^2}\right) \qquad i = 1, 2, \ldots, m; \quad j = 1, 2, \ldots, J \qquad (6.1.8)$$

with the parameters $\boldsymbol{\mu}_j$ and σ_j^2 assumed to have been computed using the earlier described methods.

For "strict" interpolation problems, it is desired that an interpolation function be found that is constrained to "exactly" map the sample points $\mathbf{x}^i$ into their associated targets d^i, for $i = 1, 2, \ldots, m$. It is well known that a polynomial with finite order $r = m - 1$ is capable of performing strict interpolation on m samples $\{\mathbf{x}^i, d^i\}$, assuming distinct vectors $\mathbf{x}^i$ in R^n (see Problem 1.3.4). A similar result is available for RBF nets. This result states that there is a class of radial basis functions that guarantee that an RBF net with m such functions is capable of strict interpolation of m sample points in R^n (Micchelli, 1986; Light, 1992b); the Gaussian function in Equation (6.1.3) is one example. Furthermore, there is no need to search for the centers $\boldsymbol{\mu}_j$; one can just set $\boldsymbol{\mu}_j = \mathbf{x}^j$ for $j = 1, 2, \ldots, m$. Thus, for strict interpolation, the $\mathbf{Z}$ matrix in Equation (6.1.8) becomes the $m \times m$ matrix

$$\mathbf{Z}_{ji} = K\left(\frac{\|\mathbf{x}^i - \mathbf{x}^j\|}{\sigma_j^2}\right) \qquad i = 1, 2, \ldots, m; \quad j = 1, 2, \ldots, m \qquad (6.1.9)$$

which we refer to as the *interpolation matrix*. Note that the appropriate width parameters σ_j still need to be found; the choice of these parameters affects the interpolation quality of the RBF net.[2]

According to the preceding discussion, an exact solution $\mathbf{w}^*$ is ensured. This requires $\mathbf{Z}$ to be nonsingular. Hence $\mathbf{w}^*$ can be computed as

$$\mathbf{w}^* = (\mathbf{Z}^{\mathrm{T}})^{-1}\mathbf{d} \qquad (6.1.10)$$

Although, in theory, Equation (6.1.10) always ensures a solution to the strict interpolation problem, in practice, the direct computation of $(\mathbf{Z}^{\mathrm{T}})^{-1}$ can become ill-conditioned when $\mathbf{Z}^{\mathrm{T}}$ is nearly singular. Alternatively, one may resort to Equation (6.1.6) for an adaptive computation of $\mathbf{w}^*$.

Receptive field properties play an important role in the quality of an RBF network's approximation capability. To see this, consider a single-input/single-output RBF network for approximating a continuous function $f: R \to R$. Approximation error, due to error in the "fit" of the RBF network to that of the target function f, occurs when the receptive fields (e.g., Gaussians) are either too broad and/or too widely spaced relative to the fine spatial structure of f. In other words, these factors act to locally limit the high-frequency content of the approximating network. According to Nyquist's sampling criterion, the highest frequency that may be recovered from a sampled signal is one-half the sampling frequency. Therefore, when the receptive field density is not high enough, the high-frequency fine structure in the function being approximated is lost. The high-frequency fine structure of f also can be "blurred" when the receptive fields are excessively wide. By employing the Taylor series expansion, it can be shown (Hoskins et al., 1993) that when the width parameter is large, the RBF net exhibits polynomial behavior with an order successively decreasing as the RBF widths increase. In other words, the net's output approaches that of a polynomial function whose order is decreasing in σ. Therefore, it is important that receptive

2. This can be demonstrated as follows: Assume that a smooth nonlinear function is to be approximated from a finite set of noiseless samples. Also, assume that K is Gaussian and that all σ_j values approach zero. This makes the matrix $\mathbf{Z}$ approach the identity matrix, which from Equation (6.1.10) gives the simple solution $\mathbf{w}^* = \mathbf{d}$. Therefore, the RBF net will output the correct value of the function being approximated if the input to the net is one of the training samples. On the other hand, the net will output a near-zero output for all points between the sample points. This is because the output of all hidden units is practically zero, due to the negligible size of their receptive fields. This analysis suggests that successful interpolation requires some degree of overlap between the receptive fields, which can be accomplished by properly setting the σ_j parameters.

field densities and widths be chosen to match the frequency-transfer characteristics imposed by the function f (Mel and Omohundro, 1991). These results also suggest that even for moderately high dimensional input spaces, a relatively large number of RBFs must be used if the training data represent high-frequency content mappings (functions) and if low approximation error is desired. These observations can be generalized to the case of RBF network approximation of multivariate functions.

Example 6.1.1 This example illustrates application of the RBF net for approximating the function $g(x) = [(x - 2)(2x + 1)]/(1 + x^2)$ (refer to the solid line plot in Figure 6.1.2) from the 15 noise-free samples $(x^j, g(x^j))$, $j = 1, 2, \ldots, 15$, in Figure 6.1.2. We will employ the method of strict interpolation for designing the RBF net. Hence 15 Gaussian hidden units are used (all having the same width parameter σ), with the jth Gaussian unit having its center μ^j equal to x^j. The design is completed by computing the weight vector $\mathbf{w}$ of the output linear unit using Equation (6.1.10). Three designs are generated which correspond to the values $\sigma = 0.5$, 1.0 and 1.5. These networks are then tested with 200 inputs, x, uniformly sampled in the interval $[-8, 12]$. The output

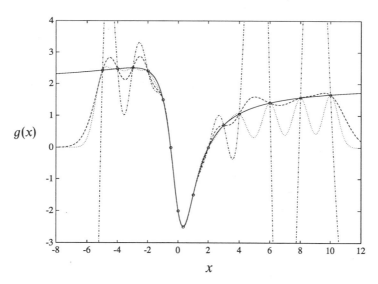

Figure 6.1.2
RBF net approximation of the function $g(x) = [(x - 2)(2x + 1)]/(1 + x^2)$ (*solid line*), based on strict interpolationusing the 15 samples shown (*small circles*). The RBF net employs 15 Gaussian hidden units, and its output is shown for three hidden unit widths: $\sigma = 0.5$ (*dotted line*), $\sigma = 1.0$ (*dashed line*), and $\sigma = 1.5$ (dotted-dashed line). (Compare these results with those in Figures 5.2.2 and 5.2.3.)

of the RBF net is shown in Figure 6.1.2 for $\sigma = 0.5$ (dotted line), $\sigma = 1.0$ (dashed line), and $\sigma = 1.5$ (dotted-dashed line). The value of $\sigma = 1.0$ is close to the average distance among all 15 sample points, and it resulted in better interpolation of $g(x)$ compared with $\sigma = 0.5$ and $\sigma = 1.5$. As expected, these results show poor extrapolation capabilities by the RBF net, regardless of the value of σ (check the net output in Figure 6.1.2 for $x > 10$ and $x < -5$). It is interesting to note the excessive overfit by the RBF net for relatively high σ (compare with the polynomial-based strict interpolation of the same data shown in Figure 5.2.2). Finally, by comparing these results with those in Figure 5.2.3, one can see that more accurate interpolation is possible with sigmoidal hidden-unit nets; this is attributed mainly to the ability of feedforward multilayer sigmoidal unit nets to approximate the first derivative of $g(x)$.

6.1.1 RBF Networks versus Backprop Networks

RBF networks have been applied with success to function approximation (Broomhead and Lowe, 1988; Lee and Kil, 1988; Casdagli, 1989; Moody and Darken, 1989a, 1989b) and classification (Niranjan and Fallside, 1988; Nowlan, 1990; Lee, 1991; Wettschereck and Dietterich, 1992; Vogt, 1993). On difficult approximation/prediction tasks [e.g., predicting the Mackey-Glass chaotic series of Problem 5.4.1 T time steps ($T > 50$) in the future], RBF networks that employ clustering for locating hidden-unit receptive field centers can achieve a performance comparable with backprop networks (backprop-trained feedforward networks with sigmoidal hidden units) while requiring orders of magnitude less training time than backprop. However, the RBF network typically requires 10 times or more data to achieve the same accuracy as a backprop network. The accuracy of RBF networks may be further improved if supervised learning of receptive field centers is used (Wettschereck and Dietterich, 1992), but then the speed advantage over backprop networks is compromised. For difficult classification tasks, RBF networks or their modified versions (see Section 6.1.2) employing sufficient training data and hidden units can lead to better classification rates (Wettschereck and Dietterich, 1992) and smaller false-positive classification errors (Lee, 1991) compared with backprop networks. In the following, qualitative arguments are given for the preceding simulation-based observations on the performance of RBF and backprop networks.

Some of the reasons for the training speed advantage of RBF networks have been presented earlier in this section. Basically, since the receptive field representation is well localized, only a small fraction of the hidden units in an RBF network respond to any particular input vector. This allows the use of efficient self-organization (clustering) algorithms for adapting such units in a training mode that does not involve the network's output units. On the other hand, all units in a backprop network must be evaluated and their weights updated for every input vector. Another important reason for the faster training speed of RBF networks is the hybrid two-stage training scheme employed, which decouples the learning task for both hidden and output layers, thus eliminating the need for the slow back error propagation.

The RBF network with self-organized receptive fields needs more data and more hidden units to achieve similar precision to that of the backprop network. When used for function approximation, the backprop network performs global fit to the training data, whereas the RBF network performs local fit. This results in greater generalization by the backprop network from each training example. It also utilizes the network's free parameters more efficiently, which leads to a smaller number of hidden units. Furthermore, the backprop network is a better candidate net when extrapolation is desired. This is due primarily to the ability of feedforward nets with sigmoidal hidden units to approximate a function and its derivatives (see Section 5.2.5). On the other hand, the local nature of the hidden-unit receptive fields in RBF nets prevents them from being able to "see" beyond the training data. This makes the RBF net a poor extrapolator.

When used as a classifier, the RBF net can lead to low false-positive classification rates. This property is due to the same reason that makes RBF nets poor extrapolators. Regions of the input space which are far from training vectors are usually mapped to low values by the localized receptive fields of the hidden units. By contrast, the sigmoidal hidden units in the backprop network can have high output even in regions far away from those populated by training data. This causes the backprop network/classifier to indicate high-confidence classifications to meaningless inputs. False-positive classification may be reduced in backprop networks by employing the "training with rubbish" strategy discussed at the end of Section 5.3.3. However, when dealing with high dimensional input spaces, this strategy generally requires an excessively large training set due to the large number of possible rubbish pattern combinations.

Which network is better to use for which tasks? The backprop network is better to use when training data are expensive (or hard to generate) and/or retrieval speed, assuming a serial machine implementation, is critical (the smaller backprop network size requires less storage and leads to faster retrievals compared with RBF networks). However, if the data are cheap and plentiful, and if on-line training is required (e.g., the case of adaptive signal processing or adaptive control where data are acquired at a high rate and cannot be saved), then the RBF network is superior.

6.1.2   RBF Network Variations

In their work on RBF networks, Moody and Darken (1989a) suggested the use of normalized hidden-unit activities according to

$$z_j(\mathbf{x}) = \frac{K\left(\dfrac{\|\mathbf{x} - \boldsymbol{\mu}_j\|}{\sigma_j^2}\right)}{\displaystyle\sum_{i=1}^{J} K\left(\dfrac{\|\mathbf{x} - \boldsymbol{\mu}_j\|}{\sigma_i^2}\right)} \tag{6.1.11}$$

based on empirical evidence of improved approximation properties. The use of Equation (6.1.11) implies that $\displaystyle\sum_{j=1}^{J} z_j = 1$ for all inputs $\mathbf{x}$; i.e., the unweighted sum of all hidden-unit activities in an RBF network results in the unity function. Here, the RBF network realizes a "partition of unity," which is a desired mathematical property in function decomposition/approximation (Werntges, 1993), the motivation being that a superposition of basis functions that can represent the unity function $[f(\mathbf{x}) = 1]$ "exactly" would also suppress spurious structures when fitting a nontrivial function. In other words, the normalization in Equation (6.1.11) leads to a form of "smoothness" regularization.

Another justification for the normalization of hidden-unit outputs may be given based on statistical arguments. If one interprets z_j in Equation (6.1.1) as the probability $P_j(\mathbf{x}^k)$ of observing $\mathbf{x}^k$ under Gaussian distribution j:

$$P_j(\mathbf{x}^k) = \frac{1}{a\sigma_j} e^{-\|\mathbf{x}^k - \boldsymbol{\mu}_j\|^2/2\sigma_j^2} \tag{6.1.12}$$

(where a is a normalization constant and $\sigma_j = \sigma$ for all j) and also assumes that all Gaussians are selected with equal probability, then the probability of Gaussian j having generated $\mathbf{x}^k$, given that we have observed $\mathbf{x}^k$, is

$$P(j|\mathbf{x}^k) = \frac{P_j(\mathbf{x}^k)}{\displaystyle\sum_{i=1}^{J} P_i(\mathbf{x}^k)} = \frac{z_j(\mathbf{x}^k)}{\displaystyle\sum_{i=1}^{J} z_i(\mathbf{x}^k)} \tag{6.1.13}$$

Therefore, the normalization in Equation (6.1.11) now has a statistical significance: It represents the conditional probability of unit j generating $\mathbf{x}^k$.

Another variation of RBF networks involves the so-called *soft competition* among Gaussian units for locating the centers $\boldsymbol{\mu}_j$ (Nowlan, 1990). The clustering of the vectors $\boldsymbol{\mu}_j$ according to the incremental k-means algorithm is equivalent to a "hard" competition winner-take-all operation where, upon the presentation of input $\mathbf{x}^k$, the RBF unit with the highest output z_j updates its mean $\boldsymbol{\mu}_j$ according to Equation (6.1.5). This in effect realizes an iterative version of the "approximate" maximum likelihood estimate (Nowlan, 1990):

$$\boldsymbol{\mu}_j = \frac{\sum\limits_{k \in S_j} \mathbf{x}^k}{N_j} \tag{6.1.14}$$

where S_j is the set of exemplars closest to Gaussian j, and N_j is the number of vectors contained in this set. Rather than using the approximation in Equation (6.1.14), the "exact" maximum likelihood estimate for $\boldsymbol{\mu}_j$ is given by (Nowlan, 1990)

$$\boldsymbol{\mu}_j = \frac{\sum\limits_{k} P(j|\mathbf{x}^k)\mathbf{x}^k}{\sum\limits_{k} P(j|\mathbf{x}^k)} \tag{6.1.15}$$

where $P(j|\mathbf{x}^k)$ is given by Equation (6.1.13). In this "soft" competitive model, all hidden-unit centers are updated according to an iterative version of Equation (6.1.15).[3] One drawback of this soft clustering method is the computational requirements, in that all centers $\boldsymbol{\mu}_j$ rather than the mean of the winner, are updated for each input. However, the high performance of RBF networks employing soft competition

---

3. An "on-line" (incremental) implementation of this learning rule has been proposed by Benaim and Tomasini (1992). Here, at each time step, a training exemplar $\{\mathbf{x}^k, \mathbf{d}^k\}$ is randomly chosen from the training set and the centers of the hidden units (radial basis functions) are updated according to the recursion

$$\Delta\boldsymbol{\mu}_j = \rho_h(\mathbf{x}^k - \boldsymbol{\mu}_j)z_j(\mathbf{x}^k)$$

where $0 < \rho_h \ll 1$. The term $z_j(\mathbf{x}^k)$ in this equation represents the output of the jth hidden unit and is given by the normalized function in Equation (6.1.11). Here, the kernels K are selected as Gaussians with identical width σ.

Note that when the width parameter σ tends to zero, $z_j(\mathbf{x}^k)$ performs a winner-take-all function: The only unit that becomes active is the one whose center $\boldsymbol{\mu}$ best matches the input vector $\mathbf{x}^k$. In this case, the incremental learning rule approximates the simple competitive learning rule given in Equation (6.1.5), where only the "winner" unit is updated. For a nonzero σ, the competition can be referred to as "soft" competition where multiple units are updated in response to a new input $\mathbf{x}^k$. This learning rule for updating $\boldsymbol{\mu}_j$ may now be combined with the LMS rule (assuming linear output units)

$$\Delta w_{lj} = \rho_o(d_l^k - y_l^k)z_j(\mathbf{x}^k)$$

to form a complete on-line learning algorithm for the RBF net. This algorithm takes the form of a "cascade" of two dynamical systems. Benaim (1994) proved the asymptotic convergence of this (stochastic) learning algorithm by employing statistical averaging techniques and using a theorem due to Hirsch (1989) on the convergence of cascade dynamical systems.

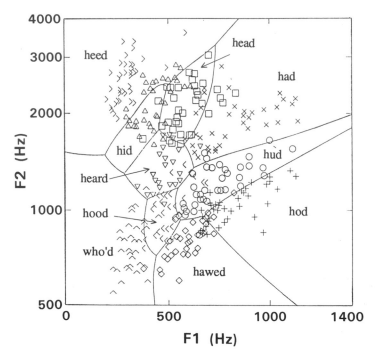

Figure 6.1.3
A plot of the test samples for the 10-vowel problem of Peterson and Barney
(1952). The lines are class boundaries generated by a two-layer feedforward
net trained with backprop on training samples. (Adapted from Huang and
Lippmann, 1988, with permission of the American Institute of Physics.)

may justify this added training computational cost. For example, consider the classic
vowel recognition task of Peterson and Barney (1952). Here, the data are obtained by
spectrographic analysis and consist of the first and second formant frequencies of 10
vowels contained in words spoken by a total of 67 men, women, and children. The
spoken words consisted of 10 monosyllabic words each beginning with the letter *h*
and ending with *d* and differing only in the vowel. The words used to obtain the data
were *heed, hid, head, had, hud, hod, heard, hood, who'd,* and *hawed.* These vowel data
are randomly split into two sets, resulting in 338 training examples and 333 test
examples. A plot of the test examples is shown in Figure 6.1.3. An RBF network
employing 100 Gaussian hidden units and soft competition for locating the Gaussian
means is capable of 87.1 percent correct classification on the 333-example test set of
the vowel data after being trained with the 338 training examples (Nowlan, 1990).

This performance exceeds the 82.0, 82.0, and 80.2 percent recognition rates reported for a 100-unit k-means-trained RBF network (Moody and Darken, 1989b), k-nearest-neighbor network (Huang and Lippmann, 1988), and backprop network (Huang and Lippmann, 1988), respectively (the decision boundaries shown in Figure 6.1.3 are those generated by the backprop network). A related general framework for designing optimal RBF classifiers can be found in Fakhr (1993).

This section concludes with consideration of a network of "semilocal activation" hidden units (Hartman and Keeler, 1991a). This network has been found to retain comparable training speeds to RBF networks, with the advantages of requiring a smaller number of units to cover high-dimensional input spaces and producing high approximation accuracy. Semilocal activation networks are particularly advantageous when the training set has irrelevant input exemplars.

An RBF unit responds to a localized region of the input space. Figure 6.1.4a shows the response of a two-input Gaussian RBF. On the other hand, a sigmoid unit responds to a semi-infinite region by partitioning the input space with a "sigmoidal" hypersurface, as shown in Figure 6.1.4b. RBFs have greater flexibility in discriminating finite regions of the input space, but this comes at the expense of a great increase in the number of required units. To overcome this tradeoff, "Gaussian-bar" units with the response depicted in Figure 6.1.4c may be used to replace the RBFs. Analytically, the output of the jth Gaussian-bar unit is given by

$$z_j(\mathbf{x}) = \sum_i w_{ji} \exp\left[-\frac{(x_i - \mu_{ji})^2}{2\sigma_{ji}^2} \right] \qquad (6.1.16)$$

where i indexes the input dimension and w_{ji} is a positive parameter signifying the ith weight of the jth hidden unit. For comparison purposes, we write the Gaussian RBF as a product

$$z_j(\mathbf{x}) = \exp\left[-\frac{\|\mathbf{x} - \boldsymbol{\mu}_j\|^2}{2\sigma_j^2} \right] = \prod_i \exp\left[-\frac{(x_i - \mu_{ji})^2}{2\sigma_j^2} \right] \qquad (6.1.17)$$

According to Equation (6.1.16), the Gaussian-bar unit responds if any of the i Gaussians is activated (assuming the scaling factors w_{ji} are nonzero), while a Gaussian RBF requires all component Gaussians to be activated. Thus a Gaussian-bar unit is more like an "ORing" device, and a pure Gaussian is more like an "ANDing" device. Note that a Gaussian-bar network has significantly more free parameters to adjust compared with a Gaussian RBF network of the same size (number of units). The output units in a Gaussian-bar network can be linear or Gaussian-bar.

Because of their semilocal receptive fields, the centers $\boldsymbol{\mu}_j$ of the hidden units cannot be determined effectively using competitive learning as in RBF networks. Therefore,

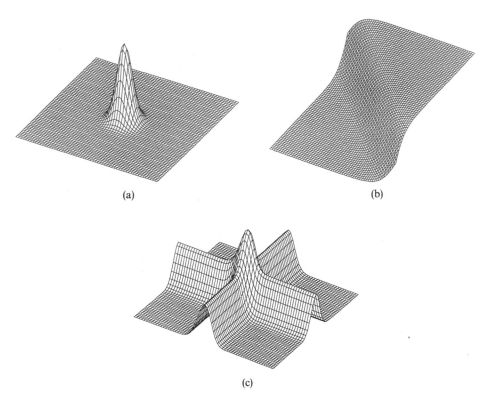

(a)   (b)

(c)

Figure 6.1.4
Response characteristics for two-input (*a*) Gaussian, (*b*) sigmoidal, and (*c*) Gaussian-bar units.

supervised gradient-descent-based learning is normally used to update all network parameters.

Since the preceding Gaussian-bar network employs parameter-update equations that are nonlinear in their parameters, one might suspect that the training speed of such a network is compromised. However, on the contrary, simulations involving difficult function prediction tasks have shown that training Gaussian-bar networks is significantly faster than training sigmoidal networks and slower but of the same order as training RBF networks. One possible explanation for the training speed of Gaussian-bar networks could be their built-in automatic dynamic reduction of the network architecture (Hartman and Keeler, 1991b), as explained next.

A Gaussian-bar unit can effectively "prune" input dimension i by one of the following mechanisms: w_{ji} becoming zero, μ_{ji} moving away from the data, and/or σ_{ji} shrinking to a very small value. These mechanisms can occur completely independently for each input dimension. On the other hand, moving any one of the μ_{ji} values away from the data or shrinking σ_{ji} to zero deactivates a Gaussian unit completely. Sigmoidal units also may be pruned (according to the techniques of Section 5.2.5), but such pruning is limited to synaptic weights. Therefore, Gaussian-bar networks have greater pruning flexibility than sigmoidal or Gaussian RBF networks. Training time also can be reduced by monitoring pruned units and excluding them from the calculations. Since pruning may lead to very small σ_{ji} values, which, in turn, create a spike response at μ_{ji}, it is desirable to move such μ_{ji} to a location far away from the data in order to eliminate the danger of these spikes on generalization. Here, one may avoid this danger, reduce storage requirements, and increase retrieval speed by postprocessing trained networks to remove the pruned units of the network.

Many other versions of RBF networks can be found in the literature (Moody, 1989; Jones et al., 1990; Saha and Keeler, 1990; Bishop, 1991; Kadirkamanathan et al., 1991; Mel and Omohundro, 1991; Platt, 1991; Musavi et al., 1992; Wettschereck and Dietterich, 1992; Lay and Hwang, 1993). Roy and Govil (1993) presented a method based on linear programming models that simultaneously adds RBF units and trains the RBF network in polynomial time for classification tasks. This training method is described in detail in Section 6.3.1 in connection with a hyperspherical classifier net similar to the RBF network.

6.2   Cerebellar Model Articulation Controller (CMAC)

Another neural network model that uses hidden units with localized receptive fields and which allows for efficient supervised training is the cerebellar model articulation controller (CMAC). This network was developed by Albus (1971) as a model of the cerebellum and was later applied to the control of robot manipulators (Albus, 1975, 1979, 1981). A similar model for the cerebellum also was developed independently by Marr (1969).

There exist many variants of and extensions to Albus's CMAC. This section describes the CMAC version reported by Miller et al. (1990c). The CMAC consists of two mappings (processing stages). The first is a nonlinear transformation that maps the network input $\mathbf{x} \in R^n$ into a higher-dimensional vector $\mathbf{z} \in \{0, 1\}^J$. The vector $\mathbf{z}$ is a sparse vector in which at most c of its components are nonzero (c is called a *generalization parameter* and is user-specified). The second mapping generates the CMAC output $\mathbf{y} \in R^L$ through a linear matrix-vector product $\mathbf{Wz}$, where $\mathbf{W}$ is an $L \times J$ matrix of modifiable real-valued weights.

The CMAC has a built-in capability of local generalization: Two similar (in terms of Euclidean distance) inputs $\mathbf{x}$ and $\hat{\mathbf{x}}$ are mapped by the first mapping stage to similar binary vectors $\mathbf{z}$ and $\hat{\mathbf{z}}$, respectively, while dissimilar inputs map into dissimilar vectors. In addition to this local generalization feature, the first mapping transforms the n-dimensional input vector $\mathbf{x}$ into a J-dimensional binary vector $\mathbf{z}$, with $J \gg n$.

This mapping is realized as a cascade of three layers: a layer of input sensor units that feeds its binary outputs to a layer of logical AND units which, in turn, is sparsely interconnected to a layer of logical OR units. The output of the OR layer is the vector $\mathbf{z}$. Figure 6.2.1 shows a schematic diagram of the CMAC with the first processing stage (mapping) shown inside the dashed rectangle. The specific interconnection patterns between adjacent layers of the CMAC are considered next.

In addition to supplying the generalization parameter c, the user also must specify a discretization of the input space. Each component of the input vector $\mathbf{x}$ is fed to a series of sensor units with overlapping receptive fields. Each sensor unit produces a 1 if the input falls within its receptive field and a 0 otherwise. The width of the receptive field of each sensor controls input generalization, while the offset of the adjacent fields controls input quantization. The ratio of receptive field width to receptive field offset defines the generalization parameter c.

The binary outputs of the sensor units are fed into the layer of logical AND units. Each AND unit receives an input from a group of n sensors, each sensor corresponds to one distinct input variable, and thus the unit's input receptive field is the interior of a hypercube in the input space (the interior of a square in the two-dimensional input space of Figure 6.2.1). The AND units are divided into c subsets. The receptive fields of the sensor units connected to each of the subsets are organized so as to span the input space without overlap. Each input vector excites one AND unit from each subset, for a total of c excited units for any input. There exist many ways of organizing the receptive fields of the individual subsets which produce the preceding excitation pattern [e.g., see Miller et al. (1990c), Parks and Militzer (1991), Lane et al. (1992)]. Miller et al. employ an organization scheme similar to Albus's original scheme, where each of the subsets of AND units is identical in its receptive field organization, but each subset is offset relative to the others along hyperdiagonals in the input space. Here, adjacent subsets are offset by the quantization level of each input.

The resulting number of AND units (also called *state space detectors*) resulting from the preceding organization can be very large for many practical problems. For example, a system with 10 inputs, each quantized into 100 different levels, would have $100^{10} = 10^{20}$ vectors (points) in its input space and would require a correspondingly

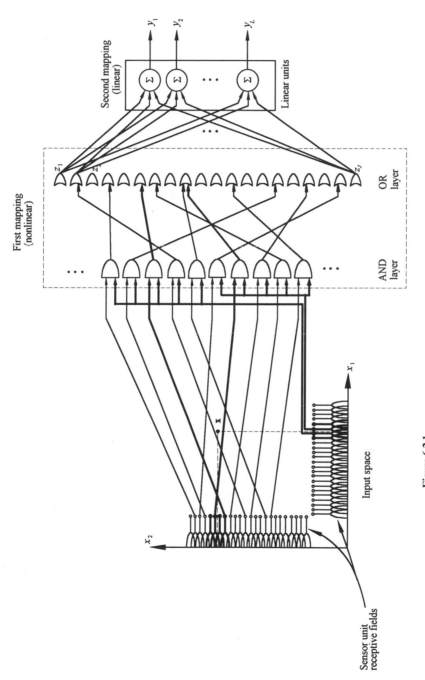

Figure 6.2.1
Schematic illustration of a CMAC for a two-dimensional input.

large number of AND units. However, most practical problems do not involve the whole input space; most of the possible input vectors would never be encountered. Therefore, one can significantly reduce the size of the adaptive output layer and hence reduce storage requirements and training time by transforming the binary output vector generated by the AND layer into a lower-dimensional vector $\mathbf{z}$ (however, the dimension of $\mathbf{z}$ is still much larger than n). This is accomplished in the CMAC by randomly connecting the AND unit outputs to a smaller set of OR units, as shown in Figure 6.2.1. Since exactly c AND units are excited by any input, at most c OR units will be excited by any input. This leads to a highly sparse vector $\mathbf{z}$.

The final output of the CMAC is generated by multiplying the vector $\mathbf{z}$ by the weight matrix of the output layer. The lth row of this weight matrix (corresponding to the lth output unit) is adaptively and independently adjusted (e.g., using LMS learning rule) in order to approximate a given function $f_l(\mathbf{x})$ implemented by the lth output unit. We also may use the CMAC as a classifier by adding nonlinear activations such as sigmoids or threshold activation functions to the output units and employing the delta rule or the perceptron rule (or adaptive Ho-Kashyap rule), respectively. The high degree of sparsity of the vector $\mathbf{z}$ typically leads to fast learning. Additional details on the learning behavior of the CMAC can be found in Wong and Sideris (1992).

Because of its intrinsic local generalization property, the CMAC can most successfully approximate functions that are slowly varying. The CMAC will fail to approximate functions that oscillate rapidly or which are highly nonlinear (Cotter and Guillerm, 1992; Brown et al., 1993). Thus the CMAC does not have universal approximation capabilities like those of multilayer feedforward nets of sigmoidal units or RBF nets.

One appealing feature of the CMAC is its efficient realization in software in terms of training time and real-time operation. The CMAC also has practical hardware realizations using logic cell arrays in VLSI technology (Miller et al., 1990b). Examples of applications of CMAC include real-time robotics (Miller et al., 1990d), pattern recognition (Glanz and Miller, 1987), and signal processing (Glanz and Miller, 1989).

6.2.1   CMAC Relation to Rosenblatt's Perceptron and Other Models

One of the earliest adaptive artificial neural network models is Rosenblatt's perceptron (Rosenblatt, 1961). In its most basic form, this model consists of a hidden layer of a large number of units which computes random Boolean functions connected to an output layer of one or more LTGs, as illustrated in Figure 6.2.2. (Historically speaking, the term *perceptron* was originally coined for the architecture of Figure 6.2.2 or its variants. However, in the current literature, the term *perceptron* is usually used to refer to the unit in Figure 3.1.1 or 3.1.7).

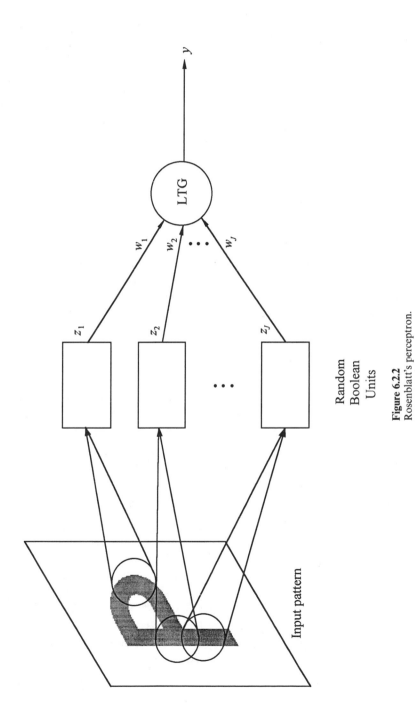

Figure 6.2.2
Rosenblatt's perceptron.

In Rosenblatt's perceptron, each hidden unit is restricted to receive a small number of inputs relative to the total number of inputs in a given input pattern. Here, the input pattern is typically assumed to be a two-dimensional binary image formed on a "retina." As shown in Figure 6.2.2, each hidden unit "sees" only a small piece of the binary input image. The idea here is that some of the many random hidden units might get "lucky" and detect "critical features" of the input image, thus allowing the output LTG(s) to perfectly classify the input image, after being trained with the perceptron rule. Ultimately, the hidden random Boolean units are intended to map a given nonlinearly separable training set of patterns onto vectors $\mathbf{z} \in \{0, 1\}^J$ of a high-dimensional feature space such that the training set becomes linearly separable. Note that these ideas are similar to those discussed in relation to polynomial threshold gates (PTGs) in Chapter 1 (refer to Figure 1.3.4). The basic difference here is that a binary-input PTG employs AND gates as its hidden units, as opposed to the potentially more powerful Boolean units employed in Rosenblatt's perceptron. Another important difference is that a PTG allows one of the hidden AND units to "see" (cover) the whole input pattern, with the other AND units covering substantial portions of the input.

Rosenblatt's perceptron also has common features with the CMAC model discussed earlier. Both models restrict the amount of input information seen by each hidden unit, employ a nonlinear Boolean transformation via the hidden units, and allow for adaptive computation of the output-layer weights. Taking a second look at the CMAC architecture in Figure 6.2.1 reveals that the first mapping (represented by the circuitry inside the dashed rectangle) is realized by a Boolean AND-OR network. Here, the jth OR unit and the set of AND units feeding into it can be thought of as generating a random Boolean function and may be compared with a random Boolean unit in Figure 6.2.2. The Boolean functions z_j in the CMAC acquire their random nature from the random interconnectivity pattern assumed between the two layers of AND and OR units. However, because of the sparsity of connections between these two layers, the class of Boolean functions realized by the CMAC hidden outputs z_j does not have the richness nor diversity of the uniformly random Boolean function z_j in Rosenblatt's perceptron. These two models also have a minor difference in that the CMAC normally uses linear output units with LMS training, while the perceptron uses LTGs trained with the perceptron rule. This difference is due to the different nature of intended applications for each model: The CMAC is used primarily as a continuous, smooth function approximator, whereas Rosenblatt's perceptron was intended originally as a pattern classifier. One also may note the more structured receptive field organization in the CMAC compared with the perceptron. Later in this section it will be seen that Rosenblatt's perceptron does not have the intrinsic local generalization feature of the CMAC.

The nonuniversality of the CMAC is also shared by Rosenblatt's perceptron. This limitation is due to the localized nature of the hidden-unit receptive fields defined on the input image. For example, it has been shown (Minsky and Papert, 1969) that this particular perceptron model cannot determine whether or not all the parts of its input image (geometric figure) are connected to one another, nor can it determine whether or not the number of "on" pixels in a finite input image is odd. The later task is equivalent to the parity problem and can only be solved by Rosenblatt's perceptron if at least one hidden unit is allowed to have its receptive field span the entire input image.

The limitations of Rosenblatt's model can be relaxed by allowing every hidden unit to see all inputs. However, this becomes impractical when the dimension n of the input is large, since there would be 2^{2^n} possible Boolean functions for each hidden random Boolean unit to choose from. Therefore, there is very little chance for the hidden units to randomly become a detector of "critical features" unless one starts with an exponentially large number of hidden units. This requirement, however, renders the model impractical.

Yet another weakness of Rosenblatt's perceptron is that it is not "robustness preserving." In other words, it does not allow for good local generalization. To see this, consider two similar unipolar binary input patterns (vectors) $\mathbf{x}'$ and $\mathbf{x}''$. Here we use the similarity measure of the normalized Hamming distance $D_\mathbf{x}$ between the two input patterns:

$$D_\mathbf{x} = D(\mathbf{x}', \mathbf{x}'') = \frac{1}{n} \sum_{i=1}^{n} |x_i' - x_i''| \qquad (6.2.1)$$

If $\mathbf{x}'$ is similar to $\mathbf{x}''$, then $D(\mathbf{x}', \mathbf{x}'')$ is much smaller than 1. Now, because of the uniform random nature of the hidden Boolean units, the output of any hidden unit z_j is one (or zero) with a probability of 0.5 regardless of the input. Thus the activation patterns $\mathbf{z}$ at the output of the hidden layer are completely uncorrelated. In particular, the normalized Hamming distance $D_\mathbf{z}$ between the two $\mathbf{z}$ vectors corresponding to any two input vectors is approximately equal to $\frac{1}{2}$. Therefore, this model is not "robustness preserving."

Gallant and Smith (1987) and, independently, Hassoun (1988) have proposed a practical classifier model inspired by Rosenblatt's perceptron that solves some of the problems associated with Rosenblatt's model. This model, the *Gallant-Smith-Hassoun (GSH) model*, is also similar to a version of an early model studied by Gamba (1961) and referred to as the *Gamba perceptron* (Minsky and Papert, 1969). The main distinguishing features of the GSH model are that every hidden unit sees the whole input pattern **x** and that the hidden units are random LTGs. For the trainable output units, the GSH model uses Ho-Kashyap learning in Hassoun's version and the pocket algorithm [a modified version of the perceptron learning rule that converges for nonlinearly separable problems; for details, see Gallant (1993)] in the Gallant and Smith version. The hidden LTGs assume fixed integer weights and bias (threshold) generated randomly in some range $[-a, +a]$.

The use of random LTGs as opposed to random Boolean units as hidden units has the advantage of a "rich" distributed representation of the critical features in the hidden activation vector **z**. This distributed representation coupled with the ability of hidden LTGs to see the full input pattern makes the GSH model a universal approximator of binary mappings. However, an important question here is how many hidden random LTGs are required to realize any arbitrary n-input binary mapping of m points/vectors? This question can be answered easily for the case where the hidden LTGs are allowed to have arbitrary (not random) parameters (weights and thresholds). In this case, and recalling Problem 2.1.3 and Theorem 1.4.1, we find that m hidden LTGs are sufficient to realize any binary function of m points in $\{0, 1\}^n$. Now, if we assume hidden LTGs with random parameters, we might intuitively expect that the required number of hidden units in the GSH model for approximating any binary function of m points will be much greater than m. Empirical results show that this intuitive answer is not correct! Simulations with the 7-bit parity function, random functions, and other completely as well as partially specified Boolean functions reveal that the required number of random LTGs is between $\frac{2}{3}m$ and m (Gallant and Smith, 1987). Note that for the worst case scenario of a complex, completely specified n-input Boolean function where $m = 2^n$, the number of hidden LTGs in the GSH model still scales exponentially in n.

The preceding result on the size of the hidden layer in the GSH model may be explained in part in terms of the mapping properties of the random LTG layer. Consider two n-dimensional binary input vectors **x**′ and **x**″ that are mapped by the random LTG layer of the GSH model into the J-dimensional binary vectors **z**′ and **z**″, respectively. It is assumed that n is large. Also assume that the weights and thresholds of the LTGs are generated according to the normal distributions $N(0, \sigma_w^2)$ and $N(0, \sigma_T^2)$, respectively. Using a result of Amari (1974, 1990), the normalized Hamming distances D_z and D_x may be related according to

$$D_z = \frac{2}{\pi} \sin^{-1}(\sqrt{AD_x}) \qquad (6.2.2)$$

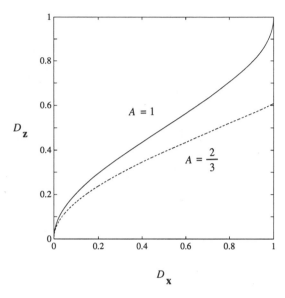

Figure 6.2.3
Normalized Hamming distance between two-hidden-layer
activation vectors versus the distance between the two
corresponding input vectors.

where

$$A = \frac{n\sigma_\mathbf{w}^2}{n\sigma_\mathbf{w}^2 + \sigma_T^2} \tag{6.2.3}$$

The parameter A is close to unity if the weights and thresholds are identically distributed or as long as $n\sigma_\mathbf{w}^2 \gg \sigma_T^2$. Figure 6.2.3 shows a plot of Equation (6.2.2) for $A = 1$
and $A = \frac{2}{3}$.

For small values of $D_\mathbf{x}$, $D_\mathbf{z}$ is small, so the output activity of the hidden layer is
similar for similar inputs. Therefore, the random LTG layer exhibits robustness-
preserving features. Also, since $\dfrac{dD_\mathbf{z}}{dD_\mathbf{x}} \approx \dfrac{1}{\pi\sqrt{AD_\mathbf{x}}}$ approaches infinity when $D_\mathbf{x}$ approaches zero, the differences among similar vectors in a small neighborhood of the
input space are amplified in the corresponding **z** vectors. Such a property is useful for
recognizing differences among very similar input vectors, as is often desired when
dealing with Boolean mappings (e.g., parity) or highly nonlinear functions. Equation
(6.2.2) also implies that very different inputs map into very different outputs when
$A \approx 1$. This richness of a distributed representation of input features at the hidden

layer's output helps increase the probability of the output unit(s) to find good approximations to arbitrary mappings. In addition to these desirable features, the GSH model is very appealing from a hardware realization point of view. Here, the restricted dynamic range integer parameters of the hidden LTGs allow for their simple realization in VLSI technology. Also note that the range $[-a, +a]$ of the hidden LTGs integer parameters can be made as small as $[-1, +1]$; however, this desirable reduced dynamic range is paid for by having to increase the number of hidden LTGs. This phenomenon is intuitively justifiable and has been verified empirically by Hassoun (1988).

6.3 Unit-Allocating Adaptive Networks

Chapter 4 (Section 4.9) indicated that training a multilayer feedforward neural network with fixed resources requires, in the worst case, exponential time. On the other hand, polynomial time training is possible, in the worst case, if one is willing to use unit-allocating nets that are capable of allocating new units, as needed, as more patterns are learned (Baum, 1989).

In the context of pattern classification, the classical k-nearest-neighbors classifier (Fix and Hodges, 1951; Duda and Hart, 1973) is an extreme example of a unit-allocating machine with $O(1)$ learning complexity. The k-nearest-neighbors classifier assigns to any new input the class most heavily represented among its k-nearest neighbors. This classifier represents an extreme unit-allocating machine because it allocates a new unit for every learned example in a training set. There are no computations involved in adjusting the "parameters" of allocated units: Each new allocated unit stores exactly the current example (vector) presented. In other words, no transformation or abstraction of the examples in the training set is required, and one can proceed immediately to use this machine for classification regardless of the size of the training set. Therefore, the training time of this classifier does not scale with the number of examples m, which means that the complexity is $O(1)$. Surprisingly, it has been shown (Cover and Hart, 1967) that in the limit of an infinite training set, this simple classifier has a probability of classification error less than twice the minimum achievable error probability of the optimal Bayes classifier[4] for any integer value of

---

4. The following theorem is due to Cover and Hart (1967): For multiclass decision problems in the infinite sample (training set) limit, the probability of error P_{NN} of a nearest-neighbor classifier satisfies

$$P_B \leq P_{NN} \leq 2P_B(1 - P_B)$$

where P_B is the probability of error of a Bayes classifier. The Bayes classifier is optimal in the sense that it minimizes the probability of classification error. For details, see Duda and Hart (1973). For asymptotic results on the behavior of P_{NN} for a sufficiently large but finite training set, the reader is referred to Cover (1968) and Snapp et al. (1991) for one- and n-dimensional data, respectively.

$k \geq 1$. Unfortunately, the performance of the nearest-neighbor classifier deteriorates for training sets of small size. Also, the convergence to the preceding asymptotic performance can be arbitrarily slow, and the classification error rate need not even decrease monotonically with m (Duda and Hart, 1973).

Even when utilizing a large training set, k-nearest-neighbors classifiers are impractical as on-line classifiers because of the large number of computations required in classifying a new input. Thus one is forced to use far fewer than one unit for every training sample; i.e., one must create and load an abstraction of the training data. This obviously leads to higher learning complexity than $O(1)$.

Practical trainable networks should have a number of desirable attributes. The most significant of these attributes are fast learning speed, accurate learning, and compact representation of training data. The reason for desiring the first two attributes is obvious. On the other hand, the formation of a compact representation is important for two reasons: good generalization (fewer free parameters leads to less overfitting) and feasibility of hardware (VLSI) realization, since silicon surface area is at a premium.

The following subsections consider three practical unit-allocating networks. These networks are capable of forming compact representations of data easily and rapidly. Two of the networks considered are classifier networks. The third network is capable of classification as well as approximation of continuous functions.

6.3.1   Hyperspherical Classifiers

Pattern classification in n-dimensional space consists of partitioning the space into category (class) regions with decision boundaries and assigning an unknown point in this space to the class in whose region it falls. The typical geometrical shapes of the decision boundaries for classical pattern classifiers are hyperplanes and hypersurfaces. This subsection discusses two unit-allocating adaptive networks/classifiers that employ hyperspherical boundary forms.

Hyperspherical classifiers were introduced by Cooper (1962, 1966), Batchelor and Wilkins (1968) and Batchelor (1969) [see Batchelor (1974) for a summary of early work]. Like the nearest-neighbor classifier, a hyperspherical classifier is based on the storage of examples represented as points in a metric space (e.g., Euclidean space). The metric defined on this space is a measure of the distance between an unknown input pattern and a known category. Each stored point has associated with it a finite "radius" that defines the point's region of influence. The interior of the resulting hypersphere represents the decision region associated with the center point's category. This region of influence makes a hyperspherical classifier typically more conservative in terms of storage than the nearest-neighbor classifier. Furthermore, the finite radii of the regions of influence can make a hyperspherical classifier abstain from classifying patterns from unknown categories (these patterns are typically represented as points in the input space that are far away from any underlying class regions). This later feature enhances the classifier's ability to reject "rubbish."

Restricted Coulomb Energy (RCE) Classifier   The following is a description of a specific network realization of a hyperspherical classifier proposed by Reilly et al. (1982) and Reilly and Cooper (1990). This model is named the *restricted Coulomb energy (RCE) network*. The name is derived from the form of the "potential function" governing the mapping characteristics, which has been interpreted (Scofield et al., 1988) as a restricted form of a "high-dimensional Coulomb potential" between a positive test charge and negative charges placed at various sites.

The architecture of the RCE network contains two layers: a hidden layer and an output layer. The hidden layer is fully interconnected to all components of an input pattern (vector) $\mathbf{x} \in R^n$. The output layer consists of L units. The output layer is sparsely connected to the hidden layer; each hidden unit projects its output to one and only one output unit. The architecture of the RCE net is shown in Figure 6.3.1.

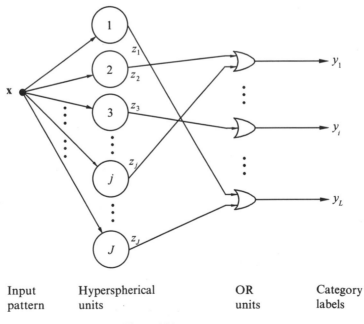

Figure 6.3.1
RCE network architecture.

Each unit in the output layer corresponds to a pattern category. The network assigns an input pattern to a category l if the output cell y_l is activated in response to the input. The decision of the network is *unambiguous* if one and only one output unit is active upon the presentation of an input; otherwise, the decision is said to be *ambiguous*.

The transfer characteristics of the jth hidden unit are given by

$$z_j(\mathbf{x}) = f[r_j - D(\boldsymbol{\mu}_j, \mathbf{x})] \qquad (6.3.1)$$

where $\boldsymbol{\mu}_j \in R^n$ is a parameter vector called *center*, $r_j \in R$ is a threshold or "radius," and D is some predefined distance metric between vectors $\boldsymbol{\mu}_j$ and $\mathbf{x}$ (e.g., Euclidean distance between real-valued vectors or Hamming distance between binary-valued vectors). Here, f is the threshold activation function given by

$$f(\xi) = \begin{cases} 1 & \text{if } \xi \geq 0 \\ 0 & \text{otherwise} \end{cases} \qquad (6.3.2)$$

On the other hand, the transfer function of a unit in the output layer is the logical OR function. The jth hidden unit in the RCE net is associated with a hyperspherical region of the input space that defines the unit's region of influence. The location of this region is defined by the center $\boldsymbol{\mu}_j$, and its size is determined by the radius r_j. According to Equation (6.3.1), any input pattern falling within the influence region of a hidden unit will cause this unit to fire. Thus the hidden units define a collection of hyperspheres in the space of input patterns. Some of these hyperspheres may overlap. When a pattern falls within the regions of influence of several hidden units, they will all "fire" and switch on the output units they are connected to.

Training the RCE net involves two mechanisms: unit commitment and modification of hidden unit radii. Units may be committed to the hidden and output layers. When committed, units are interconnected so that they do not violate the RCE interconnectivity pattern described above.

Initially, the network starts with no units. An arbitrary sample pattern $\mathbf{x}^1$ is selected from the training set, and one hidden unit and one output unit are allocated. The allocated hidden-unit center $\boldsymbol{\mu}_1$ is set equal to $\mathbf{x}^1$, and its radius r_1 is set equal to a user-defined parameter r_{max} (r_{max} is the maximum size of the region of influence ever assigned to a hidden unit). This unit is made fully interconnected to the input pattern and projects its output z_1 to the allocated output unit (OR gate). This output unit represents the category of the input $\mathbf{x}^1$. Next, a second arbitrary example $\mathbf{x}^2$ is chosen and fed into the current network. Here, one of three scenarios emerges. First, if $\mathbf{x}^2$ causes the output unit to fire, and if $\mathbf{x}^2$ belongs to the category represented by this unit, then nothing is done, and training is continued with a new input. In general, this scenario might occur at a point during training where the network has multiple hidden and output units representing various categories. In this case, if the input pattern causes only the output unit representing the correct category to fire, then nothing is done, and the training session is continued with a new input. On the other hand, the correct output unit may fire along with one or more other output units. This indicates that the regions of influence of hidden units representing various categories overlap and that the present input pattern lies inside the overlap region. Here, one proceeds by reducing the threshold values (radii) of all active hidden units that are associated with categories other than the correct one until they become inactive.

The second scenario involves the case when the input x^2 happens to belong to the same category as x^1 but does not cause the output unit to fire. Here, a new hidden unit is allocated with center at $\mu_2 = x^2$ and radius r_{max}, and the output z_2 of this unit is connected to the output unit. The general version of this scenario occurs when the network has multiple output units. Now, if the input pattern causes no output units (including the one representing the category of the input) to fire, then a new hidden unit centered at the current input vector/pattern is allocated, and it is assigned a radius $r = \min(r_{max}, d_{min})$, where d_{min} is the distance from this new center to the nearest center of a hidden unit representing any category different from that of the current input pattern. The new allocated unit is connected to the output unit representing the category of the input pattern. Note that this setting of r may cause one or more output units representing the wrong category to fire. This should not be a problem, since the shrinking of the region of influence mechanism described under the first scenario will ultimately rectify the situation. If, under this scenario, some hidden units representing the wrong category fire, then the radii of such units are shrunk as described earlier under the first scenario.

Finally, the third scenario represents the case of an input with a new category that is not represented by the network. Here, as in the first step of the training procedure, a hidden unit centered at this input is allocated, and its radius is set as in the second scenario. Also, a new output unit representing the new category is added that receives an input from the newly allocated hidden unit. Again, if existing hidden units become active under this scenario, then their radii are shrunk until they become inactive. The training phase continues (by cycling through the training set or by updating in response to a stream of examples) until no new units are allocated and the size of the regions of influence of all hidden units converges.

The RCE net is capable of developing proper separating boundaries for nonlinearly separable problems. The reader is referred to Figure 6.3.2 for a schematic representation of separating boundaries realized by the regions of influence for a nonlinearly separable two-class problem in two-dimensional pattern space. The RCE net also can handle the case where a single category is contained in several disjoint regions. In

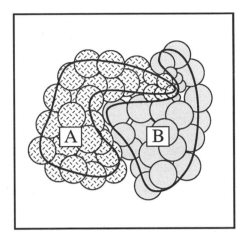

Figure 6.3.2
Schematic diagram for an RCE classifier in two-dimensional space solving a nonlinearly separable problem.

principle, an arbitrary degree of accuracy in the separating boundaries can be achieved if no restriction is placed on the size of the training set. Dynamic category learning is also possible with the RCE network. That is, new classes of patterns can be introduced at arbitrary points in training without always involving the need to retrain the network on all its previously trained data. Note that in its present form, the RCE network is not suitable for handling overlapping class regions. Here, the learning algorithm will tend to drive the radii of all hidden-unit regions of influence to zero. It also leads to allocating a large number of hidden units approximately equal to the number of training examples coming from the regions of overlap.

Several variations of the RCE network are possible. For example, one might employ mechanisms that allow the centers of the hyperspheres to drift to more optimal locations in the input space. A second variation would be to allow the hyperspheres to grow. These two mechanisms have been considered for more general hyperspherical classifiers than RCE classifiers (Batchelor, 1974). Modifications to the RCE network for handling overlapping class regions can be found in Reilly and Cooper (1990). Empirical examination of RCE classifiers appear in Lee and Lippmann (1990) and Hudak (1992).

Polynomial-Time-Trained Hyperspherical Classifier This subsection describes a classifier network with an architecture identical to the RCE network (see Figure 6.3.1) but which employs a training algorithm that is shown to construct and train the classifier network in polynomial time. This polynomial-time classifier (PTC) uses clustering and linear programming models to incrementally generate the hidden layer. Our description of the PTC net is based on the work of Roy and Mukhopadhyay (1991), Mukhopadhyay et al. (1993), and Roy et al. (1993).

As in the RCE net, the PTC net uses hidden units to cover class regions. However, the region of influence of each hidden unit need not be restricted to the hypersphere. A quadratic region of influence is assumed that defines the transfer characteristics of a hidden unit according to

$$z(\mathbf{x}) = f\left(w_0 + \sum_{i=1}^{n} w_i x_i + \sum_{i=1}^{n} \sum_{j=i}^{n} w_{ij} x_i x_j\right) \qquad (6.3.3)$$

where

$$f(\xi) = \begin{cases} 1 & \text{if } \xi \geq \varepsilon \\ 0 & \text{otherwise} \end{cases} \qquad (6.3.4)$$

and w_0, w_i, and w_{ij} are modifiable real-valued parameters to be learned. Here, ε is greater than or equal to a small positive constant (say 0.001), and its value is computed as part of the training procedure described below. With the transfer characteristics as in Equation (6.3.3), one may view each hidden unit as a quadratic threshold gate (QTG), as introduced in Chapter 1. A quadratic region of influence includes the hypersphere as a special case but allows for the realization of hyperellipsoids and hyperboloids. This enables the PTC to form more accurate boundary regions than the RCE classifier. Other regions of influence may be used in the PTC as long as they are represented by functions that are linear in the parameters to be learned: w_0, w_i, and w_{ij}. For example, $z(\mathbf{x}) = f\left[\sum_{i=1}^{n} w_i |x_i| + \sum_{i=1}^{n} \sum_{j=i}^{n} w_{ij} \sin(x_i x_j)\right]$ is also an acceptable function describing the regions of influence.

The learning algorithm determines the parameters of the hidden units in such a way that only sample patterns of a designated class are "covered" by a hidden unit representing this class. The algorithm also attempts to minimize the number of hidden units required to accurately solve a given classification problem.

Initially, the learning algorithm attempts to use a single hidden unit to cover a whole class region. If this fails, the sample patterns in that class are split into two or more clusters using a clustering procedure (e.g., the k-means procedure described in Section 6.1), and then attempts are made to adapt separate hidden units to cover each of these clusters. If this fails, or if only some clusters are covered, then the uncovered clusters are further split to be separately covered until covers are provided for each ultimate cluster. The idea here is to allow a hidden unit to cover (represent) as many of the sample patterns within a given class as is feasible (without including sample patterns from any other class), thereby minimizing the total number of hidden units needed to cover that class.

The parameters of each hidden unit are computed by solving a linear programming problem [for an accessible description of linear programming, the reader is referred to Chapter 5 in Duda and Hart (1973)]. The linear program is used to adjust the location and boundaries of the region of influence of a hidden unit representing a given class cluster such that sample patterns from this cluster cause the net inputs to the hidden unit [the argument of f in Equation (6.3.3)] to be at least slightly positive and those from all other classes to be at least slightly negative. Linear programming is appropriate here because the regions of influence are defined by quadratics that are linear functions of their parameters. Formally put, the linear program set up for adjusting the parameters of the jth hidden unit is as follows: Minimize ε^j subject to the following set of constraints:

$$
\begin{cases}
z_j(\mathbf{x}^k) \geq \varepsilon^j & \text{for all samples } \mathbf{x}^k \text{ belonging to the} \\
& \text{cluster to be covered by hidden unit } j \\
z_j(\mathbf{x}^k) \leq -\varepsilon^j & \text{for all samples } \mathbf{x}^k \text{ from classes other} \\
& \text{than those represented by unit } j
\end{cases}
\tag{6.3.5}
$$

The positive margin ε^j ensures a finite separation between the classes and prevents the formation of common boundaries. Unit j becomes a permanent fixed unit of the PTC net if and only if the solution to the preceding problem is feasible. Roy et al. (1993) gave an extension to this training method that enhances the PTC performance for data with outlier patterns. An alternative to linear programming is to use the Ho-Kashyap algorithm described in Section 3.1.4, which guarantees class separation (with finite separation between classes) if a solution exists or, otherwise, gives an indication of nonlinear separability.

Similar to the RCE net, all hidden units in the PTC whose respective regions of influence cover clusters of the same class have their outputs connected to a unique logical OR unit (or an LTG realizing the OR function) in the output layer.

The polynomial complexity of the preceding training algorithm is shown next. For each class label $c = 1, 2, \ldots, L$, let m_c be the number of pattern vectors (for a total of $m = \sum_{c=1}^{L} m_c$ patterns) to be covered. Consider the worst-case scenario (from a computational point of view) where a separate cover (hidden unit) is required for each training pattern. Thus, in this case, all the linear programs from Equation (6.3.5) for a class will be infeasible until the class is broken up into m_c single-point clusters. All single-point clusters will produce feasible solutions, which implies that a PTC with perfect recall on the training set has been designed (note, however, that such a design will have poor generalization). Further, the worst-case scenario is assumed, in which the m_c pattern vectors are broken up into one extra cluster at each clustering stage. Using simple counting arguments, it can be shown readily that for successful training, a total of $\frac{1}{2} \sum_{c=1}^{L} m_c(m_c + 1)$ linear programs (feasible and infeasible combined) are solved and clustering is performed m times. Now, since each linear program can be solved in polynomial time (Karmarkar, 1984; Khachian, 1979) and each clustering operation to obtain a specified number of clusters also can be performed in polynomial time (Everitt, 1980; Hartigan, 1975), it follows that the preceding learning algorithm is of polynomial complexity.

What remains to be seen is the generalization capability of PTC nets. As for most artificial neural nets, only empirical studies of generalization are available. One such study (Roy et al., 1993) reported comparable classification performance of a PTC net to the k-nearest-neighbors classifier and backprop nets on relatively small sample classification tasks. In general, a PTC net allocates a much smaller number of hidden units compared with the RCE net when trained on the same data. However, the PTC training procedure requires simultaneous access to all training examples, which makes the PTC net inapplicable for on-line implementations.

6.3.2 Cascade-Correlation Network

The cascade-correlation network (CCN) proposed by Fahlman and Lebiere (1990) is yet another example of a unit-allocating architecture. The CCN was developed in an attempt to solve the so-called *moving-target problem*, which is attributed to the slowness of backprop learning. Because all the weights in a backprop net are changing at once, each hidden unit sees a constantly changing environment. Therefore, instead of moving quickly to assume useful roles in the overall problem solution, the hidden units engage in a complex "dance" with much wasted motion (Fahlman and Lebiere, 1990).

The CCN differs from all networks considered so far in two major ways: (1) It builds a deep net of cascaded units (as opposed to a net with a wide hidden layer), and (2) it can allocate more than one type of hidden unit; e.g., sigmoidal units and Gaussian units may coexist in the same network. This network is suited for classification tasks or approximation of continuous functions. The CCN has a significant learning-speed advantage over backprop nets, since units are trained individually without requiring backpropagation of error signals.

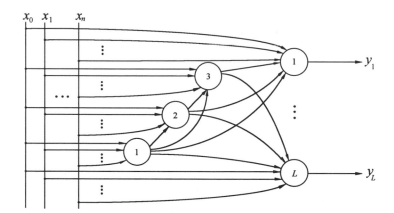

Figure 6.3.3
The cascade-correlation network architecture with three hidden units. The
number of each hidden unit represents the order in which it has been allocated.

The CCN architecture after allocating three hidden units is illustrated in Figure
6.3.3. The number of output units is dictated by the application at hand and by the
way the designer chooses to encode the outputs. The hidden units can be sigmoidal
units, Gaussian units, etc. or a mixture of such units. An important requirement on a
candidate hidden unit is that it has a differentiable transfer function. The original
CCN uses sigmoidal units as hidden units. The output units also can take various
forms, but typically, a sigmoidal (or hyperbolic tangent) activation unit is employed
for classification tasks. Linear output units are employed when the CCN is used
for approximating mappings with real-valued outputs (e.g., function approximation/
interpolation).

Every input (including a bias $x_0 = 1$) is connected to every output unit by a connection with an adjustable weight. Each allocated hidden unit receives a connection from
each preexisting hidden unit. Therefore, each added hidden unit defines a new one-
unit layer. This may lead to a very deep network with high fan-in for the hidden and
output units.

The learning algorithm consists of two phases: output-unit training and hidden-
unit training. Initially, the network has no hidden units. In the first phase, output-unit
weights are trained (e.g., using the delta rule) to minimize the usual sum of squared
error (SSE) measure at the output layer. At the completion of training, if the SSE
remains above a predefined threshold, the residual errors E_l^k (the difference $y_l^k - d_l^k$
between the actual and desired output) is recorded for each output unit l on each
training pattern $\mathbf{x}^k$, $k = 1, 2, \ldots, m$. Also, a new hidden unit is inserted whose weights

are determined by the hidden-unit training phase described below. Note that if the first training phase converges (SSE error is very small) with no hidden units, then training is stopped (this convergence would be an indication that the training set is linearly separable, assuming one is dealing with a classification task).

In the hidden-unit training phase, a pool of randomly initialized candidate hidden units (typically four to eight units) is trained in parallel. Later, one trained unit from this pool, the one that best optimizes some performance measure, is selected for permanent placement in the net. This multiple-candidate training strategy minimizes the chance that a useless unit will be permanently allocated because an individual candidate has gotten stuck at a poor set of weights during training. Each candidate hidden unit receives trainable input connections from all the network's external inputs and from all preexisting hidden units, if any. During this phase, the outputs of these candidate units are not yet connected to any output units in the network. Next, the weights of each candidate unit are adjusted, independently of other candidates in the pool, in the direction of maximizing a performance measure E. Here, E is chosen as the sum, over all output units, of the magnitude of the covariance[5] between the candidate unit's output z^k and the residual output error E_l^k, observed at unit l. Formally, the criterion E is defined as

$$E = \sum_{l=1}^{L} \left| \sum_{k=1}^{m} (z^k - \langle z \rangle)(E_l^k - \langle E_l \rangle) \right| \tag{6.3.6}$$

where $\langle z \rangle$ and $\langle E_l \rangle$ are average values taken over all patterns x^k. The maximization of E by each candidate unit is done by incrementing the weight vector $\mathbf{w}$ for this unit by an amount proportional to the gradient $\nabla_{\mathbf{w}} E$, i.e., performing steepest gradient ascent on E. Note that $\langle z \rangle$ is recomputed every time $\mathbf{w}$ is incremented by averaging the unit's outputs due to all training patterns. During this training phase, the weights of any preexisting hidden units are frozen. In fact, once allocated, a hidden unit never changes its weights. After the training reaches an asymptote, the candidate unit that achieves the highest covariance score E is added to the network by fanning out its output to all output-layer units through adjustable weights. The motivation here is that by maximizing covariance, a unit becomes tuned to the features in the input pattern that have not been captured by the existing net. This unit then becomes a permanent feature detector in the network, available for producing outputs or for creating other, more complex feature detectors. At this point, the network repeats the

---

5. The word *correlation* in *cascade-correlation net* in fact refers to the covariance maximization mechanism driving the training process. Therefore, to be precise, we may want to rename this net as the *cascade-covariance net*.

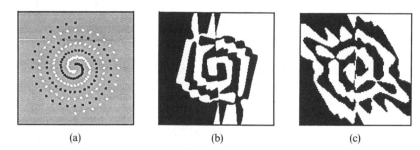

(a)   (b)   (c)

Figure 6.3.4
(a) Training samples for the two-spiral problem. (b) Solution found by a cascade-correlation network. (c) Solution found by a three-hidden-layer backprop network that employs "short-cut" connections. (Parts a and b are from Fahlman and Lebiere, 1990, and part c is from Lang and Witbrock, 1989, with permission of Morgan Kaufmann.)

output-layer training phase using the delta learning rule, and the residual output errors E_l^k are recomputed. The two training phases continue to alternate until the output SSE is sufficiently small, which is almost always possible.

The CCN has been shown empirically to be capable of learning some hard classification-type tasks 10 to 100 times faster than backprop. Fahlman and Lebiere (1990) have estimated empirically the learning time in epochs to be roughly $J \log (J)$, where J is the number of hidden units ultimately needed to solve the given task. Unfortunately, though, a precise value of J is almost impossible to determine. In addition, the CCN is capable of learning difficult tasks on which backprop nets have been found to get stuck in local minima. One of these difficult tasks is the n-bit parity problem. Another is the two-spiral problem shown in Figure 6.3.4a.

The two-spiral problem was proposed by Alex Wieland as a benchmark that is extremely hard for a standard backprop net to solve. The task requires a network with two real-valued inputs and a single output to learn a mapping that distinguishes between points on two intertwined spirals. The associated training set consists of 194 point coordinates (x_1, x_2), half of which come from each spiral. The output should be $+1$ for the first spiral and -1 for the other spiral. Figure 6.3.4b shows a solution to this problem generated by a trained CCN (Fahlman and Lebiere, 1990). This task requires, typically, 12 to 19 sigmoidal hidden units and an average of 1700 training cycles when a pool of 8 candidate hidden units is used during training. For comparison purposes, Figure 6.3.4c shows a solution generated by a backprop network employing 3 hidden layers of 5 units each and with "shortcut" connections between layers (Lang and Witbrock, 1989). Here, each unit receives incoming connections from every unit in every earlier layer, not just from the immediately preceding layer.

The backprop net requires about 20,000 training cycles and about 8000 cycles if Fahlman's version of backprop (see Section 5.2.3) is used. Therefore, the CCN outperforms standard backprop in training cycles by a factor of 10 while building a network of about the same complexity. In terms of actual computation on a serial machine, however, the CCN shows 50-fold speedup over standard backprop on the two-spiral task. This is due to the lower number of computations constituting a single CCN training cycle compared with that of standard backprop. Note also that the solution generated by the CCN is qualitatively better than that generated by backprop (the reader might have already noticed a difference in the spiral directions between Figure 6.3.4b and c. This is simply because the simulation in Part c used training spirals that have the opposite direction to those shown in Figure 6.3.4a.

On the other hand, when used for function approximation, backprop outperforms the CCN. Simulations with the Mackey-Glass time-series prediction task show poor generalization performance for the CCN (Crowder, 1991); in this case, the CCN suffers from overfitting. Another undesirable feature of the CCN is its inefficient hardware implementation: The deep-layered architecture leads to a delay in response proportional to the number of layers. Also, the high fan-in of the hidden units imposes additional implementation constraints for VLSI technology; high device fan-in leads to increased device capacitance and thus slower devices. Finally, it should be noted that the CCN requires that all training patterns be available for computing the averages $\langle z \rangle$ and $\langle E_l \rangle$ after each training cycle, which makes the CCN inappropriate for on-line implementations.

6.4 Clustering Networks

The task of pattern clustering is to automatically group unlabeled input vectors into several categories (clusters) so that each input is assigned a label corresponding to a unique cluster. The clustering process is normally driven by a similarity measure. Vectors in the same cluster are similar, which usually means that they are "close" to each other in the input space. A simple clustering net that employs competitive learning was covered in Section 3.4. In this section, two additional clustering neural networks are described which have more interesting features than the simple competitive net of Chapter 3. Either network is capable of automatic discovery (estimation) of the underlying number of clusters.

There are various ways to represent clusters. The first network described uses a simple representation in which each cluster is represented by the weight vector of a prototype unit (this is also the prototype representation scheme adapted by the simple competitive net). The first network is also characterized by its ability to allocate clusters incrementally. Networks with incremental clustering capability can handle an infinite stream of input data. They do not require large memory to store training data because their cluster prototype units contain implicit representation of all the inputs previously encountered.

The second clustering network described in this section has a more complex architecture than the first net. It employs a distributed representation as opposed to a single-prototype-unit cluster representation. This network is nonincremental in terms of cluster formation. However, the highly nonlinear multiple-layer architecture of this clustering net enables it to perform well on very difficult clustering tasks. Another interesting property of this net is that it does not require an explicit user-defined similarity measure. The network develops its own internal measure of similarity as part of the training phase.

6.4.1   Adaptive Resonance Theory (ART) Networks

Adaptive resonance architectures are artificial neural networks that are capable of stable categorization of an arbitrary sequence of unlabeled input patterns in real time. These architectures are capable of continuous training with nonstationary inputs. They also solve the *stability-plasticity dilemma*; namely, they let the network adapt yet prevent current inputs from destroying past training. The basic principles of the underlying theory of these networks, known as *adaptive resonance theory* (ART), were introduced by Grossberg (1976). ART networks are biologically motivated and were developed as possible models of cognitive phenomena in humans and animals.

A class of ART architectures, called *ART1*, is characterized by a system of ordinary differential equations (Carpenter and Grossberg, 1987a), with associated theorems proving its self-stabilization property and the convergence of its adaptive weights. ART1 embodies certain simplifying assumptions that allow its behavior to be described in terms of a discrete-time clustering algorithm. A number of interpretations/simplifications of the ART1 net have been reported in the literature (Lippmann, 1987; Pao, 1989; Moore, 1989). In the following, Moore's abstraction of the clustering algorithm from the ART1 architecture is adopted, and this algorithm is discussed in conjunction with a simplified architecture.

The basic architecture of the ART1 net consists of a layer of linear units representing prototype vectors whose outputs are acted on by a winner-take-all network (described in Section 3.4.1). This architecture is identical to that of the simple competitive net in Figure 3.4.1 with one major difference: The linear prototype units are allocated dynamically, as needed, in response to novel input vectors. Once a prototype unit is allocated, appropriate lateral-inhibitory and self-excitatory connections are introduced so that the allocated unit may compete with preexisting prototype units. Alternatively, one may assume a prewired architecture as in Figure 3.4.1 with a large number of inactive (zero weight) units. Here, a unit becomes active if the training algorithm decides to assign it as a cluster prototype unit, and its weights are adapted accordingly.

The general idea behind ART1 training is as follows. Every training iteration consists of taking a training example $\mathbf{x}^k$ and examining existing prototypes (weight vectors $\mathbf{w}_j$) that are sufficiently similar to $\mathbf{x}^k$. If a prototype $\mathbf{w}_i$ is found to "match" $\mathbf{x}^k$ (according to a "similarity" test based on a preset matching threshold), example $\mathbf{x}^k$ is added to the cluster represented by $\mathbf{w}_i$, and $\mathbf{w}_i$ is modified to make it better match $\mathbf{x}^k$. If no prototype matches $\mathbf{x}^k$, then $\mathbf{x}^k$ becomes the prototype for a new cluster. The details of the ART1 clustering procedure are considered next.

The input vector (pattern) $\mathbf{x}$ in ART1 is restricted to binary values, $\mathbf{x} \in \{0, 1\}^n$. Each learned cluster, say, cluster j, is represented by the weight vector $\mathbf{w}_j \in \{0, 1\}^n$ of the jth prototype unit. Every time an input vector $\mathbf{x}$ is presented to the ART1 net, each existing prototype unit computes a normalized output (the motivation behind this normalization is discussed later)

$$y_j = \frac{\mathbf{w}_j^\mathsf{T}\mathbf{x}}{\|\mathbf{w}_j\|^2} \tag{6.4.1}$$

and feeds it to the winner-take-all net for determining the winner unit.[6] Note that y_j is the ratio of the overlap between prototype $\mathbf{w}_j$ and $\mathbf{x}$ to the size of $\mathbf{w}_j$. The winner-take-all net computes a "winner" unit i. Subject to further verification, the weight vector of the winner unit $\mathbf{w}_i$ now represents a potential prototype for the input vector. The verification comes in the form of passing two tests.

In order to pass the first test, the input $\mathbf{x}$ must be "close enough" to the winner prototype $\mathbf{w}_i$; i.e.,

$$y_i = \frac{\mathbf{w}_i^\mathsf{T}\mathbf{x}}{\|\mathbf{w}_i\|^2} > \frac{\|\mathbf{x}\|^2}{n} \tag{6.4.2}$$

Here, $\|\mathbf{x}\|^2$ and $\|\mathbf{w}_i\|^2$ are equal to the number of 1s in $\mathbf{x}$ and $\mathbf{w}_i$, respectively. Passing this test guarantees that a sufficient fraction of the $\mathbf{w}_i$ and $\mathbf{x}$ bits is matched.

The second test is a match verification test between $\mathbf{w}_i$ and $\mathbf{x}$. This test is passed if

---

6. In practice, a small positive constant, say, 0.5, is added to the denominator in Equation (6.4.1) in order to avoid division by zero.

$$\frac{\mathbf{w}_i^T \mathbf{x}}{\|\mathbf{x}\|^2} \geq \rho \tag{6.4.3}$$

where $0 < \rho < 1$ is a user-defined *vigilance parameter*. Here, $\mathbf{w}_i$ is declared to "match" $\mathbf{x}$ if a significant fraction (determined by ρ) of the 1s in $\mathbf{x}$ appears in $\mathbf{w}_i$. Note that Equation (6.4.3) causes more differentiation among input vectors of smaller magnitude. This feature of ART1 is referred to as *automatic scaling, self-scaling*, or *noise insensitivity*.

If these two tests are passed by the winner unit i for a given input $\mathbf{x}$ (here, the network is said to be in *resonance*), then $\mathbf{x}$ joins cluster i, and this unit's weight vector $\mathbf{w}_i$ is updated according to

$$\mathbf{w}_i^{\text{new}} = \mathbf{w}_i \wedge \mathbf{x} \tag{6.4.4}$$

where "$\wedge$" stands for the logical AND operation applied component-wise to the corresponding components of vectors $\mathbf{w}_i$ and $\mathbf{x}_i$. According to Equation (6.4.4), a new prototype $\mathbf{w}_i$ can only have fewer and fewer 1s as training progresses. Note that it is possible for a training example to join a new cluster but eventually to leave that cluster because other training examples have joined it.

The second scenario corresponds to unit i passing the first test but not the second one. Here, the ith unit is deactivated (its output is clamped to zero until a new input arrives) and the tests are repeated with the unit with the next highest normalized output. If this scenario persists even after all existing prototype units are exhausted, then a new unit representing a new cluster j is allocated and its weight vector $\mathbf{w}_j$ is initialized according to

$$\mathbf{w}_j = \mathbf{x} \tag{6.4.5}$$

In a third scenario, unit i does not pass the first test. Here, $\mathbf{w}_i$ is declared "too far" from the input $\mathbf{x}$, and a new unit representing a new cluster, j, is allocated with its weight vector $\mathbf{w}_j$ initialized as in Equation (6.4.5). Hence, initially, $\mathbf{w}_j$ is a binary vector. And since, $\mathbf{w}_j$ is updated according to Equation (6.4.4), the vector $\mathbf{w}_j$ preserves its binary nature. This is true for any unit in the ART1 net, since all units undergo the initialization in Equation (6.4.5) upon being allocated.

Note that the learning dynamics in the second scenario described above constitute a search through the prototype vectors, looking at the closest, next closest, etc., according to the criterion $(\mathbf{w}_j^T \mathbf{x})/\|\mathbf{w}_j\|^2$. This search is continued until a prototype vector is found that satisfies the matching criteria in Equation (6.4.3). These criteria are different. The first criterion measures the fraction of the bits in $\mathbf{w}_j$ that are also in $\mathbf{x}$, whereas the second criterion measures the fraction of the bits in $\mathbf{x}$ that are also in $\mathbf{w}_j$.

Therefore, going further away by the first measure may actually bring us closer by the second. It also should be noted that this search only occurs before stability is reached for a given training set. After that, each prototype vector is matched on the first attempt, and no search is needed.

The normalization factor $\|\mathbf{w}_j\|^2$ in Equation (6.4.1) is used as a "tie breaker." It favors smaller-magnitude prototype vectors over vectors that are supersets of them (i.e., have 1s in the same places) when an input matches them equally well.[7] This mechanism of favoring small prototype vectors helps maintain prototype vectors apart. It also helps compensate for the fact that in the updating step of Equation (6.4.4), the prototype vectors always move to vectors with fewer 1s.

The vigilance parameter ρ in Equation (6.4.3) controls the granularity of the clusters generated by the ART1 net. Small ρ values allow for large deviations from cluster centers and hence lead to a small set of clusters. On the other hand, a higher vigilance leads to a larger number of tight clusters. Regardless of the setting of ρ, the ART1 network is stable for a finite training set; i.e., the final clusters will not change if additional training is performed with one or more patterns drawn from the original training set. A key feature of the ART1 network is its continuous learning ability. This feature, coupled with the preceding stability result, allows the ART1 net to follow nonstationary input distributions.

The clustering behavior of the ART1 network is illustrated for a set of random binary vectors. Here, the task of ART1 is to cluster 24 uniformly distributed random vectors $\mathbf{x} \in \{0, 1\}^{16}$. Simulation results are shown in Figure 6.4.1a and b for $\rho = 0.5$ and $\rho = 0.7$, respectively (here, the vectors are shown as 4×4 patterns of "on" and "off" pixels for ease of visualization). The resulting prototype vectors are also shown. Note the effect of the vigilance parameter setting on the granularity of the generated clusters.

The family of ART networks also includes more complex models such as ART2 (Carpenter and Grossberg, 1987b) and ART3 (Carpenter and Grossberg, 1990). These ART models are capable of clustering binary and analog input patterns. However, these models are inefficient from a computational point of view. A simplified model of ART2, ART2-A, has been proposed that is two to three orders of magnitude faster than ART2 (Carpenter et al., 1991b). Also, a supervised real-time learning ART model called *ARTMAP* has been proposed (Carpenter et al., 1991a).

---

7. For example, the vector $\mathbf{w}_1 = [1 \quad 0 \quad 1 \quad 0]^T$ is favored over its superset $\mathbf{w}_2 = [1 \quad 1 \quad 1 \quad 0]^T$ when matching the example $\mathbf{x} = [1 \quad 0 \quad 1 \quad 1]^T$. Here, $\mathbf{w}_1^T\mathbf{x} = \mathbf{w}_2^T\mathbf{x} = 2$, while

$$\frac{\mathbf{w}_1^T\mathbf{x}}{\|\mathbf{w}_1\|^2} = 1 > \frac{\mathbf{w}_2^T\mathbf{x}}{\|\mathbf{w}_2\|^2} = \tfrac{2}{3}.$$

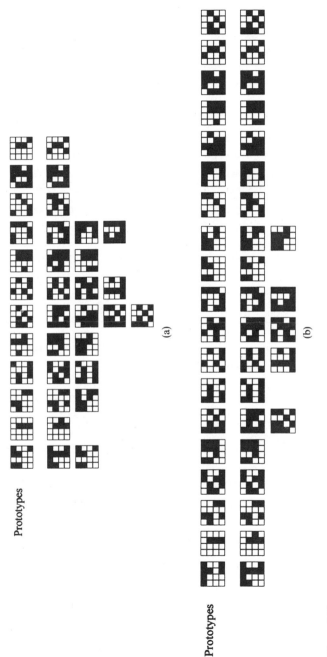

Figure 6.4.1

Random binary pattern clustering employing the ART1 net. Different vigilance values cause different numbers of categories (clusters) to form (*a*) $\rho = 0.5$ and (*b*) $\rho = 0.7$. For each case, the top row shows prototype vectors extracted by the ART1 network.

An example of ART2 clustering is shown in Figure 6.4.2 (Carpenter and Grossberg, 1987b). Here, the problem is to cluster a set of fifty 25-dimensional real-valued input signals (patterns). The results are shown for two different vigilance levels. It is left to the reader to check (subjectively) the consistency of the formed clusters. Characterization of the clustering behavior of ART2 was given by Burke (1991), who draws an analogy between ART-based clustering and k-means-based clustering.

ART networks are sensitive to the presentation order of the input patterns; they may yield different clustering on the same data when the presentation order of patterns is varied (with all other parameters kept fixed). Similar effects are also present in incremental versions of classical clustering methods such as k-means clustering (i.e., k-means is also sensitive to the initial choice of cluster centers).

6.4.2 Autoassociative Clustering Network

Other data-clustering networks can be derived from *concept-forming cognitive models* (Anderson, 1983; Knapp and Anderson, 1984; Anderson and Murphy, 1986). A *concept* describes the situation where a number of different objects are categorized together by some rule or similarity relationship. For example, a person is able to recognize that physically different objects are really "the same" (e.g., a person's concept of "tree").

A simple concept-forming model consists of two basic interrelated components. First, it consists of a prototype-forming component, which is responsible for generating category prototypes via an autoassociative learning mechanism. The second component is a retrieval mechanism where a prototype becomes an attractor in a dynamical system. Here, the prototype and its surrounding basin of attraction represent an individual concept.

Artificial neural networks based on the preceding concept-forming model have been proposed for data clustering of noisy, superimposed patterns (Anderson et al., 1990; Spitzer et al., 1990; Hassoun et al., 1992, 1994a, 1994b). Here, a feedforward (single- or multiple-layer) net is trained in an autoassociative mode (recall the discussion on autoassociative nets in Section 5.3.6) with the noisy patterns. The training is supervised in the sense that each input pattern to the net serves as its own target. However, these targets are not the "correct answers" in the general sense of supervised training. The strategy here is to force the network to develop internal representations during training so as to better reconstruct the noisy inputs. In the prototype-extraction phase, the trained feedforward net is transformed into a dynamical system by using the output-layer outputs as inputs to the net, thus forming an external feedback loop. Now, and with proper stabilization, when initialized with one of the input patterns, the dynamical system will evolve and eventually converge to the "closest"

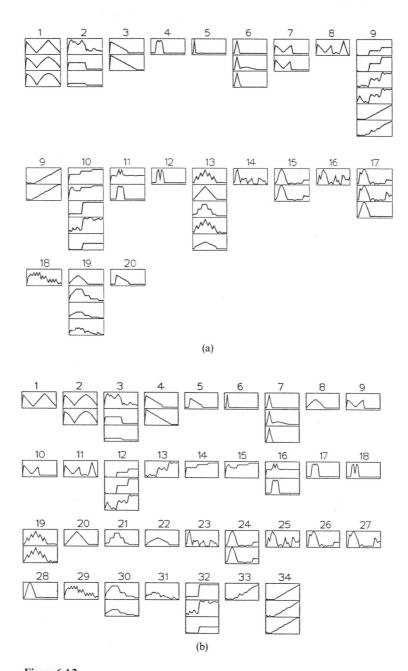

Figure 6.4.2
ART2 clustering of analog signals for two vigilance levels. The vigilance value in part *a* is smaller than that in part *b*. Note that cluster number 9 has eight signals and is broken down into two separate columns for display reasons only. (From Carpenter and Grossberg, 1987b; © 1987 Optical Society of America.)

attractor state. Hopefully, these attractors may be identified with the prototypes derived from the training phase.

Next, these ideas are described in the context of a simple single-layer network (Hassoun and Spitzer, 1988; Anderson et al., 1990), and then a more general auto-associative clustering architecture is presented. Consider an unlabeled training set of vectors $\hat{x} \in R^n$ representing distorted and/or noisy versions of a set $\{x^k; k = 1, 2, \ldots, m\}$ of m unknown prototype vectors. Also assume a single-layer net of n linear units each having an associated weight vector w_i, $i = 1, 2, \ldots, n$. Let us denote by $\mathbf{W}$ the $n \times n$ matrix whose ith row is the weight vector w_i^T. This simple network outputs the vector $y \in R^n$ upon the presentation of an input $\hat{x}$ where $y = \mathbf{W}\hat{x}$. Now the connection matrix $\mathbf{W}$ is updated in response to the presentation of a sample $\hat{x}^k$ according to the matrix form of the Widrow-Hoff (LMS) rule

$$\Delta \mathbf{W} = \rho(\hat{x}^k - y^k)\hat{x}^{k^T} \tag{6.4.6}$$

which realizes a gradient-descent minimization of the criterion function

$$J(\mathbf{W}) = \tfrac{1}{2} \sum_k \|\hat{x}^k - \mathbf{W}\hat{x}^k\|^2 \tag{6.4.7}$$

Therefore, the trained net will be represented by a connection matrix $\mathbf{W}$ that approximates the mapping

$$\mathbf{W}x = x \tag{6.4.8}$$

for all m prototype vectors x. This approximation results from minimizing J in Equation (6.4.7), and it requires that the clusters of noisy samples $\hat{x}$ associated with each prototype vector be sufficiently uncorrelated. In addition, it requires that the network be incapable of memorizing the training autoassociations and that the number of underlying prototypes m to be learned be much smaller than n.

According to Equation (6.4.8), the autoassociative training phase attempts to estimate the unknown prototypes and encode them as eigenvectors of $\mathbf{W}$ with eigenvalues of 1. A simple method for extracting these eigenvalues (prototypes) is to use the "power" method of eigenvector extraction. This is an iterative method that can be used to pick out the eigenvector with the largest-magnitude eigenvalue of a matrix $\mathbf{A}$ by repeatedly passing an initially random vector c^0 through the matrix according to (also refer to footnote 6 in Chapter 3)

$$c^{k+1} = \mathbf{A}c^k \qquad k = 0, 1, 2, \ldots \tag{6.4.9}$$

After a number of iterations, the eigenvector with the largest-magnitude eigenvalue will dominate.[8] This eigenvector extraction method can be readily implemented by adding external feedback to our simple net, with A represented by W and c by y or x.

Once initialized with one of the noisy vectors $\hat{x}$, the resulting dynamical system evolves its state (the n-dimensional output vector y) in such a way that this state moves toward the prototype vector x "most similar" to $\hat{x}$. This is possible because the prototype vectors x approximate the dominating eigenvectors of W (with eigenvalues close to 1). Note that the remaining eigenvectors of W arise from learning uncorrelated noise and tend to have small eigenvalues compared with 1. The ability of the auto-associative dynamical net to selectively extract a learned prototype/eigenvector from a "similar" input vector, as opposed to always extracting the most dominant eigen-vector, is due to the fact that all learned prototypes have comparable eigenvalues close to unity. Thus the extracted prototype is the one that is "closest" to the initial state (input vector) of the net.

The stability of the dynamic autoassociative net is an important design issue. Sta-bility is determined by the network weights and network architecture. Care must be taken in matching the learning algorithm for prototype encoding in the feedforward net to the dynamic architecture that is ultimately used for prototype extraction. One would like to design an autoassociative clustering net that minimizes an associated energy or Liapunov function; i.e., starting from any initial state, the system's state always evolves along a trajectory for which the energy function is monotonically decreasing (the reader may refer to Section 7.1.2 for further details on Liapunov functions and stability). Anderson et al. (1990) reported a stable autoassociative clus-tering net based on the brain-state-in-a-box (BSB) concept-forming model (Anderson et al., 1977) (see also Section 7.4.1).

A serious limitation of the autoassociative linear net just described is that it does not allow the user to control the granularity of the formed clusters; i.e., the number of learned prototypes. This network will tend to merge different clusters that are "close" to each other in the input space due to the lack of cluster competition mechanisms (recall the similarity and vigilance tests employed in the ART1 net for controlling cluster granularity). When two different clusters are merged by the linear net, they become represented by a distorted prototype that is a linear combination of the two correct (but unknown) prototypes. Introducing nonlinearity into the autoassociative net architecture can help the net overcome this limitation by allowing control of the granularity of the clusters. This feature is discussed in connection with the dynamic

8. The power method is discussed in more detail in many books, including Householder (1964), Wilkinson (1965), and Hornbeck (1975). An easy-to-follow discussion of an application of the power method to the analysis of simple autoassociative nets can be found in Anderson (1993).

nonlinear multilayer autoassociative network (Spitzer et al., 1990; Wang, 1991; Hassoun et al., 1992, 1994a) considered next.

Consider a two-hidden-layer feedforward net with an output layer of linear units. All hidden-layer units employ the hyperbolic tangent activation function

$$f(\xi) = \tanh(\beta\xi) \tag{6.4.10}$$

where β controls the slope of the activation. The activation slopes of the second-hidden-layer units (the layer between the first hidden and output layers) are fixed (typically set to 1). On the other hand, the activation slopes for the units in the first hidden layer are made monotonically increasing during training, as explained below. Each hidden unit in the first layer receives inputs from all components of an n-dimensional input vector and an additional bias input (held fixed at 1). Similarly, each unit in the second hidden layer receives inputs from all units in the first hidden layer plus a bias input of 1. Finally, each linear output unit receives inputs from all second-hidden-layer units plus a bias.

This layered network functions as an autoassociative net, as described above. Therefore, the n-output-layer units serve to reconstruct (decode) the n-dimensional vector presented at the input. The network is to discover a limited number of representations (prototypes) of a set of noisy input vectors to describe the training data. An essential feature of the network's architecture is therefore a restrictive "bottleneck" in the hidden layer; the number of units in each hidden layer (especially the first hidden layer) is small compared to n. The effect of this bottleneck is to restrict the degrees of freedom of the network and constrain it to discovering a limited set of unique prototypes that describes (clusters) the training set. The network does not have sufficient capacity to memorize the training set. This clustering is further enhanced by aspects of the learning algorithm, described below. Autoassociative multilayer nets with hidden-layer bottleneck have been studied by Bourlard and Kamp (1988), Baldi and Hornik (1989), Funahashi (1990), Kramer (1991), Oja (1991), and Usui et al. (1991), among others. In these studies, such nets have been found to implement principal-component analysis (PCA) and nonlinear PCA when one hidden layer and three or more hidden layers are used, respectively. The reader is referred to Section 5.3.6 for details.

The learning algorithm employed is essentially the incremental backprop algorithm of Section 5.1.1 with simple heuristic modifications. These heuristics significantly enhance the network's tendency to discover the best prototypical representations of the training data. These modifications include a dynamic slope for the first-hidden-layer activations that saturates during learning and damped learning-rate coefficients. As a result of learning, the first hidden layer in this net discovers a set of bipolar binary distributed representations that characterize the various input vectors. The second hidden and the output layers perform a nonlinear mapping that decodes these representations into reduced-noise versions of the input vectors.

In order to enhance separation of clusters and promote grouping of similar input vectors, the slope β of the activation functions of first-hidden-layer units is made dynamic; it increases monotonically during learning, according to

$$\beta(k) = \gamma^k \tag{6.4.11}$$

where γ is greater than but close to 1 and k is the learning-step index. As a result, the nonlinearity gradually (over a period of many cycles through the whole training set) becomes the sgn (sign) function, and the outputs of the first hidden layer become functionally restricted to bipolar binary values. As these activations saturate, a limited number of representations for "features" of the input vectors are available. This gradually forces "similar" inputs to activate a unique distributed representation at this layer. The larger the value of γ, the faster is the saturation of the activations, which, in turn, increases the sensitivity of the first-hidden-layer representations to differences among the input vectors. This increased sensitivity increases the number of unique representations at this layer, thus leading the rest of the network to reconstruct an equal number of prototypes. Hence the slope saturation parameter γ controls cluster granularity and may be viewed as a vigilance parameter similar to that in the ART nets.

The mapping characteristics of this highly nonlinear first hidden layer also may be thought to emerge from a kind of nonlinear principal-component analysis (PCA) mechanism where unit activities are influenced by high-order statistics of the training set. The other modification to backprop is the use of exponentially damped learning coefficients. The tendency is for the network to best remember the most recently presented training data. A decaying learning coefficient helps counteract this tendency and balance the sensitivity of learning for all patterns. The learning-rate coefficient used is therefore dynamically adjusted according to

$$\rho(k) = \lambda^k \tag{6.4.12}$$

where λ is a predefined constant less than but close to unity. As a result of this exponentially decaying learning rate, learning initially proceeds rapidly, but then the declining rate of learning produces a deemphasis of the most recently learned input vectors, which reduces "forgetting" effects and allows the repeating patterns to be learned evenly.

In the prototype-extraction phase, a dynamic net is generated by feeding the preceding trained net's output back to the input. A pass is now made over the training set, but this time no learning occurs. The primary objective of this pass is to classify the vectors in the training data and extract the prototype discovered by the network for each cluster. As each vector is presented, an output is generated and is fed back to the input of the network. This process is repeated iteratively until convergence. When the network settles into a final state, the outputs of the first hidden layer converge to a bipolar binary state. This binary state gives an intermediate distributed representation (activity pattern) of the particular cluster containing the present input. The intermediate activity pattern is mapped by the rest of the net into a real-valued activity pattern at the output layer. This output can be taken as a "nominal" representation of the underlying cluster "center," i.e., a prototype of the cluster containing the current input. Therefore, the network generates two sets of prototypes (concepts): abstract binary-valued concepts and explicit real-valued concepts. The network also supplies the user with parallel implementations of the two mappings from one concept representation to the other; the first hidden layer maps the input vectors into their corresponding abstract concepts, while the second hidden layer and the output layer implement the inverse of this mapping.

Proving the stability of this dynamic multilayer autoassociative clustering net is currently an open problem. The highly nonlinear nature of this dynamical system makes the analysis difficult. More specifically, it would be difficult to find an appropriate Liapunov function, if one exists, to prove stability. However, empirical evidence suggests a high degree of stability when the system is initialized with one of the training vectors and/or a new vector that is sufficiently similar to any one of the training vectors.

This section concludes by presenting two simulation results that illustrate the capability of the preceding autoassociative clustering net. In the first simulation, the net is used to cluster the 50 analog patterns of Figure 6.4.2. These patterns are repetitively presented to the net until the slopes (β) in the first hidden layer rise to 200, according to Equation (6.4.11). Two experiments were performed with $\gamma = 1.0003$ and 1.0005. The network used had eight units in each of the first and second hidden layers. Figures 6.4.3a and b shows the learned prototypes (top row) and their associated cluster members (in associated columns) for $\gamma = 1.0003$ and $\gamma = 1.0005$, respectively ($\gamma = 1.0003$ required about 350 training cycles to saturate β at 200, while $\gamma = 1.0005$ required about 210 cycles). A typical setting for λ in Equation (6.4.12) is 0.9999.

It is interesting to note that the choices of network size and parameters γ and λ were not optimized for this particular clustering problem. In fact, these parameters were also found to be appropriate for clustering motor unit potentials in the electromyogram (EMG) signal (Wang, 1991). It is left to the reader to compare the clustering results in Figure 6.4.3 with those due to the ART2 net shown in Figure 6.4.2. Note how the level of γ controls cluster granularity.

In the second simulation, the autoassociative clustering net (with comparable size and parameters as in the first simulation) is used to decompose a 10-sec. recording of an EMG signal obtained from a patient with a diagnosis of myopathy (a form of

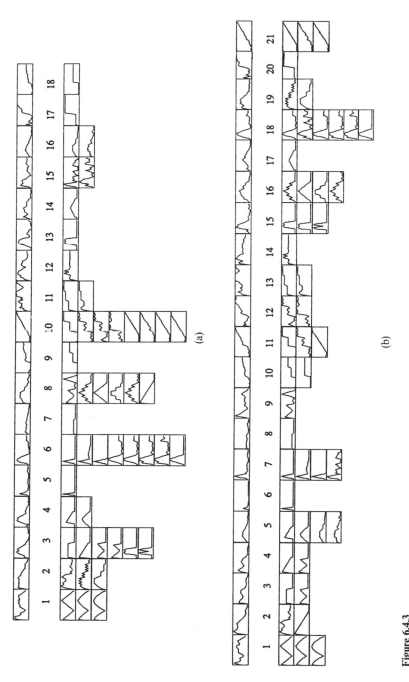

Figure 6.4.3
Clusters of patterns formed by the multilayer autoassociative clustering net: (a) $\gamma = 1.0003$ and (b) $\gamma = 1.0005$. The top row shows the learned prototype for each cluster.

50µV|
    10ms

muscle disease). A segment of this signal (about 0.8 sec.) is shown in the top window in Figure 6.4.4. The objective here is to extract prototype motor unit potentials (MUPs) comprising this signal and to associate each noisy MUP in the signal with its correct prototype. A preprocessing algorithm detected 784 candidate MUPs (each MUP pattern is uniformly sampled and is represented by a 50-dimensional vector centered at the highest peak in the MUP signal) in the 10-sec. EMG recording shown. These detected noisy MUPs were used to train the autoassociative clustering net. The clustering results are shown in Figure 6.4.4. A total of 24 unique prototype MUPs are identified by the network. The figure shows the prototypes associated with the 11 most significant clusters in small windows; i.e., a significant number of noisy input MUPs converged to these prototypes. Examples of MUPs from each cluster are shown to the right of discovered cluster prototypes. This result is superior to those of existing automated EMG decomposition techniques. For a detailed description and analysis of this problem, the reader may consult Wang (1991) and Hassoun et al. (1994a, 1994b).

6.5   Summary

This chapter starts by introducing the radial basis function (RBF) network as a two-layer feedforward net employing hidden units with locally tuned response characteristics. This network model is motivated by biologic nervous systems as well as by early results on the statistical and approximation properties of radial basis functions. The most natural application of RBF networks is in approximating smooth, continuous multivariate functions of few variables.

RBF networks employ a computationally efficient training method that decouples learning at the hidden layer from that at the output layer. This method uses a simple clustering (competitive learning) algorithm to locate hidden unit receptive field centers. It also uses the LMS or delta rule to adjust the weights of the output units.

These networks have comparable prediction/approximation capabilities to those of backprop networks but train by orders of magnitude faster. Another advantage of RBF nets is their lower false-positive classification error rates. However, by a factor of at least one order of magnitude, RBF nets require more training data and more hidden units compared with backprop nets for achieving the same level of accuracy.

Figure 6.4.4
Decomposition of an EMG signal by the autoassociative clustering net. One segment of an EMG (about 0.8 s) is shown in the top window. The extracted MUP waveform prototypes are shown in small windows. Examples of classified waveforms are shown to the right.

Two major variations to the RBF network are given that lead to improved accuracy (though at the cost of reduced training speed). The first variation involves replacing the k-means-clustering-based training method for locating hidden-unit centers by a "soft competition" clustering method. The second variation to the RBF net substitutes semilocal activation units for the local activation hidden units and employs gradient-descent-based learning for adjusting all unit parameters.

The CMAC is another example of a localized receptive field net that is considered in this chapter. The CMAC was originally developed as a model of the cerebellum. This network model shares several of the features of the RBF net, such as fast training and the need for a large number of localized receptive field hidden units for accurate approximation. It also has common features (and limitations) to those found in classical perceptrons (e.g., Rosenblatt's perceptron). One distinguishing feature of the CMAC, though, is its built-in capability of local generalization. The CMAC has been applied successfully in the control of robot manipulators.

Three unit-allocating adaptive multilayer feedforward networks are also described in this chapter. The first two networks belong to the class of hyperspherical classifiers. They employ hidden units with adaptive localized receptive fields. They also have sparse interconnections between the hidden units and the output units. These networks are easily capable of forming arbitrarily complex decision boundaries, with rapid training times. In fact, for one of these networks (PTC net), the training time was shown to be of polynomial complexity.

The third unit-allocating network (cascade-correlation net) differs from all previous networks in its ability to build a deep net of cascaded units and in its ability to utilize more than one type of hidden unit, coexisting in the same network. The motivation behind unit-allocating nets is two fold: (1) the elimination of the guesswork involved in determining the appropriate number of hidden units (network size) for a given task and (2) training speed.

Finally, two examples of dynamic multilayer clustering networks are discussed: the ART1 net and the autoassociative clustering net. These networks are intended for tasks involving data clustering and prototype generation. The ART1 net is characterized by its on-line capability of clustering binary patterns, its stability, and its ability to follow nonstationary input distributions. Generalizations of this network allow the extension of these desirable characteristics to the clustering of analog patterns. These ART networks are biologically motivated and were developed as possible models of cognitive phenomena in humans and animals.

The second clustering net is motivated by "concept-forming" cognitive models. It is based on two interrelated mechanisms: prototype formation and prototype extraction. A slightly modified backprop training method is employed in a customized autoassociative net of sigmoidal units in an attempt to estimate and encode cluster prototypes in such a way that they become attractors of a dynamical system. This dynamical system is formed by taking the trained feedforward net and feeding its output back to its input. Results of simulations involving data clustering with these nets are given. In particular, results of motor unit potential (MUP) prototype extraction and noisy/distorted MUP categorization (clustering) for a real EMG signal are presented.

It is hoped that the different network models presented in this chapter and the motivations for developing them give the reader an appreciation of the diversity and richness of these networks and the way their development has been influenced by biologic, cognitive, and/or statistical models.

Problems

6.1.1 Consider the RBF network in Figure 6.1.1, and assume the Gaussian basis function in Equation (6.1.3). Employ gradient-descent-based minimization of the instantaneous SSE criterion function [Equation (5.1.1)], and derive update rules for the hidden-unit receptive-field centers μ_j and widths σ_j and for the output layer weights w_{lj}.

6.1.2 Repeat Problem 6.1.1 using the basis function form in Equation (6.1.4).

6.1.3 Consider the Gaussian bar network of Section 6.1.2. Derive expressions for updating the hidden unit weights w_{ji}, centers μ_{ji}, and widths σ_{ji} employing gradient-descent-based minimization of the instantaneous SSE error function. Assume an output layer of L linear units whose weights are designated as w_{lj}.

6.1.4 Show that for large σ the one-dimensional Gaussian basis function $z(x) = \exp[-(x-\mu)^2/(2\sigma^2)]$ exhibits polynomial behavior. Also show that by increasing σ, polynomial models of successively decreasing degree are obtained. [*Hint*: Start by expanding $z(x)$ using Taylor series expansion at $x = \mu$.] Based on these observations, comment on the interpolation capability of an RBF network with very large RBF widths.

*__6.1.5__ Consider the problem of approximating an unknown "smooth" function $f(x)$ by a network with input $x \in R$ and output $y(x)$, given the training pairs $\{x^i, f(x^i)\}$, $k = 1, 2, \ldots, m$. We desire the approximating network to minimize the criterion function J given by

$$J(y) = \sum_{i=1}^{m} [f(x^i) - y(x^i)]^2 + \lambda J_R$$

which represents the SSE criterion function with regularization. Assume a regularization term J_R that penalizes "nonsmooth" approximations of $f(x)$, given by

$$J_R = \sum_{r=0}^{\infty} \frac{\sigma^{2r}}{r!2^r} \int_{-\infty}^{+\infty} \left[\frac{d^r y(x)}{dx^r} \right]^2 dx$$

Show that the best approximator network in the sense of minimizing J is an m-hidden-unit Gaussian RBF network with the transfer characteristics

$$y(x) = \sum_{i=1}^{m} w_i \exp\left[-\frac{(x - x^i)^2}{2\sigma^2} \right]$$

*6.1.6 Find the function $y(x)$ which minimizes the criterion functional

$$J(y) = \sum_{i=1}^{m} [f(x^i) - y(x^i)]^2 + \lambda \int_{-\infty}^{+\infty} \left[\frac{d^2 y(x)}{dx^2} \right]^2 dx$$

with respect to $\{x^i, f(x^i)\};\ i = 1, 2, \ldots, m$.

6.1.7 Employ an RBF net with two Gaussian hidden units, parameterized by $\{\boldsymbol{\mu}_1 = [0 \quad 0]^T, \sigma_1^2 = \frac{1}{4}\}$ and $\{\boldsymbol{\mu}_2 = [1 \quad 1]^T, \sigma_2^2 = \frac{1}{4}\}$, to solve the XOR problem. Assume a linear output unit with a bias input of $+1$, and compute its three-component weight vector using Equation (6.1.7). Generate a three-dimensional plot for the output of the RBF net versus the inputs x_1 and x_2, for $x_1, x_2 \in [-1, 2]$. Repeat with $\boldsymbol{\mu}_1 = [0 \quad 1]^T$ and $\boldsymbol{\mu}_2 = [1 \quad 0]^T$, and study via simulation the effect of σ ($\sigma = \sigma_1 = \sigma_2$) on the RBF net's output.

†6.1.8 Design a Gaussian RBF net to "strictly" fit the data given in Problem 5.2.13. [These data represent noise-free samples of the function $g(x) = [(x - 2)(2x + 1)]/(1 + x^2)$ plotted in Figure 5.2.3.] Verify your design by plotting the output of this net. Study, via simulation, the effect of varying the hidden-unit widths σ_j on the interpolation capability of the RBF net (assume $\sigma_j = \sigma$ for all j). How does the RBF net compare, in terms of the quality of interpolation and extrapolation, with the 12-hidden-unit feedforward neural net with backprop training whose output is shown as the dashed line in Figure 5.2.3? Interested readers may want to consider repeating this problem for the case of noisy samples, as in Problem 5.2.14. In this case, "strict" fitting should be avoided (why?).

6.2.1 Illustrate geometrically the receptive fields organization for a two-input CMAC with $c = 4$, based on the organization scheme described in Section 6.2.

6.2.2 Give qualitative arguments in support of the ability of Rosenblatt's perceptron to solve the parity problem if at least one of its hidden units is allowed to "see" all inputs.

6.3.1 Synthesize by inspection an RCE classifier net that solves the two-class problem in Figure P3.1.7 with the minimal number of hidden units. Draw a figure that superimposes the regions of influence of these hidden units on Figure P3.1.7.

†**6.3.2** Invoke the RCE classifier training procedure (with $r_{max} = 0.5$) to solve the classification problem in Figure P5.1.5. Assume that the training set consists of 1000 uniformly (randomly) generated samples from the region defined by $-1 < x_1 < +1$ and $-1 < x_2 < +1$. Plot the regions of influence of all hidden units associated with class B. Repeat for class A. Give a sketch of the resulting decision boundary.

6.3.3 Show that, in the worst-case scenario, the PTC training procedure converges after solving $\frac{1}{2} \sum_{c=1}^{L} m_c(m_c + 1)$ linear programs and after performing m clustering procedures.

†**6.3.4** Implement the PTC network using the direct Ho-Kashyap (DHK) algorithm (refer to Section 3.1.4) to solve for hidden-unit parameters and using k-means clustering for breaking up class clusters. Assume that the samples from a given class are split into two clusters at each stage, if splitting is needed. Verify your implementation by classifying the two-class problem depicted in Figure P3.1.7. Plot the resulting covers (hidden-unit regions of influence). Is the number of synthesized covers optimal? (Answer this question by trying to construct an optimal set of covers by inspection.)

6.3.5 Show that the PTC network (also the RCE network) can be realized using a two-layer feedforward net of LTGs preceded by a preprocessing layer that computes higher-order terms.

6.3.6 Derive a learning rule for updating candidate-hidden-unit weights in a single-output cascade-correlation net based on gradient ascent on the criterion function given by Equation (6.3.6). Assume a sigmoidal hidden unit with a hyperbolic tangent activation function. Also assume that the candidate hidden unit is the first unit to be allocated.

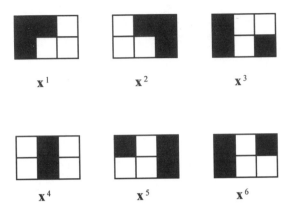

Figure P6.4.1
Training patterns for the ART1 net in Problem 6.4.1.

6.4.1 Cluster (using hand calculations) the patterns in Figure P6.4.1 using an ART1 net with vigilance $\rho = 0.6$. Use unipolar binary encoding of the patterns (e.g., $\mathbf{x}^1 = [1 \quad 1 \quad 0 \quad 1 \quad 0 \quad 0]^T$). Repeat the clustering with vigilance $\rho = 0.1$, and 0.9. For each case, draw the two-dimensional 2×3 patterns (as in the figure) of all generated cluster prototypes. Make a subjective decision on which vigilance value is more appropriate for this problem.

† **6.4.2** Generate a set of 24 uniform random binary vectors $\mathbf{x}^k \in \{0, 1\}^{16}$, $k = 1, 2, \ldots, 24$ (i.e., probability of a '1' bit is equal to 0.5). Employ the ART1 net with $\rho = 0.7$ to cluster this set. Generate a table that lists each generated prototype vector and its associated input vectors. Use a two-dimensional 4×4 pattern representation for each vector in this table. Does the number of clusters change with the permutation of the training patterns? (Answer this question by repeating the preceding simulation with the training patterns presented in reverse order.)

† **6.4.3** Apply k-means clustering to the random binary vectors generated in Problem 6.4.2. Set k to the number of prototypes generated by the ART1 net in the first simulation of Problem 6.4.2. Compare the results of k-means clustering with those of the ART1 net. (Note that the cluster prototypes discovered by the k-means clustering algorithm are real-valued. Also, it should be noted that the clustering of the k-means algorithm is sensitive to the initial selection of the k cluster centers.)

6.4.4 The power method of Equation (6.4.9) diverges if the dominating eigenvector c_{max} of matrix A has a corresponding eigenvalue $\lambda_{max} > 1$. Suggest a simple way of modifying this method so that it converges to the vector c_{max} when started from an arbitrary random initial vector c^0. Verify your modified method with

$$A = \begin{bmatrix} 1 & 0 & 0 & 0 \\ 0 & 2 & 0 & 0 \\ 0 & 0 & 3 & 0 \\ 0 & 0 & 0 & 4 \end{bmatrix} \quad \text{and} \quad c^0 = \begin{bmatrix} 1 \\ 1 \\ 1 \\ 1 \end{bmatrix}$$

6.4.5 Based on the way you would cluster the patterns in Figure 6.4.2 into 20 and 21 categories, compare and contrast the consistency of the clustering results produced by the ART2 net in Figure 6.4.2a and the autoassociative clustering net in Figure 6.4.3b.

† **6.4.6** Apply the k-means clustering algorithm with $k = 20$ prototypes to cluster the 50 analog patterns of Figure 6.4.2. Figure P6.4.6 gives a numerical representation for all 50 patterns. Compare the results from this clustering method with those in Figure 6.4.2a. Repeat with $k = 21$, and compare your results with those in Figure 6.4.3b.

† **6.4.7** Repeat Problem 6.4.6 using the incremental version of k-means clustering [Equation (6.1.5)] with a learning rate $\rho = 0.05$. Assume the same initial setting of prototypes (cluster centers) as in Problem 6.4.6. Which version of the algorithm gives better results? Why?

† **6.4.8** Compare the autoassociative clustering net–generated prototypes in Figure 6.4.3a (top row) with their respective average patterns generated by averaging all input patterns (vectors) belonging to a unique cluster. Use the data in Figure P6.4.6 for computing these averages.

6.4.9 One advantage of the ART2 net over the autoassociative clustering network is the ability of the former to learn continuously. Can you find other advantages? What about advantages of the autoassociative clustering net over the ART2 net?

```
10 80 70 60 50 40 30 20 10 20 30 40 50 60 70 80 90 80 70 60 50 40 30 20 10
10 80 74 67 59 50 40 29 17 29 40 50 59 67 74 80 85 80 74 67 59 50 40 29 17
10 80 76 70 62 52 40 26 10 26 40 50 62 70 76 80 82 80 76 70 62 50 40 26 10
10 62 85 92 75 82 74 62 64 74 89 74 63 24 35 22 22 24 39 36 25 28 23 22 23
10 50 50 50 50 50 50 50 50 50 50 50 50 10 10 10 10 10 10 10 10 10 10 10 10
10 80 75 70 65 60 55 50 45 40 35 30 25 10 10 10 10 10 10 10 10 10 10 10 10
10 10 10 10 65 60 55 50 45 40 35 30 25 10 10 10 10 10 10 10 10 10 10 10 10
10 10 90 10 10 10 10 10 10 10 10 10 10 10 10 10 10 10 10 10 10 10 10 10 10
10 10 50 90 50 10 10 10 10 10 10 10 10 10 10 10 10 10 10 10 10 10 10 10 10
10 20 20 20 20 20 20 20 20 20 20 20 10 10 10 10 10 10 10 10 10 10 10 10 10
10 20 30 39 47 54 60 60 54 47 39 30 20 10 10 10 10 10 10 10 10 10 10 10 10
10 60 54 47 39 30 20 20 30 39 47 54 60 10 10 10 10 10 10 10 10 10 10 10 10
10 70 60 50 40 30 20 20 30 40 50 60 10 10 10 10 10 10 10 10 10 10 10 10 10
10 70 60 50 40 30 20 20 30 40 50 60 15 8 16 18 12 8 30 60 90 60 30 4 2
10 0 0 0 0 0 0 0 0 30 30 30 30 30 30 30 30 50 50 50 50 50 50 50 50
10 0 0 0 0 0 0 0 0 50 50 50 50 50 50 50 50 90 90 90 90 90 90 90 90
10 10 5 14 18 8 16 10 5 45 60 52 46 58 59 42 49 89 95 83 92 90 87 89 95
10 30 50 30 18 8 16 10 5 45 60 52 46 58 59 42 49 89 95 83 92 90 87 89 95
10 60 60 60 60 60 60 60 60 80 80 80 80 80 80 80 80 90 90 90 90 90 90 90 90
10 65 80 80 65 60 60 60 60 80 80 80 80 80 80 80 80 90 90 90 90 90 90 90 90
10 51 55 53 48 60 90 60 90 60 54 53 51 56 55 54 55 52 51 54 55 52 55 53 53
10 10 10 10 10 80 90 80 90 80 10 10 10 10 10 10 10 10 10 10 10 10 10 10 10
10 10 10 10 80 90 80 90 80 10 10 10 10 10 10 10 10 10 10 10 10 10 10 10 10
10 10 10 10 80 90 30 90 80 10 10 10 10 10 10 10 10 10 10 10 10 10 10 10 10
10 10 30 50 30 50 70 50 70 90 70 50 70 50 30 50 30 10 13 11 14 12 13 11 10
10 10 20 30 40 50 60 70 80 90 80 70 60 50 40 30 20 10 10 10 10 10 10 10 10
10 20 20 20 50 50 50 80 80 80 80 50 50 50 20 20 20 10 10 10 10 10 10 10 10
10 10 30 50 30 50 70 50 70 90 70 50 70 50 30 50 30 10 3 15 8 2 12 2 14
10 10 24 28 32 36 40 44 48 52 48 44 40 36 32 28 24 10 10 10 10 10 10 10 10
10 10 50 90 50 18 20 22 24 26 24 22 20 18 16 14 12 10 10 10 10 10 10 10 10
10 10 50 90 50 18 1 1 1 1 1 1 1 1 1 1 1 1 1 1 1 1 1 1 1
10 20 80 95 52 8 40 28 39 36 3 22 25 39 10 3 6 2 40 36 30 20 25 4 6
10 10 30 65 85 99 85 65 30 10 5 10 12 7 6 10 12 9 10 11 30 30 30 30 30
10 10 60 35 80 95 78 69 32 5 14 18 3 28 59 20 30 6 4 60 55 30 35 30 55
10 10 30 68 90 99 85 62 30 10 10 10 12 7 6 10 12 9 10 11 35 30 33 30 30
10 10 80 68 90 99 85 62 30 5 15 20 4 13 6 10 12 9 10 11 35 35 33 30 30
10 10 80 68 99 85 62 40 5 15 20 4 13 6 10 12 9 10 11 60 50 30 40 40
10 10 40 68 90 99 85 62 40 10 10 10 12 10 10 10 10 10 10 10 10 10 10 10 10
10 50 60 70 60 80 60 80 60 80 40 60 40 60 40 20 40 20 40 20 40 20 10 20 10
10 40 50 60 70 80 80 80 80 80 60 40 40 40 40 20 20 20 20 20 20 10 10 10 10
10 20 25 30 35 40 40 40 40 40 30 20 20 20 20 10 10 10 10 10 10 5 5 5 5
10 30 25 32 28 45 40 46 35 42 35 15 24 25 20 15 13 9 8 2 18 10 5 2 8
10 20 20 20 20 20 20 20 20 90 90 90 90 90 90 90 90 90 90 90 90 90 90 90 90
10 20 10 35 22 24 40 33 18 23 85 96 90 88 95 99 99 82 80 86 89 93 85 88 93
10 3 3 3 3 3 3 3 3 3 40 40 40 40 40 40 40 40 40 40 40 40 40 40 40
10 95 90 85 80 75 70 65 60 55 50 45 40 35 30 25 20 15 10 5 5 5 5 5 5
10 5 5 5 5 5 5 10 15 20 25 30 35 40 45 50 55 60 65 70 75 80 85 90 95
10 7 5 7 8 2 10 14 12 21 38 30 30 38 48 45 54 62 67 75 75 85 82 91 95
10 8 4 10 3 5 4 13 16 21 24 30 38 41 45 53 56 59 63 70 74 82 86 91 96
10 10 3 5 4 13 16 21 24 30 38 41 45 53 56 59 63 70 74 82 86 91 96 95 98
```

Figure P6.4.6
Numerical representation of the 50 analog patterns shown in Figure 6.4.2. Each row represents a distinct 25-dimensional pattern. (Courtesy of Gail Carpenter and Steven Grossberg, Boston University.)

7 Associative Neural Memories

This chapter is concerned with associative learning and retrieval of information (vector patterns) in neural-like networks. These networks are usually referred to as *associative neural memories* (or *associative memories*), and they represent one of the most extensively analyzed class of artificial neural networks. Various associative memory architectures are presented, with emphasis on dynamic (recurrent) associative memory architectures. These memories are treated as nonlinear dynamical systems where information retrieval is realized as an evolution of the system's state in a high-dimensional state space. *Dynamic associative memories* (DAMs) are a class of recurrent artificial neural networks that utilize a learning/recording algorithm to store vector patterns (usually binary patterns) as stable memory states. The retrieval of these stored "memories" is accomplished by first initializing the DAM with a noisy or partial input pattern (key) and then allowing the DAM to perform a collective relaxation search to arrive at the stored memory that is best associated with the input pattern.

The chapter starts by presenting some simple networks that are capable of functioning as associative memories and derives the necessary conditions for perfect storage and retrieval of a given set of memories. The chapter continues by presenting additional associative memory models, with particular attention given to DAMs. The characteristics of high-performance DAMs are defined, and stability, capacity, and retrieval dynamics of various DAMs are analyzed. Finally, the application of a DAM to the solution of combinatorial optimization problems is described.

7.1 Basic Associative Neural Memory Models

Several associative neural memory models have been proposed over the last two decades [e.g., Amari (1972a), Anderson (1972), Nakano (1972), Kohonen (1972, 1974), Kohonen and Ruohonen (1973), Hopfield (1982), Kosko (1987), Okajima et al. (1987), Kanerva (1988), Chiueh and Goodman (1988), Baird (1990); for an accessible reference on various associative neural memory models, the reader is referred to the edited volume by Hassoun (1993)]. These memory models can be classified in various ways depending on their architecture (static versus recurrent), their retrieval mode (synchronous versus asynchronous), the nature of the stored associations (autoassociative versus heteroassociative), the complexity and capability of the memory storage/recording algorithm, etc. This section presents a simple static synchronous associative memory along with appropriate memory storage recipes. Then this simple associative memory is extended into a recurrent autoassociative memory by employing feedback. These two basic associative memories will help define some terminology and serve as a building ground for some additional associative memory models presented in Section 7.4.

7.1.1 Simple Associative Memories and Their Associated Recording Recipes

One of the earliest associative memory models is the correlation memory (Anderson, 1972; Kohonen, 1972; Nakano, 1972). This correlation memory consists of a single layer of L noninteracting linear units, with the lth unit having a weight vector $\mathbf{w}_l \in R^n$. It associates real-valued input column vectors $\mathbf{x}^k \in R^n$ with corresponding real-valued output column vectors $\mathbf{y}^k \in R^L$ according to the transfer equation

$$\mathbf{y}^k = \mathbf{W}\mathbf{x}^k \qquad (7.1.1)$$

Here, $\{\mathbf{x}^k, \mathbf{y}^k\}$, $k = 1, 2, \ldots, m$, is a collection of desired associations, and $\mathbf{W}$ is an $L \times n$ interconnection matrix whose lth row is given by $\mathbf{w}_l^{\mathrm{T}}$. A block diagram of the simple associative memory expressed in Equation (7.1.1) is shown in Figure 7.1.1. Note that this associative memory is characterized by linear matrix-vector multiplication retrievals. Hence it is referred to as a *linear associative memory* (LAM). This LAM is said to be *heteroassociative* because $\mathbf{y}^k$ is different (in encoding and/or dimensionality) from $\mathbf{x}^k$. If $\mathbf{y}^k = \mathbf{x}^k$ for all k, then this memory is called *autoassociative*.

Correlation Recording Recipe   The correlation memory is a LAM that employs a simple *recording/storage recipe* for loading the m associations $\{\mathbf{x}^k, \mathbf{y}^k\}$ into memory. This recording recipe is responsible for synthesizing $\mathbf{W}$ and is given by

$$\mathbf{W} = \sum_{k=1}^{m} \mathbf{y}^k (\mathbf{x}^k)^{\mathrm{T}} \qquad (7.1.2)$$

In other words, the interconnection matrix $\mathbf{W}$ is simply the correlation matrix of m association pairs. Another way of expressing Equation (7.1.2) is

$$\mathbf{W} = \mathbf{Y}\mathbf{X}^{\mathrm{T}} \qquad (7.1.3)$$

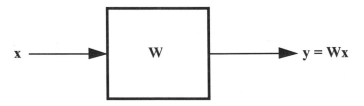

Figure 7.1.1
A block diagram of a simple linear heteroassociative memory.

where $\mathbf{Y} = [\mathbf{y}^1 \quad \mathbf{y}^2 \quad \cdots \quad \mathbf{y}^m]$ and $\mathbf{X} = [\mathbf{x}^1 \quad \mathbf{x}^2 \quad \cdots \quad \mathbf{x}^m]$. Note that for the auto-associative case where the set of association pairs $\{\mathbf{x}^k, \mathbf{x}^k\}$ is to be stored, one may still employ Equation (7.1.2) or Equation (7.1.3) with $\mathbf{y}^k$ replaced by $\mathbf{x}^k$.

One appealing feature of correlation memories is the ease of storing new associations or deleting old ones. For example, if after recording the m associations $\{\mathbf{x}^1, \mathbf{y}^1\}$ through $\{\mathbf{x}^m, \mathbf{y}^m\}$ it is desired to record one additional association $\{\mathbf{x}^{m+1}, \mathbf{y}^{m+1}\}$, then one simply updates the current $\mathbf{W}$ by adding to it the matrix $\mathbf{y}^{m+1}(\mathbf{x}^{m+1})^\mathrm{T}$. Similarly, an already recorded association $\{\mathbf{x}^i, \mathbf{y}^i\}$ may be "erased" by simply subtracting $\mathbf{y}^i(\mathbf{x}^i)^\mathrm{T}$ from $\mathbf{W}$. However, as is seen next, the price paid for simple correlation recording is that to guarantee successful *retrievals*, one must place stringent conditions on the set $\{\mathbf{x}^k; k = 1, 2, \dots, m\}$ of input vectors.

What are the requirements on the $\{\mathbf{x}^k, \mathbf{y}^k\}$ associations that will guarantee the successful retrieval of all recorded vectors (memories) $\mathbf{y}^k$ from their associated "perfect key" $\mathbf{x}^k$? Substituting Equation (7.1.2) in Equation (7.1.1) and assuming that the key $\mathbf{x}^h$ is one of the $\mathbf{x}^k$ vectors, one gets an expression for the retrieved pattern $\tilde{\mathbf{y}}^h$ as

$$\tilde{\mathbf{y}}^h = \left[\sum_{k=1}^m \mathbf{y}^k(\mathbf{x}^k)^\mathrm{T} \right] \mathbf{x}^h = \|\mathbf{x}^h\|^2 \mathbf{y}^h + \sum_{k \neq h}^m \mathbf{y}^k(\mathbf{x}^k)^\mathrm{T} \mathbf{x}^h \tag{7.1.4}$$

The second term on the right-hand side of Equation (7.1.4) represents the "cross-talk" between the key $\mathbf{x}^h$ and the remaining $(m-1)$ patterns $\mathbf{x}^k$. This term can be reduced to zero if the $\mathbf{x}^k$ vectors are orthogonal. The first term on the right-hand side of Equation (7.1.4) is proportional to the desired memory $\mathbf{y}^h$, with a proportionality constant equal to the (energy) square of the norm of the key vector $\mathbf{x}^h$. Hence a sufficient condition for the retrieved memory to be the desired perfect recollection is to have orthonormal vectors $\mathbf{x}^k$ independent of the encoding of the $\mathbf{y}^k$ (note, though, how the $\mathbf{y}^k$ affects the cross-talk term if the memory vectors $\mathbf{x}^k$ are not orthogonal). If nonlinear units replace the linear ones in the correlation LAM, perfect recall of binary $\{\mathbf{x}^k, \mathbf{y}^k\}$ associations is, in general, possible even when the vectors $\mathbf{x}^k$ are only pseudo-orthogonal. This can be seen in the following analysis.

A Simple Nonlinear Associative Memory Model   The assumption of binary-valued associations $\mathbf{x}^k \in \{-1, +1\}^n$ and $\mathbf{y}^k \in \{-1, +1\}^L$ and the presence of a clipping non-linearity F operating component-wise on the vector $\mathbf{W}\mathbf{x}$ (i.e., each unit now employs a sgn or sign activation function) according to

$$\mathbf{y} = F[\mathbf{W}\mathbf{x}] \tag{7.1.5}$$

relaxes some of the constraints imposed by correlation recording of a LAM. Here, $\mathbf{W}$ needs to be synthesized with the requirement that only the sign of the corresponding components of $\mathbf{y}^k$ and $\mathbf{W}\mathbf{x}^k$ agree. Next, consider the normalized correlation recording recipe given by

$$\mathbf{W} = \frac{1}{n} \sum_{k=1}^{m} \mathbf{y}^k (\mathbf{x}^k)^{\mathrm{T}} \tag{7.1.6}$$

which automatically normalizes the $\mathbf{x}^k$ vectors (note that the square of the norm of an n-dimensional bipolar binary vector is n). Now, if one of the recorded *key patterns* $\mathbf{x}^h$ is presented as input, then the following expression for the retrieved memory pattern can be written:

$$\tilde{\mathbf{y}}^h = F\left[\mathbf{y}^h + \frac{1}{n} \sum_{k \neq h}^{m} \mathbf{y}^k (\mathbf{x}^k)^{\mathrm{T}} \mathbf{x}^h\right] = F[\mathbf{y}^h + \Delta^h] \tag{7.1.7}$$

where Δ^h represents the cross-talk term. For the ith component of $\tilde{\mathbf{y}}^h$, Equation (7.1.7) gives

$$\tilde{y}_i^h = \operatorname{sgn}\left(y_i^h + \frac{1}{n} \sum_{j=1}^{n} \sum_{k \neq h}^{m} y_i^k x_j^k x_j^h\right) = \operatorname{sgn}(y_i^h + \Delta_i^h)$$

from which it can be seen that the condition for perfect recall is given by the requirements

$$\Delta_i^h > -1 \qquad \text{for } y_i^h = +1$$

and

$$\Delta_i^h < +1 \qquad \text{for } y_i^h = -1$$

for $i = 1, 2, \ldots, L$. These requirements are less restrictive than the orthonormality requirement of the vectors $\mathbf{x}^k$ in a LAM.

Uesaka and Ozeki (1972) and later Amari (1977a, 1990) [see also Amari and Yanai (1993)] analyzed the error correction capability of the preceding nonlinear correlation associative memory when the memory is loaded with m independent, uniformly distributed, and random bipolar binary associations $\{\mathbf{x}^k, \mathbf{y}^k\}$. Based on this analysis, the relation between the output and input error rates D_{out} and D_{in}, respectively, in the limit of large n is given by

$$D_{\text{out}} = \Phi\left[\frac{1 - 2D_{\text{in}}}{\sqrt{\dfrac{2m}{n}}}\right] \tag{7.1.8}$$

where Φ is defined as

$$\Phi(u) = \frac{1}{2}\left(1 - \frac{2}{\sqrt{\pi}}\int_0^u e^{-\xi^2}\,d\xi\right) \approx \frac{1}{2}\left[1 - \tanh\left(\frac{2u}{\sqrt{\pi}}\right)\right] \tag{7.1.9}$$

Here, D_{in} is the normalized Hamming distance, $D_{\text{in}} = D_{\text{in}}(\mathbf{x}^k, \hat{\mathbf{x}}^k) = \frac{1}{2n}\sum_{i=1}^{n}|x_i^k - \hat{x}_i^k|$, between a perfect key vector $\mathbf{x}^k$ and a noisy version $\hat{\mathbf{x}}^k \in \{-1, +1\}^n$ of $\mathbf{x}^k$. D_{in} also may be related to the "overlap" between $\mathbf{x}^k$ and $\hat{\mathbf{x}}^k$, $(1/n)(\mathbf{x}^k)^T\hat{\mathbf{x}}^k$, as $1 - 2D_{\text{in}} = (1/n)(\mathbf{x}^k)^T\hat{\mathbf{x}}^k$. Similarly, D_{out} is the normalized Hamming distance between $\mathbf{y}^k$ and the output $\hat{\mathbf{y}}^k$ of the associative memory due to the input $\hat{\mathbf{x}}^k$. The error rates D_{in} and D_{out} also may be viewed as the probability of error of an arbitrary bit in the input and output vectors, respectively [for an insight into the derivation of Equations (7.1.8) and (7.1.9), the reader is referred to the analysis in Section 7.2.1]. Equation (7.1.8) is plotted in Figure 7.1.2 for several values of the pattern ratio r, $r = m/n$. Note how the ability of the correlation memory to retrieve stored memories from noisy inputs is reduced

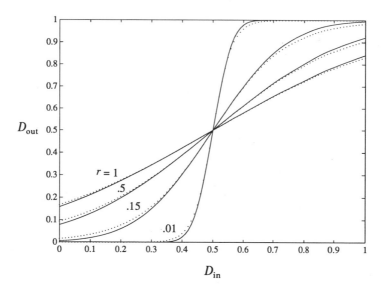

Figure 7.1.2
Output versus input error rates for a correlation memory with clipping (sgn) nonlinearity for various values of pattern ratio $r = m/n$. Bipolar binary association vectors are assumed that have independent, random, and uniformly distributed components. Dotted lines correspond to the approximation in Equation (7.1.9).

as the pattern ratio r approaches and exceeds the value 0.15. For low loading levels ($r < 0.15$), the error-correction capabilities of memory improve, and for $r \ll 1$, the memory can correct up to 50 percent error in the input patterns with a probability approaching 1. For large n with $n \gg m$, it can be shown that a random set of m key vectors $\mathbf{x}^k$ becomes mutually orthogonal with probability approaching unity (Kanter and Sompolinsky, 1987). Hence the loading of the m associations $\{\mathbf{x}^k, \mathbf{y}^k\}$, with arbitrary $\mathbf{y}^k$, is ensured using the normalized correlation recording recipe of Equation (7.1.6).

Optimal Linear Associative Memory (OLAM) The correlation recording recipe does not make optimal use of the LAM interconnection weights. A more optimal recording technique can be derived which guarantees perfect retrieval of stored memories $\mathbf{y}^k$ from inputs $\mathbf{x}^k$ as long as the set $\{\mathbf{x}^k; k = 1, 2, \dots, m\}$ is linearly independent (as opposed to the more restrictive requirement of orthogonality required by the correlation-recorded LAM). This recording technique leads to the optimal linear associative memory (OLAM) (Kohonen and Ruohonen, 1973) and is considered next.

For perfect storage of m associations $\{\mathbf{x}^k, \mathbf{y}^k\}$, a LAM's interconnection matrix $\mathbf{W}$ must satisfy the matrix equation given by

$$\mathbf{Y} = \mathbf{WX} \qquad (7.1.10)$$

with $\mathbf{Y}$ and $\mathbf{X}$ as defined earlier in this section. Equation (7.1.10) can always be solved exactly if all m vectors $\mathbf{x}^k$ (columns of $\mathbf{X}$) are linearly independent, which implies that m must be smaller or equal to n. For the case $m = n$, the matrix $\mathbf{X}$ is square, and a unique solution for $\mathbf{W}$ in Equation (7.1.10) exists, giving

$$\mathbf{W}^* = \mathbf{Y}\mathbf{X}^{-1} \qquad (7.1.11)$$

which requires that the matrix inverse $\mathbf{X}^{-1}$ exists; i.e., the set $\{\mathbf{x}^k\}$ is linearly independent. Thus this solution guarantees the perfect recall of any $\mathbf{y}^k$ on the presentation of its associated key $\mathbf{x}^k$.

Now, returning to Equation (7.1.10) with the assumption $m < n$ and that the $\mathbf{x}^k$ are linearly independent, it can be seen that an exact solution $\mathbf{W}^*$ may not be unique. In this case, one is free to choose any of the $\mathbf{W}^*$ solutions satisfying Equation (7.1.10). In particular, the minimum Euclidean norm solution (Rao and Mitra, 1971) see Problem 7.1.6 for further details) given by

$$\mathbf{W}^* = \mathbf{Y}(\mathbf{X}^\mathrm{T}\mathbf{X})^{-1}\mathbf{X}^\mathrm{T} \qquad (7.1.12)$$

is desirable because it leads to the best error-tolerant (optimal) LAM (Kohonen, 1984). Equation (7.1.12) will be referred to as the *projection recording recipe* because the matrix-vector product $(\mathbf{X}^T\mathbf{X})^{-1}\mathbf{X}^T\mathbf{x}^k$ transforms the kth stored vector $\mathbf{x}^k$ into the kth column of the $m \times m$ identity matrix. Note that for an arbitrary $\mathbf{Y}$, if the set $\{\mathbf{x}^k\}$ is orthonormal, then $\mathbf{X}^T\mathbf{X} = \mathbf{I}$ and Equation (7.1.12) reduces to the correlation recording recipe of Equation (7.1.3). An iterative version of the projection recording recipe in Equation (7.1.12) exists (Kohonen, 1984) based on Greville's theorem (Albert, 1972), which leads to the exact weight matrix $\mathbf{W}$ after exactly one presentation of each one of the m vectors $\mathbf{x}^k$. This method is convenient because a new association can be learned (or an old association can be deleted) in a single update step without involving other earlier-learned memories. Other adaptive versions of Equation (7.1.12) can be found in Hassoun (1993).

OLAM Error-Correction Capabilities   The error-correcting capabilities of OLAMs [with the projection recording in Equation (7.1.12)] has been analyzed by Kohonen (1984) and Casasent and Telfer (1987), among others, for the case of real-valued associations. The following is a brief account of the key points of such analysis. Let $\hat{\mathbf{x}}^k = \mathbf{x}^k + \mathbf{n}$, where $\mathbf{x}^k$ is the key of one of the m stored associations $\{\mathbf{x}^k, \mathbf{y}^k\}$. Also assume $\mathbf{x}^k \in R^n$ and $\mathbf{y}^k \in R^L$. The vector $\mathbf{n}$ is a noise vector of zero mean with a covariance matrix $\sigma_{in}^2\mathbf{I}$. Denote the variance of the input and output noise by σ_{in}^2 and σ_{out}^2, respectively. That is, $\sigma_{in}^2 = \langle(\hat{x}_i^k - x_i^k)^2\rangle$ and $\sigma_{out}^2 = \langle(\hat{y}_i^k - y_i^k)^2\rangle$, where $\hat{y}_i^k$ is the ith component of the retrieved vector $\hat{\mathbf{y}}^k = \mathbf{W}\hat{\mathbf{x}}^k$. Here, the expectation $\langle\cdot\rangle$ is taken over the elements of the argument vector, not over k (note that for zero-mean data, $\sigma_z^2 = \langle z^2\rangle$, which is the case for the input and output noise, since the LAM retrieval operation is linear). For an autoassociative OLAM ($\mathbf{y}^k = \mathbf{x}^k$, for all k) with a linearly independent set $\{\mathbf{x}^k\}$, the error-correction measure $\sigma_{out}^2/\sigma_{in}^2$ is given by (Kohonen, 1984)

$$\frac{\sigma_{out}^2}{\sigma_{in}^2} = \frac{m}{n} \qquad (7.1.13)$$

Thus, for linearly independent key vectors (requiring $m \le n$), the OLAM always reduces the input noise (or in the worst case when $m = n$, the input noise is not amplified). Also note that the smaller m is relative to n, the better is the noise-suppression capability of the OLAM.

For the heteroassociative case ($\mathbf{y}^k \ne \mathbf{x}^k$), it can be shown (Casasent and Telfer, 1987) that the OLAM error correction is given by

$$\frac{\sigma_{out}^2}{\sigma_{in}^2} = \langle y_{ij}^2\rangle\langle\text{Tr}(\mathbf{X}^T\mathbf{X})^{-1}\rangle \qquad (7.1.14)$$

where y_{ij} is the ijth element of matrix $\mathbf{Y}$, and $\text{Tr}(\cdot)$ is the trace operator (which simply sums the diagonal elements of the argument matrix). The first expected value operator is taken over all elements of $\mathbf{Y}$; also, both expectation operators are taken over the entire ensemble of possible recollection and key vectors, respectively. Also, it is assumed that $\mathbf{y}^k$ and $\mathbf{x}^k$ are not correlated and that the recollection vectors $\mathbf{y}^k$ have equal energy $E(\mathbf{y})$, defined as $E(\mathbf{y}) = \langle y_i^2 \rangle - \langle y_i \rangle^2$. Equation (7.1.14) shows that the error correction in a heteroassociative OLAM depends on the choice of not only the key vectors $\mathbf{x}^k$ but also the recollection vectors. Poor performance is to be expected when the matrix $\mathbf{X}^T\mathbf{X}$ is nearly singular [which leads to a large value for $\mathrm{Tr}\,(\mathbf{X}^T\mathbf{X})^{-1}$]. The reader should be warned, though, that the $\sigma_{\mathrm{out}}^2/\sigma_{\mathrm{in}}^2$ error-correction measure is not suitable for heteroassociation OLAMs because it is not normalized against variation in key/recollection vector magnitudes, also called *vector energies*; one can artificially reduce the value of this measure by merely reducing the energy of the recollection vectors $\mathbf{y}^k$ (i.e., reducing $\langle y_{ij}^2 \rangle$). The reader is referred to Problem 7.1.11 for a more appropriate error-correction measure for heteroassociative LAMs.

Error-correction characteristics of nonlinear associative memories whose transfer characteristics are described by Equation (7.1.5) and employing projection recording with uniformly distributed random bipolar binary key/recollection vectors have also been analyzed. The reader is referred to the theoretical analysis by Amari (1977a) and the empirical analysis by Stiles and Denq (1987) for details.

Strategies for Improving Memory Recording   The encoding and dimension of the input memory vectors $\mathbf{x}^k$, the total number of such memories to be stored, and the recording recipe employed highly affect the performance of an associative memory. Assuming that an associative memory architecture and a suitable recording recipe are identified, how can one improve associative retrieval and memory loading capacity? There are various strategies for enhancing associative memory performance. In the following, two example strategies are presented.

One strategy involves the use of a multiple training method (Wang et al., 1990) that emphasizes those unsuccessfully stored associations by introducing them to the weight matrix $\mathbf{W}$ through multiple recording passes until all associations are recorded. This strategy is potentially useful when correlation recording is employed. In this case, the interconnection matrix is equivalent to a weighted correlation matrix with different weights on different association pairs. Here, it is assumed that there exists a weighted correlation matrix that can store all desired association pairs.

User-defined specialized associations also may be used in a strategy for improving associative memory performance. For instance, one way to enhance the error-correction capability of an associative memory is to augment the set of association pairs $\{\mathbf{x}^k, \mathbf{y}^k\}$ to be stored with a collection of associations of the form $\{\hat{\mathbf{x}}^k, \mathbf{y}^k\}$, where $\hat{\mathbf{x}}^k$

represents a noisy version of $\mathbf{x}^k$. Here, several instances of noisy key vector versions for each desired association pair may be added. This strategy arises naturally in training pattern classifiers and is useful in enhancing the robustness of associative retrieval. The addition of specialized association pairs also may be employed when specific associations must be introduced (or eliminated). One possibility of employing this strategy is when a "default memory" is required. For example, for associations encoded such that sparse input vectors $\mathbf{s}^i$ have low information content, augmenting the original set of associations with associations of the form $\{\mathbf{s}^i, \mathbf{0}\}$ during recording leads to the creation of a default "no-decision" memory $\mathbf{0}$. This memory is retrieved when highly corrupted noisy input key vectors are input to the associative memory, thus preventing these undesirable inputs from causing the associative memory to retrieve the "wrong" memories.

The strategy of adding specialized associations increases the number of associations m to be stored and may result in $m > n$. Therefore, this strategy is not well suited for correlation LAMs. Here, one may employ a recording technique that synthesizes $\mathbf{W}$ such that the association error is minimized over all m association pairs. Mathematically speaking, the desired solution is the one that minimizes the SSE criterion function $J(\mathbf{W})$ given by

$$J(\mathbf{W}) = \|\mathbf{Y} - \mathbf{WX}\|^2 = \sum_{k=1}^{m} \sum_{i=1}^{L} (y_i^k - \tilde{y}_i^k)^2 \tag{7.1.15}$$

where y_i^k and $\tilde{y}_i^k$ are the ith components of the desired memory $\mathbf{y}^k$ and that of the estimated one, respectively. Now, by setting the gradient of $J(\mathbf{W})$ to zero and solving for $\mathbf{W}$, one arrives at the following memory storage recipe:

$$\mathbf{W} = \mathbf{Y}\mathbf{X}^{\mathrm{T}}(\mathbf{X}\mathbf{X}^{\mathrm{T}})^{-1} = \mathbf{Y}\mathbf{X}^{\dagger} \tag{7.1.16}$$

where $\mathbf{X}^{\dagger}$ is the psuedoinverse of matrix $\mathbf{X}$ (Penrose, 1955). This solution assumes that the inverse of the matrix $\mathbf{X}\mathbf{X}^{\mathrm{T}}$ exists.

7.1.2   Dynamic Associative Memories (DAMs)

Associative memory performance can be improved by using more powerful architectures than the simple ones considered above. As an example, consider the auto-associative version of the single-layer associative memory employing units with the sign-activation function and whose transfer characteristics are given by Equation (7.1.5). Now assume that this memory is capable of associative retrieval of a set of m bipolar binary memories $\{\mathbf{x}^k\}$. Upon the presentation of a key $\hat{\mathbf{x}}^k$, which is a noisy version of one of the stored memory vectors $\mathbf{x}^k$, the associative memory retrieves (in a single pass) an output $\mathbf{y}$ that is closer to stored memory $\mathbf{x}^k$ than to $\hat{\mathbf{x}}^k$. In general, only a fraction of the noise (error) in the input vector is corrected in the first pass (presentation). Intuitively, we may proceed by taking the output $\mathbf{y}$ and feeding it back as an input to the associative memory, hoping that a second pass would eliminate more of the input noise. This process could continue with more passes until we eliminate all errors and arrive at a final output $\mathbf{y}$ equal to $\mathbf{x}^k$. The retrieval procedure just described amounts to constructing a recurrent associative memory with the synchronous (parallel) dynamics given by

$$\mathbf{x}(t + 1) = F[\mathbf{W}\,\mathbf{x}(t)] \tag{7.1.17}$$

where $t = 0, 1, 2, 3, \ldots$, and $\mathbf{x}(0)$ is the initial state of the dynamical system, which is set equal to the noisy key $\hat{\mathbf{x}}^k$. For proper associative retrieval, the set of memories $\{\mathbf{x}^k\}$ must correspond to stable states (attractors) of the dynamical system in Equation (7.1.17). In this case, $\mathbf{W}$ (which is the set of all free parameters w_{ij} of the dynamical system in this simple case) should be synthesized so that starting from any initial state $\mathbf{x}(0)$, the dynamical associative memory converges to the "closest" memory state $\mathbf{x}^k$. Note that a necessary requirement for such convergent dynamics is system stability.

In the following subsections, several variations of the preceding dynamical associative memory are presented, and their stability is analyzed.

Continuous-Time, Continuous-State Model   Consider the nonlinear active electronic circuit shown in Figure 7.1.3. This circuit consists of resistors, capacitors, ideal current sources, and identical nonlinear amplifiers. Each amplifier provides an output voltage x_i given by $f(u_i)$, where u_i is the input voltage and f is a differentiable monotonically increasing nonlinear activation function, such as $\tanh(\beta u_i)$. Each amplifier is also assumed to provide an inverting terminal for producing output $-x_i$. The resistor R_{ij} connects the output voltage x_j (or $-x_j$) of the jth amplifier to the input of the ith amplifier. Since, as will be seen later, the conductances R_{ji}^{-1} play the role of interconnection weights, positive as well as "negative" resistors are required. Connecting a resistor R_{ij} to $-x_j$ helps avoid the complication of actually realizing negative resistive elements in the circuit. R and C are positive quantities and are assumed equal for all n amplifiers. Finally, the current I_i represents an external input signal (or bias) to amplifier i.

The circuit in Figure 7.1.3 is known as the *Hopfield net*. It can be thought of as a single-layer neural net of continuous nonlinear units with feedback. The ith unit in this circuit is shown in Figure 7.1.4. The dynamical equations describing the evolution of the ith state x_i, $i = 1, 2, \ldots, n$, in the Hopfield net can be derived by applying Kirchoff's current law to the input node of the ith amplifier as

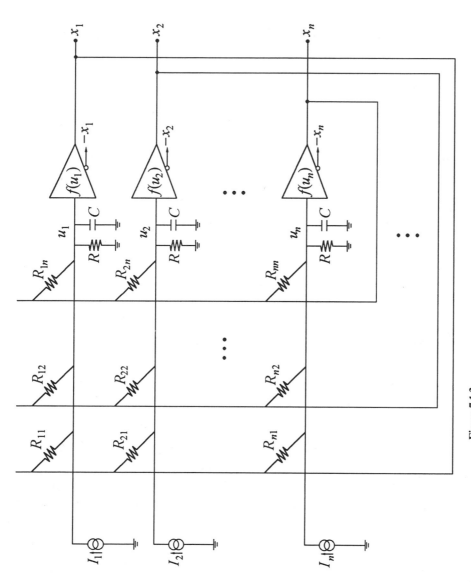

Figure 7.1.3
Circuit diagram for an electronic dynamic associative memory.

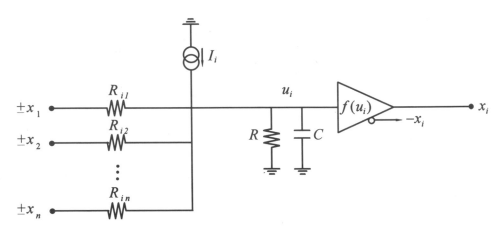

Figure 7.1.4
Circuit diagram for the ith unit of the associative memory in Figure 7.1.3.

$$C\frac{du_i}{dt} = \sum_{j=1}^{n}\frac{1}{R_{ij}}(x_j - u_i) - \frac{u_i}{R} + I_i \qquad (7.1.18)$$

which can also be written as

$$C\frac{du_i}{dt} = -\alpha_i u_i + \sum_{j=1}^{n} w_{ij} f(u_j) + I_i \qquad (7.1.19)$$

where

$$\alpha_i = \sum_{j=1}^{n}\frac{1}{R_{ij}} + \frac{1}{R} \qquad \text{and} \qquad w_{ij} = \frac{1}{R_{ij}}$$

(or $w_{ij} = -1/R_{ij}$ if the inverting output of unit j is connected to unit i). The preceding Hopfield net can be considered as a special case of a more general dynamical network developed and studied by Cohen and Grossberg (1983) that has an ith state dynamics expressed by:

$$\tau_i \frac{du_i}{dt} = -\alpha_i u_i + (\gamma_i - \beta_i u_i)\left[\sum_{j=1}^{n} w_{ij} f_j(u_j) + I_i\right] \qquad (7.1.20)$$

The overall dynamics of the Hopfield net can be described in compact matrix form as

$$\mathbf{C}\frac{d\mathbf{u}}{dt} = -\alpha\mathbf{u} + \mathbf{W}\mathbf{x} + \boldsymbol{\theta} \qquad (7.1.21)$$

where $\mathbf{C} = C\mathbf{I}$ ($\mathbf{I}$ is the identity matrix), $\boldsymbol{\alpha} = \text{diag}(\alpha_1, \alpha_2, \ldots, \alpha_n)$, $\mathbf{x} = F(\mathbf{u}) = [f(u_1) \quad f(u_2) \quad \cdots \quad f(u_n)]^T$, $\boldsymbol{\theta} = [I_1 \quad I_2 \quad \cdots \quad I_n]^T$, and $\mathbf{W}$ is an interconnection matrix defined as

$$\mathbf{W} = \begin{bmatrix} w_{11} & w_{12} & \cdots & w_{1n} \\ w_{21} & w_{22} & \cdots & w_{2n} \\ \vdots & \vdots & \ddots & \vdots \\ w_{n1} & w_{n2} & \cdots & w_{nn} \end{bmatrix}$$

The equilibria of the dynamics in Equation (7.1.21) are determined by setting $\dfrac{d\mathbf{u}}{dt} = \mathbf{0}$, giving

$$\boldsymbol{\alpha}\mathbf{u} = \mathbf{W}\mathbf{x} + \boldsymbol{\theta} = \mathbf{W}F(\mathbf{u}) + \boldsymbol{\theta} \tag{7.1.22}$$

A sufficient condition for the Hopfield net to be stable is that the interconnection matrix $\mathbf{W}$ be symmetric (Hopfield, 1984). Furthermore, Hopfield showed that the stable states of the network are the local minima of the bounded Liapunov function

$$E(\mathbf{x}) = -\tfrac{1}{2}\mathbf{x}^T\mathbf{W}\mathbf{x} - \mathbf{x}^T\boldsymbol{\theta} + \sum_{j=1}^{n} \alpha_j \int_0^{x_j} f^{-1}(\xi)\,d\xi \tag{7.1.23}$$

where $\mathbf{x} = [x_1 \quad x_2 \quad \cdots \quad x_n]^T$ is the net's output state, and $f^{-1}(x_j)$ is the inverse of the activation function $x_j = f(u_j)$. Note that the value of the right-most term in Equation (7.1.23) depends on the specific shape of the nonlinear activation function f. In the limit of high-gain (β approaching infinity), $f(u_j)$ approaches the sign function; i.e., the amplifiers in the Hopfield net become threshold elements. In this case, the Liapunov function [also known as the *computational energy* for the system given in Equation (7.1.22)] becomes approximately the quadratic function

$$E(\mathbf{x}) = -\tfrac{1}{2}\mathbf{x}^T\mathbf{W}\mathbf{x} - \mathbf{x}^T\boldsymbol{\theta} \tag{7.1.24}$$

It has been shown (Hopfield, 1984) that the only stable states of the high-gain, continuous-time, continuous-state system in Equation (7.1.21) are the corners of the hypercube; i.e., the local minima of Equation (7.1.24) are states $\mathbf{x}^* \in \{-1, +1\}^n$. For large but finite amplifier gains, the third term in Equation (7.1.23) begins to contribute. The sigmoidal nature of $f(u)$ leads to a large positive contribution near hypercube boundaries but negligible contribution far from the boundaries. This causes a slight drift of the stable states toward the interior of the hypercube.

Another way of looking at the Hopfield net is as a gradient system. To see this, simply take the gradient of E with respect to the state $\mathbf{x}$ and compare with Equation (7.1.21). Hence, by equating terms, we have the following gradient system:

$$\frac{d\mathbf{u}}{dt} = -\boldsymbol{\rho}\nabla E(\mathbf{x}) \tag{7.1.25}$$

where $\boldsymbol{\rho} = \text{diag}(1/C, 1/C, \ldots, 1/C)$. Now the gradient system in Equation (7.1.25) converges asymptotically to an equilibrium state that is a local minimum or a saddle point of the energy E (Hirsch and Smale, 1974) (fortunately, the unavoidable noise in practical applications prevents the system from staying at the saddle points, and convergence to a local minimum is achieved). To see this, we first note that the equilibria of the system described by Equation (7.1.25) correspond to local minima (or maxima or points of inflection) of $E(\mathbf{x})$, since $\dfrac{d\mathbf{u}}{dt} = \mathbf{0}$ means that $\nabla E(\mathbf{x}) = \mathbf{0}$. For each isolated local minimum $\mathbf{x}^*$, there exists a neighborhood Σ over which the candidate function $V(\mathbf{x}) = E(\mathbf{x}) - E(\mathbf{x}^*)$ has continuous first partial derivatives and is strictly positive except at $\mathbf{x}^*$, where $V(\mathbf{x}^*) = 0$. Additionally,

$$\frac{dV}{dt} = \frac{dE}{dt} = \nabla E(\mathbf{x})^{\mathrm{T}}\dot{\mathbf{x}}(t) = \sum_{j=1}^{n}\frac{\partial E}{\partial x_j}\frac{dx_j}{dt} = -C\sum_{j=1}^{n}\frac{du_j}{dt}\frac{dx_j}{dt} = -C\sum_{j=1}^{n}\frac{dx_j}{du_j}\left(\frac{du_j}{dt}\right)^2 \tag{7.1.26}$$

is always negative [since $\dfrac{dx_j}{du_j}$ is always positive because of the monotonically nondecreasing nature of the relation $x_j = f(u_j)$] or zero at $\mathbf{x}^*$. Hence V is a Liapunov function, and $\mathbf{x}^*$ is asymptotically stable.[1]

---

1. The second, or direct, method of Liapunov (see D'Azzo and Houpis, 1988) provides a means for determining the stability of a system without explicitly computing the solution trajectories in state space. This method comes in the form of two theorems which are stated next. It differs from Liapunov's first method, which requires determination of the eigenvalues from the linearized equations about an equilibrium point (see footnote 4 in Chapter 4). Liapunov's second method is very general in that it may be generalized to systems which may be linear or nonlinear, time-invariant or time-varying, forced or unforced, deterministic or stochastic, and continuous or discrete.

The Liapunov Asymptotic Stability Theorem   A system of the form $\dot{\mathbf{x}} = f(\mathbf{x})$ has an asymptotically stable equilibrium point $\mathbf{x}^*$ if there exists a scalar function $V(\mathbf{x})$ such that

1. $V(\mathbf{x})$ is continuous and has continuous first partial derivatives in a neighborhood Σ containing $\mathbf{x}^*$.
2. $V(\mathbf{x}) > 0$ in $\Sigma - \mathbf{x}^*$ (i.e., in the neighborhood Σ excluding $\mathbf{x}^*$).
3. $V(\mathbf{x}^*) = 0$.
4. $\dfrac{dV(\mathbf{x})}{dt} < 0$ in $\Sigma - \mathbf{x}^*$. (If $\dfrac{dV}{dt} \leq 0$ in $\Sigma - \mathbf{x}^*$, then $\mathbf{x}^*$ is stable but not asymptotically stable.)

The operation of the Hopfield net as an autoassociative memory is straightforward; given a set of memories $\{\mathbf{x}^k\}$, the interconnection matrix $\mathbf{W}$ is encoded such that the vectors $\mathbf{x}^k$ become local minima of the Hopfield net's energy function $E(\mathbf{x})$. Then, when the net is initialized with a noisy key $\hat{\mathbf{x}}$, its output state evolves along the negative gradient of $E(\mathbf{x})$ until it reaches the closest local minima, which, hopefully, is one of the fundamental memories $\mathbf{x}^k$. In general, however, $E(\mathbf{x})$ will have additional local minima other than the desired ones encoded in $\mathbf{W}$. These additional undesirable stable states are referred to as *spurious memories*.

When used as a DAM, the Hopfield net is operated with very high activation function gains and with binary-valued stored memories. The synthesis of $\mathbf{W}$ can be done according to the correlation recording recipe of Equation (7.1.3) or the more optimal recipe in Equation (7.1.12). These recording recipes lead to symmetric $\mathbf{W}$'s (since autoassociative operation is assumed; i.e., $\mathbf{y}^k = \mathbf{x}^k$ for all k), which guarantees the stability of retrievals. Note that the external bias may be eliminated in such DAMs. The elimination of bias, the symmetric $\mathbf{W}$, and the use of high gain amplifiers in such DAMs lead to the truncated energy function

$$E(\mathbf{x}) = -\tfrac{1}{2}\mathbf{x}^T\mathbf{W}\mathbf{x} \tag{7.1.27}$$

Additional properties of these DAMs are explored in Problems 7.1.13 through 7.1.15.

The Liapunov Global Asymptotic Stability Theorem   A system is globally asymptotically stable if there is only one equilibrium point $\mathbf{x}^*$ and there exists a scalar function $V(\mathbf{x})$ such that

1. $V(\mathbf{x})$ is continuous and has continuous first partial derivatives in the entire state space.
2. $V(\mathbf{x}) > 0$ for all $\mathbf{x} \neq \mathbf{x}^*$.
3. $V(\mathbf{x}^*) = 0$.
4. $V(\mathbf{x}) \to \infty$ at $\|\mathbf{x}\| \to \infty$.
5. $\dfrac{dV(\mathbf{x})}{dt} \leq 0$.
6. Either $\dfrac{dV(\mathbf{x})}{dt} \neq 0$ except at $\mathbf{x} = \mathbf{x}^*$ or any locus in the state space where $\dfrac{dV(\mathbf{x})}{dt} = 0$ is not a trajectory of the system.

For discrete-time systems, the derivative $\dfrac{dV(\mathbf{x})}{dt}$ in the preceding theorems is replaced by the first difference, $\Delta V(\mathbf{x}) = V[\mathbf{x}(k + 1)] - V[\mathbf{x}(k)]$. Note that the Liapunov theorems give no indication as to how a Liapunov function might be found. In practice, an appropriate $V(\mathbf{x})$ is formulated either by pure guess or tempered by physical insight and energy-like considerations (for an example of the latter, see Problem 7.5.6). For linear systems, a quadratic $V(\mathbf{x})$ may be assumed (see Problem 7.5.7). On the other hand, finding an appropriate Liapunov function for general nonlinear systems is difficult [methods for synthesizing $V(\mathbf{x})$ have been reported in the literature but are generally elaborate. For example, see the variable gradient method proposed by Schultz and Gibson (1962)].

Discrete-Time, Continuous-State Model   An alternative model for retrieving the stable states (attractors) can be derived by employing the relaxation method (also known as the *fixed-point method*) for iteratively solving Equation (7.1.22) (Cichocki and Unbehauen, 1993). Here, an initial guess $\mathbf{x}(0)$ for an attractor state is used as the initial search point in the relaxation search. Starting from Equation (7.1.22) with $\boldsymbol{\alpha} = \mathbf{I}$ (without loss of generality) and recalling that $\mathbf{u} = F^{-1}(\mathbf{x})$, one may write the relaxation equation

$$F^{-1}[\mathbf{x}(k + 1)] = \mathbf{W}\mathbf{x}(k) + \boldsymbol{\theta} \qquad k = 0, 1, 2, \dots \qquad (7.1.28)$$

or, by solving for $\mathbf{x}(k + 1)$,

$$\mathbf{x}(k + 1) = F[\mathbf{W}\mathbf{x}(k) + \boldsymbol{\theta}] \qquad (7.1.29)$$

Equation (7.1.29) describes the dynamics of a discrete-time, continuous-state, synchronously updated DAM. For $\boldsymbol{\theta} = \mathbf{0}$, Equation (7.1.29) is identical to Equation (7.1.17), which was derived intuitively, except that the unit activations in the preceding relaxation model are of sigmoid type as opposed to the threshold type (sgn) assumed in Equation (7.1.17). Also, when the unit activations are piece-wise linear, Equation (7.1.29) leads to a special case of the BSB model discussed in Section 7.4.1. The parallel update nature of this DAM is appealing because it leads to faster convergence (in software simulations) and easier hardware implementations as compared with the continuous-time Hopfield model.

Most current implementations of continuous-time neural networks are done using computer simulations that are necessarily discrete-time implementations. However, the stability results obtained earlier for the continuous-time DAM do not necessarily hold for the discrete-time versions. Thus it is important to have a rigorous discrete-time analysis of the stability of the dynamics in Equation (7.1.29). Marcus and Westervelt (1989) showed that the function

$$E(\mathbf{x}) = -\frac{1}{2}\sum_{i=1}^{n}\sum_{j=1}^{n} w_{ij}x_i x_j - \sum_{j=1}^{n} I_j x_j + \sum_{j=1}^{n} G(x_j) \qquad (7.1.30)$$

where

$$G(x_j) \triangleq \int_0^{x_j} f^{-1}(x)\,dx \qquad (7.1.31)$$

is a Liapunov function for the DAM in Equation (7.1.29) when $\mathbf{W}$ is symmetric and the activation gain β [e.g., assume $f(x) = \tanh(\beta x)$] satisfies the condition

$$\frac{1}{\beta} > -\lambda_{\min} \qquad (7.1.32)$$

Here, λ_{min} is the smallest eigenvalue of the interconnection matrix $\mathbf{W}$. Equation (7.1.30) is identical to Equation (7.1.23), since it is assumed that $\alpha_j = 1, j = 1, 2, \ldots, n$. If $\mathbf{W}$ has no negative eigenvalues, then Equation (7.1.32) is satisfied by any value of β, since $\beta > 0$. On the other hand, if $\mathbf{W}$ has one or more negative eigenvalues, then λ_{min}, the most negative of them, places an upper limit on the gain for stability.

To prove that E in Equation (7.1.30) is a Liapunov function when Equation (7.1.32) is satisfied, consider the change in E between two discrete time steps:

$$\Delta E(k) = E(k+1) - E(k)$$

$$= -\frac{1}{2} \sum_i \sum_j w_{ij} x_i(k+1) x_j(k+1) + \frac{1}{2} \sum_i \sum_j w_{ij} x_i(k) x_j(k) \qquad (7.1.33)$$

$$- \sum_i I_i[x_i(k+1) - x_i(k)] + \sum_i \{G[x_i(k+1)] - G[x_i(k)]\}$$

Using the update equation for x_i from Equation (7.1.29) and the symmetry property of $\mathbf{W}$, Equation (7.1.33) becomes

$$\Delta E(k) = -\frac{1}{2} \sum_i \sum_j w_{ij} \Delta x_i(k) \Delta x_j(k) - \sum_i f^{-1}[x_i(k+1)] \Delta x_i(k)$$

$$+ \sum_i \{G[x_i(k+1)] - G[x_i(k)]\} \qquad (7.1.34)$$

when $\Delta x_i(k) = x_i(k+1) - x_i(k)$. The last term in Equation (7.1.34) is related to $\Delta x_i(k)$ by the inequality (Marcus and Westervelt, 1989)

$$G[x_i(k+1)] - G[x_i(k)] \le \dot{G}[x_i(k+1)] \Delta x_i(k) - \frac{1}{2\beta} [\Delta x_i(k)]^2 \qquad (7.1.35)$$

where $\dot{G}(x) = \dfrac{dG(x)}{dx}$ or, by using Equation (7.1.31), $\dot{G}(x) = f^{-1}(x)$. Combining Equations (7.1.34) and (7.1.35) leads to

$$\Delta E(k) \le -\frac{1}{2} \sum_i \sum_j \left(w_{ij} + \delta_{ij} \frac{1}{\beta} \right) \Delta x_i(k) \Delta x_j(k) = -\frac{1}{2} \Delta \mathbf{x}(k)^\mathrm{T} \left(\mathbf{W} + \frac{1}{\beta} \mathbf{I} \right) \Delta \mathbf{x}(k) \quad (7.1.36)$$

where $\Delta \mathbf{x}(k) = \mathbf{x}(k+1) - \mathbf{x}(k)$, and $\delta_{ij} = 1$ for $i = j$ and $\delta_{ij} = 0$ otherwise. Now if the matrix $\mathbf{W} + (1/\beta)\mathbf{I}$ is positive definite, then $\Delta E(k) \le 0$ [equality holds only when $\Delta \mathbf{x}(k) = \mathbf{0}$, which implies that the network has reached an attractor].[2] The require-

---

2. A real symmetric matrix $\mathbf{A}$ is positive definite if the quadratic form $\mathbf{x}^\mathrm{T}\mathbf{A}\mathbf{x}$ is strictly positive for all $\mathbf{x} \ne \mathbf{0}$ or, equivalently, if all eigenvalues of $\mathbf{A}$ are strictly positive.

ment that $\mathbf{W} + (1/\beta)\mathbf{I}$ be positive definite is satisfied by the inequality of Equation (7.1.32).[3] This result, combined with the fact that $E(k)$ is bounded, shows that the function in Equation (7.1.30) is a Liapunov function for the DAM in Equation (7.1.29), and thus the DAM is stable. If, on the other hand, the inequality of Equation (7.1.32) is violated, then it can be shown that the DAM can develop period-2 limit cycles (Marcus and Westervelt, 1989).

Discrete-Time, Discrete-State Model   Starting with the dynamical system in Equation (7.1.29) and replacing the continuous activation function by the sign function, one arrives at the discrete-time, discrete-state, parallel (synchronous) updated DAM model where all states $x_i(k)$, $i = 1, 2, \ldots, n$, are updated simultaneously according to

$$x_i(k + 1) = \mathrm{sgn}\left[\sum_{j=1}^{n} w_{ij} x_j(k) + I_i \right] \tag{7.1.37}$$

Another version of this DAM operates in a serial (asynchronous) mode. It assumes the same dynamics as Equation (7.1.37) for the ith unit, but only one unit updates its state at a given time. The unit that updates its state is chosen randomly and independently of the times of firing of the remaining $(n - 1)$ units in the DAM. This asynchronously updated discrete-state DAM is commonly known as the *discrete Hopfield net*, which was originally proposed and analyzed by Hopfield (1982). In its original form, this net was proposed as an associative memory that employed the correlation recording recipe for memory storage.

It can be shown (see Problem 7.1.17) that the discrete Hopfield net with a symmetric interconnection matrix ($w_{ij} = w_{ji}$) and with nonnegative diagonal elements ($w_{ii} \geq 0$) is stable with the same Liapunov function as that of a continuous-time Hopfield net in the limit of high amplifier gain; i.e., it has the Liapunov function in Equation (7.1.24). Hopfield (1984) showed that both nets (discrete and continuous nets with the preceding assumptions) have identical energy maxima and minima. This implies that there is a one-to-one correspondence between the memories of the two models. Also, since the two models may be viewed as minimizing the same energy function E, one would expect that the macroscopic behavior of the two models is very similar; i.e., both models will perform similar memory retrievals.

---

3. Let $\lambda_{\min}$ be the smallest eigenvalue of $\mathbf{W}$; then the matrix $\mathbf{W} + (1/\beta)\mathbf{I}$ is positive definite if all eigenvalues of $\mathbf{W} + (1/\beta)\mathbf{I}$ are strictly positive, which is the case if $\lambda_{\min} + 1/\beta > 0$ or $1/\beta > -\lambda_{\min}$.

7.2   DAM Capacity and Retrieval Dynamics

In this section, the capacity and retrieval characteristics of the autoassociative DAMs introduced in the preceding section are analyzed. Correlation-recorded DAMs are considered first, followed by projection-recorded DAMs.

7.2.1   Correlation DAMs

DAM capacity is a measure of the ability of a DAM to store a set of m unbiased random binary patterns $\mathbf{x}^k \in \{-1, +1\}$ (i.e., the vector components x_i^k are independent random variables taking values 1 or -1 with probability $\frac{1}{2}$) and at the same time be capable of associative recall (error correction). A commonly used capacity measure, known as *absolute capacity*, takes the form of an upper bound on the pattern ratio m/n in the limit $n \to \infty$ such that all stored memories are equilibrium points, with a probability approaching 1. This capacity measure, though, does not assume any error-correction behavior; i.e., it does not require that the fundamental memories $\mathbf{x}^k$ be attractors with associated basins of attraction. Another capacity measure, known as *relative capacity*, has been proposed that is an upper bound on m/n such that the fundamental memories or their "approximate" versions are attractors (stable equilibria).

It has been shown (Amari, 1977a; Hopfield, 1982; Amit et al., 1985) that if most of the memories in a correlation-recorded discrete Hopfield DAM, with $w_{ii} = 0$, are to be remembered approximately (i.e., nonperfect retrieval is allowed), then m/n must not exceed 0.15. This value is the relative capacity of the DAM. Another result on the capacity of this DAM for the case of error-free memory recall by one-pass parallel convergence is (in probability) given by the absolute capacity (Weisbuch and Fogelman-Soulié, 1985; McEliece et al., 1987; Amari and Maginu, 1988; Newman, 1988), expressed as the limit

$$\max\left(\frac{m}{n}\right) \to \frac{1}{4\ln n} \qquad \text{as } n \to \infty \tag{7.2.1}$$

Equation (7.2.1) indicates that the absolute capacity approaches zero as n approaches infinity! Thus the correlation-recorded discrete Hopfield net is an inefficient DAM model. The absolute-capacity result in Equation (7.2.1) is derived below.

Assuming $\mathbf{y}^k = \mathbf{x}^k$ (autoassociative case) in Equation (7.1.7) and $w_{ii} = 0$, $i = 1, 2, \ldots, n$, then by direct recall from initial input $\mathbf{x}(0) = \mathbf{x}^h$ with $\mathbf{x}^h \in \{\mathbf{x}^k\}$, the ith bit of the retrieved state $\mathbf{x}(1)$ is given by

$$x_i(1) = \text{sgn}\left[\frac{(n-1)}{n}x_i(0) + \frac{1}{n}\sum_{\substack{j \neq i}}^{n}\sum_{\substack{k \neq h}}^{m} x_i^k x_j^k x_j(0)\right]$$

$$\approx \text{sgn}\left[x_i(0) + \Delta_i(0)\right] \tag{7.2.2}$$

Consider the quantity $C_i(0) = -x_i(0)\Delta_i(0)$. Now, if $C_i(0)$ is negative, then $x_i(0)$ and $\Delta_i(0)$ have the same sign, and the cross-talk term $\Delta_i(0)$ does no harm. On the other hand, if $C_i(0)$ is positive and larger than 1, then the one-pass retrieved bit $x_i(1)$ is in error. Next, assume that the stored memories are random, with equal probability for $x_i^k = +1$ and for $x_i^k = -1$, independently for each k and i. Hence, for large m and n, the $C_i(0)$ term is approximately distributed according to a normal distribution $N(\mu, \sigma^2) = N(0, m/n)$. To see this, first note that $\Delta_i(0)$, and equivalently $C_i(0)$, is $1/n$ times the sum of $(n-1)(m-1)$ independent and uniformly distributed random bipolar binary numbers, and thus it has a binomial distribution with zero mean and variance $\sigma^2 = [(n-1)(m-1)]/n^2$. Thus, by the central limit theorem, $C_i(0)$ approaches $N(0, m/n)$ asymptotically as m and n become large (Mosteller et al., 1970). Therefore, we may compute the probability that $x_i(1)$ is in error, $P_{error} = \text{Prob}(C_i(0) > 1)$, by integrating $N(0, m/n)$ from 1 to ∞, giving

$$P_{error} = \left(\frac{2\pi m}{n}\right)^{-1/2} \int_1^\infty e^{-\xi^2/(2m/n)}\, d\xi = \frac{1}{2}\left[1 - \text{erf}\left(\sqrt{\frac{n}{2m}}\right)\right] \qquad (7.2.3)$$

where $\text{erf}(x) = (2/\sqrt{\pi})\int_0^x e^{-\xi^2}\, d\xi$ is the error function. Note that Equation (7.2.3) is a special case of Equation (7.1.8) where D_{in} in Equation (7.1.8) is set to zero. Now, using the fact that for a random variable x distributed according to $N(0, \sigma^2)$, $\text{Prob}(x > 3\sigma) = 0.0014$, and if the ith bit $x_i(1)$ in Equation (7.2.2) is required to be retrievable with error probability less than 0.0014, then the condition $3\sigma < 1$ or $m/n < 1/9$ must be satisfied. Therefore, $m < 0.111n$ is required for $P_{error} \leq 0.0014$. Similarly, Equation (7.2.3) can be solved for the requirement $P_{error} \approx 0.005$, which gives $m/n = 0.15$.

On the other hand, if all memories $\mathbf{x}^k$ are required to be equilibria of the DAM with a probability close to 1, say 0.99, then an upper bound on m/n can be derived by requiring that all bits of all memories $\mathbf{x}^k$ be retrievable with less than a 1 percent error; i.e., $(1 - P_{error})^{mn} > 0.99$. Employing the binomial expansion, this inequality may be approximated as $P_{error} < 0.01/(mn)$. Noting that this stringent error-correction requirement necessitates small m/n values, Equation (7.2.3) can be approximated using the asymptotic $(x \to \infty)$ expansion $1 - \text{erf}(x) \cong [1/(\sqrt{\pi}x)]e^{-x^2}$. This approximation can then be used to write the inequality $P_{error} < 0.01/(mn)$ as

$$P_{error} \cong \frac{1}{2}\frac{e^{-n/(2m)}}{\sqrt{\pi n/(2m)}} < \frac{0.01}{mn} \qquad (7.2.4)$$

Now, taking the natural logarithm (ln) of both sides of the inequality in Equation (7.2.4) and eliminating all constants and the $\ln(n/m)$ factor (since they are dominated by higher-order terms) results in the bound

$$\frac{m}{n} < \frac{1}{2 \ln(mn)} \qquad n \to \infty \qquad (7.2.5)$$

By noting that $\ln(mn) < \ln n^2$ (since $n > m$), a more stringent requirement on m/n in Equation (7.2.5) becomes

$$\frac{m}{n} < \frac{1}{2 \ln n^2} = \frac{1}{4 \ln n} \qquad n \to \infty \qquad (7.2.6)$$

which represents the absolute capacity of a zero-diagonal, correlation-recorded DAM. The effects of a nonzero diagonal on DAM capacity are treated in Section 7.4.3.

Another, more useful DAM capacity measure gives a bound on m/n in terms of error correction and memory size (Weisbuch and Fogelman-Soulié, 1985; McEliece et al., 1987). According to this capacity measure, a correlation-recorded discrete Hopfield DAM must have its pattern ratio m/n satisfy

$$\frac{m}{n} < \frac{(1 - 2\rho)^2}{4 \ln n} \qquad n \to \infty \qquad (7.2.7)$$

in order that error-free one-pass retrieval of a fundamental memory (say $\mathbf{x}^k$) from random key patterns lying inside the Hamming hypersphere (centered at $\mathbf{x}^k$) of radius ρn ($\rho < \frac{1}{2}$) is achieved with probability approaching 1. Here, ρ defines the radius of attraction of a fundamental memory. In other words, ρ is the largest normalized Hamming distance from a fundamental memory within which almost all the initial states reach this fundamental memory in one-pass. The inequality in Equation (7.2.7) can be derived by starting with an equation similar to Equation (7.2.2) with one difference that the input $\mathbf{x}(0)$ is not one of the stored memories. Rather, a random input $\mathbf{x}(0)$ is assumed that has an overlap $(1/n)(\mathbf{x}^h)^T\mathbf{x}(0) = 1 - 2\rho$ with one of the stored memories, say $\mathbf{x}^h$. Here, one can readily show that the ith retrieved bit $x_i(1)$ is in error if and only if $C_i(0) > 1 - 2\rho$. The error probability for the ith bit is then given by Equation (7.2.3), with the lower limit on the integral replaced by $1 - 2\rho$. This leads to $P_{\text{error}} = \frac{1}{2}\left\{ 1 - \text{erf}\left[(1 - 2\rho)\sqrt{\frac{n}{2m}} \right] \right\}$ which, by using a similar derivation to the one leading to Equation (7.2.6), leads us to Equation (7.2.7).

The capacity analysis leading to Equations (7.2.6) and (7.2.7) assumed a single parallel retrieval iteration, starting from $\mathbf{x}(0)$ and retrieving $\mathbf{x}(1)$. This same analysis cannot be applied if one starts the DAM at $\mathbf{x}(k)$, $k = 1, 2, \ldots$; i.e., Equations (7.2.6) and (7.2.7) are not valid for the second or higher DAM iterations. In this case, the analysis is more complicated due to the fact that $\mathbf{x}(k)$ becomes correlated with the stored memory vectors, and hence the statistical properties of the noise term $\Delta_i(k)$ in Equation (7.2.2) are more difficult to determine [in fact, such correlations depend on the whole history of $\mathbf{x}(k-T)$, $T = 0, 1, 2, \ldots$]. Amari and Maginu (1988) [see also Amari and Yanai (1993)] analyzed the transient dynamical behavior of memory recall under the assumption of a normally distributed $\Delta_i(k)$ [or $C_i(k)$] with mean zero and variance $\sigma^2(k)$. This variance was calculated by taking the direct correlations up to two steps between the bits of the stored memories and those in $\mathbf{x}(k)$. Under these assumptions, the relative capacity was found to be equal to 0.16. This theoretical value is in good agreement with early simulations reported by Hopfield (1982) and with the theoretical value of 0.14 reported by Amit et al. (1985) using a method known as the *replica method*.

Komlós and Paturi (1988) showed that if Equation (7.2.6) is satisfied, then the DAM is capable of error correction when multiple-pass retrievals are considered. In other words, they showed that each of the fundamental memories is an attractor with a basin of attraction surrounding it. They also showed that once initialized inside one of these basins of attraction, the state converges (in probability) to the basin's attractor in order $\ln(\ln n)$ parallel steps. Burshtien (1993) took these results a step further by showing that the radius of the basin of attraction for each fundamental memory is $\rho n = n/2$, independent of the retrieval mode (serial or parallel). He also showed that a relatively small number of parallel iterations, asymptotically independent of n, is required to recover a fundamental memory even when ρ is very close to $\frac{1}{2}$ (e.g., for $\rho = 0.499$, at most 20 iterations are required).

When initialized with a key input $\mathbf{x}(0)$ lying outside the basins of attraction of fundamental memories, the discrete Hopfield DAM converges to one of an exponential (in n) number of spurious memories. These memories are linear combinations of fundamental memories (Amit et al., 1985; Gardner, 1986; Komlos and Paturi, 1988). Thus a large number of undesirable spurious states that compete with fundamental memories for basins of attraction "volumes" are intrinsic to correlation-recorded discrete Hopfield DAMs.

Next, the capacity and retrieval characteristics of two analog (continuous-state) correlation-recorded DAMs (one continuous-time and the other discrete-time parallel updated) based on models introduced in the preceding section are analyzed. The first analog DAM considered here will be referred to as the *continuous-time DAM* in the remainder of this section. It is obtained from Equation (7.1.21) by setting $\mathbf{C} = \boldsymbol{\alpha} = \mathbf{I}$ and $\boldsymbol{\theta} = \mathbf{0}$. Its interconnection matrix $\mathbf{W}$ is defined by the autocorrelation version of Equation (7.1.6) with zero diagonal. The second analog DAM is obtained from Equation (7.1.29) with $\boldsymbol{\theta} = \mathbf{0}$. It employs the normalized correlation recording recipe for $\mathbf{W}$

with zero diagonal as for the continuous-time DAM. This latter analog DAM will be referred to as the *discrete-time DAM* in this section. Both DAMs employ the hyperbolic tangent activation function with gain β.

The dynamics of these two DAMs have been studied in terms of the gain β and the pattern ratio m/n for unbiased random bipolar stored memories (Amit et al., 1985, 1987; Marcus et al., 1990; Shiino and Fukai, 1990; Kühn et al., 1991; Waugh et al., 1993). Figure 7.2.1 shows two analytically derived *phase diagrams* for the continuous-time and discrete-time DAMs, valid in the limit of large n (Marcus et al., 1990; Waugh et al., 1993). These diagrams indicate the type of attractors as a function of activation function gain β and pattern ratio m/n. For the continuous-time DAM, the diagram (Figure 7.2.1a) shows three regions labeled origin, spin glass, and recall. In the recall region, the DAM is capable of either exact or approximate associative retrieval of stored memories. In other words, a set of $2m$ attractors exist, each having a large overlap (inner product) with a stored pattern or its inverse (the stability of the inverse of a stored memory is explored in Problem 7.1.13). This region also contains attractors corresponding to spurious states that have negligible overlaps with the stored memories (or their inverse). In the spin-glass region [so named because of the similarity to dynamical behavior of simple models of magnetic material (spin glasses) in statistical physics], the desired memories are no longer attractors; hence the only attractors are spurious states. Finally, in the origin region, the DAM has the single attractor state $\mathbf{x} = \mathbf{0}$.

The boundary separating the recall and spin-glass regions determines the relative capacity of the DAM. For the continuous-time DAM, and in the limit of high-gain β ($\beta > 10$), this boundary asymptotes at $m/n \approx 0.14$, which is essentially the relative capacity of the correlation-recorded discrete Hopfield DAM analyzed earlier in this section. This result supports the arguments presented at the end of Section 7.1.2 on the equivalence of the macroscopic dynamics of the discrete Hopfield net and the continuous-time, high-gain Hopfield net.

The phase diagram for the discrete-time DAM is identical to the one for the continuous-time DAM except for the presence of a fourth region marked oscillation in Figure 7.2.1b. In this region, the stability condition in Equation (7.1.32) is violated (note that the zero-diagonal autocorrelation weight matrix can have negative eigenvalues; see Problem 7.2.1). Associative retrieval and spurious states may still exist in this region (especially if m/n is small), but the DAM can also become trapped in period-2 limit cycles (oscillations). In both DAMs, error-correction capabilities cease to exist at activation gains close to or smaller than 1 even as m/n approaches zero.

The boundary separating the recall and spin-glass regions has been computed by methods that combine the Liapunov function approach with the statistical

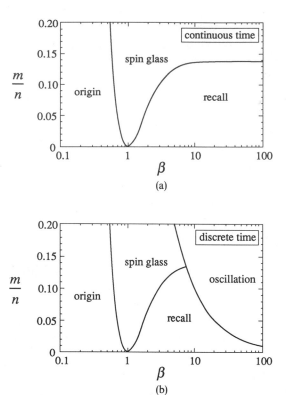

Figure 7.2.1
Phase diagrams for correlation-recorded analog DAMs
with activation function $f(u) = \tanh(\beta u)$ for (a) continuous-time and (b) parallel discrete-time updating. (Adapted
from Marcus et al., 1990, with permission of the American
Physical Society.)

mechanics of disordered systems. The boundary between the spin-glass and origin regions in Figure 7.2.1*a* and *b* is given by the expression

$$\beta = \frac{1}{1 + 2\sqrt{m/n}} \tag{7.2.8}$$

This expression can be derived by performing local stability analysis about the equilibrium point $\mathbf{x}^* = \mathbf{0}$ that defines the origin region. This method is explored in Problems 7.2.2 and 7.2.3 for the continuous-time and discrete-time DAMs, respectively.

The associative retrieval capability of the preceding analog DAMs can vary considerably even within the recall region. It has been shown analytically and empirically that the basin of attraction of fundamental memories increases substantially as the activation function gain decreases with fixed pattern ratio m/n for values of $m/n \leq$ 0.15. Waugh et al. (1991, 1993) showed that the number of local minima (and thus spurious states) in the energy function of the preceding DAMs increases exponentially as $\exp(ng)$, where $g = g(m/n, \beta)$. Here, g is monotonically increasing in β. Therefore, even a small decrease in β can lead to substantial reduction in the number of local minima, especially the shallow ones which correspond to spurious memories. The reason behind the improved DAM performance as gain decreases is that the energy function becomes smoother so that shallow local minima are eliminated. Since the fundamental memories tend to lie in wide, deep basins, essentially all the local minima eliminated correspond to spurious memories. This phenomenon is termed *deterministic annealing*, and it is reminiscent of what happens as temperature increases in simulated annealing (the reader is referred to the next chapter for a discussion of annealing methods in the context of neural networks).

7.2.2   Projection DAMs

The capacity and performance of autoassociative correlation-recorded DAMs can be greatly improved if projection recording is used to store the desired memory vectors [recall Equation (7.1.12), with $\mathbf{Y} = \mathbf{X}$]. Here, any set of memories can be memorized without errors as long as they are linearly independent (note that linear independence restricts m to be less than or equal to n). In particular, projection DAMs are well suited for memorizing unbiased random vectors $\mathbf{x}^k \in \{-1, +1\}^n$, since it can be shown that the probability of m ($m < n$) of these vectors being linearly independent approaches 1 in the limit of large n (Komlós, 1967). In the following, the retrieval properties of projection-recorded discrete-time DAMs are analyzed. More specifically, the two versions of discrete-state DAMs, serially updated and parallel updated, and the parallel-updated continuous-state DAM are discussed. For the remainder of this section, these three DAMs will be referred to as the *serial-binary*, *parallel-binary*, and *parallel-analog projection DAMs*, respectively. The following analysis assumes the usual unbiased random bipolar binary memory vectors.

The relation between the radius of attraction of fundamental memories ρ and the pattern ratio m/n is a desirable measure of DAM retrieval/error-correction characteristics. For correlation-recorded binary DAMs, such a relation has been derived analytically for single-pass retrieval and is given by Equation (7.2.7). On the other hand, deriving similar relations for multiple-pass retrievals and/or more complex recording recipes (such as projection recording) is a much more difficult problem. In such cases, numerical simulations with large n values (typically equal to several hundred) are a viable tool [e.g., see Kanter and Sompolinsky (1987), Amari and Maginu (1988)]. Figure 7.2.2, reported by Kanter and Sompolinsky (1987), shows plots of the

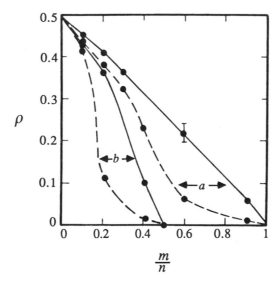

Figure 7.2.2
Measurements of ρ as a function of m/n by computer simulation for projection-recorded binary DAMs. The lines are guides to the eye. The typical size of the statistical fluctuations is indicated. Lines tagged by a refer to a zero-diagonal projection matrix **W**. Lines tagged by b refer to a standard projection matrix. Solid lines refer to serial update with a specific order of updating as described in the text. Dashed lines refer to parallel update. (Adapted from Kanter and Sompolinsky, 1987, with permission of the American Physical Society.)

radius of attraction of fundamental memories versus pattern ratio generated by numerical simulation for serial-binary and parallel-binary projection DAMs (multiple-pass retrieval is assumed).

There are two pairs of plots, labeled a and b, in this figure. The pair labeled a corresponds to the case of a zero-diagonal projection weight matrix $\mathbf{W}$, whereas pair b corresponds to the case of a projection $\mathbf{W}$ matrix with preserved diagonal. The solid and dashed lines in Figure 7.2.2 represent serial and parallel retrievals, respectively.

According to these simulations, forcing the self-coupling terms w_{ii} in the diagonal of $\mathbf{W}$ to zero has a drastic effect on the size of the basin of attraction. Note that the error-correction capability of fundamental memories ceases as m/n approaches and then exceeds $\frac{1}{2}$ for both serial and parallel DAMs for the nonzero-diagonal case (Problem 7.2.8 explores this phenomenon). On the other hand, the corresponding DAMs with zero-diagonal projection matrix continue to have substantial error-correction capabilities even after m/n exceeds $\frac{1}{2}$ but ultimately lose these capabilities at $m/n = 1$. A common feature of these discrete projection DAMs is the monotonic decrease of ρ from 0.5 to 0 as m/n increases from 0 to 1. Empirical results show that inside the basin of attraction of stable states, the flows to the states are fast, with a maximum of 10 to 20 parallel iterations (corresponding to starting at the edge of the basin). These results are similar to the theoretical ones reported for parallel-updated correlation-recorded DAMs (Burshtien, 1993).

For the preceding parallel-updated zero-diagonal projection DAM, simulations show that in almost all cases where the retrieval did not result in a fundamental memory, it resulted in a limit cycle of period 2 as opposed to spurious memories. For the preserved-diagonal projection DAM, simulations with finite n and $m/n < \frac{1}{2}$ show that no oscillations exist (Youssef and Hassoun, 1989). (The result of Problem 7.2.10 taken in the limit of $\beta \to \infty$ can serve as an analytical proof for the nonexistence of oscillations for the case of large n.)

The zero-diagonal serial projection DAM has the best performance depicted by the solid line a in Figure 7.2.2. In this case, an approximate linear relation between ρ and m/n can be deduced from this figure as

$$\rho \approx \frac{1}{2}\left(1 - \frac{m}{n}\right) \qquad 0 \leq \frac{m}{n} \leq 1 \tag{7.2.9}$$

Here, the serial update strategy used employs an updating such that the initial updates are more likely to reduce the Hamming distance (i.e., increase the overlap) between the DAM's state and the closest fundamental memory rather than increase it. In the simulations, the initial state $\mathbf{x}(0)$ tested had its first ρn bits identical to one of the stored vectors, say, $\mathbf{x}^1$, while the remaining bits were chosen randomly. Thus the region $\rho n < i \leq n$ represents the bits where errors are more likely to occur. The serial update strategy used above allowed the units corresponding to the initially random bits $\{x_i(0), \rho n < i \leq n\}$ to update their states before the ones having the correct match with $\mathbf{x}^1$ [i.e., units corresponding to $\{x_i(0), 1 < i \leq \rho n\}$. However, in practical applications, this update strategy may not be applicable (unless we have partial input keys that match a segment of one of the stored memories such as a partial image), and hence a standard serial update strategy (e.g., updating the n states in some random or unbiased deterministic order) may be employed. Such standard serial updating leads to reduced error-correction behavior compared with the particular serial update employed in the preceding simulations. The performance, though, would still be better than that of a parallel-updated DAM. Spurious memories do exist in the preceding projection DAMs. These spurious states are mixtures of the fundamental memories (just as in the correlation-recorded discrete Hopfield DAM) at very small m/n values. Above $m/n \approx 0.1$, mixture states disappear. Instead, most of the spurious states have very little overlap with individual fundamental memories.

Lastly, consider the parallel analog projection DAM with zero-diagonal interconnection matrix $\mathbf{W}$. This DAM has the phase diagram shown in Figure 7.2.3 showing origin, recall, and oscillation phases but no spin-glass phase (Marcus et al., 1990). The absence of the spin-glass phase does not imply that this DAM does not have spurious memories; just as for the correlation-recorded discrete Hopfield DAM, there are many spurious memories within the recall and oscillation regions that have small

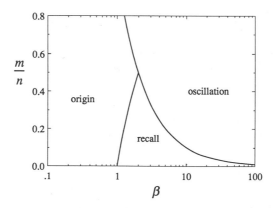

Figure 7.2.3
Phase diagram for the parallel updated analog projection DAM (with zero-diagonal $\mathbf{W}$). (Adapted from Marcus et al., 1990, with permission of the American Physical Society.)

overlap with fundamental memories, especially for large m/n. However, there is no region where only spurious memories exist. Note also that in the oscillation region, all fundamental memories exist as stable equilibria states with basins of attraction defined around each of them. The radius of this basin decreases (monotonically) as m/n increases until, ultimately, all such memories lose their basins of attraction.

According to Equation (7.1.32), oscillations are possible in the dynamics of the present analog DAM when $1/\beta < -\lambda_{\min}$, where $\lambda_{\min}$ is the minimal eigenvalue of the interconnection matrix $\mathbf{W}$. It can be shown (Kanter and Sompolinsky, 1987) that a zero-diagonal projection matrix which stores m unbiased random memory vectors $\mathbf{x}^k \in \{-1, +1\}^n$ has the extremal eigenvalues $\lambda_{\min} = -m/n$ and $\lambda_{\max} = 1 - (m/n)$. Therefore, the oscillation region in the phase diagram of Figure 7.2.3 is defined by $\beta > n/m$. Also, by following an analysis similar to the one outlined in Problem 7.2.3, it can be shown that the origin point loses its stability when $\beta > 1/[1 - (m/n)]$ for $0 \le m/n \le 0.5$ and $\beta > n/m$ for $m/n > 0.5$. With these expressions, it can be easily seen that oscillation-free associative retrieval is possible up to $m/n = 0.5$ if the gain β is equal to 2. Adding a positive diagonal element $w_{ii} = \gamma > 0$ to $\mathbf{W}$ shifts the extremal eigenvalues $\lambda_{\min}$ and $\lambda_{\max}$ to $\gamma - (m/n)$ and $1 + \gamma - (m/n)$, respectively, and thus

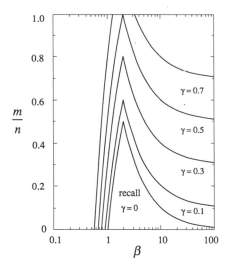

Figure 7.2.4
The recall region of a parallel updated analog projection DAM for various values of diagonal element γ. (Adapted from Marcus et al., 1990, with permission of the American Physical Society.)

increases the value of m/n for oscillation-free associative retrieval of fundamental memories to a maximum value of $\frac{1}{2} + \gamma$, which exists at $\beta = 2$. The recall regions for several values of γ are shown in Figure 7.2.4. Here, one should note that the increase in the size of the recall region does not necessarily imply increased error correction. On the contrary, a large diagonal term greatly reduces the size of the basins of attraction of fundamental memories, as was seen earlier for the binary projection DAM. The reader is referred to Section 7.4.3 for further exploration into the effects of the diagonal term on DAM performance.

7.3   Characteristics of High-Performance DAMs

Based on the preceding analysis and comparison of DAM retrieval performance, a set of desirable performance characteristics can be identified. Figure 7.3.1a and b presents conceptual diagrams of the state space for high- and low-performance DAMs, respectively (Hassoun, 1993).

The high-performance DAM in Figure 7.3.1a has large basins of attraction around all fundamental memories. It has a relatively small number of spurious memories, and each spurious memory has a very small basin of attraction. This DAM is stable in the sense that it exhibits no oscillations. The shaded background in this figure represents

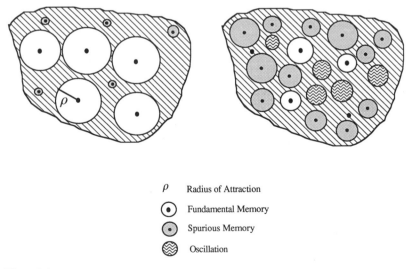

ρ Radius of Attraction

   Fundamental Memory

   Spurious Memory

   Oscillation

Figure 7.3.1
A conceptual diagram comparing the state space of (a) high-performance and (b) low-performance autoassociative DAMs.

the region of state space for which the DAM converges to a unique ground state (e.g., zero state). This ground state acts as a default "no-decision" attractor state where unfamiliar or highly corrupted initial states converge.

A low-performance DAM has one or more of the characteristics depicted conceptually in Figure 7.3.1*b*. It is characterized by its inability to store all desired memories as fixed points; those memories which are stored successfully end up having small basins of attraction. The number of spurious memories is very high for such a DAM, and they have relatively large basins of attraction. This low-performance DAM also may exhibit oscillations. Here, an initial state close to one of the stored memories has a significant chance of converging to a spurious memory or to a limit cycle.

To summarize, high-performance DAMs must have the following characteristics (Hassoun and Youssef, 1989): (1) high capacity, (2) tolerance to noisy and partial inputs (this implies that fundamental memories have large basins of attraction), (3) the existence of only relatively few spurious memories and few or no limit cycles with negligible size of basins of attraction, (4) provision for a "no-decision" default memory/state (inputs with very low "signal-to-noise" ratios are mapped, with high probability, to this default memory), and (5) fast memory retrievals. This list of high-performance DAM characteristics can act as performance criteria for comparing various DAM architectures and/or DAM recording recipes.

The capacity and performance of DAMs can be improved by employing optimal recording recipes (such as the projection recipe) and/or using proper state updating schemes (such as serial updating), as was seen in Section 7.2. One also may improve the capacity and performance of DAMs by modifying their basic architecture or components. Such improved DAMs and other common DAM models are presented in the next section.

7.4   Other DAM Models

As compared with the preceding models, a number of more sophisticated DAMs have been proposed in the literature. Some of these DAMs are improved variations of the ones just discussed. Others, though, are substantially different models with interesting behavior. The following is a sample of such DAMs [for a larger sample of DAM models and a thorough analysis, the reader is referred to Hassoun (1993)].

7.4.1   Brain-State-in-a-Box (BSB) DAM

The *brain-state-in-a-box* (*BSB*) *model* (Anderson et al., 1977) is one of the earliest DAM models. It is a discrete-time, continuous-state parallel-updated DAM whose dynamics are given by

$$\mathbf{x}(k + 1) = F[\gamma \mathbf{x}(k) + \alpha \mathbf{W} \mathbf{x}(k) + \delta \boldsymbol{\theta}] \tag{7.4.1}$$

where the input key is presented as the initial state $\mathbf{x}(0)$ of the DAM. Here, $\gamma \mathbf{x}(k)$, with $0 \leq \gamma \leq 1$, is a decay term of the state $\mathbf{x}(k)$, and α is a positive constant that represents feedback gain. The vector $\boldsymbol{\theta} = [I_1 \quad I_2 \quad \cdots \quad I_n]^{\mathrm{T}}$ represents a scaled external input (bias) to the system, which persists for all time k. Some particular choices for δ are $\delta = 0$ (i.e., no external bias) or $\delta = \alpha$. The operation $F(\xi)$ is a piece-wise linear operator that maps the ith component ξ_i of its argument vector ξ according to

$$f(\xi_i) = \begin{cases} 1 & \text{if } \xi_i \geq 1 \\ \xi_i & \text{if } -1 < \xi_i < +1 \\ -1 & \text{if } \xi_i \leq -1 \end{cases} \tag{7.4.2}$$

The BSB model gets its name from the fact that the state of the system is continuous and constrained to be in the hypercube $[-1, +1]^n$.

When operated as a DAM, the BSB model typically employs an interconnection matrix $\mathbf{W}$ given by the correlation recording recipe to store a set of m n-dimensional bipolar binary vectors as attractors (located at corners of the hypercube $[-1, +1]^n$). Here, one normally sets $\delta = 0$ and assumes the input to the DAM [i.e., $\mathbf{x}(0)$] to be a noisy vector that may be anywhere in the hypercube $[-1, +1]^n$. The performance of this DAM with random stored vectors, large n, and $m \ll n$ has been studied through numerical simulations by Anderson (1993). These simulations particularly address the effects of model parameters γ and α on memory retrieval.

The stability of the BSB model in Equation (7.4.1) with symmetric $\mathbf{W}$, $\delta = 0$, and $\gamma = 1$ has been analyzed by several researchers including Golden (1986), Greenberg (1988), Hui and Żak (1992), and Anderson (1993). In this case, this model reduces to

$$\mathbf{x}(k + 1) = F[\mathbf{x}(k) - \alpha \mathbf{W} \mathbf{x}(k)] \tag{7.4.3}$$

Golden (1986, 1993) analyzed the dynamics of the system in Equation (7.4.3) and found that it behaves as a gradient system that minimizes the energy

$$E(\mathbf{x}) = -\tfrac{1}{2} \mathbf{x}^{\mathrm{T}} \mathbf{W} \mathbf{x} \tag{7.4.4}$$

He also proved that the dynamics in Equation (7.4.3) always converge to a local minimum of $E(\mathbf{x})$ if $\mathbf{W}$ is symmetric and $\lambda_{\min} \geq 0$ (i.e., $\mathbf{W}$ is positive semidefinite) or $\alpha < 2/|\lambda_{\min}|$, where $\lambda_{\min}$ is the smallest eigenvalue of $\mathbf{W}$. With these conditions, the

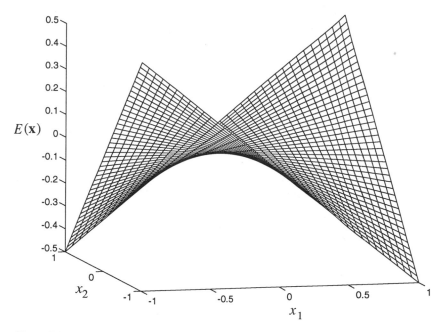

Figure 7.4.1
A plot of the energy function $E(\mathbf{x})$ for the BSB DAM of Example 7.4.1. There are two minima with energy $E = -0.5$ at states $[+1 \quad -1]^T$ and $[-1 \quad +1]^T$ and two maxima with energy $E = 0.5$ at $[+1 \quad +1]^T$ and $[-1 \quad -1]^T$.

stable equilibria of this model are restricted to the surface and/or vertices of the hypercube. It is interesting to note here that when this BSB DAM employs correlation recording (with preserved diagonal of $\mathbf{W}$), it always converges to a minimum of $E(\mathbf{x})$ because of the positive semidefinite symmetric nature of the autocorrelation matrix. The following example illustrates the dynamics for a two-state zero-diagonal correlation-recorded BSB DAM.

Example 7.4.1   Consider the problem of designing a simple BSB DAM that is capable of storing the memory vector $\mathbf{x} = [+1 \quad -1]^T$. One possible way to record this DAM with $\mathbf{x}$ is to employ the normalized correlation recording recipe of Equation (7.1.6). This recording results in the symmetric weight matrix

$$\mathbf{W} = \begin{bmatrix} 0 & -0.5 \\ -0.5 & 0 \end{bmatrix}$$

after setting the diagonal elements to zero. This matrix has the two eigenvalues $\lambda_{\min} = -0.5$ and $\lambda_{\max} = 0.5$. The energy function for this DAM is given by Equation (7.4.4)

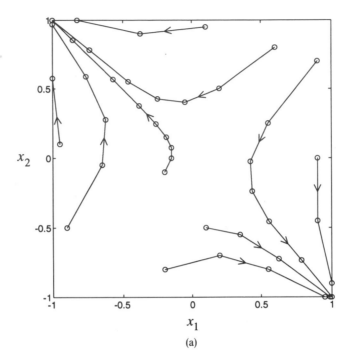

Figure 7.4.2
State-space trajectories of a two-state BSB DAM that employs a zero-diagonal autocorrelation weight matrix to store the memory vector $\mathbf{x} = [+1 \quad -1]^T$. The resulting weight matrix is symmetric with $\lambda_{min} = -0.5$ and $\lambda_{max} = +0.5$: (a) $\alpha = 1$, and (b) $\alpha = 0.3$. Circles indicate state transitions. The lines are used as guides to the eye.

and is plotted in Figure 7.4.1. The figure shows two minima of equal energy at the state $[+1 \quad -1]^T$ and its complement state $[-1 \quad +1]^T$ and two maxima of equal energy at $[+1 \quad +1]^T$ and $[-1 \quad -1]^T$. Simulations using the BSB dynamics of Equation (7.4.3) are shown in Figure 7.4.2 for a number of initial states $\mathbf{x}(0)$. Using $\alpha = 1$ and $\alpha = 0.3$ resulted in convergence to one of the two minima of $E(\mathbf{x})$, as depicted in Figure 7.4.3a and b, respectively. The basins of attraction of these stable states are equal in size and are separated by the line $x_2 = x_1$. Note that the values of α used here satisfy the condition $\alpha < 2/|\lambda_{min}| = 4$. The effects of violating this condition on the stability of the DAM are shown in Figure 7.4.3, where α was set equal to 5. The figure depicts a limit cycle or an oscillation between the two states of maximum energy, $[-1 \quad -1]^T$ and $[+1 \quad +1]^T$. This limit cycle was generated by starting from $\mathbf{x}(0) = [0.9 \quad 0.7]^T$. Starting from $\mathbf{x}(0) = [0.9 \quad 0.6]^T$ leads to convergence to the

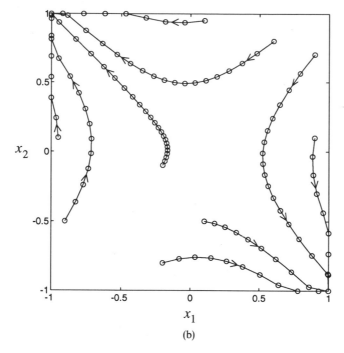

x_2

x_1

(b)

Figure 7.4.2 (continued)

desired state $[+1 \quad -1]^T$, as depicted by the lower state trajectory in Figure 7.4.3. It is interesting to note how this state was reached by bouncing back and forth off the boundaries of the state space, $[-1, +1]^2$.

Greenberg (1988) showed the following interesting BSB DAM property. He showed that all vertices $\{-1, +1\}^n$ of a BSB DAM are attractors (asymptotically stable equilibria) if

$$w_{ii} > \sum_{\substack{j=1 \\ j \neq i}}^{n} |w_{ij}| \qquad i = 1, 2, \ldots, n \tag{7.4.5}$$

Equation (7.4.5) defines what is referred to as a "strongly" *row diagonal dominant* matrix $\mathbf{W}$. As an example, it is noted that the BSB DAM with $\mathbf{W} = \mathbf{I}$ has its vertices as attractors. For associative memories, though, it is not desired to have all vertices (2^n of them) of the hypercube as attractors. Therefore, a row diagonally dominant

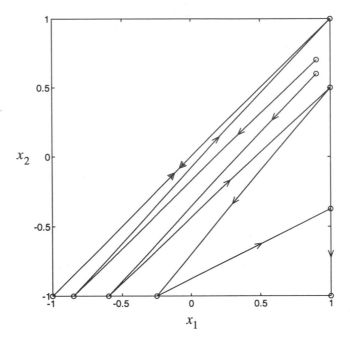

Figure 7.4.3
State-space trajectories of the BSB DAM of Figure 7.4.2 but with
$\alpha = 5$. The limit cycle (top trajectory) was obtained by starting from
$\mathbf{x}(0) = [0.9 \quad 0.7]^T$. The converging dynamics (bottom trajectory) was
obtained by starting from $\mathbf{x}(0) = [0.9 \quad 0.6]^T$.

weight matrix is to be avoided (recall that the interconnection matrix in a DAM is
usually treated by forcing its diagonal to zero).

A more general result concerning the stability of the verticies of the BSB model in
Equation (7.4.1), with $\gamma = 1$ and $\alpha = \delta$, was reported by Hui and Żak (1992) and Hui
et al. (1993). They showed that if $w_{ii} > \sum\limits_{\substack{j=1 \\ j \neq i}}^{n} |w_{ij}| + |I_i|$ for $i = 1, 2, \ldots, n$, then all vertices
of the bipolar hypercube are asymptotically stable equilibrium points. Here, $\mathbf{W}$ need
not be symmetric, and I_i is an arbitrary constant bias input to the ith unit. Hui and
Żak (1992) also showed that if $\mathbf{W}$ is symmetric, a hypercube vertex $\mathbf{x}^*$ that satisfies the
condition

$$[(\mathbf{I} + \alpha\mathbf{W})\mathbf{x}^* + \alpha\boldsymbol{\theta}]_i x_i^* > 1 \qquad i = 1, 2, \ldots, n \qquad (7.4.6)$$

is a stable equilibrium. Here, $[\cdot]_i$ signifies the ith component of the argument vector.
Equation (7.4.6) is particularly useful in characterizing the capacity of a zero-diagonal

correlation-recorded BSB DAM where m unbiased and independent random vectors $\mathbf{x}^k \in \{-1, +1\}^n$ are stored. Let $\mathbf{x}^h$ be one of these vectors, and substitute it in Equation (7.4.6). Assuming the DAM is receiving no bias ($\boldsymbol{\theta} = \mathbf{0}$), the inequality in Equation (7.4.6) becomes

$$(x_i^h)^2 + \alpha[\mathbf{W}\mathbf{x}^h]_i x_i^h > 1 \qquad i = 1, 2, \ldots, n \tag{7.4.7}$$

or

$$[\mathbf{W}\mathbf{x}^h]_i x_i^h > 0 \qquad i = 1, 2, \ldots, n \tag{7.4.8}$$

since $(x_i^h)^2 = 1$ and $\alpha > 0$. Thus the vertex $\mathbf{x}^h$ is an attractor if

$$\left(\sum_{j=1}^{n} w_{ij} x_j^h \right) x_i^h \approx (x_i^h)^2 + \frac{1}{n} \left[\sum_{\substack{j=1 \\ j \neq i}}^{n} \sum_{\substack{k=1 \\ k \neq h}}^{m} x_i^k x_j^k x_j^h \right] x_i^h > 0 \qquad i = 1, 2, \ldots, n \tag{7.4.9}$$

or, equivalently,

$$-x_i^h \left[\frac{1}{n} \sum_{\substack{j=1 \\ j \neq i}}^{n} \sum_{\substack{k=1 \\ k \neq h}}^{m} x_i^k x_j^k x_j^h \right] < 1 \qquad i = 1, 2, \ldots, n \tag{7.4.10}$$

where the term inside the parentheses is the cross-talk term. In Section 7.2.1, it was determined that the probability of the n inequalities in Equation (7.4.10) being more than 99 percent correct for all m memories approaches 1, in the limit of large n, if $m/n < 1/(4 \ln n)$. Hence it is concluded that the absolute capacity of the BSB DAM for storing random bipolar binary vectors is identical to that of the discrete Hopfield DAM when correlation recording is used with zero self-coupling (i.e., $w_{ii} = 0$ for all i). In fact, the present capacity result is stronger than the absolute capacity result of Section 7.2.1; when m/n is smaller than $1/(4 \ln n)$, the condition of Equation (7.4.6) is satisfied, and therefore, all $\mathbf{x}^k$ vectors are stable equilibria (attractors).

7.4.2   Nonmonotonic Activations DAM

As indicated in Section 7.3, one way of improving DAM performance for a given recording recipe is by appropriately designing the DAM components. Here, the idea is to design the DAM retrieval process so that the DAM dynamics exploit certain known features of the synthesized interconnection matrix $\mathbf{W}$. This section presents correlation-recorded DAMs whose performance is significantly enhanced as a result of modifying the activation functions of their units from the typical sgn- or sigmoid-type activation to more sophisticated nonmonotonic activations. Two DAMs are considered: a discrete-time, discrete-state, parallel-updated DAM and a continuous-time, continuous-state DAM.

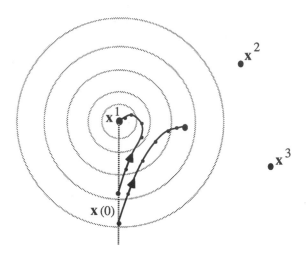

Figure 7.4.4
Schematic representation of converging trajectories in a correlation-recorded discrete Hopfield DAM. When the distance
(overlap) between $\mathbf{x}(0)$ and $\mathbf{x}^1$ is larger (smaller) than some
critical value, the DAM converges to a spurious memory
(right-hand side trajectory). Otherwise, the DAM retrieves
the fundamental memory $\mathbf{x}^1$. (From Morita, 1993; © 1993 by
Pergamon Press.)

Discrete Model   First, consider the zero-diagonal correlation-recorded discrete Hopfield DAM discussed earlier in this chapter. The retrieval dynamics of this DAM show
some strange dynamic behavior. When initialized with a vector $\mathbf{x}(0)$ that has an
overlap p with one of the stored random memories, say, $\mathbf{x}^1$, the DAM state $\mathbf{x}(k)$
initially evolves toward $\mathbf{x}^1$ but does not always converge or stay close to $\mathbf{x}^1$, as shown
in Figure 7.4.4. It has been shown (Amari and Maginu, 1988) that the overlap
$p(k) = (1/n)(\mathbf{x}^1)^{\mathrm{T}}\mathbf{x}(k)$, when started with $p(0)$ less than some critical value p_c, initially
increases but soon starts to decrease and ultimately stabilizes at a value less than 1. In
this case, the DAM converges to a spurious memory, as depicted schematically by the
trajectory on the right in Figure 7.4.4. The value of p_c increases (from zero) monotonically with the pattern ratio m/n and increases sharply from about 0.5 to 1 as m/n
becomes larger than 0.15, the DAM's relative capacity (note that p_c also can be
written as $1 - 2\rho$, where ρ is the radius of attraction of a fundamental memory as in
Section 7.2.1). This peculiar phenomenon can be explained by first noting the effects
of the overlaps $p(k)$ and $q_h(k) = (1/n)(\mathbf{x}^h)^{\mathrm{T}}\mathbf{x}(k)$, $h = 2,\dots,m$, on the ith unit weighted
sum $u_i(k)$ given by

$$u_i(k) = \sum_{j=1}^{n} w_{ij} x_j(k) = x_i^1 \left[\frac{1}{n} (\mathbf{x}^1)^{\mathsf{T}} \mathbf{x}(k) \right] + \sum_{h=2}^{m} x_i^h \left[\frac{1}{n} (\mathbf{x}^h)^{\mathsf{T}} \mathbf{x}(k) \right] \qquad (7.4.11)$$

or, when written in terms of $p(k)$ and $q_h(k)$,

$$u_i(k) = x_i^1 p(k) + \sum_{h=2}^{m} x_i^h q_h(k) \qquad (7.4.12)$$

Note the effects of the overlap terms $q_h(k)$ on the value of $u_i(k)$. The higher the overlaps with memories other than $\mathbf{x}^1$, the larger the value of the cross-talk term [the summation term in Equation (7.4.12)], which, in turn, drives $|u_i(k)|$ to large values. Morita (1993) showed, using simulations, that both the sum of squares of the overlaps with all stored memories except $\mathbf{x}^1$, defined as

$$s(k) = \sum_{h=2}^{m} q_h^2(k) = \frac{1}{n^2} \sum_{h=2}^{m} [(\mathbf{x}^h)^{\mathsf{T}} \mathbf{x}(k)]^2 \qquad (7.4.13)$$

and $p^2(k)$ initially increase with k. Then one of two scenarios might occur. In the first scenario, $s(k)$ begins to decrease, and $p^2(k)$ continues to increase until it reaches 1; i.e., $\mathbf{x}(k)$ stabilizes at $\mathbf{x}^1$. In the second scenario, $s(k)$ continues to increase and may attain values larger than 1 while $p^2(k)$ decreases.

This phenomenon suggests a method for improving DAM performance by modifying the dynamics of the Hopfield DAM such that the state is forced to move in such a direction that $s(k)$ is reduced but not $p^2(k)$. One such method is to reduce the influence of units with large $|u_i|$ values. Such neurons actually cause the increase in $s(k)$. The influence of a unit i with large $|u_i|$, say, $|u_i| > \alpha > 0$, can be reduced by reversing the sign of x_i. This method can be implemented using the "partial-reverse" dynamics (Morita, 1993) given by

$$\mathbf{x}(k+1) = F[\mathbf{W}\{\mathbf{x}(k) - \lambda G[\mathbf{W}\mathbf{x}(k)]\}] \qquad (7.4.14)$$

where $\lambda > 0$ and F and G are activation functions that operate component-wise on their vector arguments. Here, F is the sgn activation function and G is defined by

$$G(u) = \begin{cases} -1 & \text{if } u < -\alpha \\ 0 & \text{if } -\alpha \le u \le \alpha \\ +1 & \text{if } u > \alpha \end{cases} \qquad (7.4.15)$$

where u is a component of the vector $\mathbf{u} = \mathbf{W}\mathbf{x}(k)$. The values of parameters α and λ must be determined with care. Empirically, $\lambda = 2.7$ and $\alpha = 1 + 2\sqrt{m/n}$ may be chosen. These parameters are chosen so that the number of units which satisfy $|u_i| > \alpha$ is small when $\mathbf{x}(k)$ is close to any of the stored memories, provided m/n is not too large. It should be noted that Equation (7.4.14) does not always converge to a stable equilibrium. Numerical simulations show that a DAM employing this partial-reverse method has several advantages over the same DAM but with pure sgn activations. These advantages include a smaller critical overlap p_c (i.e., wider basins of attraction for fundamental memories), faster convergence, lower rate of convergence to spurious memories, and error-correction capability for pattern ratios up to $m/n \approx 0.27$.

Continuous Model   Consider the continuous-time DAM in Equation (7.1.21) with $\mathbf{C} = \boldsymbol{\alpha} = \mathbf{I}$, and $\boldsymbol{\theta} = \mathbf{0}$. Namely,

$$\frac{d\mathbf{u}}{dt} = -\mathbf{u} + \mathbf{W}F(\mathbf{u}) \tag{7.4.16}$$

where $\mathbf{W}$ is the usual zero-diagonal normalized autocorrelation matrix $[\mathbf{W} = (1/n) \sum\limits_{k=1}^{m} \mathbf{x}^k (\mathbf{x}^k)^{\mathrm{T}} - (m/n)\mathbf{I}]$. Here, the partial-reverse method just described

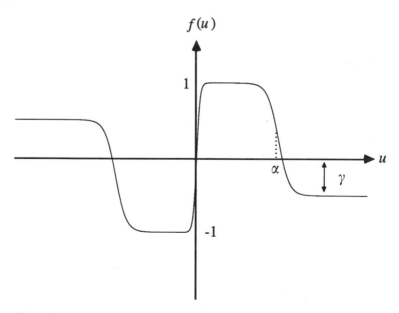

Figure 7.4.5
Nonmonotonic activation function generated from Equation (7.4.17) with $\beta = 50$, $\beta' = 15$, $\alpha = 1$, and $\gamma = 0.5$.

cannot be applied directly due to the continuous DAM dynamics. One can still capture the essential elements of this method, though, by designing the activation function such that it reduces the influence of unit i if $|u_i|$ is very large. This can be achieved by employing the nonmonotonic activation function shown in Figure 7.4.5 with the following analytical form (Morita et al., 1990a, b):

$$f(u) = \frac{1 - e^{-\beta u}}{1 + e^{-\beta u}} \frac{1 - \gamma e^{\beta'(|u| - \alpha)}}{1 + e^{\beta'(|u| - \alpha)}} \tag{7.4.17}$$

where β, β', α, and γ are positive constants with typical values of 50, 15, 1, and 0.5, respectively. This nonmonotonic activation function operates to keep the variance of $|u_i|$ from growing too large and hence implements a similar effect to the one implemented by the partial-reverse method. Empirical results show that this DAM has an absolute capacity that is proportional to n with substantial error-correction capabilities. Also, this DAM almost never converges to spurious memories when retrieval of a fundamental memory is not successful; instead, the DAM state continues to wander (chaotically) without reaching any equilibrium (Morita, 1993).

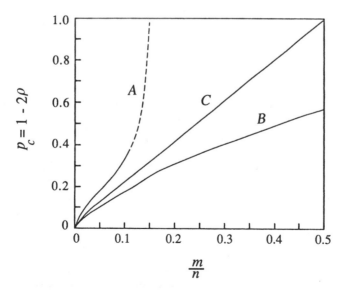

Figure 7.4.6
Simulation-generated capacity/error correction curves for the continuous-time DAM of Equation (7.4.16). Curves A and B represent the cases of zero-diagonal correlation-recorded DAM with sigmoidal activation function and nonmonotonic activation function, respectively. Curve C is for a projection-recorded (preserved diagonal) DAM with sigmoidal activation function and is given for comparison purposes. (From Yoshizawa et al., 1993a; © 1993 by Pergamon Press.)

Figure 7.4.6 gives simulation-based capacity curves (Yoshizawa et al., 1993a) depicting plots of the critical overlap p_c (i.e., $1 - 2\rho$, where ρ is the radius of attraction of a fundamental memory) versus pattern ratio for three DAMs with the dynamics in Equation (7.4.16). Two of the DAMs (represented by curves A and B) employ a zero-diagonal autocorrelation interconnection matrix with sigmoidal activation function and the activation function in Equation (7.4.17), respectively. The third DAM (curve C) employs projection recording with preserved $\mathbf{W}$ diagonal and sigmoid activation. As expected, the DAM represented by curve A loses its associative retrieval capabilities and the ability to retain the stored memories as fixed points (designated by the dashed portion of curve A) as m/n approaches 0.15. On the other hand, and with the same interconnection matrix, the nonmonotonic activation DAM exhibits good associative retrieval for a wide range of pattern ratios even when m/n exceeds 0.5 [e.g., Figure 7.4.6 (curve B) predicts a basin of attraction radius $\rho \approx 0.22$ at $m/n = 0.5$; this means that proper retrieval is possible from initial states having 22 percent or less random errors with any one of the stored memories]. It is interesting to note that this performance exceeds that of the projection-recorded DAM with sigmoidal activation function, represented by curve C. Note, though, that the performance of the zero-diagonal projection-recorded discrete DAM with serial update of states (refer to Section 7.2.2 and Figure 7.2.2) has $\rho \approx \frac{1}{2}[1 - (m/n)]$ (or $p_c \approx m/n$), which exceeds that of the nonmonotonic activations correlation-recorded DAM. Still, the demonstrated retrieval capabilities of the nonmonotonic activations DAM are impressive. The nonmonotonic dynamics can thus be viewed as extracting and using intrinsic information from the autocorrelation matrix which the "sigmoidal dynamics" are not capable of utilizing. For a theoretical treatment of the capacity and stability of the nonmonotonic activations DAM, the reader is referred to Yoshizawa et al. (1993a, b). Nishimori and Opris (1993) reported a discrete-time, discrete-state version of this model where the nonmonotonic activation function in Figure 7.4.5 is used with $\beta = \beta' \to \infty$, $\gamma = 1.0$, and arbitrary $\alpha > 0$. They showed that a maximum capacity of $m/n = 0.22$ is possible with $\alpha = 1.75$ and gave a complete characterization of this model's capacity versus the parameter α.

7.4.3 Hysteretic Activations DAM

Associative recall of DAMs can be improved by introducing hysteresis to the units' activation function. This phenomenon is described next in the context of a discrete Hopfield DAM. Here, the interconnection matrix $\mathbf{W}$ is the normalized zero-diagonal autocorrelation matrix with the ith DAM state updated according to

$$x_i(k+1) = f_i\left[\sum_{\substack{j=1 \\ j \neq i}}^{n} w_{ij}x_j(k), x_i(k)\right] = f_i[u_i(k+1), x_i(k)] \qquad (7.4.18)$$

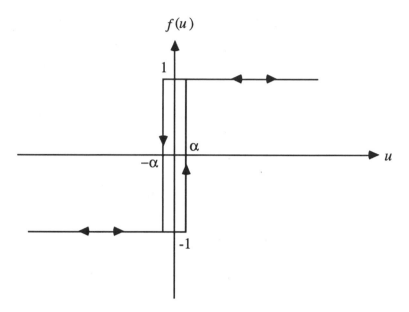

Figure 7.4.7
Transfer characteristics of a unit with hysteretic activation function.

where the activation function f_i is given by

$$f_i[u_i(k + 1), x_i(k)] = \text{sgn}\,[u_i(k + 1) + \alpha_i x_i(k)] \tag{7.4.19}$$

The following discussion assumes a hysteretic parameter $\alpha_i = \alpha$ for all units $i = 1$, $2,\ldots, n$. A plot of this activation function is given in Figure 7.4.7, which shows a hysteretic property controlled by the parameter $\alpha > 0$. Qualitatively speaking, the hysteresis term $\alpha x_i(k)$ in Equation (7.4.19) favors a unit to stay in its current state $x_i(k)$; the larger the value of α, the higher the tendency of unit i to retain its current state.

   In the preceding subsection, it was noted that when the state of a DAM is not far from a fundamental memory, degradation of the associative retrieval process is caused by the units moving from the right states to the wrong ones. The motivation behind the hysteretic property is that it causes units with proper response to preserve their current state longer, thus increasing the chance for the DAM to correct its "wrong" states and ultimately converge to the closest fundamental memory. However, simultaneously, there are units moving from the wrong states to the right ones, and hysteresis tends to prevent these transitions as well. It has been shown (Yanai and Sawada, 1990) that, for the proper choice of α, the former process is more effective than the later, and associative retrieval can be enhanced. For small α, Yanai and Sawada (1990) showed that the absolute capacity of a zero-diagonal correlation-recorded DAM with hysteretic units is given by the limit

$$\max\left(\frac{m}{n}\right) \rightarrow \frac{(1 + \alpha)^2}{4\ln n} \qquad n \rightarrow \infty \qquad (7.4.20)$$

This result can be derived by first noting that the ith bit transition for the preceding DAM may be described by Equation (7.2.2) with $x_i(0)$ replaced by $(1 + \alpha)x_i(0)$ and following a derivation similar to that in Equations (7.2.3) through (7.2.6). By comparing Equations (7.4.20) and (7.2.6), we find that hysteresis leads to a substantial increase in the number of memorizable vectors as compared with using no hysteresis at all. Yanai and Sawada also showed that the relative capacity increases with α (e.g., the relative capacity increases from 0.15 at $\alpha = 0$ to about 0.25 at $\alpha = 0.2$). This implies that the basin of attraction of fundamental memories increases when hysteresis is employed. Empirical results suggest that a value of α slightly higher than m/n (with $m/n \ll 1$) leads to the largest basin of attraction size around fundamental memories.

Hysteresis can arise from allowing a nonzero diagonal element (self connections) w_{ii}, $i = 1, 2, \ldots, n$. To see this, consider a discrete DAM with a normalized auto-correlation matrix $\mathbf{W} = (1/n) \sum_{k=1}^{m} \mathbf{x}^k(\mathbf{x}^k)^{\mathrm{T}}$. You should note that this matrix has diagonal elements $w_{ii} = m/n$, $i = 1, 2, \ldots, n$. Now, the update rule for the ith unit is

$$x_i(k + 1) = \mathrm{sgn}\left[\sum_{\substack{j=1 \\ j \neq i}}^{n} w_{ij}x_j(k) + \frac{m}{n}x_i(k) \right] \qquad (7.4.21)$$

Comparing Equation (7.4.21) with Equation (7.4.19) of a hysteretic activation DAM reveals that the two DAMs are mathematically equivalent if α is set equal to m/n (it is interesting to note that m/n is, approximately, the empirically optimal value for the hysteretic parameter α). Therefore, it is concluded that preserving the original diagonal in a correlation-recorded DAM is advantageous in terms of the quality of associative retrieval when $m/n \ll 1$ (see Problem 7.4.8 for further explanation).

The advantages of small positive self-connections also have been demonstrated for projection-recorded discrete DAMs. Krauth et al. (1988) have demonstrated that using a small positive diagonal element with the projection-recorded discrete DAM increases the radius of attraction of fundamental memories if the DAM is substantially loaded (i.e., m/n is approximately greater than 0.4). For example, they found numerically that for $m/n = 0.5$, using a diagonal term of about 0.075 instead of zero increases the basins of attraction of fundamental memories by about 50 percent. For the projection DAM, though, retaining the original diagonal leads to relatively large values for the self-connections if the pattern ratio m/n is large (for m unbiased random memories $\mathbf{x}^k \in \{-1, +1\}^n$, one has $w_{ii} \approx m/n$, $i = 1, 2, \ldots, n$). This greatly reduces the basin of attraction size for fundamental memories, as shown empirically in Section 7.2.2. All this suggests that the best approach is to give all self-connections a small positive value $\alpha \ll 1$.

7.4.4   Exponential-Capacity DAM

Up to this point, the best DAM considered has a capacity proportional to n, the number of units in the DAM. However, very high capacity DAMs (e.g., m exponential in n) can be realized if one is willing to consider more complex memory architectures than the ones considered thus far. An exponential capacity DAM was proposed by Chiueh and Goodman (1988, 1991). This DAM can store up to c^n ($c > 1$) random vectors $\mathbf{x}^h \in \{-1, +1\}^n$, $h = 1, 2, \ldots, m$, with substantial error-correction abilities. The exponential DAM is described next.

Consider the architecture in Figure 7.4.8. This architecture describes a two-layer dynamic autoassociative memory. The dynamics are nonlinear due to the nonlinear operations G and F. The output nonlinearity F implements sgn activations which give the DAM a discrete-state nature. The matrix $\mathbf{X}$ is the matrix whose columns are the desired memory vectors $\mathbf{x}^h$, $h = 1, 2, \ldots, m$. This DAM may update its state $\mathbf{x}(k)$ in either serial or parallel mode. The parallel-updated dynamics are given in vector form as

$$\mathbf{x}(k + 1) = F[\mathbf{X}G[\mathbf{X}^T\mathbf{x}(k)]] \tag{7.4.22}$$

and in component form as

$$x_i(k + 1) = \text{sgn}\left\{\sum_{h=1}^{m} g[(\mathbf{x}^h)^T\mathbf{x}(k)]x_i^h\right\} \tag{7.4.23}$$

where g is the scalar version of the operator G. Here, g is normally assumed to be a continuous monotonic nondecreasing function over $[-n, +n]$. The recording of a new memory vector $\mathbf{x}^h$ is simply done by augmenting the matrices $\mathbf{X}^T$ and $\mathbf{X}$ with $(\mathbf{x}^h)^T$ and $\mathbf{x}^h$, respectively (this corresponds to allocating two new n-input units, one in each

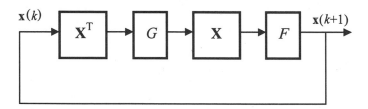

Figure 7.4.8
Architecture of a very high capacity discrete DAM.

layer, in the network of Figure 7.4.8). The choice of the first-layer activation functions g plays a critical role in determining the capacity and dynamics of this DAM. To see this, assume first a simple linear activation function $g(\xi) = \xi$. This assumption reduces the dynamics in Equation (7.4.22) to

$$\mathbf{x}(k + 1) = F[\mathbf{X}\mathbf{X}^{\mathrm{T}}\mathbf{x}(k)] \qquad (7.4.24)$$

which is simply the dynamics of the correlation-recorded discrete DAM.

On the other hand, if one chooses $g(\xi) = (n + \xi)^q$, q is an integer greater than 1, a higher-order DAM results with polynomial capacity $m \propto n^q$ for large n (Psaltis and Park, 1986). Exponential capacity is also possible with proper choice of g. Such choices include $g(\xi) = (n - \xi)^{-a}$, $a > 1$ (Dembo and Zeitouni, 1988; Sayeh and Han, 1987) and $g(\xi) = a^{\xi}$, $a > 1$ (Chiueh and Goodman, 1988).

The choice $g(\xi) = a^{\xi}$ results in an "exponential" DAM with capacity $m = c^n$ and with error-correction capability. Here, c is a function of a and the radius of attraction ρ of fundamental memories, as depicted in Figure 7.4.9. According to this figure, the exponential DAM is capable of achieving the ultimate capacity of a binary-state DAM, namely, $m = 2^n$, in the limit of large a. As one might determine intuitively, though, this DAM has no error-correction abilities at such loading levels. For rela-

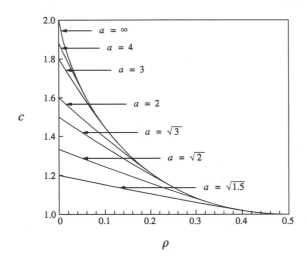

Figure 7.4.9
Relation between the base constant c and fundamental memories basins of attraction radius ρ for various values of the nonlinearity parameter a for an exponential DAM. This DAM has a storage capacity of c^n. (Adapted from Chiueh and Goodman, 1991; © 1991 by IEEE.)

tively small a, one may come up with an approximate linear relation between c and ρ. For example, Figure 7.4.9 gives $c \approx 1.2 - 0.4\rho$ for $a = \sqrt{1.5}$. Hence an exponential DAM with nonlinearity $g(\xi) = 1.5^{\xi/2}$ can store up to $(1.2 - 0.4\rho)^n$ random memories if it is desired that all such memories have basins of attraction of size ρ, $0 \le \rho < \frac{1}{2}$ (here, one-pass retrieval is assumed).

Chiueh and Goodman (1991) showed that a sufficient condition for the dynamics in Equation (7.4.23) to be stable in both serial and parallel update modes is that the activation function $g(\xi)$ be continuous and monotonic nondecreasing over $[-n, +n]$. This condition can be easily shown to be true for all choices of $g(\xi)$ indicated above.

7.4.5   Sequence-Generator DAM

Autoassociative DAMs can be synthesized to act as sequence generators. In fact, no architectural changes are necessary for a basic DAM to behave as a sequence generator. Furthermore, a simple correlation recording recipe may be used for storing sequences. Here, a simple *sequence-generator* DAM (also called *temporal associative memory*) is described whose dynamics are given by Equation (7.1.37) operating in a parallel mode with $I_i = 0$, $i = 1, 2, \ldots, n$. Consider a sequence S_i of m_i distinct patterns $S_i: \mathbf{x}_i^1 \to \mathbf{x}_i^2 \to \cdots \to \mathbf{x}_i^{m_i}$ with $\mathbf{x}_i^j \in \{-1, +1\}^n$, $j = 1, 2, \ldots, m_i$. The length of this sequence is m_i. This sequence is a cycle if $\mathbf{x}_i^1 = \mathbf{x}_i^{m_i}$ with $m_i > 2$. Here, the subscript i on $\mathbf{x}_i$ and m_i refers to the ith sequence. An autoassociative DAM can store the sequence S_i when the DAM's interconnection matrix $\mathbf{W}$ is defined by

$$\mathbf{W} = \frac{1}{n} \sum_{j=1}^{m_i-1} \mathbf{x}_i^{j+1}(\mathbf{x}_i^j)^{\mathrm{T}} + \frac{1}{n}\mathbf{x}_i^{m_i}(\mathbf{x}_i^{m_i})^{\mathrm{T}} \tag{7.4.25}$$

Note that the first term on the right-hand side of Equation (7.4.25) represents the normalized correlation recording recipe of the heteroassociations $\{\mathbf{x}_i^j, \mathbf{x}_i^{j+1}\}$, $j = 1, 2, \ldots, m_i - 1$, whereas the second term is an autocorrelation that attempts to terminate the recollection process at the last pattern of sequence S_i, namely, $\mathbf{x}_i^{m_i}$. Similarly, a cycle (i.e., S_i with $\mathbf{x}_i^1 = \mathbf{x}_i^{m_i}$ and $m_i > 2$) can be stored using Equation (7.4.25) with the autocorrelation term removed.

This DAM is also capable of storing autoassociations by treating them as sequences of length 1 and using Equation (7.4.25) [here, the first term in Equation (7.4.25) vanishes]. Finally, Equation (7.4.25) can be extended for storing s distinct sequences S_i by summing it over i, $i = 1, 2, \ldots, s$. Hence this sequence-generator DAM is capable of simultaneous storage of sequences with different lengths and cycles with different periods. However, associative retrieval may suffer if the loading of the DAM

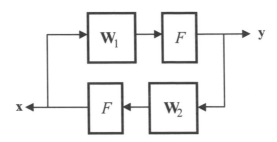

Figure 7.4.10
Block diagram of a heteroassociative DAM.

exceeds its capacity. Also, the asymmetric nature of **W** in Equation (7.4.25) will generally lead to spurious cycles (oscillations) of period 2 or higher.

Generally speaking, the capacity of the sequence-generator DAM is similar to that of an autoassociative DAM if unbiased independent random vectors/patterns are assumed in all stored sequences. This implies that the effective number of stored vectors $m = \sum_{i=1}^{s} m_i$ must be very small compared with n, in the limit of large n, for proper associative retrieval.

7.4.6   Heteroassociative DAM

A heteroassociative DAM (HDAM) is shown in the block diagram of Figure 7.4.10 (Okajima et al., 1987). It consists of two processing paths that form a closed loop. The first processing path computes a vector $\mathbf{y} \in \{-1, +1\}^L$ from an input $\mathbf{x} \in \{-1, +1\}^n$ according to the parallel update rule

$$\mathbf{y} = F[\mathbf{W}_1 \mathbf{x}] \tag{7.4.26}$$

or its serial (asynchronous) version, where one and only one unit updates its state at a given time. Here, F is usually the sgn activation operator. Similarly, the second processing path computes a vector $\mathbf{x}$ according to

$$\mathbf{x} = F[\mathbf{W}_2 \mathbf{y}] \tag{7.4.27}$$

or its serial version. The vector $\mathbf{y}$ in Equation (7.4.27) is the same vector generated by Equation (7.4.26). Also, because of the feedback employed, $\mathbf{x}$ in Equation (7.4.26) is given by (7.4.27).

The HDAM can be operated in either parallel or serial retrieval modes. In the parallel mode, the HDAM starts from an initial state $\mathbf{x}(0)$ [$\mathbf{y}(0)$], computes its state $\mathbf{y}$

(**x**) according to Equation (7.4.26) [Equation (7.4.27)], and then updates state **x** (**y**) according to Equation (7.4.27) [Equation (7.4.26)]. This process is iterated until convergence; i.e., until state **x** (or equivalently **y**) ceases to change. On the other hand, in the serial-update mode, only one randomly chosen component of the state **x** or **y** is updated at a given time.

Various methods have been proposed for storing a set of heteroassociations $\{\mathbf{x}^k, \mathbf{y}^k\}$, $k = 1, 2, \ldots, m$, in the HDAM. In most of these methods, the interconnection matrices $\mathbf{W}_1$ and $\mathbf{W}_2$ are computed independently by requiring that all one-pass associations $\mathbf{x}^k \to \mathbf{y}^k$ and $\mathbf{y}^k \to \mathbf{x}^k$, respectively, are perfectly stored. Here, it is assumed that the set of associations to be stored forms a one-to-one mapping; otherwise, perfect storage becomes impossible. Examples of such HDAM recording methods include the use of projection recording (Hassoun, 1989a, b) and Householder transformation-based recording (Leung and Cheung, 1991). These methods require the linear independence of the vectors $\mathbf{x}^k$ (also $\mathbf{y}^k$) for which a capacity of $m = \min(n, L)$ is achievable. One drawback of these techniques, though, is that they do not guarantee the stability of the HDAM; i.e., convergence to spurious cycles is possible. Empirical results show (Hassoun, 1989b) that parallel-updated projection-recorded HDAMs exhibit significant oscillatory behavior only at memory loading levels close to the HDAM capacity.

Kosko (1987, 1988) independently proposed a heteroassociative memory with the architecture of the HDAM but with the restriction $\mathbf{W}_2^T = \mathbf{W}_1 = \mathbf{W}$. This memory is known as a *bidirectional associative memory (BAM)*. The interesting feature of a BAM is that it is stable for any choice of the real-valued interconnection matrix **W** and for both serial and parallel retrieval modes. This can be shown by starting from the BAM's bounded Liapunov (energy) function

$$E(\mathbf{x}, \mathbf{y}) = -\tfrac{1}{2}\mathbf{x}^T\mathbf{W}\mathbf{y} - \tfrac{1}{2}\mathbf{y}^T\mathbf{W}^T\mathbf{x}$$
$$= -\mathbf{x}^T\mathbf{W}\mathbf{y} \geq -\sum_i \sum_j |w_{ij}| \tag{7.4.28}$$

and showing that each serial or parallel state update decreases E (see Problem 7.4.14). One also can prove BAM stability by noting that a BAM can be converted to a discrete autoassociative DAM (discrete Hopfield DAM) with state vector $\mathbf{x}' = [\mathbf{x}^T \quad \mathbf{y}^T]^T$ and interconnection matrix $\mathbf{W}'$ given by

$$\mathbf{W}' = \begin{bmatrix} \mathbf{0} & \mathbf{W} \\ \mathbf{W}^T & \mathbf{0} \end{bmatrix} \tag{7.4.29}$$

Now, since $\mathbf{W}'$ is a symmetric zero-diagonal matrix, the autoassociative DAM is stable if serial update is assumed, as was discussed in Section 7.1.2 (also see Problem

7.4.15). Therefore, the serially updated BAM is stable. One also may use this equivalence property to show the stability of the parallel-updated BAM [note that a parallel-updated BAM is not equivalent to the (nonstable) parallel-updated discrete Hopfield DAM; this is so because either states $\mathbf{x}$ or $\mathbf{y}$, but not both, are updated in parallel at each step].

From the preceding, it can be concluded that the BAM always converges to a local minimum of its energy function defined in Equation (7.4.28). It can be shown (Wang et al., 1991) that these local minima include all those which correspond to associations $\{\mathbf{x}^k, \mathbf{y}^k\}$ which are successfully loaded into the BAM (i.e., associations which are equilibria of the BAM dynamics.)

The most simple storage recipe for storing the associations as BAM equilibrium points is the correlation recording recipe of Equation (7.1.2). This recipe guarantees the BAM requirement that the forward path and backward path interconnection matrices $\mathbf{W}_1$ and $\mathbf{W}_2$ are the transpose of each other, since

$$\mathbf{W}_1 = \sum_{k=1}^{m} \mathbf{y}^k (\mathbf{x}^k)^{\mathrm{T}} \tag{7.4.30}$$

and

$$\mathbf{W}_2 = \sum_{k=1}^{m} (\mathbf{x}^k)^{\mathrm{T}} \mathbf{y}^k \tag{7.4.31}$$

However, some serious drawbacks of using the correlation recording recipe are low capacity and poor associative retrievals; when m random associations are stored in a correlation-recorded BAM, the condition $m \ll \min(n, L)$ must be satisfied if good associative performance is desired (Hassoun, 1989b; Simpson, 1990). Heuristics for improving the performance of correlation-recorded BAMs can be found in Wang et al. (1990).

Before leaving this section, it should be noted that the preceding models of associative memories are by no means exclusive. A number of other interesting models have been reported in the literature [interested readers may find the volume edited by Hassoun (1993) useful in this regard]. Some of these models are particularly interesting because of connections to biologic memories [e.g., see Kanerva (1988, 1993) and Alkon et al. (1993)].

7.5   The DAM as a Gradient Net and Its Application to Combinatorial Optimization

In the preceding presentation, the DAM is generally viewed as a stable monlinear dynamical system that performs associative retrievals of stored vectors/memories from noisy initial states. The fundamental idea is to store a set of desired memories as local minima of an energy function which is minimized by the DAM's dynamics. Memory storage is achieved by using recording recipes that result in the proper synthesis of DAM parameters (weights).

The notion of minimizing an energy function by a dynamical system (especially a physically realizable one) has important implications to the solution of optimization problems. Here, a stable dynamical system is designed whose energy function $E(\mathbf{x})$ matches the cost/objective function J of a given optimization problem. Then this dynamical system is initialized at a random state $\mathbf{x}(0)$ and is allowed to relax to a solution $\mathbf{x}^*$. This solution may be viewed as a solution to the optimization problem. The degree of optimality of the solution $\mathbf{x}^*$ does not depend on the initial state $\mathbf{x}(0)$ if the dynamical system used has global search capability. Unfortunately, no design methodology is available for designing such a stable dynamical system for optimization problems of practical significance.

Gradient dynamical systems are often used to generate solutions to optimization problems (Cichocki and Unbehauen, 1993) because of their potential realization via physical systems and their intrinsic stability. However, gradient systems are only capable of local (gradient-based) search, and thus the quality of the solutions they generate depends greatly on the initial state of the system. This problem may be partially treated if fast analog hardware (or a fast parallel computer) is used to implement the gradient system; this leads to fast convergence time ranging from nanoseconds to microseconds and allows running the system many times from different initial conditions within a short period of time and may eventually lead to high-quality solutions.

One particular class of optimization problems frequently encountered in many branches of science and technology consists of problems with combinatorial complexity. Such problems have a finite set of possible solutions but scale exponentially or factorially in problem size n (dimension of $\mathbf{x}$). Because of the combinatorial nature of these problems, the time needed to solve any one of them scales exponentially, thus making the solution intractable for large n (for an example, the reader is referred to the traveling salesman problem described at the end of Section 3.5.2; see also Problem 7.5.3). These problems are known as *nondeterministic polynomial-time complete* (*NP complete*), for which no algorithm is known that provides the global minimal solution in a polynomial computational time (Papadimitriou and Steiglitz, 1982; Garey and Johnson, 1979). Heuristic algorithms with polynomial-time complexity have been developed which provide suboptimal solutions to NP-complete problems [e.g., see Simeone (1989)]. Unfortunately, these heuristic algorithms are problem-specific, and their sequential-search nature prevents their implementation on fast parallel computers or in hardware.

Many combinatorial optimization problems can be cast as a problem of minimizing the sum of a cost term and a constraints satisfaction term according to

$$J = (\text{cost term}) + (\text{constraints satisfaction terms}) \qquad (7.5.1)$$

Furthermore, for a wide range of practical problems, the objective function J can be put in the form of or approximated by the quadratic function (Hopfield and Tank, 1985)

$$J(\mathbf{x}) = \tfrac{1}{2}\mathbf{x}^T\mathbf{W}\mathbf{x} - \mathbf{x}^T\boldsymbol{\theta} \qquad (7.5.2)$$

where $\mathbf{W}$ is a symmetric zero-diagonal real-valued matrix, and $\boldsymbol{\theta} = \begin{bmatrix} I_1 & I_2 & \cdots & I_n \end{bmatrix}^T$ is a bias vector. Here, $\mathbf{W}$ and $\boldsymbol{\theta}$ are determined by the optimization problem to be solved. The vector $\mathbf{x}$ usually has binary components, $\mathbf{x} \in \{-1, +1\}^n$ (or $\{0, 1\}^n$), reflecting the combinatorial nature of the problem.

The cost function J in Equation (7.5.2) has the same functional form as the energy function in Equation (7.1.24) minimized by the discrete Hopfield DAM. The cost function J is also approximately equal to the energy function of the continuous-time, continuous-state Hopfield net [Equation (7.1.23)] in the limit of large amplifier gain β. This suggests that one may map the cost function in Equation (7.5.2) onto a Hopfield DAM and let the DAM relax to a local minimum of this cost function, hoping that such a local minimum is a good solution to the optimization problem at hand. In practice, the continuous model is more preferable than the discrete model because it can avoid some of the numerous poor local minima of J (located at vertices of the hypercube $\{-1, +1\}^n$) encountered by the discrete model. When the continuous Hopfield net is used, the amplifier gains are initially set to a value close to 1 so that sufficient time is given for the net to "explore" the solution space before converging to a vertex solution. After some time, though, the gains should be increased gradually in order to force all local minima of the network's energy to move to corners of the hypercube where the desired solutions are located. This gradual increase in gain β is known as *hardware annealing* (Lee and Shen, 1991) (also see Section 8.4.1). Another technique is to add to the cost function J (and thus to the energy function E) an additional quadratic constraint satisfaction (penalty) term $\sum_{i=1}^{n} (1 - x_i^2)$ that is equal to zero only if $x_i \in \{-1, +1\}$ for all i.

With finite gain, the continuous Hopfield net may be viewed as a gradient system in terms of the energy function $E(\mathbf{x})$ of Equation (7.1.23). Formally,

$$\frac{du_i}{dt} = \rho\left(-\alpha_i u_i + \sum_{j=1}^{n} w_{ij} x_j + I_i\right)$$

$$= -\rho\frac{\partial E(\mathbf{x})}{\partial x_i} \qquad i = 1, 2, \ldots, n \qquad (7.5.3)$$

where $\rho, \alpha_i > 0$ are as defined in Section 7.1.2. Writing Equation (7.5.3) in terms of the cost function J to be minimized gives

$$\frac{du_i}{dt} = \rho\left[-\alpha_i u_i - \frac{\partial J(\mathbf{x})}{\partial x_i}\right] \qquad i = 1, 2, \ldots, n \qquad (7.5.4)$$

Solving for the partial derivative term in Equation (7.5.4) leads to

$$\frac{\partial J(\mathbf{x})}{\partial x_i} = -\frac{1}{\rho}\frac{du_i}{dt} - \alpha_i u_i \qquad (7.5.5)$$

Now, the time derivative of $J(\mathbf{x})$ is

$$\frac{\partial J}{\partial t} = \nabla J(\mathbf{x})^T \dot{\mathbf{x}}(t) = \sum_{i=1}^{n} \frac{\partial J}{\partial x_i}\frac{dx_i}{dt} = -\frac{1}{\rho}\sum_{i=1}^{n}\frac{dx_i}{du_i}\left(\frac{du_i}{dt}\right)^2 - \sum_{i=1}^{n} \alpha_i u_i \frac{dx_i}{dt} \qquad (7.5.6)$$

where Equation (7.5.5) was used. The first term on the right-hand side of Equation (7.5.6) is always positive. However, the second term can become positive, and therefore, $\frac{\partial J}{\partial t}$ may become positive. This means that Equation (7.5.3) is not a gradient system in J unless the decay terms $\alpha_i u_i$ are eliminated (Takefuji and Lee, 1991). This can be physically accomplished by assuming lossless amplifiers in the Hopfield net. With all $\alpha_i = 0$, the Hopfield net's dynamics reduce to the stable gradient system

$$\frac{du_i}{dt} = -\rho\frac{\partial J(\mathbf{x})}{\partial x_i} = \sum_{j=1}^{n} w_{ij} x_j + I_i \qquad i = 1, 2, \ldots, n \qquad (7.5.7)$$

To summarize, the lossless amplifier Hopfield net whose energy function is exactly matched to a quadratic objective function $J(\mathbf{x})$ is guaranteed to converge to a local minimum of J. It should be noted here that the cost and the constraint satisfaction terms comprising J compete with each other and may develop local minima in J which may violate one or more constraints (in which case the solution is not acceptable) or may satisfy all constraints at the expense of suboptimal solutions.

This section is concluded by an illustrative example of mapping an objective function representing a simple computational task onto a continuous Hopfield net.

Problems 7.5.2 and 7.5.3 further explore the ideas of this section. A large body of research on and applications of the Hopfield net have appeared since the original introduction of the idea of optimization via gradient neural-like nets by Hopfield and Tank (1985) [see also Tank and Hopfield (1986)]. A good sample of this research can be found in the books by Hertz et al. (1991) and Cichocki and Unbehauen (1993). See also Watta (1994) and Watta and Hassoun (1995) for an extension of the Hopfield net idea to constrained mixed-integer optimization problems.

Example 7.5.1: Design of a 2-Bit A/D Converter   The objective in this example is to demonstrate via a specific simple example the procedure for mapping a computational (optimization) task onto a continuous Hopfield net, thus resulting in a fast parallel analog implementation of the desired task. The computational task here is to convert a continuous analog signal $z(t) \in [0, 3]$ into its 2-bit binary representation (x_0, x_1), where x_0 is the least significant bit. First, the problem is expressed in terms of a quadratic objective function $J(x_0, x_1)$. The main objective here is for the equivalent decimal value of the desired digital representation of z to be as close as possible to the analog value of z. In other words, it is desired to minimize the quantity $\frac{1}{2}\left(z - \sum_{i=0}^{1} 2^i x_i\right)^2$. Furthermore, it is important that the variables x_0 and x_1 take on unipolar binary values. This can be accomplished by minimizing the constraint satisfaction terms $x_1(1 - x_1)$ and $x_0(1 - x_0)$. Therefore, a suitable objective function is given by (note the intentional quadratic nature of J)

$$J(x_0, x_1) = \frac{1}{2}\left(z - \sum_{i=0}^{1} 2^i x_i\right)^2 + \lambda_0 x_0(1 - x_0) + \lambda_1 x_1(1 - x_1) \qquad (7.5.8)$$

Equation (7.5.8) should now be minimized. Expanding J gives

$$J(x_0, x_1) = \frac{1}{2}z^2 + 2x_0 x_1 + x_0(\lambda_0 - z) + x_1(\lambda_1 - 2z) + x_0^2(\frac{1}{2} - \lambda_0) + x_1^2(2 - \lambda_1) \qquad (7.5.9)$$

Since J should ultimately match a Hopfield net's energy function, which has no x_0^2 and x_1^2 terms, the last two terms on the right-hand side of Equation (7.5.9) must vanish. This is accomplished by choosing $\lambda_0 = \frac{1}{2}$ and $\lambda_1 = 2$. The term $\frac{1}{2}z^2$ is not a function of the states x_0 and x_1, and its presence only shifts J by a positive amount. Thus the term $\frac{1}{2}z^2$ can be deleted without affecting the local minima of J. Hence the following alternative objective function may be used:

$$J(x_0, x_1) = 2x_0 x_1 + x_0(\frac{1}{2} - z) + 2x_1(1 - z) \qquad (7.5.10)$$

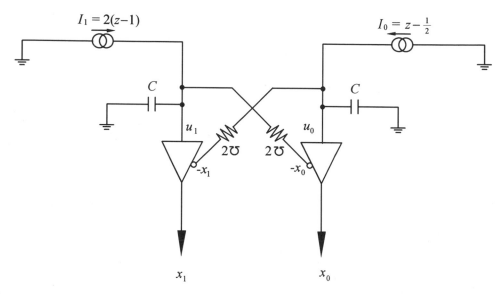

Figure 7.5.1
A circuit realization of the 2-bit A/D converter in Example 7.5.1.

Because of the unipolar nature of x_0 and x_1, the transfer function of the Hopfield net amplifiers will be assumed to have the following unipolar sigmoidal form:

$$f(\xi) = \tfrac{1}{2}[\tanh(\beta\xi) + 1] \tag{7.5.11}$$

Now, by matching the net's energy function given by (here, $w_{00} = w_{11} = 0$, $w_{01} = w_{10}$ and high amplifier gain are assumed)

$$E(x_0, x_1) = -w_{01}x_0x_1 - I_0x_0 - I_1x_1 \tag{7.5.12}$$

to J in Equation (7.9.10), one gets $w_{10} = w_{01} = -2$, $I_0 = z - \tfrac{1}{2}$, and $I_1 = 2(z - 1)$. According to Equations (7.5.7) and (7.5.10), the network dynamics are given by (assuming $\rho = 1/C$)

$$C\begin{bmatrix} \dot{u}_0 \\ \dot{u}_1 \end{bmatrix} = \begin{bmatrix} -2x_1 + z - \tfrac{1}{2} \\ -2x_0 + 2z - 2 \end{bmatrix} \tag{7.5.13}$$

Finally, a circuit realization of this system is given in Figure 7.5.1. [Actually, this circuit does not exactly model the dynamics in Equation (7.5.13). See Problem 7.5.1 for further exploration into this matter.]

7.6 Summary

This chapter introduces a variety of associative neural memories and characterizes their capacity and their error-correction capability. In particular, attention is given to recurrent associative nets with dynamic recollection of stored information.

The most simple associative memory is the linear associative memory (LAM) with correlation recording of real-valued memory patterns. Perfect storage in the LAM requires associations whose key patterns (input patterns) are orthonormal. Further-more, one only needs to have linearly independent key patterns if the projection recording technique is used. This results in an optimal linear associative memory (OLAM) that has noise-suppression capabilities. If the stored associations are binary patterns, and if a clipping nonlinearity is used at the output of the LAM, then the orthonormal requirement on the key patterns may be relaxed to a pseudo-orthogonal requirement. In this case, the associative memory is nonlinear.

Methods for improving the performance of LAMs, such as multiple training and adding specialized associations to the training set, are also discussed. The remainder of the chapter deals with DAMs (mainly single-layer autoassociative DAMs) that have recurrent architectures.

The stability, capacity, and associative retrieval properties of DAMs are character-ized. Among the DAM models discussed are the continuous-time, continuous-state model (the analog Hopfield net), the discrete-time, continuous-state model, and the discrete-time, discrete-state model (Hopfield's discrete net). The stability of these DAMs is shown by defining appropriate Liapunov (energy) functions. A serious shortcoming with the correlation-recorded versions of these DAMs is their inefficient memory storage capacity, especially when error correction is required. Another disadvantage of these DAMs is the presence of too many spurious attractors (or false memories), whose number grows exponentially with the size (number of units) of the DAM.

Improved capacity and error correction can be achieved in DAMs that employ projection recording. Several projection DAMs are discussed which differ in their state update dynamics and/or the nature of their state: continuous versus discrete. It is found that these DAMs are capable of storing a number of memories that can approach the number of units in the DAM. These DAMs also have good error-correction capabilities. Here, the presence of self-coupling (diagonal weights) is gen-erally found to have a negative effect on DAM performance; substantial improve-ments in capacity and error-correction capability are achieved when self-coupling is eliminated.

In addition to the preceding DAMs, the following models are discussed: brain-state-in-a-box (BSB) model, nonmonotonic activations model, hysteretic activations model, exponential-capacity model, sequence-generator model, and heteroassociative model. Some of these models still employ simple correlation recording for memory storage, yet the retrieval dynamics employed result in substantial improvement in DAM performance; this is indeed the case when nonmonotonic or hysteretic activations are used. A generalization of the basic correlation DAM into a model with higher nonlinearities allows for storage of an exponential (in memory size) number of associations with "good" error correction. It is also shown how temporal associations (sequences) and heteroassociations can be handled by simple variation of the recording recipe and intuitive architectural extension, respectively.

The chapter concludes by showing how a single-layer, continuous-time, continuous-state DAM can be viewed as a gradient net and applied to search for solutions to combinatorial optimization problems.

Problems

7.1.1 Verify Equation (7.1.7) by substituting Equation (7.1.6) into Equation (7.1.5).

† 7.1.2 Consider a set of m uniformly distributed random vectors $\mathbf{x}^k \in \{-1, +1\}^n$. Assume large n values (e.g., $n = 200$) and $m \ll n$ (e.g., $m = 10$). Compute the inner products $(\mathbf{x}^i)^\mathrm{T}\mathbf{x}^j$ for $i, j = 1, 2, \ldots, m$. What can you say about the degree of orthogonality of this set of vectors? Repeat with $m = n/2$.

7.1.3 Consider the autoassociative version of the recording recipe in Equation (7.1.11), and assume that $|\mathbf{X}| \neq 0$. Show that the LAM employing this recording recipe has no error-correction capabilities. [Note that Equation (7.1.11) assumes $m = n$.]

7.1.4 Show that the LAM with the projection recording recipe in Equation (7.1.12) and with linearly independent vectors $\mathbf{x}^k \in R^n$ is capable of perfect storage of all associations $\{\mathbf{x}^k, \mathbf{y}^k\}$, $k = 1, 2, \ldots, m$, with $m < n$. Also show that in the autoassociative case the matrix $\mathbf{W} = \mathbf{X}(\mathbf{X}^\mathrm{T}\mathbf{X})^{-1}\mathbf{X}^\mathrm{T}$ projects onto the m-dimensional subspace spanned by the vectors $\mathbf{x}^k$, which are the columns of matrix $\mathbf{X}$.

7.1.5 Consider the autoassociative LAM recording recipe given by

$$\mathbf{W} = \mathbf{X}\mathbf{D}(\mathbf{X}^\mathrm{T}\mathbf{X})^{-1}\mathbf{X}^\mathrm{T}$$

where $\mathbf{D} = \mathrm{diag}(\lambda_1, \lambda_2, \ldots, \lambda_m)$ with $\lambda_i > 0$, $i = 1, 2, \ldots, m$ and $\mathbf{X} = [\mathbf{x}^1 \quad \mathbf{x}^2 \quad \cdots \quad \mathbf{x}^m]$. Assume the vectors $\mathbf{x}^k$, $k = 1, 2, \ldots, m$, are linearly independent. Show that the m vectors $\mathbf{x}^k$ are stored as eigenvectors of $\mathbf{W}$ with corresponding eigenvalues λ_k.

*7.1.6 Show that Equation (7.1.12) is the solution of the following constrained optimization problem:

$$\text{Minimize} \quad \|\mathbf{W}\|_E = \sqrt{\text{Tr}\,(\mathbf{W}^T\mathbf{W})}$$

$$\text{Subject to} \quad \mathbf{WX} = \mathbf{Y}$$

with the assumption that the columns of matrix $\mathbf{X}$ are linearly independent.

*7.1.7 Consider an autoassociative memory defined by Equation (7.1.5). Assume that a set of m orthogonal vectors $\{\mathbf{x}^k; k = 1, 2, \ldots, m\}$ has already been loaded into this memory according to Equation (7.1.6) with $\mathbf{y}^k \equiv \mathbf{x}^k$. Show that any input vector $\hat{\mathbf{x}}$ lying within a Hamming distance of $n/(2m)$ from a stored memory $\mathbf{x}^k$ leads to the perfect retrieval of this memory in one step (Personnaz et al., 1986).

*7.1.8 Using the notation of Section 7.1.1, show that for any LAM with interconnection matrix $\mathbf{W}$,

$$\frac{\sigma_{\text{out}}^2}{\sigma_{\text{in}}^2} = n\langle w_{ij}^2 \rangle$$

where w_{ij} is an element of $\mathbf{W}$ and the expectation is over all elements of $\mathbf{W}$.

*7.1.9 For an autoassociative LAM, show that by employing the projection recording recipe and recording with linearly independent memories $\mathbf{x}^k \in R^n$, $k = 1, 2, \ldots, m$, the error-correction behavior is given by

$$\frac{\sigma_{\text{out}}^2}{\sigma_{\text{in}}^2} = \frac{m}{n}$$

(*Hint*: First, show that $\langle w_{ij}^2 \rangle = m/n^2$ and then substitute this result into the expression of $\sigma_{\text{out}}^2/\sigma_{\text{in}}^2$ from Problem 7.1.8).

7.1.10 Simplify Equation (7.1.14) for the case of orthonormal vectors $\mathbf{x}^k, k = 1, 2, \ldots, m$, and where $\mathbf{y}^k$ are the columns of the $m \times m$ identity matrix $\mathbf{I}$. Repeat for $\mathbf{y} = c\mathbf{I}$ with $|c| < 1$. What do these results say about the appropriateness of $\sigma_{\text{out}}^2/\sigma_{\text{in}}^2$ in measuring the error-correction capabilities of heteroassociative OLAMs?

*7.1.11 A properly normalized performance measure for a heteroassociative OLAM is the signal-to-noise (SNR) ratio, given by

$$SNR = \frac{(s^2_{out}/s^2_{in})}{(\sigma^2_{out}/\sigma^2_{in})}$$

where $(\sigma^2_{out}/\sigma^2_{in})$ is given by Equation (7.1.14), and s^2_{in} and s^2_{out} are signal "energies" given by

$$s^2_{in} = \langle (x^k_i)^2 \rangle - \langle x^k_i \rangle^2$$

and

$$s^2_{out} = \langle (y^k_i)^2 \rangle - \langle y^k_i \rangle^2$$

where the averaging is over all elements i and all vectors k. Show that for zero-mean orthonormal key vectors $\mathbf{x}^k$, $k = 1, 2, \ldots, m$, and zero-mean recollection vectors $\mathbf{y}^k$, this measure gives

$$SNR = \frac{1}{m}$$

Compare this result to those in Problem 7.1.10.

7.1.12 Show that the Hopfield net is a gradient system by verifying Equation (7.1.25).

7.1.13 Show that for the Hopfield DAM with the computational energy in Equation (7.1.27), states $\mathbf{x}$ and $-\mathbf{x}$ have equal energy, $E(\mathbf{x}) = E(-\mathbf{x})$. Also show that if $\mathbf{x}^k$ is a local minimum of E, then $-\mathbf{x}^k$ is also a local minimum of E.

7.1.14 Consider the Hopfield DAM with the computational energy function

$$E(\mathbf{x}) = -\tfrac{1}{2}\mathbf{x}^T\mathbf{W}\mathbf{x} \tag{1}$$

The idea of the energy function as something to be minimized in the stable states gives us a way to derive a learning recipe for this DAM. If we desire a single memory $\mathbf{x}^k$ to be stored as a local minimum of the energy, we would require that the overlap between an arbitrary DAM state $\mathbf{x}$ and the vector $\mathbf{x}^k$ is maximized. Thus we choose

$$E(\mathbf{x}) = -\tfrac{1}{2}(\mathbf{x}^T\mathbf{x}^k)^2 \tag{2}$$

If it is desired that m memories be stored as local minima, then we may minimize the energy function

$$E(\mathbf{x}) = -\tfrac{1}{2}\sum_{k=1}^{m}(\mathbf{x}^T\mathbf{x}^k)^2 \tag{3}$$

Show that the computational energy function in Equation (3) is that of the DAM in Equation (1) when correlation recording is used.

7.1.15 Consider the high-gain, zero-bias continuous-time Hopfield net with symmetric **W**. This net may be described by the gradient system

$$\frac{d\mathbf{u}}{dt} = -\nabla E(\mathbf{x})$$

where

$$E(\mathbf{x}) = -\tfrac{1}{2}\mathbf{x}^T\mathbf{W}\mathbf{x}$$

a. Find the equilibria for this system.
b. Compute the Hessian $\mathbf{H}(\mathbf{x}) = \nabla\nabla E(\mathbf{x})$, and employ it to study the stability of the equilibria of part a.
*c. Show that if **W** is positive definite, then the only attractors are corners of the hypercube.

7.1.16 Verify inequality (7.1.35) for the activation function $f(x) = \tanh(\beta x)$. [*Hint*: Note that $1/\beta$ is the minimum curvature of $G(x)$ in Equation (7.1.31).]

7.1.17 Consider the discrete-time, discrete-state DAM operated in a serial mode (discrete Hopfield net). Suppose that only one $x_i(k)$ changes its value to $x_i(k + 1) = x_i(k) + \Delta x_i$ according to Equation (7.1.37). Show that if $w_{ij} = w_{ji}$, for $i, j = 1, 2, \ldots, n$, the resulting change in the net's computational energy [Equation (7.1.24)] can be expressed as

$$\Delta E = E(k + 1) - E(k)$$

$$= -\Delta x_i\left[\sum_{j=1}^{n} w_{ij}x_j(k) + I_i\right] - (\Delta x_i)^2 w_{ii}$$

Next show that $\Delta E \leq 0$ if $w_{ii} \geq 0$ for $i = 1, 2, \ldots, n$, with $\Delta E = 0$ only when an attractor is reached.

†**7.1.18** Consider the ten 7×5 pixel patterns shown in Figure P7.1.18. Generate a set of ten 35-dimensional bipolar column vectors from these patterns. Here, each vector is obtained by scanning its corresponding pattern starting from the top left corner and scanning each row from left to right (e.g., the vector corresponding to the pattern "0" would be $\mathbf{x} = [-1 \quad -1 \quad +1 \quad +1 \quad -1 \quad -1 \quad +1 \quad -1 \quad -1 \quad +1 \quad \cdots]^T$. Design a static nonlinear associative memory having the input/output relation in Equation (7.1.5) to store these patterns.

Figure P7.1.18
A set of 10 memory patterns used in Problem 7.1.18.

Use the autoassociative version of the correlation recording recipe in Equation (7.1.6). Repeat using the autoassociative version of the projection recording recipe in Equation (7.1.12). Is the correlation-recorded associative memory capable of storing all 10 patterns simultaneously? Compare the noise-correction capabilities of both designs. Here, test with noisy input vectors which are obtained by flipping each bit of an original pattern with a probability P. Experiment with $P = 0.1$, 0.2, 0.3, and 0.4. From these simulations, determine the least and the most "stable" pattern/fundamental memory for each of the two designs.

* **7.2.1** Consider the correlation matrix in Equation (7.1.6) with vanishing diagonal and assume unbiased, independent random vectors $\mathbf{y}^k = \mathbf{x}^k \in \{-1, +1\}^n$, $k = 1, 2, \ldots, m$. Show that in the limit of large n with $m < n$, the extreme eigenvalues of this matrix are $\lambda_{\min} = -(m/n)$ and $\lambda_{\max} = 1 + 2\sqrt{m/n}$ (Geman, 1980; Crisanti and Sompolinsky, 1987; Le Cun et al., 1991b).

  7.2.2 Show that the boundary between the spin-glass and origin regions in the phase diagram of Figure 7.2.1 for the continuous-time, zero-diagonal, correlation-recorded DAM, in the limit of large n with $m < n$, is given by

$$\beta = \frac{1}{1 + 2\sqrt{m/n}}$$

[*Hint*: Perform local stability analysis about the equilibrium $\mathbf{x}^* = \mathbf{0}$ that defines the origin region. First, linearize the DAM dynamics at $\mathbf{x}^* = \mathbf{0}$ to get

$$\frac{d\mathbf{x}}{dt} = -\mathbf{x} + \beta\mathbf{W}\mathbf{x} = (-\mathbf{I} + \beta\mathbf{W})\mathbf{x}$$

Then use the result of Problem 7.2.1 and the fact that $\mathbf{x}^* = \mathbf{0}$ is destabilized when at least one eigenvalue of the matrix $\beta\mathbf{W} - \mathbf{I}$ has a positive real part to establish the desired transition condition on the stability of the origin.]

7.2.3 Repeat Problem 7.2.2 for the discrete-time, zero-diagonal, correlation-recorded analog DAM. [*Hint*: The linearized dynamics at $\mathbf{x}^* = \mathbf{0}$ are given by

$$\mathbf{x}(k + 1) = \beta\mathbf{W}\mathbf{x}(k)$$

and the transition point between stability and instability of $\mathbf{x}^*$ occurs when at least one eigenvalue of $\beta\mathbf{W}$ has a magnitude of 1.]

7.2.4 Show that the boundary of the oscillation region for the discrete-time, zero-diagonal, correlation-recorded analog DAM (refer to Figure 7.2.1*b*) is given by $\beta = n/m$.

*7.2.5 Show that if the diagonal elements of the autocorrelation interconnection matrix $\mathbf{W}$ in the analog DAMs (both continuous-time and discrete-time versions) of Section 7.2 are retained [i.e., $\mathbf{W} = (1/n) \sum_{k=1}^{m} \mathbf{x}^k(\mathbf{x}^k)^\mathsf{T}$], then the spin-glass/origin region boundary becomes

$$\beta = \frac{1}{1 + (m/n) + 2\sqrt{m/n}}$$

Plot and compare this boundary to the one in Figure 7.2.1.

7.2.6 Consider a correlation-recorded DAM with analog activation $f(x) = \tanh(\beta x)$ and pattern ratio $m/n = 0.1$. Calculate the reduction (in percent) in the number of local minima of the energy function when β is reduced from 100 to 10 for $n = 100$. Use the theoretical values of $g(0.1, 100)$ and $g(0.1, 10)$ given by 0.059 and 0.040, respectively. Repeat for $n = 1,000$.

*7.2.7 Consider the autoassociative version of the projection-recorded interconnection matrix in Equation (7.1.12) and assume unbiased, independent random bipolar variables for the components of the $n \times m$ matrix $\mathbf{X}$. Show that in the limit as

$n \to \infty$, the expected value of a diagonal element w_{ii} of $\mathbf{W}$ approaches m/n and that the fluctuations of w_{ii} around this value are small and are of order $1/\sqrt{n}$.

*7.2.8 Self-coupling in a discrete-state, projection-recorded DAM greatly reduces the basins of attraction of fundamental memories, especially for large m/n. Show that the basin of attraction of a fundamental memory vanishes when $m/n > 0.5$. (*Hint*: Equivalently, you may show that for $m/n > 0.5$ if one starts from a key input $\hat{\mathbf{x}}$ which differs from a stored memory $\mathbf{x}^k \in \{-1, +1\}^n$ by only 1 bit does not converge to $\mathbf{x}^k$. The results of Problem 7.2.7 also should be helpful.)

7.2.9 Derive the analytical expressions for the phase diagram boundaries in Figure 7.2.3 for the parallel-updated, analog projection DAM with zero-diagonal $\mathbf{W}$.

7.2.10 Show that the parallel-updated, projection-recorded analog DAM of Section 7.2 has the phase diagram shown in Figure P7.2.10 when the diagonal elements of the $\mathbf{W}$ matrix are retained. (*Hint*: Use the results of Problem 7.2.7.)

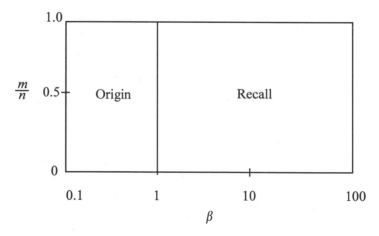

Figure P7.2.10
Phase diagram for the projection-recorded analog DAM with preserved diagonal of $\mathbf{W}$.

7.3.1 Consider the Hamming autoassociative memory shown in Figure P7.3.1. This memory consists of three cascaded modules: a max selector module sandwiched between two LAMs. Matrices $\mathbf{W}_1$ and $\mathbf{W}_2$ are given by

$$\mathbf{W}_2 = \mathbf{W}_1^T = \mathbf{X} = [\mathbf{x}^1 \quad \mathbf{x}^2 \quad \cdots \quad \mathbf{x}^m]$$

Figure P7.3.1
Hamming associative memory.

where $x^k \in \{-1, +1\}^n$, $k = 1, 2, \ldots, m$, are stored memory patterns. The first LAM takes the input key $\hat{x}$ and produces the vector $z = W_1 \hat{x}$, which becomes the input to the max selector module. The max selector generates an output vector $y \in \{0, 1\}^m$ whose ith component y_i is given by

$$y_i = \begin{cases} 1 & \text{if } z_i \geq z_j \quad j \neq i = 1, 2, \ldots, n \\ 0 & \text{otherwise} \end{cases}$$

Finally, the second LAM generates the output vector $x = W_2 y$. [*Note*: This associative memory is based on the Hamming net of Lippmann (1987). A more general dynamical associative memory where the max selector module is replaced by a nonlinear dynamical network that allows for the storage and retrieval of temporal and other complex memory trajectories is described in Baird (1990) and analyzed theoretically in Baird and Eeckman (1993).]

a. Show that if $y_i = 1$, then the Hamming distance between the input $\hat{x}$ and stored memory x^i must be less than or equal to that between $\hat{x}$ and any stored memory x^k, $k \neq i$.

b. Show that for any input, the output x is either one of the stored memories or the sum of two or more stored memories.

c. What is the maximum number of distinct vectors $x^k \in \{-1, +1\}^n$ this memory can store? Does the memory have error-correction capability when loaded with this maximum number of memories? Why?

†d. Let the components of the X matrix assume uncorrelated random values of $+1$ or -1 equally likely, and assume large n. Use simulations to generate a plot relating $(2/n)\log_2 m$ to the radius of attraction ρ, $0 \leq \rho \leq \frac{1}{2}$, of fundamental memories. Assume $n = 500$. Here, an input $\hat{x}$ is within the radius of attraction of a stored memory x^k if the Hamming DAM recovers x^k from $\hat{x}$ in one iteration.

e. Assume that the max selector module in Figure P7.3.1 is implemented using the winner-take-all net described in Section 3.4.1. Find the total number of interconnection weights required for implementation of the Hamming autoassociative memory as a function of m and n.

    f. Based on the preceding results, compare and contrast the performance and implementation efficiency of the Hamming associative memory and the DAMs of Section 7.2.

    g. How would you modify the Hamming associative memory so that it becomes heteroassociative?

7.4.1 Consider a correlation-recorded discrete Hopfield net loaded with m random sparse *binary* vectors $\mathbf{x}^k \in \{0, 1\}^n$. The ith component of vector $\mathbf{x}^k$, x_i^k, is set to 1 with probability a_n (or is set to zero with probability $1 - a_n$). Here, the parameter a_n is equal to $\frac{1}{2}n^{-\alpha}$, $0 \le \alpha < 1$, and it controls the degree of sparcity of vector $\mathbf{x}^k$ (when $\alpha = 0$, each vector $\mathbf{x}^k$ will be random with an equal expected number of 1s and 0s, and as α increases, the vector $\mathbf{x}^k$ becomes increasingly sparse with approximately $\frac{1}{2}n^{1-\alpha}$ ones). It has been shown (Amari, 1989) that the absolute capacity of this sparsely encoded DAM is given by

$$
\text{Absolute Capacity} = \begin{cases} \dfrac{n^{3\alpha-1}}{(1 + 3\alpha)\ln n} & \text{for } 0 \le \alpha \le 0.5 \\[4mm] \dfrac{n^\alpha}{4(2 + \alpha)\ln n} & \text{for } 0.5 < \alpha < 1 \end{cases}
$$

Plot the absolute capacity versus α for $n = 1000$. Show that the capacity of this DAM when loaded with nonsparse ($\alpha = 0$) unipolar binary vectors is much worse than that of the same DAM loaded with nonsparse *bipolar* binary vectors [recall Equation (7.2.1)]. Also show that for the sparse case with $\alpha > \frac{1}{3}$, the preceding sparsely encoded DAM has a substantial storage capacity where m grows faster than linear in n.

7.4.2 Consider a set of m unbiased and independent random vectors $\mathbf{x} \in \{-1, +1\}^n$ with large n. Find the range of values α for which the BSB DAM in Equation (7.4.3) is stable assuming that the DAM's interconnection matrix $\mathbf{W}$ is formed by storing the vectors $\mathbf{x}$ according to

    a. Normalized correlation recording.

    b. Normalized correlation recording with zero-diagonal $\mathbf{W}$.

    c. Projection recording.

    d. Projection recording with zero-diagonal $\mathbf{W}$.

7.4.3 Consider the discrete-time, parallel-updated, linear dynamical system

$$\mathbf{x}(k + 1) = \mathbf{x}(k) + \alpha\mathbf{W}\mathbf{x}(k) \qquad k = 0, 1, 2, \ldots$$

with symmetric **W**. Find all equilibria states. Show that no finite equilibrium inside the hypercube $[-1, +1]^n$ is stable if either $\lambda_{max} > 0$ or $\lambda_{max} < 0$ with $\alpha > 2/|\lambda_{min}|$, where λ_{min} and λ_{max} are the smallest and largest eigenvalues of **W**, respectively. Employ this result in a BSB DAM to show that all trajectories starting at a state inside the hypercube $[-1, +1]^n$, other than the origin, flow toward the surface of the hypercube (note that this analysis says nothing about the convergence of the BSB DAM to a vertex or a point on the surface of the hypercube).

† **7.4.4** Consider a two-state BSB DAM with the following parameters:

$$\mathbf{W} = \begin{bmatrix} 1.2 & -0.4 \\ -0.4 & 1.8 \end{bmatrix} \qquad \mathbf{\theta} = \begin{bmatrix} -0.9 \\ 0 \end{bmatrix} \qquad \alpha = 0.3$$

Find all attractor states. Does this DAM have any attractors inside the hypercube $[-1, +1]^n$? Why? Show that the points $(0.81, 0.18)$, $(0.42, -1)$, and $(-1, -0.22)$ are unstable equilibrium points. Plot the trajectories $\mathbf{x}(k)$ for $\mathbf{x}(0) = [0.9 \quad 0.5]^T$ and $\mathbf{x}(0) = [0.4 \quad -0.25]^T$. Estimate (numerically) and plot the boundaries of the basins of attraction for all attractors found.

† **7.4.5** Consider a BSB DAM with the following parameters:

$$\mathbf{W} = \begin{bmatrix} 2 & -0.8 \\ -0.5 & 1 \end{bmatrix} \qquad \mathbf{\theta} = \begin{bmatrix} I_1 \\ I_2 \end{bmatrix} = \begin{bmatrix} 0.4 \\ -0.2 \end{bmatrix} \qquad \alpha = 0.3$$

Show that **W** satisfies the inequality

$$w_{ii} > \sum_{\substack{j=1 \\ j \neq i}}^{2} |w_{ij}| + |I_i| \qquad i = 1, 2$$

and thus the four vertices of the square $[-1, +1]^2$ are stable equilibria (attractors). Estimate and plot the basins of attraction boundaries for all vertices. Solve for the equilibrium state inside $[-1, +1]^2$, and study its stability. Use the estimated basin boundaries to estimate the four unstable equilibria which lie on the edges of the square $[-1, +1]^2$.

* **7.4.6** Show that if

$$w_{ii} > \sum_{\substack{j=1 \\ j \neq i}}^{n} |w_{ij}| + |I_i| \qquad i = 1, 2, \ldots, n$$

in a BSB DAM with symmetric $\mathbf{W}$, $\gamma = 1$, and $\alpha = \delta$, then any vertex of the hypercube $[-1, +1]^n$ is a stable equilibrium. [*Hint*: Employ the vertex stability criterion in Equation (7.4.6).]

7.4.7 Derive the absolute capacity given in Equation (7.4.20) for the correlation-recorded hysteretic DAM. [*Hint*: Follow the derivation in Section 7.2.1 for the capacity of a correlation-recorded DAM. Start from Equation (7.2.2) but account for the hysteresis term $\alpha x_i(0)$.]

7.4.8 Show that in the limit of large n, a correlation-recorded DAM with preserved diagonal is capable of correcting ρn random errors through single-pass retrieval when loaded with up to $\dfrac{n(1 - 2\rho + m/n)^2}{(4 \ln n)}$ unbiased random bipolar binary memories for small m/n values. Compare this result to the one in Equation (7.2.7).

*7.4.9 Consider the dynamic version of the Hamming autoassociative memory of Problem 7.3.1. This Hamming DAM is shown in Figure P7.4.9. Note that this architecture is similar to that of the exponential DAM of Section 7.4.4 with the nonlinear transformation G taking the form of a "max selector." Here, F is the sgn nonlinearity.

a. Assume that the following three vectors are stored as memories in this Hamming DAM.

$$\mathbf{x}^1 = \begin{bmatrix} 1 \\ -1 \\ 1 \\ -1 \end{bmatrix} \qquad \mathbf{x}^2 = \begin{bmatrix} -1 \\ -1 \\ 1 \\ 1 \end{bmatrix} \qquad \mathbf{x}^3 = \begin{bmatrix} 1 \\ 1 \\ -1 \\ -1 \end{bmatrix}$$

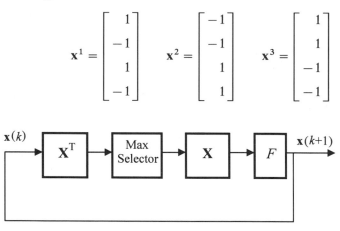

Figure P7.4.9
Hamming DAM.

Compute the DAM state transitions which result from initializing the
DAM with any one of the 16 possible vectors $x(0) \in \{-1, +1\}^4$.

b. Does this Hamming DAM have exponential capacity? (The answer to this
question can be deduced from the answers to Problem 7.3.1, parts c and d.)

c. Study the stability of this DAM.

d. Is it possible for this DAM to have spurious memories?

e. Show that this DAM is equivalent to the exponential DAM of Section
7.4.4 if the activation function $g(\xi) = a^\xi$ with $a \to \infty$ is employed in the
exponential DAM.

7.4.10 A sufficient condition for the stability of the DAM dynamics in Equation
(7.4.23) is that the activation function $g(\xi)$ be continuous, monotonically nondecreasing over $[-n, n]$. Verify the stability of this DAM if

a. $g(\xi) = \xi$.

b. $g(\xi) = (n + \xi)^a, a > 1$.

c. $g(\xi) = (n - \xi)^{-a}, a \geq 1$.

d. $g(\xi) = a^\xi, a > 1$.

7.4.11 Consider the following vectors:

$$
\mathbf{x}^1 = \begin{bmatrix} 1 \\ 1 \\ -1 \\ 1 \\ -1 \\ -1 \end{bmatrix}
\qquad
\mathbf{x}^2 = \begin{bmatrix} -1 \\ 1 \\ 1 \\ -1 \\ -1 \\ 1 \end{bmatrix}
\qquad
\mathbf{x}^3 = \begin{bmatrix} -1 \\ 1 \\ -1 \\ -1 \\ 1 \\ -1 \end{bmatrix}
$$

Employ the recording recipe in Equation (7.4.25), with appropriate modifications, to store the following transitions in the sequence-generator DAM of
Section 7.4.5

$$\mathbf{x}^1 \to \mathbf{x}^2 \to \mathbf{x}^1 \qquad \text{and} \qquad \mathbf{x}^3 \to \mathbf{x}^3$$

Verify that the preceding dynamics are realized by the DAM (assume paral-
lel-state update). Is $\mathbf{x}^3$ an attractor? If yes, what is the maximum number of
errors in $\mathbf{x}^3$ that can be tolerated? Does the cycle $\mathbf{x}^1 \to \mathbf{x}^2 \to \mathbf{x}^1$ have a basin
of attraction?

7.4.12 Consider the sequence-generator DAM discussed in Section 7.4.5. Can this DAM retrieve sequences that intersect each other at a common intermediate state? Why?

7.4.13 Express the interconnection matrices $\mathbf{W}_1$ and $\mathbf{W}_2$ of a projection-recorded HDAM in terms of the matrices $\mathbf{X} = [\mathbf{x}^1 \ \mathbf{x}^2 \ \cdots \ \mathbf{x}^m]$ and $\mathbf{Y} = [\mathbf{y}^1 \ \mathbf{y}^2 \ \cdots \ \mathbf{y}^m]$, where $\{\mathbf{x}^k, \mathbf{y}^k\}, k = 1, 2, \ldots, m$, is a set of associations to be stored. Assume $\mathbf{x}^k \in \{-1, +1\}^n$ and $\mathbf{y}^k \in \{-1, +1\}^L$. What are the conditions on the vectors $\mathbf{x}^k$ and $\mathbf{y}^k$ for perfect storage?

7.4.14 Starting from the energy function $E(\mathbf{x}, \mathbf{y}) = -\mathbf{x}^T\mathbf{W}\mathbf{y} = -\sum_i \sum_j w_{ij}x_iy_j$, show that a parallel-updated BAM always evolves its state $\mathbf{x}$ (also $\mathbf{y}$) such that energy E is monotonically nonincreasing. Combine this result with the fact that E is bounded from below to deduce the stability of the BAM. Repeat the analysis by assuming a serial update mode.

7.4.15 Starting from the Liapunov function $E(\mathbf{x}') = -\frac{1}{2}(\mathbf{x}')^T\mathbf{W}'\mathbf{x}'$ for a discrete Hopfield DAM, and using the equivalence property between this DAM and a BAM that was pointed out in Section 7.4.6, show that $E(\mathbf{x}, \mathbf{y}) = -\mathbf{x}^T\mathbf{W}\mathbf{y}$ is a Liapunov function for the BAM.

7.5.1 Derive the dynamical equations for the circuit in Figure 7.5.1 by applying Kirchoff's current law at nodes u_0 and u_1 [your answer should be similar to Equation (7.5.13) but with extra decay terms]. Explain the discrepancy between your answer and Equation (7.5.13). Can you suggest circuit modifications that eliminate this discrepancy?

7.5.2 Extend the design of the 2-bit A/D converter of Example 7.5.1 to an n-bit A/D converter. Show that an appropriate set of weights and inputs is given by

$$w_{ij} = \begin{cases} -2^{i+j} & \text{for } i \neq j = 0, 1, 2, \ldots, n-1 \\ 0 & \text{for } i = j \end{cases} \quad \text{and}$$

$$I_i = -2^{2i-1} + 2^i x \quad \text{for } i = 0, 1, 2, \ldots, n-1$$

[*Note:* Proper operation of the preceding Hopfield net as an A/D converter requires the reinitialization of all states to zero every time a new analog input x is to be converted (Tank and Hopfield, 1986). This makes it impractical for the on-line conversion of time-varying analog inputs $x(t)$.]

7.5.3 The traveling salesman problem is an example of a constrained combinatorial optimization problem. Here, you are given n cities (points) in a region of R^2 as well as the distances d_{ij} between them. The task is to find the minimum-length closed tour that visits each city once and returns to its starting point. Hopfield and Tank (1985) suggested the use of a continuous Hopfield net for finding solutions to this problem. This net has $n \times n$ unipolar sigmoidal activation units where the iath unit has output $x_{ia} = 1$ if and only if city i is the ath stop on the tour. Figure P7.5.3 shows one possible network activity pattern and the corresponding tour for a four-city problem. Now, consider the following objective function:

$$J = \tfrac{1}{2} \sum_{i=1}^{n} \sum_{j \neq i}^{n} \sum_{a=1}^{n} d_{ij} x_{ia}(x_{j,a+1} + x_{j,a-1})$$

$$+ \frac{\lambda}{2}\left[\sum_{a=1}^{n}\left(1 - \sum_{i} x_{ia}\right)^2 + \sum_{i=1}^{n}\left(1 - \sum_{a} x_{ia}\right)^2 \right]$$

Verify that J is an appropriate objective function for this problem (this can be done by identifying the cost term and verifying its validity and by verifying that all the necessary constraint satisfaction terms are accounted for). In this context of an energy minimizing net, write an expression for the dynamics of unit x_{ia} assuming lossless amplifiers. Write an equation for the weight $w_{ia,jb}$ that connects unit x_{jb} to unit x_{ia}, $i, j, a, b = 1, 2, \ldots, n$.

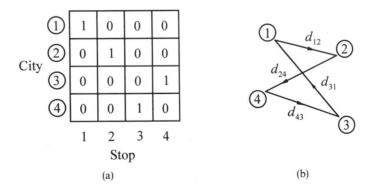

(a)   (b)

Figure P7.5.3
Four-city traveling salesman problem. (a) Hopfield net activity pattern; (b) its corresponding tour.

7.5.4 Use Liapunov's second method (refer to footnote 1, page 358) to show that the origin $x = 0$ is globally asymptotically stable for the following system:

$$\dot{x} = \begin{bmatrix} x_2 - x_1(x_1^2 + x_2^2) \\ -x_1 - x_2(x_1^2 + x_2^2) \end{bmatrix}$$

[*Hint*: Assume a Liapunov function of the form $V(x) = a_1 x_1^2 + a_2 x_2^2$.]

7.5.5 Show that $V(x) = x_1^2 + x_2^2/(2 \sin t)$ is a Liapunov function for the time-varying linear system

$$\dot{x} = \begin{bmatrix} x_2 \\ -x_2 - (2 + \sin t)x_1 \end{bmatrix}$$

7.5.6 Consider the damped pendulum system

$$\dot{x} = \begin{bmatrix} x_2 \\ -\dfrac{g}{L}\sin x_1 - f(x_2) \end{bmatrix}$$

where L is the length of the pendulum, g is the gravitational constant, and the function $f(x_2)$ arises from a damping force depending on the angular velocity $\dot{\theta}(t) = x_2(t)$. Assume that f is continuous and that the damping force satisfies $x_2 f(x_2) \geq 0$. Show that the function

$$V(x) = \tfrac{1}{2}L^2 x_2^2 + gL(1 - \cos x_1)$$

obtained by adding the kinetic and potential energies of the system (assuming unit mass) is a Liapunov function for this system.

7.5.7 Study the stability of the linear system

$$\dot{x} = Ax = \begin{bmatrix} 0 & 1 \\ -2 & -3 \end{bmatrix} x$$

using Liapunov's second method. A systematic way of finding an appropriate Liapunov function for the linear case is to set $V(x) = x^T Q x$, where Q is the solution to the equation $A^T Q + QA = -I$ (I is the identity matrix).

*7.5.8 Consider the discrete-time gradient system

$$x(k + 1) = x(k) - \rho \nabla E[x(k)]$$

with positive ρ. Let $\mathbf{x}^*$ be a local minimum of E. Show that $V(k) = \|\mathbf{x}(k) - \mathbf{x}^*\|$ is a candidate Liapunov function. Employ Liapunov's theorem to show that the asymptotic stability of $\mathbf{x}^*$ is guaranteed if

$$(\mathbf{x} - \mathbf{x}^*)^{\mathrm{T}} \frac{\nabla E(\mathbf{x})}{\|\nabla E(\mathbf{x})\|^2} > \frac{\rho}{2} \qquad \text{for } \mathbf{x} \neq \mathbf{x}^*$$

*7.5.9   Consider the dynamical system described by

$$\dot{u}_i = -\alpha u_i + \frac{1}{n} \sum_{j=1}^{n} w_{ij} f(u_j) \qquad i = 1, 2, \ldots, n$$

where α is a positive constant, and f is a sigmoid function. Show that when the weights $\{w_{ij}\}$ are independent and identically distributed random variables with mean $\bar{w}$ and n is very large, then the dynamical behavior of the system can be approximated by the system of n decoupled equations

$$\dot{u}_i = -\alpha u_i + \bar{w} f(u_i) \qquad i = 1, 2, \ldots, n$$

as $t \to \infty$. [*Hint*: Employ the *chaos hypothesis* in analogy to statistical mechanics (Rozonoer, 1969; Amari, 1972b; Geman, 1982), which states that when n is large, the system behaves as if the variables $u_1(t), \ldots, u_n(t)$ were independent of each other and of the random variables $\{w_{ij}\}$.] Next, let $f(x) = \tanh(\beta x)$, $\beta > 0$, and establish a relation between α, β, and $\bar{w}$ such that the dynamical system is stable.

8 Global Search Methods for Neural Networks

In Chapter 4, learning in neural networks was viewed as a search mechanism for a minimum of a multidimensional criterion function or error function. There, and in subsequent chapters, gradient-based search methods were used for discovering locally optimal weight configurations for single- and multiple-unit nets. Also, in Section 7.5, gradient search was employed for descending on a computational energy function to reach points/states that may represent locally optimal solutions to combinatorial optimization problems.

This chapter discusses search methods which are capable of finding global optima of multimodal multidimensional functions. In particular, it discusses search methods that are compatible with neural network learning and retrieval. These methods are expected to lead to "optimal" or "near-optimal" weight configurations by allowing the network to escape local minima during training. Also, these methods can be used to modify the gradient-type dynamics of recurrent neural nets (e.g., Hopfield's energy-minimizing net) so that the network is able to escape "poor" attractors.

First, a general discussion on the difference between local and global search is presented. A stochastic gradient-descent algorithm is introduced that extends local gradient search to global search. This is followed by a general discussion of stochastic simulated annealing search for locating globally optimal solutions. Next, simulated annealing is discussed in the context of stochastic neural nets for improved retrieval and training. A mean-field approximation of simulated annealing for networks with deterministic units is presented that offers a substantial speedup in convergence compared with stochastic simulated annealing. The chapter also reviews the fundamentals of genetic algorithms and their application in the training of multilayer neural nets. Finally, an improved hybrid genetic algorithm/gradient-search method for feedforward neural net training is presented along with simulations and comparisons with backprop.

8.1 Local versus Global Search

Consider the optimization problem of finding the extreme point(s) of a real-valued multidimensional scalar function (objective function) of the form $y: \Sigma \to R$, where the search space Σ is a compact subset of R^n. An extreme point is a point $\mathbf{x}^*$ in Σ such that $y(\mathbf{x}^*)$ takes on its maximum (or minimum) value. In the following discussion, it will be assumed, without loss of generality, that by *optimization* we mean minimization. Thus an extreme point in Σ produces the "global" minimum of y. Multiple extreme points may exist. In addition to the global minimum (minima), the function y may also admit local minima. A point $\mathbf{x}^*$ is a local minimum of y if $y(\mathbf{x}^*) < y(\mathbf{x})$ for all $\mathbf{x}$ such that

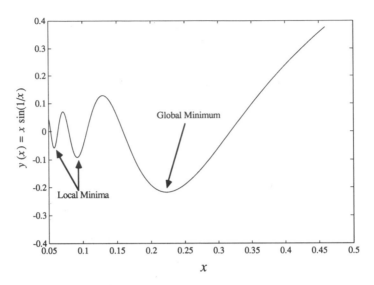

Figure 8.1.1
Local and global minima for the function $y(x) = x \sin(1/x)$.

$\|\mathbf{x}^* - \mathbf{x}\| \leq \varepsilon$, for some $\varepsilon > 0$. Figure 8.1.1 illustrates the concepts of global and local minima for the univariate scalar function $y(x) = x \sin(1/x)$ for $x \in [0.05, 0.5]$.

There are several ways to determine the minima of a given function. Analytical techniques exploit *Fermat's stationarity principle*, which states that the gradient (or derivative in the univariate case) of y with respect to $\mathbf{x}$ is zero at all minima (and maxima). Thus one can find these minima (and maxima) by solving the set of equations (possibly nonlinear) of the form $\nabla y(\mathbf{x}) = \mathbf{0}$. Here, a solution $\mathbf{x}^*$ is a minimum of y if the Hessian matrix $\mathbf{H}(\mathbf{x}) = \nabla\nabla y(\mathbf{x})$ evaluated at $\mathbf{x}^*$ is positive definite [i.e., $\mathbf{x}^T\mathbf{H}(\mathbf{x}^*)\mathbf{x} > 0$ for all $\mathbf{x} \neq 0$), or if $\left.\dfrac{d^2 y}{dx^2}\right|_{x=x^*} > 0$ in the univariate case. The global minimum may then be identified by direct evaluation of $y(\mathbf{x}^*)$. This method is theoretically sound as long as the function y is twice differentiable. In practical situations, though, this approach is inefficient due to the computational overhead involved in its implementation on a digital computer.

Other, more efficient optimization techniques do exist. One example is the simple (steepest) gradient-descent algorithm introduced in Chapter 3 [e.g., see Equation (3.1.21)], which formed the basis for most of the learning rules discussed so far in this book. Assuming y is differentiable, gradient descent can be expressed according to the recursive rule:

$$\mathbf{x}(t + 1) = \mathbf{x}(t) - \rho \nabla y(\mathbf{x})|_{\mathbf{x}(t)} \qquad (8.1.1)$$

where ρ is a small positive constant, and t is a positive integer representing the iteration number. Given an initial "guess" $\mathbf{x}(0)$ (e.g., a random point in Σ), the recursive rule in Equation (8.1.1) implements a search strategy, whereby a sequence of vectors

$$\mathbf{x}(0), \mathbf{x}(1), \mathbf{x}(2), \ldots, \mathbf{x}(t), \ldots$$

is generated such that

$$y[\mathbf{x}(0)] \geq y[\mathbf{x}(1)] \geq y[\mathbf{x}(2)] \geq \cdots \geq y[\mathbf{x}(t)] \geq \cdots$$

and hence at each iteration we move closer to an optimal solution.[1] Although computationally efficient (its convergence properties and some extensions were considered in Section 5.2.3), gradient search methods may lead only to local minima of y that happen to be "close" to the initial search point $\mathbf{x}(0)$.[2] As an example, consider the one-dimensional function $y(\mathbf{x}) = x \sin(1/x)$ shown in Figure 8.1.1. It is clear from this figure that given any initial search point $\mathbf{x}(0) \in [0.05, 0.12]$, the gradient-descent algorithm will always converge to one of the two local minima shown. In this case, the region of search space Σ containing the global solution will never be explored. Hence, for local search algorithms, such as gradient descent, the quality (optimality) of the final solution is highly dependent on the selection of the initial search point.

Global minimization (optimization) requires a global search strategy, a strategy that cannot be easily fooled by local minima. Sections 8.2, 8.4, and 8.5 will discuss three commonly used global search strategies. For a survey of global optimization methods, the reader is referred to the book by Törn and Žilinskas (1989). The remainder of this section will discuss extensions that help transform a simple gradient search into a global search.

8.1.1   A Gradient Descent/Ascent Search Strategy

Using intuition and motivated by the saying, "There is a valley behind every mountain," gradient descent/ascent may be employed in a simple search strategy that will allow the discovery of global minima. Assuming a univariate objective function $y(x)$, $x \in [a, b]$ with $a < b$, start with $\mathbf{x}(0) = a$, and use gradient-descent search to reach the

---

1. To be precise, the step size ρ must be readjusted at each iteration in order not to jump over a minimum point and to ensure that the search is consistently moving "down hill."

2. It is conceivable that the search might reach a solution at a saddle point of y. In practice, however, noise in the system is sufficient to deviate the solution from a saddle point, and once away, the solution diverges from this unstable equilibrium point and moves toward a local minimum.

first local minimum x^{*^1}. Next, save the value $y(x^{*^1})$, and proceed by ascending the function y [using Equation (8.1.1) with the negative sign replaced by a positive sign] starting from the initial point $x(0) = x^{*^1} + \varepsilon_x$, where ε_x is a sufficiently small positive constant. Continue ascending until a local maximum is reached. Now switch back to gradient descent, starting from the current point (maximum) perturbed by ε_x until convergence to the second local minimum x^{*^2}, and save the value $y(x^{*^2})$. This full-search cycle is repeated until the search reaches the point $x = b$. At this point, all minima of y over $x \in [a, b]$ have been obtained, and the global minimum is the point

x^* satisfying $y(x^*) = \min_j \{y(a), y(b), y(x^{*^j})\}$. This strategy will always lead to the global minimum when y is a function of a single variable; i.e., when the search space is one-dimensional.

One also may use this strategy for multidimensional functions, though the search is not guaranteed to find the global minimum. This is because when the search space has two or more dimensions, the perturbation ε_x is now a vector, and it is unclear how to set the direction of ε_x so that the search point visits all existing minima. Also, in the multidimensional case, the preceding gradient-descent/ascent strategy may get caught in a repeating cycle, where the same local minimum and maximum solutions are found repeatedly. The reader is encouraged to stare at Figure 8.1.2, which depicts a plot of a two-dimensional function, to see how (starting from a local minimum point) the choice of ε_x affects the sequence of visited peaks and valleys.

For such differentiable multivariate functions, an example of a search strategy that would be useful for finding some "good" (sufficiently deep) local minima may be given as follows: Start the initial search point at a corner of the search region (Σ), and randomly vary the direction of the perturbation ε_x after each local minimum (maximum) is found, such that ε_x points in a random direction, away from the current

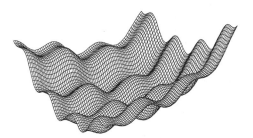

Figure 8.1.2
A plot of a two-variable function showing multiple minima, maxima, and saddle points.

minimum (maximum). A similar global search strategy is one that replaces the gradient-ascent step in the preceding descent/ascent search strategy by a "tunneling step." Here, tunneling is used to move the search point away from the current minimum to another point in its vicinity such that the new point is (hopefully) on a surface of that search landscape that leads into a deeper minimum. This idea is similar to the one embodied in the global-descent search strategy discussed in Section 5.1.2.

8.1.2   Stochastic Gradient Search: Global Search via Diffusion

The preceding search methods are deterministic in nature. Stochastic (nondeterministic) ideas also may be incorporated in gradient-search-based optimization, thus leading to stochastic gradient algorithms. In fact, for problems of moderate to high dimensions, the only feasible methods for global optimization are stochastic in nature (Schoen, 1991). These methods use noise to perturb the function $y(\mathbf{x})$ being minimized in order to avoid being trapped in "bad" local minima, though, in order for the stochastic method to converge to a "good" solution, this noise should be introduced appropriately and then subsequently removed. That is, during the search process, the perturbations to y are gradually removed so that the effective function being minimized will become exactly y prior to reaching the final solution.

In its most basic form, the stochastic gradient algorithm performs gradient-descent search on a perturbed form $\tilde{y}(\mathbf{x}, \mathbf{N})$ of the function $y(\mathbf{x})$, where the perturbation is additive in nature:

$$\tilde{y}(\mathbf{x}, \mathbf{N}) = y(\mathbf{x}) + c(t) \sum_{i=1}^{n} x_i N_i(t) \qquad (8.1.2)$$

Here, $\mathbf{N} = [N_1 \quad N_2 \quad \cdots \quad N_n]^{\mathrm{T}}$ is a vector of independent noise sources, and $c(t)$ is a parameter that controls the magnitude of noise. To achieve the gradual reduction in noise mentioned above, $c(t)$ must be selected in such a way that it approaches zero as t tends to infinity. A simple choice for $c(t)$ is given by (Cichocki and Unbehauen, 1993)

$$c(t) = \beta e^{-\alpha t} \qquad (8.1.3)$$

with $\beta \neq 0$ and $\alpha > 0$. Substituting the perturbed function $\tilde{y}$ in the gradient-descent rule in Equation (8.1.1) gives the stochastic gradient rule:

$$\mathbf{x}(t + 1) = \mathbf{x}(t) - \rho[\nabla y(\mathbf{x})|_{\mathbf{x}(t)} + c(t)\mathbf{N}(t)] \qquad (8.1.4)$$

The stochastic gradient algorithm in Equation (8.1.4) is inspired by the dynamics of the diffusion process in physical phenomena such as atomic migration in crystals or chemical reactions. The dynamics of the diffusion process across potential barriers involve a combination of gradient descent and random motion according to the Smoluchowski-Kramers equation (Aluffi-Pentini et al., 1985):

$$\dot{\mathbf{x}} = -\mu \left[\nabla E(\mathbf{x}) + \sqrt{\frac{2kT}{m}} \mathbf{N} \right] \tag{8.1.5}$$

where $E(\mathbf{x})$ is the potential energy, T is the absolute temperature, k is the Boltzmann constant, and m is the reduced mass. The term $\sqrt{2kT/m}\,\mathbf{N}$ is a stochastic force. Geman and Hwang (1986) [see also Chiang et al. (1987)] developed a method for global optimization which is essentially the simulation of an annealed diffusion process. This method is based on Equation (8.1.5) with the temperature T made inversely proportional to the logarithm of positive time t for almost guaranteed convergence to the global minimum. The discrete-time version of Equation (8.1.5) with annealed temperature leads to the stochastic gradient rule in Equation (8.1.4). Convergence analysis of a slightly modified version of Equation (8.1.4) can be found in Gelfand and Mitter (1991).

The search rule in Equation (8.1.4) may be applied to any function y as long as the gradient information can be determined or estimated. Unlike the gradient search rule in Equation (8.1.1), the stochastic rule in Equation (8.1.4) may allow the search to escape local minima. Note that for zero-mean statistically independent noise, the present search method will follow, on average, the gradient of y.

The probability that stochastic gradient search leads to the global minimum solution critically depends on the functional form of the noise amplitude schedule $c(t)$. In the exponential schedule in Equation (8.1.3), the coefficient β controls the amplitude of noise, and α determines the rate of damping. A sufficiently large β should be used in order for the search to explore a large range of the search space. For large α, the stochastic effects decay very rapidly and prematurely reduce the search to the simple deterministic gradient search, thus increasing the probability of reaching a local suboptimal solution. Small values for α are desirable because they allow the stochastic search to explore a sufficiently large number of points on the search surface, which is necessary for global optimization. However, very small values of α lead to a very slow convergence process. Thus the coefficient α needs to be chosen such that a balance is struck between the desire for fast convergence and the need to ensure an optimal (or near-optimal) solution. The following is an example of the application of stochastic gradient search for finding the global solution.

Example 8.1.1   Let us use the stochastic gradient rule in Equation (8.1.4) to search for minima of the function $y(x) = x \sin(1/x)$ near the origin. The function $y(x)$ has an infinite number of local minima that become very dense in the region closest to $x = 0$.

The function has three minima in the region $x \in [0.05, 0.5]$, as is shown in Figure 8.1.1, which are located approximately at 0.058, 0.091, and 0.223. This function is even; thus, for each minimum $x^* > 0$, there exists a symmetric (with respect to the vertical axis) minimum at $-x^*$. The global minima of y are approximately at 0.223 and -0.223.

Differentiating $y(x)$ and substituting in Equation (8.1.4) leads to the search rule

$$x(t + 1) = x(t) - \rho \left[\sin\left(\frac{1}{x}\right) - \frac{1}{x} \cos\left(\frac{1}{x}\right) + c(t)N(t) \right]$$

where $c(t) = \beta \exp(-\alpha t)$, $N(t)$ is normally distributed random noise with zero mean and unity variance, and $\rho = 10^{-4}$. Initial simulations are performed to test for proper setting of the parameters of $c(t)$. Values of $\beta > 100$ and $\alpha < 0.05$ allowed the search to converge to "deep" minima of $y(x)$. Figure 8.1.3 shows two trajectories of the search point x for $\beta = 50$ (dashed line) and $\beta = 200$ (solid line) with $\alpha = 0.02$, and $x(0) = 0.07$. The same noise sequence $N(t)$ is used in computing these trajectories. In most simulations with $x(0)$ close to zero, searches with large β lead to "deeper" minima

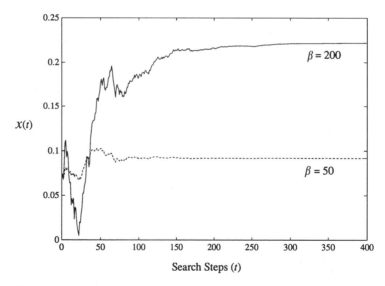

Figure 8.1.3
Search trajectories generated by the stochastic gradient search method of Equation (8.1.4) for the function $y(x) = x \sin(1/x)$. The search started at $x(0) = 0.07$ and converged to the local minimum $x^* \approx 0.091$ for a noise gain coefficient $\beta = 50$ (*dashed line*) and to the global minimum $x^* \approx 0.223$ for $\beta = 200$ (*solid line*).

compared with searches with small β ($\beta < 100$). For $\beta = 0$, the search becomes a pure gradient-descent search, and with $x(0) = 0.07$, the local minima at 0.058 will always be reached. On the other hand, for $\beta > 200$, the search has a very good chance of converging to the global minimum at 0.223 or its neighboring minimum at $x^* \approx 0.091$ (some simulations also led to the minima at 0.058, -0.058, -0.091, and -0.223).

The stochastic gradient rule in Equation (8.1.4) can be applied to all the gradient-descent-based learning rules for both single and multilayer feedforward neural nets. This type of weight update is sometimes referred to as *Langevin-type learning* (Heskes and Kappen, 1993b). For example, the Langevin-type backprop is easily formulated by adding the decaying noise terms $c_l(t)N(t)$ and $c_j(t)N(t)$ to the right-hand side of the batch version of Equations (5.1.2) and (5.1.9), respectively. The subscripts l and j imply the possibility for using different noise magnitude schedules for the output and hidden layers and/or units. The training of multilayer nets according to Langevin-type backprop can be more computationally effective than deterministic gradient descent (i.e., batch backprop). This is because a fast suboptimal schedule for $c(t)$ can be used and still lead (on average) to better solutions than gradient descent. Also, stochastic gradient search has a better chance of escaping local minima and areas of shallow gradient, which may allow it to converge faster (Hoptroff and Hall, 1989). It should be noted here that the incremental update version of backprop [Equations (5.1.2) and (5.1.9)] also may be viewed as a stochastic gradient rule, though the stochasticity is intrinsic to the gradient itself, due to the nature of the minimization of an "instantaneous" error and the random presentation order of the training vectors, as opposed to being artificially introduced, as in Langevin-type learning.[3]

8.2   Simulated Annealing–Based Global Search

The success of global search methods in locating a globally optimal solution (say, a global minimum) of a given function $y(\mathbf{x})$ over $\mathbf{x} \in \Sigma$ hinges on a balance between an *exploration process*, a *guidance process*, and a *convergence-inducing process*. The exploration process gives the search a mechanism for sampling a sufficiently diverse set of points $\mathbf{x}$ in Σ. This exploration process is usually stochastic in nature. The guidance

---

3. For Langevin-type backprop, the noise is homogeneous, i.e., the same at each minimum. On the other hand, for incremental backprop, the noise is inhomogeneous, since it is related to the intrinsic fluctuations due to the random pattern presentation, which are a function of the weights. In incremental backprop, the higher the error, the more there is to learn, the larger the weight fluctuations, the higher the noise level, and the easier to escape local minima. The inhomogeneous stochastic noise in incremental backprop gives it an edge over Langevin-type backprop in escaping local minima, and this has been demonstrated in simulations by Heskes and Kappen (1993b).

process is an explicit or implicit process that evaluates the relative "quality" of search points (e.g., two consecutive search points) and biases the exploration process to move toward regions of high-quality solutions in Σ . Finally, the convergence-inducing process ensures the ultimate convergence of the search to a fixed solution $\mathbf{x}^*$. The dynamic interaction among these three processes is thus responsible for giving the search process its global optimizing character. As an exercise, one might consider identifying these three processes in the global optimization method of stochastic gradient descent presented in the preceding section. Here, the exploration process is realized by the noise term in Equation (8.1.4). The convergence-inducing process is realized effectively by the noise amplitude schedule $c(t)$ and by the gradient term $\nabla y(\mathbf{x})$. On the other hand, the search guidance process is not readily identifiable. In fact, this method lacks an effective guidance process, and the only guidance available is the local guidance due to the gradient term. Note that gradient-based guidance is only effective when the function $y(\mathbf{x})$ being minimized has its global minimum (or a near-optimal minimum) located at the bottom of a wide "valley" relative to other shallow local minima. A good example of such a function is $y(x) = x \sin (1/x)$.

Another stochastic method for global optimization is (stochastic) simulated annealing (Kirkpatrick et al., 1983; Kirkpatrick, 1984; Aart and Korst, 1989). This method does not use gradient information explicitly and thus is applicable to a wider range of functions (specifically, functions whose gradients are expensive to compute or functions that are not differentiable) than the stochastic gradient method.

Simulated annealing is analogous to the physical behavior of annealing a molten metal (Metropolis et al., 1953; Kirkpatrick et al.,1983). Above its melting temperature, a metal enters a phase where atoms (particles) are positioned at random according to statistical mechanics. As with all physical systems, the particles of the molten metal seek minimum energy configurations (states) if allowed to cool. A minimum energy configuration means a highly ordered state such as a defect-free crystal lattice. In order to achieve the defect-free crystal, the metal is annealed: First, the metal is heated above its melting point and then cooled slowly until it solidifies into a "perfect" crystalline structure. Slow cooling (as opposed to quenching) is necessary to prevent dislocations of atoms and other crystal lattice disruption. The defect-free crystal state corresponds to the global minimum energy configuration.

Next, a brief presentation of related statistical mechanics concepts is given that will help us understand the underlying principles of the simulated annealing global optimization method. Statistical mechanics is the central discipline of condensed-matter physics, which deals with the behavior of systems with many degrees of freedom in thermal equilibrium at a finite temperature [for a concise presentation of the basic ideas of statistical mechanics, see Shrödinger (1946)]. The starting point of statistical mechanics is an energy function $E(\mathbf{x})$ that measures the thermal energy of a physical system in a given state $\mathbf{x}$, where $\mathbf{x}$ belongs to a set of possible states Σ. If the system's absolute temperature T is not zero (i.e., $T > 0$), then the state $\mathbf{x}$ will vary in time, causing E to fluctuate. Being a physical system, the system will evolve its state in an average direction corresponding to that of decreasing energy E. This continues until no further decrease in the average of E is possible, which indicates that the system has reached thermal equilibrium. A fundamental result from physics is that at thermal equilibrium each of the possible states $\mathbf{x}$ occurs with probability

$$P(\mathbf{x}) = \frac{e^{-\frac{E(\mathbf{x})}{kT}}}{\displaystyle\sum_{\mathbf{x}\in\Sigma} e^{-\frac{E(\mathbf{x})}{kT}}} \tag{8.2.1}$$

where k is Boltzmann's constant, and the denominator is a constant that restricts $P(\mathbf{x})$ between zero and one. Equation (8.2.1) is known as the *Boltzmann-Gibbs distribution*.

Now define a set of transition probabilities $W(\mathbf{x} \to \mathbf{x}')$ from a state $\mathbf{x}$ into $\mathbf{x}'$. What is the condition on $W(\mathbf{x} \to \mathbf{x}')$ so that the system may reach and then remain in thermal equilibrium? A sufficient condition for maintaining equilibrium is that the average number of transitions from $\mathbf{x}$ to $\mathbf{x}'$ and from $\mathbf{x}'$ to $\mathbf{x}$ be equal:

$$P(\mathbf{x})W(\mathbf{x} \to \mathbf{x}') = P(\mathbf{x}')W(\mathbf{x}' \to \mathbf{x}) \tag{8.2.2}$$

or, by dividing by $W(\mathbf{x} \to \mathbf{x}')$ and using Equation (8.2.1),

$$\frac{W(\mathbf{x} \to \mathbf{x}')}{W(\mathbf{x}' \to \mathbf{x})} = \frac{P(\mathbf{x}')}{P(\mathbf{x})} = e^{-\frac{\Delta E}{kT}} \tag{8.2.3}$$

where $\Delta E = E(\mathbf{x}') - E(\mathbf{x})$. In simulating physical systems, a common choice for $W(\mathbf{x} \to \mathbf{x}')$ is the Metropolis algorithm (Metropolis et al., 1953), where

$$W(\mathbf{x} \to \mathbf{x}') = \begin{cases} 1 & \text{if } \Delta E < 0 \\ e^{-\frac{\Delta E}{kT}} & \text{otherwise} \end{cases} \tag{8.2.4}$$

This has the advantage of making more transitions to lower-energy states than those in Equation (8.2.3) and therefore reaches equilibrium more rapidly. Note that transitions from low- to high-energy states are possible except when $T = 0$.

Simulated annealing optimization for finding global minima of a function $y(\mathbf{x})$ borrows from the preceding theory. Two operations are involved in simulated annealing: a thermostatic operation that schedules decreases in the "temperature" and a stochastic relaxation operation that iteratively finds the equilibrium solution at the new temperature using the final state of the system at the previous temperature as a starting point. Here, a function y of discrete or continuous variables can be thought of as the energy function E in the preceding analysis. Simulated annealing introduces artificial thermal noise that is gradually decreased over time. This noise is controlled by a new parameter T that replaces the constant kT in Equation (8.2.4). Noise allows occasional hill climbing interspersed with descents. The idea is to apply uniform random perturbations $\Delta\mathbf{x}$ to the search point $\mathbf{x}$ and then to determine the resulting change $\Delta y = y(\mathbf{x} + \Delta\mathbf{x}) - y(\mathbf{x})$. If the value of y is reduced (i.e., $\Delta y < 0$), the new search point $\mathbf{x}' = \mathbf{x} + \Delta\mathbf{x}$ is adopted. On the other hand, if the perturbation leads to an increase in y (i.e., $\Delta y > 0$), the new search point $\mathbf{x}'$ may or may not be adopted. In this case, the determination of whether to accept $\mathbf{x}'$ is stochastic, with probability $\exp(-\Delta y/T)$. Hence, for large values of T, the probability of an uphill move in y is large. However, for small T, the probability of an uphill move is low; i.e., as T decreases, fewer uphill moves are allowed. This leads to an effective guidance of search, since the uphill moves are done in a controlled fashion, and thus there is no danger of jumping out of a local minimum and falling into a worse one.

The following is a step-by-step statement of a general-purpose simulated annealing optimization algorithm for finding the global minimum of a multivariate function $y(\mathbf{x})$, $\mathbf{x} \in \Sigma$:

1. Initialize $\mathbf{x}$ to an arbitrary point in Σ. Choose a "cooling" schedule for T. Initialize T at a sufficiently large value.

2. Compute $\mathbf{x}' = \mathbf{x} + \Delta\mathbf{x}$, where $\Delta\mathbf{x}$ is a small uniform random perturbation.

3. Compute $\Delta y = y(\mathbf{x}') - y(\mathbf{x})$.

4. Use the Metropolis algorithm [Equation (8.2.4)] for deciding whether to accept $\mathbf{x}'$ as the new search point (or else remain at $\mathbf{x}$). That is, if $\Delta y < 0$, the search point becomes $\mathbf{x}'$, otherwise, accept $\mathbf{x}'$ as the new point with a transition probability $W(\mathbf{x} \to \mathbf{x}') = \exp(-\Delta y/T)$. For this purpose, select a uniform random number a between zero and one. If $W(\mathbf{x} \to \mathbf{x}') > a$, then $\mathbf{x}'$ becomes the new search point, otherwise, the search point remains at $\mathbf{x}$.

5. Repeat steps 2 through 4 until the system reaches an equilibrium. Equilibrium is reached when the number of accepted transitions becomes insignificant, which happens when the search point is at or very close to a local minimum. In practice, steps 2 through 4 may be repeated for a fixed prespecified number of cycles.

6. Update T according to the annealing schedule chosen in step 1, and repeat steps 2 through 5. Stop when T reaches zero or a prespecified small positive value.

The effectiveness of simulated annealing in locating global minima and its speed of convergence critically depend on the choice of the cooling schedule for T. Generally speaking, if the cooling schedule is too fast, a premature convergence to a local minimum might occur, and if it is too slow, the algorithm will require an excessive amount of computation time to converge. Unfortunately, it has been found theoretically (Geman and Geman, 1984) that T must be reduced very slowly in proportion to the inverse log of time (processing cycle)

$$T(t) = \frac{T_0}{1 + \ln t} \qquad t = 1, 2, 3, \ldots \tag{8.2.5}$$

to guarantee that the simulated annealing search converges almost always to the global minimum. The problem of accelerating simulated annealing search has received increased attention, and a number of methods have been proposed to accelerate the search (Szu, 1986; Salamon et al., 1988). In practice, a suboptimal solution is sometimes sufficient, and faster cooling schedules may be employed. For example, one may even try a schedule of the form $T(t) = \alpha T(t - 1)$, where $0.85 \leq \alpha \leq 0.98$, which reduces the temperature exponentially fast.

Because of its generality as a global optimization method, simulated annealing has been applied to many optimization problems. Example applications can be found in Geman and Geman (1984), Sontag and Sussann (1985), Ligthart et al. (1986), Romeo (1989), Rutenbar (1989), and Johnson et al. (1989, 1991).

By now the reader might be wondering about the applicability of simulating annealing to neural networks. As is shown in the next section, it turns out that simulated annealing can be naturally mapped onto recurrent neural networks with stochastic units for the purpose of global retrieval and/or optimal learning. Simulated annealing may also be easily applied to the training of deterministic multilayer feedforward nets. Here, one can simply interpret the error function $E(\mathbf{w})$ [e.g., the SSE function in Equation (5.1.13) or the "batch" version of the entropy function in Equation (5.2.16)] as the multivariate scalar function $y(\mathbf{x})$ in the preceding algorithm. However, because of its intrinsic slow search speed, simulated annealing should only be considered in the training of deterministic multilayer nets if a global or near-global solution is desired and if one suspects that E is a complex multimodal function.

8.3   Simulated Annealing for Stochastic Neural Networks

In a stochastic neural network, the units have nondeterministic activation functions, as discussed in Section 3.1.6. Here, units behave stochastically, with the output (assumed to be bipolar binary) of the ith unit taking the value $x_i = +1$ with probability $f(net_i)$ and value $x_i = -1$ with probability $1 - f(net_i)$, where net_i is the weighted sum (net input) of unit i and

$$P(x_i) = f(net_i x_i) = \frac{1}{1 + e^{-2\beta\, net_i x_i}} = \frac{e^{\beta\, net_i x_i}}{e^{\beta\, net_i} + e^{-\beta\, net_i}} = \tfrac{1}{2}[1 + \tanh(\beta\, net_i x_i)] \quad (8.3.1)$$

where $P(x_i)$ represents the probability distribution of x_i. There are several possible choices of f which could have been made in Equation (8.3.1), but the choice of the sigmoidal function is motivated by statistical mechanics [Glauber (1963), Little (1974); see also Amari (1971)], where the units behave stochastically exactly like the spins in an Ising model of a magnetic material in statistical physics [for more details on the connections between stochastic units and the Ising model, the reader is referred to Hinton and Sejnowski (1983), Peretto (1984), Amit (1989), and Hertz et al., (1991)]. Equation (8.3.1) also may be derived based on observations relating to the stochastic nature of the post-synaptic potential of biological neurons (Shaw and Vasudevan, 1974). Here, the neuron may be approximated as a linear threshold gate (LTG) [recall Equation (1.1.1)] with zero threshold, signum activation function, and the net input (postsynaptic potential) being a Gaussian random variable as explored in Problem 8.3.1.

The parameter β in Equation (8.3.1) controls the steepness of the sigmoid $f(net)$ at $net = 0$. We may think of β as the reciprocal pseudotemperature, $\beta \triangleq 1/T$. When the "temperature" approaches zero, the sigmoid becomes a step function, and the stochastic unit becomes deterministic. As T increases, this sharp threshold is "softened" in a stochastic way, thus making the unit stochastic. Next, it is shown how stochastic neural nets with units described by Equation (8.3.1) and with controllable temperature T form a natural substrate for the implementation of simulated annealing–based optimization.

8.3.1   Global Convergence in a Stochastic Recurrent Neural Net: The Boltzmann Machine

Since simulated annealing is a global optimization method, one might be tempted to consider its use to enhance the convergence to optimal minima of gradient-type nets such as the Hopfield net used for combinatorial optimization.[4] In combinatorial optimization problems, one is interested in finding a solution vector $\mathbf{x} \in \{-1, 1\}^n$ (or $\{0, 1\}^n$) that best minimizes an objective function $y(\mathbf{x})$. When $y(\mathbf{x})$ is quadratic, the continuous Hopfield net may be used to search for local minimizers of $y(\mathbf{x})$. This is

---

4. Other more traditional methods for the solution of combinatorial optimization problems exist [e.g., branch-and-bound methods (Lawler and Wood, 1966) and Lagrangian relaxation (Fisher, 1981)] but will not be considered here.

achieved by first mapping $y(\mathbf{x})$ onto the quadratic energy function of the Hopfield net and then using the net as a gradient-descent algorithm to minimize $E(\mathbf{x})$, thus minimizing $y(\mathbf{x})$ (see Section 7.5 for details).

Rather than using the suboptimal Hopfield net approach, the desired global minimum of $y(\mathbf{x})$ may be obtained by a direct application of the simulated annealing method of Section 8.2. However, the promise of fast analog hardware implementations of the Hopfield net leads us to take another look at the network optimization approach, but with modifications that improve convergence to global solutions. The following is an optimization method based on an efficient way of incorporating simulated annealing search in a discrete Hopfield net.

Consider the discrete-state, discrete-time recurrent net (discrete Hopfield model) with ith unit dynamics described by Equation (7.1.37), repeated here for convenience:

$$x_i(k+1) = \mathrm{sgn}\,(net_i) = \mathrm{sgn}\left[\sum_{j=1}^{n} w_{ij}x_j(k) + I_i\right] \qquad i = 1, 2, \ldots, n \qquad (8.3.2)$$

This deterministic network has a quadratic Liapunov function (energy function) if its weight matrix is symmetric with positive (or zero) diagonal elements and if serial state update is used (recall Problem 7.1.17). In other words, this net will always converge to one of the local minima of its energy function $E(\mathbf{x})$ given by

$$E(\mathbf{x}) = -\tfrac{1}{2}\sum_{i=1}^{n}\sum_{j=1}^{n} w_{ij}x_i x_j - \sum_{i=1}^{n} I_i x_i \qquad (8.3.3)$$

Next, consider a stochastic version of this net, referred to as the *stochastic Hopfield net*, where we replace the deterministic threshold units by stochastic units according to Equation (8.3.1). By employing Equation (8.3.1) and assuming "thermal" equilibrium [note that here $W(x_i \to -x_i) = 1 - W(-x_i \to x_i)$], one may find the transition probability from x_i to $-x_i$ (i.e., the probability to flip unit i from $+1$ to -1 or vice versa) as

$$W(x_i \to -x_i) = \frac{1}{1 + e^{\frac{2\,net_i x_i}{T}}} = \frac{1}{1 + e^{\frac{\Delta E}{T}}} \qquad (8.3.4)$$

The right-most term in Equation (8.3.4) is obtained by using Equation (8.3.3), which gives $\Delta E_i = E(x_1, x_2, \ldots, -x_i, \ldots, x_n) - E(x_1, x_2, \ldots, x_i, \ldots, x_n) = 2\,net_i x_i$. The transition probabilities in Equation (8.3.4) give a complete description of the stochastic sequence of states in the stochastic Hopfield net. Note that if $T = 0$, the probability of a transition that increases the energy $E(\mathbf{x})$ becomes zero and that of a transition that decreases $E(\mathbf{x})$ becomes one; hence the net reduces to the stable deterministic

Hopfield net. On the other hand, for $T > 0$, a transition that increases $E(\mathbf{x})$ is allowed, but with a probability that is smaller than that of a transition that decreases $E(\mathbf{x})$. This last observation, coupled with the requirement that one and only one stochastic unit (chosen randomly and uniformly) is allowed to flip its state at a given time, guarantees that "thermal" equilibrium will be reached for any $T > 0$.

It may now be concluded that the serially updated stochastic Hopfield net with the stochastic dynamics in Equation (8.3.1) is stable (in an average sense) for $T \geq 0$ as long as its interconnection matrix is symmetric with positive diagonal elements. In other words, this stochastic net will reach an equilibrium state where the average value of E is a constant when T is held fixed for a sufficiently long period of time. Now, if a slowly decreasing temperature T is used with an initially large value, the stochastic Hopfield net becomes equivalent to a simulated annealing algorithm; i.e., when initialized at a random binary state $\mathbf{x}(0)$, the net will perform a stochastic global search seeking the global minimum of $E(\mathbf{x})$. As discussed in Section 8.2, at the beginning of the computation, a higher temperature should be used so that it is easier for the states to escape from local minima. Then, as the computation proceeds, the temperature is gradually decreased according to a prespecified cooling schedule. Finally, as the temperature approaches zero, the state, now placed (hopefully) near the global minimum, will converge to this minimum.

The preceding stochastic net is usually referred to as the *Boltzmann machine* because, at equilibrium, the probability of the states of the net is given by the Boltzmann-Gibbs distribution of Equation (8.2.1) or, equivalently,

$$\frac{P(\mathbf{x}')}{P(\mathbf{x})} = \frac{e^{-E(\mathbf{x}')/T}}{e^{-E(\mathbf{x})/T}} = e^{-\Delta E/T} \tag{8.3.5}$$

where $\mathbf{x}$ and $\mathbf{x}'$ are two states in $\{-1, 1\}^n$ that differ in only one bit. Equation (8.3.5) can be easily derived by employing Equations (8.3.1) and (8.3.3).

8.3.2 Learning in Boltzmann Machines

In the following, statistical mechanics ideas are extended to learning in stochastic recurrent networks, or *Boltzmann learning* (Hinton and Sejnowski, 1983, 1986; Ackley et al., 1985). These networks consist of n arbitrarily interconnected stochastic units where the state x_i of the ith unit is 1 or -1 with probability $f(net_i x_i)$, as in Equation (8.3.1). The units are divided into visible and hidden units, as shown in Figure 8.3.1. The hidden units have no direct inputs from, nor do they supply direct outputs to, the outside world. The visible units may (but need not) be further divided into input units and output units. The units are interconnected in an arbitrary way, but whatever the

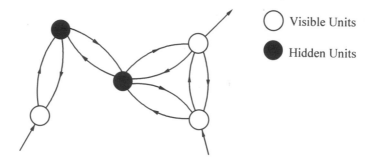

Visible Units

Hidden Units

Figure 8.3.1
A stochastic net with visible and hidden units. Connections between any
two units (if they exist) must be symmetric. The visible units may be further
divided into input and output units as illustrated.

interconnection pattern, all connections must be symmetric, $w_{ij} = w_{ji}$, with $w_{ii} = 0$.
The net activity at unit i is given by $net_i = \sum_{j \neq i} w_{ij} x_j$, where thresholds (biases) are
omitted for convenience and self-feedback is not allowed. This leads to an energy
function for this net given by

$$E(\mathbf{x}) = -\tfrac{1}{2} \sum_{\substack{i,j=1 \\ i \neq j}}^{n} w_{ij} x_i x_j \qquad (8.3.6)$$

whose minima are the stable states $\mathbf{x}^*$ characterized by $x_i^* = \mathrm{sgn}(net_i)$, $i = 1, 2, \dots, n$.
According to the discussion in Section 8.3.1, and because of the existence of an energy
function, it is seen that the states of the present stochastic net are governed by the
Boltzmann-Gibbs distribution of Equation (8.2.1), which may be adapted for the
present network/energy function as

$$P(\mathbf{x}) = \frac{e^{-\beta E(\mathbf{x})}}{\sum_{\mathbf{x} \in \Sigma} e^{-\beta E(\mathbf{x})}} = \frac{e^{-\beta E(\mathbf{x})}}{Z} \qquad (8.3.7)$$

where $\Sigma = \{-1, +1\}^n$ is the set of all possible states. Thus far a stable stochastic net
(Boltzmann machine) has been designed that is capable of reaching the global minimum (or a good suboptimal minimum) of its energy function by slowly decreasing the
pseudotemperature $T = 1/\beta$ starting from a sufficiently high temperature. Therefore,
this net may be viewed as an extension of the stochastic Hopfield net to include
hidden units. The presence of hidden units has the advantage of theoretically allowing
the net to represent (learn) arbitrary mappings/associations. In Boltzmann learning,

the weights w_{ij} are adjusted to give the states of the visible units a particular desired probability distribution.

Next, the derivation of a Boltzmann learning rule is presented. This rule is derived by minimizing a measure of the difference between the probability of finding the states of visible units in the freely running net and a set of desired probabilities for these states. Before proceeding any further, the states of the visible units are denoted by the activity pattern α and those of the hidden units by γ. Let N and K be the numbers of visible and hidden units, respectively. Then the set A of all visible patterns has a total of 2^N members (state configurations), and the set G of all hidden patterns has 2^K members. The vector $\mathbf{x}$ still represents the state of the whole network, and it belongs to the set Σ of $2^{N+K} = 2^n$ possible network states. The probability $P(\alpha)$ of finding the visible units in state α irrespective of γ is then obtained as

$$P(\alpha) = \sum_{\gamma \in G} P(\mathbf{x}) = \frac{1}{Z} \sum_{\gamma \in G} e^{-\beta E(\mathbf{x})} \tag{8.3.8}$$

Here, $P(\mathbf{x}) = P(\alpha, \gamma)$ denotes the joint probability that the visible units are in state α and the hidden units are in state γ, given that the network is operating in its clamped condition. Also, $E(\mathbf{x}) = E(\alpha, \gamma)$ is the energy of the network when the visible units are in state α and the hidden units are jointly in state γ. The term Z is the denominator in Equation (8.3.7) and should be interpreted as $\sum_{\alpha} \sum_{\gamma} \exp[-\beta E(\alpha, \gamma)]$. Equation (8.3.8) gives the actual probability $P(\alpha)$ of finding the visible units in state α in the freely running network at "thermal" equilibrium. This probability is determined by the weights w_{ij}. Now, assume that a set of desired probabilities $R(\alpha)$ is given, independent of the weights w_{ij}, for the visible states. Then the objective is to bring the distribution $P(\alpha)$ as close as possible to $R(\alpha)$ by adjusting the w_{ij} values. A suitable measure of the difference between $P(\alpha)$ and $R(\alpha)$, is the relative-entropy H (see Section 5.2.7):

$$H = \sum_{\alpha \in A} R(\alpha) \ln \frac{R(\alpha)}{P(\alpha)} \tag{8.3.9}$$

which is positive or zero [H is zero only if $R(\alpha) = P(\alpha)$ for all α]. Therefore, a learning equation may be arrived at by performing gradient descent on H:

$$\Delta w_{ij} = -\rho \frac{\partial H}{\partial w_{ij}} = \rho \sum_{\alpha \in A} \frac{R(\alpha)}{P(\alpha)} \frac{\partial P(\alpha)}{\partial w_{ij}}$$

$$i \neq j = 1, 2, \ldots, n \tag{8.3.10}$$

where ρ is a small positive constant. Using Equations (8.3.6) through (8.3.8) and recalling that $w_{ij} = w_{ji}$, one finds

$$\frac{\partial P(\alpha)}{\partial w_{ij}} = \frac{\beta}{Z} \sum_{\gamma \in G} e^{-\beta E(\mathbf{x})} x_i x_j - \frac{\beta}{Z^2} \left(\sum_{\gamma \in G} e^{-\beta E(\mathbf{x})} \right) \left(\sum_{\mathbf{x} \in \Sigma} e^{-\beta E(\mathbf{x})} x_i x_j \right) \qquad (8.3.11)$$

where $\sum\limits_{\mathbf{x} \in \Sigma}$ denotes $\sum\limits_{\alpha} \sum\limits_{\gamma}$, and x_i (x_j) should be interpreted as the state of unit i (j), given that the visible units are in state α and the hidden units are jointly in state γ.

Next, using Equation (8.3.8) and noting that the quantity $(1/Z) \sum\limits_{\mathbf{x} \in \Sigma} e^{-\beta E(\mathbf{x})} x_i x_j = \sum\limits_{\mathbf{x} \in \Sigma} P(\mathbf{x}) x_i x_j = \sum\limits_{\alpha} \sum\limits_{\gamma} P(\alpha, \gamma) x_i x_j$ is the average $\langle x_i x_j \rangle$ gives

$$\frac{\partial P(\alpha)}{\partial w_{ij}} = \beta \left[\sum_{\gamma \in G} P(\alpha, \gamma) x_i x_j - P(\alpha) \langle x_i x_j \rangle \right] \qquad (8.3.12)$$

Thus substituting Equation (8.3.12) in Equation (8.3.10) leads to the Boltzmann learning rule:

$$\Delta w_{ij} = \rho \beta \left[\sum_{\alpha} \frac{R(\alpha)}{P(\alpha)} \sum_{\gamma} P(\alpha, \gamma) x_i x_j - \sum_{\alpha} R(\alpha) \langle x_i x_j \rangle \right]$$

$$i \neq j = 1, 2, \ldots, n$$

$$= \rho \beta [\overline{\langle x_i x_j \rangle}_{\text{clamped}} - \langle x_i x_j \rangle] \qquad (8.3.13)$$

where $\sum\limits_{\alpha} R(\alpha) = 1$ is used and

$$\overline{\langle x_i x_j \rangle}_{\text{clamped}} \triangleq \sum_{\alpha} \frac{R(\alpha)}{P(\alpha)} \sum_{\gamma} P(\alpha, \gamma) x_i x_j = \sum_{\alpha} R(\alpha) \sum_{\gamma} P(\gamma | \alpha) x_i x_j \qquad (8.3.14)$$

represents the value of $\langle x_i x_j \rangle$ when the visible units are clamped in state α, averaged over all α according to their desired probabilities $R(\alpha)$. Note that in Equation (8.3.14), the term $P(\alpha, \gamma)/P(\alpha)$ was replaced by $P(\gamma | \alpha)$ according to Bayes' rule.

The first term on the right-hand side of Equation (8.3.13) is essentially a Hebbian learning term, with the visible units clamped, while the second term corresponds to anti-Hebbian learning, with the system free-running. Note that learning converges when the free unit-unit correlations are equal to the clamped ones. It is very important that the correlations in the Boltzmann learning rule be computed when the system is in thermal equilibrium at temperature $T = 1/\beta > 0$, since the derivation of this rule hinges on the Boltzmann-Gibbs distribution of Equation (8.3.7). At equilibrium, the state $\mathbf{x}$ fluctuates, and one measures the correlations $\langle x_i x_j \rangle$ by taking a time average of $x_i x_j$. This must be done twice, once with the visible units clamped in each of their states α for which $R(\alpha)$ is nonzero and once with the state α unclamped. Thermal equilibrium must be reached for each of these computations.

As the reader may have already suspected by examining Equations (8.3.13) and (8.3.14), Boltzmann learning is very computationally intensive. Usually, one starts with a high temperature (very small β) and chooses a cooling schedule. At each of these temperatures, the network is allowed to follow its stochastic dynamics according to Equation (8.3.1), or equivalently, many units are sampled and are updated according to Equation (8.3.4). The temperature is lowered slowly according to the preselected schedule until T approaches zero and equilibrium is reached. This simulated annealing search must be repeated with clamped visible units in each desired pattern α and with unclamped visible units. In the computation of $\langle x_i x_j \rangle_{\text{clamped}}$, the states α are clamped to randomly drawn patterns from the training set according to a given probability distribution $R(\alpha)$. For each such training pattern, the network seeks equilibrium following the same annealing schedule. The weights are updated only after enough training patterns are taken. This whole process is repeated many times to achieve convergence to a good set of weights w_{ij}.

The learning rule just described is compatible with pattern completion, in which a trained net is expected to fill in missing bits of a partial pattern when such a pattern is clamped on the visible nodes. This is reminiscent of retrieval in the dynamic associative memories of Chapter 7. Note that the presence of hidden units allows for high memory capacity. During retrieval, the weights derived in the training phase are held fixed, and simulated annealing–based global retrieval is used as discussed in Section 8.3.1. Here, the visible units are clamped at corresponding known bits of a noisy/partial input pattern. Starting from a high temperature, the net follows the stochastic dynamics in Equation (8.3.1), or equivalently, state transitions are made according to Equation (8.3.4). The temperature is gradually lowered according to an appropriate schedule until the dynamics become deterministic at $T = 0$, and convergence to the "closest" pattern (global solution) is (hopefully) achieved.

We also may extend Boltzmann learning to handle the association of input/output pairs of patterns, as in supervised learning in multilayer perceptron nets. Here, we need to distinguish between two types of visible units: input and output. Let us represent the input units, the output units, and the hidden units by the states σ, α, and γ, respectively. In this case, the network is to learn the desired associations $\sigma \rightarrow \alpha$. The problem may be posed as follows: For each σ, the w_{ij} values must be adjusted such that the conditional probability distribution $P(\alpha|\sigma)$ is as close as possible to a desired distribution $R(\alpha|\sigma)$. Assuming that the σ occur with probability $p(\sigma)$, a suitable error measure is

$$H = \sum_{\sigma} p(\sigma) \sum_{\alpha} R(\alpha|\sigma) \ln \frac{R(\alpha|\sigma)}{P(\alpha|\sigma)} \tag{8.3.15}$$

which leads to the Boltzmann learning rule (Hopfield, 1987):

$$\Delta w_{ij} = \rho\beta[\overline{\langle x_i x_j \rangle}_{\text{I, O clamped}} - \overline{\langle x_i x_j \rangle}_{\text{I clamped}}] \tag{8.3.16}$$

In Equation (8.3.16), both the inputs and outputs are clamped in the Hebbian term, while only the input states are clamped in the anti-Hebbian (unlearning) term, with averages over the inputs taken in both cases. Examples of applications of learning Boltzmann machines can be found in Ackley et al. (1985), Parks (1987), Sejnowski et al. (1986), Kohonen et al. (1988), and Lippmann (1989). Theoretically, Boltzmann machines with learning may outperform gradient-based learning such as backprop. However, the demanding computational overhead associated with these machines would usually render them impractical in software simulations. Specialized electronic (Alspector and Allen, 1987) and optoelectronic (Farhat, 1987; Ticknor and Barrett, 1987) hardware has been developed for the Boltzmann machine. However, such hardware implementations are still experimental in nature. Variations and related networks can be found in Derthick (1984), Hopfield et al. (1983), Smolensky (1986), van Hemman et al. (1990), Galland and Hinton (1991), and Apolloni and De Falco (1991).

8.4 Mean-Field Annealing and Deterministic Boltzmann Machines

Mean-field annealing (Soukoulis et al., 1983; Bilbro et al., 1989) is a deterministic approximation to simulated annealing that is significantly more computationally efficient (faster) than simulated annealing (Bilbro et al., 1992). Instead of directly simulating the stochastic transitions in simulated annealing, the mean (or average) behavior of these transitions is used to characterize a given stochastic system. Because computations using the mean transitions attain equilibrium faster than those using the corresponding stochastic transitions, mean-field annealing relaxes to a solution at each temperature much faster than does stochastic simulated annealing. This leads to a significant decrease in computational effort. The idea of using a deterministic mean-valued approximation for a system of stochastic equations to simplify the analysis has been adopted at various instances in this book (e.g., see Section 4.3). Generally speaking, such approximations are adequate in high-dimensional systems of many interacting units (states), where each state is a function of all or a large number of other states, allowing the central limit theorem to be used (see Problem 7.5.9). This section restricts the discussion of mean-field annealing to the Boltzmann machine, which was introduced in the preceding section.

8.4.1   Mean-Field Retrieval

Consider a stochastic Hopfield net with the stochastic dynamics given in Equation (8.3.1). The evolution of the stochastic state x_i of unit i depends on net_i, which involves variables x_j that themselves fluctuate between -1 and $+1$. Let us transform the set of n stochastic equations in x_i to n deterministic equations in $\langle x_i \rangle$ governing the means of the stochastic variables. If the focus is on a single variable x_i, and its average is computed by assuming no fluctuations of the other x_j values (this allows us to replace net_i by its average $\langle net_i \rangle$), the result is

$$\langle x_i \rangle = P(x_i = +1)(+1) + P(x_i = -1)(-1)$$

$$= \tfrac{1}{2}[1 + \tanh(\beta \langle net_i \rangle)] - \tfrac{1}{2}[1 + \tanh(-\beta \langle net_i \rangle)]$$

$$= \tanh(\beta \langle net_i \rangle)$$

$$= \tanh\left(\beta \sum_{j=1}^{n} w_{ij} \langle x_j \rangle + \beta I_i \right) \qquad i = 1, 2, \ldots, n \qquad (8.4.1)$$

The system is now deterministic and is approximated by the n mean-field equations represented by Equation (8.4.1). It is important to point out that Equation (8.4.1) is meaningful only when the network is at thermal equilibrium, which means that all the quantities $\langle x_i \rangle$ converge (become time-independent). Luckily, the stochastic Hopfield net is guaranteed to reach thermal equilibrium, as was discussed in Section 8.3.1.

At thermal equilibrium, the stochastic Hopfield net fluctuates about the constant average values in Equation (8.4.1). The mean state $\langle \mathbf{x} \rangle$ is thus one of the local minima of the quadratic energy function $E(\mathbf{x})$ at temperature $T = 1/\beta$. The location of this minimum may then be computed by solving the set of n nonlinear mean-field equations. An alternative approach is to solve for $\langle \mathbf{x} \rangle$ by gradient descent on $E(\mathbf{x})$ from an initial random state. This is exactly what the deterministic continuous Hopfield net with hyperbolic tangent activations does [recall Equation (7.1.25)]. In fact, Equation (8.4.1) has the same form as the equation governing the equilibrium points of the Hopfield net (Bilbro et al., 1989). To see this, recall from Equation (7.1.19) the dynamics of the ith unit in a continuous-state electronic Hopfield net, namely,

$$C \frac{du_i}{dt} = -\alpha_i u_i + \sum_{j=1}^{n} w_{ij} x_j + I_i \qquad (8.4.2)$$

The equilibria of Equation (8.4.2) are given by setting $\dfrac{du_i}{dt}$ to zero, giving

$$u_i = \frac{1}{\alpha_i} \left(\sum_{j=1}^{n} w_{ij} x_j + I_i \right) \tag{8.4.3}$$

Assuming the common choice $x = f(u) = \tanh(\beta u)$ in Equation (8.4.3) gives

$$x_i = \tanh \left(\frac{\beta}{\alpha_i} \sum_{j=1}^{n} w_{ij} x_j + \beta I_i \right) \tag{8.4.4}$$

which becomes identical in form to Equation (8.4.1) after setting $\alpha_i = 1$ and thinking of x_i as $\langle x_i \rangle$.

The electronic continuous-state (deterministic) Hopfield net must employ high-gain amplifiers (large β) in order to achieve a binary-valued solution, as is normally generated by the original stochastic net. However, starting with a deterministic net having large β may lead to a poor local minimum, as is the case with a stochastic net whose "temperature" T is quenched. Since annealing a stochastic net increases the probability that the state will converge to a global minimum, one may try to reach this minimum by annealing the approximate mean-field system. This approach is known as *mean-field annealing*. Mean-field annealing can be realized very efficiently in electronic (analog) nets like the one in Figure 7.1.3, where dynamic amplifier gains allow for a natural implementation of continuous cooling schedules (Lee and Shen, 1993). This is referred to as *hardware annealing*.

The deterministic Boltzmann machine is applicable only to problems involving quadratic cost functions. However, the principles of mean-field annealing may still be applied to more general cost functions with substantial savings in computing time by annealing a steady-state average system as opposed to a stochastic one. In addition to being faster than simulated annealing, mean-field annealing has proved to lead to better solutions in several optimization problems (van den Bout and Miller, 1988, 1989; Cortes and Hertz, 1989; Bilbro and Snyder, 1989).

8.4.2 Mean-Field Learning

The excessive number of calculations required by Boltzmann machine learning may be circumvented by extending the preceding mean-field method to adapting the weights w_{ij} (Peterson and Anderson, 1987). Here, the correlations $\langle x_i x_j \rangle$ are approximated by $s_i s_j$, where s_i is given by the average equation:

$$s_i = \langle x_i \rangle = \tanh \left(\beta \sum_{j=1}^{n} w_{ij} \langle x_j \rangle \right) = \tanh \left(\beta \sum_{j=1}^{n} w_{ij} s_j \right) \tag{8.4.5}$$

as in Equation (8.4.1), but with $I_i = 0$ for convenience. Equation (8.4.5) applies for free units (hidden units and unclamped visible units). For a clamped visible unit i, s_i is set to ± 1 (the value that the unit's output is supposed to be clamped at). As required by

Boltzmann learning, the correlations $\langle x_i x_j \rangle$ should be computed at thermal equilibrium. This means that approximation terms $s_i s_j$ must be used, where the s_i values (s_j values) are solutions to the n nonlinear equations represented by Equation (8.4.5). One may employ an iterative method to solve for the unclamped states s_i according to

$$s_i^{\text{new}} = \tanh\left(\beta \sum_{j=1}^{n} w_{ij} s_j^{\text{old}} \right) \tag{8.4.6}$$

combined with annealing (gradual increasing of β). Peterson and Anderson (1987) reported that this mean-field learning is 10 to 30 times faster than simulated annealing on some test problems with somewhat better results.

8.5   Genetic Algorithms in Neural Network Optimization

Genetic algorithms are global optimization algorithms based on the mechanics of natural selection and natural genetics. They employ a structured yet randomized parallel multipoint search strategy that is biased toward reinforcing search points of "high fitness," i.e., points at which the function being minimized has relatively low values. Genetic algorithms are similar to simulated annealing (Davis, 1987) in that they employ random (probabilistic) search strategies. However, one of the apparent distinguishing features of genetic algorithms is their effective implementation of parallel multipoint search. This section presents the fundamentals of genetic algorithms and shows how they may be used for neural networks training.

8.5.1   Fundamentals of Genetic Algorithms

The *genetic algorithm (GA)*, as originally formulated by Holland (1975), was intended to be used as a modeling device for organic evolution. Later, De Jong (1975) demonstrated that the GA also may be used to solve optimization problems and that globally optimal results may be produced. Although there has been a lot of work done on modifications and improvements to the method, this section will present the standard genetic algorithm, and the analysis will follow the presentation given in Goldberg (1989).

In its simplest form, the standard genetic algorithm is a method of stochastic optimization for discrete programming problems of the form

$$\begin{aligned} &\text{Maximize} \quad f(s) \\ &\text{subject to} \quad \mathbf{s} \in \Omega = \{0, 1\}^n \end{aligned} \tag{8.5.1}$$

In this case, $f : \Omega \to R$ is called the *fitness function*, and the n-dimensional binary vectors in Ω are called *strings*. The most noticeable difference between the standard genetic algorithm and the methods of optimization discussed earlier is that at each stage (iteration) of the computation, genetic algorithms maintain a collection of samples from the search space Ω rather than a single point. This collection of samples is called a *population* of strings.

To start the genetic search, an initial population of, say, M binary strings $S(0) = \{s_1, s_2, \ldots, s_M\} \subset \Omega$, each with n bits, is created. Usually, this initial population is created randomly because it is not known a priori where the globally optimal strings in Ω are likely to be found. If such information is given, though, it may be used to bias the initial population toward the most promising regions of Ω. From this initial population, subsequent populations $S(1), S(2), \ldots S(t), \ldots$ will be computed by employing the three genetic operators of *selection*, *crossover*, and *mutation*.

The standard genetic algorithm uses a roulette wheel method for selection, which is a stochastic version of the survival-of-the-fittest mechanism. In this method of selection, candidate strings from the current generation $S(t)$ are selected to survive to the next generation $S(t + 1)$ by designing a roulette wheel where each string in the population is represented on the wheel in proportion to its fitness value. Thus those strings which have a high fitness are given a large share of the wheel, while those strings with low fitness are given a relatively small portion of the roulette wheel. Finally, selections are made by spinning the roulette wheel M times and accepting as candidates those strings which are indicated at the completion of the spin.

Example 8.5.1   As an example, suppose $M = 5$, and consider the following initial population of strings: $S(0) = \{(10110), (11000), (11110), (01001), (00110)\}$. For each string s_i in the population, the fitness may be evaluated: $f(s_i)$. The appropriate share of the roulette wheel to allot the ith string is obtained by dividing the fitness of the ith string by the sum of the fitnesses of the entire population:

$$\frac{f(s_i)}{\sum_{j=1}^{M} f(s_j)}$$

Figure 8.5.1 shows a listing of the population with associated fitness values and the corresponding roulette wheel.

To compute the next population of strings, the roulette wheel is spun five times. The strings chosen by this method of selection, though, are only candidate strings for the next population. Before actually being copied into the new population, these strings must undergo crossover and mutation.

Pairs of the M (assume M even) candidate strings which have survived selection are next chosen for crossover, which is a recombination mechanism. The probability that

String s_i	Fitness $f(s_i)$	Relative Fitness
s_1 10110	2.23	0.14
s_2 11000	7.27	0.47
s_3 11110	1.05	0.07
s_4 01001	3.35	0.21
s_5 00110	1.69	0.11

(a)

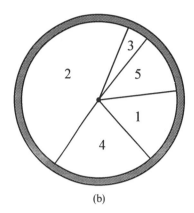

(b)

Figure 8.5.1
(a) A listing of the five-string population and the associated fitness values. (b) Corresponding roulette wheel for string selection. The integers shown on the roulette wheel correspond to string labels.

1 1 0 1 0 1	1 1 0 1 0 1	1 1 0 1 0 0
1 0 0 1 0 0	1 0 0 1 0 0	1 0 0 1 0 1
(a)	(b)	(c)

Figure 8.5.2
An example of a crossover for two 6-bit strings. (a) Two strings are selected for crossover. (b) A crossover site is selected at random. In this case, $k = 4$. (c) Now swap the two strings after the kth bit.

the crossover operator is applied will be denoted by P_c. Pairs of strings are selected randomly from $S(t)$, without replacement, for crossover. A random integer k, called the *crossing site*, is chosen from $\{1, 2, \ldots, n - 1\}$, and then the bits from the two chosen strings are swapped after the kth bit with a probability P_c. This process is repeated until $S(t)$ is empty. For example, Figure 8.5.2 illustrates a crossover for two 6-bit strings. In this case, the crossing site k is 4, so the bits from the two strings are swapped after the fourth bit.

Finally, after crossover, mutation is applied to the candidate strings. The mutation operator is a stochastic bit-wise complementation applied with uniform probability P_m. That is, for each single bit in the population, the value of the bit is flipped from 0 to 1 or from 1 to 0 with probability P_m. As an example, suppose $P_m = 0.1$, and the string $s = 11100$ is to undergo mutation. The easiest way to determine which bits, if any, to flip is to choose a uniform random number $r \in [0, 1]$ for each bit in the string. If $r \le P_m$, then the bit is flipped; otherwise, no action is taken. For the string s above, suppose the random numbers (0.91, 0.43, 0.03, 0.67, 0.29) were generated, then the resulting mutation is shown below. In this case, the third bit was flipped.

$$\text{Before mutation:} \quad 1 \; 1 \; ① \; 0 \; 0$$
$$\text{After mutation:} \quad \; 1 \; 1 \; 0 \; 0 \; 0$$

After mutation, the candidate strings are copied into the new population of strings $S(t + 1)$, and the whole process is repeated by calculating the fitness of each string, using a roulette wheel method of selection, and applying the operators of crossover and mutation.

Before pursuing an analytical analysis of the action of the genetic operators, some qualitative comments may be helpful first. In the roulette wheel method of selection, it is clear that only the above-average strings will tend to survive successive populations. Applying only selection to a population of strings results in a sort of MAX operation, i.e., the operation of selecting the maximum from a set of numbers. It has been shown (Suter and Kabrisky, 1992) that a MAX operation may be implemented by successive application of a theorem by Hardy et al. (1952), which states that for a set of nonnegative real numbers $Q \subset R$, then

$$\min(Q) < \text{ave}(Q) < \max(Q) \tag{8.5.2}$$

(where it is assumed that not all the elements of Q are equal). Therefore, the maximum value may be obtained by simply averaging the elements of Q and excluding all elements that are below average. The remaining subset may be averaged and the process repeated until only the maximum value survives. The roulette wheel method of selection may be thought of as a "soft" stochastic version of this MAX operation, where strings with above-average strengths tend to survive successive roulette wheel spins.

The reason that the stochastic version is used, rather than just deterministically always choosing the best strings to survive, gets at the crux of the underlying theory and assumptions of genetic search. This theory is based on the notion that even strings with very low fitness may contain some useful partial information to guide the search. For this reason, though the survival probability is small, these lowly fit strings are not altogether discarded during the search.

Of the three genetic operators, the crossover operator is the most crucial in obtaining global results. Crossover is responsible for mixing the partial information contained in the strings of the population. In the next section it will be conjectured that this type of mixing will lead to the formation of optimal strings. Based on empirical evidence, it has been found (De Jong, 1975; Grefenstette, 1986; Schaffer et al., 1989) that reasonable values for the probability of crossover are $0.6 \leq P_c \leq 0.99$.

Unlike the previous two operators, which are used to fully exploit and possibly improve the structure of the best strings in the current population, the purpose of the mutation operator is to diversify the search and introduce new strings into the population in order to fully explore the search space. The creation of these new strings is usually required because of the vast differences between the number of strings in the population M and the total number of strings in the entire search space Ω, 2^n. Typically, M is chosen to be orders of magnitude smaller than 2^n, so by selecting and recombining (crossing) the M strings in a given population, only a fraction of the total search space Ω is explored. Thus mutation forces diversity in the population and allows more of the search space to be sampled, thus allowing the search to overcome local minima.

Mutation, though, cuts with a double-edged sword. Applying mutation too frequently will result in destroying the highly fit strings in the population, which may slow and impede convergence to a solution. Hence, although necessary, mutation is usually applied with a small probability. Empirically, it has been found (De Jong, 1975; Grefenstette, 1986; Schaffer et al., 1989) that reasonable values for the probability of mutation are $0.01 \leq P_m \leq 0.001$. Bäck (1993) presented a theoretical analysis where he showed that $P_m = 1/n$ is the best choice when the fitness function f is unimodal. However, for a multimodal fitness function, Bäck shows that a dynamic mutation rate may overcome local minima, whereas a fixed mutation rate may not. The dynamic mutation rate may be implemented by following a schedule where P_m is slowly decreased toward $1/n$ from an initial value $P_m(0)$ such that $1 > P_m(0) \gg 1/n$. This is analogous to decreasing the temperature in simulated annealing. Davis and Principe (1993) showed that the asymptotic convergence of a GA with a suitable mutation probability schedule can be faster than that of simulated annealing.

The Fundamental Theorem of Genetic Algorithms   The mechanisms of the standard genetic algorithm have just been described. Later, it will be demonstrated by example that the GA actually works; i.e., global solutions to multimodal functions may be obtained. The question here is, *Why* does the standard GA work? Surprisingly, although the literature abounds with applications that demonstrate the effectiveness of GA search, the underlying theory is far less understood. The theoretical basis that has been established thus far (Goldberg, 1989; Thierens and Goldberg, 1993), though, will be described next.

To analyze the convergence properties of the GA, it is useful to define the notion of *schema* (plural, *schemata*). A schema H is a structured subset of the search space Ω. The structure in H is provided by string similarities at certain fixed positions of all the strings in H. The string positions that are not fixed in a given schema are usually denoted by *. For example, the schema $H = *11*0$ is the collection of all 5-bit binary strings that contain a 1 in the second and third string positions and a 0 in the last position, that is,

$$H = \{(01100), (01110), (11100), (11110)\}$$

In total, there are 3^n different schemata possible: all combinations of the symbols $\{0, 1, *\}$. Since there are only 2^n different strings in Ω, it is clear that a given string in Ω will belong to several different schemata. More precisely, each string in Ω will belong to 2^n different schemata.

To prove the fundamental theorem of genetic algorithms, it is necessary to investigate the effect that selection, crossover, and mutation has on a typical population of strings. More generally, it is possible to determine the effect of these genetic operators on the schemata of a typical population. The following notation will be useful: The *order* of a schema H is the number of fixed positions over the strings in H, and the *defining length* of a schema is the distance between the first and last fixed positions of the schema. The order and defining length are denoted by $o(H)$ and $\delta(H)$, respectively. For example, for the schema $*11**0$, $o(H) = 3$ because there are 3 fixed positions in H, and $\delta(H) = 6 - 2 = 4$, because 2 and 6 are the indices of the first and last fixed string positions in H, respectively.

Consider $S(t)$, the population of strings at time t, and consider the collection of schemata that contain one or more of the strings in this population. For each such schema H, denote by $m(H, t)$ the number of strings in the population at time t which are also in H. We want to study the long-term behavior of $m(H, t)$ for those schemata H which contain highly fit strings.

Using the roulette wheel method of selection outlined in the preceding section, the expected number of strings in $H \cap S(t + 1)$ given the quantity $m(H, t)$ is easily seen to be

$$m(H, t + 1) = \frac{f(H)}{\bar{f}} m(H, t) \qquad (8.5.3)$$

where $f(H)$ is the average fitness of the strings in $H \cap S(t + 1)$, and $\bar{f} = (1/M) \sum_{j=1}^{M} f(\mathbf{s}_j)$ is the average fitness of all the strings in the population at time t. Assuming $f(H)/\bar{f}$ remains relatively constant, the preceding equation has the form of a linear difference equation: $x(t + 1) = ax(t)$. The solution of this equation is well known and given by $x(t) = a^t x(0)$, $t = 0, 1, 2, \ldots$, which explodes if $a > 1$ and decays if $a < 1$. By comparing with Equation (8.5.3), it is seen that the number of strings in the population represented by H is expected to grow exponentially if $f(H) > \bar{f}$, i.e., if the average fitness of the schema is higher than the average fitness of the entire population. Conversely, the number of strings in the population represented by H will decay exponentially if $f(H) < \bar{f}$.

Now consider the effect of crossover on a schema H with $m(H, t)$ samples in the population at time t. If a string belonging to H is selected for crossover, one of two possibilities may occur: (1) the crossover preserves the structure of H (in this case, the schema is said to have *survived crossover*), or (2) the crossover destroys the structure (and hence the resulting crossed string will not belong to H at time $t + 1$). It is easy to see by example which schemata are likely to survive crossover. Consider the two schemata A and B shown below:

$$A = 1{*}{*}{*}1{*} \qquad B = {*}01{*}{*}{*}$$

Claim: Schema A will not survive crossover if the cross site k is 1, 2, 3, or 4. To see this, just take a representative example from A, say, 100011. Making the reasonable assumption that the mating string is not identical to the example string at precisely the fixed string positions of A (i.e., the first and fifth positions), then upon crossover with cross site 1, 2, 3, or 4, the fixed 1 at the fifth string position will be lost, and the resulting string will not belong to A.

On the other hand, schema B may be crossed at sites 1, 3, 4, and 5 and still preserve the structure of B, because, in this case, the 01 fixed positions will lie on the same side of the crossing site and will be copied into the resulting string. The only crossing site that will destroy the structure of schema B would be $k = 2$.

By noticing the difference in defining length for these two schemata, $\delta(A) = 4$ and $\delta(B) = 1$, the following conclusion may be made: A schema survives crossover when the cross site is chosen outside its defining length. Hence the probability that a schema H will survive crossover is given by $[1 - \delta(H)]/(n - 1)$. However, since the crossover operator is only applied with probability P_c, the following quantity is a lower bound for the crossover survival probability:

$$\frac{1 - P_c \delta(H)}{n - 1}$$

Finally, the mutation operator destroys schema only if it is applied to the fixed positions in the schema. Hence the probability that a schema H will survive mutation is given by $(1 - P_m)^{o(H)}$. For small values of P_m, the binomial theorem may be employed to obtain the approximation $(1 - P_m)^{o(H)} \approx 1 - o(H)P_m$. The *fundamental theorem of genetic algorithms* may now be given.

THEOREM 8.5.1 (Goldberg, 1989)   By using the selection, crossover, and mutation of the standard genetic algorithm, then short, low-order, and above-average schemata receive exponentially increasing trials in subsequent populations.

Proof   Since the operations of selection, crossover, and mutation are applied independently, the probability that a schema H will survive to the next generation may be obtained by a simple multiplication of the survival probabilities derived above:

$$m(H, t + 1) \geq \frac{f(H)}{\bar{f}} \left[1 - P_c \frac{\delta(H)}{n - 1} \right] [1 - o(H)P_m] m(t, H) \qquad (8.5.4)$$

By neglecting the cross-product terms, the desired result is obtained:

$$m(H, t + 1) \geq \frac{f(H)}{\bar{f}} \left[1 - P_c \frac{\delta(H)}{n - 1} - o(H)P_m \right] m(t, H) \qquad (8.5.5)$$

The short, low-order, and above-average schemata are called *building blocks*, and the fundamental theorem indicates that building blocks are expected to dominate the population. Is this good or bad in terms of the original goal of function optimization? The preceding theorem does not answer this question. Rather, the connection between the fundamental theorem and the observed optimizing properties of the genetic algorithm is provided by the following conjecture.

THE BUILDING BLOCK HYPOTHESIS   The globally optimal strings in Ω may be partitioned into substrings that are given by the bits of the fixed positions of building blocks.

Stated another way, the hypothesis is that the partial information contained in each of the building blocks may be combined to obtain globally optimal strings. If this hypothesis is correct, then the fundamental theorem implies that the GA is doing the right thing in allocating an exponentially increasing number of trials to the building blocks, because some arrangement of the building blocks is likely to produce a globally optimal string.

Unfortunately, although the building block hypothesis seems reasonable enough, it does not always hold true. Cases where the hypothesis fails can be constructed. It is believed (Goldberg, 1989), though, that such cases are of "needle in the haystack" type, where the globally optimal strings are surrounded (in a Hamming distance sense) by the worst strings in Ω. Such problems are called *GA-deceptive* because by following the building block hypothesis, the GA is lead away from the globally optimal solutions rather than toward them. Current trends in GA research (Kuo and

Hwang, 1993; Qi and Palmieri, 1993) include modifying the standard genetic operators in order to enable the GA to solve such "needle in the haystack" problems and
hence shrink in size the class of GA-deceptive problems.

The preceding analysis is based entirely on the schemata in the population rather
than the actual strings in the population. The GA, though, processes strings—not
schemata. This type of duality is called *implicit parallelism* by Holland (1975). The
implicit parallelism notion means that a larger amount of information is obtained and
processed at each generation by the GA than would appear by simply looking at the
processing of the M strings. This additional information comes from the number of
schemata that the GA is processing per generation. The next question is, How many
schemata are actually processed per generation by the GA? Clearly, in every population of M strings, there are between 2^n and $2^n M$ schemata present (if all the strings in
the population are the same, then there are 2^n schemata; if all the strings are different,
there may be at most $2^n M$ schemata). Because the selection, crossover, and mutation
operations tend to favor certain schemata, not all the schemata in the population will
be processed by the GA. Holland (1975) estimated that $O(M^3)$ schemata per generation are actually processed in a useful manner (see also Goldberg, 1989). Hence implicit parallelism implies that by processing M strings, the GA actually processes
$O(M^3)$ schemata for free!

To apply the standard genetic algorithm to an arbitrary optimization problem of
the form

$$\text{Minimize} \quad y(\mathbf{x})$$
$$\text{subject to} \quad \mathbf{x} \in \Sigma \subset R^n \tag{8.5.6}$$

it is necessary to establish the following:

1. A correspondence between the search space Σ and some space of binary strings Ω,
   i.e., an invertible mapping of the form $D: \Sigma \to \Omega$.

2. An appropriate fitness function $f(\mathbf{s})$ such that the maximizers of f correspond to
   the minimizers of y.

This situation is shown schematically in Figure 8.5.3.

Example 8.5.2   As an example of the solution process, consider the function shown in
Figure 8.1.1 and the following optimization problem:

$$\text{Minimize} \quad y(\mathbf{x}) = x \sin\left(\frac{1}{x}\right)$$
$$\text{subject to} \quad x \in [0.01, 0.5] \tag{8.5.7}$$

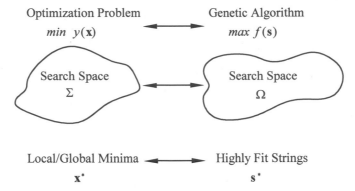

Figure 8.5.3
A schematic representation of the process of matching an optimization
problem with the genetic algorithm framework.

This is the same function considered earlier in Example 8.1.1 and plotted in Figure
8.1.1. This function has two local minima, $x \approx 0.058$ and $x \approx 0.091$, as well as a global
minimum at $x^* \approx 0.223$. The standard genetic algorithm will be used to obtain the
global minimum of this function.

The first thing to notice is that the search space here is real-valued: $\Sigma = [0.05, 0.5]$.
As mentioned earlier, some transformation is needed in order to encode/decode the
real-valued search space Σ into some space of binary strings Ω. In this example, a
binary search space consisting of 6-bit strings, i.e., $\Omega = \{0, 1\}^6$, was used, with the
decoding transformation given by

$$D(\mathbf{s}) = 0.05 + \frac{d(\mathbf{s})}{64}(0.5 - 0.05) \tag{8.5.8}$$

where $d(\mathbf{s})$ is the ordinary decimal representation of the 6-bit binary string $\mathbf{s}$. For
example, the decimal representation of 000011 is 3, so $D\,(000011) \approx 0.071$; as would
be expected, the two endpoints are mapped in the following way: $D\,(000000) = 0.05$
and $D\,(111111) = 0.5$.

To establish an appropriate fitness function for this problem, recall that the problem is to minimize $y(\mathbf{x})$ but maximize the fitness function $f(\mathbf{s})$. Thus some sort of
inverting transformation is required here. In this example, the following fitness function is used:

$$f(\mathbf{s}) = 1 - z \sin\left(\frac{1}{z}\right) \tag{8.5.9}$$

where $z = D(\mathbf{s})$.

Before applying the standard genetic algorithm, values for M, P_c, and P_m must be chosen. The values for these parameters are usually determined empirically by running some trial simulations. However, one may first try to choose P_c and P_m in the ranges $0.6 \leq P_c \leq 0.99$ and $0.01 \leq P_m \leq 0.001$, respectively, as mentioned earlier. As for the value of M, empirical results suggest that $n \leq M \leq 2n$ is a good choice (Alander, 1992) [see also Reeves (1993)]. Besides the preceding parameters, some stopping or convergence criterion is required. Although several different convergence criteria may be used, the criterion used here is to stop when the population is sufficiently dominated by a single string. In this case, convergence is obtained when a single string comprises 80 percent or more of the population.

Two simulations will be described below. In the first simulation, an initial population of strings was generated uniformly over the search space, and then, as usual, the genetic operators of selection, crossover, and mutation were applied until the convergence criterion was met. The following parameters were used: $M = 10$, $P_c = 0.8$, and $P_m = 0.01$, and the results of this simulation are shown in Table 8.5.1. In this table, a

Table 8.5.1
A Listing of the First Four Populations in the First Simulation for Example 8.5.2

	Population $S(t) = \{s_1, \ldots, s_{10}\}$	Decoded Value $x = D(s)$	Fitness $1 - y(x)$
$t = 0$	000010 (1)	0.064	0.994
	000110 (1)	0.092	1.091
	001010 (1)	0.120	0.892
	010001 (1)	0.170	1.063
	011001 (1)	0.226	1.217
	100000 (1)	0.275	1.131
	100111 (1)	0.324	0.981
	101110 (1)	0.373	0.833
	110101 (1)	0.423	0.704
	111100 (1)	0.472	0.597
$t = 1$	010101 (1)	0.198	1.185
	110101 (1)	0.423	0.704
	101010 (1)	0.345	0.916
	001010 (1)	0.120	0.892
	011001 (3)	0.226	1.217
	010001 (3)	0.170	1.064
$t = 2$	101001 (1)	0.338	0.938
	011001 (4)	0.226	1.217
	111001 (1)	0.451	0.640
	010001 (3)	0.170	1.063
	110101 (1)	0.423	0.704
$t = 3$	010001 (4)	0.170	1.063
	011001 (6)	0.226	1.217

Note: The numbers in parenthesis show the multiplicity of the string in the total population of 10 strings.

listing of the population is shown for the generations at times $t = 0, 1, 2$, and 3. The decoded real value for each string is also shown, as well as the associated fitness values. The number in parentheses beside each string shows the number of multiplicities of the string appearing in the total population of 10 strings. Notice how the population converges to populations dominated by highly fit strings. After the fourth iteration ($t = 4$), the population is dominated by the string $\mathbf{s}^* = 011001$, and the population has converged. The string $\mathbf{s}^*$ is decoded to the value $x^* = 0.23$, which is close to the globally optimal solution of $x^* \approx 0.223$. Note that better accuracy may be obtained by using a more accurate encoding of the real-valued search space. That is, by using a GA search space with strings of higher dimension, e.g., $\Omega = \{0, 1\}^{10}$, or $\Omega = \{0, 1\}^{20}$, whatever accuracy is required.

The second simulation of this problem demonstrates a case where mutation is necessary to obtain the global solution. In this simulation, the initial population was created with all strings near the left endpoint $x = 0.05$. The following parameters were used here: $M = 10$, $P_c = 0.9$, and $P_m = 0.05$. The increased mutation and crossover rates were used to encourage diversity in the population. This helps the genetic algorithm branch out to explore the entire space. In fact, if mutation were not used (i.e., $P_m = 0$), then the global solution could never be found by the GA. This is because the initial population is dominated by the schema $00000**$, which is not a desirable building block because the fitness of this schema is relatively small. Applying selection and crossover will not help because no new schemata would be generated. The results of the simulation are shown in Table 8.5.2. This time, the GA took 44 iterations to converge to the solution $\mathbf{s}^* = 011000$, with corresponding real value $x^* = 0.219$.

Although the preceding example used a one-dimensional objective function, multidimensional objective functions $y: R^n \to R$ also may be mapped onto the genetic algorithm framework by simply extending the length of the binary strings in Ω to represent each component of the points $\mathbf{x} = (x_1, \ldots, x_n)$ in Σ. That is, each string $\mathbf{s}$ will consist of n substrings $\mathbf{s} = (\mathbf{s}^1, \ldots, \mathbf{s}^n)$, where $\mathbf{s}^i$ is the binary encoding for the ith component of $\mathbf{x}$. A decoding transformation may then be applied to each substring separately: $D(\mathbf{s}) = [D_1(\mathbf{s}^1), \ldots, D_n(\mathbf{s}^n)]$. Although not necessary, decoding each component separately might be desirable in certain applications. For example, suppose $\mathbf{x} = (x_1, x_2)$ and $\Sigma = [0, 1] \times [0, 100]$. To obtain the same level of accuracy for the two variables, then more bits would have to be allotted the substring representing the second component of $\mathbf{x}$ because it has a much larger range of values than the first component. Hence, in this case, the decoding transformations $D_1(\mathbf{s}^1)$ and $D_2(\mathbf{s}^2)$ would be different.

The crossover operator also may be slightly modified to exploit the structure of the substring decomposition of $\mathbf{s}$. Instead of choosing a single crossing site over the entire

Table 8.5.2
A Listing of the Population at Various Stages of the Computation for the Second Simulation of Example 8.5.2

	Population $P(t) = \{s_1, \ldots, s_{10}\}$	Decoded Value $x = D(s)$	Fitness $1 - y(x)$
$t = 0$	000000 (3)	0.050	0.954
	000001 (1)	0.057	1.055
	000010 (3)	0.064	0.994
	000011 (3)	0.071	0.929
$t = 5$	000010 (2)	0.064	0.994
	000110 (1)	0.922	1.091
	011010 (2)	0.233	1.213
	001011 (1)	0.127	0.873
	100010 (1)	0.289	1.090
	010010 (1)	0.177	1.103
	001000 (1)	0.106	0.999
	001110 (1)	0.148	0.935
$t = 30$	111000 (1)	0.444	0.656
	010010 (4)	0.177	1.103
	000010 (1)	0.064	0.994
	011010 (2)	0.233	1.213
	010000 (2)	0.163	1.021
$t = 44$	010100 (1)	0.191	1.164
	011000 (9)	0.219	1.217

Note: In this simulation, the initial population of strings was concentrated at the left endpoint of the search space Σ.

string as shown below for a string of the form $s = (s^1, s^2, s^3, s^4)$:

$$
\begin{array}{ccc|cc}
1\,1\,0\,1 & 1\,1\,0\,1\,0\,1 & 1\,1\,0\,1 & 0\,0 & 1\,0\,0\,1\,1 \\
1\,0\,0\,0 & 1\,0\,1\,1\,1\,1 & 0\,1\,0\,1 & 0\,1 & 0\,1\,1\,1\,0
\end{array}
$$

crossing sites may be chosen for each of the substrings, and the crossover occurs locally at each substring. This type of crossover (known as *multiple-point crossover*) is shown below:

$$
\begin{array}{c|c|c|c|c|c}
1\,1 & 0\,1 & 1\,1 & 0\,1\,0\,1 & 1\,1\,0\,1 & 0\,0 & 1 & 0\,0\,1\,1 \\
1\,0 & 0\,0 & 1\,0 & 1\,1\,1\,1 & 0\,1\,0\,1 & 0\,1 & 0 & 1\,1\,1\,0
\end{array}
$$

A large number of other variations of and modifications to the standard GA have been reported in the literature. For example, the reader is referred to Chapter 5 in Goldberg (1989) and to the *Proceedings of the International Conference on Genetic Algorithms* (1989–1994).

The general-purpose nature of GAs allows them to be used in many different optimization tasks. As was discussed earlier, an arbitrary optimization problem with objective function $y(\mathbf{x})$ can be mapped onto a GA as long as one can find an appropriate fitness function that is consistent with the optimization task. In addition, one needs to establish a correspondence (an invertible mapping) between the search space in $\mathbf{x}$ (Σ) and the GA search space (Ω), which is typically a space of binary strings. Both these requirements are possible to satisfy in many optimization problems. For example, one may simply use any positive monotonically increasing function in y as the fitness function if $y(\mathbf{x})$ is to be maximized, or any positive monotonically decreasing function in y may be used if $y(\mathbf{x})$ is to be minimized. On the other hand, the mapping between the original search space and the GA space can vary from a simple real-to-binary encoding to more elaborate encoding schemes. Empirical evidence suggests that different choices/combinations of fitness functions and encoding schemes can have significant effect on the GA's convergence time and solution quality (Bäck, 1993). Unfortunately, theoretical results on the specification of the space to be explored by a GA are lacking (De Jong and Spears, 1993).

8.5.2   Application of Genetic Algorithms to Neural Networks

There are various ways of using GA-based optimization in neural networks. The most obvious way is to use a GA to search the weight space of a neural network with a predefined architecture (Caudell and Dolan, 1989; Miller et al., 1989; Montana and Davis, 1989; Whitley and Hanson, 1989). The use of GA-based learning methods may be justified for learning tasks that require neural nets with hidden units (e.g., nonlinearly separable classification tasks, nonlinear function approximation, etc.), since the GA is capable of global search and is not easily fooled by local minima. Also, GAs are useful for training nets consisting of units with nondifferentiable activation functions (e.g., LTGs), since the fitness function need not be differentiable.

In supervised learning, one may readily identify a fitness function as $-E$, where $E = E(\mathbf{w})$ may be the sum of squared error criterion as in Equation (5.1.13) or the entropy criterion of Equation (5.2.16). As for specifying the search space for the GA, the complete set of network weights is coded as a binary string $\mathbf{s}_i$ with associated fitness $f(\mathbf{s}_i) = -E[D(\mathbf{s}_i)]$. Here, $D(\mathbf{s}_i)$ is a decoding transformation.

An example of a simple two-input, two-unit feedforward net is shown in Figure 8.5.4. In this example, each weight is coded as a 3-bit signed-binary substring where the left-most bit encodes the sign of the weight (e.g., 110 represents -2 and 011 represents $+3$).

Now we may generate an appropriate GA-compatible representation for the net in Figure 8.5.4 as a contiguous sequence of substrings $\mathbf{s} = (101010001110011)$ that corresponds to the real-valued weight string $(w_{11}, w_{12}, w_{13}, w_{21}, w_{22}) = (-1, 2, 1, -2, 3)$. Starting with a random population of such strings (population of random nets), suc-

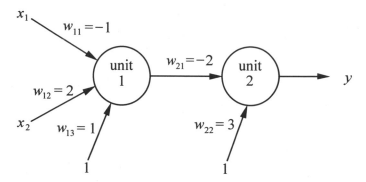

Figure 8.5.4
A simple two-layer feedforward net used to illustrate weight coding in a GA.

cessive generations are constructed using the GA to evolve new strings out of old ones. Thus strings with fitnesses above average (more specifically, strings that meet the criteria of the fundamental theorem of GAs) tend to survive, and ultimately, the population converges to the "fittest" string. This string represents, with a high probability, the optimal weight configuration for the learning task at hand for the predefined net architecture and predefined admissible weight values. It is interesting to note here how the crossover operation may be interpreted as a swapping mechanism where parts (individual units, group of units, and/or a set of weights) of fit networks are interchanged in the hope of producing a network with even higher fitness.

GAs are also able to deal with learning in generally interconnected networks, including recurrent nets. Recurrent networks pose special problems for gradient-descent learning techniques (refer to Section 5.4) that are not shared by GAs. With gradient-descent learning, it is generally necessary to correlate causes and effects in the network so that units and weights that cause the desired output are strengthened. However, with recurrent networks, the cause of a state may have occurred arbitrarily far in the past. On the other hand, the GA evolves weights based on a fitness measure of the whole network (a global performance measure), and the question of what caused any particular network state to occur is considered only in that the resulting state is desirable (Wieland, 1991). This inherent strength of GAs is in some ways also a weakness. By ignoring gradient (or more generally cause and effect) information when it does exist, the GAs can become slow and inefficient. There are also large costs in speed and storage for working with a whole population of networks, which can make standard GAs impractical for evolving optimal designs for large networks.

Thus, when gradient information exists, particularly if it is readily available, one can use such information to speed up the GA search. This leads to hybrid GA/

gradient search, where a gradient-descent step may be included as one of the genetic operators (Montana and Davis, 1989). A more general view of the advantages of the marriage of GA and gradient descent can be seen based on the relationship between evolution and learning. Belew et al. (1990) have demonstrated the complementary nature of evolution and learning: The presence of learning facilitates the process of evolution [see also Smith (1987); Hinton and Nowlan (1987); Nolfi et al. (1990); Keesing and Stork (1991)]. In the context of this discussion, genetic algorithms can be used to provide a model of evolution, and supervised learning (or some other learning paradigm, e.g., reinforcement or unsupervised learning) may be used to provide simple but powerful learning mechanisms. Thus the presence of learning makes evolution much easier; all evolution has to do is to evolve (find) an appropriate initial state of a system, from which learning can do the rest (much like teaching a child who already has an "evolved" potential for learning). These ideas motivate the use of hybrid learning methods that employ GA and gradient-based searches. A specific example of such a method is presented in the next section.

Potential applications of GAs in the context of neural networks include evolving appropriate network structures and learning parameters (Harp et al., 1989, 1990) that optimize one or more network performance measure. These measures may include fast response (requires minimizing network size), VLSI hardware implementation compatibility (requires minimizing connectivity), and real-time learning (requires optimizing the learning rate). Another interesting application of GAs is to evolve learning mechanisms (rules) for neural networks. In other words, evolution is recruited to discover a process of learning. Chalmers (1991) reported an interesting experiment where a GA with proper string representation applied to a population of single-layer neural nets evolved the LMS learning rule [Equation (3.1.35)] as an optimal learning rule.

8.6 Genetic Algorithm–Assisted Supervised Learning

In the preceding section, a method for training multilayer neural nets was described that uses a GA to search for optimal weight configurations. Here, an alternative learning method is described that performs global search for finding optimal targets for hidden units based on a hybrid GA/gradient-descent search strategy. This method is a supervised learning method that is suited for arbitrarily interconnected feedforward neural nets. In the following, this hybrid learning method is described in the context of a multilayer feedforward net having a single hidden layer.

In Section 2.3, the universal approximation capabilities of single-hidden-layer feedforward nets was established for a wide variety of hidden-unit activation functions, including the threshold activation function. This implies that an arbitrary nonlinearly separable mapping can always be decomposed into two linearly separable mappings that are realized as the cascade of two single-layer neural nets as long as the first layer (hidden layer) has a sufficient number of nonlinear units (e.g., sigmoids or LTGs).

In supervised learning, a desired target vector (pattern) is specified for each input vector in a given training set. A linearly separable set of training input/target pairs can be learned efficiently in a single-layer net using the gradient-based LMS or delta learning rules [See Equations (3.1.35) and (3.1.53)]. On the other hand, a general complex training set may not be linearly separable, which necessitates the use of a hidden layer. Thus more sophisticated learning rules must be used that are usually far less efficient (slower) than the LMS or delta rules and, as in the case of backprop, may not always lead to satisfactory solutions. Ideally, one would like to "decouple" the training of a multiple-layer network into the training of two (or more) single-layer networks. This could be done if some method for finding an appropriate set of hidden-unit activations could be found. These hidden-unit activations will be called *hidden targets* because they can be used as target vectors to train the first layer. This approach would be useful if it could be guaranteed that the mapping from the input to the hidden targets and that from those hidden targets to the desired output targets are linearly separable. Now, once these hidden targets are found, efficient learning of the weights can proceed independently for the hidden and output layers using the delta rule. In fact, backprop may be thought of as employing a dynamic version of the preceding method where hidden targets are estimated according to Equation (5.1.10) for each training pair. However, because of its gradient-descent nature, backprop's estimate of the hidden targets does not guarantee finding an optimal hidden-target configuration. The following is a more efficient method for training multilayer feedforward neural nets which utilizes the preceding hidden-target-based supervised learning strategy. Here, a GA is used to "evolve" proper hidden targets, and a gradient-descent search (LMS or delta rule) is used to learn optimal network interconnection weights (Song, 1992; Hassoun and Song, 1993a, b).

8.6.1   Hybrid GA/Gradient-Descent Method for Feedforward Multilayer Net Training

The basics of the hybrid GA/gradient-descent (GA/GD) learning method for a multilayer feedforward net are described next. The GA/GD method consists of two parts: genetic search in hidden-target space and gradient-based weight update at each layer. Consider the fully interconnected feedforward single-hidden-layer net of Figure 8.6.1 with LTG hidden units and training set $\{\mathbf{x}^k, \mathbf{d}^k\}$, $k = 1, 2, \ldots, m$. The output units can be linear units, sigmoid units, or LTGs, depending on the nature of the target vector $\mathbf{d}$.

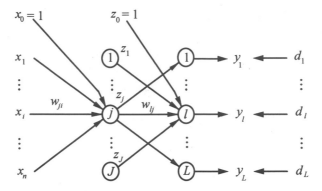

Figure 8.6.1
A two-layer fully interconnected feedforward neural network.

Now if we are given a set of hidden-target column vectors $\{\mathbf{h}^1, \mathbf{h}^2, \ldots, \mathbf{h}^m\}$, $\mathbf{h}^j \in \{0, 1\}^J$ (or $\{-1, +1\}^J$), such that the mappings $\mathbf{x}^k \to \mathbf{h}^k$ and $\mathbf{h}^k \to \mathbf{d}^k$, for $k = 1, 2, \ldots, m$, are linearly separable, then gradient-descent-based search (e.g., perceptron rule, LMS, delta rule, or Ho-Kashyap rule) may be employed to independently and quickly learn the optimal weights for both hidden and output layers. Initially, though, we do not know the proper set $\{\mathbf{h}^k\}$ of hidden targets that solves the problem. Therefore, a GA will be used to evolve such a set of hidden targets. In other words, a GA search is used to explore the space of possible hidden targets $\{\mathbf{h}\}$ (hidden target space) and converge to a global solution that renders the mappings $\mathbf{x} \to \mathbf{h}$ and $\mathbf{h} \to \mathbf{d}$ linearly separable. Since the hidden targets are binary-valued, a natural coding of a set of hidden targets is the string $\mathbf{s} = (\mathbf{s}^1 \quad \mathbf{s}^2 \quad \cdots \quad \mathbf{s}^m)$, where $\mathbf{s}^i$ is a string formed from the bits of the vector $\mathbf{h}^i$. Equivalently, the search "point" may be represented as a $J \times m$ array (matrix) $\mathbf{H} = [\mathbf{h}^1 \quad \mathbf{h}^2 \quad \cdots \quad \mathbf{h}^m]$. This representation is particularly useful in the multipoint crossover described next.

A population of M random binary arrays $\{\mathbf{H}_j\}$, $j = 1, 2, \ldots, M$, is generated as the initial population of search "points." Each array has an associated network labeled j whose architecture is shown in Figure 8.6.1, with all M nets initialized with the same set of random weights. The fitness of the jth search point (array $\mathbf{H}_j$) is determined by the output SSE of network j:

$$E_j = \tfrac{1}{2} \sum_{k=1}^{m} \sum_{l=1}^{L} [d_l^k - (y_l^k)_j]^2 \tag{8.6.1}$$

Here, $(y_l^k)_j$ is the output of the lth output unit in network j due to the input $\mathbf{x}^k$. Now any one of a number of fitness functions may be used. Examples are $f(\mathbf{H}_j) = -E_j$,

$f(\mathbf{H}_j) = 1 - (E_j/\max E)$, or even $f(\mathbf{H}_j) = 1/(E_j + \varepsilon)$, where ε is a very small positive number. However, different fitness functions may lead to different performance.

Initially, starting from random weight values and random hidden targets, LMS is used to adapt the weights of the hidden layer in each of the M networks subject to the training set $\{\mathbf{x}^k, \mathbf{h}^k\}$, $k = 1, 2, \ldots, m$. Here, the threshold activation is removed during weight adaptation, and the hidden units are treated as linear units. Alternatively, an adaptive version of the Ho-Kashyap algorithm or the perceptron rule may be employed directly to the hidden LTGs. Similarly, the weights of the output layer units are adapted subject to the training set $\{\mathbf{h}^k, \mathbf{d}^k\}$, independent of the first hidden layer.

After the weights are updated, each network is tested by performing feedforward computations, and its fitness is computed. In these computations, the outputs of the hidden units (as opposed to the hidden targets) serve as the inputs to the output layer. Next, the GA operators of reproduction, crossover, and mutation are applied to evolve the next generation of hidden target sets $\{\mathbf{H}_j\}$. In reproduction, the $M/2$ hidden target sets $\mathbf{H}_j$ with the highest fitness are duplicated and are entered into a temporary pool for crossover. Crossover is applied with a probability P_c (P_c is set close to 1). A pair $\{\mathbf{H}_i, \mathbf{H}_j\}$ is selected randomly without replacement from the temporary pool just generated. If a training pair $\{\mathbf{x}^k, \mathbf{d}^k\}$ is poorly learned by network i (network j) during the preceding learning phase [i.e., if the output error due to this pair is substantially larger than the average output error of network i (network j) on the whole training set], then the corresponding column $\mathbf{h}^k$ of $\mathbf{H}_i$ is replaced by the kth column of $\mathbf{H}_j$. Here, crossover can affect multiple pairs of columns in the hidden-target arrays. The preceding reproduction and crossover operations differ from those employed by the standard GA and are motivated by empirical results (Hassoun and Song, 1993b). On the other hand, the standard mutation operation is used here, where each bit of the $\mathbf{H}_i$ array, after crossover, is flipped with a probability P_m (typically, $P_m = 0.01$ is used).

The preceding is a description of a single cycle of the GA/GD learning method. This cycle is repeated until the population $\{\mathbf{H}_i\}$ converges to a dominant representation or until at least one network is generated that has an output SSE less than a prespecified value. During GA/GD learning, the weights of all M networks are re-initialized at the beginning of each cycle to small random values (one set of random weights may be used for all networks and for all cycles). Hassoun and Song (1993b) reported several variations of this method, including the use of sigmoidal hidden units, using the outputs of the hidden layer instead of the hidden targets to serve as the input pattern to the output layer during the training phase, and using different fitness functions. However, the present GA/GD method showed better overall performance on a range of benchmark problems.

One of the main motivations behind applying GA to the hidden-target space as opposed to the weight space is the possibility of the existence of a more dense set of solutions for a given problem. That is, there may be many more optimal hidden-target sets {$\mathbf{H}^*$} in hidden-target space that produce zero SSE error than optimal weights {$\mathbf{w}^*$} in weight space. This hypothesis was validated on a number of simple problems designed so that the weight space and the hidden-target space had the same dimensions. However, further and more extensive testing is still required in this area.

In the architecture of Figure 8.6.1, the preceding GA/GD method involves a GA search space of dimension mJ. On the other hand, the GA search in weight space involves a search space of dimension $[(n + 1)J + (J + 1)L]b$, where b is the number of binary bits chosen to encode each weight in the network (see Problem 8.5.6). Since one would normally choose a population size M proportional to the dimension of the binary search space in GA applications, one may conclude that the GA/GD method has a speed advantage over the other method when the following condition is satisfied:

$$mJ < [(n + 1)J + (J + 1)L]b \qquad (8.6.2)$$

Equation (8.6.2) implies that the GA/GD method is preferable over GA-based weight search in neural network learning tasks when the size of the training set m is small compared with the product of the dimension of the training patterns and the bit accuracy nb (here it is assumed that $n \gg L$). Unfortunately, many practical problems (such as pattern-recognition, system identification, and function approximation problems) lead to training sets characterized by $m \gg n$, which makes the GA/GD method less advantageous in terms of computational speed. However, one may alleviate this problem (e.g., in pattern-recognition applications) by partial preprocessing of the training set using a fast clustering method, which would substantially reduce the size of the training set (refer to Section 6.1 for details) and thus make the GA/GD method regain its speed advantage.

As in the case of the simulated annealing global search method in the weight space, the GA/GD method may not compete with backprop in computational speed. However, the GA/GD method is an effective alternative to backprop in learning tasks that involve complex multimodal criterion (error) functions, if optimal solutions are at a premium.

8.6.2 Simulations

The GA/GD method is tested on the 4-bit parity binary mapping and a continuous mapping that arises from a nonlinear system identification problem. The 4-bit parity (refer to the K-map in Figure 2.1.2) is chosen because it is known to pose a difficult problem to neural networks using gradient-descent-based learning due to multiple local minima. On the other hand, the nonlinear system identification problem is chosen to test the ability of the GA/GD method with binary hidden targets to approximate continuous nonlinear functions.

In both simulations, a two-layer feedforward net was used with sigmoidal hidden units employing the hyperbolic tangent activation. For the binary mapping problem, bipolar training data, bipolar hidden targets, and bipolar output targets are assumed. Also, a single sigmoidal unit is used for the output layer. On the other hand, the system identification problem used one linear output unit. The delta rule with a learning rate of 0.1 is used to learn the weights at both hidden and output layers. Only 10 delta rule learning steps are allowed for each layer per full GA/GD training cycle.

The 4-bit parity is a binary mapping from 4-dimensional binary-valued input vectors to one binary-valued (desired) output. The desired output is taken as $+1$ if the number of 1 bits in the input vector is odd and -1 otherwise. The networks used in the following simulations employ four hidden units. The GA/GD method is tested with population sizes of 8, 32, and 64 strings. For each population size, 50 trials are performed (each trial re-randomizes all initial weights and hidden target sets), and learning cycles statistics (mean value, standard deviation, maximum, and minimum) are computed. Simulation results are reported in Table 8.6.1 for the GA/GD method and three other methods: (1) a method similar to GA/GD but with the GA process replaced by a process where the search is reinitialized with random hidden targets and random weights at the onset of every learning cycle [this method is referred to as the *random hidden target/gradient-descent (RH/GD) method*; it should be noted here that sufficient iterations of the delta rule are allowed for each cycle in order to rule out nonconvergence], (2) incremental backprop (BP), and (3) standard GA learning in weight space (SGA).

In all simulations, the GA/GD method led to successful convergence, with population sizes of 64, 32, and 8, in an average of a few hundred learning cycles or less. The RH/GD method could not find a single solution with 10^6 trials. This shows clearly the difficulty of the task and verifies the effectiveness of the GA/GD method. As for backprop, only 4 of 100 runs resulted in a solution, with the remaining 96 solutions reaching a high error plateau and/or a local minima. Finally, the SGA method neither converged nor was able to find a solution within 1000 generations, with population sizes of 64 and 132, this being the case for codings of 8 and 16 binary bits for each weight.

The second simulation involves the identification of a nonlinear plant described by the discrete-time dynamics of Equation (5.4.4). A feedforward neural network with 20 hidden units is used and is trained using the GA/GD method on a training set that is

Table 8.6.1
Simulation Results for the Four-Bit Parity Problem Using the GA/Gradient-Descent (GA/GD) Method, the Random Hidden Target/Gradient-Descent (RH/GD) Method, Backprop (BP), and the Standard GA (SGA) in Weight Space Method

Learning method:	Learning Cycle Statistics:	Population Size											
		8				32				64			
		Mean	Standard Deviation	Max	Min	Mean	Standard Deviation	Max	Min	Mean	Standard Deviation	Max	Min
GA/GD		437	530	1882	14	159	195	871	8	105	335	2401	5
RH/GD		Does not converge within 1 million trials											
BP		96 out of 100 runs do not converge within 1 Million backprop cycles. The remaining 4 runs converged in an average of 3644 cycles..											
SGA		Does not converge within 1000 generations with population sizes of 64 and 132.											

Note: A four-hidden-unit feedforward neural net is used.

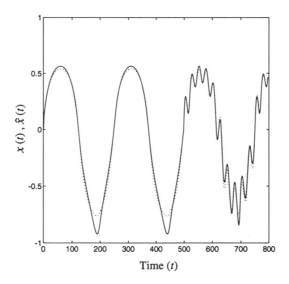

Figure 8.6.2
Nonlinear system identification results (*dotted line*)
employing a single-hidden-layer feedforward neural net
trained with the GA/GD method. The exact dynamics are
given by the solid line.

generated according to a random input signal in a similar fashion as described in
Section 5.4.1. The size of the training set used here, though, is $m = 100$. Figure 8.6.2
shows a typical simulation result after 20 learning cycles with a population of 50
hidden-target sets. The test input signal in this case is the one given in Equation
(5.4.5). This result compares favorably with those in Figure 5.4.4a and b for a two-
hidden-layer feedforward net and a single-hidden-layer feedforward net, respectively,
which required on the order of 10^5 to 10^6 training iterations of incremental backprop.

This chapter concludes by pointing out that genetic algorithms also may be used as
the evolutionary mechanism in the context of more general learning systems. Holland
(1986) and Holland and Reitman (1978) introduced a classifier system that is an
adaptive parallel rule-based system that learns syntactically simple string rules (called
classifiers) to guide its performance in an arbitrary environment. The classifier system
develops a sequence(s) of actions or decisions so that a particular objective is achieved
in a dynamically evolving environment. As an example, one may think of the classifier
system as a controller whose objective is to regulate or control the state of a dynamical system. Here, the fitness of a particular classifier (rule) is a function of how
well an individual classifier complements others in the population. The heart of the

classifier system is a reinforcement-type learning mechanism assisted with GA exploration [see Goldberg (1989) for an accessible reference on classifier systems and their applications]. Recently, Abu Zitar (1993) and Abu Zitar and Hassoun (1993, 1995) have developed a framework for synthesizing multilayer feedforward neural net controllers for robust nonlinear control from binary string rules generated by a classifier-like system.

8.7 Summary

This chapter discusses probabilistic global search methods that are suited for neural network optimization. Global search methods, as opposed to deterministic gradient-based search methods, must be used in optimization problems where reaching the global minimum (or maximum) is at a premium. However, the price one pays for using global search methods is increased computational and/or storage requirements as compared with that of local search. The intrinsic slowness of global search methods is mainly due to the slow but crucial exploration mechanisms employed.

Global search methods may be used as optimal learning algorithms for neural networks. Some global search methods also may be mapped onto recurrent neural networks such that the retrieval dynamics of these networks escape local minima and evolve toward global minimum.

Two major probabilistic global search methods are covered in this chapter. The first method is stochastic simulated annealing, which is motivated by statistical mechanics, and the second method is genetic algorithms, which are motivated by the mechanics of natural selection and natural genetics. The exploration mechanism in simulated annealing is governed by the Boltzmann-Gibbs probability distribution, and its convergence is determined by a "cooling" schedule of slowly decreasing "temperature." This method is especially appealing because it can be naturally implemented by a stochastic neural network known as the Boltzmann machine. The Boltzmann machine is a stochastic version of Hopfield's energy-minimizing net that is capable of almost guaranteed convergence to the global minimum of an arbitrary bounded quadratic energy function. Simulated annealing is also applied to optimal weight learning in generally interconnected multilayer Boltzmann machines, thus extending the applicability of the Boltzmann machine from combinatorial optimization to optimal supervised learning of complex binary mappings. However, these desirable features of Boltzmann machines come with slow learning and/or retrieval.

Mean-field annealing is a deterministic approximation (based on mean-field theory) to stochastic simulated annealing where the mean behavior of the stochastic state transitions is used to characterize the Boltzmann machine. This approximation is found to preserve the optimal characteristics of the Boltzmann machine but with one to two orders of magnitude speed advantage. Mean-field annealing is applied in the context of retrieval dynamics and weights learning in a Boltzmann machine. It is interesting to see that applying mean-field theory to a single-layer Boltzmann machine leads to the deterministic continuous Hopfield net.

Genetic algorithms (GAs) are introduced as another method for optimal neural network design. They employ a parallel multipoint probabilistic search strategy that is biased toward reinforcing search points of high fitness. The most distinguishing feature of GAs is their flexibility and applicability to a wide range of optimization problems. In the domain of neural networks, GAs are useful as global search methods for synthesizing the weights of generally interconnected networks, optimal network architectures and learning parameters, and optimal learning rules.

It is argued that in order to make global search methods more speed efficient, local gradient information (if available) could be used advantageously. In the context of GA optimization, it is possible to think of the GA as an evolutionary mechanism that could be accelerated by simple learning processes. This observation motivates the hybrid GA/gradient-descent method for feedforward multilayer net training introduced at the end of the chapter.

Problems

† **8.1.1** Plot and find analytically the global minima of the following functions:

a. $y(x) = x \sin\left(\dfrac{1}{x}\right)$ $x \in [0.05, 0.5]$

b. $y(x) = (x^2 + 2x) \cos(x)$ $|x| < 5$

c. $y(x) = 10 \sin^2 x + 0.2(x + 3)^2$ $|x| < 20$

d. $y(x) = x^6 - 15x^4 + 27x^2 + 250$ $|x| < 3.7$

e. $y(x_1, x_2) = \dfrac{x_1^4}{4} - \dfrac{x_1^2}{2} + 0.1x_1 + \dfrac{x_2^2}{2}$ $|x_1| < 1.5$ and $|x_2| < 1.5$

f. $y(x_1, x_2) = 0.5x_1^2 + 0.5[1 - \cos(2x_1)] + x_2^2$ $|x_1| < 2$ and $|x_2| < 2$

† **8.1.2** Plot and count the number of minima, maxima, and saddle points for the following functions:

a. $y(x_1, x_2) = -2x_1^4 + 4x_1^2 + x_1 x_2 - 4x_2^2 + 4x_2^4$
with $|x_1| \leq 1.25$ and $|x_2| \leq 1.5$

b. $y(x_1, x_2) = x_1^3 + x_1^2 + 2x_2^2 - x_1 x_2 - 0.3 \cos(3\pi x_1) - 0.4 \cos(4\pi x_2) + 0.7$
with $|x_1| \leq 0.3$ and $|x_2| \leq 0.5$

c. $y(x_1, x_2) = (4 - 2.1x_1^2) \cos(40x_1) + x_1 x_2 + (-4 + 4x_2) \sin(3x_2)$
with $|x_1| \leq 0.12$ and $-2 \leq x_2 \leq 0.8$

†**8.1.3** Employ the gradient-descent search rule given by

$$x(t + 1) = x(t) - \rho \left.\frac{dy(x)}{dx}\right|_{x(t)} \qquad t = 0, 1, 2, \ldots$$

to find a minimum of the function $y(x) = x \sin(1/x)$ starting from the initial search point (a) $x(0) = 0.05$, (b) $x(0) = 0.1$, (c) $x(0) = 0.15$. Assume $\rho = 10^{-4}$.

†**8.1.4** Repeat Problem 8.1.3 for the function in Problem 8.1.1 part c with $x(0) = -20$ and $\rho = 0.01$.

†**8.1.5** Employ the gradient-descent/ascent global search strategy described in Section 8.1 to find the global minima of the functions a through d in Problem 8.1.1.

†**8.1.6** *Global descent* is a global search method that was discussed in Section 5.1.2. Implement the global-descent method to search for the global minimum of the function $y(x)$ given in Problem 8.1.1 part c. Assume $x(0) = -20$, $\rho = 0.005$, $\varepsilon_x = 0.01$, $\sigma = 2$, and experiment with different values of the repeller parameter $k \geq 0$.

†**8.1.7** For the univariate case $y = y(x)$, the global minimum can be reached by gradient descent on the noisy function

$$\tilde{y}(x) = y(x) + c(t)N(t)x$$

where $N(t)$ is a "noise signal," and $c(t)$ is a parameter that controls the magnitude of noise. Apply the gradient-descent rule (with $\rho = 0.01$) of Problem 8.1.3 to $\tilde{y}(x)$. Use the resulting stochastic gradient rule to find the global minimum of $y(x)$ in Problem 8.1.1 part c. Assume that $N(t)$ is a normally distributed sequence with a mean of zero and a variance of one and that $c(t) = 150 \exp(-\alpha t)$. Start from $x(0) = -20$, and experiment with different values of α, $\alpha \in [0.01, 0.001]$. Plot $x(t)$ versus t ($t = 0, 1, 2, \ldots$). What range of values of α are likely to lead to the global minimum of $y(x)$?

†**8.2.1** Use the simulated annealing algorithm described in Section 8.2 with the temperature schedule in Equation (8.2.5) to find the global minima of the functions in Problem 8.1.1 parts a through c and Problem 8.1.2 parts a and b. Make intelligent choices for the variance of the random perturbation Δx, taking into account the domain of the function being optimized. Also make use of the plots of these functions to estimate the largest possible change in y due to Δx, max Δy, and use this information to guide your estimate of T_0.

*8.3.1 Consider the simple model of a biologic neuron with output x given by $x(net) = \text{sgn}(net)$, where net is the postsynaptic potential. Experimental observations (Katz, 1966) show that this postsynaptic potential is normally distributed; i.e.,

$$p(net) = \frac{1}{\sqrt{2\pi}\,\sigma}\, e^{-\frac{(net - \overline{net})^2}{2\sigma^2}}$$

where $\overline{net}$ is the mean potential. The distribution width σ is determined by the parameters of the noise sources associated with synaptic junctions. Show that the probability that the neuron fires (i.e., the probability of its output to be equal to one) is given by

$$P(x = +1) = \tfrac{1}{2}\left(1 + \frac{2}{\sqrt{\pi}} \int_0^{\beta\,\overline{net}} e^{-\xi^2}\, d\xi\right)$$

where $\beta = 1/(\sqrt{2}\sigma)$. Note how the pseudotemperature $T = 1/\beta$ now has the physical interpretation as being proportional to the fluctuation σ of the postsynaptic potential of a real neuron. Next, show that the preceding probability can be roughly approximated by

$$\tfrac{1}{2}\left[1 + \tanh\left(\frac{2\beta}{\sqrt{\pi}}\,\overline{net}\right)\right]$$

Hint: Compare the Taylor series expansion of $\int_0^x e^{-\xi^2}\, d\xi$ with that of $\tanh(x)$.

8.3.2 Derive Equation (8.3.4). [*Hint*: Employ the thermal equilibrium condition of Equation (8.2.3) and Equation (8.3.1), and assume that all units have equal probability of being selected for updating and that only one unit updates its state at a given time.] Show that according to Equation (8.3.4) the probability of a transition (bit-flip) that increases the energy E is always less than 0.5.

8.3.3 Show that the relative-entropy H in Equation (8.3.9) is positive or zero.

8.3.4 Derive Equation (8.3.12) starting from Equation (8.3.8).

*8.3.5 Derive Equation (8.3.16) by performing a gradient descent on H in Equation (8.3.15).

8.5.1 Employ Hardy's theorem [see Equation (8.5.2) and associated discussion] in a simple iterative procedure to find the largest number in the set $Q = \{1, 3, 4.5, 1.5, 4.2, 2\}$.

8.5.2 Consider the 10 strings in population $S(0)$ in Table 8.5.1 and the two schemata $H_1 = *11***$ and $H_2 = *01**0$. Which schemata are matched by which strings in the population $S(0)$? What are the order and defining length of both H_1 and H_2?

8.5.3 Consider the problem of finding the global minimum of the function $y(x) = x \sin(1/x)$, $x \in [0.05, 0.5]$, using a GA. Assume the initial population $S(0)$ as in Table 8.5.1, and let $P_c = 0.8$ and $P_m = 0.01$ as in the first simulation of Example 8.5.2. Use Equation (8.5.4) to compute a lower bound for the expected number of schemata of the form $*11***$ in the generation at $t = 1$. Repeat using the approximation of Equation (8.5.5). Next, compare these two bounds to the actual number of schemata of the form $*11***$ in population $S(1)$ in Table 8.5.1.

8.5.4 Repeat Problem 8.5.3 with the schema $*01**0$.

† **8.5.5** Find the global minimum of the functions in Problem 8.1.1 parts a through c and Problem 8.1.2 parts a and b using the standard genetic algorithm of Section 8.5.1. Use binary strings of dimension $n = 8$. Assume $P_c = 0.85$, $P_m = 0.02$, and a uniformly distributed initial population of 10 strings. Compare your results to those in Problem 8.2.1.

8.5.6 Consider the two-layer feedforward net shown in Figure 8.6.1. Assume that a binary coding of weights is used where each weight is represented by a b-bit substring for the purpose of representing the network as a GA string **s** of contiguous weight substrings. Show that the dimension of **s** is equal to $[(n + 1)J + (J + 1)L]b$, where n, J, and L are the input vector dimension, number of hidden units, and number of output units, respectively.

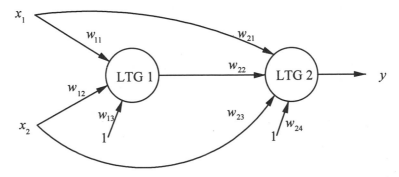

Figure P8.5.7
A simple two-layer feedforward net for problem 8.5.7.

†**8.5.7** Use the standard genetic algorithm to find integer weights in the range $[-15, +15]$ for the neural network in Figure P8.5.7 such that the network solves the XOR problem. Assume a signed-binary coding of 5 bits (sign bit plus four magnitude bits) for each weight. Also assume $P_c = 0.85$ and $P_m = 0.01$, and experiment with population sizes of $M = 10, 20, 30, 40$, and 50. The total number of correct responses (over the training set) may be used as the fitness function.

References

Aart, E., and Korst, J. (1989). *Simulated Annealing and Boltzmann Machines*. Wiley, New York.

Abu-Mostafa, Y. S. (1986a). Neural networks for computing? in *Neural Networks for Computing*, J. S. Denker, ed., pp. 1–6. American Institute of Physics, New York.

Abu-Mostafa, Y. S. (1986b). Complexity of random problems, in *Complexity in Information Theory*, Y. Abu-Mostafa, ed., pp. 115–131. Springer-Verlag, Berlin.

Abu-Mostafa, Y. S., and Psaltis, D. (1987). Optical neural computers, *Scientific American*, **256**(3), 88–95.

Abu Zitar, R. A. (1993). Machine Learning with Rule Extraction by Genetic Assisted Reinforcement (REGAR): Application to Nonlinear Control. Ph.D. dissertation, Department of Electrical and Computer Engineering, Wayne State University, Detroit, Mich.

Abu Zitar, R. A., and Hassoun, M. H. (1993). Regulator control via genetic search assisted reinforcement, in *Proceedings of the Fifth International Conference on Genetic Algorithms* (Urbana-Champaign, 1993), S. Forrest, ed., pp. 254–262. Morgan Kaufmann, San Mateo, Calif.

Abu Zitar, R. A., and Hassoun, M. H. (1995). Neurocontrollers trained with rules extracted by a genetic assisted reinforcement learning system, *IEEE Transactions on Neural Networks*. In press.

Ackley, D. H., and Littman, M. S. (1990). Generalization and scaling in reinforcement learning, in *Advances in Neural Information Processing II* (Denver, 1989), D. S. Touretzky, ed., pp. 550–557. Morgan Kaufmann, San Mateo, Calif.

Ackley, D. H., Hinton, G. E., and Sejnowski, T. J. (1985). A learning algorithm for Boltzmann machines, *Cognitive Science*, **9**, 147–169.

Alander, J. T. (1992). On optimal population size of genetic algorithms, in *Proceedings of CompEuro 92* (The Hague, Netherlands, 1992), pp. 65–70. IEEE Computer Society Press, New York.

Albert, A. (1972). *Regression and the Moore-Penrose Pseudoinverse*. Academic Press, New York.

Albus, J. S. (1971). A theory of cerebellar functions, *Mathematical Biosciences*, **10**, 25–61.

Albus, J. S. (1975). A new approach to manipulator control: The cerebellar model articulation controller (CMAC), *Journal of Dynamic Systems Measurement and Control, Transactions of the ASME*, **97**, 220–227.

Albus, J. S. (1979). A model of the brain for robot control, Part 2: A neurological model, *BYTE*, **4**, 54–95.

Albus, J. S. (1981). *Brains, Behavior, and Robotics*. BYTE/McGraw-Hill, Peterborough, N.H.

Alkon, D. L., Blackwell, K. T., Vogl, T. P., and Werness, S. A. (1993). Biological plausibility of artificial neural networks: Learning by non-Hebbian synapses, in *Associative Neural Memories: Theory and Implementation*, M. H. Hassoun, ed., pp. 31–49. Oxford University Press, New York.

Almeida, L. B. (1987). A learning rule for asynchronous perceptrons with feedback in a combinatorial environment, in *IEEE First International Conference on Neural Networks* (San Diego, 1987), M. Caudill and C. Butler, eds., vol. II, pp. 609–618. IEEE, New York.

Almeida, L. B. (1988). Backpropagation in perceptrons with feedback, in *Neural Computers* (Neuss, 1987), R. Eckmiller and C. von der Malsburg, eds., pp. 199–208. Springer-Verlag, Berlin.

Alspector, J., and Allen, B. B. (1987). A neuromorphic VLSI learning system, in *Advanced Research in VLSI: Proceedings of the 1987 Stanford Conference*, P. Losleben, ed., pp. 313–349. MIT Press, Cambridge Mass.

Aluffi-Pentini, F., Parisi, V., and Zirilli, F. (1985). Global optimization and stochastic differential equations, *Journal of Optimization Theory and Applications*, **47**(1), 1–16.

Amari, S.-I. (1967). Theory of adaptive pattern classifiers, *IEEE Transactions on Electronic Computers*, **EC-16**, 299–307.

Amari, S.-I. (1968). *Geometrical Theory of Information* (in Japanese). Kyoritsu-Shuppan, Tokyo.

Amari, S.-I. (1971). Characteristics of randomly connected threshold-element networks and network systems, *IEEE Proceedings*, **59**(1), 35–47.

Amari, S.-I. (1972a). Learning patterns and pattern sequences by self-organizing nets of threshold elements, *IEEE Transactions on Computers*, **C-21**, 1197–1206.

Amari, S.-I. (1972b). Characteristics of random nets of analog neuron-like elements, *IEEE Transactions on Systems, Man, and Cybernetics*, **SMC-2**(5), 643–657.

Amari, S.-I. (1974). A method of statistical neurodynamics, *Kybernetik*, **14**, 201–215.

Amari, S.-I. (1977a). Neural theory of association and concept-formation, *Biological Cybernetics*, **26**, 175–185.

Amari, S.-I. (1977b). Dynamics of pattern formation in lateral-inhibition type neural fields, *Biological Cybernetics*, **27**, 77–87.

Amari, S.-I. (1980). Topographic organization of nerve fields, *Bulletin of Mathematics and Biology*, **42**, 339–364.

Amari, S.-I. (1983). Field theory of self-organizing neural nets, *IEEE Transactions on Systems, Man, Cybernetics*, **SMC-13**, 741–748.

Amari, S.-I. (1989). Characteristics of sparsely encoded associative memory, *Neural Networks*, **2**(6), 451–457.

Amari, S.-I. (1990). Mathematical foundations of neurocomputing, *Proceedings of the IEEE*, **78**(9), 1443–1463.

Amari, S.-I. (1993). A universal theorem on learning curves, *Neural Networks*, **6**(2), 161–166.

Amari, S.-I., Fujita, N., and Shinomoto, S. (1992). Four types of learning curves, *Neural Computation*, **4**(2), 605–618.

Amari, S.-I., and Maginu, K. (1988). Statistical neurodynamics of associative memory, *Neural Networks*, **1**(1), 63–73.

Amari, S.-I., and Murata, N. (1993). Statistical theory of learning curves under entropic loss criterion, *Neural Computation*, **5**(1), 140–153.

Amari, S.-I., and Yanai, H.-F. (1993). Statistical neurodynamics of various types of associative nets, in *Associative Neural Memories: Theory and Implementation*, M. H. Hassoun, ed., pp. 169–183. Oxford University Press, New York.

Amit, D. J. (1989). *Modeling Brain Function: The World of Attractor Neural Networks*. Cambridge University Press, Cambridge.

Amit, D. J., Gutfreund, H., and Sompolinsky, H. (1985). Storing infinite numbers of patterns in a spin-glass model of neural networks, *Physical Review Letters*, **55**(14), 1530–1533.

Amit, D. J., Gutfreund, H., and Sompolinsky, H. (1987). Statistical mechanics of neural networks near saturation, *Annals of Physics, New York*, **173**, 30–67.

Anderberg, M. R. (1973). *Cluster Analysis for Applications*. Academic Press, New York.

Anderson, I. (1989). *A First Course in Combinatorial Mathematics*. Oxford University Press, Oxford.

Anderson, J. A. (1972). A simple neural network generating interactive memory, *Mathematical Biosciences*, **14**, 197–220.

Anderson, J. A. (1983). Neural models for cognitive computations, *IEEE Transactions on Systems, Man, and Cybernetics*, **SMC-13**, 799–815.

Anderson, J. A. (1993). The BSB model: A simple nonlinear autoassociative neural network, in *Associative Neural Memories: Theory and Implementation*, M. H. Hassoun, ed., pp. 77–103. Oxford University Press, New York.

Anderson, D. Z., and Erie, M. C. (1987). Resonator memories and optical novelty filters, *Optical Engineering*, **26**, 434–444.

Anderson, J. A., Gately, M. T., Penz, P. A., and Collins, D. R. (1990). Radar signal categorization using a neural network, *Proceedings of the IEEE*, **78**, 1646–1657.

Anderson, J. A., and Murphy, G. L. (1986). Psychological concepts in a parallel system, *Physica*, **22-D**, 318–336.

Anderson, J. A., Silverstien, J. W., Ritz, S. A., and Jones, R. S. (1977). Distinctive features, categorical perception, and probability learning: Some applications of a neural model, *Psychological Review*, **84**, 413–451.

Angeniol, B., Vaubois, G., and Le Texier, Y.-Y. (1988). Self-organizing feature maps and the traveling salesman problem, *Neural Networks*, **1**(4), 289–293.

Apolloni, B., and De Falco, D. (1991). Learning by asymmetric parallel Boltzmann machines. *Neural Computation*, **3**(3), 402–408.

Apostol, T. M. (1957). *Mathematical Analysis: A Modern Approach to Advanced Calculus*. Addison-Wesley, Reading, Mass.

Bachmann, C. M., Cooper, L. N., Dembo, A., and Zeitouni, O. (1987). A relaxation model for memory with high storage density, *Proceedings of the National Academy of Sciences, USA*, **84**, 7529–7531.

Bäck, T. (1993). Optimal mutation rates in genetic search, *Proceedings of the Fifth International Conference on Genetic Algorithms* (Urbana-Champaign, 1993), S. Forrest, ed., pp. 2–8. Morgan Kaufmann, San Mateo, Calif.

Baird, B. (1990). Associative memory in a simple model of oscillating cortex, in *Advances in Neural Information Processing Systems 2* (Denver, 1989) D. S. Touretzky, ed., pp. 68–75. Morgan Kaufmann, San Mateo, Calif.

Baird, B., and Eeckman, F. (1993). A normal form projection algorithm for associative memory, in *Associative Neural Memories: Theory and Implementation*, M. H. Hassoun, ed., pp. 135–166. Oxford University Press, New York.

Baldi, P. (1991). Computing with arrays of bell-shaped and sigmoid functions, in *Neural Information Processing Systems 3* (Denver, 1990), R. P. Lippmann, J. E. Moody, and D. S. Touretzky, eds., pp. 735–742. Morgan Kaufmann, San Mateo, Calif.

Baldi, P., and Chauvin, Y. (1991). Temporal evolution of generalization during learning in linear networks, *Neural Computation*, **3**(4), 589–603.

Baldi, P., and Hornik, K. (1989). Neural networks and principal component analysis: Learning from examples without local minima, *Neural Networks*, **2**(1), 53–58.

Barto, A. G. (1985). Learning by statistical cooperation of self-interested neuron-like computing elements, *Human Neurobiology*, **4**, 229–256.

Barto, A. G., and Anandan, P. (1985). Pattern recognizing stochastic learning automata, *IEEE Transactions on Systems, Man, and Cybernetics*, **SMC-15**, 360–375.

Barto, A. G., and Jordan, M. I. (1987). Gradient following without backpropagation in layered networks, in IEEE *First International Conference on Neural Networks* (San Diego, 1987), M. Caudill and C. Butler, eds., vol. II, pp. 629–636. IEEE, New York.

Barto, A. G., and Singh, S. P. (1991). On the computational economics of reinforcement learning, in *Connectionist Models: Proceedings of the 1990 Summer School* (Pittsburgh, 1990), D. S. Touretzky, J. L. Elman, T. J. Sejnowski, and G. E. Hinton, eds., pp. 35–44, Morgan Kaufmann, San Mateo, Calif.

Barto A. G., Sutton, R. S., and Anderson, C. W. (1983). Neuronlike adaptive elements that can solve difficult learning control problems, *IEEE Transactions System. Man, and Cybernetics*, **SMC-13**(5), 834–846.

Batchelor, B. G. (1969). Learning Machines for Pattern Recognition. Ph.D. thesis, University of Southampton, Southampton, England.

Batchelor, B. G. (1974). *Practical Approach to Pattern Classification*. Plenum Press, New York.

Batchelor, B. G., and Wilkins, B. R. (1968). Adaptive discriminant functions, *Pattern Recognition*, IEEE Conference Publication **42**, 168–178.

Battiti, R. (1992). First- and second-order methods for learning: Between steepest descent and Newton's method, *Neural Computation*, **4**(2), 141–166.

Baum, E. B. (1988). On the capabilities of multilayer perceptrons, *Journal of Complexity*, **4**, 193–215.

Baum, E. (1989). A proposal for more powerful learning algorithms, *Neural Computation*, **1**(2), 201–207.

Baum, E., and Haussler, D. (1989). What size net gives valid generalization? *Neural Computation*, **1**(1), 151–160.

Baum, E. B., and Wilczek, F. (1988). Supervised learning of probability distributions by neural networks, in *Neural Information Processing Systems* (Denver, 1987), D. Z. Anderson, ed., pp. 52–61, American Institute of Physics, New York.

Baxt, W. G. (1990). Use of artificial neural network for data analysis in clinical decision-making: The diagnosis of acute coronary occlusion, *Neural Computation*, **2**(4), 480–489.

Becker, S., and Le Cun, Y. (1989). Improving the convergence of back-propagation learning with second order methods, in *Proceedings of the 1988 Connectionist Models Summer School* (Pittsburgh, 1988), D. Touretzky, G. Hinton, and T. Sejnowski, ed., pp. 29–37. Morgan Kaufmann, San Mateo, Calif.

Beckman, F. S. (1964). The solution of linear equations by the conjugate gradient method, in *Mathematical Methods for Digital Computers*, A. Ralston and H. S. Wilf, eds., pp. 62–72, Wiley, New York.

Belew, R., McInerney, J., and Schraudolph, N. N. (1990). Evolving Networks: Using the Genetic Algorithm with Connectionist Learning, CSE Technical Report CS90-174, University of California, San Diego.

Benaim, M. (1994). On functional approximation with normalized Gaussian units, *Neural Computation*, **6**(2), 319–333.

Benaim, M., and Tomasini, L. (1992). Approximating functions and predicting time series with multi-sigmoidal basis functions, in *Artificial Neural Networks*, J. Aleksander and J. Taylor, eds., vol. 1, pp. 407–411. Elsevier Science Publishers, Amsterdam.

Bilbro, G. L., Mann, R., Miller, T. K., Snyder, W. E., van den Bout, D. E., and White, M. (1989). Optimization by mean field annealing, in *Advances in Neural Information Processing Systems I* (Denver, 1988), D. S. Touretzky, ed., pp. 91–98. Morgan Kaufmann, San Mateo, Calif.

Bilbro, G. L., and Snyder, W. E. (1989). Range image restoration using mean field annealing, in *Advances in Neural Information Processing Systems I* (Denver, 1988), D. S. Touretzky, ed., pp. 594–601. Morgan Kaufmann, San Mateo, Calif.

Bilbro, G. L., Snyder, W. E., Garnier, S. J., and Gault, J. W. (1992). Mean field annealing: A formalism for constructing GNC-like algorithms, *IEEE Transactions on Neural Networks*, **3**(1), 131–138.

Bishop, C. (1991). Improving the generalization properties of radial basis function neural networks, *Neural Computation*, **3**(4), 579–588.

Bishop, C. (1992). Exact calculation of the Hessian matrix for the multilayer perceptron, *Neural Computation*, **4**(4), 494–501.

Block, H. D., and Levin, S. A. (1970). On the boundedness of an iterative procedure for solving a system of linear inequalities, *Proceedings of the American Mathematical Society*, **26**, 229–235.

Blum, A. L., and Rivest, R. (1989). Training a 3-node neural network is NP-complete, *Proceedings of the 1988 Workshop on Computational Learning Theory*, pp. 9–18. Morgan Kaufmann, San Mateo, Calif.

Blum, A. L., and Rivest, R. (1992). Training a 3-node neural network is NP-complete, *Neural Networks*, **5**(1), 117–127.

Blumer, A., Ehrenfeucht, A., Haussler, D., and Warmuth, M. (1989). Learnability and the Vapnik-Chervonenkis dimension, *J. of American Computing Machinery*, **36**(4), 929–965.

Boole, G. (1854). *An Investigation of the Laws of Thought*. Macmillan. Republished in 1958 by Dover, New York.

Bounds, D. G., Lloyd, P. J., Mathew, B., and Wadell, G. (1988). A multilayer perceptron network for the diagnosis of low back pain, in *Proceedings of the IEEE International Conference on Neural Networks* (San Diego, 1988), vol. II, pp. 481–489. IEEE, New York.

Bourlard, H., and Kamp, Y. (1988). Auto-association by multilayer perceptrons and singular value decomposition, *Biological Cybernetics*, **59**, 291–294.

van den Bout, D. E., and Miller, T. K. (1988). A traveling salesman objective function that works, in *IEEE International Conference on Neural Networks* (San Diego, 1988), vol. II, pp. 299–303. IEEE, New York.

van den Bout, D. E., and Miller, T. K. (1989). Improving the performance of the Hopfield-Tank neural network through normalization and annealing, *Biological Cybernetics*, **62**, 129–139.

Bromley, J., and Denker, J. S. (1993). Improving rejection performance on handwritten digits by training with "rubbish," *Neural Computation*, **5**(3), 367–370.

Broomhead, D. S., and Lowe, D. (1988). Multivariate functional interpolation and adaptive networks, *Complex Systems*, **2**, 321–355.

Brown, R. R. (1959). A generalized computer procedure for the design of optimum systems, parts I and II, *AIEE Transactions, Part I:* Communications and Electronics, **78**, 285–293.

Brown, R. J. (1964). Adaptive Multiple-Output Threshold Systems and Their Storage Capacities. Ph.D. thesis, Technical Report 6771-1, Stanford Electronics Labs, Stanford University, Calif.

Brown, M., Harris, C. J., and Parks, P. (1993). The interpolation capabilities of the binary CMAC, *Neural Networks*, **6**(3), 429–440.

Bryson, A. E., and Denham, W. F. (1962). A steepest-ascent method for solving optimum programming problems, *Journal of Applied Mechanics*, **29**(2), 247–257.

Bryson, A. E., and Ho, Y.-C. (1969). *Applied Optimal Control*. Blaisdell, New York.

Burke, L. I. (1991). Clustering characterization of adaptive resonance, *Neural Networks*, **4**(4), 485–491.

Burshtien, D. (1993). Nondirect convergence analysis of the Hopfield associative memory, in *Proceedings of the World Congress on Neural Networks* (Portland, 1993), vol. II, pp. 224–227. LEA and INNS Press, Hillsdale, N.J.

Butz, A. R. (1967). Perceptron type learning algorithms in nonseparable situations, *Journal of Mathematical Analysis and Applications*, **17**, 560–576. Also see Ph.D. dissertation, University of Minnesota, 1965.

Cameron, S. H. (1960). An Estimate of the Complexity Requisite in a Universal Decision Network, Wright Air Development Division, Report 60-600, pp. 197–212.

Cannon, R. H., Jr. (1967). *Dynamics of Physical Systems*. McGraw-Hill, New York.

Carnahan, B., Luther, H. A., and Wilkes, J. O. (1969). *Applied Numerical Methods*. Wiley, New York.

Carpenter, G. A., and Grossberg, S. (1987a). A massively parallel architecture for a self-organizing neural pattern recognition machine, *Computer Vision, Graphics, and Image Processing*, **37**, 54–115.

Carpenter, G. A., and Grossberg, S. (1987b). ART2: Self-organization of stable category recognition codes for analog input patterns, *Applied Optics*, **26**(23), 4919–4930.

Carpenter, G. A., and Grossberg, S. (1990). ART3: Hierarchical search using chemical transmitters in self-organizing pattern recognition architectures, *Neural Networks*, **3**(2), 129–152.

Carpenter, G. A., Grossberg, S., and Reynolds, J. H. (1991a). ARTMAP: Supervised real-time learning and classification of nonstationary data by a self-organizing neural network, *Neural Networks*, **4**(5), 565–588.

Carpenter, G. A., Grossberg, S., and Rosen, D. B. (1991b). ART2-A: An adaptive resonance algorithm or rapid category learning and recognition, *Neural Networks*, **4**(4), 493–504.

Casasent, D., and Telfer, B. (1987). Associative memory synthesis, performance, storage capacity, and updating: New heteroassociative memory results, *Proceedings of SPIE, Intelligent Robots and Computer Vision*, **848**, 313–333.

Casdagli, M. (1989). Nonlinear prediction of chaotic time series, *Physica*, **35D**, 335–356.

Cater, J. P. (1987). Successfully using peak learning rates of 10 (and greater) in back-propagation networks with the heuristic learning algorithm, in *Proceedings of the IEEE First International Conference on Neural Networks* (San Diego, 1987), M. Caudill and C. Butler, eds., vol. II, pp. 645–651. IEEE, New York.

Cauchy, A. (1847). Méthod génerale pour la résolution des systémes d'e'quations simultanées, *Comptes Rendus Hebdomadaires des Séances del l'Académie des Sciences*, **25**, 536–538.

Caudell, T. P., and Dolan, C. P. (1989). Parametric connectivity: Training of constrained networks using genetic algorithms, in *Proceedings of the Third International Conference on Genetic Algorithms* (Arlington, 1989), J. D. Schaffer, ed., pp. 370–374. Morgan Kaufmann, San Mateo, Calif.

Cetin, B. C., Burdick, J. W., and Barhen, J. (1993a). Global descent replaces gradient descent to avoid local minima problem in learning with artificial neural networks, in *IEEE International Conference on Neural Networks* (San Francisco, 1993), vol. II, pp. 836–842. IEEE, New York.

Cetin, B. C., Barhen, J., and Burdick, J. W. (1993b). Terminal repeller unconstrained subenergy tunneling (TRUST) for fast global optimization, *Journal of Optimization Theory and Applications*, **77**, 97–126.

Chalmers, D. J. (1991). The evolution of learning: An experiment in genetic connectionism, in *Connectionist Models: Proceedings of the 1990 Summer School* (Pittsburgh, 1990), D. S. Touretzky, J. L. Elman, and G. E. Hinton, eds., pp. 81–90. Morgan Kaufmann, San Mateo, Calif.

Chan, L. W., and Fallside, F. (1987). An adaptive training algorithm for backpropagation networks, *Computer Speech and Language*, **2**, 205–218.

Changeux, J. P., and Danchin, A. (1976). Selective stabilization of developing synapses as a mechanism for the specification of neural networks, *Nature (London)*, **264**, 705–712.

Chauvin, Y. (1989). A back-propagation algorithm with optimal use of hidden units, in *Advances in Neural Information Processing Systems 1* (Denver, 1988), D. S. Touretzky, ed., pp. 519–526. Morgan Kaufmann, San Mateo, Calif.

Chen, D. S., and Jain, R. C. (1994). A robust back propagation learning algorithm for function approximation, *IEEE Transactions on Neural Networks*, **5**(3), 467–479.

Chiang, T.-S., Hwang, C.-R., and Sheu, S.-J. (1987). Diffusion for global optimization in R^n, *SIAM Journal on Control Optimization*, **25**(3), 737–752.

Chiueh, T. D., and Goodman, R. M. (1988). High capacity exponential associative memory, in *Proceedings of the IEEE International Conference on Neural Networks* (San Diego, 1988), vol. I, pp. 153–160. IEEE, New York.

Chiueh, T. D., and Goodman, R. M. (1991). Recurrent correlation associative memories, *IEEE Transactions on Neural Networks*, **2**(2), 275–284.

Cichocki, A., and Unbehauen, R. (1993). *Neural Networks for Optimization and Signal Processing*. Wiley, New York.

Cohen, M. A., and Grossberg, S. (1983). Absolute stability of global pattern formation and parallel memory storage by competitive neural networks, *IEEE Transactions on Systems, Man, and Cybernetics*, **SMC-13**, 815–826.

Cohn, D., and Tesauro, G. (1991). Can neural networks do better than the Vapnik-Chervonenkis bounds? in *Neural Information Processing Systems 3* (Denver, 1990), R. P. Lippmann, J. E. Moody, and D. S. Touretzky, eds., pp. 911–917. Morgan Kaufmann, San Mateo, Calif.

Cohn, D., and Tesauro, G. (1992). How tight are the Vapnik-Chervonenkis bounds? *Neural Computation*, **4**(2), 249–269.

Cooper, P. W. (1962). The hypersphere in pattern recognition, *Information and Control*, **5**, 324–346.

Cooper, P. W. (1966). A note on adaptive hypersphere decision boundary, *IEEE Transactions on Electronic Computers* (December 1966), 948–949.

Cortes, C., and Hertz, J. A. (1989). A network system for image segmentation, in *International Joint Conference on Neural Networks* (Washington, 1989), vol. I, pp. 121–127. IEEE, New York.

Cotter, N. E., and Guillerm, T. J. (1992). The CMAC and a theorem of Kolmogorov, *Neural Networks*, **5**(2), 221–228.

Cottrell, G. W. (1991). Extracting features from faces using compression networks: Face, identity, emotion, and gender recognition using holons, in *Connectionist Models: Proceedings of the 1990 Summer School* (Pittsburgh, 1990), D. S. Touretzky, J. L. Elman, T. J. Sejnowski, and G. E. Hinton, eds., pp. 328–337. Morgan Kaufmann, San Mateo, Calif.

Cottrell, M., and Fort, J. C. (1986). A stochastic model of retinotopy: A self-organizing process, *Biological Cybernetics*, **53**, 405–411.

Cottrell, G. W., and Munro, P. (1988). Principal component analysis of images via backpropagation, invited talk, in *Proceedings of the Society of Photo-Optical Instrumentation Engineers* (Cambridge, 1988), vol. 1001, pp. 1070–1077. Bellingham, Washington, D.C.

Cottrell, G. W., Munro, P., and Zipser, D. (1987). Learning internal representations from gray-scale images: An example of extensional programming, in *Ninth Annual Conference of the Cognitive Science Society* (Seattle, 1987), pp. 462–473. Erlbaum, Hillsdale.

Cottrell, G. W., Munro, P., and Zipser, D. (1989). Image compression by back propagation: An example of extensional programming, in *Models of Cognition: A Review of Cognitive Science*, vol. 1, N. Sharkey, ed., pp. 208–240. Ablex, Norwood.

Cover, T. M. (1964). Geometrical and Statistical Properties of Linear Threshold Devices. Ph.D. dissertation, Technical Report 6107-1, Stanford Electronics Labs, Stanford University, Calif.

Cover, T. M. (1965). Geometrical and statistical properties of systems of linear inequalities with applications in pattern recognition, *IEEE Transactions on Electronic Computers*, **EC-14**, 326–334.

Cover, T. M. (1968). Rates of convergence of nearest neighbor decision procedures, *Proceedings of the Hawaii International Conference on Systems Sciences*, B. K. Kinariwala and F. F. Kuo, eds., pp. 413–415. University of Hawaii Press, Honolulu.

Cover, T. M., and Hart, P. E. (1967). Nearest neighbor pattern classification, *IEEE Transactions on Information Theory*, **IT-13**(1), 21–27.

Crisanti, A., and Sompolinsky, H. (1987). Dynamics of spin systems with randomly asymmetric bounds: Langevin dynamics and a spherical model, *Physiological Reviews A*, **36**, 4922.

Crowder, R. S., III (1991). Predicting the Mackey-Glass time series with cascade-correlation learning, in *Connectionist Models: Proceedings of the 1990 Summer School* (Pittsburgh, 1990), D. S. Touretzky, J. L. Elman, T. J. Sejnowski, and G. E. Hinton, eds., pp. 117–123. Morgan Kaufmann, San Mateo, Calif.

Cybenko, G. (1989). Approximation by superpositions of a sigmoidal function, *Mathematical Control Signals Systems*, **2**, 303–314.

Darken, C., and Moody, J. (1991). Note on learning rate schedules for stochastic optimization, in *Neural Information Processing Systems 3* (Denver, 1990), R. P. Lippmann, J. E. Moody, and D. S. Touretzky, eds., pp. 832–838. Morgan Kaufmann, San Mateo, Calif.

Darken, C., and Moody, J. (1992). Towards faster stochastic gradient search, in *Neural Information Processing Systems 4* (Denver, 1991), J. E. Moody, S. J. Hanson, and R. P. Lippmann, eds., pp. 1009–1016. Morgan Kaufmann, San Mateo, Calif.

Davis, L. (1987). *Genetic Algorithms and Simulated Annealing*. Pitman, London.

Davis, T. E., and Principe, J. C. (1993). A Markov chain framework for the simple genetic algorithm, *Evolutionary Computation*, **1**(3), 269–288.

D'Azzo, J. J., and Houpis, C. H. (1988). *Linear Control Systems Analysis and Design* (3d ed.). McGraw-Hill, New York.

De Jong, K. (1975). An Analysis of the Behavior of a Class of Genetic Adaptive Systems. Ph.D. thesis, Department of Computer and Communications Sciences, University of Michigan, Ann Arbor.

De Jong, K., and Spears, W. (1993). On the state of evolutionary computation, in *Proceedings of the Fifth International Conference on Genetic Algorithms* (Urbana-Champaign, 1993), S. Forrest, ed., pp. 618–623. Morgan Kaufmann, San Mateo, Calif.

Dembo, A., and Zeitouni, O. (1988). High density associative memories, in *Neural Information Processing Systems* (Denver, 1987), D. Z. Anderson, ed., pp. 211–212. American Institute of Physics, New York.

DeMers, D., and Cottrell, G. (1993). Non-linear dimensionality reduction, in *Advances in Neural Information Processing Systems 5* (Denver, 1992), S. J. Hanson, J. D. Cowan, and C. L. Giles, eds., pp. 550–587. Morgan Kaufmann, San Mateo, Calif.

Dennis, J. E., Jr., and Schnabel, R. B. (1983). *Numerical Methods for Unconstrained Optimization and Nonlinear Equations*. Prentice-Hall, Englewood Cliffs, N.J.

Denoeux, T., and Lengellé, R. (1993). Initializing back propagation networks with prototypes, *Neural Networks*, **6**(3), 351–363.

Derthick, M. (1984). Variations on the Boltzmann Machine, Technical Report CMU-CS-84-120, Department of Computer Science, Carnegie Mellon University, Pittsburgh, Pa.

Dertouzos, M. L. (1965). *Threshold Logic: A Synthesis Approach*. MIT Press, Cambridge, Mass.

Dickinson, B. W. (1991). *Systems: Analysis, Design, and Computation*. Prentice-Hall, Englewood Cliffs, N.J.

Dickmanns, E. D., and Zapp, A. (1987). Autonomous high speed road vehicle guidance by computer vision, in *Proceedings of the 10th World Congress on Automatic Control* (Munich, West Germany, 1987), vol. 4, pp. 221-226. Pergamon Press, New York.

Drucker, H., and Le Cun, Y. (1992). Improving generalization performance using double backpropagation, *IEEE Transactions on Neural Networks*, **3**(6), 991–997.

Duda, R. O., and Hart, P. E. (1973). *Pattern Classification and Scene Analysis*. Wiley, New York.

Duda, R. O., and Singleton, R. C. (1964). Training a threshold logic unit with imperfect classified patterns, in *IRE Western Electric Show and Convention Record*, Paper 3.2. Institute of Radio Engineers, New York.

Durbin, R., and Willshaw, D. (1987). An analogue approach to the traveling salesman problem using an elastic net method, *Nature (London)*, **326**, 689–691.

Efron, D. (1964). The Perceptron Correction Procedure in Non-Separable Situations, Technical Report. No. RADC-TDR-63-533. Rome Air Development Center, Rome, N.Y.

Elamn, J. L., and Zipser, D. (1988). Learning the hidden structure of speech, *Journal of Acoustical Society of America*, **83**, 1615–1626.

Everitt, B. S. (1980). *Cluster Analysis* (2d ed.). Heinemann Educational Books, London.

Fahlman, S. E. (1989). Fast learning variations on back-propagation: An empirical study, in *Proceedings of the 1988 Connectionist Models Summer School* (Pittsburgh, 1988), D. Touretzky, G. Hinton, and T. Sejnowski, eds., pp. 38–51. Morgan Kaufmann, San Mateo, Calif.

Fahlman, S. E., and Lebiere, C. (1990). The cascade-correlation learning architecture, in *Advances in Neural Information Processing Systems 2* (Denver, 1989), D. S. Touretzky, ed., pp. 524–532. Morgan Kaufmann, San Mateo, Calif.

Fakhr, W. (1993). Optimal Adaptive Probabilistic Neural Networks for Pattern Classification. Ph.D. thesis, Department of Electrical and Computer Engineering, University of Waterloo, Waterloo, Canada.

Fang, Y., and Sejnowski, T. J. (1990). Faster learning for dynamic recurrent backpropagation, *Neural Computation*, **2**(3), 270–273.

Farden, D. C. (1981). Tracking properties of adaptive signal processing algorithms, *IEEE Transactions on Acoustics and Speech Signal Processing*, **ASSP-29**, 439–446.

Farhat, N. H. (1987). Optoelectronic analogs of self-programming neural nets: Architectures and methods for implementing fast stochastic learning by simulated annealing, *Applied Optics*, **26**, 5093–5103.

Feigenbaum, M. (1978). Quantitative universality for a class of nonlinear transformations, *Journal of Statistical Physics*, **19**, 25–52.

Fels, S. S., and Hinton, G. E. (1993). Glove-Talk: A neural network interface between a data-glove and a speech synthesizer, *IEEE Transactions on Neural Networks*, **4**(1), 2–8.

Finnoff, W. (1993). Diffusion approximations for the constant learning rate backpropagation algorithm and resistance to local minima, in *Advances in Neural Information Processing Systems 5* (Denver, 1992), S. J. Hanson, J. D. Cowan, and C. L. Giles, eds., pp. 459–466. Morgan Kaufmann, San Mateo, Calif.

Finnoff, W. (1994). Diffusion approximations for the constant learning rate backpropagation algorithm and resistance to local minima, *Neural Computation*, **6**(2), 285–295.

Finnoff, W., Hergert, F., and Zimmermann, H. G. (1993). Improving model selection by nonconvergent methods, *Neural Networks*, **6**(5), 771–783.

Fisher, M. L. (1981). The Lagrangian relaxation method for solving integer programming problems, *Management Sciences*, **27**(1), 1–18.

Fix, E., and Hodges, J. L. Jr. (1951). Discriminatory Analysis: Non-parametric Discrimination, Report 4, Project 21-49-004, USAF School of Aviation Medicine, Randolph Field, Texas.

Franzini, M. A. (1987). Speech recognition with back propagation, in *Proceedings of the Ninth Annual Conference of the IEEE Engineering in Medicine and Biology Society* (Boston, 1987), pp. 1702–1703. IEEE, New York.

Frean, M. (1990). The upstart algorithm: A method for constructing and training feedforward neural networks, *Neural Computation*, **2**(2), 198–209.

Fritzke, B. (1991). Let it grow—Self-organizing feature maps with problem dependent cell structure, in *Artificial Neural Networks, Proceedings of the 1991 International Conference on Artificial Neural Networks* (Espoo, 1991), T. Kohonen, K. Mäkisara, O. Simula, and J. Kangas, eds., vol. I, 403–408. Elsevier Science Publishers, Amsterdam.

Funahashi, K.-I. (1989). On the approximate realization of continuous mappings by neural networks, *Neural Networks*, **2**(3), 183–192.

Funahashi, K.-I. (1990). On the approximate realization of identity mappings by 3-layer neural networks (in Japanese), *Transactions of the IEICE A*, **J73-A**, 139–145.

Funahashi, K.-I., and Nakamura, Y. (1993). Approximation of dynamical systems by continuous time recurrent neural networks, *Neural Networks*, **6**(6), 801–806.

Galland, C. C., and Hinton, G. E. (1991). Deterministic Boltzmann learning in networks with asymmetric connectivity, in *Connectionist Models: Proceeding of the 1990 Summer School* (Pittsburgh, 1990), D. S. Touretzky, J. L. Elman, T. J. Sejnowski, and G. E. Hinton, eds., pp. 3–9. Morgan Kaufmann, San Mateo, Calif.

Gallant, S. I. (1993). *Neural Network Learning and Expert Systems*. MIT Press, Cambridge, Mass.

Gallant, S. I., and Smith, D. (1987). Random cells: An idea whose time has come and gone ... and come again? in *Proceedings of the IEEE International Conference on Neural Networks* (San Diego, 1987), vol. II, pp. 671–678. IEEE, New York.

Gamba, A. (1961). Optimum performance of learning machines, *Proceedings of the IRE*, **49**, 349–350.

Gantmacher, F. R. (1990). *The Theory of Matrices*, vol. 1 (2d ed.). Chelsea, New York.

Gardner, E. (1986). Structure of metastable states in Hopfield model, *Journal of Physics A*, **19**, L1047–1052.

Garey, M. R., and Johnson (1979). *Computers and Intractability: A Guide to the Theory of NP-Completeness*. Freeman, New York.

Gelfand, S. B., and Mitter, S. K. (1991). Recursive stochastic algorithms for global optimization in R^d, *SIAM Journal of Control and Optimization*, **29**(5), 999–1018.

Geman, S. (1979). Some averaging and stability results for random differential equations, *SIAM Journal of Applied Mathematics*, **36**, 86–105.

Geman, S. (1980). A limit theorem for the norm of random matrices, *Annals of Probability*, **8**, 252–261.

Geman, S. (1982). Almost sure stable oscillations in a large system of randomly coupled equations, *SIAM Journal of Applied Mathematics*, **42**(4), 695–703.

Geman, S., and Geman, D. (1984). Stochastic relaxation, Gibbs distributions, and the Bayesian restoration of images, *IEEE Transactions on Pattern Analysis and Machine Intelligence*, **6**, 721–741.

Geman, S., and Hwang, C. R. (1986). Diffusions for global optimization, *SIAM Journal of Control and Optimization*, **24**(5), 1031–1043.

Gerald, C. F. (1978). *Applied Numerical Analysis* (2d ed.). Addison-Wesley, Reading, Mass.

Geszti, T. (1990). *Physical Models of Neural Networks*. World Scientific, Singapore.

Gill, P. E., Murray, W., and Wright, M. H. (1981). *Practical Optimization*. Academic Press, New York.

Girosi, F., and Poggio, T. (1989). Representation properties of networks: Kolmogorov's theorem is irrelevant, *Neural Computation*, 1(4), 465–469.

Glanz, F. H., and Miller, W. T. (1987). Shape recognition using a CMAC based learning system, *Proceedings of SPIE, Robotics and Intelligent Systems*, **848**, 294–298.

Glanz, F. H., and Miller, W. T. (1989). Deconvolution and nonlinear inverse filtering using a neural network, in *Proceedings of the International Conference on Acoustics, Speech, and Signal Processing*, (Glasgow, 1989), vol. 4, pp. 2349–2352. IEEE, New York.

Glauber, R. J. (1963). Time dependent statistics of the Ising model, *Journal of Mathematical Physics*, **4**, 294–307.

Goldberg, D. (1989). *Genetic Algorithms*. Addison-Wesley, Reading, Mass.

Golden, R. M. (1986). The "brain-state-in-a-box" neural model is a gradient descent algorithm, *Journal of Mathematical Psychology*, **30**, 73–80.

Golden, R. M. (1993). Stability and optimization analysis of the generalized brain-state-in-a-box neural network model, *Journal of Mathematical Psychology*, **37**, 282–298.

Goldman, L., Cook, E. F., Brand, D. A., Lee, T. H., Rouan, G. W., Weisberg, M. C., Acampora, D., Stasiulewicz, C., Walshon, J., Gterranova, G., Gottlieb, L., Kobernick, M., Goldstein-Wayne, B., Copen, D., Daley, K., Brandt, A. A., Jones, D., Mellors, J., and Jakubowski, R. (1988). A computer protocol to predict myocardial infarction in emergency department patients with chest pain, *New England Journal of Medicine*, **318**, 797–803.

Gonzalez, R. C., and Wintz, P. (1987). *Digital Image Processing* (2d ed.). Addison-Wesley, Reading, Mass.

Gordon, M. B., Peretto, P., and Berchier, D. (1993). Learning algorithms for perceptrons from statistical physics, *Journal Physique I*, **3**, 377–387.

Gorse, D., and Shepherd, A. (1992). Adding stochastic search to conjugate gradient algorithms, in *Proceedings of 3rd International Conference on Parallel Applications in Statistics and Economics*. Tiskărenfkě Zacody, Prague.

Gray, R. M. (1984). Vector quantization, *IEEE ASSP Magazine*, **1**, 4–29.

Greenberg, H. J. (1988). Equilibria of the brain-state-in-a-box (BSB) neural model, *Neural Networks*, 1(4), 323–324.

Grefenstette, J. J. (1986). Optimization of control parameters for genetic algorithms, *IEEE Transactions on Systems, Man and Cybernetics*, **SMC-16**, 122–128.

Grossberg, S. (1969). On learning and energy-entropy dependence in recurrent and nonrecurrent signed networks, *Journal of Statistical Physics*, **1**, 319–350.

Grossberg, S. (1976). Adaptive pattern classification and universal recording: I. Parallel development and coding of neural feature detectors, *Biological Cybernetics*, **23**, 121–134.

Grossberg, S. (1976). Adaptive pattern classification and universal recording, II. Feedback, expectation, olfaction, and illusions, *Biological Cybernetics*, **23**, 187–202.

Hampel, F. R., Rousseuw, P. J., Ronchetti, E. M., and Stahel, W. A. (1986). *Robust Statistics: The Approach Based on Influence Function*. Wiley, New York.

Hanson, S. J., and Burr, D. J. (1987). Knowledge representation in connectionist networks, Bellcore Technical Report. Bellcore, Livingston, N.J.

Hanson, S. J., and Burr, D. J. (1988). Minkowski-*r* back-propagation: Learning in connectionist models with non-Euclidean error signals, in *Neural Information Processing Systems* (Denver, 1987), D. Z. Anderson, ed., pp. 348–357. American Institute of Physics, New York.

Hanson, S. J., and Pratt, L. (1989). A comparison of different biases for minimal network construction with back-propagation, in *Advances in Neural Information Processing Systems 1* (Denver, 1988), D. S. Touretzky, ed., pp. 177–185. Morgan Kaufmann, San Mateo, Calif.

Hardy, G., Littlewood, J., and Polya, G. (1952). *Inequalities.* Cambridge University Press, Cambridge, England.

Harp, S. A., Samad, T., and Guha, A. (1989). Towards the genetic synthesis of neural networks, in *Proceedings of the Third International Conference on Genetic Algorithms* (Arlington, 1989), J. D. Schaffer, ed., pp. 360–369. Morgan Kaufmann, San Mateo, Calif.

Harp, S. A., Samad, T., and Guha, A. (1990). Designing application-specific neural networks using the genetic algorithms, in *Advances in Neural Information Processing Systems 2* (Denver, 1989), D. S. Touretzky, ed., pp. 447–454. Morgan Kaufmann, San Mateo, Calif.

Hartigan, J. A. (1975). *Clustering Algorithms.* Wiley, New York.

Hartman, E. J., and Keeler, J. D. (1991a). Semi-local units for prediction, in *Proceedings of the International Joint Conference on Neural Networks* (Seattle, 1991), vol. II, pp. 561–566. IEEE, New York.

Hartman, E. J., and Keeler, J. D. (1991b). Predicting the future: Advantages of semilocal units, *Neural Computation*, 3(4), 566–578.

Hartman, E. J., Keeler, J. D., and Kowalski, J. M. (1990). Layered neural networks with Gaussian hidden units as universal approximators, *Neural Computation*, 2(2), 210–215.

Hassoun, M. H. (1988). Two-level neural network for deterministic logic processing, *Proceedings of the SPIE, Optical Computing and Nonlinear Materials*, 881, 258–264.

Hassoun, M. H. (1989a). Adaptive dynamic heteroassociative neural memories for pattern classification, in *Proceedings of the SPIE, Optical Pattern Recognition*, 1053, 75–83.

Hassoun, M. H. (1989b). Dynamic heteroassociative neural memories, *Neural Networks*, 2(4), 275–287.

Hassoun, M. H., ed. (1993). *Associative Neural Memories: Theory and Implementation.* Oxford University Press, New York.

Hassoun, M. H., and Clark, D. W. (1988). An adaptive attentive learning algorithm for single-layer neural networks, in *Proceedings of the IEEE Annual Conference on Neural Networks*, vol. I, pp. 431–440. IEEE, New York.

Hassoun, M. H., and Song, J. (1992). Adaptive Ho-Kashyap rules for perceptron training, *IEEE Transactions on Neural Networks*, 3(1), 51–61.

Hassoun, M. H., and Song, J. (1993a). Multilayer perceptron learning via genetic search for hidden layer activations, in *Proceedings of the World Congress on Neural Networks* (Portland, 1993), vol. III, pp. 437–444. LEA/INNS Press, N.J.

Hassoun, M. H., and Song, J. (1993b). Hybrid genetic/gradient search for multilayer perceptron training. *Optical Memory and Neural Networks, Special Issue on Architectures, Designs, Algorithms and Devices for Optical Neural Networks* (part 1), 2(1), 1–15.

Hassoun, M. H., and Spitzer, A. R. (1988). Neural network identification and extraction of repetitive superimposed pulses in noisy 1-D signals, *Neural Networks*, 1, Supplement 1: *Abstracts of the First Annual Meeting of the International Neural Networks Society* (Boston, 1988), p. 443. Pergamon Press, New York.

Hassoun, M. H., and Youssef, A. M. (1989). A high-performance recording algorithm for Hopfield model associative memories, *Optical Engineering*, 28(1), 46–54.

Hassoun, M. H., Song, J., Shen, S.-M., and Spitzer, A. R. (1990). Self-organizing autoassociative dynamic multiple-layer neural net for the decomposition of repetitive superimposed signals, in *Proceedings of the International Joint Conference on Neural Networks* (Washington, 1990), vol. I, pp. 621–626. IEEE, New York.

Hassoun, M. H., Wang, C., and Spitzer, A. R. (1992). Electromyogram decomposition via unsupervised dynamic multi-layer neural network, in *Proceedings of the International Joint Conference on Neural Networks* (Baltimore, 1992), vol. II, pp. 405–412. IEEE, New York.

Hassoun, M. H., Wang, C., and Spitzer, A. R. (1994a). NNERVE: Neural network extraction of repetitive vectors for electromyography: I. Algorithm, *IEEE Transactions on Biomedical Engineering* 41(11), 1039–1052.

Hassoun, M. H., Wang, C., and Spitzer, A. R. (1994b). NNERVE: Neural network extraction of repetitive vectors for electromyography: II. Performance analysis, *IEEE Transactions on Biomedical Engineering* **41**(11), 1053–1061.

Haussler, D., Kearns, M., Opper, M., and Schapire, R. (1992). Estimating average-case learning curves using Bayesian, statistical physics and VC dimension methods, in *Neural Information Processing Systems 4* (Denver, 1991), J. E. Moody, S. J. Hanson, and R. P. Lippmann, eds., pp. 855–862. Morgan Kaufmann, San Mateo, Calif.

Hebb, D. (1949). *The Organization of Behavior*. Wiley, New York.

Hecht-Nielsen, R. (1987). Kolmogorov's mapping neural network existence theorem, in *Proceedings of the International Conference on Neural Networks* (San Diego, 1987), vol. III, pp. 11–14, IEEE, New York.

Hecht-Nielsen, R. (1990). *Neurocomputing*. Addison-Wesley, Reading, Mass.

van Hemman, J. L., Ioffe, L. B., and Vaas, M. (1990). Increasing the efficiency of a neural network through unlearning, *Physica*, **163A**, 368–392.

Hergert, F., Finnoff, W., and Zimmermann, H. G. (1992). A comparison of weight elimination methods for reducing complexity in neural networks, in *Proceedings of the International Joint Conference on Neural Networks* (Baltimore, 1992), vol. III, pp. 980–987. IEEE, New York.

Hertz, J., Krogh, A., and Palmer, R. G. (1991). *Introduction to the Theory of Neural Computation*. Addison-Wesley, Reading, Mass.

Heskes, T. M., and Kappen, B. (1991). Learning processes in neural networks, *Physical Review A*, **44**(4), 2718–2726.

Heskes, T. M., and Kappen, B. (1993a). Error potentials for self-organization, in *IEEE International Conference on Neural Networks* (San Francisco, 1993), vol. III, pp. 1219–1223. IEEE, New York.

Heskes, T. M., and Kappen, B. (1993b). On-line learning processes in artificial neural networks, in *Mathematical Approaches to Neural Networks*, J. G. Taylor, ed., pp. 199–233. Elsevier Science Publishers, Amsterdam.

Hestenes, M. R., and Stiefel, E. (1952). Methods of conjugate gradients for solving linear systems, *Journal of Research of the National Bureau of Standards*, **49**, 409–436.

Hinton, G. E. (1986). Learning distributed representations of concepts, in *Proceedings of the 8th Annual Conference of the Cognitive Science Society* (Amherst, 1986), pp. 1–12. Erlbaum, Hillsdale.

Hinton, G. E. (1987a). Connectionist Learning Procedures, Technical Report CMU-CS-87-115, Carnegie-Mellon University, Computer Science Department, Pittsburgh, Pa.

Hinton, G. E. (1987b). Learning translation invariant recognition in a massively parallel network, in *PARLE: Parallel Architectures and Languages, Europe Lecture Notes in Computer Science*, G. Goos and J. Hartmanis, eds., pp. 1–13. Springer-Verlag, Berlin.

Hinton, G. E., and Nowlan, S. J. (1987). How learning can guide evolution, *Complex Systems*, **1**, 495–502.

Hinton, G. E., and Sejnowski, T. J. (1983). Optimal perceptual inference, in *Proceedings of the IEEE Conference on Computer Vision and Pattern Recognition* (Washington, 1983), pp. 448–453. IEEE, New York.

Hinton, G. E., and Sejnowski, T. J. (1986). Learning and relearning in Boltzmann machines, in *Parallel Distributed Processing: Explorations in the Microstructure of Cognition*, vol. I, D. E. Rumelhart, J. L. McClelland, and the PDP Research Group, eds., pp. 282–317. MIT Press, Cambridge, Mass.

Hirsch, M. W. (1989). Convergent activation dynamics in continuous time networks, *Neural Networks*, **2**(5), 331–349.

Hirsch, M., and Smale, S. (1974). *Differential Equations, Dynamical Systems, and Linear Algebra*. Academic Press, New York.

Ho, Y.-C., and Kashyap, R. L. (1965). An algorithm for linear inequalities and its applications, *IEEE Transactions on Electronic Computers*, **EC-14**, 683–688.

Holland, J. H. (1975). *Adaptation in Natural and Artificial Systems*. The University of Michigan Press, Ann Arbor, Mich.; reprinted as a second edition (1992), MIT Press, Cambridge, Mass.

Holland, J. H. (1986). Escaping brittleness: The possibilities of general-purpose learning algorithms applied to parallel rule based systems, in *Machine Learning: An Artificial Intelligence Approach*, vol. 2, R. Michalski, J. Carbonell, and T. Mitchell, eds., pp. 593–623. Morgan Kaufmann, San Mateo, Calif.

Holland, J. H., and Reitman, J. S. (1978). Cognitive systems based on adaptive algorithms, in *Pattern Directed Inference Systems*, D. A. Waterman and F. Hayes-Roth, eds., pp. 313–329. Academic Press, New York.

Hopfield, J. J. (1982). Neural networks and physical systems with emergent collective computational abilities, *Proceedings of the National Academy of Sciences, USA*, **79**, 2445–2558.

Hopfield, J. J. (1984). Neurons with graded response have collective computational properties like those of two-state neurons, *Proceedings of the National Academy of Sciences, USA*, **81**, 3088–3092.

Hopfield, J. J. (1987). Learning algorithms and probability distributions in feed-forward and feed-back networks, *Proceedings of the National Academy of Sciences, USA*, **84**, 8429–8433.

Hopfield, J. J. (1990). The effectiveness of analogue "Neural Network" hardware, *Network: Computation in Neural Systems*, **1**(1), 27–40.

Hopfield, J. J., and Tank, (1985). Neural computation of decisions in optimization problems, *Biological Cybernetics*, **52**, 141–152.

Hopfield, J. J., Feinstein, D. I., and Palmer, R. G. (1993). "Unlearning" has a stabilizing effect in collective memories, *Nature (London)*, **304**, 158–159.

Hoptroff, R. G., and Hall, T. J. (1989). Learning by diffusion for multilayer perceptron, *Electronic Letters*, **25**(8), 531–533.

Hornbeck, R. W. (1975). *Numerical Methods*. Quantum, New York.

Hornik, K. (1991). Approximation capabilities of multilayer feedforward networks, *Neural Networks*, **4**(2), 251–257.

Hornik, K. (1993). Some new results on neural network approximation, *Neural Networks*, **6**(8), 1069–1072.

Hornik, K., Stinchcombe, M., and White, H. (1989). Multilayer feedforward networks are universal approximators, *Neural Networks*, **2**(5), 359–366.

Hornik, K., Stinchcombe, M., and White, H. (1990). Universal approximation of an unknown mapping and its derivatives using multilayer feedforward networks, *Neural Networks*, **3**(5), 551–560.

Horowitz, L. L., and Senne, K. D. (1981). Performance advantage of complex LMS for controlling narrow-band adaptive arrays, *IEEE Transactions on Circuits Systems*, **CAS-28**, 562–576.

Hoskins, J. C., Lee, P., and Chakravarthy, S. V. (1993). Polynomial modeling behavior in radial basis function networks, in *Proceedings of the World Congress on Neural Networks* (Portland, 1993), vol. IV, pp. 693–699. LEA/INNS Press, Hillsdale, N.J.

Householder, A. S. (1964). *The Theory of Matrices in Numerical Analysis*. Blaisdel, New York; reprinted (1975) by Dover, New York.

Hu, S. T. (1965). *Threshold Logic*. University of California Press, Berkeley, Calif.

Huang, W. Y., and Lippmann, R. P. (1988). Neural nets and traditional classifiers, in *Neural Information Processing Systems* (Denver, 1987), D. Z. Anderson, ed., pp. 387–396. American Institute of Physics, New York.

Huang, Y., and Schultheiss, P. M. (1963). Block quantization of correlated Gaussian random variables, *IEEE Transactions on Communications Systems*, **CS-11**, 289–296.

Huber, P. J. (1981). *Robust Statistics*. Wiley, New York.

Hudak, M. J. (1992). RCE classifiers: Theory and practice, *Cybernetics and Systems: An International Journal*, **23**, 483–515.

Hueter, G. J. (1988). Solution of the traveling salesman problem with an adaptive ring, in *IEEE International Conference on Neural Networks* (San Diego, 1988), vol. I, pp. 85–92. IEEE, New York.

Hui, S., and Żak, S. H. (1992). Dynamical analysis of the brain-state-in-a-box neural models, *IEEE Transactions on Neural Networks*, **3**, 86–89.

Hui, S., Lillo, W. E., and Żak, S. H. (1993). Dynamics and stability analysis of the brain-state-in-a-box (BSB) neural models, in *Associative Neural Memories: Theory and Implementation*, M. H. Hassoun, ed., pp. 212–224. Oxford University Press, New York.

Hush, D. R., Salas, J. M., and Horne, B. (1991). Error surfaces for multi-layer perceptrons, in *International Joint Conference on Neural Networks* (Seattle, 1991), vol. I, pp. 759–764, IEEE, New York.

Irie, B., and Miyake, S. (1988). Capabilities of three-layer perceptrons, in *IEEE International Conference on Neural Networks*, vol. I, pp. 641–648. IEEE, New York.

Ito, Y. (1991). Representation of functions by superpositions of step or sigmoid function and their applications to neural network theory, *Neural Networks*, **4**(3), 385–394.

Jacobs, R. A. (1988). Increased rates of convergence through learning rate adaptation, *Neural Networks*, **1**(4), 295–307.

Johnson, D. S., Aragon, C. R., McGeoch, L. A., and Schevon, C. (1989). Optimization by simulated annealing: An experimental evaluation: I. Graph partitioning, *Operations Research*, **37**(6), 865–892.

Johnson, D. S., Aragon, C. R., McGeoch, L. A., and Schevon, C. (1991). Optimization by simulated annealing: An experimental evaluation: II. Graph coloring and number partitioning, *Operations Research*, **39**(3), 378–406.

Johnson, R. A., and Wichern, D. W. (1988). *Applied Multivariate Statistical Analysis* (2d ed.). Prentice-Hall, Englewood Cliffs, N.J.

Jones, R. D., Lee, Y. C., Barnes, C. W., Flake, G. W., Lee, K., Lewis, P. S., and Qian, S. (1990). Function approximation and time series prediction with neural networks, in *Proceedings of the International Joint Conference on Neural Networks* (San Diego, 1990), vol. I, pp. 649–666. IEEE, New York.

Judd, J. S. (1987). Learning in networks is hard, in *IEEE First International Conference on Neural Networks* (San Diego, 1987), M. Caudill and C. Butler, eds., vol. II, pp. 685–692. IEEE, New York.

Judd, J. S. (1990). *Neural Network Design and the Complexity of Learning*. MIT Press, Cambridge, Mass.

Kadirkamanathan, V., Niranjan, M., and Fallside, F. (1991). Sequential adaptation of radial basis function neural networks and its application to time-series prediction, in *Advances in Neural Information Processing Systems 3* (Denver, 1990) R. P. Lippmann, J. E. Moody, and D. S. Touretzky, eds., pp. 721–727. Morgan Kaufmann, San Mateo, Calif.

Kamimura, R. (1993). Minimum entropy method for the improvement of selectivity and interpretability, in *Proceedings of the World Congress on Neural Networks* (Portland, 1993), vol. III, pp. 512–519. LEA/INNS Press, Hillsdale, N.J.

Kanerva, P. (1988). *Sparse Distributed Memory*. Bradford/MIT Press, Cambridge, Mass.

Kanerva, P. (1993). Sparse distributed memory and other models, in *Associative Neural Memories: Theory and Implementation*, M. H. Hassoun, ed., pp. 50–76. Oxford University Press, New York.

Kanter, I., and Sompolinsky, H. (1987). Associative recall of memory without errors, *Physical Review A*, **35**, 380–392.

Karhunen, J. (1994). Optimization criteria and nonlinear PCA neural networks, in *IEEE International Conference on Neural Networks*, (Orlando, 1994), vol. II, pp. 1241–1246. IEEE, New York.

Karhunen, K. (1947). Uber lineare methoden in der Wahrscheinlichkeitsrechnung, *Annales Academiae Scientiarium Fennicae*, **A37**(1), 3–79 (translated by RAND Corp., Santa Monica, Calif., report T-131, 1960).

Karmarkar, N. (1984). A new polynomial time algorithm for linear programming, *Combinatorica*, **1**, 373–395.

Karnaugh, M. (1953). A map method for synthesis of combinatorial logic circuits, *Transactions AIEE, Communications and Electronics*, **72**, part I, 593–599.

Kashyap, R. L. (1966). Synthesis of switching functions by threshold elements, *IEEE Transactions on Electronic Computers*, **EC-15**(4), 619–628.

Kaszerman, P. (1963). A nonlinear summation threshold device, *IEEE Transactions on Electronic Computers*, **EC-12**, 914–915.

Katz, B. (1966). *Nerve, Muscle and Synapse*. McGraw-Hill, New York.

Keeler, J., and Rumelhart, D. E. (1992). A self-organizing integrated segmentation and recognition neural network, in *Advances in Neural Information Processing Systems 4* (Denver, 1991), J. E. Moody, S. J. Hanson, and R. P. Lippmann, eds., pp. 496–503. Morgan Kaufmann, San Mateo, Calif.

Keeler, J. D., Rumelhart, D. E., and Leow, W.-K. (1991). Integrated segmentation and recognition of handprinted numerals, in *Advances in Neural Information Processing Systems 3* (Denver, 1990), R. P. Lippmann, J. E. Moody, and D. S. Touretzky, eds., pp. 557–563. Morgan Kaufmann, San Mateo, Calif.

Keesing, R., and Stork, D. G. (1991). Evolution and learning in neural networks: The number and distribution of learning trials affect the rate of evolution, in *Advances in Neural Information Processing Systems 3* (Denver, 1990), R. P. Lippmann, J. E. Moody, and D. S. Touretzky, eds., pp. 804–810. Morgan Kaufmann, San Mateo, Calif.

Kelley, H. J. (1962). Methods of gradients, in *Optimization Techniques with Applications to Aerospace Systems*, G. Leitmann, ed., pp. 206–254. Academic Press, New York.

Khachian, L. G. (1979). A polynomial algorithm in linear programming, *Soviet Mathematika Doklady*, **20**, 191–194.

Kirkpatrick, S. (1984). Optimization by simulated annealing: Quantitative studies, *Journal of Statistical Physics*, **34**, 975–986.

Kirkpatrick, S., Gilatt, C. D., and Vecchi, M. P. (1983). Optimization by simulated annealing, *Science*, **220**, 671–680.

Kishimoto, K., and Amari, S. (1979). Existence and stability of local excitations in homogeneous neural fields, *Journal of Mathematical Biology*, **7**, 303–318.

Knapp, A. G., and Anderson, J. A. (1984). A theory of categorization based on distributed memory storage, *Journal of Experimental Psychology: Learning, Memory, and Cognition*, **9**, 610–622.

Kohavi, Z. (1978). *Switching and Finite Automata*. McGraw-Hill, New York.

Kohonen, T. (1972). Correlation matrix memories, *IEEE Transactions on Computers*, **C-21**, 353–359.

Kohonen, T. (1974). An adaptive associative memory principle, *IEEE Transactions on Computers*, **C-23**, 444–445.

Kohonen, T. (1982a). Self-organized formation of topologically correct feature maps, *Biological Cybernetics*, **43**, 59–69.

Kohonen, T. (1982b). Analysis of simple self-organizing process, *Biological Cybernetics*, **44**, 135–140.

Kohonen, T. (1984). *Self-Organization and Associative Memory*. Springer-Verlag, Berlin.

Kohonen, T. (1988). The "Neural" phonetic typewriter, *IEEE Computer Magazine* (March 1988), 11–22.

Kohonen, T. (1989). *Self-Organization and Associative Memory* (3d ed.). Springer-Verlag, Berlin.

Kohonen, T. (1990). Improved versions of learning vector quantization, in *Proceedings of the International Joint Conference on Neural Networks* (San Diego, 1990), vol. I, pp. 545–550. IEEE, New York.

Kohonen, T. (1991). Self-organizing maps: Optimization approaches, in *Artificial Neural Networks*, T. Kohonen, K. Makisara, O. Simula, and J. Kanga, eds., pp. 981–990. North-Holland, Amsterdam.

Kohonen, T. (1993a). Things you haven't heard about the self-organizing map, *IEEE International Conference on Neural Networks* (San Francisco, 1993), vol. III, pp. 1147–1156. IEEE, New York.

Kohonen, T. (1993b). Physiological interpretation of the self-organizing map algorithm, *Neural Networks*, **6**(7), 895–905.

Kohonen, T., and Ruohonen, M. (1973). Representation of associated data by matrix operators, *IEEE Transactions on Computers*, **C-22**, 701–702.

Kohonen, T., Barna, G., and Chrisley, R. (1988). Statistical pattern recognition with neural networks: Benchmarking studies, in *IEEE International Conference on Neural Networks* (San Diego, 1988), vol. I, pp. 61–68. IEEE, New York.

Kolen, J. F., and Pollack, J. B. (1991). Back propagation is sensitive to initial conditions, in *Advances in Neural Information Processing Systems 3* (Denver, 1990). R. P. Lippmann, J. E. Moody, and D. S. Touretzky, eds., pp. 860–867. Morgan Kaufmann, San Mateo, Calif.

Kolmogorov, A. N. (1957). On the representation of continuous functions of several variables by superposition of continuous functions of one variable and addition, *Doklady Akademii Nauk USSR*, **114**, 679–681.

Komlós, J. (1967). On the determinant of (0, 1) matricies. *Studia Scientarium Mathematicarum Hungarica*, **2**, 7–21.

Komlós, J., and Paturi, R. (1988). Convergence results in an associative memory model, *Neural Networks*, **3**(2), 239–250.

Kosko, B. (1987). Adaptive bidirectional associative memories, *Applied Optics*, **26**, 4947–4960.

Kosko, B. (1988). Bidirectional associative memories, *IEEE Transactions on Systems, Man, and Cybernetics*, **SMC-18**, 49–60.

Kosko, B. (1992). *Neural Networks and Fuzzy Systems: A Dynamical Systems Approach to Machine Intelligence*. Prentice-Hall, Englewood Cliffs, N.J.

Kramer, A. H., and Sangiovanni-Vincentelli, A. (1989). Efficient parallel learning algorithms for neural networks, in *Advances in Neural Information Processing Systems 1* (Denver, 1988) D. S. Touretzky, ed., pp. 40–48. Morgan Kaufmann, San Mateo, Calif.

Kramer, M. (1991). Nonlinear principal component analysis using autoassociative neural networks, *AICHE Journal*, **37**, 233–243.

Krauth, W., Mézard, M., and Nadal, J.-P. (1988). Basins of attraction in a perceptron like neural network, *Complex Systems*, **2**, 387–408.

Krekelberg, B., and Kok, J. N. (1993). A lateral inhibition neural network that emulates a winner-takes-all algorithm, in *Proceedings of the European Symposium on Artificial Neural Networks* (Brussels, 1993), M. Verleysen, ed., pp. 9–14. D facto, Brussels, Belgium.

Krishnan, T. (1966). On the threshold order of Boolean functions, *IEEE Transactions on Electronic Computers*, **EC-15**, 369–372.

Krogh, A., and Hertz, J. A. (1992). A simple weight decay can improve generalization, in *Advances in Neural Information Processing Systems 4* (Denver, 1991), J. E. Moody, S. J. Hanson, and R. P. Lippmann, eds., pp. 950–957. Morgan Kaufmann, San Mateo, Calif.

Kruschke, J. K., and Movellan, J. R. (1991). Benefits of gain: Speeded learning and minimal hidden layers in back-propagation networks, *IEEE Transactions on Systems, Man, and Cybernetics*, **SMC-21**(1), 273–280.

Kuczewski, R. M., Myers, M. H., and Crawford, W. J. (1987). Exploration of backward error propagation as a self-organizational structure, *IEEE International Conference on Neural Networks* (San Diego, 1987), M. Caudill and C. Butler, eds., vol. II, pp. 89–95. IEEE, New York.

Kufudaki, O., and Horejs, J. (1990). PAB: Parameters adapting backpropagation, *Neural Network World*, **1**, 267–274.

Kühn, R., Bös, S., and van Hemmen, J. L. (1991). Statistical mechanics for networks of graded response neurons, *Physical Review A*, **43**, 2084–2087.

Kullback, S. (1959). *Information Theory and Statistics*. Wiley, New York.

Kung, S. Y. (1993). *Digital Neural Networks*. PTR Prentice-Hall, Englewood Cliffs, N.J.

Kuo, T., and Hwang, S. (1993). A genetic algorithm with disruptive selection, in *Proceedings of the Fifth International Conference on Genetic Algorithms* (Urbana-Champaign, 1993), S. Forrest, ed., pp. 65–69. Morgan Kaufmann, San Mateo, Calif.

Kůrková, V. (1992). Kolmogorov's theorem and multilayer neural networks, *Neural Networks*, **5**(3), 501–506.

Kushner, H. J. (1977). Convergence of recursive adaptive and identification procedures via weak convergence theory, *IEEE Transactions on Automatic Control*, **AC-22**(6), 921–930.

Kushner, H. J., and Clark, D. (1978). *Stochastic Approximation Methods for Constrained and Unconstrained Systems*. Springer, New York.

Lane, S. H., Handelman, D. A., and Gelfand, J. J. (1992). Theory and development of higher order CMAC neural networks, *IEEE Control Systems Magazine* (April 1992), 23–30.

Lang, K. J., and Witbrock, M. J. (1989). Learning to tell two spirals apart, in *Proceedings of the 1988 Connectionists Models Summer Schools* (Pittsburgh, 1988), D. Touretzky, G. Hinton, and T. Sejnowski, eds., pp. 52–59. Morgan Kaufmann, San Mateo, Calif.

Lapedes, A. S., and Farber, R. (1987). Nonlinear Signal Processing Using Neural Networks: Prediction and System Modeling, Technical Report, Los Alamos National Laboratory, Los Alamos, New Mexico.

Lapedes, A., and Farber, R. (1988). How neural networks works, in *Neural Information Processing Systems* (Denver, 1987), D. Z. Anderson, ed., pp. 442–456. American Institute of Physics, New York.

Lapidus, L. E., Shapiro, E., Shapiro, S., and Stillman, R. E. (1961). Optimization of process performance, *AICHE Journal*, **7**, 288–294.

Lawler, E. L., and Wood, D. E. (1966). Branch-and-bound methods: A survey, *Operations Research*, **14**(4), 699–719.

Lay, S.-R., and Hwang, J.-N. (1993). Robust construction of radial basis function networks for classification, in *Proceedings of the IEEE International Conference on Neural Networks* (San Francisco, 1993), vol. III, pp. 1859–1864. IEEE, New York.

Le Cun, Y., Boser, B., Denker, J. S., Henderson, D., Howard, R. E., Hubbard, W., and Jackel, L. D. (1989). Backpropagation applied to handwritten ZIP code recognition, *Neural Computation*, **1**(4), 541–551.

Le Cun, Y., Boser, B., Denker, J. S., Henderson, D., Howard, R. E., Hubbard, W., and Jackel, L. D. (1990). Handwritten digit recognition with a backpropagation network, in *Advances in Neural Information Processing Systems 2* (Denver, 1989), D. S. Touretzky, ed., pp. 396–404. Morgan Kaufmann, San Mateo, Calif.

Le Cun, Y., Kanter, I., and Solla, S. A. (1991a). Second order properties of error surfaces: Learning time and generalization, in *Advances in Neural Information Processing Systems 3* (Denver, 1990), R. P. Lippmann, J. E. Moody, and D. S. Touretzky, eds., pp. 918–924. Morgan Kaufmann, San Mateo, Calif.

Le Cun, Y., Kanter, I., and Solla, S. A. (1991b). Eigenvalues of covariance matrices: Application to neural network learning, *Physical Review Letters*, **66**, 2396–2399.

Le Cun, Y., Simard, P. Y., and Pearlmutter, B. (1993). Automatic learning rate maximization by on-line estimation of the Hessian's eigenvectors, in *Advances in Neural Information Processing Systems 5* (Denver, 1992), S. J. Hanson, J. D. Cowan, and C. L. Giles, eds., pp. 156–163. Morgan Kaufmann, San Mateo, Calif.

Lee, B. W., and Shen, B. J. (1991). Hardware annealing in electronic neural networks, *IEEE Transactions on Circuits and Systems*, **38**, 134–137.

Lee, B. W., and Shen, B. J. (1993). Parallel hardware annealing for optimal solutions on electronic neural networks, *IEEE Transactions on Neural Networks*, **4**(4), 588–599.

Lee, S., and Kil, R. (1988). Multilayer feedforward potential function networks, in *Proceedings of the IEEE Second International Conference on Neural Networks* (San Diego, 1988), vol. I, pp., 161–171. IEEE, New York.

Lee, Y. (1991). Handwritten digit recognition using *k*-nearest neighbor, radial-basis functions, and backpropagation neural networks, *Neural Computation*, **3**(3), 440–449.

Lee, Y., and Lippmann, R. P. (1990). Practical characteristics of neural networks and conventional pattern classifiers on artificial and speech problems, in *Advances in Neural Information Processing Systems 2* (Denver, 1989), D. S. Touretzky, ed., pp. 168–177. Morgan Kaufmann, San Mateo, Calif.

Lee, Y., Oh, S.-H., and Kim, M. W. (1991). The effect of initial weights on premature saturation in back-propagation learning, in *International Joint Conference on Neural Networks* (Seattle, 1991), vol. I, pp. 765–770. IEEE, New York.

von Lehman, A., Paek, E. G., Liao, P. F., Marrakchi, A., and Patel, J. S. (1988). Factors influencing learning by back-propagation, in *IEEE International Conference on Neural Networks* (San Diego, 1988), vol. I, pp. 335–341. IEEE, New York.

Leshno, M., Lin, V. Y., Pinkus, A., and Schocken, S. (1993). Multilayer feedforward networks with a nonpolynomial activation function can approximate any function, *Neural Networks*, 6(6), 861–867.

Leung, C. S., and Cheung, K. F. (1991). Householder encoding for discrete bidirectional associative memory, in *Proceedings of the International Joint Conference on Neural Networks* (Singapore, 1991), vol. I, pp. 237–241. IEEE, New York.

Levin, A. V., and Narendra, K. S. (1992). Control of Nonlinear Dynamical Systems Using Neural Networks: II. Observability and Identification, Technical Report 9116, Center for Systems Science, Yale University, New Haven.

Lewis, P. M., II, and Coates, C. L. (1967). *Threshold Logic*. Wiley, New York.

Light, W. A. (1992a). Ridge functions, sigmoidal functions and neural networks, in *Approximation Theory VII*, E. W. Cheney, C. K. Chui, and L. L. Schumaker, eds., pp. 163–206. Academic Press, New York.

Light, W. A. (1992b). Some aspects of radial basis function approximation, in *Approximation Theory, Spline Functions, and Applications*, S. P. Singh, ed., NATO ASI series 256, pp. 163–190. Klawer Academic Publishers, Boston, Mass.

Ligthart, M. M., Aarts, E. H. L., and Beenker, F. P. M. (1986). Design-for-testability of PLA's using statistical cooling, in *Proceedings of the ACM/IEEE 23rd Design Automation Conference* (Las Vegas, 1986), pp. 339-345. IEEE, New York.

Lin, J.-N., and Unbehauen, R. (1993). On the realization of a Kolmogorov network, *Neural Computation*, 5(1), 21–31.

Linde, Y., Buzo, A., and Gray, R. M. (1980). An algorithm for vector quantizer design, *IEEE Transactions on Communications*, COM-28, 84–95.

Linsker, R. (1986). From basic network principles to neural architecture, *Proceedings of the National Academy of Sciences, USA*, 83, 7508–7512, 8390–8394, 8779–8783.

Linsker, R. (1988). Self-organization in a perceptual network, *Computer* (March 1988), 105–117.

Lippmann, R. P. (1987). An introduction to computing with neural nets, *IEEE Magazine on Accoustics, Signal, and Speech Processing*, 4, 4–22.

Lippmann, R. P. (1989). Review of neural networks for speech recognition, *Neural Computation*, 1(1), 1–38.

Little, W. A. (1974). The existence of persistent states in the brain, *Mathematical Bioscience*, 19, 101–120.

Ljung, L. (1977). Analysis of recursive stochastic algorithms, *IEEE Transactions on Automatic Control*, AC-22(4), 551–575.

Ljung, L. (1978). Strong convergence of stochastic approximation algorithm, *Annals of Statistics*, 6(3), 680–696.

Lo, Z.-P., Yu, Y., and Bavarian, B. (1993). Analysis of the convergence properties of topology preserving neural networks, *IEEE Transactions on Neural Networks*, 4(2), 207–220.

Loève, M. (1963). *Probability Theory* (3d ed.). Van Nostrand, New York.

Logar, A. M., Corwin, E. M., and Oldham, W. J. B. (1993). A comparison of recurrent neural network learning algorithms, in *Proceedings of the IEEE International Conference on Neural Networks* (San Francisco, 1993), vol. II, pp. 1129–1134. IEEE, New York.

Luenberger, D. G. (1969). *Optimization by Vector Space Methods*. Wiley, New York.

Macchi, O., and Eweda, E. (1983). Second-order convergence analysis of stochastic adaptive linear filtering, *IEEE Transactions on Automatic Control*, AC-28(1), 76–85.

Mackey, D. J. C., and Glass, L. (1977). Oscillation and chaos in physiological control systems, *Science*, **197**, 287–289.

MacQueen, J. (1967). Some methods for classification and analysis of multivariate observations, in *Proceedings of the Fifth Berkeley Symposium on Mathematics, Statistics, and Probability*, L. M. LeCam and J. Neyman, eds., pp. 281–297. University of California Press, Berkeley.

Magnus, J. R., and Neudecker, H. (1988). *Matrix Differential Calculus with Applications in Statistics and Econometrics*. Wiley, New York.

Makram-Ebeid, S., Sirat, J.-A., and Viala, J.-R. (1989). A rationalized back-propagation learning algorithm, in *International Joint Conference on Neural Networks* (Washington, 1989), vol. II, pp. 373–380. IEEE, New York.

von der Malsberg, C. (1973). Self-organizing of orientation sensitive cells in the striate cortex, *Kybernetick*, **14**, 85–100.

Mano, M. M. (1979). *Digital Logic and Computer Design*, Prentice-Hall, Englewood Cliffs, N.J.

Mao, J., and Jain, A. K. (1993). Regularization techniques in artificial neural networks, in *Proceedings of the World Congress on Neural Networks* (Portland, 1993), vol. IV, pp. 75–79. LEA/INNS Press, Hillsdale, N.J.

Marchand, M., Golea, M., and Rujan, P. (1990). A convergence theorem for sequential learning in two-layer perceptrons, *Europhysics Letters*, **11**, 487–492.

Marcus, C. M., and Westervelt, R. M. (1989). Dynamics of iterated-map neural networks, *Physical Review A*, **40**(1), 501–504.

Marcus, C. M., Waugh, F. R., and Westervelt, R. M. (1990). Associative memory in an analog iterated-map neural network, *Physical Review A*, **41**(6), 3355–3364.

Marr, D. (1969). A theory of cerebellar cortex, *Journal of Physiology (London)*, **202**, 437–470.

Martin, G. L. (1990). Integrating Segmentation and Recognition Stages for Overlapping Handprinted Characters, MCC Technical Report ACT-NN-320-90, Austin, Texas.

Martin, G. L. (1993). Centered-object integrated segmentation and recognition of overlapping handprinted characters, *Neural Networks*, **5**(3), 419–429.

Martin, G. L., and Pittman, J. A. (1991). Recognizing hand-printed letters and digits using backpropagation learning, *Neural Computation*, **3**(2), 258–267.

Mays, C. H. (1964). Effects of adaptation parameters on convergence time and tolerance for adaptive threshold elements, *IEEE Transactions on Electronic Computers*, **EC-13**, 465–468.

McCulloch, J. L., and Pitts, W. (1943). A logical calculus of ideas immanent in nervous activity, *Bulletin of Mathematical Biophysics*, **5**, 115–133.

McEliece, R. J., Posner, E. C., Rodemich, E. R., and Venkatesh, S. S. (1987). The capacity of the Hopfield associative memory, *IEEE Transactions on Information Theory*, **IT-33**, 461–482.

McInerny, J. M., Haines, K. G., Biafore, S., and Hecht-Nielsen, R. (1989). Backpropagation error surfaces can have local minima, in *International Joint Conference on Neural Networks* (Washington, 1989), vol. II, pp. 627. IEEE, New York.

Mead, C. (1991). Neuromorphic electronic systems, *Aerospace and Defense Science*, **10**(2), 20–28.

Medgassy, P. (1961). *Decomposition of Superposition of Distributed Functions*. Hungarian Academy of Sciences, Budapest.

Megiddo, N. (1986). On the Complexity of Polyhedral Separability, Technical Report RJ 5252, IBM Almaden Research Center, San Jose, Calif.

Mel, B. W., and Omohundro, S. M. (1991). How receptive field parameters affect neural learning, in *Advances in Neural Information Processing Systems 3* (Denver, 1990), R. P. Lippmann, J. E. Moody, and D. S. Touretzky, eds., pp. 757–763. Morgan Kaufmann, San Mateo, Calif.

Metropolis, N., Rosenbluth, A., Teller, A., and Teller, E. (1953). Equation of state calculations by fast computing machines, *Journal of Chemical Physics*, **21**(6), 1087–1092.

Mézard, M., and Nadal, J.-P. (1989). Learning in feedforward layered networks: The tiling algorithm, *Journal of Physics A*, **22**, 2191–2204.

Micchelli, C. A. (1986). Interpolation of scattered data: Distance and conditionally positive definite functions, *Constructive Approximation*, **2**, 11–22.

Miller, G. F., Todd, P. M., and Hedg, S. U. (1989). Designing neural networks using genetic algorithms, in *Proceedings of the Third International Conference on Genetic Algorithms* (Arlington, 1989), J. D. Schaffer, ed., pp. 379–384. Morgan Kaufmann, San Mateo, Calif.

Miller, W. T., Sutton, R. S., and Werbos, P. J., eds. (1990a). *Neural Networks for Control*. MIT Press, Cambridge, Mass.

Miller, W. T., Box, B. A., and Whitney, E. C. (1990b). Design and Implementation of a High Speed CMAC Neural Network Using Programmable CMOS Logic Cell Arrays, Report No. ECE.IS.90.01, University of New Hampshire, Durham, N.H.

Miller, W. T., Glanz, F. H., and Kraft, L. G. (1990c). CMAC: An associative neural network alternative to backpropagation, *Proceedings of the IEEE*, **78**(10), 1561–1657.

Miller, W. T., Hewes, R. P., Glanz, F. H., and Kraft, L. G. (1990d). Real-time dynamic control of an industrial manipulator using a neural-network-based learning controller, *IEEE Transactions on Robotics and Automation*, **6**, 1–9.

Minsky, M., and Papert, S. (1969). *Perceptrons: An Introduction to Computational Geometry*. MIT Press, Cambridge, Mass.

Møller, M. F. (1990). A Scaled Conjugate Gradient Algorithm for Fast Supervised Learning, Technical Report PB-339, Computer Science Department, University of Aarhus, Aarhus, Denmark.

Montana, D. J., and Davis, L. (1989). Training feedforward networks using genetic algorithms, in *Eleventh International Joint Conference on Artificial Intelligence* (Detroit, 1989), N. S. Sridhara, ed., pp. 762–767. Morgan Kaufmann, San Mateo, Calif.

Moody, J. (1989). Fast learning in multi-resolution hierarchies, in *Advances in Neural Information Processing Systems I* (Denver, 1988), D. S. Touretzky, ed., pp. 29-39. Morgan Kaufmann, San Mateo, Calif.

Moody, J., and Darken, C. (1989a). Learning with localized receptive fields, in *Proceedings of the 1988 Connectionist Models Summer School* (Pittsburgh, 1988), D. Touretzky, G. Hinton, and T. Sejnowski, eds., pp. 133–143. Morgan Kaufmann, San Mateo, Calif.

Moody, J., and Darken, C. (1989b). Fast learning in networks of locally-tuned processing units, *Neural Computation*, **1**(2), 281–294.

Moody, J., and Yarvin, N. (1992). Networks with learned unit response functions, in *Advances in Neural Information Processing Systems 4* (Denver, 1991), J. E. Moody, S. J. Hanson, and R. P. Lippmann, eds., pp. 1048–1055. Morgan Kaufmann, San Mateo, Calif.

Moore, B. (1989). ART1 and pattern clustering, in *Proceedings of the 1988 Connectionists Models Summer Schools* (Pittsburgh, 1988), D. Touretzky, G. Hinton, and T. Sejnowski, eds., pp. 174–185. Morgan Kaufmann, San Mateo, Calif.

Morgan, N., and Bourlard, H. (1990). Generalization and parameter estimation in feedforward nets: Some experiments, in *Advances in Neural Information Processing Systems 2* (Denver, 1989), D. S. Touretzky, ed., 630–637. Morgan Kaufmann, San Mateo, Calif.

Morita, M. (1993). Associative memory with nonmonotone dynamics, *Neural Networks*, **6**(1), 115–126.

Morita, M., Yoshizawa, S., and Nakano, K. (1990a). Analysis and improvement of the dynamics of auto-correlation associative memory, *Transactions of the Institute of Electronics, Information and Communication Engineers*, **J73-D-III**(2), 232–242.

Morita, M., Yoshizawa, S., and Nakano, K. (1990b). Memory of correlated patterns by associative neural networks with improved dynamics, in *Proceedings of the International Neural Networks Conference*, Paris, vol. 2, pp. 868–871. Kluwer, Boston.

Mosteller, F., and Tukey, J. (1980). *Robust Estimation Procedures*. Addison-Wesley, Reading, Mass.

Mosteller, F., Rourke, R. E., and Thomas Jr., G. B. (1970). *Probability with Statistical Applications* (2d ed.). Addison-Wesley, Reading, Mass.

Mukhopadhyay, S., Roy, A., Kim, L. S., and Govil, S. (1993). A polynomial time algorithm for generating neural networks for pattern classification: Its stability properties and some test results, *Neural Computation*, **5**(2), 317–330.

Muroga, S. (1959). The principle of majority decision logical elements and the complexity of their circuits, *Proceedings of the International Conference on Information Processing*, Paris, pp. 400–407. Unesco, Paris.

Muroga, S. (1965). Lower bounds of the number of threshold functions and a maximum weight, *IEEE Transactions on Electronic Computers*, **EC-14**(2), 136–148.

Muroga, S. (1971). *Threshold Logic and its Applications*. Wiley Interscience, New York.

Musavi, M. T., Ahmed, W., Chan, K. H., Faris, K. B., and Hummels, D. M. (1992). On the training of radial basis function classifiers, *Neural Networks*, **5**(4), 595–603.

Nakano, K. (1972). Associatron: A model of associative memory, *IEEE Transactions on Systems, Man, Cybernetics*, **SMC-2**, 380–388.

Narayan, S. (1993). ExpoNet: A generalization of the multi-layer perceptron model, in *Proceedings of the World Congress on Neural Networks* (Portland, 1993), vol. III, pp. 494–497. LEA/INNS Press, Hillsdale, N.J.

Narendra, K. S., and Parthasarathy, K. (1990). Identification and control of dynamical systems using neural networks, *IEEE Transactions on Neural Networks*, **1**(1), 4–27.

Narendra, K. S., and Wakatsuki, K. (1991). A Comparative Study of Two Neural Network Architectures for the Identification and Control of Nonlinear Dynamical Systems, Technical Report, Center for Systems Science, Yale University, New Haven.

Nerrand, O., Roussel-Ragot, P., Personnaz, L., Dreyfus, G., and Marcos, S. (1993). Neural networks and nonlinear adaptive filtering: Unifying concepts and new algorithms, *Neural Computation*, **5**(2), 165–199.

Newman, C. (1988). Memory capacity in neural network models: Rigorous lower bounds, *Neural Networks*, **3**(2), 223–239.

Nguyen, D., and Widrow, B. (1989). The truck backer-upper: An example of self-learning in neural networks, in *Proceedings of the International Joint Conference on Neural Networks* (Washington, 1989), vol. II, pp. 357–362. IEEE, New York.

Nilsson, N. J. (1965). *Learning Machines*. McGraw-Hill, New York; reissued (1990) as *The Mathematical Foundations of Learning Machines*. Morgan Kaufmann, San Mateo, Calif.

Niranjan, M., and Fallside, F. (1988). Neural Networks and Radial Basis Functions in Classifying Static Speech Patterns, Technical Report CUEDIF-INFENG17R22, Engineering Department, Cambridge University.

Nishimori, H., and Opriş, I. (1993). Retrieval process of an associative memory with a general input-output function, *Neural Networks*, **6**(8), 1061–1067.

Nolfi, S., Elman, J. L., and Parisi, D. (1990). Learning and Evolution in Neural Networks, CRL Technical Report 9019, University of California, San Diego.

Novikoff, A. B. J. (1962). On convergence proofs of perceptrons, in *Proceedings of the Symposium on Mathematical Theory of Automata*, pp. 615–622. Polytechnic Institute of Brooklyn, Brooklyn, N.Y.

Nowlan, S. J. (1988). Gain variation in recurrent error propagation networks, *Complex Systems*, **2**, 305–320.

Nowlan, S. J. (1990). Maximum likelihood competitive learning, in *Advances in Neural Information Processing Systems 2* (Denver, 1989). D. Touretzky, ed., pp. 574–582. Morgan Kaufmann, San Mateo, Calif.

Nowlan, S. J., and Hinton, G. E. (1992a). Adaptive soft weight tying using Gaussian mixtures, in *Advances in Neural Information Processing Systems 4* (Denver, 1991), J. E. Moody, S. J. Hanson, and R. P. Lippmann, eds., pp. 993–1000. Morgan Kaufmann, San Mateo, Calif.

Nowlan, S. J., and Hinton, G. E. (1992b). Simplifying neural networks by soft weight-sharing, *Neural Computation*, **4**(4), 473–493.

Oja, E. (1982). A simplified neuron model as a principal component analyzer, *Journal of Mathematical Biology*, **15**, 267–273.

Oja, E. (1983). *Subspace Methods of Pattern Recognition*. Research Studies Press and Wiley, Letchworth, England.

Oja, E. (1989). Neural networks, principal components, and subspaces, *International Journal of Neural Systems*, **1**(1), 61–68.

Oja, E. (1991). Data compression, feature extraction, and autoassociation in feedforward neural networks, in *Artificial Neural Networks, Proceedings of the 1991 International Conference on Artificial Neural Networks* (Espoo, 1991), T. Kohonen, K. Mäkisara, O. Simula, and J. Kangas, eds., vol. I, pp. 737–745. Elsevier Science Publishers, Amsterdam.

Oja, E., and Karhunen, J. (1985). On stochastic approximation of the eigenvectors of the expectation of a random matrix, *Journal of Mathematical Analysis and Applications*, **106**, 69–84.

Okajima, K., Tanaka, S., and Fujiwara, S. (1987). A heteroassociative memory network with feedback connection, in *Proceedings of the IEEE First International Conference on Neural Networks* (San Diego, 1987), M. Caudill and C. Butler, eds., vol. II, pp. 711–718.

Paek, E. G., and Psaltis, D. (1987). Optical associative memory using fourier transform holograms, *Optical Engineering*, **26**, 428–433.

Pao, Y. H. (1989). *Adaptive Pattern Recognition and Neural Networks*. Addison-Wesley, Reading, Mass.

Papadimitriou, C. H., and Steiglitz (1982). *Combinatorial Optimization: Algorithms and Complexity*. Prentice-Hall, Englewood Cliffs, N.J.

Park, J., and Sandberg, I. W. (1991). Universal approximation using radial-basis-function networks, *Neural Computation*, **3**(2), 246–257.

Park, J., and Sandberg, I. W. (1993). Approximation and radial-basis-function networks, *Neural Computation*, **5**(2), 305–316.

Parker, D. B. (1985). Learning Logic, Technical Report TR-47, Center for Computational Research in Economics and Management Science, Massachusetts Institute of Technology, Cambridge, Mass.

Parker, D. B. (1987). Optimal algorithms for adaptive networks: Second order backprop, second order direct propagation, and second order Hebbian learning, in *IEEE First International Conference on Neural Networks* (San Diego, 1987), M. Caudill and C. Butler, eds., vol. II, pp. 593–600. IEEE, New York.

Parks, M. (1987). Characterization of the Boltzmann machine learning rate, in *IEEE First International Conference on Neural Networks* (San Diego, 1987), M. Caudill and C. Butler, eds., vol. III, pp. 715–719. New York, IEEE.

Parks, P. C., and Militzer, J. (1991). Improved allocation of weights for associative memory storage in learning control systems, in *Proceedings of the 1st IFAC Symposium on Design Methods of Control Systems*, vol. II, pp. 777–782. Pergamon Press, Zurich.

Parzen, E. (1962). On estimation of a probability density function and mode, *Annals of Mathematics and Statistics*, **33**, 1065–1076.

Pearlmutter, B. A. (1988). Learning State Space Trajectories in Recurrent Neural Networks, Technical Report CMU-CS-88-191, School of Computer Science, Carnegie-Mellon University, Pittsburgh, Pa.

Pearlmutter, B. A. (1989a). Learning state space trajectories in recurrent neural networks, in *International Joint Conference on Neural Networks* (Washington, 1989), vol. II, pp. 365–372. IEEE, New York.

Pearlmutter, B. A. (1989b). Learning state space trajectories in recurrent neural networks, *Neural Computation*, **1**(2), 263–269.

Penrose, R. (1955). A generalized inverse for matrices, *Proceedings of the Cambridge Philosophical Society*, **51**, 406–413.

Peretto, P. (1984). Collective properties of neural networks: A statistical physics approach, *Biological Cybernetics*, **50**, 51–62.

Personnaz, L., Guyon, I., and Dreyfus, G. (1986). Collective computational properties of neural networks: New learning mechanisms, *Physical Review A*, **34**(5), 4217–4227.

Peterson, C., and Anderson, J. R. (1987). A mean field theory learning algorithm for neural networks, *Complex Systems*, **1**, 995–1019.

Peterson, G. E., and Barney, H. L. (1952). Control methods used in a study of the vowels, *Journal of the Acoustical Society of America*, **24**(2), 175–184.

Pflug, G. Ch. (1990). Non-asymptotic confidence bounds for stochastic approximation algorithms with constant step size, *Mathematik*, **110**, 297–314.

Pineda, D. A. (1988). Dynamics and architectures for neural computation, *Journal of Complexity*, **4**, 216–245.

Pineda, F. J. (1987). Generalization of back-propagation to recurrent neural networks, *Physical Review Letters*, **59**, 2229–2232.

Platt, J. (1991). A resource-allocating network for function interpolation, *Neural Computation*, **3**(2), 213–225.

Plaut, D. S., Nowlan, S., and Hinton, G. (1986). Experiments on Learning by Back Propagation, Technical Report CMU-CS-86-126, Department of Computer Science, Carnegie-Mellon University, Pittsburgh, Pa.

Poggio, T., and Girosi, F. (1989). A Theory of Networks for Approximation and Learning, A.I. Memo 1140, MIT, Cambridge, Mass.

Poggio, T., and Girosi, F. (1990a). Networks for approximation and learning, *Proceedings of the IEEE*, **78**(9), 1481–1497.

Poggio, T., and Girosi, F. (1990b). Regularization algorithms for learning that are equivalent to multilayer networks, *Science*, **247**, 978–982.

Polak, E., and Ribiére, G. (1969). Note sur la convergence de methods de directions conjugies, *Revue Francaise d'Informatique et Recherche Operationnalle*, **3**, 35–43.

Polyak, B. T. (1987). *Introduction to Optimization*. Optimization Software, Inc., New York.

Polyak, B. T. (1990). New method of stochastic approximation type, *Automation and Remote Control*, **51**, 937–946.

Pomerleau, D. A. (1991). Efficient training of artificial neural networks for autonomous navigation, *Neural Computation*, **3**(1), 88–97.

Pomerleau, D. A. (1993). *Neural Network Perception for Mobile Robot Guidance*. Kluwer, Boston.

Powell, M. J. D. (1987). Radial basis functions for multivariate interpolation: A review, in *Algorithms for the Approximation of Functions and Data*, J. C. Mason and M. G. Cox, eds. Clarendon Press, Oxford, England.

Press, W. H., Flannery, B. P., Teukolsky, S. A., and Vetterling, W. T. (1986). *Numerical Recipes: The Art of Scientific Computing*. Cambridge University Press, Cambridge, England.

Psaltis, D., and Park, C. H. (1986). Nonlinear discriminant functions and associative memories, in *Neural Networks for Computing*, J. S. Denker, ed., pp. 370–375. American Institute of Physics, New York.

Qi, X., and Palmieri, F. (1993). The diversification role of crossover in the genetic algorithms, in *Proceedings of the Fifth International Conference on Genetic Algorithms* (Urbana-Champaign, 1993), S. Forrest, ed., pp. 132–137. Morgan Kaufmann, San Mateo, Calif.

Qian, N., and Sejnowski, T. (1989). Learning to solve random-dot stereograms of dense transparent surfaces with recurrent back-propagation, in *Proceedings of the 1988 Connectionist Models Summer School* (Pittsburgh, 1988), D. Touretzky, G. Hinton, and T. Sejnowski, eds., pp. 435–443. Morgan Kaufmann, San Mateo, Calif.

Rao, C. R., and Mitra, S. K. (1971). *Generalized Inverse of Matrices and its Applications*. Wiley, New York.

Reed, R. (1993). *Pruning algorithms—A survey, IEEE Transactions on Neural Networks*, **4**(5), 740–747.

Reeves, C. R. (1993). Using genetic algorithms with small populations, in *Proceedings of the Fifth International Conference on Genetic Algorithms* (Urbana-Champaign, 1993), S. Forrest, ed., pp. 92–99. Morgan Kaufmann, San Mateo, Calif.

Reilly, D. L., and Cooper, L. N. (1990). An overview of neural networks: Early models to real world systems, in *An Introduction to Neural and Electronic Networks*, S. F. Zornetzer, J. L. Davis, and C. Lau, eds. pp. 227–248. Academic Press, San Diego.

Reilly, D. L., Cooper, L. N., and Elbaum, C. (1982). A neural model for category learning, *Biological Cybernetics*, **45**, 35–41.

Rezgui, A., and Tepedelenlioglu, N. (1990). The effect of the slope of the activation function on the backpropagation algorithm, in *Proceedings of the International Joint Conference on Neural Networks* (Washington, 1990), M. Caudill, ed., vol. I, pp. 707–710. IEEE, New York.

Ricotti, L. P., Ragazzini, S., and Martinelli, G. (1988). Learning of word stress in a sub-optimal second order back-propagation neural network, in *IEEE First International Conference on Neural Networks* (San Diego, 1987), M. Caudill and C. Butler, eds., vol. I, pp. 355–361. IEEE, New York.

Ridgway, W. C., III (1962). An Adaptive Logic System with Generalizing Properties, Technical Report 1556-1, Stanford Electronics Labs., Stanford University, Stanford, Calif.

Riedel, H., and Schild, D. (1992). The dynamics of Hebbian synapses can be stabilized by a nonlinear decay term, *Neural Networks*, **5**(3), 459–463.

Ritter, H., and Schulten, K. (1986). On the stationary state of Kohonen's self-organizing sensory mapping, *Biological Cybernetics*, **54**, 99–106.

Ritter, H., and Schulten, K. (1988a). Kohonen's self-organizing maps: Exploring their computational capabilities, in *IEEE International Conference on Neural Networks* (San Diego, 1988), vol. I, pp. 109–116. IEEE, New York.

Ritter, H., and Schulten, K. (1988b). Convergence properties of Kohonen's topology conserving maps: Fluctuations, stability, and dimension selection, *Biological Cybernetics*, **60**, 59–71.

Robinson, A. J., and Fallside, F. (1988). Static and dynamic error propagation networks with application to speech coding, in *Neural Information Processing Systems* (Denver, 1987), D. Z. Anderson, ed., pp. 632–641. American Institute of Physics, New York.

Robinson, A. J., Niranjan, M., and Fallside, F. (1989). Generalizing the nodes of the error propagation network (abstract), in *Proceedings of the International Joint Conference on Neural Networks* (Washington, 1989), vol. II, p. 582. IEEE, New York; also printed as Technical Report CUED/F-INFENG/TR.25, Cambridge University, Engineering Department, Cambridge, England.

Rohwer, R. (1990). The "moving targets" training algorithm, in *Advances in Information Processing Systems 2* (Denver, 1989), D. S. Touretzky, ed., pp. 558–565. Morgan Kaufmann, San Mateo, Calif.

Romeo, F. I. (1989). Simulated Annealing: Theory and Applications to Layout Problems. Ph.D. thesis, Memorandum UCB/ERL-M89/29, University of California at Berkeley. Berkeley, Calif.

Rosenblatt, F. (1961). *Principles of Neurodynamics: Perceptrons and the Theory of Brain Mechanisms*. Spartan Press, Washington.

Rosenblatt, F. (1962). *Principles of Neurodynamics: Perceptrons and the Theory of Brain Mechanisms*. Spartan Press, Washington.

Roy, A., and Govil, S. (1993). Generating radial basis function net in polynomial time for classification, in *Proceedings of the World Congress on Neural Networks* (Portland, 1993), vol. III, pp. 536–539. LEA/INNS Press, Hillsdale, N.J.

Roy, A., and Mukhopadhyay, S. (1991). Pattern classification using linear programming, *ORSA Journal on Computing*, **3**(1), 66–80.

Roy, A., Kim, L. S., and Mukhopadhyay, S. (1993). A polynomial time algorithm for the construction and training of a class of multilayer perceptrons, *Neural Networks*, **6**(4), 535–545.

Rozonoer, L. I. (1969). Random logic nets I, *Automatiki i Telemekhaniki*, **5**, 137–147.

Rubner, J., and Tavan, P. (1989). A self-organizing network for principal-component analysis, *Europhysics Letters*, **10**, 693–698.

Rudin, W. (1976). *Principles of Mathematical Analysis* (3d ed.). McGraw-Hill, New York.

Rumelhart, D. E. (1989). Learning and generalization in multilayer networks, presentation given at the NATO Advanced Research Workshop on Neuro Computing, Architecture, and Applications, Les Arcs, France 1989.

Rumelhart, D. E., and Zipser, D. (1985). Feature discovery by competitive learning, *Cognitive Science*, **9**, 75–112.

Rumelhart, D. E., McClelland, J. L., and the PDP Research Group (1986a). *Parallel Distributed Processing: Exploration in the Microstructure of Cognition*, vol. 1. MIT Press, Cambridge, Mass.

Rumelhart, D. E., Hinton, G. E., and Williams, R. J. (1986b). Learning internal representations by error propagation, in *Parallel Distributed Processing: Explorations in the Microstructure of Cognition*, vol. I, D. E. Rumelhart, J. L. McClelland, and the PDP Research Group eds. MIT Press, Cambridge, Mass.

Rutenbar, R. A. (1989). Simulated annealing algorithms: An overview, *IEEE Circuits Devices Magazine*, **5**(1), 19–26.

Saha, A., and Keeler, J. D. (1990). Algorithms for better representation and faster learning in radial basis function networks, in *Advances in Neural Information Processing Systems 2* (Denver, 1989), D. Touretzky, ed., pp. 482–489. Morgan Kaufmann, San Mateo, Calif.

Salamon, P., Nulton, J. D., Robinson, J., Petersen, J., Ruppeiner, G., and Liao, L. (1988). Simulated annealing with constant thermodynamic speed, *Computer Physics Communications*, **49**, 423–428.

Sanger, T. D. (1989). Optimal unsupervised learning in a single layer linear feedforward neural network, *Neural Networks*, **2**(6), 459–473.

Sato, M. (1990). A real time learning algorithm for recurrent analog neural networks, *Biological Cybernetics*, **62**, 237–241.

Sayeh, M. R., and Han, J. Y. (1987). Pattern recognition using a neural network, *Proceedings of the SPIE, Intelligent Robots and Computer Vision*, **848**, 281–285.

Schaffer, J. D., Caruana, R. A., Eshelman, L. J., and Das, R. (1989). A study of control parameters affecting online performance of genetic algorithms for function optimization, in *Proceedings of the Third International Conference on Genetic Algorithms and their Applications* (Arlington, 1989), J. D. Schaffer, ed., pp. 51–60. Morgan Kaufmann, San Mateo, Calif.

Schoen, F. (1991). Stochastic techniques for global optimization: A survey of recent advances, *Journal of Global Optimization*, **1**, 207–228.

Schultz, D. G., and Gibson, J. E. (1962). The variable gradient method for generating Liapunov functions, *Transactions of the IEE*, **81**(II), 203–210.

Schumaker, L. L. (1981). *Spline Functions: Basic Theory*. Wiley, New York.

Schwartz, D. B., Samalam, V. K., Solla, S. A., and Denker, J. S. (1990). Exhaustive learning, *Neural Computation*, **2**(3), 374–385.

Scofield, C. L., Reilly, D. L., Elbaum, C., and Cooper, L. N. (1988). Pattern class degeneracy in an unrestricted storage density memory, in *Neural Information Processing Systems* (Denver, 1987), D. Z. Anderson, ed., pp. 674–682. American Institute of Physics, New York.

Sejnowski, T. J., and Rosenberg, C. R. (1987). Parallel networks that learn to pronounce English text, *Complex Systems*, **1**, 145–168.

Sejnowski, T. J., Kienker, P. K., and Hinton, G. (1986). Learning symmetry groups with hidden units: Beyond the Perceptron, *Physica*, **22D**, 260–275.

Shannon, C. E. (1938). A symbolic analysis of relay and switching circuits, *Transactions of the AIEE*, **57**, 713–723.

Shaw, G., and Vasudevan, R. (1974). Persistent states of neural networks and the nature of synaptic transmissions, *Mathematical Bioscience*, **21**, 207–218.

Sheng, C. L. (1969). *Threshold Logic*. Academic Press, New York.

Shiino, M., and Fukai, T. (1990). Replica-symmetric theory of the nonlinear analogue neural networks, *Journal of Physics A*, **23**, L1009–L1017.

Shrödinger, E. (1946). *Statistical Thermodynamics*. Cambridge University Press, London.

Sietsma, J., and Dow, R. J. F. (1988). Neural net pruning—Why and how, in *IEEE International Conference on Neural Networks* (San Diego, 1988), vol. I, pp. 325–333. IEEE, New York.

Silva, F. M., and Almeida, L. B. (1990). Acceleration techniques for the backpropagation algorithm, in *Neural Networks, Europe Lecture Notes in Computer Science*, L. B. Almeida and Wellekens, eds., pp. 110–119. Springer-Verlag, Berlin.

Simard, P. Y., Ottaway, M. B., and Ballard, D. H. (1988). Analysis of Recurrent Backpropagation, Technical Report 253, Department of Computer Science, University of Rochester, N.Y.

Simard, P. Y., Ottaway, M. B., and Ballard, D. H. (1989). Analysis of recurrent backpropagation, in *Proceedings of the 1988 Connectionist Models Summer School* (Pittsburgh, 1988), D. Touretzky, G. Hinton, and T. Sejnowski, eds., pp. 103–112. Morgan Kaufmann, San Mateo, Calif.

Simeone, B., ed. (1989). *Combinatorial Optimization*. Springer-Verlag, New York.

Simpson, P. K. (1990). Higher-ordered and intraconnected bidirectional associative memory, *IEEE Transactions on Systems, Man, and Cybernetics*, **20**(3), 637–653.

Slansky, J., and Wassel, G. N. (1981). *Pattern Classification and Trainable Machines*. Springer-Verlag, New York.

van der Smagt, P. P. (1994). Minimization methods for training feedforward neural networks, *Neural Networks*, **7**(1), 1–11.

Smith, J. M. (1987). When learning guides evolution, *Nature (London)*, **329**, 761–762.

Smolensky, P. (1986). Information processing in dynamical systems: Foundations of harmony theory, in *Parallel Distributed Processing: Explorations in the Microstructure of Cognition*, D. E. Rumelhart, J. L. McClelland, and the PDP Research Group eds., vol. I. MIT Press, Cambridge, Mass.

Snapp, R. R., Psaltis, D., and Venkatesh, S. S. (1991). Asymptotic slowing down of the nearest-neighbor classifier, in *Advances in Neural Information Processing Systems 3* (Denver, 1990), R. P. Lippmann, J. E. Moody, and D. S. Touretzky, eds., pp. 932–938. Morgan Kaufmann, San Mateo, Calif.

Solla, S. A., Levin, E., and Fleisher, M. (1988). Accelerated learning in layered neural networks, *Complex Systems*, **2**, 625–639.

Sonehara, N., Kawato, S., Miyake, S., and Nakane, K. (1989). Image data compression using a neural network model, *Proceedings of the International Joint Conference on Neural Networks* (Washington, 1989), vol. II, pp. 35–41.

Song, J. (1992). Hybrid Genetic/Gradient Learning in Multi-Layer Artificial Neural Networks, Ph.D. dissertation, Department of Electrical and Computer Engineering, Wayne State University, Detroit, Michigan.

Sontag, E. D., and Sussann, H. J. (1985). Image restoration and segmentation using annealing algorithm, in *Proceedings of the 24th IEEE Conference on Decision and Control* (Ft. Lauderdale, 1985), pp. 768–773. IEEE, New York.

Soukoulis, C. M., Levin, K., and Grest, G. S. (1983). Irreversibility and metastability in spin-glasses. I. Ising model, *Physical Review*, **B28**, 1495–1509.

Specht, D. F. (1990). Probabilistic neural networks, *Neural Networks*, **3**(1), 109–118.

Sperduti, A., and Starita, A. (1991). Extensions of generalized delta rule to adapt sigmoid functions, in *Proceedings of the 13th Annual International Conference IEEE/EMBS*, pp. 1393–1394. IEEE, New York.

Sperduti, A., and Starita, A. (1993). Speed up learning and networks optimization with extended back propagation, *Neural Networks*, **6**(3), 365–383.

Spitzer, A. R., Hassoun, M. H., Wang, C., and Bearden, F. (1990). Signal decomposition and diagnostic classification of the electromyogram using a novel neural network technique, in *Proceedings of the XIVth Annual Symposium on Computer Applications in Medical Care* (Washington, 1990), R. A. Miller, ed., pp. 552–556. IEEE Computer Society Press, Los Alamitos, Calif.

Spreecher, D. A. (1993). A universal mapping for Kolmogorov's superposition theorem, *Neural Networks*, **6**(8), 1089–1094.

Stent, G. S. (1973). A physiological mechanism for Hebb's postulate of learning, *Proceedings of the National Academy of Sciences, USA*, **70**, 997–1001.

Stiles, G. S., and Denq, D.-L. (1987). A quantitative comparison of three discrete distributed associative memory models, *IEEE Transactions on Computers*, **C-36**, 257–263.

Stinchcombe, M., and White, H. (1989). Universal approximations using feedforward networks with non-sigmoid hidden layer activation functions, in *Proceedings of the International Joint Conference on Neural Networks* (Washington, 1989), vol. I, pp. 613–617. SOS Printing, San Diego, Calif.

Stone, M. (1978). Cross-validation: A review, *Mathematische Operationsforschung Statistischen*, **9**, 127–140.

Sudjianto, A., and Hassoun, M. (1994). Nonlinear Hebbian rule: A statistical interpretation, in *IEEE International Conference on Neural Networks*, (Orlando, 1994), vol. II, pp. 1247–1252. IEEE, New York.

Sun, G.-Z., Chen, H.-H., and Lee, Y.-C. (1992). Green's function method for fast on-line learning algorithm of recurrent neural networks, in *Advances in Neural Information Processing 4* (Denver, 1991), J. E. Moody, S. J. Hanson, and R. P. Lippmann, eds., pp. 317–324. Morgan Kaufmann, San Mateo, Calif.

Sun, X., and Cheney, E. W. (1992). The fundamentals of sets of ridge functions, *Aequationes Mathematicae*, **44**, 226–235.

Suter, B., and Kabrisky, M. (1992). On a magnitude preserving iterative MAXnet algorithm, *Neural Computation*, **4**(2), 224–233.

Sutton, R. (1986). Two problems with backpropagation and other steepest-descent learning procedures for networks, in *Proceedings of the 8th Annual Conference on the Cognitive Science Society* (Amherst, 1986), pp. 823–831. Erlbaum, Hillsdale, N.J.

Sutton, R. S., ed. (1992). Special issue on reinforcement learning, *Machine Learning*, **8**, 1–395.

Sutton, R. S., Barto, A. G., and Williams, R. J. (1991). Reinforcement learning is direct adaptive optimal control, in *Proceedings of the American Control Conference* (Boston, 1991), pp. 2143–2146. IEEE, New York.

Szu, H. (1986). Fast simulated annealing, in *Neural Networks for Computing* (Snowbird, 1986), J. S. Denker, ed., pp. 420–425. American Institute of Physics, New York.

Takefuji, Y., and Lee, K. C. (1991). Artificial neural network for four-coloring map problems and K-colorability problem, *IEEE Transactions Circuits and Systems*, **38**, 1991, 326–333.

Takens, F. (1981). Detecting strange attractors in turbulence, in *Dynamical Systems and Turbulence, Lecture Notes in Mathematics* (Warwick, 1980), D. A. Rand and L.-S. Young, eds., vol. 898, pp. 366–381. Springer-Verlag, Berlin.

Takeuchi, A., and Amari, S.-I. (1979). Formation of topographic maps and columnar microstructures, *Biological Cybernetics*, **35**, 63–72.

Tank, D. W., and Hopfield, J. J. (1986). Simple "Neural" optimization networks: An A/D converter, signal decision circuit, and a linear programming circuit, *IEEE Transactions on Circuits and Systems*, **33**, 533–541.

Tank, D. W., and Hopfield, J. J. (1987). Concentrating information in time: Analog neural networks with applications to speech recognition problems, in *IEEE First International Conference on Neural Networks* (San Diego, 1987), M. Caudill and C. Butler, eds., vol. IV, pp. 455–468. IEEE, New York.

Tattersal, G. D., Linford, P. W., and Linggard, R. (1990). Neural arrays for speech recognition, in *Speech and Language Processing*, C. Wheddon and R. Linggard, eds., pp. 245–290. Chapman and Hall, London.

Tawel, R. (1989). Does the neuron "learn" like the synapse? in *Advances in Neural Information Processing Systems 1* (Denver, 1988), D. S. Touretzky, ed., pp. 169–176. Morgan Kaufmann, San Mateo, Calif.

Taylor, J. G., and Coombes, S. (1993). Learning higher order correlations, *Neural Networks*, 6(3), 423–427.

Tesauro, G., and Janssens, B. (1988). Scaling relationships in back-propagation learning, *Complex Systems*, 2, 39–44.

Thierens, D., and Goldberg, D. (1993). Mixing in genetic algorithms, in *Proceedings of the Fifth International Conference on Genetic Algorithms* (Urbana-Champaign, 1993), S. Forrest, ed., pp. 38–45. Morgan Kaufmann, San Mateo, Calif.

Thorndike, E. L. (1911). *Animal Intelligence*. Hafner, Darien, Conn.

Ticknor, A. J., and Barrett, H. (1987). Optical implementations of Boltzmann machines, *Optical Engineering*, 26, 16–21.

Tishby, N., Levin, E., and Solla, S. A. (1989). Consistent inference of probabilities in layered networks: Predictions and generalization, in *International Joint Conference on Neural Networks* (Washington, 1989), vol. II, pp. 403–410. IEEE, New York.

Tolat, V. (1990). An analysis of Kohonen's self-organizing maps using a system of energy functions, *Biological Cybernetics*, 64, 155–164.

Tollenaere, T. (1990). SuperSAB: Fast adaptive back propagation with good scaling properties, *Neural Networks*, 3(5), 561–573.

Tompkins, C. B. (1956). Methods of steep descent, in *Modern Mathematics for the Engineer*, E. B. Beckenbach, ed., pp. 448–479. McGraw-Hill, New York.

Törn, A. A., and Žilinskas, A. (1989). *Global Optimization*. Springer-Verlag, Berlin.

Tsypkin, Ya. Z. (1971). *Adaptation and Learning in Automatic Systems*, trans. by Z. J. Nikolic. Academic Press, New York (first published in Russian language under the title *Adaptatsia i obuchenie v avtomaticheskikh sistemakh*. Nauka, Moskow, 1968).

Turing, A. M. (1952). The chemical basis of morphogenesis, *Philosophical Transactions of the Royal Society, Series B*, 237, 5–72.

Uesaka, G., and Ozeki, K. (1972). Some properties of associative type memories, *Journal of the Institute of Electrical and Communication Engineers of Japan*, 55-D, 323–330.

Usui, S., Nakauchi, S., and Nakano, M. (1991). Internal color representation acquired by a five-layer network, in *Artificial Neural Networks, Proceedings of the 1991 International Conference on Artificial Neural Networks* (Espoo, 1991), T. Kohonen, K. Mäkisara, O. Simula, and J. Kangas, eds., vol. I, pp. 867–872. Elsevier Science Publishers, Amsterdam.

Vapnik, V. N., and Chervonenkis, A. Y. (1971). On the uniform convergence of relative frequencies of events to their probabilities, *Theory of Probability and Its Applications*, 16(2), 264–280.

Veitch, E. W. (1952). A chart method for simplifying truth functions, *Proceedings of the ACM*, 127–133. Richard Rimbach, Pittsburgh.

Villiers, J., and Barnard, E. (1993). Backpropagation neural nets with one and two hidden layers, *IEEE Transactions on Neural Networks*, 4(1), 136–141.

Vogl, T. P., Manglis, J. K., Rigler, A. K., Zink, W. T., and Alkon, D. L. (1988). Accelerating the convergence of the back-propagation method, *Biological Cybernetics*, 59, 257–263.

Vogt, M. (1993). Combination of radial basis function neural networks with optimized learning vector quantization, in *Proceedings of the IEEE International Conference on Neural Networks* (San Francisco, 1993), vol. III, pp. 1841–1846. IEEE, New York.

Waibel, A. (1989). Modular construction of time-delay neural networks for speech recognition, *Neural Computation*, 1, 39–46.

Waibel, A., Hanazawa, T., Hinton, G., Shikano, K., and Lang, K. (1989). Phoneme recognition using time-delay neural networks, *IEEE Transactions on Acoustics, Speech, and Signal Processing*, 37, 328–339.

Wang, C. (1991). A Robust System for Automated Decomposition of the Electromyogram Utilizing a Neural Network Architecture. Ph.D. dissertation, Department of Electrical and Computer Engineering, Wayne State University, Detroit, Mich.

Wang, C., Venkatesh, S.S., and Judd, J.S. (1994), Optimal stopping and effective machine complexity in learning, in *Advances in Neural Information Processing Systems*, **6** (Denver, 1993), J. D. Cowan, G. Tesauro, and J. Alspector, eds., pp. 303–310. Morgan Kaufmann, San Francisco.

Wang, Y.-F., Cruz, J. B., Jr., and Mulligan, J. H., Jr. (1990). Two coding strategies for bidirectional associative memory, *IEEE Transactions on Neural Networks*, **1**(1), 81–92.

Wang, Y.-F., Cruz, J. B., Jr., and Mulligan, J. H., Jr. (1991). Guaranteed recall of all training pairs for bidirectional associative memory, *IEEE Transactions on Neural Networks*, **2**(6), 559–567.

Wasan, M. T. (1969). *Stochastic Approximation*. Cambridge University Press, New York.

Watta, P. B. (1994). A Coupled Gradient Network Approach for Static and Temporal Mixed Integer Optimization, Ph.D. dissertation, Department of Electrical and Computer Engineering, Wayne State University, Detroit, Mich.

Watta, P. B. and Hassoun, M. H. (1995). A coupled gradient network approach for static and temporal mixed integer optimization, *IEEE Transactions on Neural Networks*. In press.

Waugh, F. R., Marcus, C. M., and Westervelt, R. M. (1991). Reducing neuron gain to eliminate fixed-point attractors in an analog associative memory, *Physical Review A*, **43**, 3131–3142.

Waugh, F. R., Marcus, C. M., and Westervelt, R. M. (1993). Nonlinear dynamics of analog associative memories, in *Associative Neural Memories: Theory and Implementation*, M. H. Hassoun, ed., pp. 197–211. Oxford University Press, New York.

Wegstein, J. H. (1958). Accelerating convergence in iterative processes, *ACM Communications,* **1**(6), 9–13.

Weigend, A. S., and Gershenfeld, N. A. (1993). Results of the time series prediction competition at the Santa Fe Institute, in *Proceedings of the IEEE International Conference on Neural Networks* (San Francisco, 1993), vol. III, pp. 1786–1793. IEEE, New York.

Weigend, A. S., and Gershenfeld, N. A., eds. (1994). *Time Series Prediction: Forecasting the Future and Understanding the Past. Proc. of the NTAO Advanced Research Workshop on Comparative Time Series Analysis (Santa Fe, 1992)*. Addison-Wesley, Reading, Mass.

Weigend, A. S., Rumelhart, D. E., and Huberman, B. A. (1991). Generalization by weight-elimination with application to forecasting, in *Advances in Neural Information Processing Systems 3* (Denver, 1990), R. P. Lippmann, J. E. Moody, and D. S. Touretzky, eds., pp. 875–882. Morgan Kaufmann, San Mateo, Calif.

Weisbuch, G., and Fogelman-Soulié, F. (1985). Scaling laws for the attractors of Hopfield networks, *Journal De Physique Letters*, **46**(14), L-623–L-630.

Werbos, P. (1974). Beyond Regression: New Tools for Prediction and Analysis in the Behavioral Sciences, Ph.D. dissertation, Committee on Applied Mathematics, Harvard University, Cambridge, Mass.

Werbos, P. J. (1988). Generalization of backpropagation with application to gas market model, *Neural Networks*, **1**, 339–356.

Werntges, H. W. (1993). Partitions of unity improve neural function approximators, in *Proceedings of the IEEE International Conference on Neural Networks* (San Francisco, 1993), vol. II, pp. 914–918. IEEE, New York.

Wessels, L. F. A., and Barnard, E. (1992). Avoiding false local minima by proper initialization of connections, *IEEE Transactions on Neural Networks*, **3**(6), 899–905.

Wettschereck, D., and Dietterich, T. (1992). Improving the performance of radial basis function networks by learning center locations, in *Advances in Neural Information Processing Systems 4* (Denver, 1991), J. E. Moody, S. J. Hanson, and R. P. Lippmann, eds., pp. 1133–1140. Morgan Kaufmann, San Mateo, Calif.

White, H. (1989). Learning in artificial neural networks: A statistical perspective, *Neural Networks*, **1**, 425–464.

White, S. A. (1975). An adaptive recursive digital filter, in *Proceedings of the 9th Asilomar Conference on Circuits, Systems, and Computers* (San Francisco, 1975), pp. 21–25. Western Periodicals, North Hollywood, Calif.

Whitley, D., and Hanson, T. (1989). Optimizing neural networks using faster, more accurate genetic search, in *Proceedings of the Third International Conference on Genetic Algorithms* (Arlington, 1989), J. D. Schaffer, ed., pp. 391–396. Morgan Kaufmann, San Mateo, Calif.

Widrow, B. (1987). ADALINE and MADALINE—1963 (plenary speech), in *Proceedings of the IEEE 1st International Conference on Neural Networks* (San Diego, 1982), vol. I, pp. 143–158. IEEE, New York.

Widrow, B., and Angell, J. B. (1962). Reliable, trainable networks for computing and control, *Aerospace Engineering*, **21**, 78–123.

Widrow, B., and Hoff, M. E., Jr. (1960). Adaptive switching circuits, *IRE Western Electric Show and Convention Record*, part 4, 96–104.

Widrow, B., and Lehr, M. A. (1990). 30 years of adaptive neural networks: Perceptron, madaline, and backpropagation, *Proceedings of the IEEE*, **78**(9), 1415–1442.

Widrow, B., and Stearns, S. D. (1985). *Adaptive Signal Processing*, Prentice-Hall, Englewood Cliffs, N.J.

Widrow, B., Gupta, N. K., and Maitra, S. (1973). Punish/reward: Learning with a critic in adaptive threshold systems, *IEEE Transactions on Systems, Man, and Cybernetics*, **SMC-3**, 455–465.

Widrow, B., McCool, J. M., Larimore, M. G., and Johnson Jr., C. R. (1976). Stationary and nonstationary learning characteristics of the LMS adaptive filter, *Proceedings of the IEEE*, **64**(8), 1151–1162.

Wieland, A. P. (1991). Evolving controls for unstable systems, in *Connectionist Models: Proceedings of the 1990 Summer School* (Pittsburgh, 1990), D. S. Touretzky, J. L. Elman, and G. E. Hinton, eds., pp. 91–102. Morgan Kaufmann, San Mateo, Calif.

Wieland, A., and Leighton, R. (1987). Geometric analysis of neural network capabilities, in *First IEEE International Conference on Neural Networks* (San Diego, 1987), vol. III, pp. 385–392. IEEE, New York.

Wiener, N. (1956). *I Am a Mathematician.* Doubleday, New York.

Wilkinson, J. H. (1965). *The Algebraic Eigenvalue Problem.* Oxford University Press, Oxford, England.

Williams, R. J. (1987). A class of gradient estimating algorithms for reinforcement learning in neural networks, in *IEEE First International Conference on Neural Networks* (San Diego, 1987), M. Caudill and C. Butler, eds., vol. II, pp. 601–608. IEEE, New York.

Williams, R. J. (1992). Simple statistical gradient-following algorithms for connectionist reinforcement learning, *Machine Learning*, **8**, 229–256.

Williams, R. J., and Zipser, D. (1989a). A learning algorithm for continually running fully recurrent neural networks, *Neural Computation*, **1**(2), 270–280.

Williams, R. J., and Zipser, D. (1989b). Experimental analysis of the real-time recurrent learning algorithm, *Connection Science*, **1**, 87–111.

Willshaw, D. J., and von der Malsburg, C. (1976). How patterned neural connections can be set up by self-organization, *Proceedings of the Royal Society of London*, **B194**, 431–445.

Winder, R. O. (1962). Threshold Logic. Ph.D. dissertation, Deptartment of Mathematics, Princeton University, Princeton, N.J.

Winder, R. O. (1963). Bounds on threshold gate realizability, *IEEE Transactions on Electronic Computers*, **EC-12**(5), 561–564.

Wittner, B. S., and Denker, J. S. (1988). Strategies for teaching layered networks classification tasks, in *Neural Information Processing Systems* (Denver, 1987), D. Z. Anderson, ed., pp. 850-859. American Institute of Physics, New York.

Wong, Y.-F., and Sideris, A. (1992). Learning convergence in the cerebellar model articulation controller, *IEEE Transactions on Neural Networks*, **3**(1), 115–121.

Xu, L. (1993). Least mean square error reconstruction principle for self-organizing neural-nets, *Neural Networks*, **6**(5), 627–648.

Xu, L. (1994). Theories of unsupervised learning: PCA and its nonlinear extensions, in *IEEE International Conference on Neural Networks* (Orlando, 1994), vol. II, pp. 1252–1257. IEEE, New York.

Yanai, H., and Sawada, Y. (1990). Associative memory network composed of neurons with hysteretic property, *Neural Networks*, **3**(2), 223–228.

Yang, L., and Yu, W. (1993). Backpropagation with homotopy, *Neural Computation*, **5**(3), 363–366.

Yoon, Y. O., Brobst, R. W., Bergstresser, P. R., and Peterson, L. L. (1989). A desktop neural network for dermatology diagnosis, *Journal of Neural Network Computing*, Summer, 43–52.

Yoshizawa, S., Morita, M., and Amari, S.-I. (1993a). Capacity of associative memory using a nonmonotonic neuron model, *Neural Networks*, **6**(2), 167–176.

Yoshizawa, S., Morita, M., and Amari, S.-I. (1993b). Analysis of dynamics and capacity of associative memory using a nonmonotonic neuron model, in *Associative Neural Memories: Theory and Implementation*, M. H. Hassoun, ed., pp. 239–248. Oxford University Press, New York.

Youssef, A. M., and Hassoun, M. H. (1989). Dynamic autoassociative neural memory performance vs. capacity, in *Proceedings of the SPIE, Optical Pattern Recognition*, H.-K. Liu, ed., pp. 52–59. SPIE, Bellingham.

Yu, X., Loh, N. K., and Miller, W. C. (1993). A new acceleration technique for the backpropagation algorithm, in *IEEE International Conference on Neural Networks* (San Francisco, 1993), vol. III, pp. 1157–1161. IEEE, New York.

Yuille, A. L., Kammen, D. M., and Cohen, D. S. (1989). Quadrature and the development of orientation selective cortical cells by Hebb rules, *Biological Cybernetics*, **61**, 183–194.

Zak, M. (1989). Terminal attractors in neural networks, *Neural Networks*, **2**(4), 258–274.

Zhang, J. (1991). Dynamics and formation of self-organizing maps, *Neural Computation*, **3**(1), 54–66.

Index